ART NOUVEAU

Gabriele Fahr-Becker

ART NOUVEAU

KÖNEMANN

Notes
Where the location of a pictured object is not given, it is either in private ownership or in a
colllection not named.
Accents on Catalan proper names in the chapter "Barcelona" follow guidelines laid down
by the Casa-Museu Gaudi, Barcelona.

Endpaper: Antoni Gaudí i Cornet, Casa Mila, Barcelona 1906-10
Ill. p. 2: Hector Guimard, Metro-Station "Porte Dauphine," Paris, 1900-01
Ill. p. 3: Josef Hoffmann, frame for a poem by Rainer Maria Rilke, in Ver Sacrum, I, Heft 9,
1989 (reproduced in original size)
Ill. p. 380: Carine Cadby, Shirley Poppies, 1901, Photograph, 27.8 x 19.9 cm, The Royal
Photography Society, Bath

For Philipp and Sittig

© 2004 KÖNEMANN*, an imprint of Tandem Verlag GmbH, Königswinter

Editing: Chistine Westphal
Design: Peter Feierabend
Layout: Peter Feierabend, Sanna Salber
Assistant: Sonja Latsch
Appendix: Regine Ermert

Original title: *Jugendstil*

© 2004 for the English edition:
KÖNEMANN*, an imprint of Tandem Verlag GmbH, Königswinter

Translation from the German: Paul Aston, Ruth Chitty, Karen Williams
Copy-editing of
the English edition: Jackie Dobbyne for Hart McLeod, Cambridge
Typesetting: Goodfellow & Egan, Cambridge

*KÖNEMANN is a registered trademark of Tandem Verlag GmbH

Printed in EU

ISBN 3-8331-1234-4

10 9 8 7 6 5 4 3 2 1
X IX VIII VII VI V IV III II I

Contents

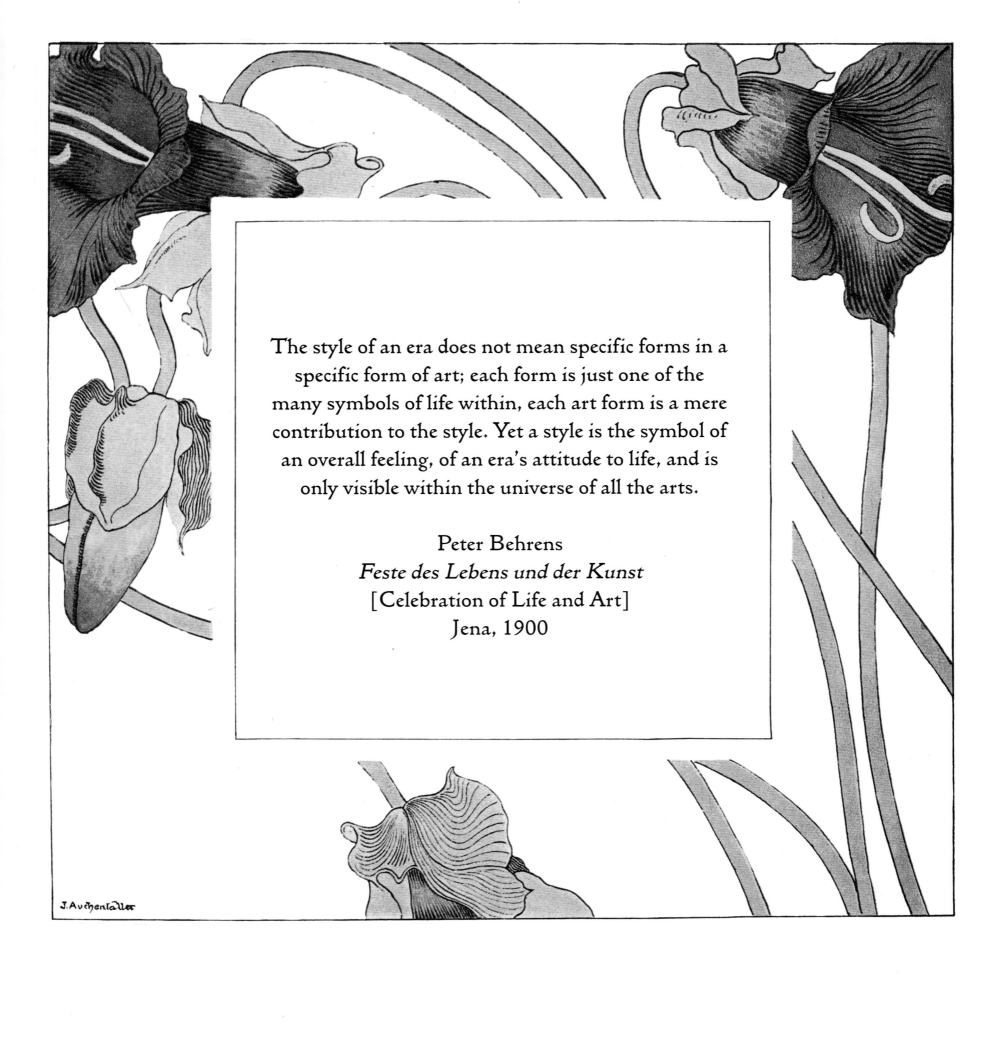

The style of an era does not mean specific forms in a specific form of art; each form is just one of the many symbols of life within, each art form is a mere contribution to the style. Yet a style is the symbol of an overall feeling, of an era's attitude to life, and is only visible within the universe of all the arts.

Peter Behrens
Feste des Lebens und der Kunst
[Celebration of Life and Art]
Jena, 1900

Introduction
The Final Chord and A New Beginning

Josef Maria Auchentaller
Book illustration
From *Ver Sacrum*, 1898
Color heliogravure,
202.2 x 202.2 cm

There are three kinds of reader: a first who enjoys without judging, a third who judges without enjoyment, and one in between, who judges with enjoyment and enjoys with judgment; it is this reader who actually produces the work of art anew.
Johann Wolfgang von Goethe[1]

Cube and arabesque

A work of art is created anew by the response of its beholder – or, if instead of Goethe we were to follow the words of Panofsky[2] – it is the beholder's knowledge and experience which cause a work of art to evolve. It is possible to perceive every object aesthetically, whether a product of man or of nature, and it is a personal decision whether we view it aesthetically or not. Yet even if its creator intended, not every work of art is seen in an aesthetic sense. This is dependent on the dominance of certain influential criteria: do I react chiefly to the shape or to the subject, to the idea or to the content, and how do I associate these elements? The artist's intentions need an opposite pole; even consciously executed works of art are dependent on the "qualifications" with which the observer is armed. The conception of a work of art is determined by the observer's visual practice and intellectual and cultural knowledge, which in turn spark off the most diverse associations of ideas.

This short digression is intended to further the understanding of Art Nouveau, on the one hand celebrated as the beginning of the Modern Style and as the first and last uniform style since the Baroque, and on the other dismissed as "ornamental hell", kitsch, and arts and crafts. The aesthetics of Art Nouveau is an aesthetics of contradiction; in order for these contradictions to

be experienced as a work of art, a sufficient understanding of the object beheld is required which reaches far beyond visual perception. "Of course, every style is unique, but Art Nouveau is unique among styles."[3] Before the incredibly high quality which Art Nouveau was to contribute to the artistic development of the 20th century can be applied as a criterion, this style, a relatively short-lived phenomenon of 25 years, must be respected as an achievement in its own right. "In the past, numerous artistic directions have called themselves 'modern'. We can disregard the fact that the builders of the first Gothic cathedrals differentiated between 'opus anti-quum' and their work, 'opus modernum'. Even Rococo was termed 'style moderne' by its contemporaries. The style we call Art Nouveau was named 'modern style' in England around 1890."[4] Art Nouveau, "New Art", was and still is modern, and was and still is historical. The violent mutation of the turn of the century – the extremes of our present day and age are no fewer – hid the lure of a beautiful death and a catalyst for all kinds of new ideas still relevant to today's world. "We were all Art Nouveau artists. There were so many wild, crazy curves to those Métro entrances and on all Art Nouveau work that I rebelled and restricted myself almost exclusively to straight lines. Yet despite this, I still took part in Art Nouveau in my own way. Even if you are against a movement, you are still part of it."[5] Cube and arabesque (ill. right and opposite page) are the pro and contra of the same movement, whose source lies in the same fund of philosophical, literary, artistic, and socio-reformative thoughts and ideas. It was these "qualifications", the cultural and political background, which shaped this principle of design. A great

Josef Hoffmann
Geometric design, ca. 1905
Pencil and Indian ink, 29.5 x 21 cm

Emile Gallé
Calla vase (detail), ca, 1900
Mold-blown flashed glass, etched
and cut, 35 cm in height
One is left in no doubt that the basic
designs for Art Nouveau's
flickering, feathery, flowing
linearism were provided by nature;
to this is added what the artist
projects on to it, a second major
factor. The natural object takes on
new permutations; it is relieved of its
elemental background and placed in
a new formal and intellectual
context. Its organic physiognomy is
absorbed by the framework of the
mind.

sense of tension is apparent when contemplating Art Nouveau, brought about by the often contrary artistic versions of the different countries and artists. These diverse interpretations and indeed their common basis are particularly well-illustrated in the large number and variety of theories and writings by artists and their contemporaries. Aesthetic Discontent and the Aesthetic Movement, decadence and the beginnings of socialism were mutual starting points for Art Nouveau, as were the manifold artistic trends evident in varying degrees of importance in the individual countries, all of which produced a hive of artistic activity whose effect is yet to be exhausted.

Japan and the West

Japanese art has turned to nature. It teaches ways of feeling and expressing the subtlest changes in nature with the different seasons. An object's beauty remains hidden from the analytical research of the mind. Beauty is revealed in the feeling that binds heart and object.
Kaii Higashiyama[6]

The influence of Japanese art on Art Nouveau and indeed on turn-of-the-century art in general is genuine and has many facets. Its various forms of adoption and orientation show themselves in many guises: in asymmetrical composition, in new motifs from nature and society, in a respect for empty spaces in composition, that is to say the love of voids instead of *horror vacui*, and in the clear beauty of the line. When Samuel Bing exhibited 725 Japanese prints and 428 illustrated books at the École des Beaux-Arts in 1890,

attracting artists from all over Europe, the Japanese model transcended from a stimulus for a handful of painters to a leitmotiv for an entire generation of artists. The first knowledge of Japanese art dates from the world exhibitions. "Japanese art is important as a teacher. From it, we once again learn to feel clearly how far we have strayed from nature's true designs through the persistent tradition of inherited forms, through the persistent imitation of fixed models; we learn how necessary it is to draw from the source; how the human spirit is able to absorb a wealth of magnificent, naive beauty from the organic forms of nature in place of pedantic, decrepit rigidity of form."[7] As Julius Lessing's words illustrate, it was neither the bizarre nor the exotic which left their mark on Western art, but naturalness and simplicity, both of which had been suppressed by the intellect in Europe (ill. right and p. 10). In an essay published in 1899 in *Ver Sacrum*, Ernst Schur brings together Europe's "art of the intellect" with Japan's "art of the nerves."[8]

Japanese art was not only viewed with perspective; it reached into the depths of the soul and was the source of poetic inspiration. The passionate late work of van Gogh, the hero of Modernism, was the product of his familiarity with Japanese color woodcuts. "Here my life becomes more and more like that of a Japanese painter,"[9] he wrote in a letter to his brother, Theo, from the south of France in 1887. Van Gogh was captivated by the light of the bright colors, the vibrant rhythm of the lines and dots, the increased power of expression of simplified outlines and the juxtaposition of decorative

Japan
Fireman's cape (detail), early 19th century
Suede, with the brigade's stenciled emblem (the patterns were made using a special 1000-year-old technique, where drifts of smoke are blown through a template), 95 x 133 cm
Mingeikan – Japan Folk Crafts Museum, Tokyo
The new styles of the Arts and Crafts Movement in England spread across the entire continent and revolutionized design. Art Nouveau refused to continue to differentiate between "lower, applied" art forms and "higher, free" art. The Japanese artist-craftsman was a paradigm for this equality. "What we are trying to do is what the Japanese have always done," proclaimed Josef Hoffmann (see note 10).

Koloman Moser
Wall decoration, December (detail), 1901
Color lithograph, 26 x 30 cm
From *Die Quelle – ein Vorlagewerk mit 71 Tafeln* [The Source: a reference work with 71 plates], edited by Martin Gerlach junior, Gerlach & Schenk, Vienna – Munich
Die Quelle was a reference work of nature's world of shapes and forms. It depicted plants, insects, crystals, stones, and the smallest organisms in detailed enlargements. The graphic work by this Viennese Art Nouveau artist betrays the great influence nature bore on Moser's principles of design. Cube and arabesque are the pro and contra of the same movement whose source lies in the same fund of philosophical, literary, artistic, and socio-reformative thoughts and ideas.

planes on the pictorial surface evident in the *ukiyo-e* [pictures of the floating world]. The bold cuts of Toulouse-Lautrec's lithographs (ill. p. 103) also originate from the decentralized arrangements and sectionalized way of seeing things characteristic of Japanese woodcuts. The French aristocrat produced his own version of *Kabuki* scenes and *shunga* [Spring pictures] from Yoshiwara, the entertainments district of Edo (modern Tokyo, ill. opposite page), imitating not only forms, but also the milieu with his motifs from the world of Montmartre. Even Cézanne, a stubborn opponent of the Japanese trend, did not escape its influence. Lurking in the distance beyond his crystalline homages to Mont Sainte-Victoire is Hokusai's equally important Fuji series (ill. p. 12). The list of painters directly and indirectly inspired by the *ukiyo-e* reads like a hit parade of art from 1860–1910: Pissarro, Monet, van Gogh (ill. p. 14–15), Gauguin, Seurat, Signac, Redon, Ensor, Munch, Hodler, Toulouse-Lautrec, Bonnard, Vallotton (ill. p. 13), Vuillard, Beardsley, Klimt, Matisse, and all those omitted from art history's Hall of Fame. The turn to pure surfaces and the moving away from edges is not a phenomenon restricted to graphic art in Art Nouveau; it was also applied to furnished spaces. The consideration of function, properties of materials and work processes – characteristics of Japanese art – was to become an archetype for the design of object art at the turn of the century (ill. above). The new styles taken from the reforms of the Arts and Crafts Movement in England spread across the entire continent and revolutionized design. Art Nouveau refused to continue to differentiate between "lower, applied" art forms and "higher, free" art. The Japanese artist-craftsman was a paradigm for this equality. "What we are trying to do is what the Japanese have always done,"[10] proclaimed Josef Hoffmann in the Wiener Werkstätte's (Vienna Workshops) work program. There was not a master studio in about 1900, whether Gallé's, Lalique's or Tiffany's, which did not produce its own personal Japanese-style articles (ill. p. 17, 23), just as book art and lithographics could not have blossomed without the spontaneity of Japanese art. In Zen, the directness of the heart replaces any kind of dogmatism; in this lies probably the deepest-reaching relationship – which is also the most difficult to describe – in an aesthetic lifestyle. "The world of objects means nothing, yet every common object is absolute. Small things are just as humble and commendable as large things. One doesn't grasp; one is grasped. A Zen work of art also means nothing; it is there. Form is void, void nothing but form. The circle is empty and full. Things and the void between them are equally valid."[11] The teachings of Zen figure in Western architecture without modification. Frank Lloyd Wright and Josef Hoffmann both achieved free-flowing movement between interior and exterior using simple constructions with suitable materials.

Post-Ruskin artists, artist-craftsmen, designers, architects and artist-architects demonstrated a ready acceptance of new forms and subjects, the result among other things of a desire for a new spirituality which would counter the threatening, unfriendly implications of a growing industrial society with a unity with nature both internal and external.

Utagawa Kunimasa
The Actor Ichikawa Ebizō, 1796
Color woodcut, *Nishiki-e* [multi-color print], 38.1 x 26.1 cm
Hiraki-Ukiyo-e Museum, Yokohama
The bold cuts of Toulouse-Lautrec's lithographs also originate from the decentralized arrangements and sectionalized way of seeing things characteristic of Japanese woodcuts. The French aristocrat produced his own version of *kabuki* scenes and the Spring pictures from Yoshiwara, the entertainments district of Edo (modern Tokyo), imitating not only forms, but also the milieu with his motifs from the world of Montmartre.

Ornamental organisms

**Seven billion years before my birth I was an iris.
Arno Holz[12]**

Art Nouveau sought to quash the exhausted clichés of historicism and naturalism not with logic, but with "bio-logic"; the magic of life and of the organic was to exorcise the ghosts of styles past (ill. p. 8). It was no longer considered important to protect oneself from elemental force, but from the noise of cities, from the violence of modern traffic, boxing in everything in its path, from industry and the mechanized masses. The animal and plant world, the incarnation of creation and of natural growth offered ways and means of regeneration (ill. p. 16). "Only three things exist for the creative mind: here am I, here is nature and here is the object I am going to embellish."[13]

The zoologist and natural philosopher Ernst Haeckel (1834–1919) was in tune with the spirit of the times with his monist teachings. In his illustrated writings, *Natürliche Schöpfungsgeschichte* [Story of the Creation, 1868] and *Kunstformen der Natur* [Art Forms of Nature, 1899], he presented the theory that reality can be put down to one single – spiritual or material – principle. Haeckel was primarily concerned with amorphous, plant-like animals – jellyfish, cnidarians, seaweed, radiolarians, algae, corals, and protozoa – whose structures were almost devoid of solid, straight lines and featured heavily in the ornamentation of Art Nouveau. He himself described these "in-between creatures" as "wonderfully ornamented". Another man concerned with natural forms was Karl Blossfeldt (1865–1932), who studied plants in their various stages of growth, enlarging them many times in his detail photographs (ill. p. 21). These served to sharpen artists' awareness of nature and were often directly worked into patterns and designs. The growing interest in natural science and advances in technology at the end of the 19th century permitted the exploration of microcosms, phenomena previously hidden from the eyes of man. Through the addition of a condenser to the microscope in 1872, Ernst Abbe (1840–1905) opened up boundless new opportunities for the natural sciences. Attention was particularly focused on the study of insects, which became incredibly popular. The curved, elastic limbs of these buzzing, fluttering, living organisms lent themselves to Art Nouveau's play of lines like cut-out patterns (ill. p. 17). The iridescent play of colors of butterfly and dragonfly wings, the changing shades of the chitin exoskeletons of beetles, crabs, spiders, and insects are mirrored in the color schemes of Art Nouveau. The plasmatic character of these "in-between creatures" has an almost secretive affinity with the swelling ornaments of the turn of the century. The bare feelers and tentacles of polyps become lamps and lights; as women's hair they entangle and entwine the art and psyche of the *fin de siècle*.

Katsushika Hokusai
The South Wind Drives Away the Clouds, from *36 Views of Mount Fuji,* 1831–34
Color woodcut, *Nishiki-e* [multi-color print], 26.1 x 38.1 cm
Hiraki-Ukiyo-e Museum, Yokohama
Even Cézanne, a stubborn opponent of the Japanese trend, did not escape its influence. Lurking in the distance beyond his crystalline homages to Mont Sainte-Victoire is Hokusai's equally important Fuji series.

Félix Vallotton
The Balloon, or *Corner of the Park
with a Child Playing with a
Balloon*, 1899
Oil on card, 48 x 61 cm
Musée d'Orsay, Paris
Vallotton, the most important wood
engraver of his time, clearly
demonstrates Japanese influences in
his work. Even in his painting, the
single figures and elements in his
pictures, reduced to their typical
movements, have something of the
woodcut about them.

Breathing life into nature – Synesthesia

*It is not the ornament ... which has "expressed" the inner
life of these strange times, but people who have led the life
of the ornament; souls themselves have become
ornaments.*
Dolf Sternberger[14]

One is left in no doubt that the basic designs for
Art Nouveau's flickering, feathery, flowing linearism were provided by nature (ill. p. 6); to this is
added what the artist projects on to it, a second
major factor. The natural object takes on new
permutations; it is relieved of its elemental

background and placed in a new formal and
intellectual context. Its organic physiognomy is
absorbed by the framework of the mind. "All
shapes suffuse into one another, driving everything equally with emotion, with the soul, moving
it 'organically'. In this way, Art Nouveau's ornamental world comes alive; it is a materialization
of the 'atmosphere of souls' of which Maeterlinck
speaks. It is this peculiarity which distinguishes
Art Nouveau from all earlier epochs and ornamental representations. According to the theories
of Art Nouveau, even the most abstract figures,
even the simplest graphic elements are allotted,

Vincent van Gogh
Irises, May 1889
Oil on canvas, 71 x 93 cm
Joan Whitney Payson Gallery of
Art, Westbrook College,
Portland/Maine
The passionate late work of van
Gogh, the hero of Modernism, was
the product of his familiarity with
Japanese color woodcuts. "Here my
life becomes more and more like that
of a Japanese painter," he wrote in a
letter to his brother, Theo, from the
south of France in 1887. Van Gogh
was captivated by the light of the
bright colors, the vibrant rhythm of
the lines and dots, the increased
power of expression of simplified
outlines and the fixing of decorative
surfaces to the picture surface evident
in the *ukiyo-e*.

indeed are inhabited by, certain feelings or 'experiences'."[15] Fantasies and emotions are fired which cannot be experienced in reality – a stylistic method the Symbolists have always employed in word, but which becomes visually transparent only with Art Nouveau. The Greek word *symbolon* describes the secret signs by which those sworn to mystic cults recognized one another. Thus the symbol as a bearer of coded messages to a chosen few has the power of revelation.

Symbolic or symbolist art is a trait of every era, yet its meaning has always been different. Art Nouveau was stamped by the decorative emblems of the French and Belgian Symbolists. "… so let's say that Charles Baudelaire must be named the true forerunner of the current movement. Stéphane Mallarmé gave it its sense of secrecy and inexpressibility …"[16] An entire host of artistic media was caught up in this *fin-de-siècle* arabesque: literature, poetry, music, fine and applied art. Proust, Debussy, Verlaine, Maeterlinck, Sibelius, Ibsen, Strauss, Hofmannsthal, Rilke, D'Annunzio, Huysmans, to name but a few authors and composers, were part of the Art Nouveau effort in this dizzy climate of sensual, poetic masterpieces. Artists in 1900 were all striving toward synesthesia, literally a "mutual sensation". Their virtuoso example was Richard Wagner (1813–83), who effected a suggestive synthesis of the senses with his fusion of music, language, and theater. Gustave Flaubert (1821–80) also uses the concept of synesthesia in his novel *Salammbô* (1863). "Her earrings were two sapphire beads bearing hollow

Josef Hoffmann
Tumbler from the Var. F set of glasses, ca. 1910
Frosted glass with black bronzite decoration, 10.4 cm in height
Made by J. and L. Lobmeyr, Vienna
Wiener Glasmuseum, Lobmeyr Collection

pearls filled with liquid perfume. Drops occasionally trickling through holes in the pearls wove patterns on her naked shoulders."[17] Smell, desire, sight – Flaubert touches on all these senses with his description. Salome, the idol of the Decadents, is herself an example of synesthesia, and often appears as a theme in painting (ill. p. 19), poetry, and music. Art Nouveau condensed synesthesia into reality: great waves of thick hair, ornamental curves and plant arabesques resemble the graphic notation of patterns of sound, and the flowers, whether deadly or innocent, give off a wonderful bouquet. For Baudelaire, the fragrance of *Fleurs du mal*[18] was a parable of the "stupidity, confusion, sin, and the soiled mind" of his contemporary world. His poetry cycle is like a compendium of turn-of-the-century floral mysticism, where one translates the age-old language of flowers into endless roundelays of blooms and blossoms.

Above:
Peking
Snuff bottles, 19th century
Cut, flashed glass, 25.5 cm in height
In retrospect, one could say that cut, flashed glass was a typical product of Art Nouveau. This complicated and yet "natural" technique of processing glass drew its inspiration from Chinese snuff bottles.

Jean-Antonin Daum
Vase with fish, ca. 1890
Flashed crystal, with oxide inclusions, glass thread and glass powder inclusions, engraved, cut and etched, painted and gilded, 21 cm in height
Tokuso Takasima attended the École Forestière in Nancy and there awoke the interest of local artists – such as the Daum brothers or Gallé – for the art of his native Japan.

Eternal femininity

Sex is very similar to torture or surgery.
Charles Baudelaire[19]

The taut span of the senses also served to stimulate the relationship between the two sexes; plants and animal symbols, more eloquent than words, became the emblems of eroticism. Burning embers were explosively rekindled by decadence, and sensuality became accepted in the salons, whereby lasciviousness and vice were aesthetically domesticated and art was used to elevate any tones of obscenity. The motto "back to nature" was a pretext for grasping and handling the concept of the body – the female body – anew. Tense, nervous lines seized the Eves decoratively and willingly wafting through all artistic walks of Art Nouveau, smothered by their manes of hair, swimming in complex waves and swirls of smoke, imprisoned and surrendering. Art Nouveau's female images are the sisters of Dante Gabriel Rossetti's embodiments of femininity (ill. p. 18). For the great Pre-Raphaelite painter, the female body was the "symbol of all beauty." The dreamy poses of his female figures created a "fusion of quivering eroticism and spiritual nobility,"[20] their full, almost greedy lips in sensuous counterpoint with the withdrawn, unfathomable eyes. Yet in Art Nouveau the word "woman" also takes on dangerous undertones, undertones of wicked witches, the man-devouring vamp, the *femme fatale*, the murderess Judith, of blood-sucking vampires, of sin and the dancing temptress, Salome – an endless procession all symbolizing the fears of the stronger sex. Figures of innocence also had their own sensory appeal; the slight figures of young girls about to blossom were smuggled into vignettes and landscapes bursting with symbolism. Puberty was painted by Edvard Munch, who, like many others, also took the Madonna (ill. p. 285) as a model of the self-abandoned female martyr, of the lover and the conceiver, often crowned with flowers and with the flame of sensuality burning behind her closed eyes (ill. p.18).

In an attempt to master this phobia, artists adopted the androgyne, the hermaphrodite, as a favorite motif of unstilled desire. Yet the phobia was inescapable, as the Sphinx, for example, demonstrated. This strange, monstrous mixture of beings was the symbol of man's sexual

Emile Gallé
Vase with a Japanese base, ca. 1900
Flashed glass with embossed and engraved levels of carving, *intercalaire* [inter-layered decoration], appliqué and marquetry-de-verre, bronze base, 16.5 cm in height
Post-Ruskin artists, artist-craftsmen, designers, architects, and artist-architects demonstrated a ready acceptance for new forms and subjects, the result among other things of a desire for a new spirituality which would counter the threatening, unfriendly implications of a growing industrial society with a unity with nature both internal and external. Art Nouveau sought to quash the exhausted clichés of historicism and naturalism not with logic, but with "bio-logic"; the magic of life and of the organic was to exorcise the ghosts of styles past.

Georges Auger
Dragonfly brooch, ca. 1895
Platinum, yellow gold, diamond roses, pink-colored ruby squares, enamel and turquoise, 11.1 x 9.3 cm
(Reproduction in the original size)
Within scientific developments, attention was particularly focused on the study of insects, which became incredibly popular. The curved, elastic limbs of these buzzing, fluttering, living organisms lent themselves to Art Nouveau's play of lines like cut-out patterns.

confusion, unable to solve its riddle. Sigmund Freud tried to offer a remedy, giving a scientific basis to hysteria and neuroticism through psychoanalysis.

"This throng of women / Which guides us, indulges us / With their flowing hair / So beautiful in dance,"[21] wrote Stefan George, associating with his poem the graphic rhythm of these nymph-like beings with the new discipline of artistic dance, which reached its climax in the flowing veils of Loïe Fuller. This sweet, heathen prototype is in harmony with Eric Bergson's Pan philosophy and Rudolf Steiner's anthroposophists. Philosophies from Nietzsche's *Zarathustra* to Schopenhauer found expression in the all-embracing art of life and experience.

The collage in 1900

If we said that beauty is idea, then beauty and truth in one sense are the same ...
Through this, beauty characterizes itself as the sensual appearance of the idea.
Georg Wilhelm Friederich Hegel[22]

Art Nouveau's countless ciphers and wealth of disparities intermingled and formed the characteristic visage of an era, which still managed to produce an overall sense of design both fascinating and – in an autonomous sense – unified. Technical components were combined with the organic. Functionalism's hymn of praise clothed itself in emphatic words and phrases. The world exhibitions vividly paraded this divergence of styles before the eyes of their visitors. "Some of the illustrations, even the exhibition catalogue, are like collages. When, fifty years ago, Max Ernst was searching for media which would disrupt the middle-classes' understanding of themselves, he

Artists in around 1900 also discovered the sensory appeal of figures of innocence; the slight figures of young girls about to blossom were smuggled into vignettes and landscapes bursting with symbolism. The Madonna was also a desired model of the self-abandoned female martyr, of the lover and the conceiver, often crowned with flowers and with the flame of sensuality burning behind her closed eyes. Sigmund Freud tried to offer a remedy in the battle of the sexes, giving a scientific basis to hysteria and neuroticism through psychoanalysis.

Gustave Flaubert also uses the concept of synesthesia in his novel *Salammbô* (1863). "Her earrings were two sapphire beads bearing hollow pearls filled with liquid perfume. Drops occasionally trickling through holes in the pearls wove patterns on her naked shoulders." Smell, desire, sight – Flaubert touches on all these senses with his description. Salome, the idol of the Decadents, is herself an example of synesthesia, and often appears as a theme in painting, poetry, and music.

For the great Pre-Raphaelite painter Rossetti, the female body was the "symbol of all beauty". The dreamy poses of his female figures created a "fusion of quivering eroticism and spiritual nobility" (Wolfram Waldschmidt, see note 20), their full, almost greedy lips in sensuous counterpoint with the withdrawn, unfathomable eyes.

Alphonse Balat, Henri Maquet
Grand Jardin d'Hiver [Great
Winter Garden] at Royal Palace at
Laeken, avenue du Parc Royal,
1875–76
The iron-and-glass constructions
made possible by technical
innovation and promoted by the
world exhibitions were the
harbingers of ecological building –
an ecology of construction which
brought with it the use of new
materials, the use of science as a
constructional foundation. The
economical deployment of new
building matter such as glass and
iron led to transparency and
lightness of construction.

stumbled across these attestations to creative diligence and discovery. The rigidity of the figures, the naive and brutal combination of familiar objects with mechanical ones was surreal *avant la lettre*."[23] The clash of *fin de siècle* and the dawning 20th century threaded through artistic achievements about 1900 like a leitmotiv, giving them their uniqueness and restricting their duration. The iron-and-glass constructions made possible by technical innovation and promoted by the world exhibitions were the harbingers of ecological building – an ecology of construction which brought with it the use of new materials, the use of science as a constructional foundation. The economical deployment of new building matter such as glass and iron led to transparency and lightness of construction (ill. opposite page). However, the growing concern at the end of the last century was that one day architecture would disintegrate into nothing with the increased

flimsiness of the buildings. The result was a kind of hybrid architecture which on the one hand was modern and practical, but on the other ornamentally decorated and heavily "made-up", as a favorite criticism put it. Yet it is this symbiosis of incompatibility which bestows upon these buildings their charm.

The Hall of Machines in Arcadia, the arabesque in *amor vacui* are not two sides of the same coin of "dream and reality"[24] but daily experience reaped from a period of change. Over-ornate, self-celebratory pomp (ill. below left), the expression of a bourgeoisie and industrial age hungry for forms of representation, coexisted alongside objects demonstrating a simple, formal balance we still consider modern today (ill. right). In France, Pierre Cécile Puvis de Chavannes painted his "island of the Blessed", faceless forms bathed in a mist of eternal light (ill. p. 23) and influenced the next generation just as

Beaker from a christening set
Vienna, 1826
Silver, 10.5 cm in height
Die Neue Sammlung, Staatliches Museum für angewandte Kunst, Munich
The 19th century produced not only a capricious mixture of eclectic styles but also objects demonstrating a simple, formal balance we still consider modern today.

Percy Holmes Dobson and Charles Westcott Dobson
Centerpiece
Silver, 250 x 93.3 cm
For Dobson & Sons, London
"Abominable household items ... flow from the inexhaustible springs of bad taste: stepped towers as ink pots, enormous crosses as lampshades ... and a pair of towers crowned by an arch calling themselves 'iron scraper after a Gothic model' ... Those who produce such abominable objects have no feeling for proportion and form, for utility and unity of style ..." wrote the British architect Augustin W. Pugin in 1841.

Left:
Karl Blossfeldt
Curcurbita [pumpkin tendrils]
Photograph enlarged four times, 1900–03
From *Urformen der Kunst* [Prototype of Art], Berlin 1928
Blossfeldt studied plants in their various stages of growth, enlarging them many times in his detailed photographs. These served to sharpen artists' awareness of nature and were often directly worked into patterns and designs.

Philipp Otto Runge
Morning from *The Times of the Day*, 1808
Oil on canvas, 109 x 85.5 cm
Kunsthalle Hamburg
Intensifying the ornamental arrangement by way of an extreme choice of frame was one of the main characteristics of Art Nouveau. Even with Runge, the impact of the picture is doubled by his filled surfaces and frame adorned with symbolic figures.

strongly as the prophetic English painter, William Blake, whose dream faces form a linear contrast of the horizontal and the vertical. The lithe bodies of his figures move to an ornamental rhythm and add a sense of spirituality to the ornamentation and events illustrated in the picture (ill. below). In the works of Philipp Otto Runge, one discovers a signal-like coloring of surfaces which paved the way for ornamental design (ill. left). The ornament is immanent as an allegory for the river of life and as a way of ordering the picture. "All forms of imitation have a beginning and an end; an ornament merely has duration. Emulation breathes life and inspires; ornamentation banishes and kills."[25]

This inspiring imitation promised by philosopher of history Oswald Sprenger (1880–1936) in his *Untergang des Abendlandes* [The Decline of the West, 1918–22] is provided by the East, by the Orient. The embellishments of Arabian art, the arabesque, the shapes of Far Eastern receptacles, the minarets of the mosques, nomad textile designs, the techniques and decorations used in Chinese glasswork (ill. p. 16), glazing and

firing processes for royal ceramics from the Middle Kingdom and in particular from Japan, the land of the rising sun, inspired and liberated the formal language of the West. Half-forgotten stylistic periods closer to home also experienced a revival, especially the Gothic period, which managed to preserve a unity of art, craft, and spirituality. The Celtic catalogue of patterns and designs was also taken as a model, as were the glass objects of antiquity. It was a puzzle of the ages, of the cultures, a collage of decadence and of the intellect: Art Nouveau.

The name of this stylistic period was in full accordance with its diverse ingredients which merged together in dramatic, often astoundingly controversial designs. In all lands and languages, these attributes were termed "new," "young," "modern," "original" and "quite unprecedented". The English name actually comes from Maison Bing, L'Art Nouveau in France, a gallery founded by Samuel Bing in 1895 as an exhibition forum for the new art. It was, however, quite by chance that the German word for Art Nouveau,

William Blake
The River of Life, 1805
Watercolor, pen on paper, 30.5 x 33.6 cm
Tate Gallery, London
Art Nouveau was also heavily influenced by the prophetic English painter, William Blake, who axialized his dream faces in a linear contrast of the horizontal and the vertical. The lithe bodies of his figures move to an ornamental rhythm and add a sense of spirituality to the ornamentation and events illustrated in the picture.

Pierre Cécile Puvis de Chavannes
The poor fisherman
Oil on canvas, 150 x 192 cm
Musée d'Orsay, Paris
In France, Puvis de Chavannes
painted his "island of the Blessed",
faceless forms bathed in a mist of
eternal light. His mood pictures
would strongly influence the next
generation of artists.

Jugendstil, came about. The first part of the compound was taken from the magazine *Jugend* which was first published in Munich in 1896. The magazine itself had nothing to do with the origins and developments of Art Nouveau. In Italy, the term *Lo Stile Liberty* was taken from Liberty's, an Art Nouveau store in London. "Stil," "style," "stile," gradually teamed up with "young" and "modern," two important Art Nouveau hallmarks, to lend voice to the conscious development of a new direction: Modern Style, *Style Guimard* and *Style Métro* are all forerunners of Art Nouveau. The terminologies *Lo Stile florale* and Floral Style paid homage to the style's floral ornamentation. Spain's word, *Modernista*, stresses the newness of the forms. Defamatory word creations such as *Style nouilles* (Noodle Style) in France, *Bandwurmstil* (Tapeworm Style) in Germany and *Brettlstil* (Plank Style) in Austria only served to enliven Art Nouveau's spectrum of modifiers.

The herbarium of different lifestyles and powers of design was fused a second time – almost incestuously – in the "complete" work of art. Turn-of-the-century aesthetics was the domain of the individual, styled down to the last detail, in today's didactics termed an "overall design".

Pride of place in this respect goes to architecture, fluently shifting its function between preserver of bodily warmth and religious building, according to Hans Hollein.[26] Artists bent on creating an *œuvre global* have left us with creations of breathtaking luxuriousness. This intensity – Art Nouveau's strength – also housed the risk of failure. "Narcissus died because he had lost himself to his own mirror image."[27] "When Narcissus died, the flowers in the meadows became so stricken with grief that they asked the river to spare them a few drops of water so they could show their sadness.

'Oh,' answered the river, 'if all my drops of water were tears, I still wouldn't have enough of them to grieve over Narcissus, so great was my love for him.'

'But of course,' said the flowers, 'how could anyone not love Narcissus, he was so beautiful!'
'Was he so beautiful?' asked the river.

'Is there anyone who knows that better than you, who mirrored his face when he bent over your rippling waters and looked at his reflection?'

'I loved him,' answered the river, 'because every time he bent over me I could see my own beauty reflected in his eyes.'"[28]

Walter Hampel
Japanese Woman, ca. 1910
Drawing colored with watercolors on art board, 21 x 13.4 cm
Barlow/Widmann Collection, Spain

ISOLDE

Ruskin, Morris and the Pre-Raphaelites
England

I confessed that I had resolved to follow the paths of
Ruskin and Morris until they had realized their prophecy:
the return of beauty on earth and the dawning of an era of
social justice and human dignity.
Henry van de Velde[1]

The Aesthetic Movement and Aesthetic Discontent

During the 18th century, Great Britain became the strongest economic and colonial power in the world. It was an epoch which saw the Age of Enlightenment and the great bourgeois revolutions; an epoch during which a young, capitalist economy swept away the old feudal system once and for all, and the Industrial Revolution triumphantly conquered in the factories. It was an age when world history was founded, an age of pathos and the battle for the civil rights and liberties of the individual, an age when culture was made accessible to the general public. In his last will and testament, Sir Hans Sloane bequeathed his art collection and library to the "people of England". Inspired by an insatiable thirst for knowledge and the French *Encyclopédie*, the major social and political reference work of the French Enlightenment, to produce a comprehensive inventory of human knowledge and experience, and embellished by King George III's collection of Egyptian antiquities, Sloane's heritage laid the foundation stone for one of the most important museums in the world. The British Museum, a universal treasure trove, was opened in 1759.

During the next century, England technologically outstripped the Continent; economic expansion reached its peak in 1850, but was unfortunately already revealing its first defects. The process of adapting historicising craftsmanship to technical methods of production was considered torturous. The phrase "Aesthetic Discontent" was coined, representing a growing dissatisfaction with eclecticism in art, with normative historicism and its cluttered decorative forms. This crisis was not restricted to the arts; it was a rebellion against social egotism and the staunchly defended privileges of the ruling class. John Ruskin (1819–1900) was the initiator of the Aesthetic Movement which grew out of this period of Aesthetic Discontent. He called for a "gospel of beauty" in his writings, and fought for a new code of ethics in industry and the creative value of arts and crafts. Ruskin talked of the dignity of work and the degradation caused by the division of labor. His remedy was that all classes should show understanding for the kinds of work that are good for people, that uplift them, that make them happy. The problem was to ensure that a place for craftsmen and artists could be secured in the world of mass production. This aesthetic revolt (to which the movement owed its initial success) was joined by artists, craftsmen, and intellectuals all over Europe. They devoted their full attention to what was happening in England.

Archibald Knox
Lidded jug, 1903
Tudric pewter, 15 cm in height
For Liberty & Co., London

Edward C. Burne-Jones, William Morris
Friends in need meet in the wild wood
From *The well at the world's end*
Wood engraving, 27.8 x 19 cm
Print in Chaucer Type, Kelmscott Press, Hammersmith
1896
In Morris' books, equal importance was attached to type, illustration, and bordering: Morris designed the three most important typefaces – Golden Type, Troy Type, and Chaucer Type – himself. Morris's edition of the works of Geoffrey Chaucer, with illustrations by Burne-Jones, is the embodiment of perfect craftsmanship.

A life of beauty – The dandy

Art is a bold attempt to put life in its proper place.
Art alone can protect us from the humiliating dangers
of real life.
Oscar Wilde[2]

Other tendencies besides the call for social reform had been simmering since the beginning of the century, all of which shared a common source: the contempt for a positivism which believed in progress and which seemed to be heading for absolute mediocrity in all things. Sensitive aesthetes saw their only ideal – which had always been beauty – threatened by the triviality of the bourgeois world. One feared one was living in an age of cultural demise. Yet in these supposed final death throes, a new, highly individualistic breed of person came into his own, characterized in England especially by his cultivation of uniqueness: he was the dandy, the snob, the incarnation of exquisite, male self-awareness, who in the form of George Bryan "Beau" Brummell stood up for an aristocracy of taste. Half a century later, imitators were to be found all over Europe. In short, without England there would have been no Art Nouveau. England paved the way, even if here Art Nouveau took on a very different guise from other European versions.

Art is not something to take its turn after other needs and desires have been satisfied; it is man's first desire after his basic animal instincts. Art is not a "beautification of life"; it is life itself. It is not art's job to distance us in solemn moments from the cares of everyday life; insofar as he considers himself a man of culture, man should constantly nurture his feeling for art and express it wherever possible. This was the quintessence of the new religion Ruskin preached. Like so many innovators, Ruskin believed that he should seek his ideal in the past. The Middle Ages was his Garden of Eden where people had true artistic ideals. He advocated a return to the Middle Ages, even in a social respect, and thus demonstrated peculiarities which caused him to leave art theory behind and branch into politics and sociology. Nevertheless, his social commitment was genuine and led him to form a close friendship with Thomas Carlyle (1795–1881), who gave him an insight into socio-economic issues. Ruskin's desire to put theory into practice was so strong that as an Oxford lecturer he demonstrated his views on the necessity for physical labor by becoming a working model. He joined the road-builders in London and broke stones; he swept streets and

William Morris
Windrush, wall decoration, after 1883
Printed linen, 165 x 247 cm
Morris reorganized his company, which had previously stood under the sign of medievalism, and now specialized in printed wallpaper and textiles, a step which also bought the company commercial success.
Natural plant and vegetable dyes, traditional weaving forms, and the revival of hand-printing all contributed to the high quality of the designs.

William Morris
Cover for Dante Gabriel Rossetti's *Sonnets and Lyrical Poems*
From *Pan*, No. 4, Vol. 2, 1896
Gravure
Besides his involvement with arts and crafts, Morris continued to write poetry. He also translated Icelandic sagas and Greek myths and published his own works. Morris – more consistent than any of his artistic predecessors – saw the book as an integral work of art, and consequently set up his own printing press and publishing house, the Kelmscott Press, in the London district of Hammersmith in 1891. When Morris died in 1896, he had published over 20 works under the name of Morris Prints.

trained as a house-painter and carpenter. At the same time, he traveled widely and wrote extensively. These literary works, in addition to a substantial inheritance, earned him financial independence. Yet, as he aged, he became peculiar, an oddball, lonely and embittered. If someone looked into his garden, hoping to catch a glimpse of the famous old man, he went "Boo!" and pulled a face. Nonetheless, the theories he expounded held true, despite so many inconsistencies. One of aesthete Ruskin's greatest merits will always be that he inspired his prize pupil, William Morris (1834–96), to act on his words, and that he vehemently supported the Pre-Raphaelite Brotherhood.

The Pre-Raphaelites

**People who dream in broad daylight learn about things which are never revealed to those who dream at night.
Dante Gabriel Rossetti[3]**

The initiators of the Brotherhood were the Scot William Dyce (1806–64) and Ford Madox Brown (1821–93). They wanted to unite art and ethics and to replace soulless routine and conventional arrangements with a reverent, vivid study of nature. Their model was Italian painting before Raphael. For them, Raphael had spoilt art with his superficial paintings which were the epitome of the High Renaissance. The great master of the Pre-Raphaelite Brotherhood was Dante Gabriel Rossetti (1828–82) who, starting from the naive simplicity of the quattrocento ideal, wandered ever further into a wonderful, neurotic land of dreams. Many characteristics of Pre-Raphaelite painting are mirrored in Art Nouveau: solemn composition, strong axial alignments riddled with symbolism, and the myth of woman. "Her choice beauty was completely harmonious, yet had a slight trace of melancholy. She appeared tortured by very bitter memories. Her smile was wistfully attractive."[4] This was mingled with a highly developed sensitivity for line and color.

May Morris
Screen for the Sanderson family's
drawing room, Bullerswood,
Chislehurst, Kent, ca. 1889
Silk embroidery, carved mahogany
frame, 184 x 186 cm
Made by William Morris & Co.

The link between the Pre-Raphaelites and Art Nouveau and William Morris was Edward C. Burne-Jones (1833–98) (ill. p. 29), the youngest of the Brotherhood, who transmuted symbolism to decoration: "Symbolic form becomes magnificent, sumptuous ornamentation."[5] The friendship between Morris and Burne-Jones dates to their student days at Exeter College, Oxford. Together they discovered the ideas of Ruskin and Carlyle, and medieval literature (ill. p. 26), particularly that of Geoffrey Chaucer (ca. 1343–1400) and Sir Thomas Malory (ca. 1408–71). They became committed medievalists and visited numerous old churches, including journeys to the cathedrals of northern France. These trips strengthened their conviction that they did not want to devote their life to the church, as they had originally intended, but to art: Morris chose architecture and Burne-Jones settled for painting.

William Morris – whom all Art Nouveau artists claim as their mentor – was like his spiritual father, Ruskin, in that he was repelled by capitalism. Yet he did not look to the past, but rather to the future, where people would be "art-loving creatures", free from the clutches of capitalism and of the industrial world.

William Morris and the Arts and Crafts Movement

My home is my castle.
William Morris

"He [Morris] came to arts and crafts in a rather unusual way. He got married and started to set up a home, yet found no furniture in any of the London stores that he wanted to have in his house. So he decided to make all his furniture and furnishings himself. This could be seen as the first step towards the founding of his company, William Morris and Co. Morris really had learned and practised a number of crafts, yet his company did not develop into any old handicraft business. It also produced beautiful printed books. One could safely say Morris's company reformed book printing, yet book printing is not a craft; far more, it is the first in a serial production of great style. ... William Morris, writer, painter, craftsman, and socialist, was totally dedicated to reform. This, or rather the desire for a complete change in human culture, was the bond which held his various activities together. ... The results stretch far into our century and far beyond the borders of England. ... Even the Deutscher Werkbund, founded in 1907 and still active, was shaped by Morris's influence; it was also to play a major role in extending the reaches of this influence."[6] In tune with the principles of medieval art as depicted by Ruskin in *The Stones of Venice* and in *The Seven Lamps of Architecture*, a group of artists came together for the building of Morris's Red House. "Morris commissioned Philip Webb to build him a house which, at the time it was built in 1858, was shockingly simple. And Morris tolerated this, for his house was designed to meet the simple needs of a middle-class citizen and craftsman. He decorated the rooms himself, together with his painter friend, Burne-Jones. ... Yet Morris packed as much decorative art as possible into the clear framework of the rooms. Morris's house can clearly be treated as the paradigm of his doctrines, of how art blossoms forth from the work of the craftsman and of how the craftsman's work is already more than just a basis for art. ... The first time I was there [at The Red House] was many long years ago. I was quite cheeky: I simply rang the bell. The architect's wife answered the door. ... I took the opportunity of asking her: 'Dear lady, with all due respect, what is it like living in the great man's slippers?' She replied: 'It's not like you think it is. This house is so human, the atmosphere is good and livable in that one can be quite happy here without even giving a thought to Morris. I am

Philip Webb
The Red House, entrance facade, Bexley Heath, Upton, 1858
"Morris commissioned Philip Webb to build him a house which, at the time it was built in 1858, was shockingly simple. And Morris tolerated this, for his house was designed to meet the simple needs of a middle-class citizen and craftsman. He decorated the rooms himself, together with his painter friend, Burne-Jones. ... Yet Morris packed as much decorative art as possible into the clear framework of the rooms. Morris's house can clearly be treated as the paradigm of his doctrines, of how art blossoms forth from the work of the craftsman and of how the craftsman's work is already more than just a basis for art." (Julius Posener, see note 7)

Christopher Dresser
Teapot, 1879
Plated, ebony handle, 12 cm in
height and diameter
Made by James Dixon & Sons
Christopher Dresser, a
contemporary of Morris, was the
first to produce work void of
ornamentation but with severe lines
where, with the minimum use of
materials, form and decoration were
secondary to the presence of the
actual substance, and where the actual
function of the object stood in logical
relation to the design. The result was
a formal discipline which has echoed
through the designs of the 20th
century.

especially happy for the children.' This Red
House was a manifesto. … And I tell you, it is a
real delight, a quite charming, habitable house. It
cries out against poor design, against shabbiness
and trash, where the true form is hidden beneath
decoration or where decoration makes the form
bearable."[7] With all the revolutionary socialism
Morris preached, art and the artist were both the
starting and finishing point. There is a famous
story of a friend who paid Morris a visit one
day and found him working hard at his bench.
He asked Morris: "What beautiful things are
you making there, William?" Morris answered:
"By the sweat of my brow I'm making simple
furniture that is so expensive only the wealthiest
capitalists will be able to buy it."[8]
Morris created a kind of sect, made up of the
artist craftsmen of the Arts and Crafts
Movement and their followers and customers.
This group did not wish to discredit the machine
entirely, however. On the contrary, they believed
that designing models and choosing materials
for industrial manufacturing processes should
be jobs designated to artists. This was not
considered a form of degradation, but as a new
task and challenge for the productive artist.

The Guilds

The beauty of form is nature's inner reason made visible.
Karl Friedrich Schinkel[9]

The Arts and Crafts Movement found concrete
expression in the various societies and organizations formed in England during the second half
of the 19th century. The Century Guild, a
workshop for interior design, was founded by
Arthur Heygate Mackmurdo (1851–1942) and
Selwyn Image (1849–1930) in London in 1882.
The association produced all kinds of decorative
work and it is often difficult to ascertain which
artist designed what as, in accordance with the
ideal of the medieval guild, work was presented
as the product of a cooperative. In 1884, the first
issue of *The Hobby Horse*, a journal which
publicized the Century Guild's ideals and
achievements, was published. "[This] was, at the
time of its appearance, a work quite unique of
its kind. Never before had modern print been
treated as a serious art, whose province was to
embrace the whole process, from the selection
and spacing of the type and the position of the
printed matter on the page, to the embellishment
of the book with appropriate initials and other
decorative ornaments."[10] *The Hobby Horse* was
the first of many magazines in England to aid the
popularization of the new art in England and on
the Continent (ill. p. 35). Apart from John Ruskin's
rather less successful St George's Guild, the
Century Guild was the first association of artist
craftsmen to put into practice methodically the
ideas of the Aesthetic Movement; it was the first

Christopher Dresser
Sugar crystals bowl and spoon, ca.
1875
Silver-plated metal and ebony
Sugar bowl: 12 x 17 x 9.5 cm
Spoon: 14.3 cm in length
Made by J. W. Hukin &
J. T. Heath, Birmingham
Musée d'Orsay, Paris

to turn away from the gothicizing devices initially so admired, and – as shown by Mackmurdo's graphics, for example – to produce early evidence of an almost Continental Jugendstil. The Art Worker's Guild was founded in 1883, the Home Arts and Industries Association in 1889 and the Wood Handicraft Society in 1892. Among the initiators and leading members of these organizations were Charles Robert Ashbee (1863–1942), Walter Crane (1845–1915), William Morris, Arthur Heygate Mackmurdo and Christopher Dresser (1834–1904). Dresser, a contemporary of Morris, was the first to produce work void of ornamentation but with severe lines where, with the minimum use of materials, form and decoration were secondary to the presence of the substance, and where the actual function of the object stood in logical relation to the design. The result was a formal discipline which has echoed through the designs of the 20th century (ill. opposite page, p. 37, p. 43). Dresser did not only contribute greatly to applied art in England; he was also one of the great protagonists of Japonisme, awakened by a journey to the Far East in 1876. He went on to organize the relatively short-lived Art Furniture Alliance, whose members manufactured furniture and metalwork in the Japanese style. He was also inspired by Pre-Columbian and Asian pottery and by the vocabulary of forms of Islam, India, China, classical antiquity and the Celts.

Morris & Co. – Merton Abbey – The Kelmscott Press

In 1861, the pioneering cooperative became a constitution, namely that of Morris, Marshall, Faulkner & Company. The company aimed to produce all sorts of ornamentation and ornamental objects. Its founder members were William Morris, Peter Paul Marshall (1830–1900), Charles J. Faulkner (1834–1892), Philip Webb (1831–1915), Dante Gabriel Rossetti, Ford Madox Brown and Edward C. Burne-Jones. In 1875, the original partnership was disbanded and the enterprise was renamed Morris & Co. Morris reorganized the company, which had previously stood under the sign of medievalism, and now specialized in printed wallpaper and textiles (ill. p. 27), a step which also bought the company commercial success. Natural plant and vegetable dyes, traditional weaving forms and the revival of hand-printing all contributed to the high quality of the designs. Morris's commitment to his new avenue of design was at its peak when he bought the textiles factory at Merton Abbey in

1881. The wall hangings printed here from cartoons by Burne-Jones are some of the most beautiful pieces of work produced at that time; Art Nouveau's rediscovery of the impact of pictures has its roots in these spectacular works of art (ill. p. 28, p. 29). Walter Crane and Charles Francis Annesley Voysey (1857–1941) also designed wall hangings for Morris, who expanded his company in various directions. In the 1890s, Morris bought the Pimlico furniture factory in the Netherlands and began making tiles and jewelry, also concentrating on working with glass. He was no longer interested, as at the beginning of his career, in antiquarian glass windows, but in simply decorated drinking glasses, manufactured at James Powell and Sons' workshop in Whitefriars, London. The elegant design of the thin glasses was a stark contrast to the "glass art" of his contemporaries and found few buyers. Today we can recognize in them the antecedents of modern glass design (ill. p. 33). Besides his involvement with arts and crafts, Morris continued to write. He also translated Icelandic sagas and Greek myths and published

Harry James Powell
Cup, before 1902
Blown optical flint, with thread inlay and cut decoration, 21 cm in height
British Museum, London
The elegant design of the thin glasses manufactured by James Powell and Sons workshop was in stark contrast to the "glass art" of his contemporaries and found few buyers. Today we can recognize in them the antecedents of modern glass design.

Charles Francis Annesley Voysey
Thank-you card, 1901
Three-color print on a colored background, 57 x 51.5 cm
Made by Essex & Co., Battersea, London
Whitworth Art Gallery, University of Manchester
The architect Charles Francis Annesley Voysey rejected the notion that architecture is an "occult being" and stressed that like any other form of art, architecture had its roots in good, quality work and should have some connection with everyday life, with the good life, where well-made objects are treasured. He consequently expanded his range of activities to include graphics, and furniture, carpet, wallpaper, and tool design. He was thus a true Art Nouveau artist in the best sense of the word, an *architecte d'art*, as his famous French colleague, Hector Guimard, liked to call himself.

his own works. Morris – more consistent than any of his artistic predecessors – saw the book as an integral work of art, and consequently set up his own printing press and publishing house, the Kelmscott Press, in the London district of Hammersmith in 1891. When Morris died in 1896, he had published over 20 works under the imprint of Morris Prints. Equal importance was attached to type, illustration, and bordering: Morris designed the three most important typefaces – Golden Type, Troy Type, and Chaucer Type – himself. Morris's edition of the works of Chaucer, with illustrations by Burne-Jones, is the embodiment of perfect craftsmanship, and his artists' printing press was to be a decisive contributory factor to the further development of book art (ill. p. 26).

The Dial – The Studio

The magazine *The Dial* was published by Charles Ricketts (1866–1931) and Charles Shannon (1863–1937) as early as 1889 in an attempt to bridge the gap between tradition – printing inspired by the Middle Ages – and Art Nouveau's graphic forms of expression (ill. opposite page). Woodcuts printed in *The Dial* in 1893 were expressly referred to as "an experiment in line". The magazine which took over the role of intermediary to the Continent was *The Studio*, established in London in 1893. Acting as a kind of representative for current trends and events in English art and the numerous craft guilds, *The Studio*'s influence spread throughout the whole of Europe, and as a reciprocal action introduced similar efforts in other countries to interested parties in England by publishing essays and illustrations from abroad. Special issues were

Charles Ricketts
The Great Worm
From *The Dial*, No. 1, 1889
Color lithograph, 24 x 16.5 cm
The magazine *The Dial* was published by Charles Ricketts and Charles Shannon as early as 1889 in an attempt to bridge the gap between tradition – printing inspired by the Middle Ages – and Art Nouveau's graphic forms of expression. Woodcuts printed in *The Dial* in 1893 were expressly referred to as "an experiment in line".

Arthur Heygate Mackmurdo
Cover for *The Hobby Horse*, 1893
Woodcut
In 1884, the first issue of *The Hobby Horse* was published, a journal which publicized the Century Guild's ideals and achievements. "[This] was, at the time of its appearance, a work quite unique of its kind. Never before had modern painting been treated as a serious art, whose province was to embrace the whole process, from the selection and spacing of the type and the position of the printed matter on the page, to the embellishment of the book with appropriate initials and other decorative ornaments." (Aymer Vallance, see note 10)

printed, devoted to the École de Nancy or the Wiener Werkstätte, for example. Without doubt, *The Studio* was the most important source of information on trends and developments in turn-of-the-century art. Other significant "trendsetters" were the regional and national exhibitions staged by the Arts and Crafts Exhibitions Society, which brought together individual communities of craftsmen. According to its rules, the exhibitions, accompanied by a full program of events, were intended to acquaint a broad section of the public with the leitmotiv of arts and crafts as a single entity.

Charles Robert Ashbee – The Guild and School of Handicraft

We are here to lead you back to the realities of life, to show you how to use your hands and your heads which your machines have already made over half of the population lose.
Charles Robert Ashbee[11]

The hidden problems behind all reformist and aesthetic ideas become evident if we take a look at the fate of the designer Charles Robert Ashbee, one of Morris's followers (ill. p. 39). The Guild and School of Handicraft grew out of a small workshop Ashbee set up in 1888 in London's East End. "Ashbee collected a group around him who thought the same way as he did. But they soon discovered that they could not afford to stay in London. They made very expensive luxury items. Ashbee himself was a

Charles Francis Annesley Voysey
House for A. Currer Briggs, Lake
Windermere, Lancashire, 1898
Watercolor
Victoria and Albert Museum,
London

year previously, the group had disbanded, and Ashbee, the man of reform, had had to ask some very rich people for help, hoping they would continue to support the experiment as a hobby. His endeavor was the tragicomical lid on the Arts and Crafts Movement."[13]

Ashbee was a generation younger than Morris; he had already become accustomed to "modern life" and had, as Lenin put it, been corrupted by reform. In the end, Ashbee's ideals boiled down to special rights for artists and craftsmen – very much out of step in the age of capitalism.

Ashbee's Guild was finally wiped out by Liberty's. The farmer craftsmen were unable to withstand competition from a company which manufactured quality products in series and sold them at low prices. Only really wealthy people could afford to buy objects like the ones Ashbee made, such as elegant Art Nouveau silverware. Liberty's was, quite simply, much cheaper. Yet despite this, the Guild of Handicraft was a father figure for the countless organizations functioning in the same spirit on the Continent. In 1902, Ashbee was made an honorary member of the Munich Art Academy and made a lasting impression on that institution. The Wiener Werkstätte was founded following the example of Ashbee's Guild; van de Velde acknowledges the influence of Ashbee, and the Deutscher Werkbund carried on the movement initiated by the English "socialist and artist craftsman", as Hermann Muthesius ironically called him.

silversmith."[12] (ill. opposite page). Nevertheless, the Guild's principles were based on non-capitalist theories; individual product designs were developed in group discussions. "As Ashbee couldn't stay in London, he and his friends moved in 1902 to Chipping Campden, a town in the countryside not far from Oxford. There they planned to set themselves up as farmers and craftsmen. There was, of course, also an ideology behind this exodus; or perhaps one would be more correct in saying that Ashbee slapped an ideology onto it. In any case, Ashbee developed his theory of the farmer craftsman down to the last detail in his book *Craftsmanship in Competitive Industry*, published in London in 1908. This was late indeed: it was, in fact, Ashbee's last attempt to save or rather to re-establish the group in Chipping Campden. The

Charles Francis Annesley Voysey – The house as a work of art

... he was just a craftsman who could know nothing of the power, majesty and splendor of that wonderful occult being we call architecture.
Richard William Lethaby[14]

The architect Charles Francis Annesley Voysey rejected the notion that architecture is an "occult being" and stressed that, like any other form of art, architecture had its roots in good, quality work and should have some connection with everyday life (ill. above), with the good life, where well-made objects are treasured. He consequently expanded his range of activities to include graphics, and furniture, carpet, wallpaper, and tool design. He was thus a true Art Nouveau artist in the best sense of the word, an *architecte d'art*, as his famous French colleague, Hector Guimard (1867–1942), liked to call himself. Voysey's development was that of Morris in reverse; whereas Morris went from literature

Christopher Dresser
Jug, 1874
Glazed Böttger stoneware, silver lid,
17.3 cm in height (with lid)
Made by Watcombe Pottery,
Torquay, Devon
Badisches Landesmuseum
Karlsruhe, Museum beim Markt –
Angewandte Kunst seit 1900

and crafts to concentrate also on architecture, Voysey came from architecture to explore other forms of artistic expression. The Red House Philip Webb built for Morris was undoubtedly the catalyst for the tremendously influential English Country House Movement. The Red House (ill. p. 31) was, however, seen as the architectural manifestation of the ideas of the Morris circle and not as the independent revival of house-building as had been originally intended. The next generation of artists united both factions of the movement, combining innovations in house-building and handicrafts, and came up with interior design, the flagship of Art Nouveau. It was the logical conclusion of the whole aesthetic process. Yet the architect now faced a much more complex range of tasks than his forefathers had. The house, a simple unit of accommodation, should become a work of art. Architects started to consider seriously the various functions of the house and in England were reminded of the medieval manor house in the process, of the estate as an intricate amalgam of necessary, functional buildings. The planning of Voysey's own house is highly concentrated yet architec-turally matches the simplicity of its medieval model. This simplicity heralded him as a pioneer of modern architecture. The various permutations of English manor house adopted by the Continent between 1900 and the 1930s were more suburban villa than manor house (the latter being a feature of the country), thus no longer effecting a strict cohesion of form and function. An interview with Voysey was published in the first issue of *The Studio* in 1893; its contents were greedily devoured and quickly put into

Charles Robert Ashbee
Dish with handle, 1905–06
Chased silver and amethyst, 18 cm in length (with handle), 10.7 cm in diameter
Made by the Guild of Handicraft
Badisches Landesmuseum
Karlsruhe, Museum beim Markt –
Angewandte Kunst seit 1900
"We are here to lead you back to the realities of life, to show you how to use your hands and your heads which your machines have already made over half of the population lose." (Charles Robert Ashbee, see note 11)

Left-hand page and right:
Mackay Hugh Baillie Scott
Chair with armrests, detail of the back (left page) and view of the back (right), 1900–01
Beech, ivory, mother-of-pearl, 82 x 61.8 x 39.5 cm; exhibited in Dresden in 1903 at the Deutsche Werkstätten für Handwerkskunst (German Workshops for Arts and Crafts)
Baillie Scott borrowed some of the sweeping decoration on his furniture designs from pictures by Burne-Jones and in his artistic euphoria often exceeded the level of ornamentation usual in England at that time. Baillie Scott received many commissions from the Continent, where his cheerful and seemingly less static creations had quickly met with an enthusiastic reception.

practice by avid "reformers" on the Continent. The architect Mackay Hugh Baillie Scott (1865–1945) also devoted himself to interior design, working as a furniture designer and in many other areas of arts and crafts. He borrowed some of the sweeping decoration on his furniture designs from pictures by Burne-Jones and in his artistic euphoria often exceeded the level of ornamentation usual in England at that time (ill. opposite page and right). Baillie Scott received many commissions from the Continent, where his cheerful and seemingly less static creations had quickly met with an enthusiastic reception.

Arthur Lasenby Liberty – Art and commerce

That beautiful child, art in its shining armor, will face the dragon of commercialism and slay him.
Henry van de Velde[15]

The craft guilds and brotherhoods in England vehemently opposed any form of commercialization, however thinly disguised, yet it was one of their own kind who was to commercialize arts and crafts on a scale previously unheard of. Arthur Lasenby Liberty (1843–1917) became *the* entrepreneur of Art Nouveau. Liberty had trained in business and, as the manager of the Farmer and Rogers department store in Regent Street in London, soon developed a commercial center for all kinds of arts and crafts, specializing in goods from the Orient. Spurred on by his success, and heeding the advice of his friend William Morris, Liberty opened his own store in 1875. He initially concentrated on increasing his stock of imports from the Middle and Far East and also designed his own collection of Oriental materials and wallpapers. His first team of employees was small and included Hara Kitsui, a Japanese man who was to become a source of reference for English artist craftsmen. Liberty's soon counted a growing number of English designers among its staff, including Dresser and Voysey, who reaped ideas from Liberty's Eastern Bazaar.

Impressed by the efforts of the Aesthetic Movement, Liberty tried in his own way to rejuvenate the applied arts, and his success was such that the words "Liberty" and "Art Nouveau" were often used interchangeably. The Liberty label was obtainable all over Europe, in Canada and in South Africa, sometimes in subsidiary branches of the store. Today, examples of this "modern English industrial production" fill the museum showcases of the world. The collection (or production) started out

Below:
Charles Robert Ashbee
Design for a cabinet, 1906
Watercolor, stamped "Handicraft Ltd. 1095, 31.12.1906"
The Guild of Handicraft was a father figure for the countless organizations functioning in the same spirit on the Continent. In 1902, Ashbee was made an honorary member of the Munich Art Academy and made a lasting impression on that institution. The Wiener Werkstätte was founded following the example of Ashbee's Guild; van de Velde acknowledges the influence of Ashbee, and the Deutscher Werkbund carried on the movement initiated by the English "socialist and artist craftsman", as Hermann Muthesius ironically called him.

Archibald Knox
Jug, 1903
Cymric; silver, cabochon stones, 18 cm in height
For Liberty & Co., London
Archibald Knox was Liberty's star designer. The admirer of
Celtic art took up a position in Dresser's studio, where he
encountered Japanese art and functionalism. His Cymric
designs adeptly and economically fused Celtic ornament with
functional line and contour. The Celtic name of the series did
not, however, tempt Knox into producing clumsy
reminiscences of past art.

with embroidery and textiles, rugs and carpets, and fashion and furniture; the Liberty Style quickly came into its own and reached its climax with Liberty's pewter, silverware and jewelry. Liberty's had its own silver hallmark in 1894, but it was not until the spring of 1899 that there was enough work in commission to launch the first Liberty silver series, Cymric. Liberty's formed a partnership with W. H. Haseler in Birmingham, who took over the main body of production. The new company needed creative impetus; it was crying out for talented, original designers. Rex Silver (1879–1965), then just 20, fitted into the scheme perfectly. With great verve, he produced forms and patterns which could be cheaply mass-produced without any loss of quality. Ornamental accents were added to the products in green-blue enamel instead of precious stones (ill. opposite page). Yet Liberty's star designer was Archibald Knox (1864–1933). The admirer of Celtic art took up a position in Dresser's studio, where he encountered Japanese art and functionalism. His Cymric designs adeptly and economically fused Celtic ornament with functional line and contour (ill. left, right and on p. 42). The Celtic name of the series did not, however, tempt Knox into producing clumsy reminiscences of past art.

Knox and Silver also provided designs for pewter objects and jewelry. Liberty's had been importing Art Nouveau pewter from Germany since 1899, primarily from the Kayser company in Krefeld. The material was especially suitable for "forming" the lines of the new style. The success of these imported items prompted Liberty's to create Tudric, its own line in pewter. From 1902 onwards, home-produced pewter objects began to feature in the Liberty catalogues. Their very individual design with modified Celtic forms and plant and flower motifs makes them easy to identify as Tudric pewter (ill. p. 25, p. 43).

The greatest advantage of Liberty's jewelry collection lay in the fact that it was financially accessible to a large section of the population. One did not need to be an expert in precious stones to enjoy Liberty's "gems"; the formal harmony of the object sufficed. The gold and silverwork of Frederick James Partridge (1877–1942), another Liberty designer, achieves a particularly masterly balance between symmetry and ornamentation (ill. opposite page).

Liberty's also provided innovative stimulus with its pottery and ceramic work, and especially with its wide range of imports from Asia. Renowned English manufacturers of ceramics, such as Royal Doulton Potteries (ill. bottom right), owed

Frederick James Partridge
Dragonfly necklace, ca. 1900
Gold, enamel, *plique-à-jour* enamel and moonstones, 40 cm in length
Sold by Liberty & Co., London
The greatest advantage of Liberty's jewelry collection lay in the fact that it was financially accessible to a large section of the population. One did not need to be an expert in precious stones to enjoy Liberty's "gems"; the formal harmony of the object sufficed. The gold and silverwork of Frederick James Partridge, another Liberty designer, achieves a particularly masterly balance between symmetry and ornamentation.

(Attributed to) Archibald Knox
Clock, 1903
Cymric; silver-plated copper, mother-of-pearl, lapis lazuli, 24.5 cm in height
For Liberty & Co., London

their international acclaim to Liberty's and its brilliant sales and marketing system. Liberty's was also the best promoter of Dresser's favored Clutha glass (ill. opposite page).

Nonetheless, there were designers who achieved recognition without the Liberty machine. These include the rather unconventional Martin brothers. Their commercial success was brought about by their "vegetable ware", containers and table-ware in the shape of vegetables with "fruity" decoration. These sales triumphs enabled the four brothers – Robert Wallace (1843–1923), Walter (1859–1912), Edwin (1860–1915) and Charles (1846–1910) Martin – to open their own store and studio in London in 1879 and manufacture objects according to their own whims and fancies. Besides typical Art Nouveau ceramics, the brothers also molded birds and animals from the bizarre to the grotesque and heterogeneous beings wildly alienated from their intended purpose, such as owls as tobacco jars (ill. left). Amorphous shapes were characterized and reduced – a trait typical of Art Nouveau graphics. The Martin brothers certainly had a sense of humor – black humor which was very British.

(Attributed to) Archibald Knox
Vase, 1899
Cymric; silver, enamel, cabochon
stones
19.5 cm in height
For Liberty & Co., London

Royal Doulton Potteries
Potpourri "Sung" vase, ca. 1900
Stoneware, underglass painting,
flambé, with wooden base and lid,
28.3 cm in height
Designed by Arthur Eaton
Liberty's also provided innovative
stimulus with its pottery and
ceramic work, and especially with its
wide range of imports from Asia.
Renowned English manufacturers of
ceramics, such as Royal Doulton
Potteries, owed their international
acclaim to Liberty's and its brilliant
sales and marketing system.

Martin Brothers
Owl, tobacco jar, April 1899
Ceramic with colored salt glaze, 32 cm in height
Besides typical Art Nouveau ceramics, the Martin brothers
also molded birds and animals from the bizarre to the
grotesque, wildly alienated from their intended purpose, such
as owls as tobacco jars. Amorphous shapes were characterized
and reduced – a trait typical of Art Nouveau graphics. The
Martin brothers certainly had a sense of humor – black
humor which was very British.

Walter Crane – Line and form

Outline drawing is, so to speak, the be-all and end-all of art. It is the oldest form of expression for civilizations on the first level of culture and for every child, and has been preserved for its powers of characterization and expression and as the highest attestation to the art of drawing by the most outstanding artists of all time.
Walter Crane[16]

Apart from the various groups and associations which together made up the Art Nouveau movement, it was basically the efforts of two artists, Walter Crane and Aubrey Vincent Beardsley (1872–98), which helped shape and further the new style. Both men began their otherwise totally adverse careers as followers of Morris and the Pre-Raphaelites. They were also fascinated by the modernist tendencies apparent in the work of William Blake (1757–1827). Blake, the romantic symbolist, had at the end of the 18th century begun to pave the way for a number of trends in art; he challenged the sterile stylistic tendencies of the day with his artistic ensembles and with the rhythmic lines of his paintings and illustrations, later also a feature of crafts designs.

Blake's floating, dreamy figures are caught up in twirling arabesques like drifts of smoke; his bequest, his sweeping line, was adopted by Art Nouveau as its hallmark. This affinity with lines, the way they intertwine and weave densely across surfaces, has been an exceptional quality of English art since the Celts.

Walter Crane belonged to a generation between the Pre-Raphaelites and Art Nouveau and was the mentor of the entire movement. A prominent theoretician, his writings were translated into many languages and exerted – together with his wide range of works – much influence in America and Europe. From 1888 onwards he was the leading member of the Arts and Crafts Exhibitions Society, having a strong hand in the organization of their international program, and was one of the most dedicated members of Morris's Kelmscott Press. Crane's tract, *Line and Form* (London 1900), is considered one of the most important ideological works written by an artist at the turn of the century. "Here we seem to be able to detect a kind of progression in the expressive possibilities of the line – the poles at both ends; the horizontal and the vertical with all

Christopher Dresser
Jug, 1880
Clutha glass with inclusions of silver leaf, 18 cm in height
Made by James Cooper & Sons, Glasgow
For his glassware Dresser used Clutha glass, developed by the Glasgow company Cooper & Sons in the 1890s and named after the River Clyde in Scotland (Clutha in Old English). This green, turquoise-brown or gray-colored glass mass mixed with copper crystals and streaked, striped or peppered with small bubbles is reminiscent of the river's dull waters.

(Attributed to) Archibald Knox
Bowl for confectionery with glass dish, 1903
Tudric pewter, Clutha glass, 17 cm in height
Made by W. H. Haseler, Birmingham
Sold by Liberty & Co., London
The success of Liberty's imported items prompted the store to create Tudric, its own line in pewter. From 1902 onwards, home-produced pewter objects began to feature in the Liberty catalogues. Their very individual design with their modified Celtic forms and plant and flower motifs makes them easy to identify as Tudric pewter.

kinds of gradation and transition between them; the line of waves which lends expression to the strong, upward spiral, the meander, the flowing line approaching the horizontal: or the sharp contrast and clash of right angles. The artist can without doubt unleash a great expressive force in his mastery of the pure line. Indeed, the line, as I mentioned above, is a language, a highly sensitive and expressive language with many dialects, which can be adjusted to suit any

purpose and which is indeed imperative for all kinds of line drawing."[17] (ill. p. 47). With his words, Crane seems to be describing the true essence of Art Nouveau, and indeed he lived the ideal of the times in his work. Crane was the personification of the artist-designer: he was a painter, graphic artist, illustrator, and book artist; he designed textiles, glass windows, ceramics (ill. p. 47), jewelry, and posters. Crane loved Florentine quattrocento art, a love he shared with

Walter Crane
Neptune's Horses, 1892
Oil on canvas, 86 x 215 cm
Bayerische
Staatsgemäldesammlungen, Neue
Pinakothek, Munich
Crane's figures are an inimitable incarnation of the spirit of the age in their fairy-tale, dream-like metamorphosis. The omnipotence of Nature is allegorical in its transcription and almost decorative in its elucidation. Neptune's horses

move both within the confines of the balanced lines and at the same time seem to break free, giving strength to the picture's almost surreal subject. The wave motif illustrates the proximity of Crane's painting to Japanese graphics. Yet whereas Hokusai's famous wave in his *The Great Wave – In the Hollow of the Wave off the Coast at Kanagawa* remains firmly rooted to the surface, Crane's wave seems to come alive and burst its bonds.

his friend Burne-Jones, and was deeply impressed by the colored woodcuts from Japan. "The Japanese, who draw with brushes, have become accustomed to executing drawings without the use of preliminary sketches; the charm of their work is evoked first and foremost by the piquant freshness of their brushstrokes which can only be affected using their direct methods. Their main aim is to create a completely intimate relationship between the

eye and the hand, so that the latter accurately records what the former perceives."[18] It is precisely this combination of stylistic methods and original symbolic language which generates the ethereal effect of Crane's book illustrations, paintings, and tapestries. His figures are an inimitable incarnation of the spirit of the age in their fairy-tale, dream-like metamorphosis (ill. p. 46). The omnipotence of Nature is allegorical in its transcription and almost decorative in its elucidation. Neptune's horses move both within the confines of the balanced lines and at the same time seem to break free, giving strength to the picture's almost surreal subject. The wave motif illustrates the proximity of Crane's painting to Japanese graphics. Yet whereas Hokusai's famous wave in his *The Great Wave – In the Hollow of the Wave off the Coast at Kanagawa* remains firmly rooted to the surface, Crane's wave seems to come alive and burst its bonds (ill. p. 44–45). "Walter Crane [was] a master of line and primarily a genius of decoration, who thus seemed to have more of an effect on handicrafts than on painting … [He] was a born teller of fairy tales…"[19]

James Abbott McNeill Whistler – Mists of Light

Only truly good painting can give children rosy cheeks.
John Ruskin[20]

Another of the great inspiring forces living at the turn of the century was James Abbott McNeill Whistler (1834–1903), who also alienated the impressions of nature in his paintings, albeit in a completely different way from Crane. Whistler's influence was restricted mainly to painting, although he occasionally dabbled in crafts, designing house interiors for his friends. His ability to transgress this line probably stems among other things from his admiration for Japanese art, which is not bound by dignity within artistic creativity. In Whistler's work we can recognize the two-dimensionality of

Walter Crane
Illustration for *A Floral Fantasy in an Old English Garden* (detail),
London 1899
Autotype, 19.9 x 14 cm

Walter Crane
Skoal (Cheers!), vase, 1898–1900
Ceramic, painted in ruby red,
23.5 cm in height
Made by Man & Cie
Iparmüvészeti Múzeum, Budapest
Crane was the personification of the
artist-designer: he was a painter,
graphic artist, illustrator, and book
artist; he designed textiles, glass
windows, ceramics, jewelry, and
posters. He loved Florentine
quattrocento art, a love he shared
with his friend Burne-Jones, and
was deeply impressed by the colored
woodcuts from Japan.

Japanese surface ornament in the contours of his figures and in his shallow silhouettes, which vanish in the diffuse light like ghosts (ill. p. 48). A cosmopolitan, equally at home in America, France or England, Whistler refused to join one of the guilds. He alienated his objects to such an extent – as an opponent of anything natural he concentrated on portraying the products of his imagination – that Ruskin condemned Whistler's pictures as sorry, inartistic efforts: according to Ruskin, painting which dispersed all lines and objects was not art. Whistler lost a court case against his critic, but held his sway on Art Nouveau painting. Art Nouveau gradually shirked any form of middle-class, academic aesthetics and became a mood medium. "London fog was nonexistent until art discovered it,"[21] said Oscar Wilde, meaning Whistler. Like Wilde, a bogey of the middle classes, full of coxcomb elegance, Whistler was the embodiment of that English phenomenon: the dandy.

Oscar Wilde and Aubrey Vincent Beardsley – The virtue of vice

As the dawn broke, Pierrot fell into his last sleep. Then upon tiptoe, silently up the stair, noiselessly into the room came the comedians Arlecchino, Pantaleone, il Dottore, and Columbina, who with much love carried away upon their shoulders, the white-frocked clown of Bergamo; whither, we know not.
Aubrey Vincent Beardsley[22]

Oscar Wilde (1854–1900) and Aubrey Vincent Beardsley, the darlings of society for only a brief period in their lives, died as outsiders. Yet especially Beardsley's short life seems to reflect all those elements which aesthetically and artistically molded the turn of the century. The dandy, that hero of total artificiality, icily rejecting anything natural and striving for ultimate self-portrayal and absolute originality in an age when rigid hierarchical patterns were beginning to give way to democratic uniformity, was an identity

Walter Crane
Flora's Feast, 1892
Illustration for Flora's Feast / A
Masque of / Flowers / Penned &
Pictured / by / Walter Crane,
25 cm in height
Cassell & Co. Ltd., London – Paris
– Melbourne
"The artist can without doubt
unleash a great expressive force in
his mastery of the pure line. Indeed,
the line, as I mentioned above, is a
language, a highly sensitive and
expressive language with many
dialects, which can be adjusted to
suit any purpose and which is indeed
imperative for all kinds of line
drawing." (Walter Crane, see
note 17)

James Abbott McNeill Whistler
Symphony in White, No. 2: The young white girl, 1864
Oil on canvas, 77.5 x 51.1 cm
Tate Gallery, London
In Whistler's work we can recognize Japanese surface ornamentation in the contours of his figures and in his shallow silhouettes, which vanish in the diffuse light like ghosts. A cosmopolitan, equally at home in America, France or England, Whistler refused to join one of the guilds. He alienated his objects to such an extent – as an opponent of anything natural he concentrated on portraying the products of his imagination – that Ruskin condemned Whistler's pictures as sorry, inartistic efforts: according to Ruskin, painting which dispersed all lines and objects was not art.

Aubrey Vincent Beardsley
Cover illustration for *The Yellow Book*, No. 2, July 1894
Line block

Page 51:
Aubrey Vincent Beardsley
Climax, 1893
Illustration for Oscar Wilde's *Salome*, 1893, plate XV
Line etching, 22.7 x 16.3 cm
Beardsley's art was too cool and classic to pay homage to the floral ornament alone. From the Japanese he had learnt to create an effect using only two dimensions without even glancing at the third.

Beardsley claimed as his own. He was not as committed to social matters as were many artists in England at the time; he was more a follower of *l'art pour l'art*, art for art's sake, predestined to do so by the aestheticism and decadence of the decade in which he lived. He had more in common with Baudelaire's *Les Fleurs du mal* than with the writings of William Morris; his theory of beauty was, like that of Baudelaire, an aesthetics of evil. "I have one aim – the grotesque. If I am not grotesque, I am nothing."[23] He even stylized and ridiculed sexuality. After having one of his teeth pulled out, Beardsley reputedly remarked: "Even my teeth are somewhat phallic". Beardsley's critics dismissed dandyism, claiming it would exhaust itself in its own superficiality and could never be conjoined with creative artistry, yet this cannot be applied to Beardsley. He was an artist of bewildering and unbelievable creative power, and in his short lifetime he managed to conceive a completely new style of drawing which was fundamental to the development of Art Nouveau and which is strongly echoed by all spheres of graphic design today.

Fred Hyland
Ophelia
From *The Savoy*, 1896
Autotype, 19.5 x 14.3 cm

Bottom right:
Aubrey Vincent Beardsley
The Wagnerians
From *The Yellow Book*, No. 3, October 1894
No. 3 of four drawings, 20.6 x 17.8 cm
The Yellow Book, published by John Lane, owes its existence to Beardsley's friendship with the author Henry Harland. The monthly publication enjoyed great success, partly caused by criticism of its supposedly lewd depictions. "London turned yellow overnight," wrote essayist Sir Max Beerbohm after the publication of the first issue in 1894 (see note 27).

Aubrey Vincent Beardsley: Symbolic lines and the eloquence of black

English Art Nouveau is surrounded by the thin air and pale light of an imaginary Elysium; its life is as if it has been tapped by Merlin's wand, bewitched into becoming static and silent.
Robert Schmutzler[24]

Beardsley offered a new understanding of the frame and pictorial plane, where the decorative line cutting across flat surfaces replaces the three-dimensionalism of reality (ill. p. 24). "All [Beardsley's] depictions lack space and perspective, based for the most part on the contrast of black-and-white surfaces which meet in symbolic lines. These lines can curl in an elegant arabesque around the figures, but can also harshly isolate the figure from its surroundings. Yet it is always that Art Nouveau line, later so famous, and so much more than a mere outline: it expresses the character and being of the figure it has drawn, and does not simply define the figure's contours but is a composite part of it."[25] Beardsley not only united the supposed paradox of artist and dandy, he also made artistic use of his dandyism, of the laws of elegance and distinction so inherent in his drawings. The dandy's motto is everything but nature – a motto which led straight to the black-

and-white style of Beardsley's drawings. Oscar Wilde thus said: "… that a later epoch will ascribe in particular the discovery of the beauty of the color black to the 19th century … The light of the sun only attains its full brilliance in contrast with black."[26]

With the aim of creating something new, Beardsley's art was fed on the stylistic currents and trends of his day. The swan song of the Pre-Raphaelites, whom Beardsley greatly admired, already echoed with the spiral tones of Art Nouveau's cantilena. Yet Beardsley's art was too cool and classic to pay homage to the floral ornament alone. From the Japanese he had learnt to create an effect using only two dimensions without even glancing at the third. Beardsley undoubtedly found the sexual emancipation of Japanese *shunga* [Spring pictures], a collection of erotic woodcuts, an enlightening contrast to prudish, Victorian England; one visitor tells of the shameless prints of Japanese courtesans with their lovers, engaged in complicated acrobatics, which adorned Beardsley's walls.

Genius cannot always be linked to certain influences, yet Beardsley's uniqueness is the result of a congenial mixture of various artists and styles: Art Nouveau, Burne-Jones, Whistler, Greek vase painting, Mantegna and Botticelli, Rococo engravings, and Japonisme. To the great disgust of established art enthusiasts, the first issue of *The Studio* was dedicated to the

drawings of an unknown 21-year-old. This scandal secured Beardsley a certain popularity, enabling him to abandon his job as a clerk and devote himself entirely to art. In the wake of that first issue, he received many commissions for book illustrations. Another periodical for art and literature, *The Yellow Book* published by John Lane, owes its existence to Beardsley's friendship with the author Henry Harland. The monthly publication enjoyed great success, partly caused by criticism of its supposedly lewd depictions. "London turned yellow overnight," wrote essayist Sir Max Beerbohm[27] after the publication of the first issue in 1894 (ill. p. 49). Despite this, Beardsley was dismissed as art editor in 1895. He then teamed up with the lawyer-turned-bookseller Leonard Smithers, who dealt mainly in pornography and erotica, and began publishing a rival journal, *The Savoy*, in 1896 (ill. p. 49). The *Sunday Times* praised the new publication as a "Yellow Book" devoid of teething problems. Soon afterwards, Beardsley was forced to abandon his work with *The Savoy* due to tuberculosis of the lung, now at an advanced stage.

Earlier, the production of a Wilde and Beardsley collaboration, *Salome* (ill. opposite page), in 1893 was the perfect consolidation of *fin-de-siècle* art. The synesthetic language of Symbolism speaks out from each illustration, from each written word. Beauty and dreams are depicted by way of an aesthetic mirroring of perversion and ugliness.

Sometimes he attains pure beauty, has an unadulterated vision, as in the best illustrations of Salome … At a first glance it is a devilish beauty which is not even a contradiction in itself. There is a constant awareness of sin, but it is sin which is first transfigured and then revealed by beauty. This sin is fully conscious of its existence, conscious of its inability to escape from itself, and which demonstrates with its ugliness which law it has broken. His [Beardsley's] world is one of ghosts, where the desire to satisfy mortal feelings, the desire for infinity, has exceeded all bounds and has bewitched these gentle, quivering feelings, longing for flight, so that they have become hopelessly rigid. They have sensitivity of the soul and that physical sensitivity which bleeds their veins and paralyzes them in their sumptuous state of dreaminess. They are too thoughtful ever to be truly natural, ever to blossom completely in flesh or spirit … Beardsley is the satirist of an age without conviction and, like Baudelaire, he cannot refrain from depicting Hell without referring to Paradise as a counterpart. He uses the same methods as Baudelaire, a kind of exaggeration, which it would be uncritical to describe as insincere. In that terrible proclamation of evil which he calls The Mysterious Rose-Garden, the angel with the lantern and feathered sandals walking among the cascading roses is whispering more than just "sweet sin" … Because he loves beauty, he is gripped by the degradation of beauty; because he captures the superiority of virtue so completely, vice can seize hold of him. And in complete contrast to the "respectable" satirists of his day and age, whose wit and intellect is exhausted in the depiction of a drunkard propped up against a lamp post, or in the lady who pays a false compliment in a salon, he is a satirist who captures the true essence of things. It is always unfulfillment of the soul and not of the flesh which stares out from those greedy eyes … They look so very sad, because they have seen beauty yet have erred from its path.

Arthur Symons, *Aubrey Beardsley's Depictions of Women*, in *Ver Sacrum*, 1903.

The blossoming of interior design
Glasgow

Margaret Macdonald Mackintosh
Tea room menu, 1901, autotype, 20.9 x 10.3 cm
The main characteristics of Anglo-Saxon form – unnaturally thin artistic figures, elongated stripes and rows in architecture, that is, stretched and linearized proportions – were very much alive in Glasgow in unbroken tradition.

Hill House is sheer poetry. I would even go as far as saying that, in our century, no other house has been built which emanates as much poetry as Hill House.
Julius Posener[1]

Elegant Scottish proportions

On the basis of their work, comparing Charles Rennie Mackintosh (1868–1928) and Antoni Gaudí (1852–1926) – even mentioning them in the same breath – seems not just erroneous, but impossible. Yet both these architects are first-class examples of Art Nouveau and have often served to appease its critics and opponents. One a Scot and the other a Catalan, both artists unleashed their creative powers far removed from the centers of the movement, although their work was shaped by contemporary trends which were also the stylistic basis for Berlin, Brussels, London, and Paris. As with Gaudí's Catalan elements, it is Scotland which gives Mackintosh's architecture its color. It is not known if he was a nationalist like Gaudí; his work does, however, suggest that he was an ardent Scot. Both Gaudí and Mackintosh belong to the Art Nouveau movement, an artistic reaction to the stylistic confusion which preceded it. With Mackintosh, we learn of his apotheosis; with Hill House, we experience how Mackintosh gloriously masters not just Art Nouveau, but also all other influences.

Charles Rennie Mackintosh – Purified architecture

He is a purifier in the field of architecture.
Ludwig Mies van der Rohe[2]

I knew the School of Art in Glasgow and saw it as the beginning of a breakthrough in architecture.
Walter Gropius[3]

The Glasgow School of Art (ill. p. 55), Mackintosh's most famous building, belongs to architecture and architects, or rather, to building and the future. This manifesto of simplicity, warding off all false pomp with its block-like, self-contained composition, has become a model for future generations of architects. It is interesting to note that in the first plans for the School of Art, the upper border demonstrated a rather unarchitectural Art Nouveau wave design, whereas the completed building restricts all Art Nouveau elements to decorative metalwork on the windows of the top floor. However radical and sober the building may appear, its overall architectural design is extremely varied; its decor is not merely an ornamental afterthought but harmonizes with the building, and even breathes life into it. The north facade of the Glasgow School of Art is an entire catalogue of surprising moments which give the structure a certain dynamism. "This front actually faces the street, yet the street isn't wide enough to allow one to stand opposite the School in such a way that one can check the front's symmetry or asymmetry. One looks *along* the facade. And looking at it sideways on, the slightly larger depth of the upper windows, twice as high as those on the ground floor, and the heavy sculpturing of the entrance building are far more impressive than any other dimensional relations in the surface projection of the front elevation."[4]

Charles Rennie Mackintosh
High-backed chair, Hill House 1, 1903
Stained ash, 141 x 41 x 35 cm

Mackintosh was a keen reader of the writings of Charles Francis Annesley Voysey and William Richard Lethaby (1857–1931) in which a ceremonial and hollow form of architecture was rejected. Theirs was one of the influences to affect Mackintosh, the influence of a new, everyday kind of building, the need which grew out of the English Country House Movement for a simple house to become a work of art. One should be aware of the fact that a house is something to be used and does not become a building only when decorated with pointed arches and pillars; it gains beauty and dignity from being lived in, from its function as a place of residence. It should also embody the service it fulfills, namely in its structure. Thus it was both the English manor house and so-called "anonymous" Scottish architecture which inspired Mackintosh. Windyhill is a model of this amalgamation of Scottish and English manor house. The severe facade of this functional building is covered with gray harling, Scottish roughcast plastering, and crowned by gables and chimneys typical of the country (ill. p. 56, p. 57). A rounded external wall encloses the staircase bay which was later to become a feature of 1920s architecture, such as demonstrated by Le Corbusier (1887–1965) in his Villa Savoie in Poissy. It was this synthesis of tradition and modernity which greatly impressed post-Mackintosh architects, and eventually offered them a way of building practically yet artistically. It was the Scottish "vernacular" of Windyhill architecture and Hill House which impressed Hermann Muthesius (1861–1927) on his visit to Scotland; he positively enthused about the unconventional language of Mackintosh's interiors. "Once the interior attains the status of a work of art, that is, when it is intended to embody aesthetic values, the artistic effect must obviously be heightened to the utmost. The Mackintosh group does this…"[5] The blossoming of interior design, a recurring theme in Art Nouveau, and here especially interior design by the Mackintosh circle, was full of magic and mysticism. Lethaby called for this magic and mysticism and believed it possible – sometime in the distant future. Muthesius was quite correct to speak of the Mackintosh group, for architecture and architects alone were not enough to lend form to this "poetry of interiors". Other components were gradually amalgamated which resulted in the Glasgow Style, shaped by artists with their own distinctive ideas, and with Margaret Macdonald Mackintosh (1865–1933) at the helm. Of his wife, Mackintosh himself said: "Margaret has genius, I have only talent."[6]

Poetry of Interiors – The Macdonald Sisters

The body was nowhere to be found. Instead of the body, there was a flower, its center as yellow as saffron, surrounded by white petals.
Ovid[7]

Mackintosh, Herbert MacNair and the two Macdonald sisters, Margaret and Frances – later The Four – got to know Aubrey Vincent Beardsley, Voysey and Jan Theodoor Toorop (1858–1928), through the magazine *The Studio*. It is indisputable that these acquaintances had a spontaneous yet long-lasting effect on the group. The Symbolist ingredients, threaded through The Four's work like a leitmotiv, probably stem from the Pre-Raphaelites, enriched, however, by the influence of the Belgian lyricist Maurice Maeterlinck (1862–1949), introduced to the group by Toorop. "[These are] tall, incorporeal figures dissolved or woven into delicate webs of stems and threads, with only their heads human or saint-like, slightly inclined, each like the next, with closed eyes and dark, cascading hair – [such are the] figures in a frieze, pale green and pink, for Cranston's Tea Rooms in Glasgow, designed by Charles Rennie Mackintosh and his wife Margaret in about 1900. These same thin sticks make up the strange chair with its painfully high back, more than twice the height of the seat. And the thin lead strips sprawled across the mirror, surrounding pale violet surfaces or nothing at all, free contours which enclose nothing, as if drawn by a tired hand. The cupboards are white and all colors are pale, washed-out. All forms and objects, whether for use or for ornamentation, are slender, thin-boned, fragile, without flesh, dreamily spiritual – a singular ghostly but not unsensual sphere, abstracted, it would appear, and filtered from the angelic figures of Pre-Raphaelite forebears: that is the physiognomy of the Scottish School."[8] The main characteristics of Anglo-Saxon form – unnaturally thin artistic figures, elongated stripes and rows in architecture, that is, stretched and linearized proportions – were very much alive in Glasgow in unbroken tradition (ill. p. 52). The rolling Celtic rhythm of lines breaks up the almost cubic severity. In its basic conception, the so-called Glasgow Style existed before The Four popularized it in Europe and embellished it with external influences. The "blending of a puritanically severe practical form with an almost lyrical disappearance of any useful value"[9] is deeply rooted both in Celtic mythology, handed down through the ages, and in the ghostly symbolic

Charles Rennie Mackintosh
Poster for *The Scottish Musical Review*, 1896
Color lithograph, 246 x 101.5 cm
Many draft versions preceded Mackintosh's finished product – the fantastic yet tectonic linear structure is monumentally captured on paper. Some of Mackintosh's most beautiful interior designs were for music rooms. They resemble symphonic arrangements, decorations with thin, vibrating lines like the strings of a harp spread out across the walls, floating over pale splashes of color filling the remaining surfaces.

Charles Rennie Mackintosh
Glasgow School of Art,
167 Renfrew Street, Glasgow,
1896–99 and 1906–09
West facade, 1907–09
However radical and sober the building may appear, its overall architectural design is extremely varied; its decor is not merely an ornamental afterthought but harmonizes with the building, and even breathes life into it. The north facade of the Glasgow School of Art is an entire catalogue of surprising moments which give the structure a certain dynamism.

Charles Rennie Mackintosh
Windyhill Cottage, Kilmacolm,
Renfrewshire, 1900
Perspective drawing, pencil and pen,
28.9 x 57.2 cm

atmosphere of the Scottish moors. The Macdonald sisters' early work includes water-colours with ghostly figures and mystical ornaments from the treasure trove of Celtic legend. These characteristics earned them the nickname "Spook School". The physiognomy and the physical, however, remain sketchy in substance and are rather Pre-Raphaelite. For Dante Gabriel Rossetti, the epitome of the Pre-Raphaelite artist, the female body was the symbol of all beauty, color and thought. He spiritualized the body, for him nothing more than the soul's clothing, and created gentle, graceful figures, airy, floating beings. All sensuousness was concentrated on the mouth, on full, almost greedy lips, in counterpoint with the un-fathomable eyes which seemed to reflect the universe. "History has known no art which represents such an extreme fusion of quivering eroticism and spiritual nobility since Leonardo da Vinci."[10]

The uniqueness and fascination of Scottish Art Nouveau lies in the coupling of almost mannered figurines with the non-representationalism of its architecture and furniture design. Angelic statuettes slot into the architectural grid, their weightless heads like halos rounding off an almost esoteric ornament, made up of the mere husks of bodies and garments and garnished with flowers (ill. p. 60). These celestial beings, created by the Macdonald sisters in metal, embroidery, mosaics, and jet pearls (ill. p. 66), "haunt" furniture, wall paneling, and material. Yet the figures always find their counterpart in the intersecting lattice lines of the furniture, architecture, and layout of the room. The critics believed that the mysticism and parallel asceti-cism of this Glasgow art form was of heathen origin and not serious in its intentions. The London Arts and Crafts Movement dismissed it as totally "unBritish" fantasy; the Continent, its senses sharpened by Symbolism, was more receptive.

The Four – The Glasgow Style

Never before has our utilitarianism had opinions voiced on it so sharply and arrogantly.
Julius Meier-Graefe[11]

In 1896, the year of William Morris's death, the Scots took part in an exhibition in London for the first time at the invitation of the Arts and Crafts Society. They were mercilessly dismissed as aesthetes, at best causing astonishment among the observers. Despite this, the editor of *The Studio* decided to travel to Glasgow; the contacts he forged were to be of great significance for The Four. However, Mackintosh's architectural biography does not begin with the Glasgow Style. In 1884, he joined John Hutchison's architects' office and a few years later, in 1889, started work with the architects John Honeyman & Keppie, who had just set up their own partnership. His

first commissions and the numerous prizes he won in competitions enabled Mackintosh to spend time studying in Italy in 1891 and to travel to Paris, Brussels, Antwerp, and London. He became friends with Herbert MacNair (1869–1945) a fellow employee at the new architects' office, a friendship which was to prove extremely fruitful for Art Nouveau. They went to evening classes together at the Glasgow School of Art, where they met the Macdonald sisters, and the congenial bond of The Four was formed, both on a professional and personal level (MacNair was later to marry Frances Macdonald [1874–1921]. In 1897, Mackintosh's design for the Glasgow School of Art was approved and the memory of The Four's rejection in London quickly faded. Building officially started in May 1898; by December of the same year the art school was almost finished. The western half of the building

Charles Rennie Mackintosh
Windyhill Cottage, Kilmacolm, Renfrewshire, 1900–01
Mackintosh was inspired by both the English manor house and so-called "anonymous" Scottish architecture. Windyhill is a model of this amalgamation of Scottish and English manor house. The severe facade of this functional building is covered with gray harling, Scottish roughcast plastering, and crowned by gables and chimneys typical of the country.

Charles Rennie Mackintosh
Chair for Miss Cranston's Argyle
Street Tea Rooms, Glasgow,
1896–97
Dark-stained oak, recessed rush seat
(reconstruction uses horsehair)
137 x 47.7 x 47 cm
The chair – still a famous piece of
furniture today – contributes to the
overall design of the room with its
high back. Although the chairs
Mackintosh designed for the Argyle
Street Tea Rooms are obviously in
keeping with the tradition of the
Arts and Crafts Movement and bear
the influence of Voysey, they also
display all the characteristics of
Mackintosh's individual style.

Charles Rennie Mackintosh
Ingram Street Tea Rooms,
Glasgow,
View from the gallery of the White
Luncheon Room, 1900, 1907,
1910–11
Reproduction from a contemporary
photograph
The nonconformist Miss Catherine
Cranston became one of
Mackintosh's main clients. She was
a strong supporter of Glasgow's
Temperance Movement and decided
to open tea salons to counterbalance
the city's pubs. Here her guests
would be served in elegant, cultivated
surroundings. Her investment paid
off, as her exclusive Tea Rooms soon
attracted a large clientele.

EMPFANGS···RAUM und MUSIK···ZIMMER PANELS VON MARGARET MACDONALD MACKINTOSH

Below:
Charles Rennie Mackintosh
Dressing chair for Miss Cranston's
blue bedroom, Hous'Hill, Nitshill,
Glasgow, 1904
Oak with upholstered gold-colored
seat, 56 cm high, 38 cm deep
In 1903, Miss Cranston
commissioned Mackintosh to
completely renovate her country
house, Hous'Hill, and allowed him
great freedom in his work. The
many pieces of furniture Mackintosh
designed for this house in particular
illustrate the vast compendium of his
ideas and at the same time point
toward a change in his style to
include a greater constructive
element.

was revised and finally completed between 1907 and 1909. "Building in his [Mackintosh's] hands becomes an abstract art, both musical and mathematical … Here the abstract artist is primarily concerned with the shaping of volume and not of space, of solids not voids."[12] Music did indeed play an important role for Mackintosh, whose vision of a complete work of art was a synesthetic one: he aimed to create an ensemble of the senses. In 1896, after rejecting many draft versions, Mackintosh designed a poster for the *Scottish Musical Review*: the fantastic yet tectonic linear structure is monumentally captured on paper. Some of Mackintosh's most beautiful interior designs were for music rooms. They resemble symphonic arrangements, decorations with thin, vibrating lines like the strings of a harp spread out across the walls, floating over pale splashes of color filling the remaining surfaces. Fritz Waerndorfer, later one of the co-founders and great patron of the Wiener Werkstätte, commissioned Mackintosh to design a music salon in 1901 (completed in

1921). Mackintosh's admiration for the Belgian poet Maeterlinck led him to describe the salon as a living space "for the souls of Maurice Maeterlinck's six princesses". Earlier, in 1900, Waerndorfer had traveled to Glasgow to invite Mackintosh to take part in the Eighth Secession Exhibition in Vienna, which opened on November 4, 1900. The Four's appearance in Vienna became something of a sensation. The Scottish Room was contrived as a tea salon, with all the furniture positioned in such a way that the middle of the room was empty. A vase with flowers arranged *ikebana*-style (a homage to Japan) was the only centerpiece. These "spiritual rooms" did not merely instill a general enthusiasm, even emotion, in the onlookers; Viennese artists also began to work The Four's ideas into their own designs. Mackintosh's friendship with Josef Hoffmann (1870–1956) dates to the Secession (the movement away from traditional Viennese style), as does the growing displeasure with the cliché forms of official Secession art which led to the founding of the Wiener Werkstätte. Besides

Charles Rennie Mackintosh
Reception room and music room, 1901
Sketch of the interior, competition entry for the *Haus eines Kunstfreundes* [House for an Art Lover]
From *Meister der Innenkunst*, II, 1901–02
Indian ink, silver, gold, 21 x 33 cm
According to Hermann Muthesius, who wrote an introduction to *Meister der Innenkunst*, Mackintosh fulfilled the entry conditions of the competition like no other with his design for the *Haus eines Kunstfreundes*: it was radically modern and uncompromisingly aesthetic

Hoffmann, the work of many other Art Nouveau artists such as Joseph Maria Olbrich (1867–1908), Peter Behrens (1868–1940), Frank Lloyd Wright (1869–1959) and the De Stijl artists, reveals the legacy of Scottish forms. Many major exhibitions contributed to the publicizing of the Glasgow Style. As well as participating in the International Exhibition of Modern Decorative Art in Turin in 1902 and their earlier triumphant success at the World Exposition in Paris in 1900, The Four were also represented at exhibitions in Munich, Budapest, Dresden, Venice, and Moscow. Although the group considered they were confronted with very disadvantageous exhibiting conditions in Turin, they managed to produce a masterpiece. They manufactured huge, stenciled banners as orientation for the public and thus created an attractive entrance to the Scottish section. Behind the banners, the rather feminine Rose Boudoir in pink, silver, and white with its skeletal structures only served to substantiate the critics' "Spook School" nickname for the Macdonald sisters.

Nonetheless, Mackintosh's influence in Germany, not to be underestimated, was not so much due to these exhibitions but to the competition launched by the German periodical, *Zeitschrift für Innendekoration* in 1901. Although the "Scottish genius" submitted an incomplete entry, he was nevertheless awarded a special prize and had his work published in a portfolio entitled *Meister der Innenkunst* [Masters of Interior Decoration] alongside designs by Mackay Hugh Baillie Scott and Leopold Bauer. According to Hermann Muthesius, who wrote an introduction to the portfolio, Mackintosh fulfilled the entry conditions of the competition like no other with his design for the *Haus eines Kunstfreundes* [House for an Art Lover]: it was radically modern and uncompromisingly aesthetic (ill. p. 59).

Tea Rooms – Stylized refinements of buildings with a purpose

It is not the body which should inhabit these chambers of thought; these are *chambres garnies* for beautiful souls.
Julius Meier-Graefe[13]

The Scots' sublime conceptual works of art, their overrefined, almost overdeveloped atmospheric interiors extracted a mild criticism from Muthesius: "... Whether such enhancement is appropriate to our everyday rooms is another question. Mackintosh's rooms are refined to a degree which the lives of even the artistically educated are still a long way from matching. The

Left:
Margaret Macdonald Mackintosh
Glass window, detail of a cabinet, 1898–99
Cabinet: oak, 159 x 202 x 42.5 cm

Charles Rennie Mackintosh
Margaret Macdonald Mackintosh
Cabinet, detail of the cabinet doors, 1902
Wood, painted white and sculpted, with glass, silver-plated metal and mosaic glass on silvered panels, 154.7 x 98.6 x 39.8 cm
Made for Mrs. Rowat, 14 Kingsborough Gardens, Glasgow
The uniqueness and fascination of Scottish Art Nouveau lies in the coupling of almost mannered figurines with the non-representationalism of its architectural and furniture design. Angelic statuettes slot into the architectural grid, their weightless heads like halos rounding off an almost esoteric ornament, made up of the mere husks of bodies and garments and garnished with flowers.

delicacy and austerity of their artistic atmosphere would tolerate no admixture of the ordinariness that fills our lives. Even a book in an unsuitable binding would disturb the atmosphere simply by lying on the table. Indeed, even the man or woman of today – especially the man in his unadorned working attire – treads like a stranger in this fairy-tale world. There is no possibility for the time being of our aesthetic cultivation playing so large a part in our lives that rooms like this could become commonplace. But they are milestones placed by a genius far ahead of us to mark the way to excellence for mankind in the future."[14] Despite his reservations, Muthesius was unable to ignore this blossoming of interior art and delegated it to the future – a bold statement, for the future was to be less aesthetic and rather sober, even martial, with time. Luckily, Mackintosh was still able to find artistically literate customers with elegant taste who gave him free rein with his creations. The Four's strengths lay in the congenial realization of the sophisticated atmosphere of Scottish tea salons. The epitome of the ideal artist-designer, Mackintosh sketched whole interiors (ill. p. 58,

p. 59, p. 64–65) and was also a gifted designer of furniture (ill. p. 53, p. 58, p. 62, p. 63), an influence still traceable today in any good furnishing house. The artistic concept as a whole was always of prime importance; a chair designed for the Willow Tea Rooms, for example, would be ineffective if it failed to fit in with the overall design of the room. The towering back is impractical and the elongated shape of the chair seems rather affected. Only when placed in the room alongside which it was conceived does it receive legitimacy and its own particular appeal. The chair back is an integral part of the structured wall; its full effect is best appreciated when viewed from the front. A chair designed six years previously for the Argyle Street Tea Rooms in 1897 also contributes to the overall interior design. Although the furniture Mackintosh designed for the Argyle Street Tea Rooms is obviously in keeping with the tradition of the Arts and Crafts Movement and bears the influence of Voysey, the chair in question – still a famous piece of furniture today (ill. p. 58) – displays all the characteristics of Mackintosh's individual style. The spatial elements in Mackintosh's

Margaret Macdonald Mackintosh
Detail of a three-part screen, 1909
Oak frame and oilcloth, painting on parchment paper, one panel measures 30 x 43.5 cm
"Tall, incorporeal figures dissolved or woven into delicate webs of stems and threads, with only their heads human or saint-like, slightly inclined, each like the next, with closed eyes and dark, cascading hair ..."
(Dolf Sternberger, see note 8)

Charles Rennie Mackintosh
Margaret Macdonald Mackintosh
Cabinet, 1902
Wood, painted white and sculpted,
with glass, silver-plated metal and
mosaic glass on silvered panels,
154.7 x 98.6 x 39.8 cm
Made for Mrs. Rowat, 14
Kingsborough Gardens, Glasgow
Further gems of Mackintosh
furniture have been preserved by
another of his female clients. The
feminine coloring of the interior
betrays the influence of Mrs. Rowat,
the lady of the house, who played a
major role in the redecorating
process.

furniture and indeed also in his architectural designs are determined by squares and cubes. Yet the architecturally lucid arrangement is increasingly broken up by delicate floral ornaments spun across the structures, giving the perpendicular form a sense of mystery. The cubic principle underpinning Mackintosh's work becomes clear only when we look beyond the linear latticework. Like Japanese artists, Mackintosh used ornaments on the surface as a kind of support; the hidden penetration of background components creates a decorative whole which does not allow elements to be perceived individually. Mackintosh primarily adopted methods employed by sinkabe kozo, using partitions and painted wooden objects to divide up the room – concepts borrowed from Japanese interior design. Individual objects are arranged in such a way that the often stiff,

severe character of his furniture and constructions is softened by the convergence of the woven lines. The attenuated design has a Japanese quality that is clearly recognizable in the treatment of window grates, fittings and door handles, which are melodically formed out of their supporting surface. Through his attention to the tiniest detail and the apparent triviality of his designs, all of Mackintosh's objects and architecture seem to diffuse a whole spectrum of impressions.

In Mackintosh's own words, the female ingredient, namely that of his wife Margaret, was a decisive factor in his work. Women played an important role in his life, both artistically and professionally. The nonconformist Miss Catherine Cranston became one of Mackintosh's main clients. She was a strong supporter of Glasgow's Temperance Movement and decided to open tea salons to counterbalance the city's pubs. Here her guests would be served in elegant, cultivated surroundings. Her investment paid off, as her exclusive Tea Rooms soon attracted a large clientele. Encouraged by the success of her first enterprise, the Argyle Street Tea Rooms (ill. p. 58), she bought two more buildings and a piece of land and opened the Ingram Street Tea Rooms (ill. p. 58), the Buchanan Street Tea Rooms and the Willow Tea Rooms.

With these commissions, Mackintosh was able to unleash his true genius without any stylistic or financial restraints. In complete artistic freedom, he created rooms which resembled his dreams come true: "... narrow panels, gray silk, very, very thin wooden supports, verticals everywhere. Small, right-angled cupboards with heavily protruding plates, smooth and plain. Upright, white and serious, they stand like girls taking their first communion – yet not quite, for somewhere a hint of decoration has been added, or a large silver fitting, like a hidden jewel; and on the inside, shyly elegant lines nestled in bas-relief, never disturbing the silhouette, like a faint, distant echo of van de Velde. The charm of these proportions, the aristocratically effortless security with which an ornament of enamel, colored glass, semiprecious stones or worked metal is inlaid"[15] lend all of Mackintosh's visions their inimitable brilliance; they owe their existence to his symbiosis with Margaret.

The Macdonald sisters had opened a studio for applied art as early as 1894; designs were supplied by Mackintosh and MacNair. Yet the two men did not merely come up with designs for materials, wall paneling, metalwork, and other commodities; they also supplied ideas. In 1899, MacNair accepted a post as Instructor for Decorative Design in Liverpool, causing the partnership to disband. In spirit, however, the style of The Four lived on. Again it was Miss Cranston who granted Mackintosh total creative freedom in 1903 with her commission for Hous'Hill. The many pieces of furniture Mackintosh designed for this house in particular illustrate the vast compendium of his ideas and at the same time point toward a change in his style to include a greater constructive element (ill. p. 59). A curved, open-work screen divided the living room into two sections; a similar screen was used by Ludwig Mies van der Rohe (1886–1969) in 1930 in the Tugendhat House in Brno. Mackintosh's acquaintance with Miss Cranston was a lucky coincidence, yet it also bore the irony of fate; Mackintosh was a heavy drinker, and Miss Cranston a teetotaler, yet he designed her private rooms and tea salons to perfection.

Charles Rennie Mackintosh
Washstand for Miss Cranston's blue bedroom, Hous'Hill, Nitshill, Glasgow, 1904
Oak with ceramic tiles and lead glazing,
160.5 x 130.5 x 51.7 cm

Charles Rennie Mackintosh
Bureau for Miss Cranston's blue bedroom, Hous'Hill, Nitshill, Glasgow, 1904
Oak with lead glazing and glass,
115.5 x 76 x 30 cm

Further gems of Mackintosh furniture have been preserved by another of his female clients. The parents of Jessie Newberry, a friend of Mackintosh's whose husband was the director of the Glasgow School of Art, owned a terraced house in Kingsborough Gardens. They commissioned Mackintosh to refurbish the property. The feminine coloring of the interior (ill. opposite page) betrays the influence of Mrs. Rowat, the lady of the house, who played a major role in the redecorating process. Mackintosh was to receive further important commissions, yet the veracity of his architectural achievements manifests itself most convincingly in Hill House (ill. p. 53, p. 64–65, p. 66).

Following double page spread:
Charles Rennie Mackintosh
Hill House, Upper Colquhoun Street, Helensburgh,
View of the master bedroom,
1902–04
"Hill House is sheer poetry. I would even go as far as saying that, in our century, no other house has been built which emanates as much poetry as Hill House."
(Julius Posener, see note 1)

Hill House – Scotland's Ultimate Artistic Whole

The composition forms an organic whole, each part fitting into the rest with the same concord as do the passages of a grand symphony.
Ludwig Hevesi[16]

Frances Macdonald MacNair
The Spirit of the Rose, ca. 1900–05
Silk embroidery on linen,
51.5 x 51.5 cm
Celestial beings, created by the Macdonald sisters in metal, embroidery, mosaics, and jet pearls (ill. p. 66), "haunt" furniture, wall paneling, and material.

During 1902 and 1903, Mackintosh built Hill House for the publisher Walter Blackie in Helensburgh, an exclusive residential area near the sea. Together with Hoffmann's Palais Stoclet in Brussels, Hill House is considered to be Art Nouveau's ultimate artistic whole in an intellectual sense. "There are architects who like to differentiate between inside and out ... this is not true of Hill House. True to the teachings of English architecture, it is possible to determine which rooms are where merely by looking at the exterior of the house; indeed, here one could even speak of a particular precision. ... One can say that here the building's functions are represented by the house's exterior with great clarity ... Looking at the interior, one will notice that Mackintosh's stylized furniture does not intrude on the general design. All parts of the room come alive. I would like to point out again the bay in the drawing room with its relief on the wall, if I may call it that, endowed with a decorative momentum with which the furniture – both fixed and movable – fits in. The furniture is also architecture in itself; squares play almost as

Charles Rennie Mackintosh
Collioure, Pyrénées-Orientales
Summer Palace of the Queens of Aragon, ca. 1924–26
Watercolor, 38.1 x 43.2 cm
During his period of "exile" in the Pyrenees, Mackintosh devoted himself almost exclusively to landscape painting. His paintings clearly bear the mark of the architect.

important a role for Mackintosh as they did a little later for Peter Behrens. The lighting (and this has been conceived with great thought), the designs of the walls, and the furniture all work together to form a single unit."[17]

Once the west wing of the Glasgow School of Art had been finished in 1909, there were increasingly fewer commissions. Whereas architects' offices in Vienna flourished and Behrens and Olbrich were able to establish themselves, Mackintosh's career took a downturn. The cause for this may have been his characteristic unwillingness to compromise and his increasing dependence on alcohol. Unlike the famous Wiener Werkstätte Fledermaus chair, Mackintosh's

Charles Rennie Mackintosh
Table and chair, Hill House, Helensburgh, May 1908
Design in ink and wash on artificial silk, 29.7 x 42.5 cm

Charles Rennie Mackintosh
Fish knife, fork and dessert spoon
for Miss Cranston's Ingram Street
Tea Rooms, Glasgow, 1905
Silver-plated metal
Knife: 21 cm long

Page 69:
Charles Rennie Mackintosh
Stairs, 78 Derngate, Northampton,
commissioned by Wynne J. Bassett-
Lowke,
1916–18/19
Wood, lead glazing and glass
It is a tragedy that Mackintosh's
personal situation, alcoholism, and
unfortunate financial circumstances
heavily influenced his work. One of
the few building projects carried out
during his London period illustrates
that it was neither lack of genius nor
waning architectural creativity which
caused him to concentrate his output
on textile design. He demonstrated
his usual excellence in the
remodeling of a Victorian terraced
house in Northampton for Wynne
J. Bassett-Lowke, a member of the
Design and Industries Association.
The sensational geometric designs of
the facade and staircase are today
considered to be the first examples of
Modern Style architecture in Britain.

furniture designs were not suited to mass production. Furthermore, his furniture was also technically deficient, as he preferred to work with simple craftsmen from the boatbuilding industry, a poor choice compared with the expensive carpenters who worked for the Art Nouveau artists in London, Nancy, Paris, and Vienna. To this was added the general economic depression which hit Glasgow in 1910. A patriotic Scot, Mackintosh must have been terribly resigned when he moved down to London in 1915. He and his wife left England in 1923 to spend a few years in the French Pyrenees, in Port-Vendres, probably for financial reasons, as the cost of living in this region was then very low. Here, Mackintosh devoted himself almost exclusively to landscape painting. His paintings clearly bear the impressive mark of the architect (ill. p. 66). It is a tragedy that Mackintosh's personal situation, alcoholism and unfortunate financial circumstances heavily influenced his work. One of the few building projects carried out during his London period illustrates that it was neither lack of genius nor waning architectural creativity which caused him to concentrate his output on textile design. He demonstrated his usual excellence in the remodeling of a Victorian terraced house in Northampton for Wynne J. Bassett-Lowke, a member of the Design and Industries Association. The sensational geometric designs of the facade and staircase are today considered to be the first examples of Modern Style architecture in Britain (ill. opposite page).

The second event was very different and could almost be described as something of a sensation: the appearance of the Glasgow architects in Vienna. (Here I refer to the related couples, Mackintosh and MacNair, husbands to the two Macdonald sisters.) At more or less the same time as the movement began on the Continent, in the year Morris died, these young Scots took part in the Arts and Crafts Society Exhibition in London for the first time. After one had spent two years hoping they would improve, they were dismissed for demonstrating totally unBritish fantasies. They do indeed effect a blending of a puritanically severe practical form (as exhibited by Charles R. Mackintosh's wonderfully simple architecture) with an almost lyrical disappearance of any useful value. The interiors are like something out of a dream: narrow panels, gray silk, very, very thin wooden supports, verticals everywhere. Small, right-angled cupboards with heavily protruding plates, smooth and plain. Upright, white and serious, they stand like girls taking their first communion – yet not quite, for somewhere a hint of decoration has been added, or a large silver fitting, like a hidden jewel; and on the inside, shyly elegant lines nestled in bas-relief, never disturbing the silhouette, like a faint, distant echo of van de Velde. The charm of these proportions, the aristocratically effortless security with which an ornament of enamel, colored glass, semi precious stones or worked metal is inlaid, delighted the artists, and especially the Viennese, who were beginning to feel a little bored with the constant, solid efficiency of English interiors. Here there was something of mysticism and asceticism, by no means in the Christian sense, with lots of heliotrope fragrance, manicured hands, and gentle sensuality, just as one would wish. Compared with previous rooms stuffed full of objects, these interiors were almost devoid of any furniture; there were simply two straight chairs on a white carpet with backs as tall as a man, gazing silently at each other across a small table, crazy, ghostly ... This slightly perfumed, decorative atmosphere was the product of the Macdonald sisters. ... Their unnaturally billowing figures kept reappearing in worked metal, embroidery, glass mosaics on walls and objects, cautiously distributed, fabulously decorated – and next to them, barren surfaces. For as I have said, the masculine foundation enables an appreciation of the sophisticated charm of the unadorned. Here the Scots delivered a lesson which continued to take effect long after their experiments with paper flowers, wire, and amethysts had been forgotten.
Ludwig Hevesi, *Altkunst – Neukunst*, Vienna, 1903.

World expositions and the bourgeoisie
Paris

Henri de Toulouse Lautrec
Yvette Guilbert or *Femme de profil (Mme. Lucy)*, 1896
Watercolor on card, 56 x 48 cm
Musée d'Orsay, Paris
"He [Toulouse-Lautrec] has a room in a brothel," wrote Jules Renard, "and gets on well with all the ladies that have unaffected feelings, who are alien to respectable women and wonderfully good at being models." The crippled painter found "unaffected feelings" in the world of Montmartre, far from the emotional hypocrisy of the bourgeoisie. Nonetheless, he did not idealize the milieu. He drew whores large and small with great affection but without sentimental gloss – and if no drawing paper happened to be available, then on tablecloths, the margins of newspapers or marble slabs: no *chronique scandaleuse* but deeply moving compositions of admirable conciseness.

Par de lentes métamorphoses,
Les marbres blancs en blanches chairs,
Les fleurs roses en lèvres roses
Se refont dans des corps divers.
Théophile Gautier[1]

L'art pour l'art – Fin de siècle

Victor Cousin (1792–1867) noted in his *Cours de Philosophie*: "il faut de la religion pour la religion, de la morale pour la morale, de l'art pour l'art. Le bien et le saint ne peuvent être la route de l'utile, ni même du beau."[2] Referring to Cousin, Théophile Gautier (1811–72) applied the catch-phrase *l'art pour l'art* – art for art's sake – to poetry, so characterizing an aestheticism that exists for its own sake, pure and on its own terms, arising solely from the idea of beauty. The splendor and texture of precious stones, sumptuous materials and metals, exquisite scents, the romance of untamed fantasies and narcotic dreams, the life of the *demimonde*, the suggestive appeal of sounds and rhythms, of line and color – these were the accessories of Art Nouveau of Parisian provenance. With their poly-chromatic word colors, glittering and gleaming like gems irrespective of their meaning, the French poets of the Decadent Movement and Symbolism created an ambience of sensuous preciousness. For Rimbaud, Baudelaire, Gautier, and Verlaine, it was not a question of conjuring up a rational language but rather of compressing hallucinations into words and images. In Symbolist poetry, aromas, sounds, and colors blend into a unity. Paul Verlaine (1844–96) wrote: "I love the word '*décadence*'. It glistens with purple and gold. It coruscates fountains of fire and the gleam of precious stones. It summons up painted courtesans, circus spectacles, panting gladiators,

the leaping of wild animals, flames consuming exhausted human races …".[3] "Exhaustion," "weariness," "over-fatigue," "boredom" are all favorite words of the Decadent Movement, and the overwroughtness of a total art of the senses does unquestionably contain the germ of decline and fall – the *fin-de-siècle* state of mind. The refined savor of decay imparted itself to the aestheticism of *fin-de-siècle* art as well, and indeed became an agent of Art Nouveau. The "charm of sweet death" and "yearnful awaken-ing" – both belong to Art Nouveau; emanci-pation, reform, and innovation were the counter-parts of an art based on an aesthetically exhausted mood of doom.

The fact that overbred *l'art-pour-l'art* beauty was initially termed "Modern Style" in France, that is, characterized as an English influence, may seem astonishing; astonishing also inasmuch as the decorative elegance of Art Nouveau creations and their originators had little in common with the tracts of John Ruskin (1819–1900) or Arts and Crafts "cottage artists". The artists of Art Nouveau did not dream of applying their creativity to a useful or social end – works of arts seemed to them free of utilitarian restrictions. Yet there are connections: in the Pre-Raphaelite cult of beauty there is a school of thought linking England with *l'art pour l'art* and the Symbolists; a further point of reference is the visual language of William Blake (ill. p. 22) for which no models exist in the real world. Blake is the illustrator of subconscious visions whose metaphors resemble the French poetry of Symbolism. *Les fleurs du mal*, the "flowers of evil", of the Frenchman Charles Baudelaire (1821–67) are subsequently personified in *fin-de-siècle* England by Oscar Wilde and Aubrey Vincent Beardsley.

Hector Guimard
Tulipe Métro
Lamp (detail), Paris, 1899–1900
Painted cast iron, glass
"Now we see springing from the asphalt sprays of metal flowers, arrays of water plants, tulips radiating light, saturated with the fruitful, bubbling sap of the Paris underground."
(Maurice Rheims, *Kunst um 1900*, Munich, 1965)

World expositions –
The "absolute bourgeoisie"

*By exploiting the global market, the bourgeoisie has
rendered production and consumption in every country
cosmopolitan.*
A contemporary witness[4]

Internationalization replaced national isolation
and self-sufficiency not only in material but also
in intellectual output. Nonetheless, though it
became common property, the latter fortunately
preserved its national individuality. Of prime
importance in bringing about such international
exchanges in the 19th century were the world
expositions, which after 1900 went out of
fashion in their turn with the growing development of communications systems. These "vanity
fairs" even managed to impress the French
dandy Gautier, for all his aesthetic introspection.
As he wrote of the Paris World Exposition of
1867: "Art stood side by side with Industry. White
statues rose between black machines. Painting
spread out alongside the rich materials of the
Orient."[5] The whole fascination is expressed in
these lines – the encounter with the exotic, the
alien, art that could keep pace with progress and
the nascent aesthetics of the machine. Modern
powered machines possess an animal character
and a peculiar beauty in their construction. Thus,
in 1867 visitors in Paris went to see not only the
World Exposition but also the New Paris – Paris
Nouveau – that had sprung up under Napoleon
III and his Prefect Baron Georges-Eugène

Haussmann (1809–91). It represented the first
gloriously successful urban design for a modern
metropolis. The Third Republic's World Exposition
of 1878 in Paris turned out less brilliantly, as
traces of the Commune insurrection of 1871 –
the Paris Commune had set itself the goal of
transforming the unified French state into a
federation of sovereign communities and making
socialism a reality – were still clearly visible. In
contrast, 1900 saw a world exhibition that
exceeded all previous exhibitions in expense and
splendor – the beginning of a new century was
being celebrated. In place of the functional steel
constructions of 1889 – with their focal point the
Eiffel Tower (ill. above) – a baroque ceremonial
architecture appeared that made no bones
about its historical borrowings. Most of the
exhibition pavilions were likewise less than
successful, their bizarre forms and abstruse
motifs belonging to an illusory fantasy world
constructed of architectural clichés (ill. opposite).
A monstrous archway adorned the entrance,
dedicated to "Electricity" and lit up with over
3,000 colored light bulbs. Moving pavements
were dreamt of, and everything was to be electrified; the Metro was already operating. The neo-
Baroque opulence of the trinity of the Grand and
Petit Palais with the Pont Alexandre III gives the
bank of the Seine even today the intensive flair of
the *Belle Époque.* It is a paradox of Art Nouveau
that it came into being within the artistic framework of the selfsame *Belle Époque* it sought to
reject. We still look back with nostalgic melancholy

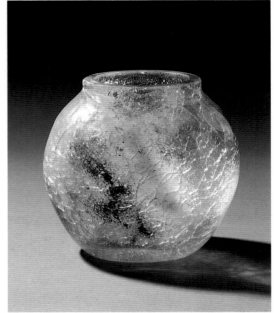

François Eugène Rousseau
Vase, between 1885 and 1891
Flashed glass, with oxide gold leaf
inclusions, 14 × 15 × 9 cm
New Collection, National Museum
of Applied Art, Munich
Like many of his colleagues,
Rousseau profited from Japanese
art. He created flashed glass with
surface effects reminiscent of the
treacle glazing used on Japanese
stoneware. Even for his thicksided,
mostly crackle, glass pieces and vases
that feature gold-leaf inclusions and
cloudy colorations produced with
metal oxides, he preferred to use
East Asian forms.

René Lalique
Corsage spray, 1905–06
Gold, *plique à jour* enamel, glass,
diamonds, 6 × 15 cm
Musée des Art Décoratifs, Paris
Lalique, who spent his
apprenticeship in England, had an
almost unlimited repertory of forms
at his disposal. Even so, his choice of
applications (corsages, necklaces,
brooches, and diadems) was
conservative.

to the era before the First World War, which is associated for us with dazzling society life, increasing prosperity, general modernization, the carefree pleasures of balls, assemblies, theaters and racecourses and a flourishing of the arts. Meanwhile, luxury and affluence were enjoyed by only a relatively small number of privileged people – the working class, peasantry, and provinces had no share in them. The *Belle Époque* was a manifestation of the bourgeoisie, which had superseded the nobility in the important positions of state and society. The "absolute bourgeoisie", as Jean Duché calls them, also owed its rise, absurdly enough, to the revolutions of 1830, 1848, and 1871, which the bourgeoisie had cleverly turned to advantage, thereby triumphing not only over the aristocracy but also over the masses. The aristocracy took refuge in pleasure, idleness, and aestheticism, which hastened its downfall; in contrast, the artists of the Decadent Movement became the embodiment of an "intellectual aristocracy", whose mortal enemy was the "bourgeois".

At the same time, those that turned the aesthetic program of Art Nouveau into reality at the turn of the century were dependent on that same bourgeoisie, as "the seeds of the iridescent flowers of this art could unfold only in the fertile,

well-prepared soil that the material culture of the grand bourgeoisie offered".[6] Moreover, toward the end of the 19th century, the bourgeoisie had, after all, put into practice what Karl Marx, with one eye on the Social Revolution, had demanded: "… that it can create its poetry not from the past but from the future. It cannot begin with itself until it has cast off the superstitious belief in the past. The Revolution must have its dead buried in order to get on with its own substance."[7] But, however much the practioners of Art Nouveau believed they had distanced themselves from the "mustiness" of the 19th century, Art Nouveau still satisfied above all a demand for luxury. Jewelry by René Lalique (ills. pp. 85, 87, 88, and above), vases by Georges de Feure or François Eugène Rousseau (ill. above) or furniture by Eugène Gaillard (ill. p. 94) carried high prices. It may be observed without irony that the philosophy that expressed itself in Art Nouveau certainly did not correspond to the opportunities and sensibilities of the rapidly growing proletariat. Attitudes to the "new art" were, however, ambivalent within the bourgeoisie itself as well. The limits of morality were still too tightly set to allow a libertine philosophy in the Decadent spirit.

Hector Guimard: Le Style Métro

Il faut arranger avec goût ce morceau de fer; il faut le disposer logiquement, avec méthode, et c'est dans cette voie seulement que vous trouverez la véritable beauté.
Hector Guimard[8]

The president of the Métro company, Adrien Bénard – a solid bourgeois – nevertheless sought out one of the "new artists" to design the surface structures and surrounds of the Metro entrances. Bénard was connected with the Art Nouveau movement and got his way over the contract with Hector Guimard (1867–1942) in the face of public opinion, which had reacted negatively to the first drafts. As we know today, it was a great achievement because Guimard's fantastic creations – a metamorphosis of architecture and nature, ornamentation with a practical application – made him immortal, and led to French Art Nouveau being sometimes called the *Style Métro* (ill. below). The reasoning of contemporary critics seems today rather odd: the green coloring of the sculptured structures was violently condemned as being "Germanic", while the lettering that Guimard designed, for the greeny yellow enamel signs fixed over the front of the entrances and closing the arch of the superstructures was attacked as unreadable and indigestible "to the honor of French taste"[9] (ill. p. 76).

In 1889, Paris reveled in the glories of iron structures, but taste later reverted to its attachment to "wedding-cake style" building. The architect and art theoretician Eugène Emmanuel Viollet-le-Duc (1814–79), advocate of the primacy of construction in architecture, exercised a decisive influence on both Guimard and also the Belgian Victor Horta. Iron was the architectural material of the future because it could also be used flexibly.[10] Unlike the "iron architects" before them, the Art Nouveau constructors Guimard and Horta invented a new Art Nouveau form, in which iron features as a slender, sinewy, statically effective element. The green-painted cast-iron stems and tropical floral pillars of the Métro entrances are an icon of Art Nouveau. "Each of the three fluted – quasi woody – stems rises from a single trunk, one helping to hold up the entrance sign, the two others, which hardly move apart, joining forces once more at the top to provide a support, frame and leaf cover for the fairy-tale glow of the lamp flower. Both below and above they become, of course, somewhat irrationally luxuriant, repeatedly knotted and cartilaginous together."[11]

An exhibition at the Musée des Arts Décoratifs in Paris in 1971 was entitled "Pionniers du XXᵉ siècle – Guimard, Horta, van der Velde." The three artists are the great inspiration of 20th-century architecture. Though line is their common means

Hector Guimard
Tulipe Métro
Lamp, Palais Royal station, Paris, 1900
Painted cast iron, glass
Guimard's Métro entrances – fantastic shapes that are almost a metamorphosis of architecture and nature, ornamentation with a practical application – made him immortal, and led to French Art Nouveau being at times called *Style Métro*.

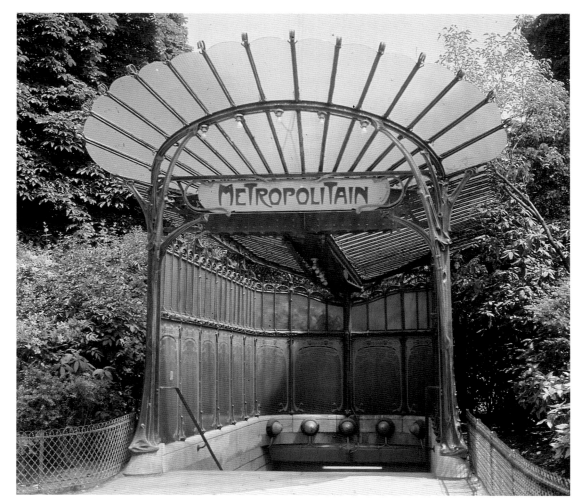

Hector Guimard
Porte Dauphine métro station, Paris, 1900–01
In his roofing for the Métro entrance porches, Guimard succeeded in creating a wonderful synthesis of glass, iron, and "air". The individual glass panes are arrayed to each other almost by suspension, permitting total transparency without compromising either the structure or its stability.

Hector Guimard
Porte Dauphine métro station
Side panels of balustrade, Paris, 1900-01
Glazed tuff

of expression, at the same time they differ in essential ways in respect of its interpretation and function. For Horta as a constructor, line was an accessory, graphic ornamentation that enlivened his light-flooded iron structures. Van de Velde meanwhile looked on dynamic, abstract line as an integral element of montage, whereas Guimard's architectural work aims for the spatialization of line. For Guimard, line is not abstract, but derived from nature without imitating it: the artist translates its structure, that is, its principle of growth. In this respect Guimard is like the great Spanish architect Antoni Gaudí, though without the latter's three-dimensional handling of line. "What is consistently avoided throughout, in everything, is anything parallel or symmetrical. 'Nature,' says Guimard, explaining his things in a booming voice and with tremendous arm movements, 'nature is the greatest builder of all and yet makes nothing parallel and nothing symmetrical.'"[12]

L'architecte d'art

"Dance of shinbones" – "Knuckle art"
Ludwig Hevesi[13]

In 1894, Guimard won a travel bursary, which he used not for the customary trip to Italy but to spend time in England, Scotland, and Belgium. "The whole ´homeliness of the interior is stamped on the exterior. Individual homes reveal themselves outwardly in orderly fashion. That is very entertaining and reasonable; it also makes it a pleasure to live there."[14] Absorbing an impression of the English Country House Movement, Guimard has here internalized its principles, that a logically conceived, modest home can likewise become a work of art on the strength of its beauty and harmony. The aim and purpose of a building are, as it were, its "decoration". The decor springs from the duty to take account of the needs of the occupants while guaranteeing them, over and above pure usefulness, an individually fashioned, cultural milieu. During his trip to Belgium, Guimard got to know Horta and the buildings of Paul Hankar (1859–1901). "Now, Horta said one day to Guimard, half in jest, 'I

Lucien Gaillard
Comb, ca. 1900
Carved ivory, gold, chalcedony,
10.6 cm long

don't use flowers as a model but their stems. '
Guimard was struck by this. At once, a jumbled
picture sprang into his mind of something that
we should like to call Stem Style. ... However,
what we have called Stem Style runs through the
whole house, inside and outside. The whole
range of grilles, banisters, wall surfaces, glazing,
mosaic floors, runners and furniture, all designed
by Guimard, display this ornamental style."[15] (ill.
p. 82–83). Guimard was not content with fashion-
ing architecture; he became the *architecte d'art*,
as he called himself, that is, a craftsman of all the
arts, in the Art Nouveau sense. Here again the
English model is evident, the architect Charles
Francis Annesley Voysey having already rejected
the elevation and special position accorded to
architecture over the applied arts. As an artist-
craftsman, Guimard thus set to work on a plate
with as much circumspection as on an architectural component (ill. p. 80). The elements are all
composed in harmony and worked out in the
tiniest detail. Preference is given to malleable
materials such as cast iron, bronze, and flexible
metals. Here, Guimard attains the greatest perfection; the poetry of Art Nouveau is wrought

more successfully here than in his work in wood.
Guimard won his first major commission from
the widowed Mme. Fournier for the construction
of Castel Béranger, a residential building with 36
units. He managed to persuade his client to alter
a first, more historicizing draft, produced before
his travels abroad, in favor of an *art du geste*, the
art of curvilinear frame. As with Mackintosh, it
was a female client who granted him carte
blanche to create an architectural masterpiece.
"And the owner, a worthy bourgeois widow
called Madame E. Fournier, has allowed her
architect a completely free hand to charge about
as he deems fit. Truly, this lady deserves
the Légion d'Honneur."[16] "The curve, the true
affective line, is the favored terrain of his ornamental imagination."[17] (ill. p. 105) Perhaps a
better appreciation of this "affective line" is the
secret of a female clientele. Thus, one may note
features shared not only with the French
rationalists of the late 18th and early 19th
centuries but also a link with the lyric poets of
Symbolism. Guimard too made use of surprising
effects in his building works. Though the various
components – even the fiercely opposed *rocaille*

Pages 78, 79:
Hector Guimard
Inner lobby and view of door to a
room, Hôtel Paul Mezzara, 60, rue
La Fontaine, Paris, 1911
The Hôtel Mezzara is laid out round
a large, two-story patio and
surrounded by a gallery that obtains
daylight via a glass window in the
ceiling. In contrast with earlier
buildings, this residential-cum-studio
building is relatively sober, but even
so, in its details it displays the typical
Style Guimard.

Hector Guimard
Plate, 1909
Bronze, gilt, diameter 36 cm
Musée des Arts Décoratifs, Paris
Guimard was not content to design
architecture. He saw himself as an
architecte d'art, an "art architect",
which in the context of Art Nouveau
means a craftsman of all the arts.
English influence can be seen in this
– the English architect Charles
Francis Annesley Voysey had
already rejected the elevation and
special position of architecture above
the applied arts. As an artist-
craftsman, Guimard set to work on a
plate with as much circumspection
as on an architectural component.
All elements are composed in
harmony and worked out in the
tiniest detail. Preference is given to
malleable materials such as cast iron,
bronze, and flexible metals. This is
where Guimard attains the greatest
perfection, and his metal works are
almost beyond comparison with his
creations in wood.

around 1900 – combine to make a whole, works of art are, unlike nature, multi-dimensional, the unity being reestablished only in the eye of the beholder (ill. p. 83). Numerous building commissions testify to Guimard's creativity. At the opening of the Humbert de Roman concert hall in 1901, critics described the gigantic steel and glass hall as a "druidic grove", since the iron ribs were perceived as the boughs of a colossal tree. (The hall was demolished a few years later.) There followed private houses, public buildings, and his own house. The Hôtel Paul Mezzara of 1911 is laid out around a large, two-story patio and surrounded by a gallery that obtains daylight via a glass window in the ceiling. In contrast with earlier buildings, this residential-cum-studio building is relatively sober, though in its detail it displays the typical *Style Guimard* (ills. pp. 78–79). "It [the patio] served the client, who was a textile manufacturer and wanted to combine home and workplace, as both reception hall and showroom. Perhaps this is why the wrought iron balustrade is relatively simple and the decoration very delicate, with free-standing structural ironwork that carries the staircase and white-painted roof."[18] The marriage of glass, iron, and "air" in the Hôtel Paul Mezzara is as successful a synthesis as the wonderful roofings over the entrance porches to the Métro. In the latter, the glass panes are arrayed to each other almost by suspension, permitting total transparency without compromising the construction or its stability (ill. p. 76). Even opponents of Art Nouveau find in Guimard's oeuvre the perfect expression of a style that, over and above all functionality, manifests qualities that have become rare in the field of modern architecture, namely, elegance and imagination, musicality and poetry. Through his formal inventions, shaped by the ornamental gesture, Guimard has remained one of the great sources of inspiration to this day (ills. pp. 71, 76, 78, 79, 82–83). It is also instructive that Guimard left a deep impression on the painters of the 20th century, particularly Picasso and Dalí. The latter could be described as Guimard's real rediscoverer while the Frenchman was still alive. Thus, parallel to a Guimard exhibition at the Museum of Modern Art in New York in 1970, Dalí organized his own exhibition at the Knoedler Gallery there under the title of "Hommage à Guimard."

Hector Guimard
Ceiling lighting, from 1909
Chased bronze, gilt, colored glass, glass beads, glass tubes, setting of brass and copper, 41 × 19 cm
Musée d'Orsay, Paris
Guimard did the design in 1909 and had it patented on August 18 1910.

La divine arabesque –
Debussy and Bergson

Il m'a dit: Cette nuit j'ai rêvé,
J'avais la chevelure autour de mon cou,
J'avais tes cheveux comme un collier noir
Autour de ma nuque et sur ma poitrine ...
Pierre Louÿs[19]

Hector Guimard
Balcony railing (detail), ca. 1909
Cast iron
"What we have termed Stem Style
runs through the whole house, inside
and outside. All the many grilles,
banisters, wall surfaces, glazings,
mosaic floors, runners, furniture –
each designed by Guimard – feature
this style of ornamentation."
(Ludwig Hevesi, see note 15)

Admirers of Guimard speak of the musicality and poetry of his architecture, thereby expressing their sensations by means of other artistic media. It is evident here how interwoven the arts had become under Art Nouveau and what inroads symbiosis and synesthesia had made. This is *l'art de geste*, that around the turn of the century manifested itself in poetry and music, as in art (ill. below). The melodic garland, the resolved ornament, Debussy's *divine arabesque*, in fact freely unfolding melismata in general, are creations of this kind. The arabesque was a form used by Claude Debussy (1862–1918) again and again – restrained and sublimated in *Pelléas et Mélisande*, and as a symbol of nature in *La mer*. Floating and transparent, sensuous and yet cool, the line of the "divine arabesque" is here the symbol of an esotericism transposed into the decorative. It is no accident that the first concert dedicated entirely to works of Debussy took place at the La Libre Esthétique Gallery in Brussels, in 1884. The "interplay of lines" united all arts, and the fact that there was also a common "cradle" is shown by the cover of *La mer* in 1905, bearing Hokusai's *View of Fuji seen from the trough of a wave in the open sea outside Kanagawa* (1831–32),

Right:
Hector Guimard
Metro cartouche, balustrade of
Abbesses station, Paris, 1900
Cast iron
Guimard was another who used
surprising effects in his structures.
Though the various components –
even the fiercely opposed *rocaille*
around 1900 – make up a whole,
works of art (unlike nature) are
multi-dimensional, and unity is only
restored in the eye and the feelings of
the beholder.

probably the most influential and most famous wave in art history.

The "divine arabesque" in the compositions of Debussy occurs in numerous variants – exactly the same variants as in the fine arts and applied art. In the setting of Mallarmé's eclogue *Prélude à l'après-midi d'un faune*, the arabesque appears as an ornamental, decorative pattern; in the "Chansons de Bilitis" from *La chevelure* by Pierre Louÿs (1870–1925), the "rocking arabesque" is a symbol for the entwinement of two lovers in the tresses of the woman. The pictorial symbolism of long female hair flows through the whole Art Nouveau style much as the arabesque does. In many of its forms, Art Nouveau appears as precisely a phenomenon of the arabesque itself. "In Art Nouveau, the arabesque becomes a

universal gesture of artistic expression … Every line generates a counterline, just as every movement calls forth a countermovement in the sense of an unending oscillation; formal oscillations expressing spiritual oscillations whose specific mood (*état d'âme*) is expressed (in the graphological, symbolic sense) through the characteristic style of lines. It is in the rhythm of the arabesque that the philosophy of this art finds form. The arabesque becomes a way of experiencing the world."[20]

The term "arabesque" long subsumed the whole formal language of the Islamic East – geometric and plant forms as much as living motifs. In his *Questions of Style* published in 1893, Alois Riegl (1858–1905) was the first to restrict the arabesque to Islamic art and its typical fork-leaved tendril, a motif rather remote from nature. The followers of Islam are of the opinion that it is not the job of the artist to record in images reality as optically perceived or experienced, that is, to confer permanence on transitory earthly forms, as it is against the divine will. Here, it is not so much in ideological respects as in the formal approach that the delight in ornamental meditation and aesthetic asceticism accords with Art Nouveau feeling.

Fin-de-siècle Europe succumbed less to the formal charm of the arabesque than to the rhythmic alternation of movement that it produces on the surface to be decorated. The French painter Odilon Redon (1840–1916) (ill. p. 100) saw events in space under the aspect of two-dimensional arabesques: "It is, without allowing a precise explanation, the reflex of a human expression which a supple imagination has woven into an interplay of arabesques; and its effect on the spirit of the beholder will, I believe, prompt him to visions whose importance will rise and fall in accordance with his sensitivity and imagination."[21]

If Debussy is to some extent the musician of arabesques and Art Nouveau, one could call Henri Bergson (1859–1941) the philosopher of these phenomena. Bergson's support for Art Nouveau was quasi-spiritual. Though he never expressed a direct opinion on Art Nouveau, or indeed on any other contemporary artistic movements, the concepts of *durée* (duration) and *élan vital* (vitality) – central to his intuition-driven "philosophy of life" – provide non-material terminology for Art Nouveau in the continuous sweep of organic lines. In his essay *La vie et l'œuvre de Ravaisson*, a contribution to *La pensée et le mouvant* of 1904, Bergson quotes Leonardo da Vinci's *Trattato della pittura*: "The secret of the art of drawing lies in discovering in every object the particular way in which a sinuous line develops as a generative axis into a whole, just as a wave spreads outwards from the centre and gives rise to numerous ripples."[22]

Developing this theme, Bergson postulates, in agreement with the French philosopher Jean Ravaisson-Mollien (1813–1900): "Living things are characterized by wave-like or serpentine lines. Every living thing snakes along in its own fashion. The aim of art is to express precisely this serpentine motion."[23]

We may justly claim that these "wave-like" or "serpentine" lines have, in terms of art history, a profound inner affinity with the *figura serpentina* or the *disegno interno* of the Mannerists. If there is a difference between the philosophy of Bergson

Paul-Elie Ranson
Tiger in the jungle, 1893
Color lithograph, 55.7 × 39.5 cm
The sinuous dragon shapes of Sino-Japanese art, motifs used there as interwoven ornamentation, are adapted by *La Revue Blanche* artist Ranson in an arabesque, Art Nouveau manner.

Left:
Julien Caussé
The Ice Fairy,
ca. 1900
Chased and patinated bronze. Base: founded opal glass, 39.3 cm high
Museum Bellerive, Zürich

and Art Nouveau, it might be described as follows: whereas Bergson aimed to comprehend the virtually existent real intention behind concrete things, Art Nouveau attempts to express wave-like or serpentine lines directly as waves or serpents. Where the main concern of the philosopher was to explore "the simple thoughts that correspond to the infinite variety of forms and colors, the concern of Art Nouveau was to understand thoroughly "the infinite variety of forms and colors" themselves and become reality thereby.

Where serpents are depicted, "woman" is never far away, and flowing tresses also feature in this context. In *La chevelure*, poetically extolled by Louÿs and set to music by Debussy, Art Nouveau seems to become immersed or sometimes even entangled in female tresses – yet without seductive, innocent and at the same time depraved woman there would be no Art Nouveau of Parisian cast.

"Her eyes and the diamonds shone in a single flame" (Gustave Flaubert)

J'ai vu le diable, l'autre nuit;
Et, dessous sa pelure,
Il n'est pas aisé de conclure
S'il faut dire: Elle, ou: Lui.
Jean Paul Toulet[24]

Femme fatale or saint, sinner or Ophelia, Chastity or *diable* – this was the question posed by a whole generation of artists, interpreting an apparently still-unsolved riddle in quite different ways, both in the answer and the stylistic devices used. The very enquiry seems at any rate to have been thoroughly stimulating, bequeathing us seductively lovely creations in almost every material imaginable (ill. p. 84). Luxury objects and jewelry, both readily associated with the fair sex, were particularly suitable media for transplanting the subject in a manner appropriate to both meaning and material, thereby also satisfying the desire for synesthesia (ill. p. 88, left). To this day the female form counts as an outstanding "selling point". In his treatise on Oscar Wilde, Enrique Gómez Carrillo (1873–1927) provides an, as it were, sensational description of Salome in which all male fears and desires are sublimated: "… Only the painting of Gustave Moreau lifted for him the veil from the

René Lalique
The Kiss, brooch, 1904–06
Silver, molded glass, 4.9 × 7 cm
Musée des Arts Décoratifs, Paris
At the 1901 exhibition of the Paris Salon, Lalique included in his collection for the first time jewelry made of crystal glass – the first move toward a new artistic creative material.

Above:
René Lalique
Diadem in the shape of a siren, 1897–98
Antique bronze, emeralds, carved opal, 9.7 × 14 × 13.3 cm
Musée des Arts Décoratifs, Paris
Diadems are among the oldest and most distinguished pieces of jewelry, and acquired immense importance for *fin-de-siècle* jewelers. With his love of plant forms and symbolic shapes, Lalique to some extent reinvented the diadem, partly in terms of shape, partly by using unusual raw materials.

soul of the legendary dancing princess of his dreams. He often repeated the famous words of Huysmans to us: 'She is almost naked. In the frenzy of the dance the veils have become undone, the brocades have fallen to the ground and only more jewels cover her body. A very small girdle embraces her hips, and between her breasts a precious jewel shines like a star; a chain of garnets coils itself lower around her loins, and over the shadow of her pudenda gleam emeralds. 'This seemed to him an unsurpassable portrayal. And five years later, in the hours of sleeplessness, fever and hunger in his prison cell, Wilde repeated the words to himself mechanically: 'Between her breasts a precious jewel shines like a star'."[25]

René Lalique: Poetic jewelry – Polished poetry

Parle moi doucement sans voix parle à mon âme.
Marceline Desbordes-Valmore[26]

"Gems" that vie with the lustre of the stars, that form a perfect reality of the poetry, music, and philosophy of life of the era – such is the fabulous jewelry created by the jeweler René Lalique (1860–1945). Lalique was one of the most celebrated artists of Art Nouveau, endowed with brilliant craft skills that mastered every challenge without effort. Like Gallé, he was able to coax truly poetic appeal from his material. "What held friend and foe, enthusiasts and vituperators, apologists and faultfinders, casual exhibition-goers and scholars alike irresistibly fast in front of Lalique's showcase and drew them under the spell of his great art was a trait in the great master's being – the secret magnet that since the beginning of time has brought the common herd crowding around the individual – a gigantic ego!"[27] These are the glowing words of a

Above:
René Lalique
Ornamental comb, ca. 1902
Iridescent horn, gold, diamonds, 6 × 12 cm
A range of new materials was added to the Art Nouveau palette of new colors: polished semiprecious stones, amber, mother-of-pearl, ivory, tortoiseshell, pearls, base metals, and horn. As an organic natural material, horn was well suited to the organic forms of Art Nouveau, and Lalique dazzled the public with ornamental combs made of horn, carved into flowers, waves, and butterflies.

Left:
Georges Fouquet
Comb, ca. 1900
Carved horn, opals, gold, enamel, 14 cm high
Georges Fouquet was a scion of the Fouquet family of jewelers. After taking over his father's business in 1895, he promptly switched over over production to the Art Nouveau style, employing designers and technicians who had previously studied with Lalique. Besides Japanese and oriental influences, Fouquet used Egyptian sources as well for decorative ensembles. Despite the "cheap" nature of horn as a raw material, work of this kind soon became fashionable, as it had exotic appeal even for the bourgeoisie.

Left:
Paul and Henri Vever
Diadem, ca. 1895
Yellow gold, diamonds, *plique à jour* enamel, diameter 12–15.6 cm

Viennese art critic, and a wood engraving called *La vitrine de Lalique* [Lalique's Showcase] by Félix Vallotton (1865–1925) documented the dense crowd of people standing in front of the "gigantic ego's" exhibition showcase at the 1900 World Exposition in Paris. The magnet that drew the public was a showcase that – like something devised by Joris-Karl Huysmans (1848–1907), a disciple of the cult of overrefined beauty – gave shape to the pictorial world of Symbolism. In front of a bronze grille of stylized butterfly women and under a firmament with suspended bats, the sensation of the World Exposition met their gaze: spirit-filled creatures of a between-world, heavy with symbolism, formed of exquisite materials. "A great dragonfly captivated the public. Its wings are made from delicate gold latticework that even moves on hinges. A threatening eye was represented by the artist with flowing enamel into which he fused little flecks of silver to enhance the effect. These very dark green surfaces are glitteringly accentuated with small diamond insets, while the other parts of the wings are filled out naturalistically with transparent enamel. The long body is studded with green chrysoprase, alternating with small fields fused with dark blue enamel. Seductive beauty turns gruesome when the menacing claws of the insect are revealed, a mixture of mole spades and cockerel's claws. The eyes of the dragonfly are formed by two dark scarabs. The green head of the insect turns out on closer inspection to be something completely new – a smiling female face that, again in an ambiguous allusion, is in the process of being either disgorged or gobbled up."[28] This exotic and "deviant" treasure was acquired in 1903 from the artist himself by the equally legendary multi-millionaire Calouste Gulbenkian (1865–1965) for his collection.

Today the collection, along with other important works by Lalique, can be seen in the museum Gulbenkian founded in Lisbon, Portugal. On the occasion of Lalique's death, he wrote to the artist's daughter: "His [Lalique's] place is among the highest in the history of art. His very personal genius, his exquisite imagination, will be admired by future *élites*. I am very proud to own what I believe is the major part of his work; it occupies a very privileged position among my collections."[29] Yet Gulbenkian was not alone; the great museums of the world snapped up Lalique's jewelry, and moreover at exorbitant prices. A museum in Leipzig, for example, acquired a dress ornament (ill. left) and an ornamental comb (ill. p. 87 top right) for several thousand gold

René Lalique
Brooch, ca. 1900
Gold, *à jour* enamel, diamonds, 6.25 cm high

francs. Lalique moved in both aesthetic and aristocratic circles and was acquainted with the eccentric Count Montesquiou (ill. p. 73), whose favor was also curried by Gallé and in whom he eventually found an admirer. The path to fame was nonetheless arduous. A gifted graphic artist, Lalique opted for gold work, completing an apprenticeship that left him, with his modest material means, hardly any time for artistic studies. After spending two years in London, the center of the new style, he returned to Paris in 1880 and designed jewelry for the great jewelry houses such as Cartier. When he had made himself independent with his own small business, he continued at first working on commissions. The breakthrough came when Lalique was able to exhibit his own creations at the annual salons, which from 1885 allowed artistic pieces from the field of applied art to be admitted as exhibits. The goldsmith of the *Belle Époque* had not spent his apprenticeship in England unprofitably. His superb design drawings – 1,500 of them survive – show the influence of the British workshops. The drafts are made to scale, on papyrin; for all their phantasmagory, they possess a geometric framework akin to the design procedure of the medieval stonemasons, who always had a – hidden – set of rules underlying their patterns (ill. opposite, right). Against this background, Lalique's immense stylistic achievement becomes palpable. His repertoire of forms was a novelty, though the jobs given to him were, of course, conservative – corsages (ill. p. 74), necklaces, brooches, and diadems. Diadems are among the oldest and most exclusive pieces of jewelry, and became extremely important for *fin-de-siècle* jewelers. With his predilection for plant forms and symbolic shapes, Lalique virtually reinvented the diadem, partly in terms of form, partly by using unusual raw materials (ill. p. 87). That artistic value is not necessarily a consequence of material value is evident from Lalique's work, but even today the fact is still not always appreciated. Whereas the fossilized jeweler's art of the Empire fiddled around with precious stones, the ornamental artists of Art Nouveau, led by Lalique, worked with simple materials with purely representational value, thereby opening up new opportunities for expression. The art of enamel technology flourished as never before; there were no limits to the skill and invention of the enamelers. In enamel, the color palette of Art Nouveau – mixed, matt tones – could be recreated almost perfectly. In addition to the nuances of color, there was a whole range of new materials: polished semiprecious stones, amber, mother-of-pearl, ivory, tortoiseshell, pearls, base metals, and horn. The natural, organic material horn fitted in well with the organic shapes of Art Nouveau, and Lalique dazzled the public with ornamental combs of horn shaped and carved into flowers, waves, and butterflies (ill. p. 87). Despite the "cheap" material, work of this kind quickly became fashionable, as it possessed exotic appeal even for the bourgeoisie. As Samuel Bing says in his work on Japanese forms: "Japanese women were the first women of all to wear combs in their hair ornamentally …"[30], so a modern air of Japonisme was adopted.

Besides Lalique, other leading ornamental artists such as Lucien Gaillard (1861–after 1945) (ill. p. 77) and Georges Fouquet (1862–1957) designed ornamental combs. The latter, a scion of the Fouquet jewelry dynasty, took over his father's business in 1895 and immediately turned over production to the Art Nouveau style, employing designers and technicians who had studied previously with Lalique. Besides Japanese and oriental influences, Fouquet used Egyptian styles for decorative ensembles (ill. p. 86). Attracted by the *genre Lalique*, numerous jewelers fell in with the Art Nouveau line, and almost all Art Nouveau artists in Paris took up the medium of jewelry, including Eugène Grasset, Alfons Maria Mucha,

Alfons Maria Mucha
Poster design for *Gismonda* (detail), 1894
Tempera on canvas, 198 × 67 cm

and Georges de Feure. The long-established jeweler Vever found in his sons, Paul and Henri, successors who were not only complete hands at the new style (ill. p. 87) but who even published in 1908 a 700-page book about French ornamental artists – a stimulating reference tome with reports on workshops, exhibitions, and production methods of this grandiose art form around 1900.

At the Paris Salon exhibition in 1901, Lalique exhibited for the first time ornamental pieces from crystal glass – the first step in a move towards a new medium for artistic creation. Where before 1900 he had been the protagonist of a new ornamental art, during the 1920s he became a celebrated artist in glass, in whose work the philosophy of an era was once again reflected.

Le Style Parisien: Alfons Maria Mucha –Jules Chéret – Eugène Grasset

Ces nymphes, je les veux perpétuer.
Stéphane Mallarmé[31]

A thematic thread that linked, indeed entwined, all these "art-makers" of around 1900 was – as already indicated – flowing hair and what came attached to it, namely woman. At the same time, allure manifested itself not just in art but also in flesh and blood. There were the great court-esans such as Bel Otéro or Cléo de Merode, indisputable "accessories" of the *Belle Époque*, and the great muses, like the tragedienne Sarah Bernhardt and the dancer Loïe Fuller. Both inspired artists in all aspects of their creation. Lalique designed diadems for the divine Bernhardt, although he had more or less rejected theatrical jewelry as artistically mediocre. Fouquet engaged the all-round genius Alfons Maria Mucha (1860–1939) as a designer, thus vicariously sharing in the immigrant Bohemian artist's fame. Mucha and Bernhardt could be relied on for bizarre notions and eccentric taste. A theatrical poster commissioned by the actress in great haste at Christmas 1894 conferred overnight on the hitherto unknown artist a halo that even now makes him seem one of the great figures of the turn of the century. The drama of the poster for *Gismonda*, a play by Victorien Sardou (1831–1908), caused a huge sensation and so entranced Sarah Bernhardt that for the next few years she gave Mucha an exclusive contract (ills. right and p. 89). Henceforth he assumed responsibility not just for all the actress's posters but also for her stage sets and costumes. Thereafter he was inundated with

Alfons Maria Mucha
Gismonda, poster, 1895
Color lithography, 217 × 74 cm
The first poster for Sarah Bernhardt and the Théatre de la Renaissance gave Mucha an artistic breakthrough virtually overnight and brought him fame. Sarah Bernhardt is portrayed in the costume of Gismonda in the last act of the play; her impressive pose and rapt facial expression became the prototype of French poster art around 1900.

Left:
Alfons Maria Mucha
Nature, bust, 1899–1900
Patinated bronze, gilt, silver-plated, 67 cm high
Execution by Pinedo, Paris
This bust shows all the features of the artist's style, and the representation of the indeterminately enigmatic character of the *Belle Époque* feminine type, which at times ruled all Paris, became an ideal outside France as well.

graphic commissions, for advertising posters, calendars, menu cards, magazine titles and *panneaux décoratifs* [decorative panels] (ill. left). Thanks to this – and his outstanding talent – Mucha developed into one of most creative artists of Art Nouveau. His work unites Byzantine traditions and contemporary stylistic features with the application of more delicate, softer colors in a new synthesis of unique individuality. Young women with dreamy expressions dressed in flowing robes are so to speak his "trademark" (ill. right). He himself never spoke about Art Nouveau and its theories and principles – "I do it my way" was his only observation.[32] Bold arabesques of thick female hair feature not only in his graphic work but also in ornamental designs and on textiles, in interiors and sculptural work. The bust entitled *Nature* (ill. opposite) incorporates all the characteristics of his style. In its representation of the indeterminately enigmatic character of the *Belle Époque* feminine type, which at times ruled all Paris, it became the ideal of female beauty outside France as well. In 1902, Mucha published *Documents décoratifs*, a pattern book of his ornamentation with suggestions for its practical application. Otherwise he remained reticent, disappearing from the art scene in Paris to live alternately in his homeland and America.

It was not just *Gismonda* that overwhelmed onlookers from the elevation of a hoarding. Never before had Paris seen so many artistic posters as it did around 1900. Visitors to the World Expositions were to be intensively courted, in order to promote the booming sales of industrial products. Posters extolled everything, ranging from bicycles through medicines to visits to the local nightspot. They caused a stir, and soon attracted collectors as well. Way back in 1868, improved printing technology had opened up new opportunities, and with the invention of color lithography in 1879 – a prerequisite for the artistic poster – the way opened for its march of triumph. Toulouse-Lautrec waxed enthusiastic about a Bonnard poster for "France Champagne" and hung it up in his workshop alongside Jules Chéret's poster for the Moulin Rouge. However, it was his own poster *La Goulue* that would revolutionise the whole genre and pioneer the development of advertising art later.

Jules Chéret (1836–1932), perhaps the most popular decorative painter and poster artist in France, represented the urbane, Parisian style within French poster art, creating as it were the "pin-up girl" of the *Belle Époque*. In an almost Rococo manner and with Impressionist coloring,

Alfons María Mucha
La Topaze, [Topaz], panneau décoratif [decorative panel], (reduced version), 1900
Color lithographie, 60 × 24 cm

he depicted figures of graceful young women of delightful radiance, which Paris loved (ill. p. 93). He made a significant contribution to the development of the poster, and considered snappy advertising texts in matching typefaces to be one of the most important parts of the poster. He felt that, to some extent, the typeface holds the key to the picture and should in every case be done by the artist himself. He drew the design on the block himself and supervised the proofs – what looked down from the hoardings of the city so light-footed and playfully had a solid crafted basis. In 1894, he designed a poster for an exhibition of Eugène Grasset (1841–1917), whom he esteemed. Grasset's rather Pre-Raphaelite, pensive young female figures are less fashionable (ill. p. 92 left). Born in Lausanne of an old artistic family, Grasset was, like the English, a reforming spirit, and in 1905 he published a textbook called *La méthode de composition*

Alfons María Mucha
Job, poster, 1897
Color lithography, 52 × 39.8 cm
Thanks to his outstanding talent, Mucha developed into one of the most creative artists of Art Nouveau. His work combines Byzantine traditions and elements of contemporary style with the application of delicate, soft colors, to create a new synthesis of unique individuality. Young women with pensive gazes wearing flowing robes are his "trademark".

Eugène Grasset
Drawing, color plaque, 1894–95
Modeled stoneware, glazed in color,
60 × 42 × 3 cm
Born of an old artistic family,
Grasset was, like the English, a
reforming spirit and, in his textbook
*La méthode de composition
ornamentale*, published in 1905, he
set out a convincing and enthusiastic
case for the principles of
democratizing art in the sense of an
aestheticism uniting all areas of art.
He put his own ideas into practice,
and set to work in all aspects of
applied art.

ornamentale, setting out a convincing and enthusiastic case for the principles of democratizing art in the sense of an aestheticism uniting all aspects of art. As a theoretician, he had already appeared in print in 1896 with his book *La plante et ses applications ornamentales*, which became a handbook of "flower mysticism". "If these reserves are used right, an infinite variety of forms and models can be found for all conceivable articles and objects," wrote Grasset in his publication, in which he included 160,000 varieties of plant. [33]

Maison Bing, L'Art Nouveau

*Art Nouveau is a nonsense; art cannot be new since
it is eternal.*
Alfons Maria Mucha[34]

Out of these manifold ingredients of the diverse stimuli and reflexes that electrified the cultural atmosphere of Paris in the 1880s and 1890s, a foaming cocktail was mixed on the threshold of the new century that, like every exclusive drink, required a name. Godfather at the christening was Siegfried (Samuel) Bing (1838–1905), a Paris-based citizen of Hamburg who is often described as the impresario and philosopher of Art Nouveau. On December 26 1895, he opened a gallery in the rue de Provence in order to give "new, young" artists in Paris a "place". The gallery was called Maison Bing, L'Art Nouveau. Bing thereby created a kind of collective term for everything, irrespective of its heterogeneity, that was distinct from the artistic taste that had ruled hitherto. The Art Nouveau idea did admittedly encounter criticism at first: "People were sorry for Bing. He was considered the victim of a treacherous coup by revolutionary artists who knew how to exploit his naivety. Edmond Goncourt, who had steeled himself to behave like a dignified gentleman at the exhibition, raised his arms as a sign of abhorrence once in the street", according to the French press.[35] In contrast, the English periodical *The Studio* celebrated the Galerie Art Nouveau as the great event of the artistic season. It honored a man who, since 1888, had published a *Treasury of Japanese Forms* in German, English, and French, thereby making a substantial contribution to a change in taste; a man who had spoken up for contemporary art, not in the least from naivety but with great commitment, and who moreover had promoted arts and crafts as well as the great Norwegian painter Edvard Munch. What roused feelings so much were the furniture and interior decorations of the Belgian Henry van de Velde – sneeringly apostrophised by the Goncourt brothers as "Yachting Style", glassware by Karl Koepping (ill. p. 263) and Louis Comfort Tiffany (p. 313 ff), the work of Otto Eckmann (ills. pp. 228, 260), glassware by Harry James Powell (ill. p. 33) and the creations of the wood sculptor François Rupert Carabin – in retrospect, heroes of Art Nouveau one and all. In the period that followed, however, under the pressure of "Parisian circumstances", Bing made concessions. He justified the compromise as attempting to revive "grace, logic, and purity", which were considered fundamental elements of French art.

Georges de Feure
Stained-glass window, ca. 1900
Leaded glass with enamel,
221 × 70 cm
Prompted by Samuel Bing, de Feure
worked in all areas of arts and crafts,
proving himself master of the
flawless, beautiful line. It adorns his
salons as filigree arabesque work;
everything is of fragilely beautiful
proportion and every object is imbued
with a feminine Art Nouveau
aestheticism. He had much success at
international exhibitions such as the
Secession Exposition in Munich in
1897 and in Turin in 1902. The high
point was, however, the one-man
exhibition staged by Bing in 1903.

Jules Chéret
Purgatif Géraudel [Géraudel purgatives], 1890
Tiled panel, iron frame, color glazed, 121.5 × 81.5 cm
Probably the most popular decorative painter and poster
artist in France, Chéret represented the urbane, Parisian style
within French poster art, creating as it were the "pin-up girl"
of the *Belle Époque*. In an almost Rococo manner and with
Impressionist coloring, he depicted figures of graceful young
women of delightful radiance, which thrilled Paris.

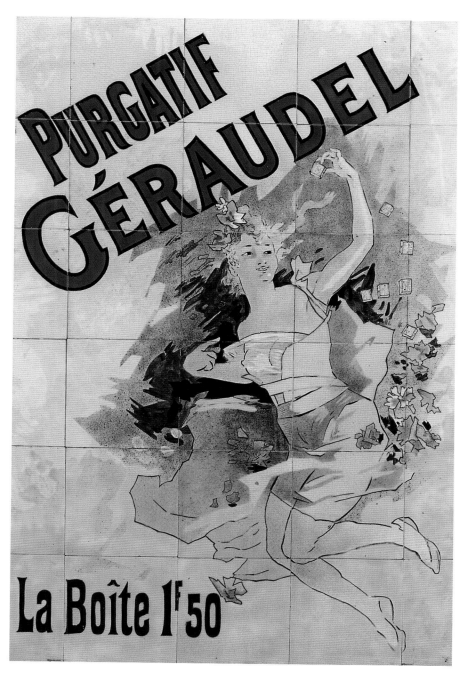

Jules Chéret
Jacket of the German edition of
Marcel Prévost's book
Pariserinnen [Parisians], Paris –
Leipzig – Munich, 1896
Color lithography, 19 × 26.5 cm

It was only with this effectively neo-Rococo
output that he appeased the public and exhibited
an "Art Nouveau style" that concurred with the
taste of the *Belle Époque*. From then on, Parisian
Art Nouveau was identified with the rich, delicate
furniture of Eugène Gaillard (ill. p. 94, right) and
Georges de Feure and the rather sculpturally
baroque work of Georges Hoentschel (ill. p. 94,
left). Despite (or perhaps because of) this,
Toulouse-Lautrec had an apartment done out in
Yachting Style.

Feminine Art Nouveau aestheticism: Georges de Feure – Eugène Gaillard

An additional aspect of the fragility of the
materials used in the arts and crafts of Parisian
Art Nouveau (glass, enamel, porcelain, horn, fruit
woods) and of the floral motifs, fragile fauna and
delicate female figures is the Rococo sentiment
reflected in many artistic products (ill. p. 95).
Eugène Gaillard (1862–1933) and George de
Feure (1868–1943) produced costly, upmarket
items of furniture in which all sharpnesses were
avoided in favor of smooth transitions and the
lines of ornamentation are sculptured and touch-
able. At the World Exposition in 1900, Bing
helped these pieces to gain the recognition
hitherto denied them. "The firm of L'Art Nouveau,

which is run by S. Bing, one of the main proponents of the style, exhibited a whole range of rooms designed by top-rank artists. We find *inter alia* a dressing room designed by de Feure; furniture made in natural ash wood, designed in refined, simple forms with really ingenious applied metal mounts and covered with a woolen material in delicate reseda colour which is embellished with stylish and extremely discreet linear patterns. There is a dining room by Gaillard with furniture designed on expansive lines; the walls are painted to match the lines on the furniture. … They are all luxury articles – every table costs several hundred francs … at any rate, these prices are low in comparison with those asked, and paid, for period furniture, where above all it is pricey material that counts. "[36]

Prompted by Bing, de Feure worked in all areas of arts and crafts, and henceforth the Art Nouveau style in Paris was virtually synonymous with de Feure's style. He proved himself to be a master of the flawless, beautiful line. It adorns his salons as filigree arabesque work; everything is of fragilely beautiful proportion (ill. p. 92) and every object is imbued with a feminine Art

Nouveau aestheticism. He had much success at international exhibitions such as the Secession Exposition of 1897 in Munich and again in Turin in 1902; the climax was Bing's one-man show for him in 1903. He supplied Limoges with designs for highly delicate porcelain, he was active as a designer of jewelry, textiles, and glassware, and made a valuable contribution to book graphics. The son of a Dutch architect and a French mother, de Feure grew up in the Netherlands and became acquainted with Symbolism while apprenticed in the book trade. His admiration for the painter Pierre Cécile Puvis de Chavannes (ill. p. 23), who helped him to the best of his ability, took him to Paris. As a watercolorist and set-designer, he began his career under the pseudonym van Feuren. He owed his profound interest in book illustration and interior decoration to his upbringing. Over and above Art Nouveau, he was also active as an Art Deco artist, and painted the interior of the Restaurant Konss in Paris, built by the Berlin architect Bruno Möhring (1863–1929). The graceful "ornamental objects" of *fin-de-siècle* art, as for example produced by André-Fernand Thesmar (1843–1912) (ill. p. 95, left),

Georges Hoentschel
Chair, 1900
Algerian plane, 102 cm high,
55 cm wide
Musée des Arts Décoratifs, Paris
The furniture of Georges Hoentschel is opulently Baroque. Though his pieces have an undeniable touch of the representational, they are to be considered primarily as "sculpture", that is, floral objects.

Eugène Gaillard
Cabinet, for Samuel Bing, L'Art Nouveau, 1901–02
Fruit wood, 184 × 107 × 37 cm
After the exhibition in Samuel Bing's gallery, the Art Nouveau style in Paris was identified with the rich, delicate pieces of furniture made by Eugène Gaillard and Georges de Feure.

belong to the delicate world of Rococo. More opulently Baroque is the furniture of Georges Hoentschel (1855–1915). Though his pieces have an undeniable touch of the representational, they are to be taken primarily as "sculpture", that is, floral objects (ill. opposite).

Symbolism in stone – Jules Aimé Lavirotte

Baroque abundance is likewise a feature of Jules Aimé Lavirotte's blend of architecture and decoration. His block of flats in the Avenue Rapp in Paris is also "Symbolism in stone". Salvador Dalí acknowledged the building as the first example of "hysterical sculpture" or "prolonged erotic ecstasy"[37], akin to his own Surrealist imagery. Thanks to its "unprecedented" nature and because of its "ornamental automatism", the facade of this "architectural sculpture" was awarded first prize in a creative competition in 1901. The jury was impressed by the masterly application of ceramic tiles on the building itself as well as in the interior. But the real appeal of this architecture lies in the manifestation of an omnipresent sexual imagery. Right in the entrance we encounter Lavirotte's almost obsessive, compulsive fetishism. The phallus on the door paneling and the vaginal surround obviously represent a sexual act – a vision that is repeated several times on the building. The provocation is nonetheless done with exquisite craft and tremendous *élan vital* (ill. p. 96). In glaring contrast is Frantz Jourdain's department store for Samaritaine, begun only two years later. It is a building that even today looks "contemporary" (ill. p. 97). In comparing the two, the words of the architect Pierre Jeanneret (1896–1967), a cousin of Le Corbusier, come to mind: "My house is practical. I am grateful, as I am grateful to the railway engineer and the telephone company. My heart you have failed to move."[38]

Masters of fire: Potters and glassmakers

Simple and yet "moving" in the haptic sense are the ceramic pieces of the artists of the "Groupe des arts du feu", as they are aptly called in French. The fame of late–19th century French pottery extends far and wide. Ever since the Vienna World Exposition of 1873, the superiority of French ceramicists has been noted without qualification

André-Fernand Thesmar
Bowl and stand, 1897
Plique à jour enamel, silver, fired gold, 13 cm high
The graceful, playful "ornamental objects" of *fin-de-siècle* art, such as those produced by André-Fernand Thesmar, for example, belong to the delicate world of Rococo.

Ernest Cardeilhac
Suger bowl with spoon, ca. 1910
Silver-plated metal, ivory, 18.7 cm high
An additional aspect of the fragility of the materials used in the arts and crafts of Parisian Art Nouveau (glass, enamel, porcelain, horn, fruit woods) and of the floral motifs, fragile fauna and delicate female figures, is the Rococo sentiment reflected in many artistic products.

in critical reports. French supremacy in the "arts of fire" dates to the establishment in Paris of a ceramics studio by the Alsatian Joseph–Théodore Deck (1823–91). Numerous Art Nouveau potters were turned out by this studio, and it was here, with the technology of new glazing processes, that the foundation was laid for the quality of work that later won such admiration. Edmond Lachenal (1855–1948) was a pupil of Deck and shared his teacher's delight in experimenting (ill. p. 99). He developed the *émaille mat velouté* process, in which acid is used to give the glazing base a velvety top coating. "Velvety" also describes the mixed, matt colors of his pottery.

The special position of the potter Jean Carriès (1855–94) is aptly summed up in the title of Arsène Alexandre's monograph: *Jean Carriès, imagier et potier, étude d'un œuvre et d'une vie* [Jean Carriès, image-maker and potter, a study of an oeuvre and a life]. Carriès was a creative spirit and inventor of genius, a protagonist of *émaux-mattes*, the matt enamels whose warm glazing tones became a hallmark of all French potters. The subtle surfaces of his pots (ill. p. 98) provide a high order of pleasure to the senses. The work of Auguste Delaherche (1857–1940) demonstrates particularly clearly how artistic creation and virtuoso mastery of materials are united in Art Nouveau. The fantastic color tones of the pots

arise in the end only during firing, which must be closely controlled by the artist throughout. Delaherche's early pots feature plant motifs (ill. p. 99), which are strongly outlined and applied with thick layers of colored pastes. Gradually, however, Delaherche gave up using figurative ornament and used nuances of color alone as decoration.

All the "masters of fire" share a reverence for Japanese stoneware. The Japanese pots exhibited within the framework of the 1878 World Exposition had left an indelible impression. The sublime glazes of Japanese pottery and the canon of plain forms shaped the work of the *arts du feu* artists, who, as Delaherche once declared, were creating works of art, not "pots" (ill. p. 99).

François Eugène Rousseau (1827–91) was both a potter and a glassmaker, and his glassware work deeply impressed and inspired Gallé. Rousseau had likewise profited from the newly discovered art of Japan; he created cased glassware with surface effects that are reminiscent of the treacle glazes of Japanese stoneware. Similarly, he preferred to use Far Eastern forms, creating thick-sided, mostly crackle, glassware that displays inclusions of gold leaf and cloudy colorations made with metal oxides (ill. p. 74). Glassmaking as an art in Paris was undoubtedly overshadowed by Nancy; nonetheless, a somewhat "light" –

Jean Carriès
Vase, ca. 1890
Stoneware, glazed in relief, crazed treacle glaze, 20 cm high
Carriès was a creative spirit and inventor of genius, a protagonist of *émaux-mattes*, matt enamels whose warm glazing tones became a hallmark of all French potters. The subtle surfaces of his pots provide a high order of pleasure to the senses.

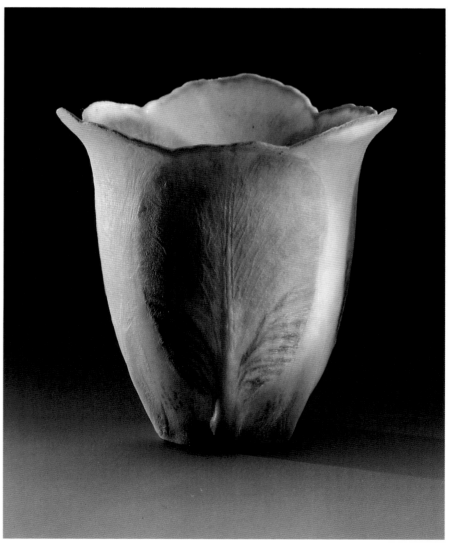

François-Emile Décorchemont
Goblet, 1907
Pâte de verre, 20.5 cm high
Pâte de verre is a mixture of colored oxides with molten glass, fired like stoneware. Besides Décorchemont, Dammouse also worked in this unusual raw material.

Albert-Louis Dammouse
Coupe iris [iris cup], ca. 1910
Pâte de verre, 8.8 cm high, 8.3 cm diameter
Musée des Arts Décoratifs, Paris
The small graceful vessels of Dammouse have a weightless transparency. They are decorated in relief with friezes from the Art Nouveau repertoire of insects, flower umbrils, and marine plants, or shaped with openwork sides filled in with translucent enamel. The rather rough surface of the glass paste forms a contrast to this delicate work, as an additional stylistic device. The result was fragile masterpieces of aloof charm.

Clément Massier
Vase, 1891
Stoneware, dark red body, luster
glaze, 21.8 cm high

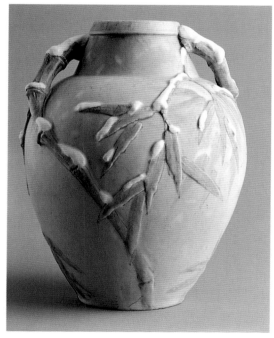

Edmond Lachenal
Snow on bamboo, vase, ca. 1900
Stoneware, decoration in relief, fired,
high-fire alkaline glaze, 32 cm high
All the "masters of fire" share a
reverence for Japanese stoneware.
The Japanese pots exhibited within
the framework of the 1878 World
Exposition had left an indelible
impression. The sublime glazes of
Japanese pottery and the canon of
plain forms shaped the work of the
arts du feu artists, who, as
Delaherche once declared, were
creating works of art, not "pots".

Auguste Delaherche
Vase with peacock-feather decoration, ca. 1889
Stoneware, 42.5 cm high
Musée des Arts Décoratifs, Paris
The early pots of Delaherche feature plant motifs, strongly
outlined with thick layers of colored pastes. Gradually,
however, he gave up using figurative ornament and used
nuances of color alone.

both in formality and in material – variant of Art Nouveau glassware was evolved, including creations in *pâte de verre* (ill. p. 98), a mixture of colored oxides with molten glass that was fired like stoneware. The artists who worked with this unusual raw material, François-Emile Décorchemont (1880–1971) and Albert-Louis Dammouse (1848–1926), were originally ceramicists. Their small, graceful vessels have a weightless transparency. They are decorated with friezes in relief from the Art Nouveau repertoire of insects, flower umbels or marine plants, or shaped with openwork sides filled in with translucent enamel. The rather rough surface of the glass paste forms a contrast to this delicate work, as an additional stylistic device. The result was fragile masterpieces of aloof charm (ill. p. 98).

A living arabesque – Loïe Fuller

In ever bolder serpentines, she waxed into a giant ornament, whose metamorphoses of turbulent flaring up, subsiding and engulfment in darkness and curtain appeared in our memories like symbols of Art Nouveau. Friedrich Ahlers-Hestermann[39]

The muse of Art Nouveau as a whole was the dancer Loïe Fuller (1862–1928). Beside the ubiquitous flora and fauna, no motif appeared so frequently in Art Nouveau as the by then legendary American (ills. right and p. 101) and her Dance of Veils. Around 1900, we encounter her figure, wreathed in high-whirling veils from which her dainty head and moving arms emerge, in almost every artistic discipline and in the work of almost every artist (ills. p. 251, 312). This "arabesque incarnate" fired the imagination. The cultured world lay at her feet, and the Loïe Fuller phenomenon became the subject of countless grave discourses. She herself viewed the matter more pragmatically: "My costume was so long that I could not avoid constantly treading on the hem and so saw myself forced to hold it up with raised arms and leap around the stage like a winged spirit. Suddenly applause broke out in the auditorium and people shouted: 'It's a butterfly! A butterfly!'"[40] This took place in an obscure little play called *Quack* in which Fuller appeared in New York in 1891. The play itself soon closed, but the Serpentine Dance conquered Art Nouveau. Her fluid movements were congenially matched to the "linear dream" of the time, and Loïe Fuller did everything to fan the flames. She shrouded herself in exquisitely thin veils, and developed a sophisticated choreography involving colored lights, thereby turning herself into "total art". With her dance, she succeeded in creating a visible connection between Symbolism, Art Nouveau, and a new conception of color and light. With shrewd business sense, she also had her ideas patented, such as the stage lit from below. She enjoyed her greatest triumph at the World Exposition in Paris in 1900. A special theater was constructed for her on the exposition site that, with her inside, represented a perfect Art Nouveau object. Just as Mucha attained stardom via Bernhardt, Fuller enabled the hitherto only modestly successful sculptor François-Raoul Larche (1860–1912) to win immortal fame. Her erotically expressive, back-lit performances gave Larche the idea of setting a lamp bulb inside the whirling veils of his bronze statue of Fuller. It was a most avant-garde inspiration for the time (ill. opposite), establishing him as the originator of a key Art Nouveau work. Yet Loïe Fuller was not just the muse of the three-dimensional arts. Toulouse-Lautrec created an unsurpassable representation of her Dance of Veils (ill. right), and she also inspired Stéphane Mallarmé (1842–98), who dedicated numerous poems to her, and Claude Debussy, who decided that his music was never more perfectly interpreted than through her. She was also a friend of the husband-and-wife physicist team Pierre and Marie Curie.

Henri de Toulouse-Lautrec

**I have set myself the task of being true, not idealistic. Perhaps this is a mistake, but it is impossible for me to overlook warts . . .
Henri de Toulouse-Lautrec[41]**

Henri de Toulouse-Lautrec (1864–1901) is not to be pigeonholed as an Art Nouveau artist – such an attribution would be unfair to this extraordinary genius. However, his influence on, and indeed his participation in, the events around 1900 was too great to pass him by unmentioned in the context of our subject. The hallmarks of his artistic creations – ornamentally simplified visual fields, the drama of detail, the contrast between empty and full fields, the delight in unexpected silhouettes, the passion for the truths of the human face, the physiognomies of clothing, attitudes, and gestures – shaped the whole graphic style of Art Nouveau (ill. p. 103).
Without becoming a mere reporter or portrait painter, he was the only one to follow the demand of Honoré Daumier (1808–79) that "il faut être de son temps" [one must be of one's

Odilon Redon
Ophelia, design for *La Revue Blanche*, ca. 1900
Pastel, 49.5 × 66.5 cm
"Le peintre comme le lithographe s'affirme Prince du Rêve." [Like lithographers, painters stand forth as Princes of Dreams.] (Thadée Natanson, in *La Revue Blanche*, June 1894)

Henri de Toulouse-Lautrec
Loïe Fuller, 1893
Color lithography, partly tinged with gold dust, 37.5 × 25.3 cm
The dancer Loïe Fuller was not only the muse of the figurative arts, such as in Toulouse-Lautrec's unsurpassable representation of her Dance of Veils. She also inspired Stéphane Mallarmé, who dedicated numerous poems to her, and Claude Debussy, who decided that his music had never been more perfectly interpreted than by her. She was also a friend of the husband-and-wife physicist team Pierre and Marie Curie.

time], and he passed beyond the succession of visual experiences to explore the psychological realm of moods and feelings, directing his attention to the enigmatic and at the same time existential, where he acted as witness and sympathizer. "He [Toulouse-Lautrec] has a room in a brothel," wrote Jules Renard (1864–1910), "and gets on well with all ladies that have unaffected feelings, that are alien to respectable women, and are wonderfully good at being models."[42] The crippled painter found "unaffected feelings" in the world of Montmartre, far from the emotional hypocrisy of the bourgeoisie. Nonetheless, he did not idealize the milieu. He drew whores large and small with great affection but without sentimental gloss, and if no drawing paper happened to be to hand, then on tablecloths, in the margins of newspapers or on marble slabs – no *chronique scandaleuse* but deeply moving compositions of admirable succinctness (ill. p. 70). Facial features almost in caricature, glaringly lit dramatic outlines – these are his stylistic devices. Like Baudelaire in his "fleurs du mal.", Lautrec in his pictures attempts to express the inexpressible by means of aesthetic shocks. Yet, that a certain Art Nouveau character exists in the composition of his posters with their linear oscillations, is undeniable. The phrase "a provoked life" may serve to describe the existence of this aristocrat of the bohemian world, a term coined by the German poet Gottfried Benn (1886–1956) to sum up the artist's extraordinarily intensive, concentrated and thereby truncated career. Toulouse-Lautrec did not take part in the epoch-making abstract discussions of his time; as befitted a risqué, intuitive way of life, he submitted his work and thereby himself for discussion. His figures, stylized in images of extreme moment, are representatives of their era but in the same moment timeless images of human disposition.

François-Raoul Larche
Loïe Fuller, table lamp, 1901
Bronze, gilt, hollow cast,
45.5 cm high
Bavarian National Museum, Munich
"In ever bolder serpentines, she grew into a giant ornament, whose metamorphoses of turbulent flaring up, subsiding and engulfment in darkness and curtain appeared in the memory like symbols of Art Nouveau." (Friedrich Ahlers-Hestermann, see note 39)

La Revue Blanche – The graphic line

Although he did not belong to any group with an avowed agenda, Toulouse-Lautrec was nonetheless a lively participant in the shaping of the important art periodical *La Revue Blanche*, first published in Belgium in 1889. The "White Review" was called thus because white is the sum of all colors and a white sheet appears unwritten and open to all opinions and trends. Moreover, its founders were under the influence of Mallarmé's theory of the mystery of the "white page", with which a poet sees himself confronted. The list of the authors published in this "trade journal" of the Nabis – one of the artistic groups devoted to Symbolism – is an almanac of *fin-de-siècle* literature, which together with the graphics of notable artists contributed toward the international fame of *La Revue Blanche*. Félix Vallotton (ill. p. 13), Toulouse-Lautrec and Pierre Bonnard (1867–1947) were the main contributors.

The poster art of Bonnard stands in a close, mutually stimulating relationship with his painting. The visual conception is developed purely from the color; everything remains open, full of drive and dynamically rhythmic. The silhouettes of Bonnard's figures have an almost collage-like effect, frankly avowing their affinity to Japanese colored woodcuts (ill. p. 102). In aesthetic circles, the horizon had long been extended beyond the world hitherto considered civilized and found both the secret code for creative form and philosophical solutions first and foremost in East Asia. The serpentine dragon shapes of Sino-Japanese art, whose motifs form interlinked ornamentation, were, for example, adapted by Paul-Elie Ranson (1861–1909), another contributor to *La Revue Blanche* in an arabesque, Art Nouveau manner.

The finale of Art Nouveau and its almost seamless transition into the following expressive Fauvist period makes it clear that all the elements of abstraction had already been worked out by about 1900. Linear diction is a principle feature of structure for the Fauvists as well, but the harmony is shattered. The euphoria of the arabesque mutates into shrill disharmony.

Pierre Bonnard
Child with sandcastle, or *Child with bucket*, ca. 1894
Oil on canvas, 167 × 50 cm
Musée d'Orsay, Paris
Bonnard's poster art stands in a close, mutually stimulating relationship with his painting. The visual conception is developed purely from the color; everything remains open, full of drive, and dynamically rhythmic. The silhouettes of Bonnard's figures have an almost collage-like effect, frankly avowing their affinity with Japanese colored woodcuts.

Henri de Toulouse-Lautrec
Divan Japonais, 1893
Color lithography, 81 × 60.5 cm
The hallmarks of Lautrec's artistic
creations – ornamentally simplified
visual fields, the drama of detail,
the contrast between empty and
full fields, the delight in
unexpected silhouettes, the passion
for the truths of the human
countenance, the physiognomies of
clothing, attitudes and gestures –
stamped themselves on the whole
graphic style of Art Nouveau.

Hector Guimard
Glass wall in stairwell, Castel
Béranger, 16, rue La Fontaine,
Paris, 1895–98
"Falconnier" tiles of blown glass,
named after the inventor. Made by
Société anonyme de verrerie à
bouteilles du Nord, Dorognie "Yet
more amazing historically is the
way of the staircase at the back, a
wall of heavy double-curved glass
panels of alternating shapes whose
very irregularity of surface does
what in terracotta panels had to be
done by the craftsman's will."
(Nikolaus Pevsner, *The Sources
of Modern Architecture and
Design*, Thames & Hudson, 1968)

However, what we have called Stem Style runs through the whole house, inside and outside. The whole range of grilles, banisters, wall surfaces, glazing, mosaic floors, runners, furniture – all designed by Guimard – display this ornamental style. He turns it into a complete decorative system such as no one before ever enterprised. The main doorway and the succeeding vestibule are at once prime examples of it. Plant stems shoot upwards, past each other, in among each other, singly or in tufts or sheaves, gracefully dipping and swaying. And for every stem there comes a moment when it is electrified. Then it zips back and forth or bends round in a great loop or – most commonly of all – darts around in the air like the crack of a whiplash. This gives rise to unexpected combinations. Large plump omega shapes emerge, the necks of cobras swelling up, hanging Persian palm fronds, egg-shaped palettes so shredded up that the edges fray into shavings and squiggles, the ends of which keep curling round and round into capricious fishhooks, in between, something like the stylized waves of the Japanese, or like large jellyfish with wide-curved tentacles, and all this with the urge to transform itself into something handwritten, a flourish, which the Italians so aptly call *ghirigoro*. It is quite peculiar. Apparently arbitrary, it yields to a harmony that does not want for decorative force. In the entrance hall, for example, when the whiplashes crack around in gleaming gold before our eyes. Or on the walls of the rooms, when the motif seems like a dense shower of shooting stars. Or on the large glazed areas, ... no, although very original, these are perhaps too anatomical. Fixed in blue, red, and yellow, they are strikingly reminiscent of anatomical diagrams of the blood system: arteries red, veins blue, lymph vessels yellow.

What is consistently avoided throughout, in everything, is anything parallel or symmetrical.

Ludwig Hevesi, *Acht Jahre Sezession, March 1897–June 1905 – Kritik, Polemik, Chronik,* [Eight Years of the Secession Movement, March 1897–June 1905 – A critique, polemic and chronicle]
Vienna, 1906

The language of flora and fauna

Nancy

Anonymous
Design for ornament, ca. 1901
From a pattern book of the École de Nancy
The thistle – the armorial flower of the city of Nancy – was the most important ornamental motif of the whole artistic output of Nancy, a symbol of Lorraine's will to resist. It was accompanied by the inscription "Qui s'y frotte, s'y pique" [Touch thistles and be pricked]. It also happened to conform with the floral character of Art Nouveau.

Je recolte en secret des fleurs mystérieuses.
Alfred de Musset[1]

Patriotism as a driving force

In the last quarter of the 19th century, in numerous countries of Europe and in North America, artists had begun to abandon the overworked recycling of historical styles of the past in favor of a self-conscious, artificial style of art. Their motivation for doing so was as varied as their artistic output, and ranged from pure *l'art-pour-l'art* thinking to social commitment. Just as often, the *zeitgeist* presupposed national purposes; pronounced patriotic tendencies, however, occur chiefly in politically oppressed regions. Even if Art Nouveau was from the first an international movement with an aversion to everything nationalistic, it is remarkable nevertheless that, precisely where patriotism was a motivating force behind attempts at reform, Art Nouveau brought forth its most brilliant achievements, namely in Nancy and in Finland.

With Paris ever more dominant as the intellectual and cultural centre of France, the provincial towns had steadily lost importance during the 19th century. To be able to understand the consequence of Nancy for Art Nouveau, account must be taken of the political situation of Lorraine, truncated after the war of 1870. Throughout its thousand-year history, the Duchy of Lorraine had remained powerful and unified. The partition of the north had a shock effect on the province, which in turn released an immense surge of artistic vitality. Strengthen the cultural heritage was the watchword. In addition, refugees from the *départements* of Meurthe-et-Moselle and Meuse-et-Vosges, and also from annexed Alsace, began to pour in. Among them were numerous artistic families such as Daum

and Muller, the designer Jacques Gruber and the *ébeniste* Herbst, all of them later leading personalities of the École de Nancy. The cross of Lorraine is not only a trade mark of numerous factories but also a favored decorative motif. Whereas the cross of Lorraine stands for the still undivided province, the thistle (ill. opposite) is the armorial flower of the city of Nancy. In the following years, it became the most important ornamental motif in the artistic output of the École de Nancy – a symbol of resistance, accompanied by the inscription "Qui s'y frotte, s'y pique" [Touch thistles and be pricked].[2] It also happened to conform with the floral character of Art Nouveau.

The close relationship of Lorraine artists with nature derives in part from the general trend of the time, but it is also due to the particular conception of art as *art naturiste*, emphasizing the love of the flora and fauna of the homeland. Reveling in floral decoration meant also attempting to win back a lost paradise. Émile Gallé, *le maître d'Art Nouveau*, decorated the doors of his furniture studio with the motto: "Ma racine est au fond des bois."[3] Consequently, Nancy became in retrospect virtually synonymous with the floral version of Art Nouveau.

Pantheism and flower mysticism

De la flore lorraine, nous avons tiré des applications à nos métiers.
From the manifesto of the École de Nancy[4]

In 1903, the English periodical *The Studio* published a report in which the critic Henri Frantz recalled "living in a city the refinement of which recalls, on a small scale, that of Athens … It must not be forgotten," he continued, "that in the

Louis Majorelle
Nénuphar lamp, ca. 1900
Patinated bronze, cast and buffed, glass shade, 59.5 cm high
Execution by Daum, Nancy
Majorelle's designs for the Daum glass factory – lamps and vase stands – belong among the most decorative works of Art Nouveau.

eighteenth century Nancy was a remarkably beautiful, indeed a brilliant city, with its rows of imposing edifices, their facades adorned in a style alike severe and pure, their entrance gates of finely chiseled ironwork, every detail thoroughly appropriate and harmonious, the whole effect forming a perfect feast to the appreciative connoisseur."[5]

Nancy possesses one of the most important creations of the Rococo style, the perfect *vue d'ensemble*, in the Place Stanislas, designed by Emmanuel Héré de Corny (1705–63) and adorned with the celebrated ironwork of Jean Lamour. Further distinguishing features of the specific art in Nancy around 1900 reveal themselves as lightness, a vibrant gracefulness, pastel tones, asymmetry, *rocaille*, and Rococo.

The patriotic character of the École de Nancy is not to be equated with narrow-minded nationalism. The psychological effectiveness of the sensitive masterpieces from Lorraine also rested on the intelligently translated self-awareness of the artists who made them. As may be gathered from the article by Henri Frantz published in England, international recognition had already been gained, but the leading capitals were likewise quickly conquered. The active colony of exiles from Lorraine in Paris, led by the art critic Roger Marx (1859–1913) from Nancy, a childhood friend of Gallé's, exploited growing national feelings to promote "their" artists. His articles about the École de Nancy, written in heavy, Symbolist language, are themselves a witness to the era. Around 1900, the poetry of both Romanticism and Symbolism played an important role in the work of all artists, alongside the symbols of naturally vegetative forces and a subtly conceived flower mysticism. Using a precise study of nature as a basis, artists developed an individual, living language of plant and animal motifs. Incontestably the favorite flowers of the *Belle Époque* were orchids and calla lilies (ills. left, opposite, pp. 115, 118). The literature of Symbolism had established its own flower mysticism in the mid-19th century, the masterpiece of which must undoubtedly be the *Les Fleurs du mal* cycle of poems by Charles Baudelaire (1821–67). The poet took flower mysticism as a parable of the bouquet of "stupidity, error, sin, and filthy minds" of the present world, which he abhorred. Following on from Symbolism, Art Nouveau subsequently established a language of flowers, which served partly to express moods and inclinations, partly to serve purely decorative points of view.

Albert Braut
Girl with calla lily, ca. 1900
Oil on canvas, 145.5 × 58.4 cm
Incontestably the favorite flowers of
the *Belle Époque* were orchids and
calla lilies, images of woman. The
literature of Symbolism had already
established its own flower mysticism
in the mid-19th century, *Les Fleurs
du mal* [Flowers of Evil] cycle of
poems by Charles Baudelaire being
considered its chef-d'œuvre.

Gallé and his "comrades-in-arms" had devoted
themselves to a form of artistic pantheism, and
carried across into their works a "nature display"
of wholly sensuous and yet at once intellectual
perceptions. The body of a vase is shaped into an
onion whose outer skin is beginning to peel; the
swirling color threads at the foot of the vase are
the source of all plant life – the roots. Night-
shades convey melancholy and renunciation,
meadow saffron stands for transitoriness. Narcotic
plants are bitter-sweet, while the secretive
atmosphere of the marsh and its vegetation
exercised a magic attraction. The writhing lines
of creepers and climbing plants were, as might
be expected, very appropriate for the new style.
Umbels and panicles fitted in well with the
decorative ordering and grading system of Art
Nouveau. Blue dahlias were properly decadent,
dahlias, wisterias, and magnolias were heavy
with scent. Fancy orchids were described by
Joris-Karl Huysmans (1848–1907) in *A rebours*
(1884), the "bible" of Art Nouveau artists: "The
gardeners brought new varieties that seemed
like artificial skins shot with red blood vessels;
and the majority, as if consumed by leprosy,
spread out their pale flesh, spotted with rash
and afflicted with lichen; … echinopses [Globe
thistles] whose wadding-wrapped blooms had
the hateful rose of a mutilated limb ..."[6] Callae
and irises in contrast were an image of woman,
callae because of their sucking bells, irises as
symbols of sexual chastity. The *fleur mystique*,
the mystic flower, is the lily, symbol of purity,
which, soaked in the blood of the martyrs, grows
up to the throne of the Virgin. We encounter the
whole vocabulary of "flower language" both
formally and artistically in every possible branch
of *fin-de-siècle* art. Facades, pictures and picture
frames all "bloom", pots grow in floral shapes on
plant-shaped étagères – it is a floral roundelay
without end (ill. p. 117). Yet, with its strong
Symbolist bias, Art Nouveau should not be
comprehended just in terms of form and art, but
as the immediate forerunner of our present. It
does not belong among the wholly concluded
eras such as the Renaissance, the Baroque
period and other art-historical periods.

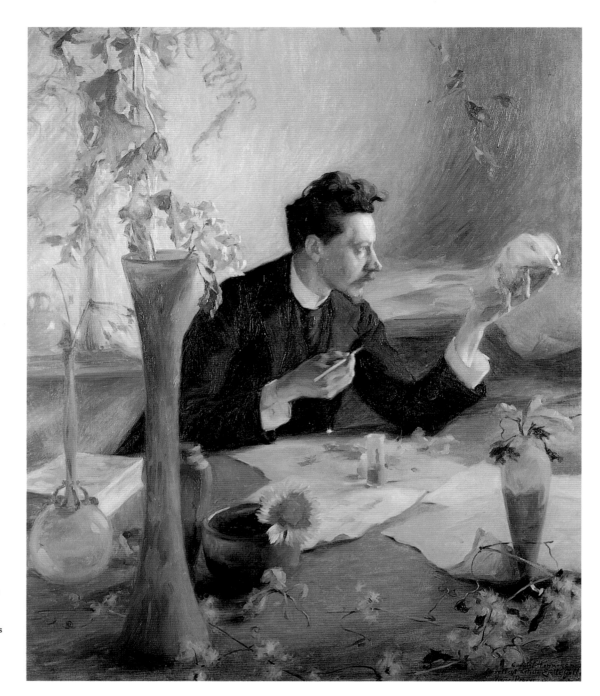

Victor Prouvé
Portrait of Émile Gallé (detail),
1892
Oil on canvas, 150 × 98 cm
Musée de l'Ecole de Nancy, Nancy
"The ambience depicts the lyrical
poetic spirit of Gallé, to which the
treatment of light also contributes as
an integrating element, forming a
kind of halo behind the head of the
subject." (Nancy 1900, exhibition
catalog)

Émile Gallé

The work of Gallé is unfathomable like a mysterious
temple, that no one enters without awe and bewilderment.
Grace and beauty are only the outer clothing. In the
depths of the consecrated area shines the flame of the
spirit.
Roger Marx[7]

The enthusiasm of the art critic Roger Marx for
the work of his friend Émile Gallé (1846–1904)
may seem today rather extravagant, but undoubtedly the quote above does sum up the essence
of Gallé's art. His wealth of ideas in the technical
aspects of glass and ceramics, and also in wood,
remain unmatched. However, the real genius of
Gallé unfolds only in the blending of poetry and
philosophy with the physical material. Émile was
born into his craft. His father, Charles Gallé,
married into a mirror business, and his rapid
successes with production encouraged him to
extend his product range to include faience
earthenware, a line that suited his inclinations.
As an ambitious, educated man, he planned the
upbringing of his son very carefully, and sent him
to a classics-biased high school where Émile's
literary and rhetorical gifts in Latin and French
could be nurtured. Brought up in a strict
Protestant household, Émile read the Bible
with his mother every day, but soon added readings more to his own taste. Molded by this

Émile Gallé

Magnolias, vase, 1901
Glass body, flashed several times,
powdered glass inclusions, cameo
cut, repoussé, intercalaire, 25 cm
high (reproduction at original size)
"The artist does not set chemical
reactions in train, nor produce the
flower, insect or landscape, but
portrays vital traits, as it were the
essence of what he sees and
experiences. A scientist may assert
that a weeping willow is no sadder
than other kinds of willow, but for a
sensitive person it is the saddest tree
there is." (Émile Gallé, see note 11)

upbringing, all his life he sought to consolidate his standing as a *bon bourgeois*, although, like the main character Jean des Esseintes in Huysman's novel *A rebours*, he lived in a world of abstract beauty far removed from the bourgeoisie. His early emotional attachment to nature showed itself not just in botanical studies and attempts at drawing but above all in contemplation of the philosophy of nature. He was still only 15 when he designed floral motifs for the family business that were translated on to glassware and pottery. The following year he left school and went to Germany, spending the years 1862 to 1866 mainly in Weimar. His studies reveal the wide range of his interests. He enrolled for lectures in art history, botany, zoology, and philosophy, took up sculpture and drawing, and devoted himself intensively to the music of contemporary composers. In 1866, he went to Meisenthal in the Saar Valley, to join the glass manufacturers Burgun, Schverer & Co. His aim was to learn all the necessary chemical processes for glassmaking. His outstanding capabilities were recognized there, providing him with confirmation that he was just the person to revolutionize arts and crafts.

From 1870, Gallé worked in the family stoneware business in Saint-Clément. The rustic tableware produced to his designs have become known as "service de ferme". The figures of cats, dogs, hens, and armorial lions that his rich imagination conjured up, are also much sought after by collectors. He had a congenial working relationship with the painter, sculptor, and designer Victor Prouvé even in these early days, Prouvé's preference for the romanticized Middle Ages making a great impression on Gallé and having a lasting influence on his first enamel decorations on glass.

At the outbreak of the First World War, Gallé was 24 and so was called up. After demobilization at the end of the war, he found himself cut off from his laboratory in Meisenthal and decided, in a fit of restlessness, to go with his father to London and then to Paris. He admired antique glass and Far Eastern art in the Victoria and Albert Museum in South Kensington and in the British Museum, and used his time for studies at Kew Gardens. His encounter with the glassware of antiquity, Venice, and Islam in the Louvre also made a vivid impression on him. Nonetheless, his stylistic borrowings from these were relatively short-lived.

Émile Gallé
Ornamental bowl (detail), ca. 1878
Faience, fired decoration on enamel containing tin, diameter 58 cm
Musée d'Orsay, Paris
Like all his skills, Gallé put the spirit of Japan to the test in his faience work before sublimating it in the unmatched quality of his art glass. "It was from Japanese art that he [Gallé] derived the general scheme, the fundamental principle of his style; but we must not infer that he imitates it in any servile manner. Nothing can be more unlike Japanese art than Monsieur Gallé's work ... Only the idea of the Japanese style is also his; and given that principle he has worked in art by the light of his own instinct and taste." (Henri Frantz, see note 9)

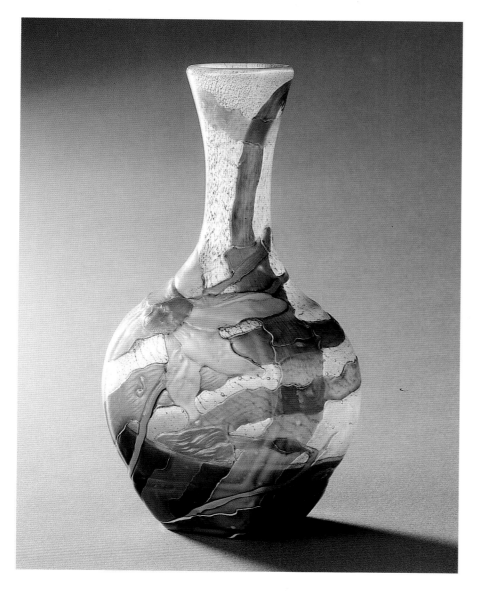

Émile Gallé
Vase with narcissus, ca. 1900
Marqueterie-de-verre, cut in relief
and incised on flashed glass sides,
oxide inclusions, 21 cm high
With the difficult *marqueterie-de-
verre* and intercalaire techniques,
colored glass plate, powdered glass or
even gold and metals are rolled on to
the still-hot glass and immediately
worked.

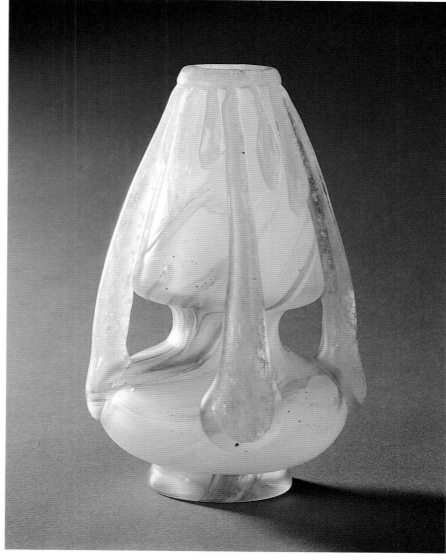

À la japonica

**Bénissons le caprice du sort qui a fait naître un
Japonais à Nancy.**
Émile Gallé[8]

Gallé's enthusiasm for Japanese art, on the other
hand, had a permanent influence on his work. His
interest had already been awakened in Paris and
London, and in the aesthetic approach of Japanese
artists he saw his own ideas put into practice. In
later years (1882–85), he established a close
friendship with the Japanese Tokuso Takasima,
who attended the École Forestière in Nancy. In
1897, the art critic Henri Frantz wrote of Gallé: "It
was from Japanese art that he derived the general
system, the fundamental principle of his style; but
we must not infer that he imitates it in any servile
manner. Nothing can be more unlike Japanese art
than Monsieur Gallé's work … only the idea of
Japanese style is also his; and given that principle
he has worked it out by the light of his own instinct

and taste. He finds constant inspiration, nay, even
collaboration, in nature. When Monsieur Émile
Gallé reproduces plant form he extracts from it its
decorative lines and colouring with the most
artistic sense. He seems to condense the whole
motive of a plant, to give it an attitude, a
movement, to draw out its individuality in a very
living way, and yet never to lose sight of the object
he is designing."[9] On numerous vases by Gallé,
one finds his homage to the *spiritus rector*
expressed in the inscription "à la japonica".
Japanese artists make no distinction between the
mineral, plant, and animal worlds. Gallé too seems
to plunge the hierarchy of all beings into chaos at
first, only to refashion it again in his own vision.
These "material powers of imagination" lend his
glassware the qualities of perfection. Like all his
skills, Gallé put the spirit of Japan in his faience
work to the test, before sublimating it in the
unmatched quality of his art glassware (ill. p. 112).

Émile Gallé
Vase, ca. 1900
Verre églomisé, intercalaire,
marbled, glass base with bubbles and
oxide inclusions, 20 cm high
Marcel Proust cites *verre églomisé*
associations in his novel *A la
recherche du temps perdu*
(1913–27): "It would soon be
winter; in the corner of the window a
white, frosty vein of snow would
appear, as on glass by Gallé," and
again: "The sea … plumed with
apparently immobile spray, as finely
painted as a feather or down by
Pisanello and fixed with the
unalterable creamy-white enamel
with which a covering of snow is
embodied on Gallé glassware."

Verres parlantes – "Talking glasses"

Tout les objets ont des contours;
Mais d'où vient la forme qui touche?
Émile Gallé[10]

In his creations, Gallé the lyric poet of glass combined botany, chemistry, art, and ethics, viewed from a poetic viewpoint. Although he was a convinced nationalist, he was at the same time an ardent devotee of Richard Wagner. The striving for beauty and unity, the symphonic in his work, the means of synesthesia, were akin to Wagner's *Gesamtkunstwerk* (synthesis of the arts). In the shaping of his vases, Gallé proceeded as one might on setting out a score; he rarely prepared clear drawings, but gave his craftsmen brief instructions that often came from a poem by Baudelaire or Mallarmé, plus a few fresh flowers and chemical formulæ. This is how the "verres parlantes", the "talking glasses", came into being. "The artist does not set chemical reactions in train, nor produce the flower, insect or landscape, but portrays vital traits, as it were the essence of what he sees and experiences. A scientist may assert that a weeping willow is no sadder than other kinds of willow, but for a sensitive person it is the saddest tree there is."[11]

"If we are to recognize any message at all in Gallé's work, it would have to be its endeavor to teach us true love – love being understood not as a false, social phenomenon but as a deep, spiritual devotion which the individual must search out in himself and further develop. Gallé was trying to tell us that we must try to understand ourselves, accept what we are. We must understand with all our senses and fulfil the role which we play in the development of the universe both as infinitely small biological units and as part of the whole. Gallé bared his innermost soul to enable others for their part to recognize their innermost beings. The language through which he makes this comprehensible is at once most expressive, diverse, and yet simple. It is a language whose vocabulary we all carry in our hearts – the language of nature and life itself."

Glass techniques

Even though Gallé looked on technique as simply the vehicle of his message, his creations are inconceivable without a multiplicity of complicated glassmaking processes (ill. opposite). Moreover, he devoted some attention to the processes in order to write *Notices sur la production du verre* (Nancy, 1884). The production processes of flashed glass with decoration cut or incised in the manner of Chinese "snuff bottles" of the Han dynasty (see also ill. p. 16) is effectively the basic method. The confusing additional wealth of techniques applied can scarcely be identified today, as the techniques were intended not to be recognized, that is, they were thrust into the background in favor of the total impression. Looking for clues can, however, be facilitated by knowing the principal methods of production.

With flashed glass, the uncolored glass body is coated, flashed with at least two layers of glaze. By means of cutting, incision or etching, parts of the additional glaze are removed at this point so that the decoration appears on the sides of the glass in relief or incised. The work of cutting, in which a little wheel set on a flywheel is used, is most closely related to working with a drawing pencil or paintbrush (ills. pp. 109, 114, 115). With etching, the "graveur à l'acide" takes over the treatment of the decoration, employing a solution of acid. With the difficult *marquetrie-de-verre* and intercalaire work, colored glass plate, powdered glass or even gold and other metals are rolled on to the still-hot glass and immediately worked (ills. p. 111, 113). Enamel is used both to paint glass and as a glaze, while the surface can be rendered iridescent and matt or

Émile Gallé
Veilleuse [night light] or incense burner, ca. 1900
Flashed glass, cameo cut, feet and mounting of bronze, silver-plated, 19 cm high

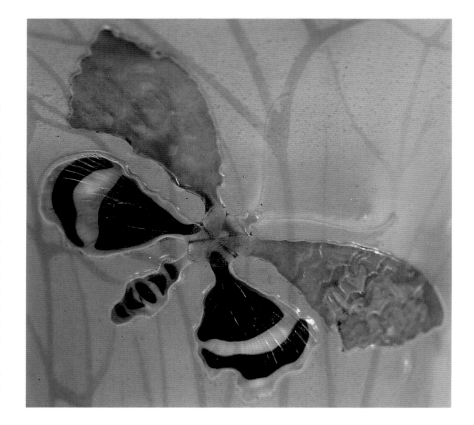

Émile Gallé
Vase (detail), ca. 1900
Flashed glass, cut in relief and incised, *marqueterie de verre*, 28 cm high

Opposite, left:
Émile Gallé
La Main [The Hand]
Glass sculpture, ca. 1900
Colored and marbled *en masse*, blown and shaped, glass embellishments, lifesize

Opposite, right:
Émile Gallé
L'Orchidée, vase, 1900
Flashed glass, cut and applied decoration, 31 cm high
Musée du Château, Boulogne-sur-Mer
Refined orchids were described in Joris-Karl Huysman's novel *A rebours* (1884), the "bible" of Art Nouveau artists: "The gardeners brought new varieties that seemed like artificial skins shot with red blood vessels; and the majority, as if consumed by leprosy, spread out their pale flesh, spotted with rash and afflicted with lichen ... echinopses whose wadding-wrapped blooms had the hateful rose of a mutilated limb ..." (see note 6)

Émile Gallé
Guéridon aux trois libellules,
dragonfly table, ca. 1900
Precious wood, carved modeling,
marquetry, 76.4 × 61 cm
The legs of this *guéridon* [pedestal
table] are three over-lifesize
dragonflies, whose naturally curved
body shape is exaggerated further.
The heads bear the top, like antique
caryatids. The original shape of the
creatures is heightened to the verge of
the grotesque.

shiny. To give a thorough insight into glass technology would require an extensive treatise. Even so, it is the very unexplained secrets and fine tunings that constitute Gallé's art. Marcel Proust (1871–1922) showed himself particularly open-minded in this respect. In his novel *A la recherche du temps perdu* [Remembrance of Things Past] (1913–27), he describes the mirror-image method of conveying ideas, and how structure and colors in nature recall Gallé's glass pieces. Proust makes an association with a *verre églomisé* (ill. p. 113): "It would soon be winter: in the corner of the window a white, frosty vein of snow would appear, as on a glass by Gallé,"[13] and again: "The sea … with a down of apparently immobile spray, which was as finely painted as a feather or down by Pisanello and fixed with the unalterable creamy-white enamel with which a covering of snow is embodied on Gallé glassware."[14]

Marvels in wood – Flora and fauna

Le décor du meuble moderne aura de l'expression, parce que l'artiste, en contact avec la nature, ne peut rester insensible à la noblesse des formes vitales.
Émile Gallé[15]

"Even more than the vases, Gallé's furniture stands out for being made entirely of elements borrowed from nature. There is nothing here that is not inspired by the immediate world, that the boundless love of the craftsman paired with the tenderness of the sensitive man, the poet and the scholar does not attest for the soil of the homeland. The woods he preferred to use came from his Lorraine homeland. He either carved them and elicited decorative motifs that became an emblem of the material or indicated the function of the furniture, or he used their diverse characteristics of color for the manifold nuances of his nature-bound marquetry motifs. His table tops and the side surfaces of his commodes and cabinets display landscapes with effortlessly integrated flowers, plants, grasses, birds, and butterflies."[16] The desire to display his creations in glass appropriately prompted Gallé to take up cabinetmaking and joinery. In 1884, he set up a furniture workshop, and by 1886 he already had a furniture factory operating, ready to astound the

Lucien Weissemburger
Steps (detail), Maison Bergeret,
Nancy, 1903–04
We encounter the whole vocabulary
of "flower language", both formally
and artistically, in every conceivable
branch of *fin-de-siècle* art. Facades,
pictures and picture frames
"bloom", pots develop florally into
plant-shaped étagères, in an
unending floral roundelay.

public visiting the World Exposition in Paris in 1889 with miracles in wood. His inspiration was the French Rococo period, examples of which his home town provided. Through the workings of his artistic genius, the étagères, tea tables and smaller pieces of the 16th and 17th centuries were transformed into asymmetrical, floral ornamental objects. Alongside these, he also wrought grander pieces whose over-refined opulence displayed a highly intricate marquetry technique that was inspired by the glass work. Exotic woods are combined with chased fittings, and often there are inscriptions with moral and ethical or symbolic contents. Bedsteads are embraced by moth's wings (ill. p. 116), and on the top of a writing desk can be found the

inscription "travail est joie" [work is pleasure]. Gallé the cabinetmaker expanded the personal repertoire of forms that nature furnished him with to include the insect world (ill. p. 116). Though this found application as decoration in his glass work as well, as a source of decorative ornament it came fully into its own only in the furniture. The general predilection of Art Nouveau for insect forms and insect-like motifs has several causes, such as the growing interest in research into nature, the improvement of microscopes by Ernst Abbé (1840–1905) and the popular interest in entomology over and above the purely scientific. There was even a periodical for applied entomology published in several languages. As stylistic models, the shimmering,

Louis Majorelle
Orchid "bureau plat" desk, 1903–05
Mahogany, amourette acacia, gilt and chased bronze, chased and beaten copper, 95 × 170 × 70 cm
Musée d'Orsay, Paris
The Frenchman Charles Cressent is accredited with the invention of the "bureau plat", the desk with a smooth, largely leather-covered, writing surface. He supplied the courts of Europe with costly furniture that was conceived almost sculpturally as unified organisms and whose woods were harmonically combined with ormolu mounts. The particular character of Cressent's work was adapted by Majorelle for his own pieces, which count among the masterpieces of Art Nouveau.

Louis Majorelle
Nénuphar mount of bedside table,
designed between 1905 and 1908
Mahogany, amourette acacia,
marquetry work in various woods,
gilt, chased bronze,
110 × 55 × 45 cm
Musée d'Orsay, Paris
Majorelle's furniture has a unity of
line, and the decoration is reduced to
just the waterlily mounts. *Nénuphar*
is the name of the Egyptian waterlily. It is an ideal fulfillment of the
contemporary yearning for a
mysterious symbolism. Since
ancient times, waterlilies have been
associated with divine majesty,
immortality, and religion, a symbol
of everlasting nature. If the color
tones and grain of the wood spoke
largely for themselves, the ormolu
mounts were carefully composed.
They became Majorelle's trademark.
Majorelle's mounts are original
works of wrought art, and were to be
seen at numerous exhibitions.

fragile nature of a type of physique that could almost be termed graphic was particularly attractive to Art Nouveau artists. The "nervousness" and the flickering manner of insects' movements are undoubtedly akin to the "nervous linear play" of Art Nouveau. On top of that, these "primitive animals" stand in close relationship to the origin of life, and their mobile, elastic limbs fit in particularly well with the principle of the curved silhouette. "All the oscillation and pulsation, sprouting and flowering acts unambiguously as organically living but amorphous. Natural forms are often reminiscent of anatomical preparations, and even more commonly triggered off are associations with that remarkable between-world of the primitive plant-like animals of the seabed, whose unpleasing, indeed repulsive, grace and elegance, and half-sucking, half-floating existence fascinated the artists."[17] Gallé noted a "strange similarity with living creatures" in his ornamentation, which is "like moths wrapped up into the dusk, slate-grey moths, beetles with striped carapaces, ladybirds with small dots, colored flecks of dust on the wings of large butterflies."[18] The legs of the dragonfly table he designed in 1900 (ill. p. 116) are larger-than-life dragonflies, whose naturally curved body shape is further exaggerated. The heads carry the top, in the manner of antique caryatids. The original shape of the animals is heightened almost to the verge of the grotesque. The hierarchy within the "levels of dignity" of decoration and art is finally abolished. Like the Japanese artist-craftsmen, Gallé seizes upon the minutest creature and is inspired, stirred by it. *Akitsu*, dragonflies, have been a symbol of the island of Japan since time immemorial.

Louis Majorelle – Les Nénuphars

Ces richesses de documentation, cette chaleur d'excitation poétique nécessaire à la composition décorative, l'artiste assembler de la ligne et du coloris ne les épuisera jamais.
From the manifesto of the École de Nancy[19]

Gallé's almost ritualistic self-abandonment to nature was shared by his loyal comrade in the struggle for the "new art", Louis Majorelle, to only a limited extent. For the other outstanding cabinetmaker of Art Nouveau alongside Gallé, nature was an "admirable colleague", supplying the decorative motifs and architectural construction of the furniture, but the structure should nonetheless remain discernable. In Majorelle's view, the *ébeniste* should never neglect the functionality of a piece, which should impress

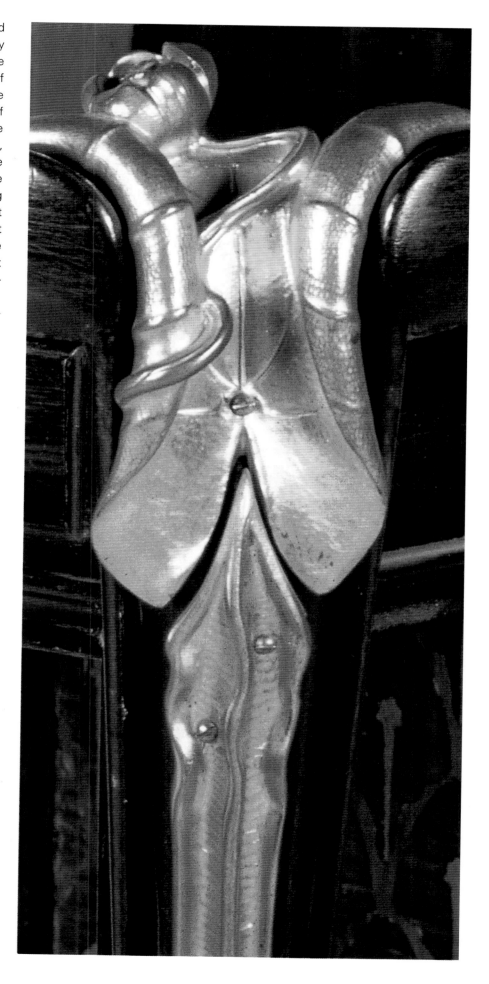

not just for its ornament but for its elegant line and proportions.

Majorelle (1859–1916) gained fame as the "Cressent of Art Nouveau". The Frenchman Charles Cressent (1685–1766) was the most important cabinetmaker of the Régence, supplying the courts of Europe with costly furniture that was conceived almost sculpturally as unified organisms, the wood being harmoniously combined with bronze mounts. He is also known as the inventor of the "bureau plat", a desk with a smooth, mostly leather-covered writing surface and drawers. Majorelle adapted the specific character of Cressent's work for his own pieces, which count among the masterpieces of Art Nouveau (ill. p. 118). His ambition to become a painter had to be abandoned with the early death of his father, when as a 20-year-old he took over the family-owned furniture and ceramics business. Influenced by Gallé, he developed the range of products it made, hitherto principally period furniture, into new fields. The characteristic Majorelle style saw the light of day as early as 1890. Assistance and support came from the designers Jacques Gruber (1870–1936) and Camille Gauthier (1870–1963). Buildings for Majorelle's expanding firm were constructed in 1898 by the leading architect of the École de Nancy, Lucien Weissemburger (1860–1929). It was a time when the suggestive power of Gallé's furniture was still clearly detectable in his marquetry, but at the 1900 World Exposition in Paris Majorelle succeeded in making a breakthrough, establishing his own distinctive style in his creations.

His "Nénuphars" studio was spontaneously acclaimed as one of the most attractive creations of Art Nouveau. The furniture, which has a unified tautness of line, is finished with a spare decoration of waterlily fittings (ill. p. 119). *Nénuphar* is the name of the Egyptian waterlily. It is an ideal fulfillment of the contemporary yearning for mysterious symbolism. Since ancient times, waterlilies have been associated with divine majesty, immortality, and religion, a symbol of everlasting nature. If the color tones and grain of the wood spoke largely for themselves, the ormolu mounts were carefully composed (ill. p. 119). They contrast in both material and color with the walnut and exotic woods Majorelle used, and they became his trademark. His mounts should be considered as wrought art in their own right, and were to be seen at numerous exhibitions. Besides bronze

Émile André
Entrance gateway, project drawing for the École de Nancy section at the Turin exhibition in 1902,
25.02.1902
Watercolor, 36 × 54.2 cm
Musée de l'Ecole de Nancy, Nancy

La Halle – Glassblowers' Hall
From the brochure *Notices & Catalogue pour l'envoi à l'Exposition Universelle de 1900* of the Verrerie et Cristaux Artistiques de Nancy, Daum Frères, Agence Générale & Exposition Permanente à Paris, 32 rue de Paradis, 1900

Le Coupage – Cutting the glass to size
From the brochure *Notices & Catalogue pour l'envoi à l'Exposition Universelle de 1900* of the Verrerie et Cristaux Artistiques de Nancy, Daum Frères, Agence Générale & Exposition Permanente à Paris, 32 rue de Paradis, 1900

and brasswork as furniture mounts, Majorelle also undertook large-scale metalwork such as the famous banisters for Galeries La Fayette in Paris. The banisters are made of wrought iron with polished copper mounts. The ornament is "monnaie du pape", that is, Judas pieces of silver. Majorelle's designs for the Daum glass factory – bases for lamps and vase settings – maintained their high quality until the 1920s (ill. p. 107). His pottery designs were produced by the Mougin brothers. A real Art Nouveau artist, Majorelle was active in numerous fields of craftwork, but his *Gesamtkunstwerk*, his grand synthesis, was the Villa Majorelle in Nancy.

Besides its sophisticated upmarket furniture products, the Villa Majorelle also offered perfectly crafted furniture at reasonable prices, thereby acceding to Gallé's early desire to "adorn the home of every Frenchman with a lovely object."[20] Putting this ambition into practice proved to be one of the most difficult tasks facing the new art. Some success was achieved by Gallé in his series productions, and by the Daum brothers with their glassware. Although in the end every Frenchman did not get his Art Nouveau object, there were nonetheless buyers outside the exclusive elite circle of the arbiters of taste.

Art for all?

They are all objects of luxury: every table by Gallé costs several hundred francs, since both the artist's design and the arduous labor of the cabinetmaker carrying out the design has to be paid for here.
Julian Marchlewski[21]

"It was absurd, but heavenly, and no one regretted admitting 'I was part of it',"[22] wrote Julius Meier-Graefe, an enthusiastic advocate of the new art, speaking of Art Nouveau. At the same time, he was one of the most keen-eyed critics, and he wrote of the Paris World Exposition in 1900: "Everything that France exhibited in the area that interests us here is luxury, sometimes extraordinarily beautiful, but in the last instance – cruel though it may sound – useless. ... Yet the key question is, can the new product be commercially possible in the modern sense, industrially useful? Does it meet modern requirements for a rational exploitation of material?"[23] Émile Gallé and the artists of the École de Nancy were thoroughly conscious of the conflict between social demands and their conversion into art. To some extent as counter-objects to his "poems in glass", in 1892 Gallé began to make sketches for pots that would be suitable for series production. This was more a matter of idealism than of commercialism. In accordance with the preachings of William Morris that not just the demand among the rich for "swinish luxury" should be satisfied, for him it was a question of educating a broad layer of the population in beauty and truth. "Art for all" was the watchword, instruction in taste from above. "To be able to manufacture at a reasonable price simple types of pot, functionality of

Jean-Antonin Daum
Base of a stem vase, ca. 1902
Flashed glass, intercalaire, color and
gold inclusions
The Daum factory created vases in
monochrome or graded coloration
devoid of ornamentation, relying on
surface effects. Forms used were of
the new simple type. The elongated
stem vases, initially unpretentious
and straight, changed in time to
almost eccentric creations of
sophisticated elegance.

Jean-Antonin Daum
Courgette flower, lamp, ca. 1905
Flashed glass, intercalaire, vitrification, iron mounting,
71.5 cm high
With the invention of the light bulb, and the general
availability of electricity, the task of supplying a basic human
need under new technical conditions released a surge of artistic
energy. The volume of output was tremendous. The
transparency of glass as a raw material could be used to great
effect, and consequently Art Nouveau lamps are among the
most appealing products of their time.

the objects and an easy-to-add decoration (such
as etching) were needed. At the same time, the
individual luxury pieces remained as models. This
then was the problem: could a work of art,
created by artists in work measured in days, be
simplified? The quality and spirit of the object – it
soon transpired – cannot be stereotyped just like
that. Verrerie Gallé succeeded only to a limited
extent in serial production, by producing its own
pots in another style.

The Daum brothers' glass factory

**D'appliquer en industriels les vrais principes de l'art
décoratif.**
Henri Clouzot[24]

Mass production of sophisticated art glassware –
alongside the production of individual pieces –
was more convincingly achieved by another glass
factory in Nancy, namely that of the Daum
brothers, because circumstances were different.
This was largely due to the aptitude of Jean-
Antonin Daum to realize that glass as a raw
material must be continually adapted to meet new
artistic demands. He believed that, as well as
over-the-top individual creations, appealing
objects that, even when produced in series,
would not degenerate into cliché, and would
retain the charm of the one-off hand-made object
in decoration and material, should be made. The
leitmotif of the brothers Jean-Louis Auguste
(1854–1909) and Jean-Antonin (1864–1930)
Daum was already explicit at the end of the 1880s:
"d'appliquer en industriels les vrais principes de
l'art décoratif" [to apply industrially the true
principles of decorative art], that is, to unite art and
industry (ill. p. 121). A lucky circumstance for the
production was the presence in the factory of a
high-quality team of glass artists, including one of
France's leading designers, Jacques Gruber (ill.
pp. 126, 127), and the potter and *pâte de verre*
master Almaric Walter (1859–1942). This is the
reason why the firm, which still exists today,
became the leading supplier of Art Deco glass,
and the factory did not pass into oblivion after the
death of its founders, in contrast to the fate of
Gallé's firm, which after his early death in 1904
experienced a sudden drop in quality. And for all
our critical reflections, we should not forget that,
even with the series products, we are still talking
about museum pieces.

The desire to convert aesthetic functionality into
practice was most easily achieved in lighting.
Lamps are in the first place necessary objects of
use, a part of interior decoration which was now

Henri Bergé
Mistletoe, after 1900
Design for mistletoe decoration of
Daum glass products
Pencil, watercolor
Daum Frères Collection, Nancy

Émile Gallé
Blackthorn lamp, ca. 1900
Glass, flashed several times, cameo
and incised decoration, engraved,
chased, 76 cm high

Jean-Antonin Daum
Four long-necked vases, 1901–05
Blown and modeled glass, flashed in
color, powdered glass technique,
47 cm to 66.3 cm high
Max Bill, a passionate collector of
stem vases, was an avowed admirer
of vases made in Nancy: "For me,
the perfect factory vases in my
collection count as the peak
achievement of creative craft in the
beauty of their material, exemplary
forms and technical perfection.
There are outstanding examples of
series productions that have
exploited to the full the possible
variations of graphics and coloring."
(see note 26)

to be reformed. The invention of the light bulb and the general availability of electricity offered new possibilities. The task of satisfying a basic human requirement under new technical conditions released artistic energies, and a remarkable volume of output was the result. The transparency of glass as a raw material could be put to good effect, as a result of which Art Nouveau lamps are among the most appealing products of their time. The motifs and repertoire of forms used for lamps were the same as for vases, facades, furniture, and paintings, namely, plants and insect motifs. Flowers, mushrooms, and trees (ill. above and p. 123) in particular blend strikingly harmoniously in their structure in lamps of all kinds. Additionally, a vase serves as an outstanding base for a lamp. A wealth of models existed for this.

But also in the vases themselves new ideas were put into practice as a consequence of the series production. The technique of etching was refined, becoming not only a means of decoration but used as decoration itself, since the improved technique had led to a separate style of surface structure. Gallé had achieved great success with etched models, but the Daum brothers went a step further. They created etched vases in monochrome or layered coloring devoid of ornament, relying on surface effects alone. Melted down or applied powdered glass between the layers of glaze achieved subtle results. Forms followed the new simplicity. Elongated flower vases (stem vases), initially unpretentious and straight, were in time transformed into almost eccentric creations of sophisticated elegance (ills. p. 122, 124–125). Art Nouveau in Nancy thus remained true to its roots, as on the one hand the vases themselves became flower stalks and on the other hand the marbled color monochromy took account of the proclamation of the poet Paul Verlaine (1844–96): "Car nous voulons, la Nuance encor,/ Pas la Couleur, rien que la nuance!"[25] Max Bill (1908–94), a passionate collector of stem vases, was smitten with vases made in Nancy: "For me, the perfect factory vases in my collection count as the peak achievement of creative craft in the beauty of their material, exemplary forms and technical perfection. There are outstanding examples of series production that have exploited to the full the possible variations of graphics and coloring." [26] (ills. pp. 124–125)

L'École de Nancy

Nous avons cherché à déduire des documents naturels les méthodes, les éléments et le caractère propres à créer un style moderne d'ornementation, un revêtement coloré ou plastique pour les usages modernes.
From the manifesto of the École de Nancy[27]

A shared enthusiasm among artist-craftsmen – almost all of them around 30 – for the sensation of beauty to be derived from observing nature, was already apparent around 1890. This unanimous movement culminated in 1901 in the founding of the École de Nancy and the formulation of a common statement of beliefs. The École de Nancy existed in name and de facto in 1894, when the leading artists of the region exhibited their works at an exposition organised by the recently founded Société Lorraine des Art Décoratifs. The first purchases for a planned museum of the shared arts were made, and the stylistic concord was tremendous. The concept of an "École de Nancy" first turns up in the writings of

the initiator of these endeavors, Émile Gallé, in 1896, in connection with his call, reiterated since 1881, for a return to nature as the sole source of motifs in art. After the overwhelming success of artists from Lorraine at the 1900 World Exposition in Paris, the necessity for an official amalgamation became obvious. Although Nancy had already overtaken Paris, as it had become clear that an independent French Art Nouveau was rooted in Nancy, the group as such did not show to advantage because its exhibits were assigned to the separate branches of art each time. The "Ecole de Nancy, Alliance provinciale des industries d'art" was thus founded on February 13 1901, with sales promotion an additional ambition. The declared goal of the Alliance was to set up joint workshops, the organization of exhibitions, the sponsorship of young trainees and a reform of the educational system in the artistic vocations. This comprised among other things the introduction of regular courses of instruction for crafts in vocational schools. Over and above that, they sought to adapt traditional arts and crafts to the new industrial production processes. Usefulness in all arts and crafts products became the supreme commandment. The flora of Lorraine remained the most important source of inspiration for Art Nouveau from Nancy (ill. p. 129).

The School's governing board consisted of Émile Gallé, Louis Majorelle, Jean-Antonin Daum and the cabinetmaker Eugène Vallin (1856–1922). After Gallé's death, Victor Prouvé (1858–1943) took over the presidency of the board. Many noted artists from the school, academics and literary figures belonged to the École's

René Wiener
Book binding of Roger Marx's *L'Estampe originale*, 1894
Inlay work in leather
Design by Camille Martin
The activities of the art critic Roger Marx, together with Eugène Corbin, publisher of the periodical *Art et Industrie*, made a decisive contribution to the École de Nancy in gaining it international recognition.

Jacques Gruber
Cabinet, ca. 1900
Mahogany, etched glass,
203 × 48.9 cm

Page 129:
Janin & Benoit, Nancy
Glazed double doors, ca. 1900
Mosaic window, leaded glass

committee. The participation of important artists in the now annual exhibitions increased the fame of their city. They included architect and painter Émile André (1871–1933), the designer Henri Bergé (1870–1937), the architect Lucien Weissemburger (1860–1929), the *ébeniste*, glass painter and sculptor Jacques Gruber (1870–1936), the bookbinder René Wiener (1855–1940) (ill. p. 127), the architect Charles André (1841–1921), father of Émile, and the decorator Camille Martin (1861–98). The art critic Roger Marx should also be mentioned again here as he and the publisher Eugène Corbin, who published the periodical *Art et Industrie*, contributed to the international recognition of the community. Among the best exponents of the École are the communal works, which bear conspicuous witness to the quality of the collective work and conferred a magnificent legitimacy on the Alliance. They include the joint furniture pieces by André, Gruber and Vallin (ill. p. 126) and the close cooperation of Daum and Majorelle (ill. p. 107).

For all its ideals, in time the community fell apart. Once again it was a war that played a decisive role. Just as the end of war in 1871 had brought together so many artistic forces, so the First World War now put an end to everything. Once more, Lorraine became a battlefield. But even before that, a capitalist economy oriented toward cheap mass production had pushed aside the demand for individual, high-quality creations. In addition, bureaucracy hindered the educational aims, and few artists of the École de Nancy were able to successfully resume their activity after 1918 in yet another new style – Art Deco.

Who will not acknowledge that the artist, endeavoring to render a flower, insect, landscape or human figure so as to display visibly its being and immanent feelings, will create a work that is more exciting and emotional than one which is only produced with a camera or a cold scalpel? A naturalistic depiction, however precise, reproduced in a scientific work does not move us because the soul is wanting, while a Japanese artist working from nature is uniquely capable of bringing out the motif of release, or the now mocking, now melancholy countenance of a living creature, an object with substance. In this way, in his passion for nature, he creates real symbols for "forest", the "joy of spring" or the "melancholy of autumn". In ornamentation, the symbol is thus a shining point in the middle of the still, deliberate meaninglessness of foliage and the arabesque. Symbols spur attentiveness on, thought, poetry, art enter the stage. Symbols are points around which ideas become concrete. There would, moreover, be no point in dissuading decorative artists from using symbols that are accepted in poetry without further ado. As long as thought directs the pen, brush or pencil, it cannot be doubted that symbols will continue to enchant people. In any case, the love of nature always brings symbolism with it: the flower loved by all, close to all, will always play an important and symbolic role ...

Employed consciously or unconsciously, symbols bring works of art to life; they are their souls.

In the dawn of the twentieth century, we may surely welcome the renewal of a national "art for all" as a herald of better times. ... And in this way, life in the twentieth century need no longer lack joy, art, and beauty.

Émile Gallé, *Le décor symbolique*, inaugural speech at a session of the Académie de Stanislas, Nancy, May 17 1900. Published in *Mémoires de l'Académie de Stanislas*, Vol. XVII, 5th series.

The new architecture
Belgium

*Ce spéctacle à je ne sais quoi de magique, de surnaturel,
qui ravir l'esprit et les sens.*
Jean Jacques Rousseau[1]

Symbolism – a Belgian tradition

If one conjures up an image of the art and culture
of Belgium – once the land between the magnificent kingdom of Burgundy and the harsh North
Sea – the painters Jan van Eyck and Roger van
der Weyden or perhaps above all the bizarre,
almost surreal world of Hieronymus Bosch and
Pieter Bruegel come to mind, a world full of
unsolved secrets that lingers on in the pictures of
contemporary painters such as René Magritte
and Paul Delvaux.

Every era has had its symbolic or symbolist art,
but the essence of the phenomenon, always an
expression of non-artistic spiritual forces as
well, has to be redefined in every period. During
the 19th century, the new science of psychoanalysis discovered the world of Bosch's
grotesques almost as textbook examples of its
theories. The artists of the Decadent Movement
appropriated his symbols of seduction such as
fish and snails, and the disproportionality of his
figures likewise found an echo in turn-of-the-
century art.

Consequently, the soil was particularly well-
prepared for symbolist tendencies from France
and England to take root in Belgium, where they
mingled with a local tradition. Symbolism always
has a literary and philosophical undertow that
delves into backgrounds, abysses, dreams. It
enjoys triggering shudders, setting puzzles,
baring inner worlds and visions. The Symbolist
Movement tinged the whole mood of the 1880s
and 1890s, and *fin-de-siècle* artists were one and
all in its grip.

The cross-connections that brought the Symbolist movement and the fine arts into contact were
established through numerous publications and
artistic societies. In his esoteric universe, the
writer Sar Mérodack Joséphin Péladan (1859-
1918) made a reality of synthesis. He founded
the Ordre Kabalistique de la Rose et la Croix, a
kind of Templar and Grail order, and wrote in the
manifesto to the first exhibition of the Rosicru-
cians: "Artist, thou art king. Art is the true kingdom. Once thy hand has written a perfect line,
the Cherubim themselves descend from Heaven
and see themselves therein, as in a looking glass.
Spiritual drawing, soulful line, charged form –
thou givest our dreams substance."[2] "The magic
of irrationalism, the seduction of organic ornament became so irresistible that whole groups
came to thank their cohesion to it and saw themselves virtually as plants that contain their own
meaning and essence within themselves without
being dependent on the external circumstances
of their existence and without knowing given
purposes outside themselves."[3] (ill. opposite)

Mallarmé – Maeterlinck – Khnopff

La chair est triste, hélas! et j'ai lu tous les livres.
Stéphane Mallarmé[4]

The poetic head of Symbolism was the poet
Stéphane Mallarmé (1842–98). "Let us say therefore that Charles Baudelaire must be designated
as the true predecessor of the present movement. Yet Stéphane Mallarmé gave it the taste
for the mysterious and the ineffable. … Meanwhile, the last enchantment has not yet been
reached: unconditional and disquieting labor
awaits newcomers."[5] Although the works of
Mallarmé were published only in limited editions

Victor Horta
Book cupboard (detail), office at the
Hôtel van Eetvelde, avenue
Palmerston 2, Brussels, 1895–97

Fernand Khnopff
I lock my door upon myself, 1891
Oil on canvas, 72 x 140 cm
Bavarian National Art Collections,
Neue Pinakothek, Munich
The painting is based on a line from
a poem called "Who shall deliver
me?" by Christina Georgina
Rossetti, sister of the painter Dante
Gabriel Rossetti.

before his death, surveys among poets in 1891 and journalists in 1893 indicated that no other poet attracted homage as commonly as he did, and in 1896 he was elected "Prince des poètes". He was taken up by the young generation of Belgian poets early on, being celebrated in Albert Mockel's periodical *La Wallonie* as the greatest contemporary poet. The appeal of his poetry lies in the foreboding, suspended singsong of the lines; it is characterized by sounds, the music of verse, the meter, as in a mist, an evanescence of the corporeal. "To name an object by its name means destroying three-quarters of the pleasure in a poem, which comes from the delight of gradual understanding; to guess step by step, to suggest – that is the dream. The complete use of this secret miracle that constitutes Symbolism lies in evoking an object little by little, to reveal a spiritual condition, an *état d'âme*, or vice versa, to derive from it a state of mind in a series of decipherings."[6] What counts is not the depiction of the object but the effect that it has.

Mallarmé had a great influence on the Belgian poet Maurice Maeterlinck (1862–1949), and again, as with Mallarmé, it was Stefan George who translated his work for German readers. Maeterlinck's fairy-tale dramas played a major part in introducing Symbolism to German-speaking areas. *La princesse Maleine* inspired Charles Rennie Mackintosh to design a music salon as a chamber for "the souls of the six princesses of Maurice Maeterlinck", in a commission for Fritz Waerndorfer in Vienna. Debussy

set *Pelléas et Mélisande* to music, and Leistikow wrote of him: "I knew of no one who painted better than this poet."[7] "The soul," wrote Maeterlinck, "has become a transparent space in which all our actions and virtues are just scurrying leaves and flowers."[8]

In translating the language of Maeterlinck, Mallarmé, Emile Verhaeren (1855–1916) and Georges Rodenbach (1855–98) into visual terms, no one surpassed the Belgian painter Fernand Khnopff. Khnofpp (1858–1921) blended his Symbolist literary associations with the *quattrocento* painterly philosophy of the Pre-Raphaelites with whom he had close ties of friendship. The painting *I lock my door upon myself* (ill. above) originated from a line in the poem "Who shall deliver me?" by Christina Georgina Rossetti, sister of the painter Dante Gabriel Rossetti. The many sphinx figures in Khnopff's work are not allegories; as Mallarmé interprets them, they are "ideas" of the senses. The sole model for the lasciviously chaste young female figures, seductive, reserved, and yet fascinating, that run through his whole work was his sister Marguerite, in whom he depicted himself as androgynous. "Khnopff thus appears to follow the commands of secret voices from eternity. Maeterlinck is fond of saying that what we speak or do is not important: that is only a simile. What is important lies behind our words and deeds."[9]

The world of figures we encounter in the work of the Belgian sculptor Georges Minne (1866–1941) is, like that of Khnopff, part of literary Symbolism.

Georges Minne
Fountain with five boy figures, 1898
Individual figure of Kneeling Youth,
1896
Marble, 83 cm high; in 1906 it was
erected by Henry van de Velde in the
lobby of the former Folkwang
Museum (today, Karl Ernst
Osthaus Museum), Hagen
The fountain is the most typical and
high-quality sculptural work of Art
Nouveau. The Flemish poet Karel
van de Woestijne (1878–1929)
called this work "Narcissus in
fivefold reflection".

Léo Jo
Pseudonym of Léontine Joris
Poster for the annual exhibition of the artists' organisation La Libre Esthétique, 1900
Color lithography, 44 x 27.5 cm
In 1894, a year after the artistic group *Les Vingt* broke up, a new channel for the work of avant-garde artists in Brussels opened with the La Libre Esthétique organization, which subsequently took over as virtual patron of the whole Art Nouveau movement in Europe. As the critic Gustave Geoffroy wrote in *La vie artistique* in 1894: "Here we are not talking about Belgian art but about the beginning of European art in Belgium."

Gisbert Combaz
A la Toison d'Or [The Golden Fleece], poster, 1895
Color lithography, 44 x 27.5 cm
Musée d'Ixelles, Brussels
The art salon La Toison d'Or was founded in Brussels in 1894 on the initiative of a group of industrialists, artists and literary figures including Octave Maus, Emile Verhaeren and Edmond Picard.

Opposite:
Victor Horta
Entrance hall, Hôtel Tassel, rue E. P. Janson 6, Brussels, 1893–97
Horta made use of painting as a supplement to the building materials, in order to extend the sense of movement in the iron components.

The simplification of outline of his figures makes the symbol act like a code. Once again, the parallelism is linked with the de-individualization of the figure. On the fountain in the former Folkwang Museum, Minne uses the fivefold repetition of the same boy-figure to express the orderliness that leads on to symbolic harmony (ill. p. 133).

Manifesto of the new style

A spokesman and the driving force of all new artistic endeavour in Belgium was the lawyer Octave Maus (1856–1919). In 1881, he founded the periodical *L'Art Moderne*. He was the initiator of *Les Vingt*, a group of 20 well-known artists; of the La Libre Esthétique organization (ill. top left); and of the La Toison d'Or art salon (ill. top right), whose numerous activities such as exhibitions, concerts, and conferences stylistically influenced the whole of Europe. By 1900, the "Belgian line" had already become synonymous with Art Nouveau. Brussels was more progressive and receptive than Paris, so that many artists who had no response there joined the organizations listed above. They included Gauguin, Toulouse-Lautrec, van Gogh, and Whistler. Thanks to the many artistic circles, the art of the poster and calligraphy enjoyed a considerable boost. A catalog by *Les Vingt* issued in 1888 is laid out so that each of the exhibiting artists had a page to himself on which to display his works. All their advertising output was similarly designed by the participating artists.

Beside these auspicious intellectual circumstances, material conditions were also favorable in Brussels. Because Brussels was a banking town there were patrons who were willing both to enthuse and to pay. Ernst Robert Curtius noted this fact with the observation that "the seeds of the iridescent flowers of this art could only unfold in the fertile, well-prepared soil offered by the material culture of the grande bourgeoisie."

Iron and glass – Victor Horta

Let the material speak for itself and appear undisguised,
in the shape and proportions that have been put to the test
by experience and science and found the most advisable.
Let brick appear as brick, wood as wood, iron as iron, each
in accordance with the laws of statics appropriate to it.
That is true simplicity.
Gottfried Semper[10]

Meanwhile, around the turn of the century, Brussels was not only the capital of Symbolism, but also a center of reformist and Socialist currents. The theories of Ruskin and Morris awoke an enthusiastic response, and helped a strongly developed aesthetic feeling to find an outlet in practice.

As a further source of inspiration for Belgian Art Nouveau the treatise "Entretiens sur l'architecture" by the French architect Eugène Viollet-le-Duc should be mentioned. His demand in the "Entretiens" for the appropriate use of materials was taken very seriously by Belgian architects, and brilliantly put into practice. One could say that, alongside Hector Guimard, the Belgian Victor Horta "invented" the new art of Art Nouveau architecture, in which iron is used as a slender, sinewy, statically effective element. In the entrance hall of the Hôtel van Eetvelde (ill. opposite), built 1895–1901, Horta (1861–1947) achieved the breakthrough into transparency and lightness in the harmonious use of glass and iron.

The result has a delicacy, even fragility, in its static perfection. Inspiration came from Viollet-le-Duc's elaborations in his *Dictionnaire raisonné de l'Architecture française* (1854– 69): "On the day when everyone is convinced that the new style is only the natural, uncontrived fragrance of a principle, of an idea that follows the logical order of things in this world; that the style develops like a plant growing in accordance with a definite law; and that it is not in any way a kind of seasoning that one plucks out of a sack to scatter on a work that in itself tastes of nothing – on that day we can be sure that posterity will award us style. The style exists because the design of the architecture is only a strict consequence of the underlying structural principles: 1. of the materials to be used, 2. of the way they are applied, 3. of the tasks that have to be carried out, 4. of the logical derivation of the detail from the whole. ... A distinguishing feature of style is above all that every object is given the form appropriate to it. If a structure clearly brings out the purpose for which it is intended, not much is lacking for it to have style; if it also forms a harmonic whole with the structures in its environment, it certainly has style. ... But why insist on the application of principles? Principles are only honesty in the use of form. Style develops more clearly in works, the less the latter deviate from the correct, true clear expression."[11]

Victor Horta
Stair railing (detail), Maison et Atelier Horta, rue Américaine 25, Saint-Gilles, Brussels, 1898
When he was building his own home, Horta felt himself free to use all the construction elements he considered important. Wood was to soar now as well. Every piece of furnishing is constructed on the same static/energetic principle, where wood – like stone – sometimes loses its natural character as material and is similarly transformed into a flowing, sculptural material. The end result is an Art Nouveau synthesis of art, a *Gesamtkunstwerk*.

Victor Horta
Balcony (detail), Maison et Atelier Horta, rue Américaine 25, Saint-Gilles, Brussels, 1898

Victor Horta
Entrance lobby, Hôtel van Eetvelde,
avenue Palmerston 2, Brussels,
1895–1901
Much more use was made of iron as
a building material in this building
than in the previous structures by
Horta. Glass partitions between
slender cast-iron struts surround the
central core of the house. The
ornaments grow out of the supports
of the glass ceiling, which pulls
together the octagonal space and
lends it a floating and yet enclosed
lightness.

A visit to the Paris World Exposition of 1889, where he admired the splendid engineering achievement of the Eiffel Tower, and an intensive study of the writings of Viollet-le-Duc led Horta to use iron in architecture undisguised. While he was discovering a new metal style, he also applied his forms to masonry. Like Antoni Gaudí, he treated stone as visibly a structural and at once a sculptural material: stone is set in motion. Alongside his splendid constructions of iron and glass, Horta also used mixed construction in which the iron (or steel) represents the moment of greatest achievement and tension. In addition, he makes use of painting in order to extend the characteristic movement of the iron (ills. pp. 134, 136). The most famous example is the staircase in the Maison et Atelier Horta in Brussels (ills. 136, 141 and 143). Wood too was supposed to soar in sympathy: every piece of furniture and every detail of it was shaped on the same static/energetic principle, whereby the wood – like stone – sometimes loses its material character and is likewise reinterpreted to become a flowing, sculptural material. The *Gesamtkunst-*

werk, the synthesis of the arts so beloved of Art Nouveau, is thus brought into being.

The Belgian line

At the bottom of what sea of mysteries do we live?
Maurice Maeterlinck[12]

Born in Ghent, Victor Horta soon abandoned his studies of music in favor of the Ghent Academy of Art. From there he went to Paris, thence to Brussels, where he resumed his studies at the Académie des Beaux-Arts. He was articled at the office of Alphonse Balat (1818–95), a noted Neoclassical architect who in the meanwhile showed his mettle in the Winter Garden of the mansion at Laeken (ills. pp. 20, 138–139). Horta got to know the early English modern style through exhibitions and readings of *Les Vingt*. Book, textile, and wallpaper designs influenced his ornamental style, which made a direct and convincing appearance after some initial conservative designs. Among Horta's first buildings is the Hôtel Tassel in Brussels (ill. p. 134), built

Following pages:
Alphonse Balat, Henry Maquet
Grand Jardin d'Hiver (Great
Winter Garden) greenhouses of the
Royal Palace at Laeken, avenue du
Parc Royal, 1875-76

1893–97. The formal elements of the facade are rather restrained, but in detail richly imaginative. With his iron staircases, Horta introduced iron as a material into residual structures (ill. p. 143). The wavy lines of the balustrade and supporting pillars, and the flowing movement between the spaces, is not limited to the horizontal axis but runs vertically through the stairwell. Horta thus not only pioneered the way for iron in domestic use but also designed the first residential ground plans with flowing transitions between spaces on both horizontal and vertical axis, as befitted the "Belgian line" – pure linear dynanism in contrary rotation. At the same time, the ornamental intricacies are not the result of a pure abstract linework but take on the form of organisms resembling bending plants or wisps of smoke (ill. opposite). And, once again, a counter-gesture develops: "The direction of this expansion is definitely from inside outwards, from the ornamental interior first to the construction of the house itself. As the formal arrangement is extended through the whole house, so the opulent profusion of the interiors diminishes. The blossom of the 'ornamental spring' fades into the architectural summer."[13]

Horta's most personal "artistic synthesis" is probably the Palais Solvay. The luxurious furnishings were designed by the artist himself and executed in the most costly materials: "… Un escalier à double volée en marbre vert auquel répondait un plafond vitré."[14] Marble, iron, and glass, in harmonic and yet contrasting combination. In the Palais Solvay, Horta showed himself to be a complete *architecte d'art*, a term that the French architect Hector Guimard coined to describe himself. Ornament whirls over the building materials like swaying wrack, swirled by the water in ever new entanglements. "At the bottom of what sea of mysteries do we live?" wonders Maeterlinck.[15] Horta designed pure Art Nouveau style in swelling, inter-knotted iron bands of almost soft plasticity. The same love of detail is as evident in the Maison Frison as in the

Above:
Paul Hankar
Window of salon, Hôtel Renkin, rue de la Loi 128, Brussels, 1897 (demolished)
Project drawing as implemented
Watercolor
Archive d'Architecture Moderne, Brussels

Paul Hankar
Maison et Atelier Ciamberlani, rue Defacqz 48, Brussels, facade, 1897–98
Hankar bestowed on the studio of the painter Ciamberlani a striking facade that shows echoes of the *quattrocento* architecture of northern Italy. This was a tribute to the client, who came from a distinguished Bolognese family. Passers-by would stop and stare at the exotic building, but the critics also indulged themselves with complacent sneers such as "a real delirum of obsessive originality." (see note 17)

"rhythmic facade" of the Maison du Peuple. With the Maison du Peuple (ill. below), an administration and conference building constructed for the Belgian Socialist Party, Horta took on a completely different sort of building commission that was bound up with the social commitment of the Morris movement. The complex, which was demolished in 1965 despite international protests, was a perfect example of Viollet-le-Duc's demand that details be logically derived from the whole. The skeleton construction with its facade of iron and glass is the forerunner of the modern curtain wall, as used today in high-rise buildings for shelter and to retain warmth. The individual members of the front seem interchangeable and lend the whole building a stunning mobility. The transparency of the glass and fragile struts arouse a desire to fold up the whole structure like a fan. In the Maison du Peuple, with its almost Spartan plainness, Art Nouveau takes on a new form. The building itself constitutes the ornament. The curved line of the

Victor Horta
Stairway, Maison et Atelier Horta, rue Américaine 25, Saint-Gilles, Brussels, 1898
The ornamental embellishments are not the result of an abstract linearity but take the form of organisms resembling inclining plants or wisps of smoke.

Victor Horta
Maison du Peuple, place Emile Vandervelde, Brussels, 1896–99 (demolished 1965)
With the Maison du Peuple, an administration and meeting building for the Belgian Socialist Party, Horta took on quite a different kind of commission, one bound up with the social commitment of the Morris movement. Demolished in 1965 despite international protests, the complex was a prime example of Viollet-le-Duc's demand for a logical derivation of the details from the whole. The skeleton construction, with its facade of iron and glass, is the precursor of the modern curtain-wall used as a covering for high-rise buildings.

facade, which reaches round without any breaks or hard transitions, is a monumental detail form, the "summer of architecture".

It took another purpose-built building, the Magasin Waucquez, built 1903–06 (ill. opposite), for the commitment to architecture to assert itself. Functional considerations came to the fore, combined with an almost classical feeling for form, which would become a characteristic of Horta's work in the following years.

Like the De Stijl Movement in the Netherlands some 20 years later, Horta extracted apparently hidden elements from traditional contexts and lent them an up-to-date character in new surroundings and explicit synthesis. He combined wood (soft), marble (hard), and iron (brittle) to make a quasi-elastic whole (ill. right). His influence on the succeeding generation is unmistakable, above all in Rudolph Schindler (1887–1953), Le Corbusier (1887–1965) and Louis H. de Konick (b. 1896).

Heyday of architecture – Brussels around 1900

This is the true simplicity, to which one may then devote oneself with all the love of chaste embroidery of decoration.
Gottfried Semper[16]

In 1893, Horta's Maison Tassel was constructed, the great architect's first pure Art Nouveau building. Almost contemporaneously, Paul Hankar built himself a residence in Brussels. Thus, almost with a roll of drums, the era of the "new architecture" opened in Belgium. Like Horta, Hankar (1859–1901) was much influenced by the writings of Viollet-le-Duc, but he was also equally enthusiastic about the English Arts and Crafts Movement, and details of his interiors are often reminiscent of the Scot Charles Rennie Mackintosh. Hankar considered it his main task to unite the fine arts with the applied arts in a decorative synthesis, and in his endeavours he developed an unmistakable style of his own. He had many contacts with artists in the fine arts. He worked closely with the sculptor Alfred Crick (b. 1858) and the painter Alphonse Crespin (1859–1944), who did a large number of sgraffiti on Hankar's buildings. Hankar's significance for Art Nouveau is not limited to his activities as an architect. His commitment to the new style as editorial secretary of the architectural periodical *L'Emulation* and as a member of numerous artistic organisations made a substantial contribution to publicizing it. His education took Hankar

Victor Horta
Stairwell, Maison et Atelier Horta, rue Américaine 25, Saint-Gilles, Brussels, 1898–1901
Horta extracted apparently concealed components from their traditional context and endowed them with an up-to-date character in new settings, in undisguised synthesis. He combined woods (soft), marble (hard), and iron (brittle) to make an almost elastic whole.

from the Academy in Brussels to the architect Henri Beyaert, with whom he shared a predilection for wrought iron and a dislike of sheet iron and cast iron. Besides his own house, Hankar build a studio for the painter Ciamberlani in Brussels (ills. pp. 140. 147). Its striking facade echoes the *quattrocento* architecture of northern Italy, by way of a tribute to his client, who came from a distinguished Bolognese family. The exotic style astonished passers-by, but the critics also thoroughly indulged themselves with complacent sneers such as "a real delirium of obsessive originality."[17] Hankar's designs for shops, restaurants, and galleries are stylistically more homogeneous – abstract Art Nouveau of Belgian stamp. His early death in 1901 robbed Belgium of one of its great inspirations and a leading light of the art scene. Broadly educated, he was involved not only in his profession but also in archaeology, and conducted major excavations in Belgium. No less original than the Maison Ciamberlani are the facades of the amateur architect Paul Cauchie (1875–1945), who trained as a painter and designer. Cauchie's studio and

Victor Horta
Ceiling bearer, Magasin Waucquez, rue des Sables 20, Brussels, 1903–06
In this building (1823–94), Horta was now fully committed to architecture. Functional purpose comes to the fore, combined with a virtually Classicist feeling for form, which would become the mark of his work in the coming years.

Victor Horta
Stairwell, Hôtel Tassel, rue E. P. Janson 6, Brussels, 1893
With the iron stairwell construction at the Hôtel Tassel, Horta introduced iron into residential buildings as a building material.

Paul Cauchie
Facade (detail), Maison et Atelier
Cauchie, rue des Francs 5, Brussels,
1905
The facade is a rare but successful
example of fresco in Art Nouveau –
"art on architecture".

Left:
Gustave Strauven
Entrance roofing (detail), business
and residential premises, avenue
Louis Bertrand 65, Brussels, 1906

Gustave Strauven
Gate, home of the painter
Saint-Cyr, square Ambiorix 11,
Brussels, 1900–03
Strauven shared Horta's stylistic
approach and his enthusiasm for
iron as a material. In his case, iron
was used not in sinewy rectilinearity
but to lend a touch of individuality
in a graceful "ornamental
undergrowth."

Ernest Blérot
Facade (detail), residential building,
place Louis Morichar 41, Brussels,
1900
An example of the "blossoming"
architecture of *fin-de-siècle* Brussels.

Paul Hamesse
Door metalwork, residential and
laboratory building, rue des
Champs-Elysées 6, Brussels

Albert Roosenboom
Drain ornamentation, residential
building (former private residence of
Roosenboom), rue Faider 83,
Brussels, 1900
Impressive detail of floral strip
ornamentation that is found all over
the "functional" parts of the
building.

Opposite:
Victor Horta
Mounts and metalwork, ca.
1895–1905
Musée Horta, Brussels

Gustave Serrurier-Bovy
Dining room, 1904
Design drawing, watercolor,
18 x 23 cm
The work of the furniture designer
Serrurier-Bovy developed
autonomously, being influenced
largely by the sober and yet vibrant
elegance of British artists.

Paul Hamesse
Interior, Hôtel Cohn-Donnay, today
the Café Restaurant Ultième
Hallucinatie, rue Royale 316,
Brussels, 1904
The interior of the present-day café
restaurant is one of the jewels of Art
Nouveau in Brussels.

home (ill. p. 144) is a rare but successful example of Art Nouveau fresco art – "art on architecture". In later years, Cauchie evolved from being the master of individuality and imagination into a builder of social homes. He designed ready-made houses that were cheap and functional. Another distinctive figure of Art Nouveau in Belgium is Gustava Strauven (1878–1919). As a collaborator with Horta, particularly on the Hôtel Eetvelde and the Maison du Peuple, he shared Horta's stylistic approach and his enthusiasm for iron as a building material (ill. p. 144). In his case, it is not used in sinewy straight lines but to give an unconventional shape as a kind of graceful "ornamental undergrowth". A significant example of this is the iron railings round the house of the painter Saint-Cyr (ill. p. 145). Another figure from the Hankar school was the architect Paul Hamesse (1877–1956), whose interior at the Hôtel Cohn-Donnay – today the Café-Restaurant Ultième Hallucinatie (ills. pp. 145, 146) is one of the jewels of Art Nouveau in the capital. Further "pearls" in the "necklace" of the city's architecture include the private residence of Albert Roosenboom, with its impressive details of floral strip ornamentation (ill. p. 145), and the flowery masonry of the architect Ernest Blérot (ill. p. 145). These examples show effectively the level of architectural design that had been achieved in *fin-de-siècle* Brussels.

Paul Hankar
Elevation and section of facade, first version, Maison et Atelier Ciamberlani, rue Defacqz 48, Brussels, 1897
Watercolor
Archive d'Architecture Moderne, Brussels

Gustave Serrurier-Bovy – Inventor of jointed furniture

We need a "joiner culture". If applied artists were to paint pictures again or sweep streets, we'd have it.
Adolf Loos[18]

The work of the furniture designer Gustave Serrurier-Bovy (1858–1910) developed as an autonomous style of its own. Its parameters were set by the sober and yet vibrant elegance of British artists. After his architectural studies at the Academy of Fine Arts in his home town of Liège, Serrurier-Bovy opened a shop there selling English furniture. His own work bears an English touch that developed into a characteristic trait – a souvenir of his trip to England, on which he embarked in his enthusiasm for the writings of William Morris.

The vital difference from his English idols such as Charles Francis Annesley Voysey or Charles Robert Ashbee lies principally in his view of the construction of furniture. The box body gave way to a body made of members. The extensive, stylized ornamental figures of his models is transposed into a new context. For example, in his chairs he breaks up the box body into its structural elements and puts them together again with individual bars (ill. opposite). The same principle applied to his interior designs (ill. p. 147). The modular system of his work and its Cubist rectilinearity recall the Wiener Werkstätte or Adolf Loos – but it was Serrurier-Bovy who came first. His sense of ornamental disposition and geometric order never led to a unified grid. Every object was developed afresh in its function from within. Like his artistic compatriots from Belgium, he too had a predilection for iron construction (ill. left), just as he got on well and collaborated with the leading established architects. Later, Henry van de Velde took over the member-system of furniture from him and made it famous as the "Van de Velde Style".

Gustave Serrurier-Bovy
Hat rack, for the Pâtisserie Marchal, Brussels, ca. 1903–04
Iron and copper bands,
204 cm high, diameter 52.5 cm
Serrurier-Bovy shared with his artistic colleagues in Brussels the Belgian preference for iron construction, just as he was always glad to collaborate with the leading architects there.

Gustave Serrurier-Bovy
Chair, ca 1902
Wood, brass mounts, enamel, ca.
120 cm high
The stylized ornamental figures of
his English models were transposed
by Serrurier-Bovy into a new
context, in which he dissolved the
box-body system for his chairs and
reconstructed them from the
individual bars. The same principle
was adopted in his interiors.

Philippe Wolfers
Day and Night, belt buckle, 1897
Chased silver, fired-gilt silver and
amethysts, 9 x 12.5 cm
(reproduction to original size)

Iron and gold – Sphinx and ivory

Tes yeux, où rien ne se révèle
De doux ni d'amer,
Sont deux bijoux froids où se mêle
L'or avec le fer.
Charles Baudelaire[19]

Belgium as a center of the avant-garde initiated unusual work not only in the field of painting, graphics, and architecture but also inspired creativity in arts and crafts. The repertoire of motifs was drained, and the new style took a whole variety of expression. In accordance with Belgian principles of form, metalwork took a leading position, as the "style" could be translated into it most credibly. Thus Fernand Dubois (1861–1939) designed lighting that appears like a quotation from Horta's iron components, demonstrating that they were as effective as stand-alone forms as they were in an architectural context (ill. p. 144). The arms of the candelabra (ill. p. 152) are like branches, representing a high point of plant design in their sculptural quality. High praise for Dubois came from the critic Octave Maus, for whose Salon de la Libre Esthétique he produced handicraft work. Like Philippe Wolfers, the giant of Belgian handicrafts, Dubois made use of "Belgian" materials such as metal and ivory from the

Congo. His chryselephantine (ivory and metal) sculptures were wrought, like those of his teacher Charles van der Stappen (1843–1910), as works of complete perfection. Stappen's bust *Le Sphinx mystérieuse* (ill. p. 153) unites all the features of *fin-de-siècle* Belgian art and constitutes a virtual incunabulum of this school of Art Nouveau. *The Sphinx* is the image of literary symbolism made flesh, the ivory underlining its mysterious aura. Chryselephantine was used in the ancient world as a material for costly statuettes for discriminating clients. The Belgian variant has, in contrast, a very pragmatic background. The commercial considerations of a king assisted Belgian Art Nouveau to some of its most brilliant achievements. Leopold II ruled the Belgian Congo as his private estate, and so was anxious to boost sales of African ivory. To bring ivory into fashion, he offered established artists the tusks free of charge. The gamble paid off – the success was overwhelming. Ivory work celebrated its first triumph at the Antwerp World Exposition in 1894, and in the display at the Belgian Congo pavilion at Tervueren, on the occasion of the Brussels World Exposition of 1897, the new branch of art stole the show. The principal works were bought by the state and remained in the African Museum in Tervueren for a long time. Today they can be seen along

Philippe Wolfers
Swan with Snakes, pendant, 1898
Opal, chased gold, rubies, diamonds,
pear-shaped pearl
Pendant 5 x 5 cm, chain 40 cm long
(reproduction of pendant to original
size)
This jewel, a one-off, was designed
by Philippe Wolfers for his wife,
Sophie.

with other Art Nouveau exhibits at the Musées Royaux d'Art et d'Histoire in Brussels. Here, too, Philippe Wolfers is the "grand master" among many grand masters.

Philippe Wolfers – Black jewels

Neiger de blancs bouquets d'étoiles parfumées. Stéphane Mallarmé[20]

Philippe Wolfers (1858–1929) created rarities in which the boundaries between sculpture and appliance, sculpture and handicraft became blurred – a pure luxury art of brilliant technique in which the object is only a medium for the symbolic content. Trained in the workshop of his father, a well-known Brussels goldsmith, in his early years Wolfers designed pricey historicizing pieces of jewelry in a Neo-Rococo style. Even at that time, he was acquainting himself with Japanese craftwork, and adapted its approach to the use of materials for his own quasi-Japanese jewelry. His later outstanding role in Belgian Art Nouveau derived from the fact that his work markedly displayed features of the new style from the mid-1880s. Wolfers had kept a sharp eye on developments in England, and became an all-round artist after the model of the English workshops. He designed bronzes, small items of furniture, lamps (ill. p. 130), glass vases (ill. p. 152), and, above all, jewelry (ill. opposite and below) decorated with enamel and gems. Only a fraction of his work has been preserved as, in contrast with other Art Nouveau goldsmiths, he had a passion for valuable stones which, when the style went out of fashion, were broken out of their settings. The gleam of precious stones and reflection of the gold ground, which evoke Byzantium and the Orient, are a sign of Symbolist inclinations. In 1899, Wolfers built himself a villa in La Hulpe, and thus became a client of Paul Hankar. Victor Horta was the architect whom he commissioned in 1909 to build him business premises in the rue d'Arenberg in Brussels. Already by 1900 he had branches of his business in Ghent, Antwerp, Liège, Budapest, Düsseldorf, London, and Paris. Besides his activities as a jeweler, he worked as a designer of glassware, in this case principally for Belgium's leading glass manufacturer Val Saint-Lambert in Seraing-sur-Meuse. The Val Saint-Lambert works occupied the site of an old Cistercian abbey, and with a daily output of around 160,000 units ranked among the biggest producers in Europe. Most of these were crystal articles, but there were also Art Nouveau flashed-glass products. The executive artist at Val Saint-Lambert was Désiré Muller, from Lunéville, who did his ornamentation in the Gallé style. Horta, van de Velde, and Serrurier-Bovy also worked for the manufacturer. Wolfers

Philippe Wolfers
Nike [Greek goddess of Victory], pendant, to be worn as a brooch or on a chain, 1902
Chased gold, *plique à jour* enamel, rubies, emeralds, diamonds, cut tourmaline, baroque pearls, 5 x 7 cm (reproduction slightly over-lifesize)

Philippe Wolfers
Large Dragonfly, pendant, to be worn as a brooch or on a chain, 1903–04
Gold, opals, enamel, rubies, diamonds, Mexican opal, 11.5 x 13 cm
Philippe Wolfers made rarities in which the border between sculpture and appliance, art and handiwork was blurred – a pure luxury art of brilliant technique, in which the object becomes just a medium for symbolic contents.

Fernand Dubois
Five-branch candelabra, ca. 1899
Bronze, gilt, 53.5 x 20.5 cm
Musée Horta, Brussels
In 1899, this candelabra, executed in pewter, was exhibited at the Salon de la Libre Esthétique and later included in a Horta display at the International Exposition in Turin in 1902.

Philippe Wolfers
Crépuscule [Dusk], vase, 1901
Crystal glass, flashed, cut,
30.5 cm high
Execution by Cristalleries du Val Saint-Lambert, Seraing-sur-Meuse
Musée d'Archéologie et d'Arts Décoratifs, Liège
The body of the glass is embraced by a bat, the creature of twilight, half-mammal, half-bird, with an almost human countenance, a synonym for the vampire. The bat plays an outstanding role in the iconography of Art Nouveau. The bizarre winged creature is perpetuated in all conceivable materials.

had his glasswork finished by gem cutters in his own workshops, each piece being unique. The vase called *Crépuscule* [Dusk] (ill. below) is a child of Symbolism in both title and representation. Twilight is the domain of ethereal souls, monochromy, and pale dreams. Encircling the body of the vessel is a bat, a creature of dusk, half-mammal, half-bird, with an almost human countenance, a synonym for the vampire. The bat here plays an outstanding role in the iconography of Art Nouveau. The bizarre, winged creatures are perpetuated in every conceivable material. The black glass has the effect of stone that glows only in artificial light. Black as a complement to shimmering color animated the Symbolists' ideas of morbidity. "The dining room was lined entirely in black ... avenues for this purpose were strewn with fine coal dust, the small wash basin bordered with basalt was filled with black ink ... the meal was served on a black tablecloth, and the guests were waited on by black negroes."[21]

Henry van de Velde – doyen of Art Nouveau

A line is a force that, like all elemental forces, is active; several lines brought into contact but in conflict with each other have the same effect as several forces working against each other.
Henry van de Velde[22]

The Maison et Atelier Horta constituted Art Nouveau's *Gesamtkunstwerk*, or synthesis of the arts. Yet, at the same time, it should be added, arose "the theory of line as an abstract medium of expression. This theory originated with van de Velde, which is no surprise as van de Velde was originally a painter. In later times, a serious quarrel blew up between van de Velde and Horta. It was said that the quarrel had personal causes, but artistic reasons certainly came into it. Horta was accused of being glued to construction, while van de Velde distorted the construction by exaggerating the primacy of abstract line. Van de Velde certainly set great store on the abstract character of line. We have met many ornamental motifs of Art Nouveau that are based on lilies, irises or female figures. In contrast, van de Velde's view was that the time for ornamentation made of tendrils, flowers, and women was over. The art of the future should be abstract."[23]
Henry van de Velde (1863–1957), the third and yet the first of the three great Belgians – Horta, Wolfers and van de Velde – did the greater part of his work in Germany. Yet his theories that held

Charles van der Stappen
The Mysterious Sphinx, 1897
Ivory, bronze, 56 x 46 x 31 cm
Musées Royaux d'Art et d'Histoire, Brussels
Van der Stappen finished his chryselephantine (ivory and metal) sculptures to the ultimate degree of craft perfection. The bust shown here unites all the features of *fin-de-siècle* Belgian art and constitutes therefore a sort of incunabulum of Art Nouveau in Belgium. *The Sphinx* is the image of literary Symbolism incarnate, while the use of exotic ivory underlines the aura of mystery.

Henry van de Velde
Above: study, exhibited at the Secession Exposition in Munich in 1897, reproduced in *L'art décoratif*, Paris, September 1899, p. 262

Right: Bureau plat writing desk and armchair, ca. 1898–99 (model dated 1896)
Bureau plat: 128 x 267 x 122 cm, Armchair: 72 cm high
Sculptured oak, bronze, copper, lamps of red copper, leather writing surface and chair upholstery
"The sinuous form and playful movement of line attempt to chain the user to the desk and ensnare him in its spell. The desk is almost saying, I can help you in your work, and with me conditions are all set for you to concentrate. The furniture is making its own statement, as it were." (Klaus-Jürgen Sembach, see note 32)

out most promise for the future were developed in his Belgian period. He may therefore be justly entitled to claim fame for helping Art Nouveau make its breakthrough on the European continent and contributing to its golden age. "At the Art Nouveau exhibition in Zürich in 1952, a desk, a chair, and a large picture had been set up together. An 89-year-old man sat there and held forth in a lively and stimulating lecture for today's artistic youth. It was Henry van de Velde. Fifty years earlier[24] he had designed the desk (ills. above and right) and Ferdinand Hodler (1853–1918) had painted the wall painting *The day*. What these two things had in common is called Art Nouveau."[25] It was the first major postwar exhibition devoted to Art Nouveau, and was opened by van de Velde as the doyen of the whole movement. The style was out of fashion and much vilified, and it would be some years yet before it came to be admired again. Van de Velde was the brightest personality, most powerful philosophical talent, and at once most striking and original phenomenon of Art Nouveau, though he rejected the term as disrespectful to the style. He was both a prophet and a shaper of a new aesthetic clarity and harmony. His path from painting to architecture and the crafts was a model for a whole generation of artists. It is therefore wrong to talk of van de Velde in his Belgian period as "van de Velde avant van de Velde"[26] Though his work in Germany is what formed his international image, we are mistaken to neglect the years up to 1901. The characteristic line was already well-formulated in the style of the painter, but took a new turn when the constructional logic was elucidated on objects and innate

power currents were channeled into them. The decision he made in 1882 to go for the applied arts certainly acted as a release from the creative straits that painting had become for him. "One would do better, in respect of the series of fine, logical interconnections of schools of painting, to heed the group of artists that suddenly switched over to industry recently. They plan an unlimited expansion of the three-dimensional arts right back to the earliest industrial beginnings, and a struggle will begin for the appropriate means and effects that they consider appropriate for reviving out-of-date ornamentation from the archives. No one can be averse to the idea of conferring an artistic character on everyday things and appli-

ances that – for how long! – have been bereft of a sense of their service and appeal."[27] At the last salon of *Les Vingt*, in 1893, van de Velde exhibited his tapestry *Angels' Vigil* (ill. above), which marks his transition within artistic disciplines. The tapestry is a translation of his theory of the reciprocal influence of colors on one another and their relationship. In form, it displays a modern insight into the rhythm of line. A contemporary critic said of the embroidery: "the composition is at once naive and solemn; it reminds one of illustrations for fairy stories by Maurice Maeterlinck."[28] With that, the circle of the specifically Belgian version of Art Nouveau closes.

Henry van de Velde
Blue tea gown, ca. 1895
Museum voor Sierkunst, Ghent
"The same forces," declared van de
Velde of his activity as a fashion
designer, "that drove me – though
not an architect – to draw up the
plans for our house, and to design
furniture, lamps, and other objects,
think up wall hangings, mats, and
carpets without ever having thought
of the production of such things,
induced me to apply the principle of
rational design, the fundamental
method of all my work, to women's
clothing as well."

Henry van de Velde
Two armchairs, for an interior for
the banker Bauer, rue de
l'Association 65, Brussels, 1896
Padauk wood (a precious wood with
colored streaks), velours upholstery,
88 x 66 cm
The later decisive features of Belgian
Art Nouveau are traceable even in
the rather plain furniture of the early
period, in the emphasis on structural
and ornamental details combining to
make an indissoluble whole.

Henry van de Velde
Bloemenwerf House, Uccle, near Brussels, 1894–96
Van de Velde's residence is distinguished for its provocatively simple forms, wholly in the manner of William Morris's Red House (1859), which Morris had constructed in the face of all conventions, in accordance with his personal ideas and requirements.

Synthesis of art

Even when I had given up painting, the demon of line did not leave me, and when I designed the first ornaments, they arose out of the dynamic interplay of their elemental forces.
Henry van de Velde[29]

In accordance with his original wish to become a painter, van de Velde, a native of Antwerp, had enrolled for the Academy there from 1881–83, and subsequently continued his studies until 1885 at the studio of the painter Durant in Paris. He admired van Gogh, Louis Anquetin, Emile Bernard and the Pointillistes, but at the same time he absorbed the influences of Japanese woodcuts and developed them in his pictures (ill. left). Fired by the exhibitions and publications

of *Les Vingt*, in 1889 he joined the group. There he made the acquaintance of the Englishman William Finch (1854–1930), who introduced him to the writings of John Ruskin and William Morris, and to English arts and crafts. The encounter with the reformist ideas of English artists lent shape to his own thoughts and objectives. Following a physical and psychological crisis in 1890, he reconsidered his situation as an artist, and ended up by following his real vocation, thanks to the deep impression that Morris had made. Measured by the conventions of his time, what he did was revolutionary. He carried out a reevaluation of all artistic disciplines, in which painting had hitherto always occupied the top position. Julius Meier-Graefe called van de Velde, after his lecture on "William Morris,

Above:
Henry van de Velde
Abstract plant composition, ca. 1893
Pastel, 47 x 49 cm
Kröller-Müller Museum, Otterlo
The study is one of the last works painted by van de Velde. It shows clearly the influence of Japanese art and the later dynamic rhythm of arts and crafts work.

Henry van de Velde
Wallpapers (detail), ca. 1897
Paper, painted

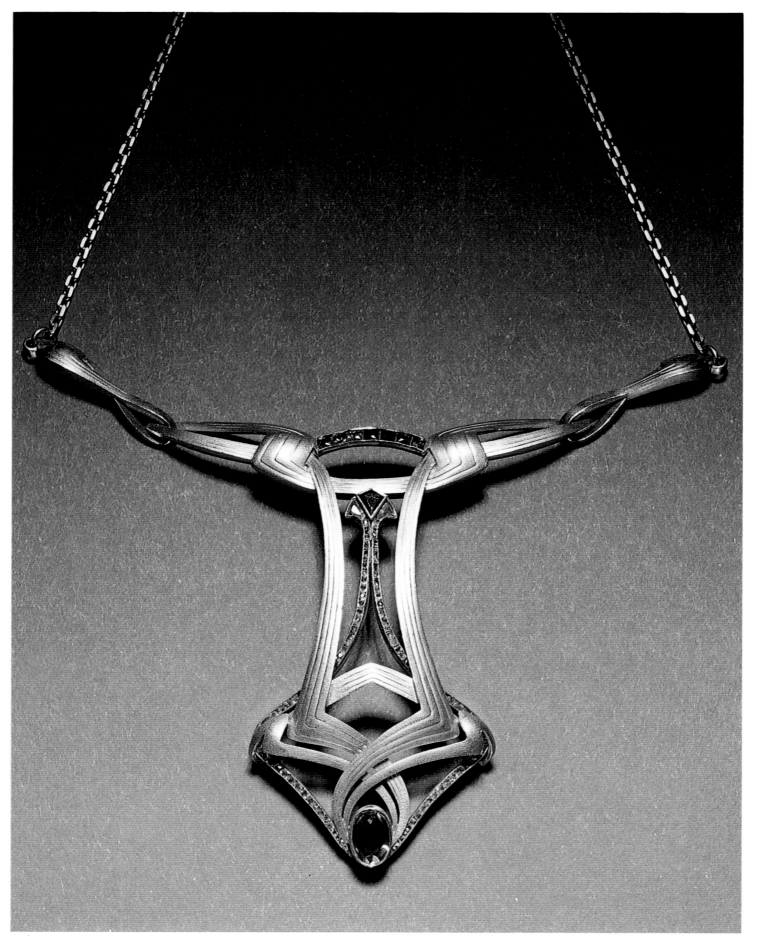

Henry van de Velde
Necklace, ca. 1900
Gold, sapphires, emeralds,
7 cm high, ca. 11 cm wide
(reproduction over-lifesize)
Neue Sammlung, Staatliches
Museum für angewandte Kunst,
Munich
"A line is a force that is active, like
all elemental forces; several lines
brought into contact but in conflict
with each other have the same effect
as several forces in conflict with each
other." (Henry van de Velde, see
note 22)

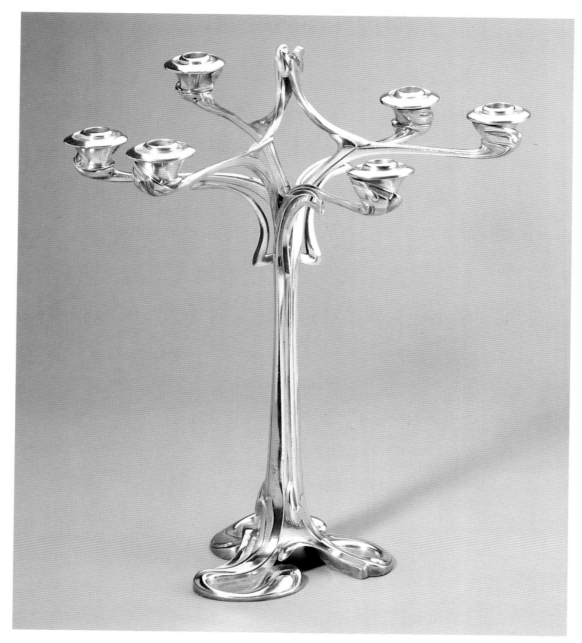

Henry van de Velde
Candelabra, 1898-99
Beaten silver, 59 cm high
Bröhan Museum, Berlin
The final conquest of the third
dimension by line was achieved by
van de Velde in exemplary fashion in
this silver candelabra. Previously
wrongly dated to 1902, it was
actually made earlier, in 1898.

Page 161:
**Henry van de Velde,
Octave van Rysselberghe**
Stairwell, Hôtel Otlet, rue de
Florence 13, Brussels, 1894
In graphic art, linear rhythm still
served as a bearer of mood. In this
respect, van de Velde found himself
in concord with the stylistic devices
of Symbolism, yet his pure Art
Nouveau work retained – in purified
form – a personal stamp. This
becomes clear in the interior design
of the Hôtel Otlet.

craftsman and socialist" in the Maison du Peuple in 1898, the "immediate succesor to Morris".[30] Van de Velde's initial enthusiasm for Morris is clear when one recalls that he selected upholstery by the English artist for his first pieces of furniture. However, he soon replaced this with his own designs, since the Victorian patterns seemed too fragmented. In 1895, van de Velde, the self-taught architect, built himself a refuge in Bloemenwerf House (ill. p. 157) in Uccle, near Brussels, entirely in the manner of the Red House by Morris (1859). Morris had had the latter built, in the face of all conventions, wholly to suit his own ideas and requirements (ill. p. 31). Van de Velde's retreat into a self-inflicted hermit's existence did not last long. His creative ambition sought influence in the external world. Through the activities of the art salon La Toison d'Or, van

de Velde came into contact with Julius Meier-Graefe (the inventor of *Pan*) and Samuel Bing, the "inventor" of Art Nouveau, which was the name of Bing's gallery in Paris. In 1896, van de Velde and four French artist colleagues – Émile Bernard (1868–1941), Maurice Denis (1870–1943), Georges Lemmen (1865–1916), and Paul Elie Ranson (1861–1909) – took on the job of fitting out four rooms at Bing's art dealer's shop. These rooms, with the addition of a rest room, were exhibited at the Dresden arts and crafts exhibition of 1897, as a result of which van de Velde became known internationally. Though these interiors may display weaknesses compared with the perfection of later designs by van de Velde, we already find here an exciting juxtaposition of the two principles of surface and space. In addition, it was the scale of the new kind of venture that constituted the significance of Bing's initiative: " ... it [the salon] corresponded so extraordinarily to an outstanding need that its opening marks a particular date in modern artistic life that will retain its importance. It is the first salon to serve both art and the public at the same time, from a single point of view that cannot be more highly conceived. Bing understood that art belongs in the home, not in large exhibitions ..."[31]

The figurative line

The rich variety of artful combinations that characterizes van de Velde's work was a result of its very range. He had proven his skill in handling two-dimensional surfaces, an art he refined in illustrations for the Flemish periodical *Van Nu en Straks* (of which he was cofounder) and posters for exhibitions and advertising purposes. Subsequently, his growing architectural and structural work developed his skills in a third dimension. In his graphics, the rhythm of line served to create atmosphere. In this, van de Velde found himself in accord with the stylistic approach of Symbolism. Nonetheless, his pure Art Nouveau creations (ill. opposite) still carried his individual signature. In the rather plain furniture of the early Belgian

style, the elements that were later decisive are already recognizable in the assertion of constructional and ornamental units to make an indivisible whole (ill. p. 156). Like Serrurier-Bovy, he broke up the English box-body furniture concept into structured bars and components. The final conquest of the third dimension by line was achieved by van de Velde in exemplary fashion in a silver candlestick (ill. p. 159), which – previously wrongly dated – was actually made as early as 1898. In his jewelry designs around 1900 (ill. p. 158), spatially hungry line is changed back into dynamic linear ornament. "Inside Belgium, van de Velde, with his particular artistic ambitions, remained an isolated figure. The most successful modern architect at the time was Victor Horta, who only once briefly engaged van de Velde as a collaborator. Less self-assured than this most practised of artists, van de Velde must have felt himself a novice beside him ... Berlin presented itself as a welcome escape ... It was an almost monitory essay by Julius Meier-Graefe that paved the way for his move. His real career had begun – brilliant, almost extravagant, but no longer so full of the fine scruples as the early, uncommonly honest things had displayed them."[32]

The difference that lies between the new and the naturalistic ornamentation is as large as that between something conscious, something right, and something wrong; between something healthy that gives strength because it is as it should be, and something else that is left to caprice, that somewhere once borrowed a motif from nature but which with the same right could have wanted the opposite; between something in accordance with the effective laws of the harmony of forms and determined by them, and something disorderly, chaotic, that proceeds from the wonderful interconnection of all things with the laws of nature. Anyone who has absorbed these laws and is imbued with the influence of lines on each other cannot feel impartial. As soon as he draws a curve, the one he places opposite it cannot be separated from the concept that lies enclosed in every part of the first; for its part, the second affects the first, changing it, and the first remodels itself in relation to the third and all others that will follow.

All lines from which forms later arise must be brought into such harmony that all effects are calculated and neutralized. This is the task of anyone who takes up the new ornamentation. Everyone knows what the various ridiculous and ridiculed names are that have been given to the new ornamentation; this evening, I can only advise them to call it "natural". ... The name does not matter, what matters is that the concept of this ornamentation should be clearly expounded, and the law of conformity will then demand that this ornamentation blend with modern architecture, that is to say, with the architecture that borrows more from the art of the engineers than from that of the contractor, and whose creative basis derives from calculations of the force and its resistance.

Henry van de Velde, inaugural speech at the Royal Academy in Antwerp, 1893.
Published in *L'Art Moderne*, 1893–94.

Abstract line and De Stijl
The Netherlands

Jan Toorop
Delftsche Slaolie [Delft Salad Oil]
Poster, 1895
Color lithography, 94.5 x 60 cm
"So possessed of his pale dream
figures is this painter that he even
consecrates Delft Salad Oil, whose
manufacturer commissioned a poster
from him, with his holy women.
Crimped into the ornamentation of
their duplicated hair, with
exaggeratedly gothicized, long-
fingered hands that protrude
chastely from huge puffed sleeves
like priceless revelations, they clutch
a bottle of oil and a serving spoon."
(Dolf Sternberger, see note 2)

The arabesque is, without being capable of precise
explanation, the reflex of a human expression that a
supple imagination has woven into a play of arabesques;
and the effect that this has on the spirit of the beholder
will, I believe, stimulate him to fantasies whose
importance will rise and fall in proportion to his
sensitivity and powers of imagination.
Odilon Redon[1]

Symbolist arabesques

In the Netherlands, two contrary developments
can be traced around the turn of the century. Both
were aiming at a formal revival, but they could
not have been more different in the character
they took. One school adopted the principle of
Mannerist line; the other manifested an intense
desire for pure form that contained the seeds of
Constructivism.

In Belgium, the Art Nouveau movement crys-
talized primarily in the two centers of Brussels
and Liège. Antwerp took part only peripherally,
but acted as a channel into the Netherlands, to
which it once belonged. Thus, currents of Dutch
art are rooted in Belgian-style Symbolism, but it
was recast with local features. The country had
been closely involved in the development of
modern art through its great artist Vincent van
Gogh (1853–90). The flowing, forceful bundles
of lines that run through his pictures (ill. pp.
14–15) derive from the same energies that
triggered off the arabesque linear gestures of Art
Nouveau. Despite the strict, insensitive Calvinism
of the country, there were forces at work that
were powerful enough to attempt a meaningful,
profoundly emotional experience of the super-
sensory. Whereas, however, the work of van
Gogh is driven to make expressive statements,
the works of the artists of Symbolist mindset

remain firmly in an introverted rhythm of linearity.
Outstanding among Dutch Symbolists is Jan
Toorop (1858–1928), in whose imagination all the
religions of the west and the Far East are fused
into unity. "… touched by the same magic spell
and always as if in a trance – the chalk paintings
of the Dutchman Jan Toorop. Half decorative
wallpaper with endless repetition of the same or
similar elements, half Symbolist representation
of legendary secrets – thin female forms, one,
two, three, six or twelve in a row, all surface and
line, in the same matt color, no light, no shadow,
long-armed, not unlike the spidery shadow-theatre
figures of Indonesia (and certainly indebted to
them as a model), all of them devoured, surrounded, entwined by endless tresses of hair, no
sky or ground, hair above and hair below, hair
even streaming out of bells, trailing up the sides,
spilling out over the edges of the picture, scored
in parallel grooves, occasionally undulating, un-
mindful of the structure of the horizontal and
vertical geometric form. So possessed of his pale
dream figures is this painter that he even consecrates Delft Salad Oil, whose manufacturer
commissioned a poster from him (ill. opposite),
with his holy women. Crimped into the ornamentation of their duplicated hair, with exaggeratedly
gothicized, long-fingered hands that protrude
chastely from the huge puffed sleeves like
priceless revelations, they clutch a bottle of oil
and a serving spoon."[2] Toorop's deftly elegant
mastery of symbol-laden arabesques make his
pictures representative of pure Art Nouveau. In
terms of content, they are marked by the tension
between Far Eastern superstition and the
Christian yearning for redemption. Toorop was
born on the island of Java as the son of a Dutch
government official. In the picture of the brides
(ill. p. 65), Javanese influences mingle with

Jacob van de Bosch
Soup tureen, 1900–1920
Stoneware, underglaze painting,
wooden knob, 31.9 cm long,
diameter 21.8 cm
Execution by Holland Fayencen
Tegelfabriek, Utrecht

mystic and lyrical components. Beside the innocent human bride in the center, in symmetrical antithesis, are placed the nun-like bride of Christ and, thirsting for human sacrifice, the bride of Satan. These are surrounded by ghostly creatures derived from Javanese art.

A meeting with Maurice Maeterlinck and Emile Verhaeren in 1890 made a deep impression on Toorop's work. As in the literature of Symbolism generally, fetishism figures largely in the work of these two poets. Wish-fantasies materialize as details of the whole, but in such a way as to condense the whole in the detail. A typical fetishist symbol is long flowing hair, a constantly recurring feature of Toorop's pictures that also became virtually a leitmotiv of Art Nouveau in general, as it had not only symbolic value but suited the decorative tendency of the style as well. The strongly expressive linear style of the painter, graphic artist and craftsman Jan Thorn-Prikker (1868–1932) opened up new ways from Art Nouveau into the art of the younger generation whom he taught. Even more than Toorop, Thorn-Prikker was a devout Catholic and created a large number of religious works of art.

Haagsche Plateelbakkerij Rozenburg

Il a taillé, limé, sculpté
Une science d'entêté,
Une science de paroisse,
Sans lumière, ni sans angoisse.
Emile Verhaeren[3]

The elements that were decisive for Toorop in his work in the fine arts were equally relevant to applied art, and they lent *fin-de-siècle* Dutch arts and crafts a wholly individual high-quality tone. The pots by the designer Jurriaan Kok (1861–1919) manifest decorative symbolic forms that also belong to the realm of fetishism. In outline, such forms take on the shape of stylized female pudenda, particularly in Art Nouveau book ornamentation. Such symbolism was applied most frequently in the Netherlands – often with erotic and sexual explicitness (ill. below). In Kok's work, the contours of the porcelain are linked with the decoration, which makes use of the whole palette of flower mysticism (ill. p. 166). Like silhouettes, the patterns stand out on the sides of vases like copies from his large collection of Javanese art. Belgium drew inspiration for its new art from the colonies, above all the Congo. The Netherlands enriched its *Nieuwe Stijl* with imports from Indonesia, which had been colonized way back in 1600. The fantastic mountain landscapes of the tropical island empire activated the imaginations of artists as much as the

Anonymous
Brooch, ca. 1910
Silver, bloodstone, diameter 5 cm

Jan Toorop
The Three Brides, 1893
Chalk on paper, 78 x 98 cm
Kröller-Müller Museum, Otterlo
In Toorop's imagery, religions fuse into unity. On each side of
the innocent human bride, in symmetrical antithesis, are the
nun-like bride of Christ and, thirsting for human sacrifice, the
bride of Satan. They are surrounded by ghostly creatures, in
the manner of Javanese art.

Jurriaan Kok, Haagsche Plateelbakkerij Rozenburg
Coffee pot, ca. 1900
Quasi or eggshell porcelain, color painted, 23 cm high, 15 cm wide, diameter 15 cm
Painting by Samuel Schellinck
Haags Gemeentemuseum, The Hague
In the Haagschen Plateelbakkerij Rozenburg Jurriaan Kok found a manufacturer capable of translating his subtle formal and decorative ideas into reality. After a long search for a porcelain that would take his unusual designs, in 1899 he finally succeeded in producing a light, thin-sided frit porcelain of ivory color and glass-like consistency.

Jurriaan Kok, Haagsche Plateelbakkerij Rozenburg
Vase, 1908
Quasi or eggshell porcelain, color painted, 40.5 cm high
Painting by Samuel Schellinck
Badisches Landesmuseum Karlsruhe, Museum beim Markt, Angewandte Kunst seit 1900

ancient traditions of Javanese craft work (ill. below). The profusion of decorative carvings covering the walls of temple buildings, *Wajang* (the art of the shadow theater) and highly developed batik techniques provided Art Nouveau with a wealth of ornamental patterns. In the Haagsche Plateelbakkerij Rozenburg, Kok found a sympathetic manufacturer who could implement his subtle formal and decorative ideas (ill. opposite). As traditional china clays proved insufficiently flexible for his out-of-the-ordinary concepts of form, Kok, who was director of Rozenburg from 1894, sought the help of the factory's chief chemist M. N. Engelden. The two of them carried out a series of complex experiments to develop a china clay that would suit his unusual designs. By 1899, they managed to produce light, thin-sided frit porcelains of ivory tone and glass-like consistency. The exact composition remains a secret, and is today described as quasi or eggshell porcelain. This stoneware mixture is extremely light. It permits sweeping outlines, curved edges and linear interlacing; it lends

Theodoros Christiaan Adriaan Colenbrander
Haagsche Plateelbakkerij Rozenburg
Lidded vase, 1887
Stoneware, polychromatic underglaze painting, 46 cm high, diameter 17.5 cm
The artistic manager of the Rozenburg factory, the architect Theodoros Christiaan Adriaan Colenbrander, had already introduced light-dark contrast-based ornamentation derived from Javanese batik before Jurriaan Kok came along. However, the vessels are still in the tradition of Dutch cupboard or fireplace decoration.

Dutch East Indies (Indonesia) pavilion, Paris World Exposition 1900
The Netherlands enriched its *Nieuwe Stijl* with imports from Indonesia, which had been colonized back in 1600. The fantastic mountain landscapes of the tropical island empire stirred the imaginations of artists, as did the ancient craft traditions of Java.

Adolf Le Comte
Delft porcelain tile, 1900
Delft faience, 13.5 cm high
Adolf Le Comte had the knack of
breathing Art Nouveau life into a
traditional pictorial medium with his
depiction of delicate, vulnerable-
looking girl figures that
corresponded to an ideal of the time
– the ideal of a frailty that is both
distressing and moving.

painted surfaces a brilliance. Besides Kok him-self, numerous other designers worked for Rozenburg, following in the path of the *spiritus rector*. Prior to Kok, the factory's architect and artistic director, Theodoros Christiaan Adriaan Colenbrander (1841–1930), had introduced light-dark contrast-based ornamentation derived from Javanese batik. These pots were nonetheless still in the tradition of Dutch cupboard and fireplace decoration (ill. p. 167).

Likewise in the Dutch tradition are artistically designed tiles. Adolf Le Comte (1850–1921) was adept at breathing new, Art Nouveau life into a traditional pictorial medium with his depictions of delicate, seemingly vulnerable girl figures that corresponded to an ideal of the time, of frailty that is both distressing and moving (ill. above).

Circumstances were very different as far as metalwork in the Netherlands was concerned. Here, the output of the English School and Guild of Handicraft found direct successors. In the late

1890s, the elder Frans Zwollo (1872–1945) created large round bowls, principally of beaten brass, and decorated them with geometric orna-mentation in which a closeness to folk art and echoes of theosophical motifs are evident (ill. opposite). A charmingly pretty variant of Benelux Art Nouveau was designed by Henri Evenepoel (1872–99), whose posters combine the extreme detail of Japanese art with French motifs (ill. above). The anti-ornamental school of Art Nouveau was represented by Jan Eissenloeffel (1876–1957) of Amsterdam in his metalwork, who soon gained an immense reputation throughout Europe. Though the gap between the two Dutch styles might seem unbridgeable – one a pro-fusion of ornament, the other purism – they are both an expression of a local artistic impetus that astonishingly manifested itself in the person of Toorop as well, when in later years he created artworks for buildings by Hendrik Petrus Berlage.

Henri Evenepoel
To the Square, 1897
Color lithography, 34.4 x 24.5 cm
Evenepoel's posters combine the
extreme detail of Japanese art with
French motifs.

Frans Zwollo senior,
Frans Zwollo junior
Fruit bowl
According to the inscription, this
was commissioned by Mr. G. J.
Verburgt, 1923/24 (reproduction
after the original by Frans Zwollo
senior, 1902)
Silver, gilt, sapphires, 21 cm high
Bowl: diameter 31.3 cm
Base: diameter 16.2 cm
Haags Gemeentemuseum, The
Hague

The non-curving line – Abstraction

*The decoration and function of an object stand once and
for all in conflict. Commonly used objects are, accordingly,
still undecorated these days, even in the hand of the
artistically minded. Only artists are greedily on the
lookout to "beautify" everything. It is the monumental
error of the new Arts and Crafts Movement – on which it
has already foundered or will founder – that it wants to
decorate everything ...*
Cornelius Gurlitt[4]

The "style" of circa 1900 lived off a formal vocabulary of curved plant and rationally rectilinear
shapes. The latter gave rise to an ascetic painting
style shortly before the First World War that
retained only the purity of geometric abstraction.
This constructivist art freed itself of figures but
nevertheless looked back to predecessors in
figurative art. The Dutch De Stijl group around
Piet Mondrian (1872–1944) (ill. p. 175) and Theo
van Doesburg (1883–1931) declared its goal to
be "a balanced relationship between the universal and the individual" (First Manifesto, 1918).[5]
That went for the participants themselves as
well – painters, sculptors, architects, and writers

all worked together. The artists of this movement
sought a harmonic balance of life through
abstraction and the reduction of colors and forms
in art and design. It was no accident that De Stijl
was formed in the Netherlands; this was not only
where their predecessors were, this was where
the main concerns of the group had already been
formulated in the works of Hendrik Petrus
Berlage and Jan Eissenloeffel. The silversmith
Eissenloeffel had already trained as a draughtsman before he entered the silverware workshop
of W. Hoeker in Amsterdam in 1896. In the same
year, he took over the management of the metals
department of the Dutch firm Amstelhoek. A
study tour to Vienna acquainted him with the
"Quadratl-Stil" [rectangle style] of Josef Hoffmann,
for which he long retained his enthusiasm. He
found another congenial community of artists
later in the Wiener Werkstätte. In 1900 he spent
a year in Russia, where he studied the craft skills
of Fabergé and refined his enamel technique. An
elegant coffee service (ill. p. 170) won him a gold
medal at the World Exposition in Turin in 1902,
and this was followed by countless international

Hendrik Petrus Berlage
Hunting lodge, Otterlo, 1914
and 1920
The striking corner tower of the
Amsterdam Exchange is, as here in
the hunting lodge of the Art
Nouveau patron Kröller-Müller in
Otterlo, a feature of a number of
buildings by Berlage. The towers
attain the same degree of simplicity
of architecture as the other
components, and again the retreating
surface is taken sculpturally into the
corners to avoid "deconstructive"
transitions. The soaring component
of towers as architectural gestures of
almost symbolic meaning occurs in
the work of many Art Nouveau
architects. Those that come to mind
include the Wedding Tower by
Joseph Maria Olbrich or the railway
station by Eliel Saarinen in
Helsinki, which leads on in an
almost direct line to American
skyscraper architecture.

awards. In the new century, Eissenloeffel
worked increasingly with base metals, preferring
brass and copper. He made plain, solid, practical
utensils that are articulated mostly only with
grooves and shaped in basic geometric forms.
The functional designs of his bowls, pots, and jars
became models for modern household utensils
(ill. opposite). At the same time Eissenloeffel
provided a convincing demonstration that strict
form and elegance are not mutually exclusive,
and that an ornamentally severe style can have
the same stimulating effect as a complicated
floral ornamental design. One might be tempted
to see him as an outsider of Art Nouveau art, but
it is precisely in his designs that the concern of
his period for the proper use of materials and for
surface art is put into effect. Eissenloeffel was
recognized as an outstanding craftsman not only
in the Netherlands but also internationally. In
1908, he was called to the Vereinigten Werkstätten für Kunst (United Workshops for Art) in
Munich, where he worked until 1909. Like
almost all Dutch artists, he collaborated with the
architect and designer Berlage.

Jan Eissenloeffel
Coffee service, ca. 1900
Silver
Coffee pot: 14.2 cm high, 20.5 cm
wide, diameter 11.5 cm
Haags Gemeentemuseum,
The Hague

Hendrik Petrus Berlage – The new architecture

So what is it about, then? It is about having a style again. Not just my kingdom but Heaven for a style! that is a cry of despair – that is the great lost fortune. Illusion-art rules, i.e., to fight the lie, to have the essence, not the illusion.
Hendrik Petrus Berlage[6]

Hendrik Petrus Berlage (1856–1934) studied architecture in Zurich, at the very polytechnic where Gottfried Semper (1803–79) taught from the founding of the institute in 1855 to 1871. As Berlage attended the college from 1875 to 1878, one may consider him at best as a pupil of Semper "once removed". Even so, Semper is one of the two masters that influenced him most. (The other was – as with the Belgian Victor Horta – Eugène Emmanuel Viollet-le-Duc.) Semper's main theoretical work was *Der Stil in den technischen und tektonischen Künsten 1860–63* [Style in the Technical and Architectural Arts, 1860–63], in which he expounds a practical aestheticism that does not start from the history of stylistic forms, as had happened hitherto, but from technical developments. This work had a formative effect on Berlage. Semper represen-

ted the view that craftsmen and architects should use materials in a manner appropriate to them. This is why, for example, he rejected Thonet's technique of bending wood – that was not appropriate to wood, that was treating it like metal. As a counter-example, he cited Egyptian seating. Here, he said, the frame was built right-angled, that is, constructively, "in the nature of timber", while the seat was inserted in this structural frame at an angle, occasionally even curved. Berlage followed this doctrine in his own furniture, tautly articulating it in the service of functional excellence (ill. p. 174). With this philosophy, he exercised a powerful influence on local furniture designers, who, deferring to the proclaimed appropriateness of materials, showed a penchant for "natural" woods. In respect of ornamentation, their designs are sober and uncompromising. In 1900, the furniture business 't Binnenhuis Inrichting tot Meubileering en Versiering der Woning (ill. p. 174) was set up with the aim of promoting the new style and binding various working artists to it in the quest for a synthesis of the arts. In pursuit of this pro-position, the business offered comprehensively designed interiors in its showroom, among others

Jan Eissenloeffel
Brass kitchenware, ca. 1900
Polished brass, carved notches and lines
Coffee pot: 22 cm high, diameter 7.5 cm (base),
large round container: 15.5 cm high, diameter 11 cm,
small round container: 10.3 cm high, diameter 6 cm
box: 9.5 x 14.5 x 14.5 cm
Die Neue Sammlung, Staatliches Museum für angewandte Kunst, Munich
After the turn of the century, Eissenloeffel worked increasingly with base metals, his preference being for brass and copper. He made plain, solid utensils that are articulated only by grooves and mostly designed in basic stereometric forms. The functional shapes of his containers, pots, and goblets served as models for modern household utensils.

Jacob van den Bosch
Chair, Opus 41, 1900–01
Oak, brass castors, upholstery in
imitation leather, 101 cm high,
75 cm wide

Hendrik Petrus Berlage
Buffet cupboard, 1898
Oak, 260 x 260 x 70 cm
Haags Gemeentemuseum,
The Hague
Gottfried Semper, the great
intellectual mentor of Berlage, held
the view that craftsmen and
architects should use each material in
a way appropriate to it. He therefore
rejected, for example, Thonet's
technique of bending wood. That
was not right for wood, that was
treating it like metal. As a counter-
example, he cited Egyptian seating.
Here, he said, the frame was built
right-angled, that is, constructively,
"in the nature of timber", while the
seat was inserted in this structural
frame at an angle or even curved. In
his own furniture, Berlage followed
this doctrine.

Previous pages:
Hendrik Petrus Berlage
Commodity Exchange, Great
Chamber, Amsterdam Exchange,
Amsterdam, 1896–1903
The clear, consistent constructional
simplicity of the building is
maintained in the furnishing. Every
detail serves to articulate the
architectural principles of Berlage.

by van de Velde, Eissenloeffel, Berlage and Jacob van den Bosch (1868–1948), a designer and member of the management (ill. p. 163 and above).

The second great influence on Berlage was Viollet-le-Duc. The latter's insistence on the primacy of construction in architecture can be traced in many buildings by Berlage, but especially in the Amsterdam Exchange. It is revealing that Berlage replaces the word "logical" in Viollet-le-Duc's writing by "functional" in respect of himself.

Berlage gained the commission for the Amsterdam Exchange, now considered his masterpiece, after a number of (unsuccessful) entries in competitions. The block design, which pulls together the individual components in surface tensions, lays the construction open to view. The individual parts do not break with tradition completely but interpret it in the context of the construction. What Berlage wanted above all was honest architecture, "honest" in the sense of social functionality and openness of design. "The main chamber is a very impressive space … (ill. pp. 172–173). Note for example the columns in the ground floor arcade of the Commodity Exchange. They are in reality not columns but pillars rounded off at the corners. The wall surface would have met a column only tangentially. That was not enough for Berlage. In

his design, the wall surface is continued as part of the surface of the pillar. And now observe with what sculptural precision the resulting problems for the transition to the base and capital are solved – if one may even term them thus! These are no frivolous matters for an architect with a gift for architectural sculpture. Each of his constructional components cut from ashlar manifests a principle, one could say. One could say it is all wall. That is why it is so appropriate that Berlage attempts to introduce metal construction into such a context. This is of course a bold venture, and I should first like to demonstrate that with a small example. You can see here short ceiling bearers made of steel that rest on the walls and support shallow barrel vaults made of brick. That fits together very well. The matter becomes more problematic when it concerns lattice girders spanning the large chamber. Berlage employs several devices to make this leap plausible: in one case, it is ornament on the rivets in the rising part of the main truss just before the bifurcation … finally, reinforcement of the wall under every truss … The ashlar block carries the joint on which the base of the framework is mounted … This is how Berlage brings off the difficult transition from the wall to the lattice girder, which is at the same time the transition from the large mass of the walls and

't Binnenhuis, Amsterdam
Invoice
Reproduction
The firm of 't Binnenhuis Inrichting
tot Meubeleering en Versiering der
Woning was established in 1900 in
Amsterdam with the purpose of
promoting the new style and
bringing together various artists in
pursuit of a synthesis of the arts.

Hendrik Petrus Berlage
Clockface, 1901
(cf. wall clock in Great Chamber,
Amsterdam Exchange)
Colored design drawing,
14.5 x 13.2 cm
Dutch Architectural Institute,
Rotterdam

the glass roof of the hall."[7] The clear and consistent constructional simplicity is continued in the furnishing of the Exchange. Every detail serves to demonstrate Berlage's principles. The striking corner tower of the Exchange is a feature that occurs in several of Berlage's buildings (ill. p. 170). The towers achieve the same degree of simplicity of architecture as the other building components, and again the retreating surface is linked sculpturally to the corners to avoid "deconstructive" transitions. The tower as an architectural gesture of almost symbolic intent is found with many Art Nouveau artists. We may recall the Wedding Tower by Joseph Maria Olbrich (ill. p. 237) or Eliel Saarinen's railway station in Helsinki (ill. p. 302), which leads on almost directly to American skyscraper architecture.

De Stijl – Concrete art

Art will disappear to the extent that life itself gains balance.
Piet Mondrian[8]

Piet Mondrian
On the Gein – Trees at Moonrise,
1907–08
Oil on canvas, 79 x 93 cm
Haags Gemeentemuseum, The
Hague

Likewise numerous were the threads that led on from Berlage to the 1920s, not only to the structures of the New Functionalism and Expressionism but also straight (in the figurative sense) to the pictorial works and objects of the Constructivists, who – and this cannot be overemphasized – also once trod a linear, organic path before pure form arose. De Stijl went in two directions, pursuing either the purity of everyday objects or the purity of pure illustrative models. Van Doesburg described this in terms of climate: "The studio of a modern painter should have the atmosphere of 3,000 meters up in the mountains of external snow; cold kills germs."[9] Gerrit Thomas Rietveld's Red and Blue Chair (ill. p. 177) is acclaimed as the manifesto of pure utilitarian objects, and indeed the cradle of De Stijl in general – clear proof that Art Nouveau in all its facets cannot be treated in terms of formal criteria alone but as a fundamental movement of the "for and against" about 1900, which in its effect remained of centennial significance. The puritanical zeal with which the principles of contemporary art were elaborated is set against Art Nouveau only in the external result. The complete working out of individual existence through style alienates from life to the same extent as Concrete Art or Suprematism.

"'Banishing man from art', against which a sagacious philosophical writer of our time (José Ortega y Gasset) has argued, targeting first and

Page 177:
Gerrit Thomas Rietveld
Red and Blue Chair, 1918
Beech, painted,
87.5 x 65 x 82.5 cm
Rietveld's Red and Blue Chair was lauded as a manifesto of pure functional objects, and today is considered as the starting point of De Stijl in general.

foremost all varieties of 'abstract' art – banishing man from art is no more than the flipside of banishing man into art. Into 'art' or into the 'realm of art' is ultimately into ornamentation. And from our point of view at least, it was introduced by Art Nouveau."[10]

The 19th century was the century of ugliness; our grandparents, parents and we ourselves lived and still live in an environment that is uglier than any before. Let us look around with sober gaze; and if we compare everything with things from earlier times, we come to the conclusion that nothing, but also nothing of everything that our parents and we ourselves commonly use, can be called beautiful, and that what still looks pretty usually dates back to an earlier century.

If we look at the interiors of our homes, we absolutely shudder at the junk we call household equipment. No chair, no table, no pot but that it only partially satisfies; and the only reason we are not vexed to the point of despair is that human beings unfortunately, or rather fortunately, get used to everything.

If we consider the homes themselves, speculation building – that mass production of the worst sort, against which a single tolerable house by an architect cannot prevail in isolation – has created a type that has probably nothing left in it that one generally calls architecture ...

Rational construction can form the basis of a new art; when that principle is not only adequately instilled but is also generally applied as well, only then will we stand at the portals of a new art, in the moment when the new cosmic feeling, the social equality of all mankind will be manifested, a cosmic feeling not with its ideal rooted in the hereafter, i.e. not in that sense religious, but with an ideal of this world, and so contrasting with it; ... Then art will once again have a spiritual basis that it needs in order to be able to manifest itself as a fully conscious utterance of this cosmic feeling ...

Hendrik Petrus Berlage, *Gedanken über den Stil in der Baukunst* [Thoughts on Style in Architecture], Leipzig, 1905

A step into the future
Italy and Russia

Richard-Ginori
Società Ceramica Italiana,
Milan, 1902
Coffee cup, 1902
Design drawing, watercolor,
16.5 x 12.5 cm
Museo della Porcellane di Doccia
Fiorentino
Richard-Ginori, a stoneware factory
with rich traditions, traded from
1896 under the name "Società
Ceramica Italiana". Its products
combined floral motifs with Tuscan
coloring.

Art! Art! That was the faithful, ever-youthful, immortal beloved, that was the source of pure delight, denied to most, reserved for the elite, that was the sumptuous food that made man godlike. How could he have drunk from other cups after putting this one to his mouth.
Gabriele D'Annunzio[1]

Neither Italy nor Russia were protagonists in the splendidly colorful drama "Art circa 1900", but in the final act both supernumaries were drawn into the limelight. To the last decade of this century, the Italian "Stile Liberty" and the Russian "Little Merchant Palaces" style have remained entertaining, sometimes autonomous interpretations of pan-European trends. We do not find a zeal for reform and full-bodied theories that the period has bequeathed us. Art Nouveau remained just an episode in both countries; energies were building up, in order to launch themselves in a sudden, unanticipated bolt from the blue as Futurism and Suprematism. Abstraction in Italy and Russia was not achieved by purifying an ornamental style. It was conceived as a singular act, carried forward by the dynamics of its inherent vision. The floral sumptuousness of architecture around the turn of the century, meanwhile, waxed into a wedding-cake building style of totalitarian pomp. These are the features that allow common treatment of otherwise divergent nations.

Italy

Expositions, the total art shows – Turin 1902

The world expositions of the 19th century were magnificent self-portrayals of economic prosperity and national yearnings for admiration. They offered, in an international context, a balance between what existed and was available on the one hand and what was wanted or hoped for on the other. From washbasins to looms, lawnmowers to adding machines, in short, from everyday articles to political models, thousands of objects were arrayed in a far-shining panorama of a world that was represented as desirable. At the same time, for artists fed up with the old clichés, they served as a cache of overseas crafts skills. Without question, expositions came into fashion reinforced. The establishment of artists' and craft workshop associations that were soon on the agenda around 1900 fueled the urge to communicate the new feeling and creativity. The term international Art Nouveau is often used because the individual Secessions, Écoles, Guilds and Schools carried on a lively interchange of ideas amongst themselves, mostly via exhibitions. In this context, Turin 1902 acted like a drum roll for expositions. For the first time, this great display of handicrafts brought together the entire creative forces of the *fin-de-siècle*. Participating countries at "Torino 1902 – Le Arti Decorative Internazionali Del Nuovo Secolo" were Austria, Belgium, Denmark, England, France, Germany, Hungary, Italy, the Netherlands, Norway, Scotland, Sweden, and the USA. It was an overwhelming performance that transformed the position of Italy, which had up to then stood rather aloof, into a focal point of international artistic forces. The Venice Biennale, which had

Raimondo D'Aronco
Galleria Degli Ambiènti
Front, Turin 1902
Contemporary photograph,
28.5 x 23 cm
Gallery of Modern Art, Udine

been founded in 1897, continues the tradition to this day. "A ghastly hubbub and yet a great act of culture, inundated with humbug and barefaced braggadocio and yet a serious testimonial, a magnificent statement of the immense progress made by humanity. … This is the first impression of the international exposition. After several visits, the spectator who came not just to gawp begins to shake off and try to forget the rackety impression, and to a certain extent he can succeed. The question arises whether one could not do without the ballast, whether an exhibition could not be put on without all this carry-on, without these attractions for the gawper, that flatter his idle curiosity. We think this is not possible, and even if it were possible, the result would be still more braggadocio. For the truth is, all the culture on show is underpinned by capitalism, and capitalism is again inconceivable without brutal competition, glittering trumpery and deceit, everything that, taken together, makes up the fun of the fair. … And yet the triumph of modern arts and crafts is the triumph of art over machines, over big industry, which now must serve it, and with that the triumph of man over machine is certain. Machine-based industry kills beauty, Ruskin rightly observes, and as a sociologist he adds: 'This same industry has turned us all today into machines, intellectual cripples, each of whom is a *specialist* …' "[2]

Magic of the Orient – D'Aronco and the Bugattis

La splendeur orientale,
Tout y parlerait
A l'âme en secret
Sa douce langue natale.
Charles Baudelaire[3]

Undoubtedly Ruskin would have delighted in the diversity of the pavilions of so many countries in Turin. Less delighted were the critics, both local and international, over the official exhibition buildings erected by Italian architects: "… uno stile uniforme, che non è altro che lo stile austrotedesco."[4] Raimondo D'Aronco (1857–1932) had emerged as victor in the competition for the construction of the main pavilion for the Turin exposition. The influence of the buildings of the Viennese architect Joseph Maria Olbrich and the Darmstadt artists' colony can clearly be discerned in his style, which is nonetheless rich in individual touches derived from his encounter with the Orient (ill. p. 179). Already successful as an architect, D'Aronco took part in the national exhibition in 1891 in Palermo where, thanks to his enthusiasm for Ottoman art, he came to meet the Turkish Sultan, Abdul Hamid. On the strength of D'Aronco's ambitious work, the Sultan summoned the Italian to his court. In June 1893, the new favorite of the cosmopolitan Ottoman ruler arrived in Constantinople (today Istanbul) and succumbed completely to its *splendeur orientale*. He took on numerous building commissions, and his work skillfully combined the essence of Arab architecture with components from European Art Nouveau. D'Aronco threw himself enthusiastically into the restoration work on Hagia Sophia and the repairs on the Great Bazaar. With such commissions under his belt, in 1899 he turned next to making good various sites of destruction left by an

earthquake in the Bosphorus area, which he filled with buildings in a neo-Oriental *Stile floreale*. In D'Aronco, this mix of cultures does not result in an exotic fairy-tale architecture but in an extravagant style that occupies a wholly individual position in architectural history. The architect returned home to undertake the pantheon of the Turin Exposition, the Rotonda d'Onore, with a design that displays all the features of *fin-de-siècle* art – a successful fusion of adapted elements reformulated in a new style. The drum and tall, light dome are reminiscent of Hagia Sophia, while the rich, painted ornamentation recalls Byzantine models combined with the cheerful lightness of Olbrich's Secession buildings (ill. opposite).

In a review of the Turin Exposition in the

Carlo Bugatti
Bench, ca. 1900
Wood, vellum, inlays of brass and white metal, beaten brass, painted decoration, tassels, 151 x 246 x 59 cm
A completely circular doorway led into one pavilion at the Turin Exposition that was without parallel. Inside, an astonishing assembly of beaten metal, repoussé leather, tattooed vellum and fine silver inlays exuded a strange, sensuous magic, further reinforced by the brown, gold, and silver tones of paint. The ornamental fantasies of Bugatti are in no way copies or adaptations but creations in the Art Nouveau sense of turning everything into a work of art.

Rembrandt Bugatti
Trained Elephant, radiator cap
figure of the Bugatti Royale
automobile, 1928 (a slightly
modified version of the 1908
sculpture *Eléphant dressé jouant*)
Cast silver, 19 cm high
Schlumpf Collection, Musée
National de l'Automobile de
Mulhouse
A joint masterpiece of the Bugatti
family was the Bugatti Royale
automobile, constructed by Ettore –
the eldest son of Carlo – and his son
Jean. It carried a small elephant
figure by Rembrandt on the radiator
cap. Between them, the Bugatti
family thus reflect a substantial
segment of Italian art history. In
1909, Marinetti wrote in the
founding manifesto of Futurism:
"A racing car whose bodywork is
decorated with great pipes
resembling snakes with explosive
breath, ... a screeching car that seems
to run on case shot, is more beautiful
than the *Nike* from Samothrace."
(see note 5)

Viennese periodical *Neue Freie Presse*, the critical observation is made that Italian arts and crafts resembles too much the gay coat of the harlequin, and it was no compensation that this coat was sometimes of superb cut and first-class workmanship. Only in the characteristics of individual exhibitors does a more thoughtful patterning occur, such as in the furnishings of Carlo Bugatti.

Bugatti's circular doorway led into a pavilion without parallel at the 1902 Exposition. Inside, an astonishing assembly of beaten metal, repoussé leather, tattooed vellum, and fine silver inlays exuded a strange sensuous magic, further reinforced by painted tones of brown, gold, and silver. The creator of this Oriental romanticism undoubtedly met all the criteria of the competition. According to the rules, any works that in any way copied or took over previous styles were disqualified. The ornamental fantasies of Bugatti (1856–1940) are in no way copies or adaptations but creations in the Art Nouveau sense of turning

everything into a work of art. Of course, influences can be traced, as in the international Art Nouveau movement generally – especially those of Joseph Maria Olbrich. Like the latter, Bugatti monumentalized objects into sculptural, architectural creations (ill. p. 180). Added to this were Turkish, Arab, and Egyptian elements (ills. p. 181 and opposite) that had, as befitted the times, a pragmatic background. The firm of Bugatti had business connections with architects from the Islamic world, and had made furniture for, among others, the Constantinople villa of the Khedive's mother (the Khedive was the former Viceroy of Egypt). Echoes of craft traditions led the Art Nouveau artist not just to his own national past but also to non-European models. Exquisite examples of handcrafted work from north Africa and Asia Minor such as tiles from Iznik had been familiar in Europe since 1867, thanks to the great world expositions. Indeed, neo-Egyptian fashions had been popular since Napoleon's campaign, and experienced a revival during the construction of the Suez Canal, which was finally commissioned in November 1869. Later still, the same trend inspired Bugatti to create a series of furniture designs featuring Oriental tassels and asymmetrical minarets for bordering. Symbolism, with its predilection for an almost sultry atmosphere, went one better – we have only to recall Louis Majorelle's *Nénuphars* furniture (ills. p. 107, 119).

Before Bugatti moved to Paris in 1904, he had already organized an extensive furniture production business in Milan, which gained international recognition. His chairs may strike one as fanciful, but they sold like hot cakes. Likewise the tables with ornamental bases and the outlandish screens, the favorite furniture of Art Nouveau. The furniture exhibited in Turin in 1902 was already more strongly marked by rounded, Cubist forms, though without forgoing the unusual materials and ornamentation. The furnishing objects of the Italian designer Eugenio Quarti (1867–1929) were created in the same decorative spirit (ill. p. 184).

As an artistic family, the Bugattis can be traced back to the 15th century, but by 1900 they had become an artistic dynasty. A brother-in-law of Carlo Bugatti was the famous painter Giovanni Segantini (1858–99). His son Rembrandt (1884–1916) was celebrated for his small-scale animal sculptures made of bronze, which he designed in the tradition of the miniature sculptures so esteemed by Art Nouveau. Rembrandt Bugatti worked direct from nature, mostly at the zoos of Paris and Amsterdam. The figures were fash-

Carlo Bugatti
Folding screen, ca. 1900
Wooden panels, vellum, inlays of
pewter and brass, hammered copper,
tassels, central panel 212 x 51 cm

Eugenio Quarti
Occasional table, overall view
(above) and view of table top
(below), ca. 1900
Wood, glass, brass, inlays of brass
and abalone, 70 cm high
Quarti's furnishings are conceived
in a decorative spirit that insisted
on unusual materials and
ornamentation.

ioned as vividly as possible, but the execution was much more impressionistic than naturalistic. A later joint masterpiece by the family was the Bugatti Royale automobile, constructed by Ettore (1882–1947), the eldest son of Carlo, and his son Jean (1909–39), which carried an elephant figure by Rembrandt on the radiator cap (ill. p. 182). The Bugatti family thus reflect a substantial portion of Italian art history. In 1909, Emilio Filippo Tommaso Marinetti (1876–1944) wrote in the founding manifesto of Futurism: "A racing car whose bodywork is decorated with great pipes resembling snakes with explosive breath ... a screeching car that seems to run on case shot, is more beautiful than the *Nike* from Samothrace."[5] The Futurists wanted to set everything in motion. As "hieroglyphs", they used zigzag and wavy-line motifs which are as much part of Cubist vocabulary as of Art Nouveau (ill. p. 193).

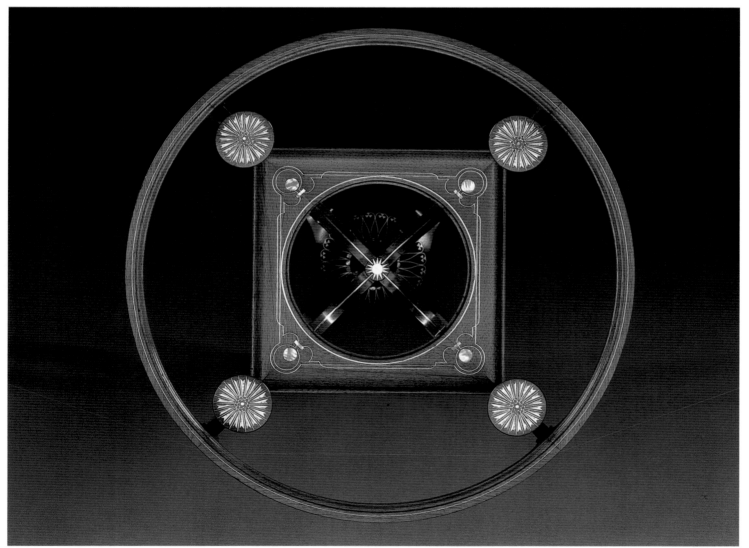

Cult of Eros and beauty –
Gabriele D'Annunzio

Artificial, like worlds carved in
Marble and gold, chimerical spaces ...
Gustave Moreau[6]

The cross-connections and also the dissonances of artistic endeavor in Europe – as in America – around the turn of the century count as one of the most interesting aspects of Art Nouveau. A large number of the artistic products constitute a virtual encyclopedia of decadence and Symbolism, stamped with the handwriting of each country. This Symbolism was a sensuously extravagant, ecstatic art whose representatives, though they followed no program, were bound by a common philosophy of life. Their aversion to the progress-worshiping positivism of the older generation amounted almost to open contempt. They saw its mass-educational optimism as heading for mediocrity. The artificial paradises created by the aesthetes as a countermeasure to the decline of culture and transformed into poetry by Baudelaire were translated by Gabriele D'Annunzio (1863–1938) into reality. Beauty was for him not just an unworldly artificiality. His Italian vitality saved him from copying the example of Des Esseintes, the hero of the Art Nouveau cult novel *A rebours*, and withdrawing into a morbid private pleasure world. D'Annunzio was Narcissus incarnate, living in style-conscious self-love, a genius of literary productivity and eroticism. His cult of Eros and beauty was in keeping with *fin-de-siècle* art. The ambivalent female type of his poetry fulfilled the Symbolist ideal of the *femme fatale*, made flesh in the Eves, Salomes, and Judiths of the art of the period. He looked on his work as a *Gesamtkunstwerk*, a synthesis of the arts, and built himself a villa as a monument to Decadent taste, filled with all the lofty *bric-à-brac* of the era. Whereas the Viennese playwright Hugo von Hofmannsthal was a great admirer of D'Annunzio, the German novelist Thomas Mann thought it necessary to warn his brother Heinrich against the "bellows poetry that has been imported from the lovely country of Italy in the last few years" and the "lush aestheticism of the Latinist D'Annunzio, the rank aestheticism of an ambitious wallower in words."[7] Decadence simply does not appeal to the German psyche. In contrast, the Irishman James Joyce envied D'Annunzio his "linguistic artistry" and his "sensuous love of words, that provided an inextinguishable delight for anyone who heard or read them."[8]

Galileo Chini
Vase, ca. 1900
Majolica, underglaze painting, 45 cm high
International Ceramics Museum, Faenza
Base diameter 14 cm, neck diameter 11.5 cm
Execution by L'Arte della Ceramica, Florence
An unmistakable embodiment of the *arte nuova*, the new art, is Galileo Chini's Arte della Ceramica factory in Florence.

Redundancy and architecture

"The marvelous sensual revelry of Baroque susceptibilities also set the parameters for a definitive version of Italian Art Nouveau."[9] Many architects of the period combined their Baroque inheritance with modern building materials, bringing a cascading, opulent architecture without compare. The buildings of Giuseppe Sommaruga (1867–1917) – for example, his Palazzo Castiglioni in Milan – have a Baroque sumptuousness whose sense of drama recalls the operas of Verdi or Puccini. Less histrionic are the mansions by Giuseppe Brega (1877–1929), which have a more floral charm, as for example the Villa Ruggeri in Pesaro shows (ill. p. 189). On closer inspection, it is not difficult to make out Italian tradition and Italian heritage under the amorphous ornamental overlay of its facade. Brega endowed the eastern wall of the house with two eye-like windows, a flowery element made of reinforced concrete that resembles a nose and an entrance doorway shaped like a mouth – all of which reminds one of the vegetable portraits of Giuseppe Arcimboldo (ca. 1527–93). Closest to D'Annunzio's approach are the "creations" of Giovanni Michelazzi (buildings from 1902), which seem like private obsessions made public. A further important figure in the Italian architectural landscape is Ernesto Basile (1857–1932), who was considered one of the most influential representatives of the Stile Liberty and devoted

as much attention to the interiors as to the buildings themselves (ill. opposite). There are unmistakable French influences in his work – soft, elegant forms and a symbiosis of painting and decoration brilliantly handled. An early follower of Sommaruga's style was the young Giulio Ulisse Arata (1881–1962), but in later years he joined forces with Antonio Sant'Elia, the inspired city planner, and other architects to form the Nueve Tendenze group. Besides the buildings of this group, which thanks to Sant'Elia represented a progressive style, there were examples of graceful Art Nouveau architecture not just in Milan but in almost all Italian towns (ill. p. 188).

Stile Liberty – Futurism

Dynamic arabesques as the only reality created by the artist in the depths of his sensibility.
Carlo Carrè[10]

In an article on the Turin Exposition of 1898 entitled "Il renascimento delle arti decorative", the art critic Enrico Thovez wrote: "… modern decoration should, like the madman in D'Annunzio's dream of a spring morning, only for more sensible reasons than in his case, slip on a green robe in order to expunge from memory the idea of the blood-red color that characterized its past." In his view, what is taking place is a "return to the expressive naturalism of medieval art" and the "redemption of decorative art by plants and animals ... in faithful naturalistic form and with unambiguously decorative intentions based on Gothic models, with instruction from the Japanese."[12] D'Annunzio might be the leading "aesthetic" light of Italy, but craftsmen were increasingly oriented toward the English and their reform of everyday objects. The English influence becomes clear when one recalls that the whole artistic activity of the *fin-de-siècle* in Italy is rarely termed *Stile floreale*, whereas the terms *Stile Inglese* or *Stile Liberty* are still used to describe Italian-style Art Nouveau. The latter name was derived from the London-based decorative business of Arthur Lasenby Liberty, whose textiles and furniture enjoyed great popularity in Italy and were sold very successfully. There is a certain irony and of course unfairness in a store being as it were godfather for the whole style of the Novecentisti, which included very individual, high-quality work in many fields. One unmistakable embodiment of the *arte nuova*, the new art, is the Arte della Ceramica factory in Florence of Galileo Chini (1873–1956) (ill. p. 185). Another is the stoneware factory Richard-Ginori. Rich in traditions, since 1896 this had been known as "Società Ceramica Italiana" and combined floral motifs and Tuscan coloring in its products (ill. p. 178). Italy had nothing to offer to counter French supremacy in Art Nouveau glassware. Nonetheless, it had a very strong tradition of glassmaking, for example in Murano, and the quality of glassmaking was continued in glass windows and other glassware. These were not very original, but their decorative and technical quality was very high (ill. left). In printing as well, Italy's role was more receptive than creative, with English and French echoes and playful symbolic motifs from Viennese Art Nouveau, which lent themselves particularly well to illustrating the literary Art Nouveau style of D'Annunzio. The painter and graphic artist Antonio Rizzi (1869–1941) was a sporadic contributor to the Munich periodical *Jugend*, so that his work shows a strong relationship with the Art Nouveau style there (ill. p. 187). A more Italian version of Art Nouveau graphics was created by Marcello Dudovich (1878–1962) in his posters (ill. p. 187). He combined the Stile Liberty with "classical" figures, as they are found in Art Nouveau facades in Milan, nudes in the tradition of Italian sculpture. The Turin Exposition was supposed to help resolve the inner conflict of Art Nouveau, whose ideology swung backwards and forwards between aesthetic exclusivity and the demand that art should

Anonymous
Doorway, Genoa, ca. 1900
There are examples of graceful Art Nouveau architecture not only in Milan but in almost all cities of Italy, like this one in Genoa.

Left:
Giovanni Beltrami
Peacocks, glass window, ca. 1900
Clear glass, enameled, 450 x 150 cm
Execution by Lindo and A. Grassi, master glaziers, Milan
Italy had nothing to offer to counter French supremacy in Art Nouveau glass. Nonetheless, the quality of glassmaking, which boasted a very strong tradition, was maintained in glass windows and glassware which, though less individual, were of a high decorative and technical quality.

become common property. It remained, nonetheless, chiefly on the side of the costly and beautiful. The most forward-looking artist of the Art Nouveau era in Italy was Antonio Sant'Elia (1888–1916). Schooled in the artistic philosophy of the Viennese architect Otto Wagner, he began to take practical steps to make art common property. He was less interested in individual buildings, more in whole complexes of buildings and city planning on a thoroughly modern technical level. As a pioneer of the Futurists' "town machine", he designed terraced houses, elevator shafts and multilevel traffic systems, thereby setting aesthetic and functional standards for the following decades. Like the painter Umberto Boccioni (ill. p. 193), who was to help Futurism make an international breakthrough, he joined up in 1914 as a volunteer in the First World War. Both of them were killed in 1916.

Russia

Art Nouveau and abstraction

I still believe that, like the cranes, nations migrate into progress …
Julian Marchlewski[13]

Just as the cradle of Futurism is to be sought in Italy, it is with the Russian artists such as Kandinsky and Malevitch that we find the beginnings of abstraction. Yet, even in Russia, Art Nouveau flowered prior to the pioneering work of these artists. As in Italy, it had its receptive aspects, but it was nonetheless a dynamic and powerful movement. The architecture of the turn of the century in Russia is nicknamed the Little Merchant Palaces style, because, here too, it was the grande bourgeoisie above all who had the desire and the financial means to support the new style.

Giovanni Brega
Villa Ruggeri, Pesaro, 1902
Oreste Ruggeri, owner of a porcelain studio and a promoter of the new style, commissioned Brega to build him a villa. On closer inspection, Italian traditions and Italian heritage can easily be made out under the amorphous ornamental overlay on the facade. Brega adorned the eastern face of the house with two eye-shaped windows, a floral component made of reinforced concrete that looks like a nose and an entrance that is shaped like a mouth. The ensemble recalls Arcimboldo's vegetable portraits.

Fyodor Osipovich Schechtel
Palais Rabushinsky (now Gorky
Museum), 2–6 A. Tolstoy Street,
Moscow. Banisters of main
staircase, 1900–02, 1906
The Palais Rabushinsky was
constructed for the Moscow banker
and owner of the *Utro Rossiyi*. It
forms a high point in the output of
the Russian Art Nouveau architect
Schechtel. The building shows him
to be a disciple of *fin-de-siècle*
Symbolism. The asymmetrical form
and severe lines of the roof constitute
an idiosyncratic contrast to the
flowing curves of the mosaic frieze,
the doorway, and window frames,
and to the wrought-iron window
grilles, which are adorned with
undulating spiral motifs. The brown
and cream tones of the frieze depict
an orchid, the favorite flower of
Symbolism.

Anonymous
Pendant, Russia, early 1900
Gold, sapphires, diamonds,
6.5 x 3 cm
Taidetcollisuusmuseo, Helsinki
The Art Nouveau jewelry of Peter
Carl Fabergé, which makes use of
mainly plant, insect, and animal
motifs and in which he incorporated
a wide range of semiprecious and
precious stones, revived
contemporary Russian gold work
and led to numerous high-quality
imitators.

Whereas in St. Petersburg the new buildings tended to fit in more with the classicizing cityscape, in Moscow Art Nouveau buildings had bulky forms with large surfaces and seem to have been influenced more by folk art and Old Russian ecclesiastical and monastic architecture. The most important Russian architect of the local Art Nouveau style was Fyodor Osipovich Schechtel (1859–1926). His representative Art Nouveau buildings are the Palais Rabushinsky in Moscow (now the Gorky Museum) and Jaroslav Station, in which he incorporated unmistakable Old Russian elements in Art Nouveau. The Palais Rabushinsky (ill. opposite) indicates that Schechtel was an adherent of *fin-de-siècle* Symbolism. The asymmetrical form and severe lines of the roof

form an idiosyncratic contrast to the flowing curves on the mosaic frieze, portals, and window frames, and to the wrought-iron window grilles, which are adorned by an undulating spiral motif. The brown and cream-colored frieze depicts an orchid, the favored flower of Symbolism.

In the hall of the Hotel Metropol that he constructed in Moscow, William Franzevich Walkot (1874–1943) was the first in Russia to use components of metal, glass, and reinforced concrete. Besides villas and hotels, cinemas and apartment blocks were also constructed in the new style. Even passenger steamers on the Volga had Art Nouveau saloons. Moscow had its own "Turin" show with an "Exposition of Architecture and Crafts of the New Style" in the winter of 1902–03, at

Ivan Yakovlevich Bilibin
Red horseman
(Midday, or the Sun)
Illustration to the fairy tale
Vassilissa the Beautiful,
St. Petersburg, 1902
Color lithography, 22.2 x 14.7 cm

Page 193:
Umberto Boccioni
Musica Futurista, book cover for
Balilla Pratella, 1912
Tempera on card, 53 x 39 cm
Civic Drawing Collection, Castello
Sforzesco, Milan
The Futurists wanted to set
everything in motion. Their
"hieroglyphs" were zigzag and
undulating motifs, which were as
much part of Cubist as of Art
Nouveau vocabulary.

which not only Russian artists were exhibited but also Mackintosh and Olbrich among others.

For a short time, even the famous Russian goldsmith and jeweler Peter Carl Fabergé (1846–1920), who came from a French Huguenot family, was a disciple of Art Nouveau. His jewelry of this period largely features adaptations of plant, insect, and animal forms. For these, he used gold, silver, and platinum, plus a wide range of semiprecious and precious stones. His Art Nouveau products revived Russian gold work, and he found numerous high-quality imitators in Russia (ill. p. 191).

The influence of the Ecole de Nancy can be recognized in the glassware produced by the factory of the Imperial Russian Court. The influential designers here around 1900 were Petushov, P. Kranovsky and J. Romanov. The last two also worked for the Imperial Russian Porcelain Factory, which closely imitated the style of the Royal Porcelain Factory in Copenhagen and in 1890 was merged with the glassworks.

Moscow proved to be the up-and-coming center competing with conservative St. Petersburg, where a more neo-Romantic pictorial style was in vogue. The fairy-tale illustrator Ivan Yakovlevich Bilibin (1876–1942) was based here, continuing the tradition of Russian popular illustrated broadsheets in an ornamental style of expressive colorfulness (ill. p. 191). He was a member of the Mir-Iskustva Group in St. Petersburg, to which Vassily Kandinsky also belonged, the most momentous talent for the development of all European art. It may be surprising that Marxist criticism of the "non-representational world" equates bourgeois Art Nouveau with abstraction. The autonomous artist does the same as the autonomous bourgeois who transforms objects aesthetically. The artist who thinks non-representationally likewise loses contact with the reality of objects in the interplay of metaphysical forms.

Absolute movement is a dynamic law anchored in objects. The visual structure of objects in this case takes the innate motion in the object into account, irrespective of whether it is stationary or in motion. I draw this distinction in order to make myself understood more easily. In reality, there is no stationary, there is only motion, as immobility is only apparent or relative. This visual structure obeys a law of motion that is characteristic for the body. It is pictorial potential that the object contains within itself and which stands in close relationship with its organic substance.

In this first condition of motion, the object is not seen in its relative motion but understood in its lifelines, which reveal how it would break up in accordance with the tendencies of its forces. Relative motion is a dynamic law anchored in the motion of the object. It is accidental because it concerns above all moving objects and the relationship between mobilized and nonmobilized objects.

The question is to understand objects not only in their innate motion but also when they are in motion. It is thus not just a matter of finding a form that is an expression of this new absolute of speed, which no really modern man can ignore. It is a question of examining how life behaves at speed and in the simultaneity that follows from it.

By lines, we mean the motive tendencies of color and form. These tendencies are the dynamic appearance of form, an illustration of the movement of matter on the course prescribed to us by the construction line of the object and its action.

Into these motive tendencies are inserted color volumes created by color and form and their endless motion.

Umberto Boccioni, "Futurist Painting and Sculpture", quoted from *Futurism 1909–1917*, exhibition catalog, Düsseldorf, 1974.

Architecture as a natural phenomenon
Barcelona

Antoni Gaudí i Cornet
Collage, bench (detail), Parc Güell, Calle de Olot, Barcelona, 1901–14
Pieces of glass, porcelain and ceramics
The Parc Güell represents a *Gesamtkunstwerk*, a synthesis of the arts, and the system of "collages", made up of fragments of stone, porcelain, ceramics, and plants, is a painting, a sculpture – the highest expression of creative imagination.

The first point: the most Catalonian Catalan of all. Hence the epigraph in this language. We called him simply "Don Antón".
The second point: the greatest architectural genius, improviser of all solutions, inexhaustible creator, always original, natural and always logical, but in a world that was entirely his own.
The third point: the most pious and devout of any architect building houses and cathedrals – faith shows through even the structures of his houses.
Joaquim Torres Garcia[1]

The "Moorish style"

Spain's position within European art history has always been unusual. The near 800-year connection between Christian and Islamic art was bound to lead to an idiosyncratic style. In the Arab parts of the "occupied" country, Christians developed a Mozarabic style, while the Moors in the Christian provinces had their own *mudéjar* fashion. The origin of both styles is to be found in the complicated surface decoration and disguise of architectural principles inherent in Islamic art. In Arab art and architecture, human images are forbidden – a major reason why ornament, the only possible form of adornment, was developed to perfection. With flat surfaces traditionally broken up into a network of arabesques, contemporary international fashions were always transformed into an individual Spanish national style. The powerful urge to decorate overcame the cerebral forms of Gothic and broadened the Baroque into "architectural sculpture". Spanish piety, which an intense reverence for saints heightened into dreamlike mysticism, reinforced the attraction towards a quasi-ecstatic art form.

Antoni Gaudí i Cornet – Catalan and world citizen

Antoni Gaudí (1852–1926) was Catalan, not Spanish, perhaps even the "most Catalonian Catalan of all". He is, therefore, by no means to be viewed as a product of Hispanic fashions in art. This is true if only for the fact that the work of a genius – Gaudí was one of the "blessed" – is always marked by an inevitable autonomy, which holds its own even though external forces may show through. External energies – they were there, hence perceivable – were interpreted by Gaudí in a wholly individual, unmistakable manner, like for example in the "Moorish style" of his first works, or again, in the progressive, anti-classicist evolution between color and form and the extreme asymmetry of his Baroque three-dimensionality. Gaudí as an outsider, being an exceptional phenomenon, was nonetheless part of the movement of the outgoing century that sought to cope with the ballast of the most recent past by probing back for "clear" styles such as Gothic. The writings of Eugène Emmanuel Viollet-le-Duc, who lauded the construction principles of Gothic cathedrals and influenced the architects of around 1900 from Horta to Sullivan via Guimard, also stirred Gaudí. However, Viollet-le-Duc parted company with Gothic structure in introducing the V-shaped pillar, that is, the double crossarm brace. "The crossarm brace is a principal feature of the practice by which Gaudí strives to master Gothic. Gaudí was an eager student of the writings of Viollet-le-Duc. However, he is closer to Gothic technology, that is, to handicrafts, than Viollet. His main objection to Gothic was directed at solid and flying buttresses. These could be dispensed with by angling the pier in the direction of the

Rafael Julio Masó i Valenti
Penholder
Design drawing, watercolor
The architect and designer Rafael Julio Masó i Valenti sought to empathize with the original creations of Gaudí. The results were rather shapeless but not unoriginal.

thrust of the vault, that is, diagonally, in the resultant of the Gothic parallelogram. The crossarm brace became a principal motif in Gaudí's constructive architecture, as did the branched brace, the tree-like pier, as in the interior of the Sagrada Familia cathedral. For this, Gaudí thought, no iron was needed, as it could be done in stone. Where Viollet trumps Gothic essentially by transferring its principles to a new material, Gaudí masters it *with its own* constructive medium. … Gaudí was a man of handicrafts who asserted that one could produce virtually everything from brick and stone. Certainly it was possible in Catalonia at that time, given the quality of Catalan craft work. In this case, stone almost looks like cast material. With Gaudí, there are no architectural drawings, only models."[2] Divergence is mostly more conspicuous than convergence. That applies without question in

the case of the great names of Art Nouveau architecture, whose common point of departure was evident but took shape in accordance with their personalities, their talents and, above all, their national characteristics. It seems nonsensical, for example, to compare Louis Sullivan's Guaranty Building in Buffalo and Gaudí's Casa Milà in Barcelona, yet the intellectual kinship of the two architects should not be overlooked. "The Sagrada Familia is the greatest work of the entire creative architecture of the last twenty-five years. It is a depiction inherent in stone that is worthy of the spirit!"[3] – these are the words of the *form follows function* architect Sullivan when an American colleague put photos of the temple church in front of him (ill. p. 207, 208). Even if Gaudí rejected iron and steel as "mechanical" building materials, he shares at the same time a starting point even with the American architect

Paco Durrio
(Francisco Durrio de Madron)
Pendant, pre-1904
Cast gold, decorated on both sides,
6.5 x 6.2 cm
Musée d'Orsay, Paris
Durrio is a representative of Spanish Art Nouveau, that is, of an internationally flavored but nonetheless local version of craft work. It is revealing that he lived mostly in Paris, where he exhibited his jewelry with great success at the Salon d'Automne in 1904. The elegant line of his creations is without question so full of expressive three-dimensionality that the Catalan inheritance of the artist cannot be denied.

Antoni Gaudí i Cornet
Palau Güell, view into the dome of the central living area, Nou-de-la-Rambla 3–5, Barcelona, 1886–89
Gaudí's first major building commission, for the Palau Güell, came from his sponsor, and later close friend, Count Eusebio Güell, a much-traveled patron of the arts. On his business trips to England, Güell had come into contact with William Morris, and had put together an extensive library of contemporary writings on art theory which Gaudí often consulted. With the Palau Güell, structure and decoration began to fuse – a feature that later became characteristic of his principal works. Gaudí made use of the varied decorative opportunities of structural iron in all their abundance. In addition, he employed flattened brick vaults of Byzantine derivation that even today are copybook examples of stereotomy.

Frank Lloyd Wright. The man of technical fantasies, who used concrete and steel to bring forth a "more plastic art", for whom paneling and frame should relate to each other like "skin and bones", walked the same path as Gaudí. His structures are also like the bones of the human body surrounded by muscles and skin, making up a unity, an organic law.

Catalonia and Europe

Catalonia with its cleons in calico and its Catalan women in cotton is the strength and weakness of Spain.
A travel writer in 1845[4]

Besides the Catalan aspect of handicrafts, there were also political and social conditions that played an important part, as in Nancy, Finland, Darmstadt, and other places. "The Catalans are neither French nor Spanish, but a nation of their own, in language and costume as much as in their way of life. Their impetuousness and energy wholly persuade the traveler that he is no longer in aristocratic, carefree Spain … and no province of the incoherent entity that makes up the official kingdom de las Españas is less connected with

the crown than this land of revolt, that is always ready to break away," remarked a travel writer in 1845.[5]

The long history of Catalonia's search for independence culminated in the rebellions of the worker movements in Barcelona and the post-1880 terror that ensued in consequence. The first real Catalan organization was the Centre Català, founded by Valenti Almirall. In 1885, Almirall presented to King Alfonso XII the "Memorial de Grèuges", known as the "Memorandum for the Defence of Moral Interests and Catalonia". The Unió Catalanista was set up in 1891 to coordinate the various Catalan entities that then existed in Catalonia. In 1892, the principles for the Catalan Regional Constitution were formulated. These contained not only political but also cultural objectives: "The fact was that Catalonia, by virtue of its Catalanism, felt it was completely and irrevocably part of Europe. If for Mañe i Flaquer [a 19th-century Catalan freedom fighter] regionalism meant the revolt of the *patres familias*, in 1892 it represented a spiritual revolution among the young. It brought with it Impressionism, the music of Wagner, the plays of Ibsen, the philosophy of

Antoni Gaudí i Cornet
Crypt, Colònia Güell, Santa Coloma de Cervelló, Barcelona, 1898–1908 and 1908–17 (unfinished)
The funicular models for the crypt, with which Gaudí worked out the arch and vaulting loadings, were a challenge both structurally and aesthetically. Gaudí identified the natural disposition of the given structural form by hanging canvas bags filled with pellets on strings, the weights being proportional to those of the loadings he had calculated. Thus weighted, the strings displayed the shape of the skeleton of the future church. The "frame" of the Colònia Güell contains all the structural forms devised by Gaudí.

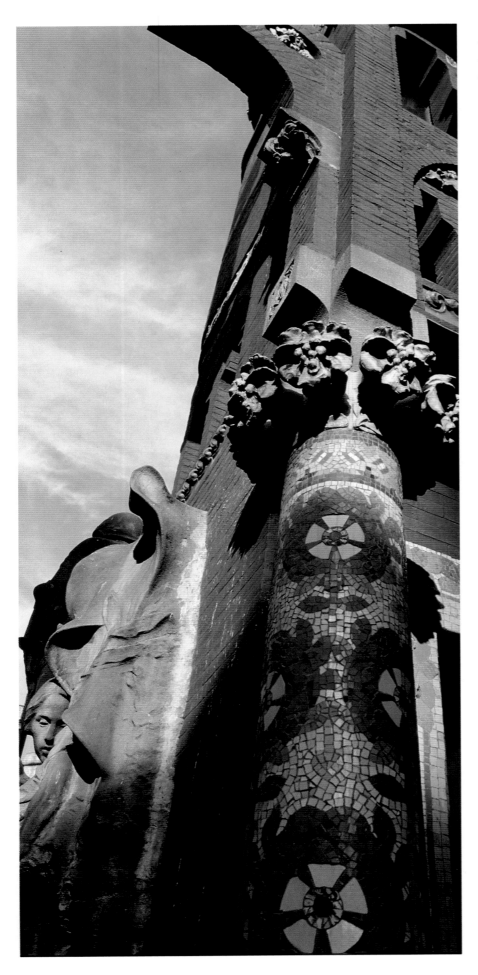

Nietzsche, Modernist aesthetics, the desire for telephones and good roads to Catalonia ..."[6] This vital fact of intellectual attachment to Europe on the part of the Catalans made *Modernisme* (the Spanish term for Art Nouveau) possible, yet it developed almost exclusively in Barcelona.

To be a Catalan had momentous consequences for European art history in the 20th century: Pablo Picasso [sic], Juan Gris, Joan Miró, Salvador Dalí, Julio González, Antonio Tàpies, Eduardo Chillida – all of them continued the traditions of their native land (ill. p. 211).

Modernisme:
Lluís Domènech i Montaner and Manuel Raspall i Mayol

I'll do you a sketch so that you can take it to the *Barcelona Cómica*, we'll see if anyone buys it. You'd laugh – it's supposed to be Modernist, like the magazine it's meant for.
Pablo Picasso[7]

The word *modernista* crops up in Catalonia for the first time in 1884 in the magazine *L'Avenç* in connection with an exhibition of European arts and crafts in Barcelona. The rapprochement to French Symbolism and the Aesthetic Movement, which affected Catalan literature first, was the breeding ground for the aesthetic movement in fine and applied art. For the occasion of the World Exposition in Barcelona in 1888, the architect Lluís Domènech i Montaner built the Grand Hotel and the Café-Restaurant popularly known as the "Castell des Tres Dragones", the "prototype" building of architectural Modernisme. In Montaner, the many facets of 19th-century Catalan style are palpably brought together. His architecture is based on a kind of late version of historicism, with a special emphasis on the formal vocabulary of Classicism and the Renaissance. The articulation of his facades, mostly on public buildings, is conceived in a rather more traditional architectural style, in contrast with which the interiors display a thoroughly individual, exciting tinge of Modernisme. Full of symbolic and structural ornamentation, the style reflects the rich range of experience of the *fin-de-siècle*. In the Café, columns carry floral capitals, while on the base remarkable Byzantine elements materialize. The virtual reversal of base and capital generates an illusionist reflection. This reflection is justified and continued in the whole "submarine decoration" of the Café, which is "flooded out" with fish and wave motifs. Here, a strong Japanese influence is evident in

Lluís Domènech i Montaner
Palau de la Música Catalana, Barcelona, 1905–08
The whole interior furnishing of the concert hall, from the lighting to the walls, is broken down into ornamental detail forms. The columns are mostly covered with polychrome pieces of glazed tile or adorned with animal sculptures. The surreal atmosphere is reinforced by the gem-like stained-glass windows and the blazing lights of the branch-like candelbras on the column capitals.

Montaner's work, as this vocabulary refers in both theme and form directly to *ukiyo-e*. Buoyed by the political independence movement, Catalan music also enjoyed a renaissance. The Catalan choir, Orfeó Català, founded in 1891, became a leading cultural force. During 1905-08, Montaner constructed for it the Palau de la Música Catalana in the heart of old Barcelona. This was now Modernist both inside and out (ill. opposite). The richly inventive decoration fuses with the organically structured body of the building in a successful symbiosis. Incorporating elements from numerous sources, Montaner's design is fronted by a facade with a double row of columns and decorated with a sculptural group symbolizing Catalan music. The rooftops recall the peculiar formations of Montserrat, a mountain in the neighborhood of Barcelona. The whole interior furnishing, from the lighting to the walls, dissolves in an abundance of ornamental detail. On the columns, the same trick of hallucination occurs as in the Café-Restaurant. The columns themselves are mostly covered with polychro-

matic glazed tile pieces or adorned with animal sculptures. The surreal atmosphere is reinforced by gem-like stained-glass windows and the blazing lighting from the branch-like candelabras of the column capitals. The importance of Montaner, who with his busy architectural practice was a major contributor to Barcelona's Modernist face, can be gauged from a first review of Gaudí's Palau Güell in *La Illustración Hispano-Americana* of February 1891: "... We shall soon be able to put Gaudí on a par with Domènech i Montaner, the initiator of the architectural renaissance."[8]

The Casa Barbey in Barcelona by architect Manuel Raspall i Mayol (1877–1937) is further evidence of the impressive variety of architectural activity in Catalonia around 1900 (ill. below).

Manuel Raspall i Mayol
Casa Barbey (detail), Barcelona, ca. 1900
"The fact was that, by virtue of its Catalanism, Catalonia felt it was completely and irrevocably part of Europe. If for Mañé i Flaquer [a Catalan freedom fighter of the 19th century] regionalism had meant the revolt of the *patres familias*, in 1892 it represented a spiritual revolution among the young. It brought with it Impressionism, the music of Wagner, the plays of Ibsen, Nietzsche's philosophy, Modernist aesthetics, and the desire for telephones and good roads to Catalonia ..."
(*Vicens Vives*, see note 6)

Antoni Gaudí i Cornet
Dragon gate, entrance to Finca
Güell, Avenida de Pedralbes 7, Les
Corts de Sarrià, Barcelona,
1884–87
Wrought iron
The dragon gate of the Finca Güell
must be considered a perfect
testimony to the artistic quality of
Catalan wrought-iron work. It is
hung between brick pillars built on
natural stone bases and swings on a
single vertical axis. The dragon
represents Ladón, the guardian of
the Garden of the Hesperides, who
at Juno's behest stood watch over the
golden apples of the garden. When
Hercules overpowered the "warder",
the fabulous beast turned itself into a
constellation. Gaudí placed the gate
under an antimony-colored orange
tree that crowns the pillar and counts
as a symbol of special wealth.

Aesthetic pluralism

... this trend indeed inspired a lively sympathy and interest to the extent that it defined the ambient magic of Barcelona; for this fact alone one must dutifully respect it. Yet these are but superficial values and variations of taste ...
Roberto Pane[9]

Basically two different trends should be distinguished: on the one hand, a trend toward sophisticated, elegant urban buildings that incorporate European fashions in a worldly but superficial way, improving the cityscape but of less interest for architectural history; on the other hand, buildings erected within the framework of a "Gaudí fashion", which, though often original and odd, lack the mastery of genius, which seems indispensible if the daring canon of forms is to be realized. In the field of arts and crafts, which in Modernisme played a subordinate role, a parallel situation obtained. In comparison with the rest of Europe, the volume of original "new" arts and crafts work is negligible. This may be connected with the Spanish – and particularly the Catalan – view that the architect is a kind of untouchable saint and therefore becomes a parable for art. The aesthetic pluralism so common on the European horizon tended in Modernisme to lead to sensual deviations. Paco Durrio, more formally Francisco Durrio de Madron (1875–1940), is a representative of Spanish Art Nouveau, that is, an internationally flavored and yet local version of handicrafts. It is revealing that he lived mostly in Paris and exhibited his jewelry there at the Salon d'Automne of 1904 with great success. The elegant line of his creations has without question such an expressive sculptural quality that the Catalan inheritance of the artist cannot be denied (ill. p. 196). In contrast, the architect and designer Rafael Julio Masó i Valenti (?1881–1935) tried to emulate the original creations of Gaudí. The results were rather shapeless but not unoriginal (ill. p. 195). Though we might be overwhelmed by the genius of Gaudí, we should not diminish the achievements of Modernisme, while not forgetting that an exceptional phenomenon is not necessarily followed by a whole style with even an approximation of the quality (ill. left). Despite all the lively inventiveness, a formal, unambiguous orientation is missing. The Modernist buildings of Barcelona, along with their interiors, in themselves very different and daring, are united only in their rejection of the historicizing legacy and the frequent borrowings from the Baroque and Liberty-style naturalism. To try at any cost to find affinities between Gaudí and the Modernists would be superficial.

Door of a residential house in Salamanca, ca. 1900
With Modernisme, sophisticated, elegant urban buildings appeared all over Spain. They incorporated European stylistic fashions in a worldly but superficial way, but improved the cityscape even so.

"God's Master Builder" – the correlation between structure, form, and space

Imagination is a power of the soul to see new forms in one's own capacity for thought and, building on what has been learnt, to know how to translate them into structures and works of art.
Juan Bassegoda Nonell[10]

Gaudí the architect and artist was an actively political person who joined several Catalan associations and voted for an independent Catalonia. He was closely attached to his homeland, but in a far-reaching sense. Besides nature, in which he found the orderliness of all things, he saw his homeland as an artistic legacy: "Let us consider," he would say, "what it means to be born in the Mediterranean. It means we are equally far from the blinding light of the tropics as from the spectral darkness of the north. We are brothers of the Italians, and that equips us more for three-dimensional work. ... Catalans have a natural sense of the three-dimensional that gives them an idea of things as a whole and of the relationship among things. The sea and light of Mediterranean lands generate this remarkable clarity, and that is why the things of reality never lead the Mediterranean peoples astray but teach them."[11] The desire for wholeness, proportion and balance breathes life into Gaudí's work. The complex architectural system he cultivated has a high position in architectural history as a one-off

phenomenon. The structuring of the buildings follows static and, as a result, geometric principles, whereby the total form that results from that leads, in its organic view of the unity of nature, that is, the archaic unity of anatomy and geometry, to an expressive appearance. This barely comprehensible principle has often called forth blank stares when, in the face of his sculptural buildings, Gaudí is depicted as an experienced structural engineer and technician. Traditionally, geometry is associated with straight lines, angles, and abstract bodies. In the literal sense, however, geometry is the branch of mathematics that deals with the patterns of planes and space; curves such as parabolas and hyperbolas, paraboloids, arches, and volutes make up Gaudí's canon and are still geometry. With the help of "natural geometry", architects can do without "vehicles" such as pillars and buttresses, as curves dynamically absorb their loads themselves. Much as he admired the construction principle – of piers and buttresses – of Gothic cathedrals, the "balance" of construction seemed to him feigned inasmuch as the thrust could only be offset through these supporting devices. Gaudí characterized Gothic architecture as "industrial" in its fundamental principle, as it was only apparently balanced by virtue of mechanics. The equilibrium that he sought he found put into practice in the *contraposto* of classic Greek statues, and, quite logically, he therefore termed

Antoni Gaudí i Cornet
Dragon lizard, steps of Parc Güell, Barcelona, 1901–14
Pieces of glazed ceramics
Besides Christian symbols, Gaudí loved classical and oriental mythology. The dragon lizard in the Parc Güell is thus a representation of Python, the guardian of the subterranean waters on the steps of the Temple of Apollo in Delphi, while the frequent motif of a tortoise on the base of columns is a Chinese symbol of order in chaos.

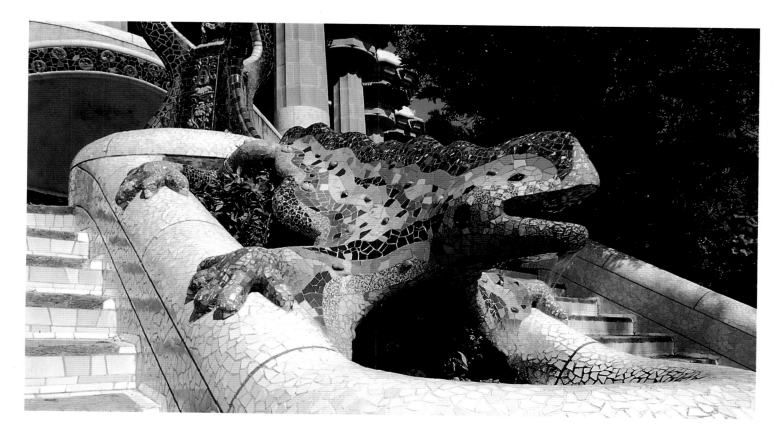

his own work as "Greek". His greatest teacher was always nature. "Do you want to know where I find my models?" Gaudí answered his own rhetorical question by pointing to a eucalyptus tree outside the windows of his studio: "An upright tree; it carries its boughs, and these carry the twigs and the twigs carry the leaves. And every single part has grown harmonically, splendidly, ever since God the artist created it. This tree needs no external assistance. All things are balanced out in themselves. All things are in balance."[12] Parabolic arches, mushroom-shaped capitals, fragile hanging vaults without visible lateral thrust – characteristics of Gaudí's architecture – reconstruct organic growth. He sought the origins of his architecture in the nature of plants, animals, and minerals, yet the architecture lacks the basic features of popular construction. One has only to think of the wall benches made of rustic stone without mortar, or the shell-shaped vaulting. "Have you ever noticed that a stick bends under the load of what it supports. Equally, my columns are stone sticks in which, as can be easily recognized, the principles of load-bearing and loading are united."[13] In Gaudí's case, "easy to recognize" hardly applies to either the constructive principle or his harmony principles, as it is mainly nurtured by a kind of aesthetic inspiration from the architect himself. The difficulty of a clear interpretation lies in two opposing factors that only a man of extraordinary wit could combine apparently effortlessly in his work. To make comprehension easier, it is of prime importance to keep in mind the ingenious "montage system" of the structures on the one hand, and on the other the contrasting intuition, which is of artistic origin. Gaudí's ideas on form and stability centered from the first on the parabolic or catenary as a linear element, which corresponded to the pressure curve most closely. He also made use of the "false arch", an extreme parabola constructed as a series of cantilevered layers of brick such as on the little houses found in Tarragonese vineyards. The arch is used to support unsupported ceilings, as for example in the roof story of the Casa Milà.

Antoni Gaudí i Cornet
Bench seat, for the Casa Calvet, Barcelona, Calle Caspe 48, 1898–1900
Sculptured oak, 180 cm long
Execution by Casas & Bardés, Barcelona
The furniture from the Casa Calvet is tailored to its functions with the minimum expenditure of material. The osseous shapes have the tension of surrounding muscle from an organic creature.

Symphonic statics

Gaudí cannot possibly be forced into stylistic pigeonholes or historic periods; his work is timeless, a great lesson in elegance, honesty, and spirituality.
Juan Bassegoda Nonell[14]

The most exciting example of both Gaudí's inventiveness and the simplicity of his solutions is the stereostatic model for the crypt of the Colònia Güell (ill. p. 197). The funicular models with which Gaudí worked out the loads of the arches and vaults in the crypt were an aesthetic as well as a structural challenge. He identified the natural disposition of the given building form by hanging up canvas bags filled with pellets, whose weight corresponded proportionally to the calculated loads. Thus weighed down, the strings demonstrated the forms of the skeleton of the future church. The "framework" of the Colònia Güell contains all the structural forms thought out by Gaudí. In his essay "Mozart and Gaudí", Juan Bassegoda Nonell has left us a charming and noteworthy comparison on the subject of artistic intention in Gaudí: "Both masters moved in a world of the Baroque; Mozart at the end of the 18th century, when neo-Classicism and Romanticism were ousting the frivolities of the Rococo; Gaudí in a time of Eclecticism, Modernisme and Novecentismo, all fashions that had virtually no influence on his work, or left at most the faintest of traces.

The common ambience of the Baroque determined the vital character of both masters. The emotion that the listener experiences on hearing the sequence of movements of the Coronation Mass corresponds to what one feels on seeing the crypt of the Colònia Güell, where every fragment radiates inventiveness, the whole an extreme unity, even though it is in fact only a half-finished work …

The compositional work of Mozart surprises us through its unexpected turns and the continuing appearance and layering of themes, each of which surpasses the last. In the same way, Gaudí surprises us with the way he plans original, absolutely new concepts in every part of his structures. …

Taking this as a starting point, knowing by virtue of effort and thorough study what the architectural work of Gaudí means, from here one can begin to set out what everyone, even a child, more or less perceives without knowing the reason why, the whirlpool, the rotor, the turmoil in which the inspiration of Antoni Gaudí was born."[15]

Louis Majorelle
Etagère, 1900
Mahogany, 86 cm high
In contrast to the pure organic furniture structures of Gaudí, Majorelle extracts – with maximum delicacy – a sinew from the organic entity and flexes it in a new, individual form.

Mythology, symbolism and functionality of the organic

Among the many impressions that contemplation of the architecture of Gaudí produces, Catholicism is certainly among the most enduring. The mystically devout framework of reference appears in numerous details, both in the iconography itself and in the symbolism. Where the saints and fathers of the Church had given voice to their religious art by means of literature, Gaudí explained the mysteries with the help of bricks and stone (ill. p. 207). When Monsignore Ragonesi, nuncio of His Holiness Pope Benedict XV in Barcelona, visited the Sagrada Familia in 1915, he called Gaudí a poet, to which the latter answered: "Who would not feel himself a poet at the side of the Church?"[16]

Besides Christian symbolism, Gaudí loved classical and oriental mythology. Thus the dragon lizard in the Parc Güell is a representation of Python, guardian of the subterranean waters on the steps of the Temple of Apollo in Delphi (ill. p. 201), while the tortoise on the base of the column is a Chinese symbol for order in chaos.

The use of allegorical images is a point of contact with Art Nouveau artists outside Spain, as are the new understanding for observing nature and the exquisite forms nature offered. The very dynamism and functional perfection of the so-called lower forms of life served Gaudí to beautify and stabilize his structures. He translated the growth structures of plants and trees directly, to fit his own message. The colors and elegance of flowers, leaves, and fruits were also used to decorate facades and interiors. How much more logical Gaudí was in doing this than, for example, Art Nouveau artists can be especially appreciated on his furniture designs. Louis Majorelle and Emile Gallé are likewise "artists of nature". However, in Gaudí's work organic form is transplanted in the original growth and not in reduction. The furnishings from the Casa Calvet are adapted to their function with the minimal expenditure of material – osseous shapes with the tension of surrounding muscle in an organic creature (ill. opposite). In contrast, Majorelle extracts – with the greatest delicacy – a sinew from the organic entity and flexes it in an individual new form (ill. left). In Gallé's work, nature "reinforces" the innate disposition of the furnishings (ill. right).

Émile Gallé
Workbox, ca. 1900
Marquetry in various fruit woods, 64.5 x 62 x 44 cm
In Gallé's work, nature "reinforces" the natural disposition of the furnishing, whereas Gaudí translates the organic form in its original growth.

Antoni Gaudí i Cornet
Casa Batlló, detail of facade with
tribune and windows, Passeig de
Gràcia 43, Barcelona, 1904–06
The flowing waves of the facade of
the Casa Batlló are decorated with
glazed mosaic pieces of different
colors and polychrome ceramic
panes. The tribune is made of
natural stone from Montjuic, which,
straightened out and rounded off,
is reminiscent of hand-molded
sculpture. The parabolic brick-built
balconies are also covered with
gleaming ceramic coloring.

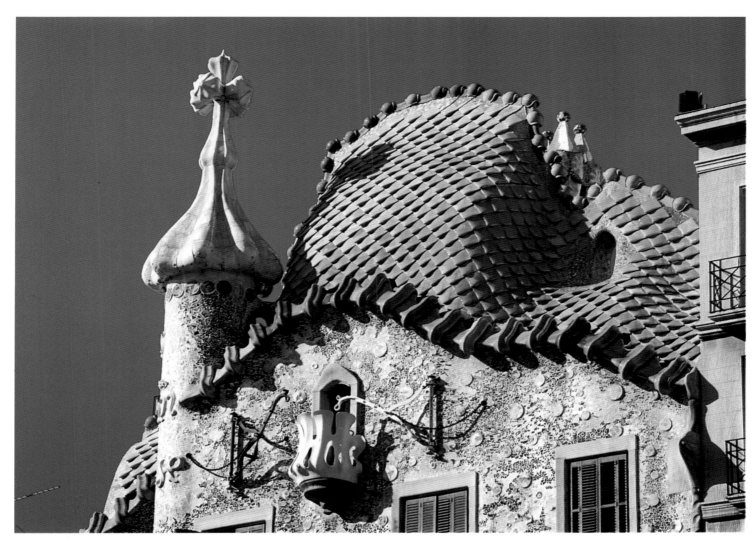

The "Dante of Architecture"

This architecture is completely different from everything that has been seen in this city before.
From a contemporary review[17]

The Casa Vicens, the Villa El Capricho and the Güell Pavilions are effectively a trio of early Gaudí works from before 1888 built in an orientalizing style. Alongside Moorish influences, the interior styling in the fashion of an English manor house shows the effects of the English Arts and Crafts Movement and William Morris's Red House. Gaudí was an eager reader of *The Studio*, a publication that interested him far more than contemporary French periodicals. These buildings, completely new in their unusual features, without forerunners even, could be described as pacesetters for the architecture of Modernisme and Art Nouveau, if they did not already contain the wholly personal autograph of Gaudí in color and structure.

His first major commission, for the Palau Güell (1885–90), came from his client, and later close friend, Count Eusebio Güell, a traveled patron of

the arts. On his business trips to England, Güell had come into contact with William Morris and had put together an extensive library of contemporary writings on art theory which Gaudí often consulted.

In the Palau Güell, structure and decoration begin to fuse, and this became a characteristic feature of Gaudí's later masterpieces. Gaudí used the varied decorative opportunities of structural iron in all their abundance. In addition, extremely flattened brick vaults of Byzantine derivation were used which are still today copybook examples of stereotomy. The frescoes of Alejo Clapés plus the sculptural and picturesque built decoration on the roof and facade link up with the inlay work of precious woods and tortoiseshell, elaborate copper work and gilt wrought iron in the furnishing, adding up to a perfect decorative system (ill. p. 200). The front of the Casa Calvet, built 1898–1900, is designed in the Baroque tradition, but nonetheless displays numerous symbolic components. In the gallery on the second floor the visitor notices various types of mushroom, artfully hewed in stone. This is a reference to the

Antoni Gaudí i Cornet
Casa Batlló, roof facing street with cylindrical lateral tower, Passeig de Gràcia 43, Barcelona, 1904–06
The play of colors, integrated into the architectural mass, is continued up to the roof of the Casa Batlló – which resembles the arched back of a lizard – and over the irregularly shaped roof structures. The flowing rhythm of the design gives away nothing of loadbearing and supports within. The whole expressiveness of the architecture lies in the three-dimensional relief and iridescence.

owner, Pere Calvet, whose hobby was mycology.
His namesake, the saint Pere Màrtir, is depicted
in the upper section of the facade. The gable is
finished off with two crosses, which are scarcely
visible from the street, prompting Countess
Güell to ask what kind of "complications" they
were. Gaudí's answer, that they were "two
crosses, complications and confusions indeed
for many", shows us a man with a ready wit.
That he could handle not only organic problems
such as the furnishings for Casa Calvet but also
the human problems of architecture is demonstrated by the manner in which he countered the
judicial complaint of neighboring nuns that the
new building would obstruct their view. His
response was an airy succession of obliquely
placed arches. These are open and therefore
leave the view unrestricted and yet screened.

Painterly and sculptural architectural composition

Amis, la nature nous fait: psst, psst!
Le Corbusier[19]

The 14-year labor on the crypt of the Colònia
Güell, begun immediately after the Casa Calvet,
was, as already mentioned, Gaudí's architectural
credo in its most creative phase. The Parc Güell,
that uniquely shaped creation with its sloping
walls, its columned halls with vertical ornamental
piers and serpentine benches on the cornice of
the Doric temple (ill. above) is virtually the
apotheosis of his work. This is no longer architecture. The park has become a *Gesamtkunstwerk*,
a synthesis of the arts. The system of "collages",
made of fragments of stone, porcelain, ceramics,
and plants, is a painting, a sculpture, the highest
expression of creative imagination (ill. p. 194).
The immense craft skills of the Catalan artists
who worked with Gaudí are evident here, as on
the Casa Batlló, the flowing waves of whose
facade are adorned with different colored pieces
of glass mosaic and polychrome ceramic panes
(ill. p. 204). The balconies have curved cast-iron
balustrades, and the balconies themselves, which
are made of brick parabolas, are covered on the
outside with shimmering ceramic coloring. The
play of color, integrated in the architectural
masses, is continued up to the roof – which resembles the arched back of a lizard – and over the
irregularly shaped roof structures (ill. p. 205). The

flowing rhythm of the design gives away none of the secrets of the supports and loads. The whole expressivity of the architecture is in the sculptural relief and iridescence. The interior spaces are a hymn to light. It floods through the changing colored windows or enters as extensive surfaces. The panes of glass in the salon on the upper first floor leading to the Passeig de Gràcia have no piers; when all the windows are open, a broad panorama opens to view.

The Casa Milà, "La Pedrera" [quarry], is often described as the greatest piece of abstract sculpture, and indeed the impression is given that a giant hand has developed to subdue and shape the great mass. The massive facade, which looks like a sea frozen in motion (ill. below and endpapers) forms – in Gaudí's words – "the highest expression of a Romantic and anti-classical will that views architecture as an event of nature."[20]

The apogee of Gaudí's roof designs is undoubtedly that of the Casa Milà. The surreal and magical atmosphere, based on the interplay of beautiful and strange three-dimensional volumes,

Antoni Gaudí i Cornet
Casa Milà, "La Pedrera" [quarry], facade, Passeig de Gràcia 92, Barcelona, 1906–10
The Casa Milà is often referred to as the greatest abstract sculpture, and indeed the impression is given of a giant hand developing to subdue and shape the mass. The immense facade, which looks like a sea frozen in motion, forms – as Gaudí himself succinctly put it – "the highest expression of a Romantic, anti-classical will that looks on architecture as a natural event." (see note 20)

Antoni Gaudí i Cornet
La Sagrada Família, general view of the east facade, Calle Mallorca 402, Barcelona, 1882–1926 ff.
When the papal nuncio in Barcelona, Monsignore Ragonesi, visited the Sagrada Família in 1915, he called Gaudí a poet, to which Gaudí replied: "Who would not feel himself a poet at the side of the Church?"

BARCELONA

is reinforced by the idiosyncratic mobility of the ground and the various levels. This dramatic creation was, in the end, highly modern. It had no brick walls, no loadbearing walls and a variable ground plan, an "underground garage" and waste disposal unit – "organic" and user-friendly living at a time long before these misused catchwords came into fashion.

La Sagrada Família

Creative forces are the result of love.
J. Hillman[21]

The Sagrada Familia, Gaudí's life's work and devotion, touches people far and beyond any architectural curiosity (ill. left and p. 207). Moreover, the Temple Expiatori de la Sagrada Familia forms a separate chapter in the cultural history of Barcelona. The conception and construction of the building in the manner of a medieval building site has involved generations of architects and clients. Gaudí's legacy is a debit to the city and at the same time an opportunity, a stroke of luck, to follow in the tradition of such historic sites as Amiens, Santiago de Compostela or Cologne, whose cathedrals are moving witnesses of human faith and religious spirituality.

In 1883, Gaudí took over from the architect Francisco Villar the job of continuing the awe-inspiring project with all its religious symbolism. Financed almost entirely from donations, building work often came to a halt as funds dried up. Nonetheless, the model and construction plan were largely complete by 1906. The organization of the nave and vaulting is extraordinary, and is designed to obtain a modulated incidence of light and optimum acoustics. Gaudí's main concern was with the arrangement of the facade on the theme of the birth of Christ, in which the four tower spires with their parabolic profile provide such dynamism and at once such stability as to compel respect from every architect. The sculptural ornamentation of the building and the decorative schemes of the three portals – of Faith, Hope, and Charity – is a gripping and vigorous declaration of Gaudí's piety and attachment to nature. Scenes from the life of Christ are combined with plant and animal allegories and motifs. The reverent amazement of the master builder at the wonder of creation is in every detail of the architecture a parable of genesis in stone.

Toward the end of his life, Gaudí scarcely ever left his workplace, the site office of the Sagrada Familia. On one of his few journeys into the city,

Antoni Gaudí i Cornet
La Sagrada Família, interior of east facade, Calle Mallorca 402, Barcelona, 1882–1926 ff.
"One looked ... straight up into a grey sky. The columns with their tortoise bases and curved palm capitals, the sculptures of the ox and the mole, the animals and the flowers and the Christmas geese, the little birds fluttering around, the rustling leaves, living statues and depictions of stars emerged and vanished like waves spraying between steep cliffs. The parabolic, three-hundred-foot bell towers loomed in pairs over the three gables like stalagmites in a cave." (Kenji Imai, see note 22)

Page 211:
Juan Gris
Le paquet de café
(The coffee packet), 1914
Gouache, collage, and charcoal on canvas, 64.8 x 47 cm
Ulmer Museum, loaned by the Ministry for Family, Women, Further Education and Arts of Baden-Württemberg
It was the Catalans' very sense of belonging intellectually to Europe that made Modernisme – the Spanish term for Art Nouveau – possible. However, the style developed almost exclusively in Barcelona. To be a Catalan had immense importance for European art history in the 20th century: Pablo Picasso [sic], Juan Gris, Joan Miró, Salvador Dalí, Julio González, Antonio Tàpies, Eduardo Chillida – all of them represented the tradition of their native land.

he was run over by a streetcar and was carried – initially unrecognized – into Santa Cruz Hospital, after first aid was denied him because of his tramp-like appearance. His wish to die in hospital like the poor and neglected was granted him.

Six months after the fatal accident to "Don Antón", the Japanese professor of architecture Kenji Imai visited the cathedral, and his description shows how Gaudí was understood beyond all frontiers: "… the melancholy atmosphere, shrouded in gloom, was to be ascribed to the absence of the master. I nodded a greeting to a lad and went back to the site, which was wet with rain. On the site, among patches of grass, were the stone sculptures of the shell and the frog, about six foot in size, and in addition there were the spherical blocks covered with gilt glass mosaics. The northeast facade of the transept and northwest walls of the apse were complete, but not the vaulting. One looked therefore straight up into a grey sky (ill. p. 208). … I went on behind this facade and looked at the walls of the apse. There too were the sculptures of the giant snake, the frog, and the shell. I bid farewell to the rainy temple with sad heart, numb with pain."[22]

To return to origins, to the beginning.

The identification of hearing as the sense organ of faith and of the eyes as those of glory.

Fear is ignorance.

Discussion does not shed light. It just creates *amour-propre*.

The incompetent are cowards. They get nothing right, and that makes them bigger cowards.

Poverty and misery are two pairs of boots. The first leads to elegance and beauty, whereas wealth leads to opulence and complication.

Scientific matters are proven and taught by means of principles, facts by means of experience.

Only one kind of person is authorized to utter stupidities – a fool.

Art is beauty and beauty is the radiance of truth, without which there is no art.

Architects are rulers in the true sense of the word, since they find no ready-made constitution but must enact one. This is why great rulers are called the architects of nations.

Work is the profit on cooperation, and the latter is possible only on a basis of love. People should therefore stop sowing hatred.

Thoughts are not free, they are the slaves of truth. Freedom is not a matter of thinking but of willing.

The recorded words and thoughts of Antoni Gaudí, quoted from Isidre PuigBoada (ed.), *El pensament de Gaudí* ..., in *Antoni Gaudí*, exhibition catalog, Barcelona – Munich, 1986.

Capital of arts and crafts
Munich

Walls which ghosts still dare to stalk
Ground not yet contaminated by twofold poison;
City of the people and of youth!
Only where Our Lady's spires soar do we think ourselves
home.
Stefan George[1]

A youthful mood in southern Germany – New Jugendstil, new lifestyle

"City of youth" – the poet Stefan George's characterization of Munich around 1900 was highly apt. It was the young generation, artists and writers not yet or only just 30, who were the source of all that was witty, frivolous, original, and exciting. George was right, too, in acknowledging Munich as the "city of the people"; of all the new movements in art around the turn of the century, that in Munich – broadly speaking, at least – remained most closely linked with popular handicraft tradition. This was undoubtedly due in part to the atmosphere of ultimately peaceful coexistence which reigned in Munich, to its comfortable relationship with the arts, and to a certain tolerance of rebellious youthfulness. When tempers grew hot, it was usually due more to the Bavarian character than to fundamental differences of opinion. Even as the Bavarian capital was pervaded by a general spirit of new departure, it never ceased to affirm the value of the traditional and the long-standing alongside the modern, eyebrow-raising and new. Munich had been spared the excesses of Wilhelminian historicist pomp, and could start calmly from the clear, refined classicism of Leo von Klenze (1784–1864) and Friedrich von Gärtner (1792–1847). The frenzy of industrialization which had gripped other areas of Germany in the 1870s had also passed by Munich. Quietly confident of its own importance, the city

instead allowed its growth to follow a careful, balanced, and unforced course. Positive factors all in all, but ones which constantly threatened to tip over into a certain complacency. The atmosphere which flowered in Munich for a while, above all in the sphere of the applied arts, was brilliant, full of energy and humor, and yet it was supplanted after just a few years by a new Biedermeier style. This boomerang in public taste was the reflection of a certain mentality: Munich lacked the private patrons from the worlds of banking and industry, the upper middle classes with their refined tastes and avant-garde sympathies. The glittering artistic heights reached under the Wittelsbach dynasty now lay in the past. The "masters" of Munich Jugendstil (the name given to the versions of Art Nouveau which flourished in German-speaking Europe) – Peter Behrens, Otto Eckmann (1865–1902), August Endell (1871–1925) and Bernhard Pankok (1872–1943) – packed their bags; if they were to realize their dream of the total work of art and of industrial design imbued with artistic value, they needed "arts managers" such as those in Berlin, and liberal-thinking potentates such as Grand Duke Ernst Ludwig of Hesse. Munich, by contrast, harbored a "latent apathy" according to the spokesman for the new style, Hermann Obrist, who also criticized the "distinctive odor of southern German leisureliness". "Munich is studded with precious stones of which it takes no more notice than gneiss its garnets. Something so far ahead of its time as the new structural and decorative art (not to be confused with modern applied art), the new psychological understanding of art, the new direction of art teaching – such passionate earnestness, in short, simply cannot flourish in the soil of southern German leisureliness[2]." Thus complained an

Richard Riemerschmid
Beer mug, ca. 1904
Stoneware, salt glaze, 22 cm high
Made by Reinhold Merkelbach,
Grenzhausen

Hof-Atelier Elvira, facade,
exhibition poster (detail),
1977
Color reconstruction
Designed by Gottfried von Haeseler

August Endell
Hof-Atelier Elvira, facade,
Von-der-Tann-Strasse 15, Munich,
1896—97
The National Socialists chipped off
the colorful facade ornament in
1937, and in 1944 the main body of
the building was bombed.
"Sometimes a building stands out
from the ranks of the ordinary, the
work of a highly imaginative young
architect, expansive and curvaceous,
adorned with bizarre ornament, full
of humor and style."
(Thomas Mann, see note 7)

abstract painting in Munich in 1910, Obrist had
already explored formal principles and theories
which lay very close to a nonrepresentational
philosophy of art.

Munich shone!

**... Her (Munich's) deep-seated artistic culture is less
intellectual than sensual; Munich is the city of the applied
and indeed the festively applied arts, and the typical
Munich artist is always a born master of ceremonies and a
reveler.**
Thomas Mann[3]

"Art is in full bloom, art holds sway, art stretches
her rose-garlanded scepter out over the city and
smiles. Prevailing on all sides is respectful
participation in her propagation, is diligent,
devoted exercise and propaganda in her service,
is faithful cultivation of line, ornament, form,
senses, beauty ... Munich shone. A brilliant
banner of blue silk spanned the skies above her
splendid squares and white-columned temples,
her antique-style monuments and Baroque
churches, and the bubbling fountains, palaces,
and parks of her Residence. Her sweeping,
harmonious vistas, flooded with light and
trimmed with green, basked in the sunny haze
of a first fine June day."[4] For Thomas Mann,
Lübeck represented the "intellectual" and
Munich the "sensual" aspects of life, in the
same principle of antithesis as found in his story
Tonio Kröger. Mann, too, felt the impact of
Munich and the Jugendstil artists based there,
with their "faithful cultivation of line". Both as a
city and above all as a center of the arts *per se*,
Munich had always represented a total work of
art, and it was eager to absorb new ideas. In his
Betrachtungen eines Unpolitischen (Obser-
vations of an Unpolitical Man), Thomas Mann
writes: "My own experience, however ... was
the 'degeneration' of middle-classness in the
genuine old-fashioned sense into the sub-
jectively artistic: an experience and a problem of
overcultivation and training, not of sclerosis ... In
short: what I experienced and created – but I
experienced it only as I created it – was also a
development and modernization of the common
man, albeit not his development into a bourgeois,
but his development into an artist."[5]

Munich had grown young, and the fact that
Jugendstil (literally "youth style") took its name
from a new Munich-based art magazine entitled
Jugend (Youth) was relatively insignificant.
Accompanying its "youth style", Munich had
created a new lifestyle (ill. opposite page). The

angry Hans Rosenhagen in his famous article of
1902, *Münchens Niedergang als Kunststadt*
(Munich's Decline as a City of Art) – an issue still
current today. To go into a decline nevertheless
implies that Munich had previously experienced
a boom as a centre of the arts. The Munich brand
of Jugendstil around 1900 was distinguished
not simply by its high standard of quality and
national, independent character, but also by its
modern, international format. Indeed, one of its
artists – Hermann Obrist – would sow the seeds
of a new art which would ultimately grow into
the *Blaue Reiter* (Blue Rider). Some 15 years
before Wassily Kandinsky arrived at his first

Ludwig von Zumbusch
Cover of *Jugend*, II, vol. 40,
1897
Color lithograph, 29 x 22.5 cm
"And of women a host / who
captivating us enslave us / One with
flowing hair / Another beautiful as
she dances."
(Stefan George, *Teppich des
Lebens*, 1900)

city owed its carnival atmosphere to the international members of Bohemian society who came here to party: budding and unrecognized geniuses, demonic Serbs, elegant Poles, brooding Russians and other extraordinary characters, above all "ladies who painted" and artist upon artist upon artist ... It had become the fashion to go to Munich. As Pablo Picasso recommended to a painter friend in a letter: "If you want to learn something, go to Munich!" Munich gave modernism a stage – a stage for modern art, modern literature, and modern living.

August Endell – "Ornamental frenzies"

The goal of all the arts is beauty. And beauty is nothing other than the intense, intoxicating joy which is produced in us by sounds, words, shapes, and colors.
August Endell[6]

The year 1896 was a magical one for Jugendstil. It was the year of *Jugend* and *Simplicissimus*, and the year in which the "cheeky monster" on the facade of the Hof-Atelier Elvira made it impossible to ignore modernism in Munich. "Sometimes a building stands out from the ranks of the ordinary, the work of a highly imaginative young architect, expansive and curvaceous, adorned with bizarre ornament, full of humor and style"[7] (ill. p. 214). Thomas Mann was not entirely accurate in assigning Endell to the architectural profession, since Endell had in fact studied philosophy and psychology. He had been particularly intrigued by Theodor Lipp's lectures on the theory of empathy, which concerned itself with the psychological impact of external impressions – the reactions prompted by lines of a different direction and shape, for example. Under the influence of Lipp's teaching, in 1896 Endell developed an entirely new theory of art, which he aired in an article about an art exhibition. "Someone, however, who has learnt to surrender to the impressions received through his eyes entirely without associations, free of

peripheral thoughts, someone who has felt, even just once, the emotional impact of shapes and colors – that person will discover therein an inexhaustible fount of extraordinary and unimagined delights. In truth, a whole new world opens up before us. And the moment at which our understanding for these things awakens for the very first time should be a major event in everyone's life. It is like an ecstasy, a delirium that comes over us. Joy threatens to obliterate us, the excess of beauty to suffocate us. Someone who has not had this experience will never understand fine art. Someone who has never been sent into raptures by the exquisite swaying of a blade of grass, the wondrous implacability of a thistle leaf, the austere youthfulness of burgeoning leaf buds, who has never been seized and touched to the core of his being by the massive shape of a tree root, the imperturbable strength of split bark, the slender suppleness of the trunk of a birch, the profound peacefulness of an expanse of leaves, knows nothing of the beauty of forms."[8]

Hof-Atelier Elvira

Endell, like so many of the great "architects" of Art Nouveau, was a self-taught architect. His "amateur" building nevertheless served to trumpet the opening of the Munich Jugendstil "season" (ill. p. 214). It was through Hermann Obrist that Endell obtained the commission for the Hof-Atelier Elvira from two unusual women: the feminists Sophia Goudstikker and Anita Augspurg. Together, the three outsiders caused a sensation in a Munich that was still dominated by the Old Masterishness of painters such as Franz von Lenbach.
There was plenty to fuel the gossip, since this free, entirely abstract creation had arisen on the instigation of two women who wore rather mannish clothing and were politically active – a scandal in every respect. It is illuminating to note

Hermann Obrist
Tree in Blossom wall hanging
(detail), ca. 1895
Satin stitch and rope stitch in silk
on silk rep, 321 x 210 cm
Made by Berthe Ruchet
Die Neue Sammlung, Staatliches
Museum für angewandte Kunst,
Munich
In 1896 Obrist fascinated the art
world with an exhibition of
embroideries designed by himself
and executed by Berthe Ruchet. The
impact of the exhibition was felt far
beyond Munich, and Obrist's works
were lauded by the critics as "the
birth of a new applied art".

Peter Behrens
Waterlilies, 1897
Color woodcut, 51.5 x 65 cm

that, once again, the so-called "weaker sex" had proved responsible for one of the most unusual artistic achievements of the late 19th century, just as was the case with Charles Rennie Mackintosh and Hector Guimard. The dragon design on the facade also contained echoes of oriental imagery, and the forms of nature described with such feeling by Endell seem here to come to life. The facade of the building was originally green, while the ornamental elements were painted a different color every year, for example, yellow or cyclamen red. The sculptor Josef Hartwig (1880–1956) describes the execution of the facade ornament in his memoirs: "... The next day I stood in front of the new building housing the highly fashionable 'Elvira' photo studio in von-der-Tann-Strasse, drew a Jugendstil dragon, 13 m wide by 7 m high, on to the facade through three levels of scaffolding, and requested a plasterer to mix the mortar for the next stage. ... Endell explained its [the design's] shapes and structures as relationships to nature, to a peach kernel, to fluttering ribbons or waves rippling over a beach, etc ... the dragon continued to shimmer for many years in ghostly silhouette, as an immortal work on the facade, so to speak."[9]

Endell's work of art would prove all too mortal, however. In 1937, Nazi Oberbürgermeister Fiehler ordered the "hideous facade disrupting the character of the rest of the street"[10] to be removed, so as not to offend the eye of the Führer on the Day of German Art, the day on which Hitler's temple of art, the Haus der Deutsche Kunst (House of German Art), was to be inaugurated. The rest of the Hof-Atelier Elvira was subsequently bombed in 1944.

Endell also designed the entire interior decor of the studio in a highly individual decorative style (ill. p. 231). He paid particular attention to the lights which, in the stairwell, for example, grow out of the banisters in the shape of flowers (ill. p. 216). Endell's furniture employs powerful, bizarre, often sinuous forms harboring a fantastical world of detail (ill. p. 217). He never copies specific models from nature, yet we seem to recognize organic structures – millipedes, waving grass, snow-capped mountains?

As well as being an artist, Endell was also an important writer on the art of the 20th century. He was closely linked with Stefan George's circle and was himself the author of works of poetry. He had few pupils, since his extremely individualistic style was hard to pass on to others. One Munich artist influenced by Endell was Gertraud von Schnellenbühel, whose extravagantly interlacing lines came close to his own. Her masterpiece, a candelabra with 24 arms, was purchased by Hermann Obrist, Endell's mentor (ill. opposite page).

Endell left Munich in 1901 and returned to his native city of Berlin. Here he executed numerous further commissions, which – after a sensational, brilliant start – remained rather more respectably conventional.

Opposite page:
Gertraud von Schnellenbühel
Candelabra, 1910–13
Silver-plated brass, 48.5 cm high
Münchner Stadtmuseum
Gertraud von Schnellenbühel was
influenced by Endell, and came close
to him in her use of extravagantly
interlacing lines. Her masterpiece,
this candelabra with 24 arms, was
purchased by Hermann Obrist,
Endell's mentor.

Hans Schmithals
Polestar and the Constellation of the Dragon, 1902
Mixed media, pastel with gold
on paper, 48 x 110 cm
Münchner Stadtmuseum
Obrist's "disciple", the painter
Hans Schmithals, translated
Obrist's ideas into his pastels: "a file
of will and yearning sweeping up the
mountain sweep and rush.
Centrifugal spiral nebulous."
(Hermann Obrist, see note 16)

"Blessed be the spiral" – Hermann Obrist

*Not just curving lines, but forms – sculptural, physical
forms whose outlines are defined by beautiful curves.
Intensification of the power of the curve by intensifying
the power of the stroke, the force of the pressure, the
crescendo of the curve thickness, the breadth of the stroke.*
Hermann Obrist[11]

"The starting point for my work was the embroidery of Hermann Obrist, where I encountered for the first time forms that were organically freely invented, not constructed from without."[12] Thus Endell fully acknowledged the visionary Obrist as the inspiration for his own art. The works which Obrist created appear to us today as ciphers of modern art; in conjunction with his brilliant rhetoric, they exerted their influence on the entire circle of Munich artists: Pankok, Paul, Eckmann, Schmithals, and even Behrens. Obrist encapsulated his artistic aims in a single elementary form, or more accurately, an elemental movement: the helix or spiral. "Beatitudinous spirals: the spiral of the blossoming tree, the spiral of the blazing tree, winding spirals, tornadoes, lianas, wisteria, wild vines, staff trees."[13] The key figure in the Munich art scene at the end of the 19th century did not restrict himself to theory, however. In 1896 Obrist fascinated the art world with an exhibition of embroideries designed by himself and executed by Berthe Ruchet. The impact of the exhibition was felt far beyond Munich, and

Obrist's designs were lauded as "the birth of a new applied art"[14] (ill. p. 218). With Berthe Ruchet, his mother's former companion, Obrist had founded an embroidery workshop in Munich with the inheritance he had received upon his mother's death. This allowed him the financial freedom to dedicate himself to his art. The son of a Swiss doctor and a Scottish noblewoman, Obrist initially studied medicine and natural sciences, devoting himself to botanical research and the writings of Darwin, Haeckel, Fechner, Schelling, and Fichte. A protracted middle-ear infection left him with a hearing impairment which at the same time encouraged him to develop his visual faculties. During a semester in Berlin, he had a visionary experience on Peacock Island in Potsdam, when an inner voice said to him: "Leave everything and fashion this."[15] The decision to devote himself entirely to art was made. Obrist notched up his first successes in 1889 at the World Exposition in Paris, where he exhibited ceramic works and furniture (ill. opposite page, below). He also attracted attention at the Munich Glass Palace exhibition of 1897, again with furniture. It is Obrist's sculptural designs and his drawings which – bordering on sheer abstraction – most convincingly embody his revolutionary aesthetic ideas, far ahead of their day (ill. opposite page, above). It is not surprising, then, that he became friends with Kandinsky. The centrifugal forces of Obrist's work, and his fundamental insistence

Hermann Obrist
Design for a monument,
ca. 1895
88 cm high
Kunstgewerbemuseum, Zurich
It is Obrist's sculptural designs and
his drawings which — bordering on
sheer abstraction — most
convincingly embody his
revolutionary aesthetic ideas, far
ahead of their day. It is not
surprising, then, that he and
Kandinsky became friends.

Hermann Obrist
Chest, metal fittings, 1897
Oak, wrought iron,
46 x 132 x 61 cm
Made by Johann Zugschwerdt and
Reinhold Kirsch, Munich
Münchner Stadtmuseum
"Every piece of furniture must be
built first and foremost in line with
its function, and any decoration
must be subordinate to construction
and functional form; it may never, as
in Renaissance and Baroque
furniture, grow profuse and exist
only as an end in itself."
(Hermann Obrist, *Neue
Möglichkeiten in der bildenden
Kunst*, Leipzig 1903)

that the goal of art was not nature, but its dynamism, are also found in the work of the great Catalan architect Antoni Gaudí – in the roof ornament of the Casa Milà, for example. Obrist's ideas thus point to the future, yet simultaneously encapsulate the spirit of the age. His "disciple", the painter Hans Schmithals (1878–1964), translated Obrist's thinking into his pastels: "a file of will and yearning sweeping up the mountain sweep and rush. Centrifugal spiral nebulous"[16] (ill. opposite page).

Munich Jugendstil was not a unanimous style, but comprised two different artistic trends which existed alongside each other and which were not in fact as divergent as they are often made out to be. "We recognize that the naturalists and the champions of absolute ornament are not two groups, since in both naturalism (floralism) and the absolute line there is an equal propensity toward stylization, and in line an equal tendency toward imaginative multiplication. Hermann Obrist can be credited with having recognized and portrayed this. He may be seen as the founder of a new theory, which showed modern art the way."[17] Both ornament as a form of individual expression and the abstract, functional line ultimately have a common contemplative starting point.

The Secession and the "snake painter"

Many paradoxes, Nietzsche in the air. Celebration of the ego and the desires. Libido without limitation. New ethos.
Paul Klee[18]

The art world of the 1870s and 1880s in Munich can be summed up in the name of Franz von Lenbach, an imperious authority whose dominion only began to be questioned with the arrival of a new "prince of painters". In 1889 Franz von Stuck exhibited his *Guardian of Paradise* in the Munich Glass Palace, eliciting a storm of applause – and indignation. Writing about the radiant angelic youth with the bared, muscular arms in his monograph on von Stuck of 1899, Otto Julius Bierbaum recalled: "It created a glaring hiatus within the room, and all eyes turned to it. Amidst the painstaking details of its naturalism, one sensed ... that here was some-thing new, something tumultuous, something fuller, promising greatness ... an angel – but at the same time Hellas, *plein air* – but not from Dachau."[19] From the sumptuous interior of his palazzo on Luisenstrasse, completed that same year, Lenbach thundered his reaction in true Bavarian fashion: "Let him publish his stupid

caricatures in the gutter press, confound it! What a brat! ..."[20] The "brat" was the highly talented son of a miller from Tettenwies in Lower Bavaria, who realized his dream of becoming an artist and who gained initial recognition with his drawings – which did indeed include some caricatures. Stuck was an unruly "natural" who succeeded nevertheless in breaking into the established art scene – a Secessionist rebel who later became a professor (in 1895) and was ultimately elevated to the nobility (in 1906). In order – after this first shock – to undermine Lenbach's all-powerful position as art dictator yet further, and to provide a mouthpiece through which to speak out against the historicism propagated by the art establish-ment, in April 1892 more than a hundred artists formed the Verein bildender Künstler Münchens (Munich Association of Fine Artists), to which title they added – so as to emphasize its separatist character – "e.V. Sezession" (Inc. Secession). The association included numerous well-established artists, as well as represen-tatives of the avant-garde such as Stuck and Behrens. Lenbach dismissed them all as "criminals" and "modern rogues". The "rogues" would subsequently give him a lot of trouble. The first international exhibition by the Secession was staged during the summer of 1893, not without difficulty. Lenbach did everything in his power to boycott the exhibition and used his position to set officialdom against the upstarts. Despite such resistance, the exhibition was an

Franz von Stuck
Faun playing the Panpipes by the Sea, 1914
Oil on wood, 70 x 79 cm
Museum Villa Stuck, Munich
Stuck also lent visual translation to
Henri Bergson's Pan philosophy.
Not only did he design the logo for
the magazine *Pan*, but he
demonstrated in his painting his
penchant for fabulous creatures,
fauns, centaurs, and Sileni.

indisputable success, and the next scandal was not far behind. That same year Stuck exhibited a painting that aroused the whole city: *Sin* (ill. opposite page). "At least five times Franz Stuck painted this luscious woman with her jet-black ringlets, her white flesh offering the viewer such a pleasurably perverse contrast to the evil gleam of the snake draping itself around her. She was variously known as *Sensuality*, *Vice* or simply *Sin*, and she documented the much-vaunted sovereignty of the artist who chooses beauty and despises middle-class morality. Strangely, it was largely the members of this latter section of society who thronged beneath her gaze in the Glass Palace."[21] *Sin* heralded the arrival of a new style, and Stuck thereby made his own contribution to the iconology of the female sex – not as worthy, upright, honest woman, but as an eternally naked, shimmering and glittering creation of nature, a prehistoric animal, closely related to the snake and the cat. Here the "Nietzsche in the air" entry in Klee's diary comes into play, with its eulogization and metaphorical discussion of the magnificent beasts. Stuck, the "creative genius in his titanic artistic powers, his healthy sensuality", the "beacon of the Secession which is opening up new worlds"[22], went on to build his own "palazzo" on Prinzregentenstrasse during 1897 and 1898. As traditional (and certainly not Jugendstil) as it may seem, the Villa Stuck is nevertheless a splendid example of a house, built by an artist, which sought to correspond to the artistic ideal of its day – perhaps Jugenstil in the ideological sense, after all. Traces of the international Art Nouveau style can be found in frieze sequences of floating, arabesque dancers, in the masonry, and in bronze statuettes (ill. right). Stuck also lent visual translation to Henri Bergson's Pan philosophy. Not only did he design the logo for the magazine *Pan*, but demonstrated in his painting his penchant for fabulous creatures, fauns, centaurs, and Sileni (ill. p. 221).

The *grand seigneur* with the paintbrush became the social hub of a self-created Arcadia in Munich, the Athens on the Isar. This frequently causes his truly groundbreaking achievements to be overlooked. "Much of what is taken for granted [in modern painting] today can be traced back to his [Stuck's] initiative and example."[23] In 1895 Stuck was appointed professor at the Munich Academy, where his pupils included Paul Klee, Wassily Kandinsky, Josef Albers and Hans Purrmann.

Franz von Stuck
Sin, ca. 1912
Oil on canvas, 88.4 x 53.4 cm, original frame
Museum Villa Stuck, Munich
This painting heralded the arrival of a new style, and Stuck thereby made his own contribution to the iconology of the female sex – not as worthy, upright, honest woman, but as an eternally naked, shimmering and glittering creation of nature, a prehistoric animal, closely related to the snake and the cat.

Munich's Montparnasse – The Decadent Movement and Symbolism

The Virgin smells the lily, the fragrant symbol of virginity, and thinks as she does so of the latest symbolic cauliflower.
The cauliflower has a paradigmatic, poetically mystical meaning: it represents the secret love of the Symbolists.
Text accompanying a caricature by Carl Strathmann[24]

The sense of a new departure pervading the fine arts manifested itself in Secessions. Similar trends can also be identified in literature, albeit under different names. The cult of beauty, aesthetic overrefinement, and satire offered alternatives to the reigning literary conventions. Although not, in Germany, the protagonist of the latest artistic trends, the art of words nevertheless also embraced various forms of expression. In the legendary Schwabing district of Munich, the poet Stefan George became a dominant figure early on. Quite apart from his own activities as a writer, he also translated from French into German the literature and poetry of the Decadent Movement and Symbolism – themselves containing all the themes of literary and visual Jugendstil – as well as some of Ruskin's writings. George thereby served as the agent of Symbolist word painting and the Pre-Raphaelite cult of beauty.

One Munich painter inspired by the Symbolists, and in particular by Bernard Khnopff (1858–1921), was Carl Strathmann. In addition to paintings rhythmically characterized by textile patterns, and as typical of so many of his Munich colleagues, he also executed satirical cartoons. His most famous picture, however, is *Salambo* (ill. p. 224), of which Lovis Corinth wrote in 1903: "Soon, however, the model was sent home, and [Strathmann] gradually covered his Salambo's nakedness with more and more rugs and fantastical garments of his own invention, so that by the end only a mystical profile and the fingers of one hand peeped out from amongst a profusion of ornamental fabrics ... Real colored stones sparkle all over the picture; the harp in particular glitters with imitation gemstones, glued or sewn on to the canvas with extraordinary skill."[25] The eccentric Strathmann fitted happily into the avant-garde set which had assembled in Munich.

Stefan George became the center of his own set on Munich's "Montparnasse". Writing about this circle some years later, Max Halbe explained: "It was as if someone had taken orchids, chrysanthemums and heliotrope, and bound

Franz von Stuck
Dancer, 1897 (cast after 1906)
Bronze, 62 cm high (with base)
Traces of the international Art Nouveau style can be found in the sequences of floating, arabesque dancers in the friezes decorating the Villa Stuck, in the masonry, and in bronze statuettes.

them up into a peculiar, disparate bouquet. But this was precisely the idea behind the programme as a whole: our goal and our declared aim was the strange, the strident, the bizarre, the grotesque, the decadent, the *fin de siècle*."[26] The George circle comprised both major names such as Karl Wolfskehl, Frank Wedekind, and Otto Julius Bierbaum, and minor figures such as the attractive youth Maximin. Virtually a group or class within themselves were the "mad Countess" Franziska zu Reventlow and Lou Andreas-Salomé. In an article entitled *Viragines oder Hetären* (Viragos or Hetaerae [courtesans]), the Countess called for the liberation of women as sexual beings and at the same time, as a child of Bohemian society, made clear her dislike of the Suffragettes. "It is only a short step from loose-fitting dresses to women breathing through gills."[27] Lou Andreas-Salomé wrote a book on Nietzsche and was a close friend of Endell, with whom she spent a summer in Wolfratshausen, staying with Rainer Maria Rilke. She and the poet became lovers. Rilke's work is to a large extent pure Jugendstil, and if one understands religion as something flowing and vague, his *Stundenbuch* (Book of Hours) can be read as a theology of Jugendstil.

Caricature and illustration – *Simplicissimus* and *Jugend*

Can we delight in life? It is so old and flat. /
We must lend our times new vigor. Youth calls on us to act. /
The world will be not be cured with blazing fire or knives, /
But painlessly improved – by being stylized.
Simplicissimus[28]

Like the circle around Stefan George, the group which formed around the publisher Albrecht Langen and his *Simplicissimus* was similarly heterogeneous. The magazine – another child of 1896 – undoubtedly owed part of its celebrity to the scandals which it regularly caused. At the same time, however, it has secured itself a prominent place in the history of caricature and Jugendstil illustration (ill. opposite page). The caricature is stylistically characterized by extreme elongations and contractions of line, and the virtuoso linear acrobatics performed by the graphic artists of Jugendstil lent enormous bite to socio-critical satire. Bruno Paul (1874–1968) and Eduard Thöny (1866–1950) were amongst the brilliant cartoonists contributing to *Simplicissimus*, while from 1902 Thomas Theodor Heine found himself rivalled for the

Bruno Paul
The Munich Fountain of Youth
Illustration from *Simplicissimus*,
no. 1250, 1897
Pencil and wash on paper,
38.1 x 60.4 cm
Staatliche Graphische Sammlung,
Munich
Simplicissimus, founded in 1896,
owed part of its celebrity to the
scandals which it regularly caused.
At the same time, however, it has
secured itself a prominent place in
the history of caricature and
Jugendstil illustration. The
caricature is stylistically
characterized by extreme elongations
and contractions of line, and the
virtuoso linear acrobatics performed
by the graphic artists of Jugendstil
lent enormous bite to socio-critical
satire. Bruno Paul was amongst the
brilliant cartoonists contributing to
Simplicissimus.

position of top caricaturist by the Norwegian Olaf Gulbransson, with the latter's unmistakable sweeping stroke and economy of outline (ill. p. 212). The extraordinarily multi-talented Heine (1867–1948) can nevertheless be considered the true inventor of the *Simplicissimus* style. Before becoming a master of satirical illustration, he had originally devoted himself to landscape painting. As a bitter opponent of Germany's radical right – something which earned him various spells in jail – he placed his artistic skills in the service of political satire (ill. p. 226). His talent for parody led him to become involved with the political cabaret *Die Elf Schafrichter* (The Eleven Executioners), for which he designed numerous posters. Heine was a consummate master of the art of reducing images to their essentials and then rendering them in what appears to be one single flowing line. This economy never resulted in a loss of elegance, however. Heine's small sculptures also

have a graphic quality and are masterpieces of succinctly soft modulation; one example is his *Devil* (ill. p. 227), one of his favorite subjects. His streamlined linear style is most clearly illustrated in his inimitable vignettes for the magazine *Pan* (ill. p. 261).

Jugend, the journal which unintentionally gave its name to the German version of Art Nouveau, did not follow an ideological agenda and was first and foremost an illustrated magazine of unfortunately anti-Semitic and nationalistic inclination. Its contribution to Jugendstil lay in its publication of color illustrations by Hans Christiansen and ornamental vignettes by Otto Eckmann, as well as drawings by French artists. Christiansen moved to Darmstadt in 1899, while Eckmann went on to become one of the leading names in the applied arts. Having begun his career as a highly regarded Symbolist painter who won numerous prizes and awards, he was subsequently

Thomas Theodor Heine
Poster for *Simplicissimus*, before 1900
Color lithograph, 79 x 59 cm
Heine was a consummate master of the art of reducing images to their essentials and then rendering them in what appears to be one single flowing line. This economy never implied a loss of elegance, however.

influenced by Japanese prints and turned first to the graphic arts and then to the applied arts. Within no time at all he was executing designs for ceramics, jewelry, metal and silverwork, furniture, glass, tapestries, and ladies' clothes. The metalwork items which he showed at the art exhibition in the Munich Glass Palace in 1897 were entirely new. In all of these fields Eckmann demonstrated his ability to shape line and plane into ever new vegetal decorative forms (ill. p. 228). As one of the most important contributors to *Pan* and the Darmstadt artists' colony, he too left Munich and devoted himself increasingly to typography; it was he who designed the Eckmann typeface and the most beautiful of the Jugendstil numbers, the seven, for the eponymous weekly paper of the same name (ill. p. 228).

Another Munich-based journal, *Die Insel* (The Island), founded in 1899, was closely linked with illustrational art right from the start. Alfred Walter von Heymel (1878–1914) and his cousin Rudolf Alexander Schröder (1878–1962) decided to publish a magazine that "would mark the start of something new in Germany[29]." They succeeded! Heymel had earned valuable experience as joint publisher of *Pan*, and now set up his own editorial offices in his apartment, exquisitely furnished by Schröder and Heinrich Vogeler – an appropriate environment for the wealthy Heymel. The quarterly appeared for only three years, but it numbers amongst the best of its day and its type. There was not a major turn-of-the-century writer who was not published in *Die Insel*, not an artist who did not contribute to its superior illustration. Peter Behrens designed the famous *Insel* logo which was adopted by the book publishers of the same name in Leipzig.

The Vereinigte Werkstätten für Kunst im Handwerk and the Munich designers

Architects, sculptors, painters, we must all return to crafts!
Walter Gropius[30]

Peter Behrens (1868–1940) ranks amongst the most outstanding artists of his day. The path followed by this universally talented designer may be said to represent the definitive biography of the Jugendstil artist: "... he was a painter, he

Thomas Theodor Heine
Devil, 1902
Modeled bronze with black patina, 44.5 cm high
Heine's small sculptures also have a graphic quality and are masterpieces of succinctly soft modulation, as here in his *Devil* — one of his favorite subjects.

Otto Eckmann
7, cover vignette for *Die Woche, Moderne Illustrierte Zeitung – Alle sieben Tage ein Heft* , Berlin 1899
It was Eckmann who designed the Eckmann typeface and the most beautiful of the Jugendstil numbers, the seven, for the weekly paper of the same name, which appeared every seven days.

Otto Eckmann
Waterlily vase, 1900
Bone china, oxblood treacle glaze, gilded bronze mounting,
54.3 cm high
The metalwork items which Eckmann showed at the art exhibition in the Munich Glass Palace in 1897 were entirely new. He demonstrated his ability to shape line and plane into ever new vegetal decorative forms in every area of the applied arts.

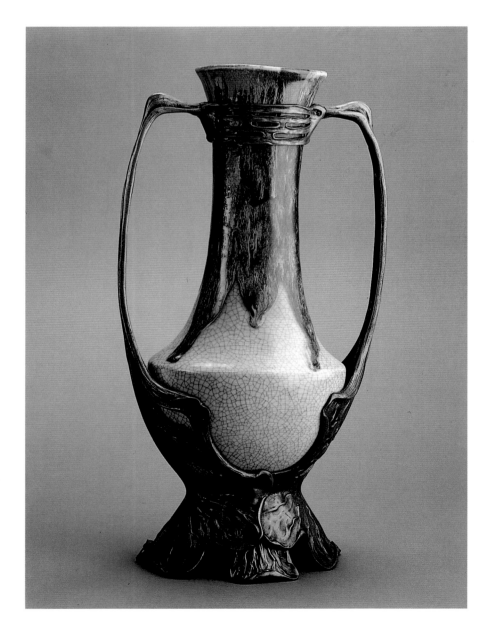

came from painting to Jugendstil painting, from there to Jugendstil ornament, and ultimately, like many others at that time, to the applied arts and from the applied arts to architecture"[31] (ill. p. 218). He embodies the metamorphosis from painter, from artist in the 19th-century sense of the word, to industrial designer (ills. pp. 270–273). Even before Behrens went to Darmstadt and later to Berlin, his influence was making itself felt in Munich, where he demonstrated his considerable talents in numerous works of art. As with Eckmann, Behrens made an abrupt break with painting; again, the "blame" lay with Japanese prints. Behrens designed his first ceramic pieces for a laid dining table exhibited in Munich's Glass Palace (ill. right). The critic Georg Fuchs praised them as "one of the most mature and sophisticated creations in the modern vein to have been produced in Germany so far."[32] Behrens' early work already anticipates the functional style of his later designs (ill. opposite page). In 1897 Behrens was amongst the founders of the Vereinigte Werkstätten für Kunst im Handwerk (Associated Workshops for Art and Handicraft) in Munich. With the formation of this association, which was widely considered a miracle of the modern age, Munich reinforced its reputation as the capital of arts and crafts. The Secessionist character of the Munich body of artists here found its true expression. Munich now assumed a significant lead over Berlin – a phenomenon true also of Nancy in regard to Paris, and of Scotland in regard to England, and one reflecting a trend characteristic of Finland and Catalonia as a whole. It would appear that Secessionist thinking went hand in hand with a general, sometimes political, sometimes national, movement towards autonomy. Despite the associations prompted by its name, and unlike the later Wiener Werkstätte (Vienna Workshops), the Vereinigte Werkstätten had very little to do with the Arts and Crafts Movement in England. No particular importance was attached to manual production; instead, top priority was given to quality, irrespective of technical means. The pioneering achievement of the Vereinigte Werkstätten was to bring together artists, craftsmen, and commercial manufacturers, both in their own interests and in the economic and national interest. As such the association prepared the ground for the later Deutscher Werkbund and brought together Munich's artist-designers, former painters and celebrated draughtsmen – Peter Behrens, Bruno Paul, Bernhard Pankok, Hermann Obrist and Richard Riemerschmid – in order to create the ultimate

Peter Behrens
Plate, 1898
Glazed and painted stoneware
26 cm diameter
Made by Villeroy & Boch, Mettlach
Behrens designed his first ceramic pieces for a laid dining table exhibited in Munich's Glass Palace. The critic Georg Fuchs praised them as "one of the most mature and sophisticated creations in the modern vein to have been produced in Germany so far" (see note 32).

Ernst Riegel
The seven ravens, goblet, 1903
Chased silver, 20 cm high
Barlow/Widmann Collection, Spain
Riegel, the "story-teller in silver", settled in Munich after living in Darmstadt. He always worked alone.

Jugendstil interior. Pankok was the daydreamer and visionary of the group, but it is precisely these qualities which lend his furniture a special magic. At the 1900 World Exposition in Paris he was awarded a gold medal for his highly original creations (ill. p. 230). Interestingly, he designed his first complete interior for Hermann Obrist, whose own canon of form can be recognized in Pankok's furniture.

Pankok was also strongly influenced by the designer and painter Hans Eduard von Berlepsch-Valendas (1849–1921). A member of the Secession, inspired by the ideals of the English guilds and highly knowledgeable about Japanese art, Berlepsch-Valendas was an individualist whose subtle ornament anticipates much of what would become so characteristic of the artists of the Vereinigte Werkstätten (ill. p. 231). Another artist working alone was the "story-teller in silver" Ernst Riegel (1871–1939), who settled in Munich after Darmstadt (ill. opposite page). Hermann Gradl the elder remained similarly independent. When the historicizing stencils used by the Nymphenburg porcelain factory to decorate their chinaware wore out, it was Gradl who helped win new fame for the company with his artistic stylization of floral motifs (ill. top right). Bruno Paul was another member of the Vereinigte Werkstätten who won a prize in Paris in 1900. He built items of furniture which constituted ornaments in themselves, and he rapidly became the master of the "rectilinear style" (ill. p. 230). His quasi fitted furniture, installed as fixed decorative ensembles, looks forward to his future development of modular furniture and add-on systems (ill. p. 230).

Richard Riemerschmid – Painter and anatomist of handicraft

In contrast to his colleagues, Richard Riemerschmid (1868–1957) never gave up painting, and his Symbolistic, decorative pictures are of high quality (ill. p. 233). Indeed, he differed from his contemporaries in many respects. "A wooden table and a metal lighting appliance (for four electric bulbs) by the German architect Richard Riemerschmid seem at first sight to fall fully into the functional category of handicraft. A small circular tabletop rests on three legs or shanks, which splay out to three sides from the center of the circle and which point their feet with a little kink just above the floor and place them straight down on the ground. From each of these three feet, however, a slender sinew of wood leads vertically upwards to reunite with the

Bruno Paul
Corner cupboard with sofa, model nos. 6076 and 6092, 1904
Lithograph/catalogue page, 22 x 17.5 cm
Archiv Vereinigte Werkstätten, Amira AG, Munich
Paul's quasi fitted furniture, installed as fixed decorative ensembles, looks forward to his future development of modular type furniture and add-on systems.

Below:
Bernhard Pankok
Free-standing closet, 1899
Walnut, spruce, and glass, 167 x 107 x 41 cm
Made by the Vereinigte Werkstätten für Kunst im Handwerk, Munich
Münchner Stadtmuseum
Pankok was the daydreamer and visionary of the Vereinigte Werkstätten artists, but it is precisely these qualities which lend his furniture a special magic. At the 1900 World Exposition in Paris he was awarded a gold medal for his highly original creations.

Bruno Paul
Seven-armed candelbra, ca. 1905
Cast brass, 29 cm high
54 cm maximum diameter
Barlow/Widmann Collection,
Spain

Bruno Paul
Armchair, 1901
Oak, leather, 87.5 x 63.5 x 69.9 cm
Made by the Vereinigte Werkstätten für Kunst im Handwerk, Munich
Bruno Paul built items of furniture which constituted ornaments in themselves, and he rapidly became the master of the "rectilinear style". He won a prize in Paris in 1900.

Above:
August Endell
Door, Hof-Atelier Elvira, Munich, 1896—97

Right:
Richard Riemerschmid
Chair for a music room, 1899
Wood, leather seat, 80.6 x 47.5 x 45 cm
"... for all their functionality, it is precisely [these pieces of furniture] which, seen through the eye of the imagination, resemble living organic beings — a leggy foal, a fantastical bird with wings outstretched — but robbed, in their anatomical structure, of soft flesh and skin."
(Dolf Sternberger, see note 33)

Richard Riemerschmid
Candlestick, 1897
Chased and gilded brass,
37 cm high
Made by the Vereinigte Werkstätten für Kunst im Handwerk, Munich
Riemerschmid was a functionalist of a highly distinctive inclination, an anatomist of handicraft.

Right:
Hans Eduard von Berlepsch-Valendas
Bookcase, 1899
Oak, oak veneer, and elm veneer; fittings of brass and steel, 254 x 100 x 57 cm
Made by Richard Braun, Munich
A member of the Secession, inspired by the ideals of the English guilds and an expert on Japan, Berlepsch-Valendas was an individualist whose subtle ornament anticipates much of what would become so characteristic of the artists of the Vereinigte Werkstätten.

Page 233:
Richard Riemerschmid
Garden of Eden, 1900
Oil on canvas; frame: wood, painted plaster,
160 x 164 (with frame)
Barlow/Widmann Collection, Spain
In contrast to his colleagues, Richard Riemerschmid never gave up painting, and his Symbolistic, decorative pictures are of high quality.

tabletop at the rim of the circle. A highly sensual and delicate object whose internal relationships can be emotionally experienced by viewer and user ... Just as the little table evokes memories of bones and sinews, here too [in the case of the lamp], in those places where the systems of bent brass wires are joined, we are inevitably reminded of elbow or knee joints ... Riemerschmid's free and light creations rank amongst the most beautiful in the exhibition. And for all their functionality, it is precisely they which, seen through the eye of the imagination, resemble living organic beings – a leggy foal, a fantastical bird with wings outstretched – but robbed, in their anatomical structure, of soft flesh and skin"[33] (ill. p. 231). Riemerschmid was a functionalist of a highly distinctive inclination, an anatomist of handicraft (ills. pp. 213, 217, 231) and a brilliant architect. The Munich Schauspielhaus theater, today the Kammerspiele, was built to his plans in 1900–01. He went on to become one of the leading designers of the Dresdner Werkstätten (Dresden Workshops) and, like many members of the Munich Vereinigte Werkstätten, was amongst the founders of the Deutscher Werkbund in 1907. The future had begun.

The rewards for our pains are enormous. There are so incredibly many beautiful things immediately accessible to us, yet seen and appreciated by so few of us, a wonderful, magnificent world right in front of our eyes, so exquisite, so colorful, and so rich that there is absolutely no need for us to invent imaginary worlds. Today, the present, reality — these are the most fantastical and incredible of all; all the wonders concocted in literature are utterly paltry by comparison. It is only our stupidity which stops us utilizing this treasure. We don't need another world above the clouds or in the past; the greatest marvels are found here in our own world, in our own day — invisible to the eye which is dull, it is true, but clear and tangible to the eye that sees.

August Endell, *Vom Sehen* [On Seeing], in *Die Neue Gesellschaft*, I, 1905

I believe it is not generally known that, in the bark of our own native trees, we possess the most rapturous symphonies of color that a painter could ever dream of. After rain, for example, when the colors are luminous and fresh, the richest and most wonderful motifs are to be found there. You need to go right up to the trunk and look hard at small areas the size of your palm. Strong colors alternate one with another. Velvety violet, fiery yellowy-red, grey with a blue shimmer, bright green — the widest possible range of color nuances are found in a rich spectrum in the boldest contrasts. Only when you have studied the colors of bark close up can you appreciate why tree trunks have such luminous colors from afar. The individual colors are garish and unbroken, but because they lie so close together in such small blotches, they tone each other down without losing their effect.

August Endell, in *Berliner Architekturwelt*, volume 4, 1902

Revolution and art
Darmstadt

*Here is the New which at last, at last we can hold up
against our oppressive inheritance.*
Friedrich Ahlers-Hestermann[1]

Art for all – "Elite art"

Ruskin's "prophesy" – that the invention of a
"New Art" was not in itself enough to ensure the
salvation of the artistic ethos, but that art needed
to form a unity with life in order to be convincing
and credible – marked a decisive shift toward the
concept of applied art. This, however, meant
teaching "style" to the ugly, ostracized world of
industry where the objects of daily use were
actually produced, and where art thus needed to
be "applied". William Morris sought to live the
commandments of his tutor Ruskin and translate
them into deeds. But while revolutionary
resolution characterized his own thinking and
personal life, the fact that he refused to
acknowledge the machine as the most important
modern means of production robbed him of the
opportunity to create a new art. The craftsmen
whom Morris employed, and the clientele who
were able to afford his products, could consider
themselves fortunate. Such craftsmanship was
of little benefit to the rest of the population,
however. This fact did not elude Morris and he
gradually switched from artist to politician,
recognizing that the way of life of the working
classes was not to be improved by an elitist form
of applied art which he himself described as
"ministering to the swinish luxury of the rich".
As a radical liberal, he joined the Democratic
Federation in 1883 and one year later founded

the Socialist League, becoming editor of the
party newspaper *Commonweal*. As a member of
these associations, he dedicated himself to the
liberation of the workforce from its dependency
upon employers.

This flashback is important insofar as the German
Jugendstil artists themselves looked back
directly to Morris in their work. They inherited
from their English forebear the belief that arts
and crafts were not two mutually exclusive areas
of activity. While they originated from the world
of art, they were not afraid to venture into the
"lower" echelons of the applied arts. Indeed,
they went decisively further than Morris by
designing objects for mass production. The
political dimension of Morris's philosophy,
however, remains absent from their work. Their
concern was the artistic enhancement of the end
product; they knew little about the details of the
manufacturing process.

This is not to dispute that there was a political
element to Jugendstil in Germany too, albeit one
less radical and always somewhat ambivalent.
As a rule, any political aims were stated at a
purely aesthetic level. Economic factors, too,
often took the emphasis away from societal
concerns. Thus one of the reasons – if not indeed
the prime reason – for the founding of the artists'
colony in Darmstadt was to secure new
commissions for the arts industry in Hesse. This
is not to belittle the achievements of this unique
initiative, once more set in the "provinces".
On the contrary, it represented the successful
attempt to make a commercial venture simultaneously an aesthetic one.

Albin Müller
Tankard, ca. 1910
Glazed stoneware, pewter,
35.5 cm high
Made by Reinhold Hanke, Höhr

Joseph Maria Olbrich
Playhouse for Princess Elisabeth, Schloss Wolfsgarten, Darmstadt, 1902
Ernst Ludwig's daughter from his first marriage died when she was just eight years old. He himself had lost his mother when he was ten. The memory of the little princess is touchingly preserved in this playhouse – pure Jugendstil – in the grounds of Wolfsgarten Palace in Darmstadt.

Deliverance from on high – Patronage around 1900

**Don't complain to me about figures. There may come a time later on when you will thank your Papa for giving you a closer acquaintance with them. Without rules, without figures, there can be no ordered existence.
The banker Osthaus to his son Karl Ernst[2]**

With his embrace of politics, Morris took the side of the working classes – something all too happily overlooked even today. In Germany, on the other hand, artists sought to "deliver" the public from "on high", that is, to improve the general standard of taste via exemplary designs for buildings and objects of everyday use. This led to the reproach that the works of applied art produced in this spirit ultimately remained confined to an ivory tower far removed from harsh reality. Such criticism addressed itself at the same time to the upper middle classes, and indeed the ruling classes themselves; in retrospect, it can be seen as a rebuke to the very people whose support for the arts made Art Nouveau possible, and not just as Jugendstil in Germany – those individuals who rallied to the side of the artists and artist groups who were initiating the new style with their progressive ideas and their break with the past. The importance of the patron of the arts had by no means dwindled; on the contrary, as far as the applied arts went, it was even greater than before. "Total works of art" began to see the light across Europe thanks to wealthy, indeed very wealthy, members of art-loving society:

Walther Rathenau of the AEG company, Karl Ernst Osthaus, Baron Eberhard von Bodenhausen, the Belgian industrialist Solvay, the banker Stoclet, the Spanish industrialist Güell, and the Viennese banker's son Fritz Waerndorfer, to name just a few. Aristocrats and millionaires were even to be found on the "production" side, as in the case of Toulouse-Lautrec and Louis Tiffany. Patrons also included art dealers such as Samuel Bing, the writer Julius Meier-Graefe, the Darmstadt publisher Alexander Koch and – last but certainly not least – Grand Duke Ernst Ludwig of Hesse (ill. left).

Grand Duke Ernst Ludwig of Hesse – Statesman and sponsor

**Incidentally, while I was in Berlin for the Kaiser's birthday, I frequently found that many of my so-called colleagues were so backward in their attitudes that I felt myself a pure Socialist by comparison.
Grand Duke Ernst Ludwig of Hesse[3]**

Ernst Ludwig of Hesse was the son of Alice, the favorite daughter of Queen Victoria of the United Kingdom. The British monarch visited Darmstadt on many occasions; her grandson was even more frequently to be found in his second home. With the cosmopolitan outlook instilled in him by his background, coupled with his engaging character, he was almost predestined to tackle the sensitive task of founding an "artists' colony". Ernst Ludwig had taken over government in 1892 at the age of just 24. His first marriage ended unhappily in divorce in 1901, and his daughter from that marriage died when she was just eight years old. Ernst Ludwig himself had lost his mother when he was ten. The memory of the little princess Elisabeth is touchingly preserved in a playhouse – pure Jugendstil – in the grounds of Wolfsgarten Palace in Darmstadt (ill. left). In 1905 Ernst Ludwig remarried. His new wife, Eleonore zu Solms-Hohensolms-Lich, supported him in his artistic ambitions, such as the Wedding Tower (ill. opposite page). The artists' colony in Darmstadt ultimately owed its foundation to the English element in the Grand Duke's background and his many visits to Britain. Extremely interested in the ideas of Ruskin and Morris, and a great enthusiast of the British revival of arts and crafts in the domestic sphere, in 1897 Ernst Ludwig commissioned Mackay Hugh Baillie Scott and Charles Robert Ashbee to decorate a number of rooms in his Darmstadt palace. He proposed plans to build a new Hesse State Museum, but the designs submitted were

Joseph Maria Olbrich
The five elongated arches crowning the Wedding Tower, Darmstadt, 1905–08
Institut Mathildenhöhe, Museum Künstlerkolonie Darmstadt
The inscription on Olbrich's magnificent Wedding Tower may have been true of the architect himself: "Have respect for the Old and the courage to attempt the New. Remain true to your own nature and true to the people you love."

Peter Behrens
Cup, ca. 1902
Chased silver, 11.6 cm high
Made by Peter Bruckmann, Heilbronn
Collection Barlow/Widmann, Spain
The domestic utensils which Behrens designed during his Darmstadt period are still subordinate to the overall principle of the house as a "cult building" and do not bear the hallmarks of prototypes destined for mass production. He nevertheless produced objects which, while still "ceremonial" in character, exhibit an ornament which is solely self-derived.

Ludwig Habich
Haus Habich, 1901
Print
Institut Mathildenhöhe, Museum Künstlerkolonie Darmstadt
"Even in 1901, the year of the remarkable exhibition at the Darmstadt artists' colony, in which each of the artists grouped around the Grand Duke – I shall name only Behrens, Huber, Habich, and Christiansen – had built a whole house to their own designs ..."
(Henry Paris, see note 11)

simply too ugly for him; he was already looking to create a total work of art, prompting Minster of State Jakob Finger to comment: "The Grand Duke is hopeless, he's just full of Utopias."[4] But the Landesmuseum project would prove to be the first of the "Utopias" that Ernst Ludwig turned into reality. "What Ernst Ludwig did for the arts in Hesse remains touching and significant, its effects lastingly felt in indirect ways. The means he used – his own, those of the capital and the province – were limited, and the rivalry of the wealthier states – nearby Frankfurt, Berlin, Dresden, Munich – was oppressive. He knew his limits only too well, but he did not allow himself to be discouraged. Money wasn't everything; initiative, imagination, and love were also capable of achieving much. If one thinks of the Grand Duke in his role of patron of the arts, as an artist himself, one thinks above all of the artists' colony that he founded in 1899, of the exhibitions of 1901, 1908, and 1914, of the thoughtful endeavors of the young generation of artists and their bold new departures, of the – at long last, truly contemporary – association of beauty with practicality, of art with a social awareness extending to handicraft, industry, and commerce."[5]

The Grand Duke's monument, the artists' colony, is still the central focus of Darmstadt today. While it undoubtedly reflected his own tastes in art, Ernst Ludwig did not create it to perpetuate his own memory, but because he was aware that, with each new day, he had to prove himself worthy of the position accorded him by divine right, and that he must carry out his duties in a responsible manner. A patriot, he fuelled the cultural and economic development of Hesse in a highly modern fashion, at the same time realizing a project of international importance with artists at the forefront of the latest trends.

The Darmstadt artists' colony

It is about creating works of art which are complete in themselves and which lend expression, with the greatest sensitivity and simplicity, to a joyous principle of life.
Joseph Maria Olbrich[6]

Grand Duke Ernst Ludwig invited "his" artists to develop the Mathildenhöhe, a park belonging to the Grand Duchy on a hill in the city. Over the following years the Mathildenhöhe would form the site of several exhibitions of architecture. The novel project was conceived as a "document of German art of enduring value". The first task facing the colony was a practical one: if they

Peter Behrens
The Kiss, 1898
Color woodcut, 27.2 x 21.7 cm
In *The Kiss*, an abstract pattern of intertwining lines is derived from the typically Symbolist motif of flowing hair, but at the same time contains echoes of the interlacing patterns of Celtic ornament. The "material" of the design is unquestionably organic, the imagery symbolic; in its artistic expression, on the other hand, it is abstract. The androgynous character of the two lovers conceals an additional element of abstraction.

Joseph Maria Olbrich
Postcards of the group of three houses designed by Olbrich on the Mathildenhöhe, Darmstadt, for the second exhibition by the Darmstadt artists' colony, July 16 to October 15 1904
Interior and exterior views of the Grey House (left and far left), the official residence of the court chaplain, 1904
Exterior view of the Corner House (below), 1904
Exterior view of the Blue House (far left, below), 1904
Lithographs
Institut Mathildenhöhe, Museum Künstlerkolonie Darmstadt
In Olbrich's group of three houses of 1904, a new stylistic trend towards structuring and functionalism can be felt, although the buildings nevertheless remain Jugendstil in their imaginative variety. The houses were commissioned by Grand Duke Ernst Ludwig and were to serve as "examples of private homes for citizens of not overly abundant means". With the exception of the chaplain's residence, the houses were for sale and were in fact bought by wealthy individuals. The Blue House was acquired by the wife of the Councillor of Commerce, Frau Knöckel, and the Corner House by Count Büdingen, who was employed by the Grand Duke.

were going to live on site, the artists needed to build homes for themselves. In December 1898 the painter Hans Christiansen (1866–1945) became the first artist to be invited to join the proposed colony. At the beginning of April the following year, a series of articles in the local paper introduced the idea of the colony to the Darmstadt population, on whose support it would naturally also rely. On July 1 1899 the appointment of the following artists was officially announced: Rudolf Bosselt (1871–1938) as sculptor and medalist, Paul Bürck (b. 1878) for book illustration and applied art, Patriz Huber (1878– 1902) for interior design and furniture and Hans Christiansen as painter and graphic artist.

The assignation of these artists to specific disciplines rapidly proved meaningless, however, as both they and later members of the colony were, without exception, active in several fields. In order to increase contact both with industrialists and the public, plans were set in motion to found an association of arts and crafts, to mount an exhibition of Hessian arts and crafts, and to construct an arts and crafts exhibition building – all in all, a massive commitment to the arts.

The first "colonists" had already taken up their posts when, in July, the highly influential appointments were made of Joseph Maria Olbrich and Peter Behrens, together with the sculptor Ludwig Habich (1872–1949) (ill. p. 238). There were now seven artists on the Mathildenhöhe committed to working in Hesse for three years. The oldest was 32, the youngest 20. Each received an annual, non-pensionable salary depending on age, personal circumstances, and previous sphere of activity; in other words, prominence. This material provision distinguished the Darmstadt colony significantly from the numerous other workshops, associations and guilds formed by Jugendstil and pre-Jugendstil artists. Although the artists were provided with free temporary accommodation while their houses were being built, they nevertheless had to pay for the land and the construction costs themselves. They were offered generous financial terms on condition that the houses were finished in time for the first exhibition in 1901. Alongside the individual contributions made by the artists, the main expenses were borne by the Grand Duke. The colony was officially opened as a private enterprise on July 1 1899.

Above:
Peter Behrens
The Behrens House, north facade, Mathildenhöhe, Darmstadt, 1901
Contemporary photograph
Institut Mathildenhöhe, Museum Künstlerkolonie Darmstadt
".... for we shall see that the house [by Peter Behrens] on the Mathildenhöhe stands right on the perimeter of Jugendstil; it is already signposting the way forward from here ..."
(Julius Posener, see note 12)

Right:
Peter Behrens
Banner, the Behrens House, 1901
Contemporary illustration
Vortices and bundles of lines are also to be found on the exterior of the house, where their "energetic lines" draw upon an additional background source: Nietzsche's *Thus spoke Zarathustra*, whose mythos of beauty had captured Behrens' imagination.

Opposite page, below:
Peter Behrens
The Behrens House, north facade, Mathildenhöhe, Darmstadt, 1901
Design drawing
Contemporary illustration

Patriz Huber
Three brooches, a button and a
pillbox (center), 1900–01
Brooches and button: silver, agate,
chrysoprase, 1.7 cm to 3.1 cm high,
2.3 cm to 5.8 cm diameter
Institut Mathildenhöhe, Museum
Künstlerkolonie Darmstadt
Pillbox: chased silver, gilt interior,
2.3 x 6.9 x 5 cm
Made by Martin Mayer, Mainz
Collection Barlow/Widmann,
Spain
Patriz Huber designed jewelry and
silverware for the Theodor Fahrner
jewelry works in Pforzheim, well-
known for its Jugendstil products.
With their spiral patterns and
simple, clear designs, Huber's
creations were such a success that
these prime examples of high-quality
serial production were exported to
England.

The home as cult building – Peter Behrens and Joseph Maria Olbrich

In days to come we will refuse to live in a room where the objects within it do not jointly attest to a common will, a single emotional effect ...
Henry van der Velde[7]

In 1901 the artists' colony was itself the object of the first exhibition on the Mathildenhöhe. It was perhaps less "A Document of German Art" (*Ein Dokument deutscher Kunst*), as it was titled, than an exhibition of grandiose, personal documents on and by the colony's artists. Behrens and Olbrich were the two architectural talents who continue to shape the face of the Mathildenhöhe today, albeit quantitatively to very different extents.

The Austrian Olbrich may be seen as the guiding spirit behind the colony, and the buildings which he designed as the most characteristic of the Mathildenhöhe. A pupil of Otto Wagner and one of the "architects" of the Secession, he had already been showered with accolades in Vienna for his Secession building with its floating laurel cupola: "... and then there is the cupola ... the crown of a colossal laurel tree, in real gold leaf ... the impression is magical ... Olbrich was the man on whom all hopes were pinned."[8]

Olbrich would not prove a disappointment in Darmstadt, either. He created total works of art free from any obligation to an ideological or stylistic standpoint: "... art is nothing other than a harmonious and aesthetic staging of life; art is nothing other than living from the point of view of a temperament and its consciousness. Can a school awaken consciousness? No!"[9] Olbrich's Wedding Tower – the vertical accent within the Mathildenhöhe complex as a whole – comes closer to a work of modern sculpture than to architecture (ill. p. 237). In the same way, his design for a studio building for the artists' colony is never a "foreign object", and is less a piece of architecture than an outsize easy chair in need of stabilizing boundaries. His Darmstadt Hall of Decorative Arts resembles a huge ocean liner, a reflection of his preference for keel-like forms. These "surface" as decorative elements on many of his buildings and lend them a sense of forward-thrusting dynamism. If we consider the catchwords defining Olbrich's architecture, it is not surprising that he became a model for probably the most popular Expressionist architect, Erich Mendelsohn (1887–1953). "Olbrich's Wedding Tower makes no allusions to the past ... Olbrich's strength employs all the ideas of his day to liberate the internal laws of

Johann Vincenz Cissarz
Poster announcing the second exhibition by the artists' colony on the Mathildenhöhe, Darmstadt, 1904
Color lithograph, 75 x 49 cm
Institut Mathildenhöhe, Museum Künstlerkolonie Darmstadt
Cissarz was chiefly active in the spheres of painting and graphics.

architecture which have been overgrown for centuries, and to reinstate them anew."[10] Olbrich was a source of inspiration not just for future generations, however, but also for his contemporaries. "Olbrich embodies modern German art in the most perfect and personal fashion. Even in 1901, the year of the remarkable exhibition at the Darmstadt artists' colony, in which each of the artists grouped around the Grand Duke – I shall name only Behrens, Huber, Habich (ill. p. 238), and Christiansen – had built a whole house to their own designs, I was struck by the elegance of the forms of Olbrich's villa and its wonderfully harmonious unity."[11]

The house by Behrens, however, attracted even greater admiration. It was more spectacular, in the best sense of the word, but also more expensive – it had cost 200,000 marks, as opposed to the 70,000 marks swallowed up by Olbrich's villa (ills. pp. 240, 241). Julius Posener took a closer look at the Behrens house in a lecture: "... for we shall see that the house [by Peter Behrens] on the Mathildenhöhe stands right on the perimeter of Jugendstil; it is already signposting the way forward from here ... What

actually remains here of Jugendstil? Really only that sweeping gable and those two sweeping gables on the roof. If you blank them out of the picture, there is no more Jugendstil. It becomes a house of strict architectural articulation, and you can see from the groundplan that it borders on being a cube. In the years after 1903 the cube becomes Behrens' chief form. This is the front facade which we saw a moment ago. Take a look at these two windows. As you will see in a moment from the plan, the strangest things are happening here: the rooms are being incorporated into the composition of the facade, a rigorous composition. A comparison with the neighboring houses on the Mathildenhöhe, by Josef Maria Olbrich, true Jugendstil houses (ill. p. 240), makes the Behrens house look a little stiff. If you look at this dining room, however, it is of course undeniably Jugendstil, both in the overall concept – see how the ceiling has been developed as if out of a whirlpool – and in the details: see how all the lamps and chairs are developed as if out of a vortex."[12] Behrens elevated the constructional and at the same time ornamental value of line to the position of highest

Hans Christiansen
Spring roundelay, tapestry, 1900
Haute lisse technique, warp: hemp,
woof: wool, 121 x 139 cm
Made by the College of Art
Weaving, Scherrebeck
Museum für Kunst and Gewerbe,
Hamburg

stylistic principle – pure Jugendstil. Since Behrens' artistic career eventually led him to industrial design, there is a temptation to look in his early work for signs of his later canon of form. Olbrich's oeuvre, on the other hand, never reached a "ripe old style", since he had only another ten years after his Secession building in which to pursue his work (he died in 1908). In the homogeneous interior of the Behrens house, we find the same linear principles as in his woodcuts. In *The Kiss* (ill. p. 239), an abstract pattern of intertwining lines is derived from the typically Symbolist motif of flowing hair, but at the same time contains echoes of the interlacing patterns of Celtic ornament. The "material" of the design is unquestionably organic, the imagery symbolic; in its artistic expression, on the other hand, it is abstract. The androgynous character of the two lovers conceals an additional element of abstraction.

Vortices and bundles of lines are also to be found on the exterior of the house (ill. p. 241), where their "energetic lines" draw upon an additional background source: Nietzsche's *Thus spoke Zarathustra*, whose mythos of beauty had captured Behrens' imagination. Rigorous and "cultured", it permitted no ornament and led to disciplined design. The domestic utensils which Behrens designed in this spirit are still subordinate to the overall principle of the Mathildenhöhe house as a "cult building" and do not bear the hallmarks of prototypes destined for mass production. He nevertheless produced objects which, while still "ceremonial" in character, exhibit an ornament which is solely self-derived (ill. p. 238).

Nietzsche's influence is also apparent in the language of Behrens' own writings. Zarathustra himself seems to be speaking of the forbidding manner of the Behrens house in contrast to the "friendliness" of Olbrich's houses when he says: "What do these houses mean? Verily, no great soul put them up as its simile! ... And these rooms and chambers – can *men* go out and in there? They seem to be made for silk dolls; or for dainty-eaters, who perhaps let others eat off them." [13]

Hans Christiansen
Pieces from a set of crystal goblets, ca. 1903
Clear glass, gold paint,
6.5 cm to 25 cm high
Institut Mathildenhöhe, Museum Künstlerkolonie Darmstadt
A characteristic feature of Hans Christiansen's work was the "Christiansen rose", as it became enduringly known in the sphere of Jugendstil. The rose motif can be found in every area of Christiansen's art, which – instantly recognizable in its style and outstanding in its quality – made him a brilliant decorative artist to some, and to others a shallow panderer to public tastes.

Hans Christiansen
Cigarette case, 1900
Silver, color enamel,
8.3 x 4 cm
Made by Luis Kuppenheim,
Darmstadt
Collection Barlow/Widmann,
Spain

Left:
Hans Christiansen
Vase, ca. 1898
Chromolithic (unglazed) stoneware, painted, 24.6 cm high
Made by Villeroy & Boch, Mettlach
Institut Mathildenhöhe, Museum Künstlerkolonie Darmstadt
"I interpret my role as an artist as broadly as possible: I want to be able to paint a portrait, but also to design a piece of furniture; I draw caricatures, but also rugs, posters, and indeed originals for every kind of printing process; I design stained-glass windows, but also occasionally a leatherwork screen. My motto is: portrayal of the characteristic in form and color, tailored to function and technique."
(Hans Christiansen, see note 14)

Friedrich Wilhelm Kleukens
Kiss, mosaic, Wedding Tower lobby,
Darmstadt, 1914
In addition to graphic works
inspired by Morris, Kleukens
designed mosaic pictures and
ornaments for the 1914 exhibition
which, like a final reprise,
summarize all of Jugendstil's
thematic and visual appeal.

Vereinte Kunstgewerbler Darmstadt
Standing hearts, pieces of a coffee and dinner service,
ca. 1903
Porcelain, underglaze painting,
5.6 cm to 19.5 cm high
At the second exhibition by the artists' colony in 1904, individual handicraft products were no longer exhibited exclusively in the context of the artists' houses, even though these continued to form the central focus as total works of art. This second exhibition actually yielded a small financial profit. From now until the outbreak of the First World War, the colony's exhibition policy became increasingly progressive.

The artists of the colony

The tension inherent in the contradiction between "court architect" and "industrial artist" – the two roles required of the Darmstadt artists – resulted in a number of highly individual creations. Olbrich's group of three houses of 1904 (ills. p. 240) indicate a stylistic shift toward structuring and functionalism, although the buildings nevertheless remain richly inventive and "Jugendstil-ish" in their variety. The inscription on Olbrich's magnificent Wedding Tower (ill. p. 237) may have been true of the architect himself: "Have respect for the Old and the courage to attempt the New. Remain true to your own nature and true to the people you love." For all his Viennese grace, Olbrich's philosophy was close to that of the English Arts and Crafts Movement, as can be seen in the solid forms of his domestic utensils and his use of simple materials. His sheer delight in design also led him to create individual pieces of an emphatically aesthetic nature, their high material value reflecting their use of costly inlay (ill. p. 253). These pieces demonstrate a typical characteristic of Jugendstil, namely its change from or transformation of one artistic discipline into another. Thus architecture – as in the case of the Wedding Tower – is understood as sculpture,

painting as the ornamental component of an overall decor, handicraft as the object of sophisticated and exquisite design. Hence full-scale buildings frequently exude the air of jewelry caskets, just as small items of handicraft are monumentalized into architecture.

Another sharp contrast to the strict linearity of Peter Behrens is provided by the works of Hans Christiansen. The luminous, painterly colorfulness of his oeuvre earnt him the nickname of the "Böcklin of decoration". If Olbrich represented the (Vienna) Secession style in the Darmstadt group, Christiansen stood for (French) Art Nouveau (ills. pp. 244, 245, 250). After studying in Hamburg and Munich, Christiansen spent three years at the Académie Julian in Paris, which remained his second home over the following years. Coming from painting, he became one of Jugendstil's classic all-rounders. "I interpret my role as an artist as broadly as possible: I want to be able to paint a portrait, but also to design a piece of furniture; I draw caricatures, but also rugs, posters, and indeed originals for every kind of printing process; I design stained-glass windows, but also occasionally a leatherwork screen. My motto is: portrayal of the characteristic in form and color, tailored to function and technique."[14] (ill. p. 245).

The author of these pithy lines on the artist-designer was also the author of the "Christiansen rose", as it became enduringly known in the sphere of Jugendstil. This characteristic rose motif can be found in every area of Christiansen's art (ill. p. 245). Instantly recognizable in its style and outstanding in its quality, the motif made him a brilliant decorative artist to some, and to others a shallow panderer to public tastes. "In Rosen" was even the name which Christiansen gave to his villa on the Mathildenhöhe. Christiansen's house offers a sort of correlation to Olbrich's neighbouring villa. Like the houses of his artist colleagues, it demonstrates the same principle of individualistic design as the expression of his own personality. As Christiansen wrote in the catalogue to the colony's exhibition of 1901: "This is no mediocre modern house, and no average person will live here, but one whose world is his own and who has built his nest in line with his own wishes and his own personality ... And I will only be happy when one day it is said: 'Here lived joy in living and in creating!'"[15]

In comparison with the houses of Christiansen, Olbrich, and Behrens, each so closely bound up with the personalities of their owner, the interiors designed by 21-year-old Patriz Huber employed a broad palette of decorative means which the artist tailored to each location. Even critics of the artists' colony acknowledged that Huber came closest to the aim of the exhibition – to present examples of an elegantly stylish form of everyday living. He also designed jewelry and silverware for the Theodor Fahrner jewelry works in Pforzheim, well-known for its Jugendstil products. With their spiral patterns and simple, clear designs, Huber's creations were such a success that these prime examples of high-quality serial production were exported to England (ill. p. 242).

Emmanuel Josef Margold
Biscuit tin for the Bahlsen company, ca. 1915
Printed tinplate, 5.5 x 19.8 x 12 cm
"... in interior ensembles, the restaurant and small *objets d'art*, [Margold] introduced the cultivated and colorful use of ornament, the perfected style of surface decoration from the circle around Josef Hoffmann."
(Paul Ferdinand Schmidt, see note 22)

Huber's prodigious talents earned him a notable commission, namely the planning of a villa colony near Posen, which he undertook with his brother, the architect Anton Huber. Before the project could be executed, however, an unhappy love affair led Huber – at the age of just 24 – to take his own life.

High-quality serial items accessible to a broad buying public were also produced by Rudolf Bosselt, including medals and plaques, practical and decorative items of bronze, and ivory and tortoiseshell jewelry. The activities of Paul Bürck, the youngest member of the colony, also centered for the most part on commercial graphics and interior decoration rather than on the "fine" arts. These, then, were the artists who were present from the start of the colony, and who from August to October 1901 put themselves on the line in the exhibition "A Document of German Art".

Ludwig Habich
Tankard, ca. 1900
Stoneware, sharp-fire glaze, treacle glaze, pewter lid with figure modeled in the round, 23.4 cm high
Made by Jakob Julius Scharvogel, Munich

Exhibitions and "documentations"

Art for the art lovers,
Handicraft for the exclusive circles
of connoisseurs
But the art industry for the people as a whole –
as a giver of bread and joie de vivre.
W. Stöffler[16]

"It is to be a large-scale public celebration and a grand festival of artists," wrote the *Darmstädter Tagblatt* in the run-up to the event.[17] A festival committee oversaw the preparations for this "documentation", and Grand Duke Ernst Ludwig "took a lively interest in all the details."[18] There was a splendid opening, an extraordinary exhibition, and at the end a certain soberness as the anticipated boost to local industry failed to materialize owing to lack of consumer interest. Reviews ranged from enthusiasm to ridicule and frank disapproval. Julius Meier-Graefe was positively venomous: "Ibsen, Goya, Thomas Theodor Heine! None of you have seen the compact majority, that black mass on the breast of one suffocating, that eternally ridiculous, as compact, as black, as ridiculous as I did on that golden morning in Darmstadt". Somewhat more specifically, he expressed his doubts "about the realistic aspects, the practical possibility of turning a town of limited means and lacking trade and industry into a center of commercial importance."[19] Alfred Lichtwark, on the other hand, reached a more positive verdict: "This exhibition will remain in my memory as the first attempt to show the German people in a real-life

example what a private house can be. Those individual things which miscarried or were even somewhat tasteless shall not count against it. The masses are being offered the bread of a new idea, a new idea for them."[20]

Despite some differences of opinion, this "new idea" maintained its momentum and the second exhibition by the artists' colony was staged in 1904, members of the colony having also taken part in various international exhibitions in the meantime, such as Paris in 1900 and Turin in 1902. Alongside financial problems, a crisis of a more personal kind was precipitated by the dominating role assumed by Olbrich. When their contracts expired in 1902, Christiansen, Bürck, and Huber resigned, followed in 1903 by Behrens and Bosselt.

The Grand Duke assumed the entire financial risk of the second exhibition, in order to spare the artists the bureaucratic miseries which had likewise contributed to their departure. As in the first exhibition, the artists' houses – as total works of art – formed the central focus, although individual handicraft products were no longer exhibited exclusively in this context (ill. p. 248). This second exhibition even yielded a small financial profit. From now until the outbreak of the First World War, the colony's exhibition policy became increasingly progressive. Alongside one-man shows, the 1908 Hesse State Exhibition

Hans Christiansen
The Lover's Tryst
ca. 1900
From *L'Estampe moderne*
Color woodcut, 34.6 x 22.1 cm
If Olbrich represented the (Vienna) Secession style in the Darmstadt group, Christiansen stood for (French) Art Nouveau.

Bernhard Hoetger
Loïe Fuller, ca. 1900
Bronze, 25.5 cm high
Institut Mathildenhöhe, Museum
Künstlerkolonie Darmstadt
The sculptor Bernhard Hoetger had
lived in Paris, where he had met
Rodin and worked in his studio. His
first bronzes were executed in a very
French, powerful Art Nouveau
style; they were Parisian, too, in
their subject, as this highly animated
figure of Loïe Fuller demonstrates.

was a great success thanks to its broad range of exhibits. The third exhibition by the artists' colony offered an impressive summary of all that had been achieved. The bombs of the Second World War destroyed for ever many of its unforgettable works.

"Artists, more than other people, are individualists"

The "Document of German Art" is most clearly documented by the artists who passed through Darmstadt during the passage of time. After the initial departures of 1902 and 1903 already mentioned, Paul Haustein (1880–1944), Johann Vincenz Cissarz (1873–1942) and Daniel Greiner (1872–1943) were appointed to the colony. Cissarz was chiefly active in the fields of painting

and graphics (ill. p. 243). Daniel Greiner was also first and foremost a "utility" artist. Talented and highly talented artists came and went over the years leading up to 1914. A number of them deserve particular mention. Albin Müller's oeuvre embraced every area of the applied arts, whereby his ceramics proved especially successful (ills. pp. 235, 248). His style of ornament is bold and original, full of strong color contrasts and characterized by an elegant "exaltedness" in its contours. In hindsight Müller (1871–1941) expressed his regret that, while the artists' colony had for a while shared and shaped the dream of the total work of art, it had failed to achieve a symbiosis of work and life. "My hopes of and efforts to achieve a friendly coalition amongst the artists of the colony were disappointed from the very start and throughout

Page 253:
Joseph Maria Olbrich
Jewelry box, ca. 1901
Mahogany, mother-of-pearl and
ivory inlay, copper fittings,
40 cm high, 20 x 14.9 cm at the
bottom,
17 x 11.7 cm at the top
Inlay by Robert Macco, Heidelberg
Institut Mathildenhöhe, Museum
Künstlerkolonie Darmstadt
In addition to practical, functional
objects, Olbrich's sheer delight in
design led him to create individual
pieces of an emphatically aesthetic
nature, their high material value
reflecting their use of costly inlay.

my time there. From my unworldly and idealistic standpoint, I had dreamed of a harmonious community of artists, of lively mutual intellectual stimulation, of taking each other's part, and saw with sadness that none of it was to be achieved in the real world. Artists, more than other people, are individualists."[21]

Their formal language was also individual. One of the most important contributions to the colony's last exhibition was the sculptural ensemble by Bernhard Hoetger (1874–1949) in the plane-tree grove. It took as its subject the circle of life – a theme which recurs in the work of artists internationally about the turn of the century. Hoetger had lived in Paris, where he had met Rodin and worked in his studio. His first bronzes were executed in a very French, powerful Art Nouveau style; they were Parisian, too, in their subject, as his highly animated figure of Loïe Fuller demonstrates (ill. p. 251). His successes in France were not without impact in Germany, and he was offered numerous one-man shows. Over the following years Hoetger abandoned his cultured Paris style in favor of an art imbued with social criticism.

A Viennese note was sounded one last time in Darmstadt by Emmanuel Josef Margold (ill. p. 249), who "in interior ensembles, the restaurant and small *objets d'art*, introduced the cultivated and colorful use of ornament, the perfected style of surface decoration from the circle around Josef Hoffmann."[22] Friedrich Wilhelm Kleukens, a member of the colony from 1907, was the first head of the Ernst Ludwig Press which did so much for book design. In addition to graphic works inspired by Morris, Kleukens designed mosaic pictures and ornaments for the 1914 exhibition which, like a final reprise, summarize all of Jugendstil's thematic and visual appeal (ill. pp. 246–247). As evidenced by the establishment of its own printing press, book design at the Darmstadt colony was of great importance, so much so that even the facades of its houses were frequently dubbed "built book illustration" (ill. p. 234) – total works of art everywhere, true "Festivals of Life and Art" (*Feste des Lebens und der Kunst*), as Behrens titled the ideological essay which he published in Jena in 1900.

They are angry, those false prophets, to find their wise words proved wrong – that there will be no new style in art, that there will never be a new style, that it can only evolve out of the old, that it cannot be invented. In this last point they are not entirely wrong. There are now indications that there will be a new style, not developed out of the old, that it is in part already here, at least in its infancy. If one keeps one's eyes open and maintains a happy optimism and a faith in beauty, one will recognize that something is in the process of becoming which resonates more profoundly with our lives than those deliberately bizarre forms which, for all their "modern" exterior, are usually just cheap goods delivered by people who seize upon the latest novelty as a means of making money. Whether one calls such goods after magazines or artist groups, one neither belittles the achievement of those who create them nor honors the efforts of those who made them. Fashion follows its ridiculous swings. The style that is currently in the process of becoming operates more at an inner level; it is neither arbitrarily invented nor playfully compiled out of the old. We have grown earnest, we take our lives seriously, we place a high value on work. We have worked a lot and evaluated a lot and we are weary of playing, of playing with the past. Through working, we have learnt to understand our age and our own lives; what good to us is the masquerade of a past long gone and impenetrable to us today? We recognize the value of our work and are creating standards of value for ourselves. We feel that we have attained something in the sphere of practical life that was never there before and which will never be lost, and this feeling makes us happy. There is a palpable sense that we are entitled to joy, to a measured tranquillity, to a well-earned wage for our work. It is surely clear that the serious man who is dedicated to hard work will find no pleasure in games and romantic dreams ... We can apply our forces to advance even further and will then have greater and higher needs; these, too, we will satisfy with powerful and beautiful forms. We are moving towards a new culture – our own.

Peter Behrens, *Feste des Lebens und der Kunst*, Jena, 1900

DIE SCHÖPFUNG DER WELT

ALS Gott anfing, den Himmel und die Erde zu schaffen, da war die Erde wüst und leer, und Dunkel deckte den Ozean, aber der Geist Gottes schwebte über dem Gewässer. Da sprach Gott: Es werde Licht! Und es ward Licht. Und Gott sah, daß das Licht gut war, und Gott trennte das Licht von dem Dunkel, und Gott nannte das Licht Tag, das Dunkel aber nannte er Nacht. Und so ward ein Abend und ein Morgen, ein erster Tag.

Dann sprach Gott: Es sei eine Feste inmitten der Gewässer, die scheide die Wasser voneinander. Und Gott

German factories and workshops
Berlin

When we arrived at the very end of the 19th century, there was no more time to lose, and those preoccupied with the idea of a new style suddenly grew restless and feverish.
Henry van de Velde[1]

Berlin – Jugendstil versus Wilhelminism

In line with the general political and social structures prevailing around 1900, Jugendstil had developed not in a centralized fashion in the capital of the German Empire, but in a number of different centers, above all Munich, Darmstadt, Dresden, Weimar, Leipzig, Hagen, and Worpswede. In each case Jugendstil assumed a clearly different form and significance. Berlin became a reservoir for all these diverging trends and remained a magnet for cultural activities of all kinds. The situation in the German metropolis at the end of the 19th century can best be summed up as Jugendstil versus Wilhelminism. Kaiser Wilhelm II appointed himself dictator of taste and arrogantly presumed to know what merited the designation of "art": "Art which goes beyond the laws and boundaries laid down by myself is no longer art; rather, it is handicraft, it is manufacturing, and that is something which art must never become."[2] With these emphatic words, the Kaiser was lashing out at the very phenomenon which was emerging in Berlin around 1900 and which would prove so influential in the future: the handicraft – the functional object of everyday use – was becoming art. The urgent desire for innovative change, the growing awareness that there was "no more time to lose", now resulted not just in decorative artistic daydreams, but in clear steps towards overcoming the problems posed by mechanical production methods and modern city life. The

slogan "art for all" now extended to the practical and functional. However diverse the face which Jugendstil – or that which was subsumed under its name – may have presented in Berlin, it was at all times a protest against the militaristic Wilhelminism and bourgeois capitalism which had flourished since the founding of the Empire in 1871. Within the arts, it was a stand against the historicism which had been perpetuated not least by the Kaiser's own attempts at painting in the style. Any deviation from the well-trodden path of heroic historicism implied a risk. Hence His Majesty denigrated not only the arts and crafts, but felt "seasick", as he put it, at the sight of a piece of van de Velde furniture, whose linear dynamism left him in a very bad way. In the face of such stuffy narrow-mindedness, it is understandable that the liberal-thinking, educated Grand Duke Ernst Ludwig of Hesse should feel the way he did: "Incidentally, while I was in Berlin for the Kaiser's birthday, I frequently found that many of my so-called colleagues were so backward in their attitudes that I felt myself a pure Socialist by comparison."[3]

The "Munch affair" – Walter Leistikow – Secession

It was against this backdrop that a scandal unprecedented in the cultural sphere now erupted. On November 5 1892 a comprehensive exhibition of works by the Norwegian artist Edvard Munch (1863–1944) opened in the Round Room in the Berlin House of Architecture, with the artist in attendance. After the vernissage, a storm of indignation broke out. "Court painter" Anton von Werner described the exhibition as an insult to art, as obscene and vulgar, and

Theodor Fontane

Auf der Kuppe der Müggelberge

(Semnonen-Vifion)

Ueber den Müggelfee fetzt mich der Ferge.
Nun erklettr' ich die Müggelberge,
Mir zu Häupten raufchen die Kronen
Wie zu Zeiten der Semnonen,
Unfrer Urahnen, die hier im Eichwaldsfchatten
Ihre Gottheitsftätten hatten.

Und die Spree hinauf, an Buchten und Seen,
Seh' ich wieder ihre Lager ftehn
Wie damals beim Aufbruch. Taufende ziehn
Hin über die Dahme . . . Der Vollmond fchien.

Am Eierhäuschen hebt es an:
Eine Vorhut, etliche dreißig Mann,
Ein Bardentrupp folgt von Friedrichshagen,
Wo jetzt noch Nachkommen die Harfe fchlagen,
Bei Kiekemal und bei Kiekebufch
Blafen Hörner den Abfchiedstufch.

Auf Flößen kommen Andre gefchwommen,
Haben den Weg bis Schmöckwitz genommen,
Bis Schmöckwitz, wo, Wandel der Epochen,
Jetzt Familien Kaffee kochen.
Aus der „Wuhlhaide" treten, wirr und verwundert,
Gefchwindfchritts immer neue Hundert
Und bei Woltersdorf und am Dämeritz-See
Sammelt fich fchon das Corps d'armée.

Jetzt aber — der Dämeritz ift überfchritten —
An des Zuges Ausgang und inmitten
Erblick' ich Mädchen, erblick' ich Fraun,
Alle thusneldifch anzufchaun,
Alle mit Butten, alle mit Hucken,
Draus blond die kleinen Germanen kucken —
So ziehen fie füdwärts mit Kiepen und Kobern,
Von der Müggel aus die Welt zu erobern.

(1)

demanded its closure. A fearsome row broke out, with whistling and yelling, and the rumpus eventually degenerated into a brawl. A week later Munch's pictures were taken down. In contrast to the flood of scathing criticism, only a few voices spoke up in Munch's favor. The consequences of the "Munch affair" were nevertheless profound: it would ultimately lead, albeit some years later, to the founding of the Berlin Secession. One painter with a highly sensitive eye for Munch's work was Walter Leistikow (1865–1908), who at the time of the scandal wrote in the *Freie Bühne*: "… that is seen, that is experienced, that is felt. Someone who can put something like that into words, or paint, or song, how shall I put it, his is a poetic nature; he looks out at the world which he loves through a poet's eyes."[4] Leistikow, who immediately became friends with Munch, was a painter of Berlin landscapes and came very close to Jugendstil in his compositions. Feelings and moods are symbolized in arabesque, mutually corresponding contours in his pictures of lakes and forests (ill. opposite page). His scenes of nature, infused with melancholy, are clearly influenced by Japanese prints in the two-dimensional reduction – at times merely to silhouette – of their pictorial elements, in their frequent use of diagonals, and in their lattice or grille-like organization of forms against an expansive landscape. Peter Behrens recognized the quality of Leistikow's work early on: "Two mutually dependent elements need mediators between them – painters who maintain the importance of contour through their mastery of the plane, draughtsmen who know how to feel in a painterly fashion. Leistikow is one of these."[5] The pebble had been tossed into the water and its ripples now began to spread. In protest against the closure of the Munch exhibition, and at Leistikow's instigation, the group *Die Elf* (The Eleven) was formed, analogous to *Les Vingt* (The Twenty) in Brussels. *Die Elf*, who included Max Liebermann (1897–1935), Max Klinger (1857–1920) and Ludwig von Hofmann (1861–1945), prepared the ground in Berlin for the new art. Subsequently, 1898 saw the foundation of the Berlin Secession. In 1906, however, this split into the New Secession and the Free Secession, a move prompted by the feeling amongst many members that Liebermann had driven the original association into the arms of Berlin art dealer Paul Cassirer. The group *Die Brücke* (The Bridge), formed in 1905, also led on from the Secession.

Left:
Theo Schmuz-Baudiss
Vase (detail), April 1903
Porcelain, underglaze painting,
30.9 cm high, 7 cm diameter
Made by the Königliche Porzellan-Manufaktur, Berlin
Badisches Landesmuseum Karlsruhe, Museum beim Markt – Angewandte Kunst seit 1900
Schmuz-Baudiss's vases, often very large, with their *pâte sur pâte* decoration, have a particular charm. *Pâte sur pâte* (lit. "paste on paste") is a difficult process in which layers of slip are carefully applied one on top of the other with a brush, until a relief pattern is achieved. Mild greens, grays and pinks further enhance the "softness" of Schmuz-Baudiss's porcelain.

Fidus (Hugo Höppener)
Waltz, from the portfolio *Dances*, 1894
Color lithograph, 35.9 x 24.1 cm
The esoteric Fidus – as his teacher Diefenbach baptized him – combined naturalistic figures, children of Helios, with abstract forms.

Walter Leistikow
Lake Schlachtensee at Dusk,
ca. 1895
Oil on canvas, 73 x 93 cm
Preussischer Kulturbesitz, Berlin
In Leistikow's pictures of lakes and
forests, feelings and moods are
symbolized in arabesque, mutually
corresponding contour lines.

Pan – Julius Meier-Graefe

**This was the true purpose of *Pan*. A sort of herbarium! It
was up to us, he argued, to make it a spawning ground for
new life … He also said all sorts of things about the serious
state of affairs in the German arts and hard work and that
Pan signified not just the cloven-hoofed god, but the
universe, the cosmos.**
Eberhard von Bodenhausen on Julius Meier-Graefe[6]

The winds of change blowing through Berlin
were coming from the north, and not just through
the works of Munch. A debate on Nietzsche's
ideas that started in Copenhagen quickly became
international. In 1892 the writers Ola Hansson
(1860–1925), Arne Garborg (1851–1924) and

August Strindberg (1849–1912), together with
the Finn Axel Gallen-Kallela, established their
own regular Scandinavian table in the *"Zum
schwarzen Ferkel"* winebar, where they were
soon joined by Berlin's entire Bohemia.
Strindberg was the uncrowned ruler of the
group, until the Germano-Polish poet Stanislaus
Przybyszewski (1868–1927) appeared and
married the beautiful Norwegian author Dagny
Juell. Dagny was the muse of the "Ferkel" set,
adored, feared and probably at one time
"possessed" by Strindberg and Munch. The
glittering couple took over the leading role in this
legendary literary circle, whose "conferences"
Meier-Graefe described in his memoirs: "The

Eckmann

reason for our meetings was first and foremost to surrender ourselves with almost holy devotion to the pleasures of alcohol, in order to attain that state of intoxication in which the soul is unloosed and reality left far behind."[7] The magazine *Pan*, published for the first time in April 1895 and quarterly from then on until the spring of 1900, was born at the very same table. Its passage was assisted by numerous midwives, but its true father was the writer, art critic and champion of Jugendstil Julius Meier-Graefe (1867-1935). And as he predicted, *Pan* became a cosmos, or more accurately a microcosm of all that was happening on the international art scene around 1900 – heterogeneous but brilliant, of high artistic and literary quality, and still the best testament to its era even today. Otto Julius Bierbaum (1865–1910) was in charge of the literature side, Meier-Graefe the fine arts. They set out their aims in the first edition: to further the arts in the spirit of an organic understanding of art, embracing the

entire sphere of artistic endeavor and seeing true artistic life only in the close proximity of all artists." *Pan* served as a direct medium of art, above all in the sphere of illustration. The quality of its printing, moreover, has never been equaled. It was available in a normal edition, a deluxe edition and an artist's proof edition, with each number containing original prints by prominent artists of the day. It was financed and published by a "Pan Cooperative Society". The editors-in-chief were Meier-Graefe and Bierbaum, and after their departure Caesar Flaischlen and Richard Graul. In contrast to the eloquent, ironic Meier-Graefe, Flaischlen was a rather more effusive type. The cosmopolitan Meier-Graefe was the most dazzling figure in the field of international arts promotion around the turn of the century, a "travelling salesman for Art Nouveau". It was to him, more than anyone, that Germany owed its links with the international art scene. Originally from an industrialist background,

Otto Eckmann
Night Herons – Three Philosophers, 1896
Color woodcut, printed in watercolor on Japanese vellum, 26.5 x 46 cm
"With Eckmann, sentimentality in ornament was perhaps extinguished for good. He was, if not its final mainstay, nevertheless the one who lent ornament enough attraction to arouse the desire to preserve it ... He always made me think of Chopin. Neither of them troubled themselves with the pure line of construction ... His fingers quiver on the line like those of a violinist on the strings."
(Henry van de Velde, see note 10)

Thomas Theodor Heine
Tailpiece
From *Pan*, no. 1, vol. 2, 1896
Heine was the master of the vignette. In *Pan* he perfected his use of the "tendril" as a means of animating the plane and of cultivating dynamic line in asymmetries, curves, and above all in the amalgamation of the organic with the functional.

Meier-Graefe rejected the family career and, after a number of study trips, chose instead to dedicate himself to writing. He was 27 when *Pan* was founded and was already acquainted with all the members of the Aesthetic Movement in England, the Parisian avant-garde and the Munich Secession. Over the following years he became friends not only with the giants of German Jugendstil, but also with Toulouse-Lautrec and Munch. He wrote passionate articles in support of Jugendstil, founded a joint company with Samuel Bing, took the side of Alfred Dreyfus – the French Jewish army officer wrongly accused and convicted of treason – and persuaded Henry van de Velde to come to Germany. In 1897 Meier-Graefe founded another magazine, *Dekorative Kunst* (Decorative Art), and two years later opened the art gallery La Maison Moderne in Paris. He also helped organize exhibitions by the Wiener Werkstätte and in 1904 published the comprehensive *Entwicklungsgeschichte der modernen Kunst* (History of Modern Art). These were just some of the incredible activities of a man who, on a trip to Russia in 1915, was imprisoned in Siberia for nine months, and who upon his release campaigned with unflagging energy on behalf of the works of Vincent van Gogh and embraced the new art of the 20th century. In 1932 Meier-Graefe left Germany for good and went to live in France. Of Jugendstil, he later wrote in hindsight: "It was crazy, but divine, and no one regrets saying they were part of it."[8]

The total work of art in print

I go to the lithograph and find life.
I am filled with courage and fear, imagination and slowness,
the desire to discover and a concern for my safety.
Who belongs to whom, the stone to me or I to it?
Paul Wunderlich[9]

The editorial committee of *Pan* included some of the most important patrons of modern German art, figures from industry and the arts, amongst them Wilhelm von Bode, Baron Eberhard von Bodenhausen, Count Harry Kessler, Alfred Lichtwark, Otto Erich Hartleben and Karl Koepping. Sitting on the board was Karl von der Heydt, whose own magnificent collection now forms the core of the museum in Wuppertal that bears his name. *Pan* was available by subscription only; copperplate printed on Japanese vellum, its mailing list included Tsar Alexander of Russia. Eventually, however, its exclusivity proved too much of a financial handicap; by 1900 it had only 500 paying readers, and the magazine ceased publication.

It would take only a few lines to list the famous and important artists and writers of the day who did not contribute to *Pan*, and a whole book to name those who did – including virtually all the artists appearing in these pages. One name which nevertheless deserves to be singled out is that of Otto Eckmann, the "giant" of lettering and ornament (ill. opposite page). Upon Eckmann's death in 1902, van de Velde wrote: "With Eckmann, sentimentality in ornament was perhaps extinguished for good. He was, if not its final mainstay, nevertheless the one who lent ornament enough attraction to arouse the desire

Melchior Lechter
Cover for *Maximin, ein Gedenkbuch*, edited by Stefan George, 1907 (design 1897)
Printed on imperial Japanese vellum in red and black, 39.7 x 30.1 cm
Printed by Otto von Holten, Berlin
Following in Morris's footsteps, Lechter arrived at an economy of lettering and image of almost epic austerity.

Thomas Theodor Heine
Dachshund tailpiece
From *Pan*, no. 3, vol. 2, 1896

to preserve it … He always made me think of Chopin. Neither of them troubled themselves with the pure line of construction … His fingers quiver on the line like those of a violinist on the strings."[10] Another major contributor to *Pan* was the master of the vignette, Thomas Theodor Heine, who perfected his use of the "tendril" as a means of animating the plane and of cultivating dynamic line in asymmetries, curves and above all in the amalgamation of the organic with the functional (ill. p. 261). Another of the outstanding *Pan* artists was Ludwig von Hofmann, a painter of archaic figures in springtime settings. His recapitulation of the content of his paintings in emblematic images on the frame served to unite picture and frame into a whole, and thereby made him the representative of the "total work of art" within painting (ill. p. 256). The esoteric Fidus – as Diefenbach baptized his pupil Hugo Höppener (1868–1948) – combined naturalistic figures, children of Helios, with abstract forms (ill. p. 258). Ephraim Mose Lilien (1874–1925) drew his inspiration from English book illustration, whereby he relinquished the latter's decorative overprofusion in favor of intertwining lines which fill the page in ornamental fashion (ill. p. 254). Melchior Lechter (1865–1937), on the other hand, also following in Morris's footsteps, arrived at an economy of lettering and image of almost epic austerity (ill. p. 261).

Dreams of flowering glass – Karl Koepping

The applied arts were represented in the pages of *Pan* by Karl Koepping (1848–1914), one of magazine's joint editors and himself an artist (ill. opposite page). Trained as a painter, he moved on to etching and ultimately to glass. Inspired by the Art Nouveau and Tiffany glassware exhibited in Paris by Bing, he drew upon his earlier qualification as a chemist and started experimenting with glass. Since his first efforts were not as successful as he had hoped, he turned to Friedrich Zitzmann (1840–1906), an experienced glassmaker who had spent a few years working in Murano – the center, near Venice, of an important glass industry since the 13th century – and who had the technical expertise necessary to realize Koepping's bizarre designs. The collaboration lasted only a few months, however, since Zitzmann failed to honor his obligation not to use Koepping's designs and specific manufacturing processes in his own glassware. Argument over the copyright is still going on today (ill. opposite page). The attractiveness of

Koepping's glassware lies in the virtuoso handling of the material, which bears no external decoration but becomes an ornament in its own right. His glasses take the shape of flowers whose wafer-thin goblets float on curved stems. Through his contacts with Bing via Meier-Graefe, Koepping was able to exhibit his works in Paris. According to a review of the annual Salon du Champ de Mars of March 1897: "There are a few things, however, deserving distinction, and I will place in the first rank the blown glass by M. Karl Koepping … M. Koepping's glass is delightfully simple and light, and supremely artistic. How infinitely preferable this plainly treated, graceful material, which is really glass, to the over-elaborate metallic complications of Tiffany."[11]

A potpourri of expressive forms

Here I sat waiting, waiting – but for nothing
On the far side of good and evil, now enjoying
the light, now the shade, the whole just a game …
Friedrich Nietzsche[12]

Light and shade, playfulness and seriousness – art in Berlin and the rest of Germany around 1900 embraced all this and more, offering the viewer an inexhaustible spectrum characterized both by its high quality and its profound formal contrasts. Many artists explored equivalent forms of expression in different media not just in theory, but also in practice. Thus, the endlessly repeated pattern of the divine arabesque was not confined to the pages of *Pan*, but expanded outwards into the sphere of three-dimensional design, spreading to furniture, glass, porcelain, pewter, and silverware. However, the opponents of ornament also began an active search for a new, "contemporary" form of expression which replaced ornament with pattern. "But even the cheapest, most worthless cotton dress can bear a print, while ornament – wherever it appears – has something distinctive about it. While there is no truly 'modern' ornament, there are certainly modern forms of 'pattern'. To take an extreme instance: a prime example of an 'abstract' pattern is the camouflage familiarly seen on military vehicles – and of which a major painter, Georges Braque, described himself the inventor with a certain pride … "[13] The luxurious jewelry by the Berlin artist Wilhelm Lucas von Cranach (1861–1918), a descendant of the famous German painter Lucas Cranach, is pure, "uncamouflaged" Art Nouveau (ill. p. 262). Cranach, too, started out as a painter before turning to jewelry. He was alone in Germany in producing works

Wilhelm Lucas von Cranach
Pendant, ca. 1900
Gold, ruby cabochons, diamonds, translucent enamel and freshwater pearls, 7 x 5.5 cm
Made by Gebrüder Friedländer, Berlin
Collection Barlow/Widmann, Spain
The luxurious items of jewelry designed by the Berlin artist Wilhelm Lucas von Cranach, a descendant of the famous German painter Lucas Cranach, are pure Art Nouveau. Wilhelm, too, started out as a painter before turning to jewelry. He was alone in Germany in producing works comparable in quality with those issuing from France – something which earned him corresponding recognition at the Paris World Exposition of 1900.

Friedrich Zitzmann
Three stemmed glasses, ca. 1899
Glass, blown and worked with a
lamp, 21.5 cm to 22.2 cm high
Kunstmuseum im Ehrenhof,
Düsseldorf

Karl Koepping
Decorative glasses
Original etching, 25 x 15 cm
From *Pan*, no. 3, vol. 2, 1896,
p. 253
"There are a few things, however,
deserving distinction, and I will
place in the first rank the blown
glass by M. Karl Koepping …
M. Koepping's glass is delightfully
simple and light, and supremely
artistic. How infinitely preferable
this plainly treated, graceful
material, which is really glass, to
the over-elaborate metallic
complications of Tiffany." (Review
of the annual Salon du Champ de
Mars exhibition, Paris 1897, see
note 11)

Left:
Max Laeuger
Vase, 1904–10
Glazed and painted earthenware,
39.5 cm high
Made by the Tonwerke Kandern,
Baden
Laeuger, who came from a
background in painting, used the
clay body of his earthenware as the
substrate for a rich, multicolored
representation of flowers, bending
branches and slender grasses which
enclasp the vessel in a sort of
framework.

Opposite page, top right:
Julius Konrad Hentschel
Items from the *Crocus* service, ca.
1899–1900
Porcelain, underglaze painting,
coffee pot: 21 high
Made by the Königlich-Sächsische
Porzellan-Manufaktur, Meissen

Centre right:
Otto Eduard Voigt
Serving plate from the *Saxonia*
service, 1904
Porcelain, sharp-fire painting,
34 cm long
Made by the Königlich-Sächsische
Porzellan-Manufaktur, Meissen
The famous porcelain works in
Meissen was initially hesitant to
embrace the new Jugendstil trend.
It nevertheless went on to produce
some of the best examples of
Jugendstil porcelain, employing
designs by Henry van de Velde,
Richard Riemerschmid, Otto
Eduard Voigt and Julius Konrad
Hentschel.

Bottom right
Königlich-Sächsische Porzellan-Manufaktur, Meissen
Flamingos, centerpiece, ca. 1900
Porcelain, underglaze painting,
18.5 cm high
Collection Barlow/Widmann,
Spain

Opposite page, far right:
Max Laeuger
Vase, 1903
Glazed and painted earthenware,
32 cm high
Made by the Tonwerke Kandern,
Baden

comparable in quality and originality with those issuing from France – something which earned him corresponding recognition at the Paris World Exposition of 1900. In order to be part of the new style, the royal porcelain works in Berlin – the Königliche Porzellan-Manufaktur (KPM) – also employed a painter, Theo Schmuz-Baudiss (1859–1942), as a designer. Schmuz-Baudiss "painted" his designs, chiefly landscapes and city panoramas, in underglaze on to the porcelain. His vases, often very large with their *pâte sur pâte* decoration, have a particular charm (ill. p. 258). *Pâte sur pâte* (lit. "paste on paste") is a difficult process in which layers of thinned clay are carefully applied one on top of the other with a brush, until a relief pattern is achieved. Mild greens, grays and pinks further enhance the "softness" of Schmuz-Baudiss's porcelain.

A pioneer in the field of porcelain manufacturing and decoration was Hermann Seger (1839–93), also employed by KPM, who gave his name to "Seger porcelain". This sintering mixture, obtained through a complex process, is particularly suitable for metal glazes, permitting an animated, abstract decor of flowing streaks of color (ill. opposite page). The famous Meissen porcelain works were initially hesitant to embrace the new Jugendstil trend. They nevertheless went on to produce some of the best examples of Jugendstil porcelain, employing designs by van de Velde, Riemerschmid, Otto Eduard Voigt (1870–1949) and Julius Konrad Hentschel (1872–1907) (ills. p. 265). At the Paris World Exposition of 1900, ceramic artist Max Laeuger (1864–1952) was awarded the Grand Prix, securing him an international reputation from that point on. His slip decor pieces rank amongst the most attractive "populist" products of Jugendstil. Laeuger, who came from a background in painting, used the clay body as the substrate for a rich, multicolored representation of flowers, bending branches, and slender grasses which enclasp the vessel in a sort of framework (ills. pp. 264, 265). This spherical style of decor, which can be found employed on practical utensils of every material, worked particularly well in metal – a natural consequence of the flexibility of the medium. The superior pewter produced by the firm of Johann Peter Kayser & Sohn AG, based in the Bockum district of Krefeld, had led Liberty to commission its own line from them. Kayser pewter was a special lead-free alloy of tin and silver which lent the material a luminous gleam (ill. right). Symbolistic and floral motifs were "processed" into functional objects with slender, elegant contours. Kayser & Sohn AG numbered amongst the German firms which boasted international success with their Jugendstil products. The WMF – Württembergische Metallwarenfabrik – in Geislingen/Steige was another manufacturer contributing to German Jugendstil with its exuberant floral and figural decors in the French Art Nouveau style (ill. left).

Johann Emil Schaudt
Armchair, 1901
Elm, embossed leather,
112 x 52 x 75 cm
Made by the Dresdner Werkstätten
für Handwerkskunst, Schmidt &
Müller
Staatliche Kunstsammlungen
Dresden, Kunstgewerbemuseum
Alongside Behrens, Obrist, Pankok,
Paul, Endell and Riemerschmid,
"local" designers such as Schaudt
also worked for the Dresdner
Werkstätten. Their furniture
encapsulated a specific "Dresden
style" which was markedly devoid of
pathos, and which struck a balance
between the strong geometry and the
exuberant Symbolism that
represented the two popular stylistic
options of the day. Clarity and
simplicity would subsequently
become synonymous with the
Deutsche Werkstätten.

Hermann Seger
Vase, ca. 1900
Porcelain, oxblood glaze,
14 cm high
Made by the Königlich-Sächsische
Porzellan-Manufaktur, Meissen
Seger was a pioneer in the field of
porcelain manufacturing and
decoration, and gave his name to
"Seger porcelain". This sintering
mixture, obtained through a
complex process, is particularly
suitable for metal glazes, permitting
an animated, abstract decor of
flowing streaks of color.

Heinrich Vogeler
Frontispiece and title page to
Der Kaiser und die Hexe [*The
Emperor and the Witch*] by Hugo
von Hofmannsthal,
Insel-Verlag, Leipzig 1900
Halftone, 20.2 x 25.3 cm
"[The illustrations to] *Der Kaiser
und die Hexe* by Hugo von
Hofmannsthal confirm that his calm
linear art, so homogeneous in its
effect and yet within itself so rich, is
suited like none other to accompany
the train of noble letters like a song."
(Rainer Maria Rilke, see note 14)

Jugendstil from Saxony

Meissen was not alone in securing the applied arts in Saxony their "positive image". In 1899, only shortly after the foundation of the Vereinigte Werkstätten für Kunst im Handwerk (Associated Workshops for Art in Handicraft) in Munich in 1898, the Dresdner Werkstätten (Dresden Workshops) were formed. The goal uppermost in the minds of the Dresden designers was to produce exemplary furniture and objects at an affordable price. Around 1902 this idea led to the foundation of the Werkstätten für deutschen Hausrat (Workshops for German Household Goods). In 1907 the Werkstätten für Wohnungs-einrichtungen, München (Munich Workshops for Interior Furnishings) amalgamated with the Dresdner Werkstätten to form the Deutsche Werkstätten Dresden-Hellerau und München (German Workshops of Dresden-Hellerau and Munich). Behrens, Obrist, Pankok, Paul, Endell and Riemerschmid all worked for the Dresdner Werkstätten, which also produced furniture in collaboration with "local" designers such as

Johann Emil Schaudt (b. 1871) (ill. p. 267). Such furniture encapsulated a specific "Dresden style" which was markedly devoid of pathos, and which struck a balance between the strong geometry and the exuberant Symbolism that represented the two popular stylistic options of the day. Clarity and simplicity would subsequently become synonymous with the Deutsche Werkstätten. The capital of Saxony reinforced its status with numerous exhibitions featuring the works of both regional and international designers.

Worpswede – lineament and plane

The far north of Germany also saw the founda-tion of design workshops. The Worpswede Werkstätten für einfache Einrichtungen und Möbel (Worpswede Workshops for Simple Interiors and Furniture) was set up in Tarmstedt, near Bremen, by Heinrich Vogeler (1872–1942), the "Morris of Germany". Like the influential Englishman, Vogeler became a committed

Lucian Bernhard
Poster advertising Adler typewriters, ca. 1909
Color lithograph, 69 x 94 cm
Printed by Hollerbaum & Schmidt, Berlin
Die Neue Sammlung, Staatliches Museum für angewandte Kunst, Munich
To the artistic spectrum which evolved, with such fascinating formal diversity, between 1900 and the beginning of the First World War in 1914, belonged the advertising poster, a favorite genre of Jugendstil and one often far ahead of it.

Peter Behrens
AEG turbine hall, Moabit, Berlin,
1909
With his appointment, in 1907, to
the AEG's artistic advisory board,
the Jugendstil "ego euphoria" of
Behrens' Darmstadt days passed
into history, and he assumed a new
role as designer of – as we say today
– the corporate identity of a modern
utility.

Socialist, and in his latter years a Communist. He is nevertheless remembered as the creator of romantic, fairytale-like etchings and drawings which added an important artistic dimension to book illustration around the turn of the century. Within the framework of the Worpswede school of painters, initiated in the village of the same name by, amongst others, Otto Modersohn and Fritz Mackensen, Vogeler ran his own printing press. The poet Rainer Maria Rilke, with whom he was acquainted, described Vogeler's "ornamental dreams" thus: "The art of encapsulating all of spring, all the wealth and abundance of the days and nights, in a flower, in the branch of a tree, a birch or a languishing girl – none was so skilled in this art as Heinrich Vogeler … [The illustrations to] *Der Kaiser und die Hexe* [The Emperor and the Witch] by Hugo von Hofmannsthal confirm that his calm linear art, so homogeneous in its effect and yet within itself so rich, is suited like none other to accompany the train of noble letters like a song."[14] The harmonious linearity of Vogeler's art attracted many imitators, resulting in a veritable Vogeler boom around 1900. His atmospheric illustrations nevertheless remained beyond compare (ill. p. 268).

To the artistic spectrum which evolved, with such fascinating formal diversity, between 1900 and the beginning of the First World War in 1914, belonged the advertising poster, a favorite genre of Jugendstil and one often far ahead of it (ill. p. 269).

Peter Behrens – From artist-designer to industrial designer

The material in itself is dead and lifeless. It is only given life by form, breathed into it by the creative will of the artist … the value of the work of art lies in the emotional satisfaction of an inner urge for redemption, not in the value of the material.
Walter Gropius[15]

The words of Bauhaus founder Walter Gropius encapsulated the new understanding of art. The artistic object was no longer the costly material, nor its ornamental cloak, but the form – the design. "The objectivity which set in from now on was essentially a further logical step in the programme, although it appeared at first sight as a countermovement, a reaction – which indeed it was as regards ornament. Although this latter did not disappear altogether, it visibly froze under the cold shower of condemnation. The rhythm, playfulness and inventiveness which had made the works of artists such as Eckmann, Pankok, Endell, Christiansen and many others so delightful, even the magnificent, wrestling lines of van de Velde – all these shriveled and dried up. Like the imaginary games played by children marching in a military 'left-right-left', it was as if someone had shouted 'Halt!'. From 1902 the dynamic and the animated, the glide and dance of line, form and color gave way to the motionless abstract figure: square and circle, rhombus and oval, an ordered juxtaposition of

Peter Behrens
Synchon, electric clock designed for
AEG, Berlin, ca. 1910
Brass, rolled metal, glass, 26 cm
diameter
"Behrens' job was not just to build
factories, but to take charge of all
aspects of formal design at the
AEG, from the lettering of its
adverts and brochures to domestic
appliances, electric kettles and arc
lamps, right up to the AEG's
buildings. Everything was entrusted
to just one person's hands, and it is
rather strange that they should have
been the hands of the painter Peter
Behrens. There must have been
some clever people at the AEG."
(Julius Posener, see note 17)

Peter Behrens
Design for a poster advertising an
AEG metal filament light, 1907
Color lithograph, 67 x 52 cm
Printed by Hollerbaum & Schmidt,
Berlin
AEG company archives,
Frankfurt/Main

compact individual motifs. It was Peter Behrens, in particular, whose austerity would establish a new yardstick and whose development towards tectonic form took place absolutely parallel to the geometricization of his ornament; thus he covered, emphasized, clarified the surfaces of his architecture by segmenting them with black rectangular or circular forms on a pale background, not dissimilar to the effect of the Baptistry in Florence."[16] In the person of Peter Behrens, we can follow the aesthetic shift – both in his work and in his career – from painter to industrial designer. The author of the quotation above omits, in the list of artists to whom he attributes the qualities of rhythm and playfulness, to include Behrens, himself the master of the vital line in his early work. The comparison between Behrens' later architecture and the Florence Baptistry is an appropriate one, and at the same time shows that Behrens did not halt on the command "Halt!", but advanced logically towards a classical style – "classical" not as a stylistic term, but in the sense of a quality of achievement, in Behrens' case a completed artistic evolution which lent his designs a fundamental definitiveness. In line with such heady terminology, the turbine hall which he built for the AEG general electricity company in Berlin was also called a "cathedral of industry" (ill. p. 270). With his appointment, in 1907, to the AEG's artistic advisory board, the Jugendstil "ego euphoria" of Behrens' Darmstadt days passed into history, and he assumed a new role as designer of – as we say today – the corporate identity of a modern utility (ills. pp. 272, 273). "Behrens' job was not just to build factories, but to take charge of all aspects of formal design at AEG, from the lettering of its adverts and brochures to domestic appliances, electric kettles and arc lamps, all the way to the company's buildings. Everything was entrusted to just one person's hands, and it is rather strange that it should have been the hands of the painter Peter Behrens. There must have been some clever people at the AEG. I have always tried to find out whether Walther Rathenau, himself an intelligent man, had a hand in it, although I suspect not. It was Walther Rathenau's opinion that art should not be mixed with everyday life, and that the two were entirely separate realms. But this was precisely what the Werkbund sought to do: to carry art into life, to create – as Peter Behrens did – the artistic factory, the artistic utensil."[17] Peter Behrens achieved the goal which the Werkbund had set itself: the unadorned functional form as art (ill. p. 271). The classicism mentioned earlier,

Peter Behrens
Three logo designs for AEG,
1908 and 1914
AEG company archives,
Frankfurt/Main

Peter Behrens
Low-consumption arc lamp for
AEG, 1907
Painted metal
AEG company archives,
Frankfurt/Main

Peter Behrens
Roof terrace of the AEG small
motors factory, Brunnenstrasse,
Berlin, 1911
AEG company archives,
Frankfurt/Main

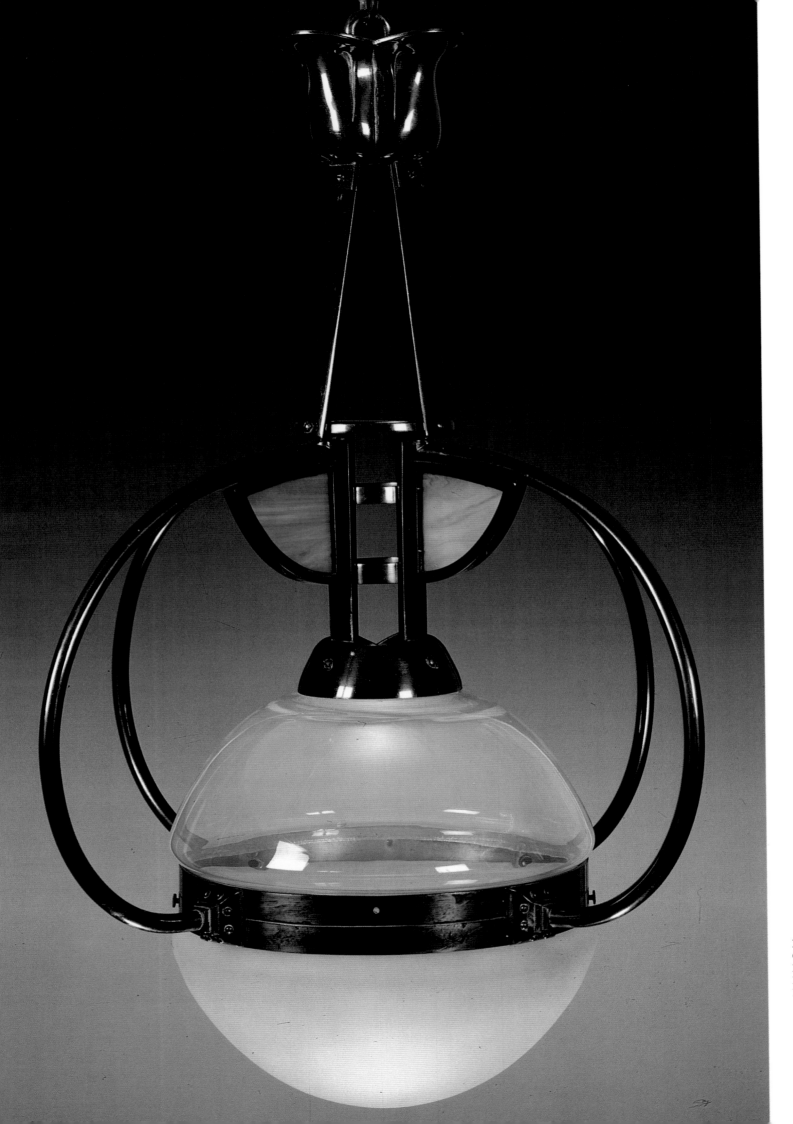

Henry van de Velde
Ceiling lamp, ca. 1906
Brass, glass, 75 cm long
Kunstsammlungen zu Weimar,
Bauhaus-Museum

Henry van de Velde
Two vases, before 1902
Stoneware, sharp-fire and flowing
glaze, 24.8 cm and 27 cm high
Made by Reinhold Hanke, Höhr

Henry van de Velde
Coffee pot, 1904
Chased silver, ivory, 16.5 cm high
Made by A. Th. Müller, Berlin

Henry van de Velde
Salon of the court hairdresser
François Haby, Mittelstrasse 7,
Berlin, 1901
Contemporary photograph
In the new interior which van de
Velde gave the salon run by court
hairdresser François Haby, he
reveals his fanciful Jugendstil side
one last time. In this connection,
Max Liebermann is alleged to have
let slip the biting remark that he
didn't actually sport his intestines as
a fob chain either.

the *reductio ad elementa* of antique form, finds its echo in Behrens' turbine hall, which is at the same time contemporary and progressive. As an indication of just how powerful an influence – both immediate and indirect – this "cathedral of industry" exerted on the future, it is interesting to note that Behrens' assistants on the project included the three leading architects of the 1920s, if not of the 20th century: Walter Gropius, Ludwig Mies van der Rohe and Charles Edouard Jeanneret, subsequently known as Le Corbusier.

Henry van de Velde – The abstract line – Karl Ernst Osthaus

Yesterday van de Velde showed me his grandiose designs for the Schelde waterside in Antwerp, which are similarly based entirely on the rhythm of enormous masses (skycrapers).
Count Harry Kessler[18]

Rathenau rejected the "artification" of everyday life, since he believed it carried the danger of rendering art banal. Henry van de Velde, one of the central figures of Jugendstil, never produced designs for industry nor tailored his art to the requirements of mass production, but his theoretical deliberations nevertheless culminated in "modernism" and the founding of the Werkbund in 1907. Van de Velde recognized early on that the era of tendrils, flowers, and the female sex as ornament was over; the art of the future would be abstract. From now on his art was dominated by the primacy of the "abstract line"

(ill. opposite page). While van de Velde also lent his support to the promotion of Thuringia's small-scale industries, he remained the urbane artist-designer favored by idealistic patrons. The aim of this symbiosis of capital, intellect and art was an "elevation", as Goethe might have termed it, to higher planes. No one was better suited to fulfill such a task than the cosmopolitan van de Velde. After early commissions in Berlin (ill. below) for Baron Eberhard von Bodenhausen, van de Velde made the acquaintance of Karl Ernst Osthaus and Count Harry Kessler, two patrons who were to play a fundamental role in shaping his career. Osthaus (1874–1921), the aesthete son of a industrialist millionaire from Hagen, was granted permission by his father to dedicate himself to what he was good at – which was not manu-facturing. In the spring of 1901 Osthaus read an article on van de Velde by Meier-Graefe. Its numerous illustrations documented the unity of a new style of life and art. The article resulted in Osthaus requesting an "audience" with van de Velde by telegraph. The fruits of their meeting were prodigious. Under Osthaus's patronage the new style took on an impressive propagandistic role. Van de Velde went on to build the Folkwang Museum in Hagen, while the Deutsches Museum in Handel und Gewerbe (German Museum of Trade and Industry) founded by Osthaus made a name for itself with lectures and touring exhibitions, as well as with the high-quality books published by its own press. The Karl Ernst Osthaus Archive in Marburg provides a wonderful document of Jugendstil in excellent

Pages 276, 277:
Henry van de Velde
Villa Hohenhof, bay window with
dressing-table in the bedroom and
winding staircase up to the second
storey, Hagen, 1908
The Villa Hohenhof for Karl Ernst
Osthaus – the home as the realm of
the individual, artistically designed
right down to the last detail, as the
synthesis of all its furnishings, and
as an "interior design" around which
everything revolved in primarily
Jugendstil style.

contemporary photographs. In 1908 Osthaus commissioned van de Velde to build the Villa Hohenhof – the home as the realm of the individual, artistically designed right down to the last detail, as the synthesis of all its furnishings, and as an "interior design" around which everything revolved in primarily Jugendstil style (ills. pp. 276, 277). Van de Velde was awarded numerous other commissions of this sort, including the Springmann house in Hagen, the Fröse house in Hanover, the Henneberg house in Weimar, and the Villa Esche in Chemnitz, to name but a few. Esche, a hosiery manufacturer, numbered amongst the impressive ranks of those "arts managers" who designed not simply their private retreats but also their environment – in this case, Chemnitz. Esche was also a patron of Edvard Munch, who painted his children (ill. left).

Weimar and Count Harry Kessler – From Goethe to the Bauhaus

Art presents itself as an outlook on life, rather like religion and science and socialism too.
Rainer Maria Rilke[19]

In 1901 the Grand Duke of Saxe-Weimar offered Henry van de Velde, the universally talented Belgian artist, a post in Weimar. It was part of a larger effort to awaken the small, forgotten city from its enchanted slumber, an ambitious plan initiated by Count Harry Kessler (1868–1937) and Elisabeth Förster Nietzsche, sister of the philosopher. Kessler was a European *par excellence*: educated at international schools, his mother was Irish and his father a banker in Paris. In Berlin Kessler hosted a salon which brought together members of Europe's cultural elite. Van de Velde furnished the interior of Kessler's Berlin apartment and that of his sister in Paris. During this period the two urbane figures developed a close friendship. Kessler lent his patronage to every sphere of Jugendstil, whereby he made a particularly outstanding contribution to typographical art, founding the Cranach Press, which published bibliographic gems designed by famous artists. He acquired unusual status as a writer and politician, and his memoirs of 1935 – *Gesichter und Zeiten* (Faces and Times) – paint the fascinating picture of an entire epoch. The support offered by the Grand Duke in Weimar fell far short of that provided by Ernst Ludwig in Darmstadt – and Kessler was robbed of some of his illusions – but Weimar was nevertheless shaken out of its sleep until the end of the Weimar Republic. Even though the commissions

Left:
Edvard Munch
The Esche Children, 1905
Oil on canvas, 147 x 153 cm
Munch Museet, Oslo
Esche, hosiery manufacturer and "arts manager", was one of Munch's patrons.

Left:
Henry van de Velde
Design for a new stairwell, part of the project to renovate the Grand-Ducal Museum in Weimar, 1908
Watercolor, 42 x 33.5 cm
Kunstsammlungen zu Weimar, Bauhaus-Museum
Following the foundation – within the rooms of the Weimar Museum in December 1903 – of the Deutscher Künstlerbund as the central organ of all the Secession movements in Germany, plans were drawn up to renovate the Grand-Ducal Museum and to build a new School of Arts and Crafts.

Opposite page, inset left, and right:
Henry van de Velde
Garden facade and stairwell, Grand-Ducal Saxon Academy of Fine Art, Weimar, 1904–11
The merger of the Grand-Ducal Saxon Academy of Fine Art and the Grand-Ducal Saxon School of Arts and Crafts resulted in the opening, on April 1 1919, of a new type of art college – the Weimar State Bauhaus headed by Walter Gropius.

Page 281:
Henry van de Velde
Doorhandle, Nietzsche Archive, Weimar, 1902–03
Van de Velde arrived at a highly successful solution for the Nietzsche Archive which he was commissioned to design within a historicizing villa. The entrance door lends a further distinguished note to the whole.

which van de Velde had hoped to receive from the government never materialized, his time in Weimar was nevertheless a fruitful one. His first commission to attract attention was the Nietzsche Archive which he redesigned on behalf of Nietzsche's sister. The highly successful solution which he implemented within a historicizing villa is dignified by the entrance door (ill. opposite page). Following the foundation – in the Weimar Museum in December 1903 – of the Deutscher Künstlerbund (German Association of Artists) as the central organ of all the Secession movements in Germany, plans were drawn up to renovate the Grand-Ducal Museum and to build a new School of Arts and Crafts (ill. p. 278). The support lent to these projects by the Grand Duchess's mother Pauline ceased upon her death in 1904. Van de Velde had already been granted teaching rooms and premises in 1902 through her patronage, but the new building housing the School of Arts and Crafts – for which van de Velde had first submitted unsolicited plans in 1904 – was finally opened in 1907. The artistic capital, too, was put up in the end: the merger of the Grand-Ducal Saxon Academy of Fine Art and the Grand-Ducal Saxon School of Arts and Crafts resulted in the opening, on April 1 1919, of a new type of art college – the Weimar State Bauhaus headed by Walter Gropius (ills. pp. 278, 279).

Most geniuses are unintelligent, while the rest are drained by the mighty taxing of their eminent organ. Van de Velde has the enormous gift of an extraordinary intellect. Without doubt a great genius, the greatest in our movement, which doesn't mean a great deal, and a manifestation which will endure through all time, which says a lot more; but at the same time an equally great intelligence, and that is a unique phenomenon. Others are instinctives, dreamers, exceptions who have made psychologists think of pathology; this one is fully conscious. A person who is well aware of his prodigious talent and has the abnormal will to exploit all of its riches. This duality, which helps only the artist craftsman to unity, is once more to be encountered in van de Velde. One is constantly surprised by the artist and at the same time constantly struck by his steely resolve, pursued with an inexorable logic which even those who dislike modern taste and modern art cannot fail to acknowledge. The two things are inseparable: even where van de Velde seems to have abandoned himself to the freest inspiration and purest ornament, one is tempted to establish a logical basis for his art; we shall see that such proof indeed exists.
Julius Meier-Graefe on Henry van de Velde in *Dekorative Kunst*, vol. 3, 1898/99

In Henry van de Velde we honor a ground-breaking pioneer and an incorruptible character. Even today, his works in Weimar, Hagen and Cologne remain in our minds as milestones in the history of modern architecture. It is with particular delight that I constantly remind my students of van de Velde as the most energetic and spirited founder of the new art of building.
Ludwig Mies van der Rohe on the occasion of Henry van de Velde's 70th birthday on April 3 1933, in *Henry van de Velde, Wegeleitung zur Ausstellung im Kunstgewerbemuseum Zürich*, Zurich, 1958

National consciousness in the "Light of the North"
Scandinavia

Norway and Finland

Be faithful to the light!
How softly
its blazing colors
all die away into white!
Only the flames
of *all* our knowledge
allow a glimpse of the pure!
Bjørnstjerne Bjørnson[1]

The light and luminosity of the North

"Light of the North" (*Licht des Nordens*) was the title of an exhibition staged in Düsseldorf in 1986 which offered, for the first time on a large scale, an overview of Scandinavian painting – an unknown and neglected factor when compared to French painting, for example. With the exception of Edvard Munch, Akseli Gallen-Kallela (1865–1931), and Anders Zorn (1860–1920), the exhibition was an introduction to strangers. These "unknowns" from the North astonished the public with the quality of their painting, their expressive use of line and their luminous palette, evoked by a light which is clearer, brighter and more intense than that of central Europe. Interest in Scandinavian art has grown since that exhibition, but it nevertheless remains largely uncharted territory with numerous blanks on the map. Even comprehensive studies on Art Nouveau still devote little attention to Finland, Norway, Sweden, and Denmark, and invariably lump them together under the heading of "Scandinavia" – with inexcusable laxity, since each of these countries made its own, substantial contribution to the art of the turn of the century, and none more so than Finland. In the present book we will discuss Norway and Finland together, followed by Denmark and Sweden. The reasons for this are artistic and at the same time political: Denmark and Sweden maintained a peaceful alliance over many centuries, and this expressed itself in a common cultural vocabulary.

Art Nouveau – Cultural heritage lent modern expression

From the 14th century, Norway was under the rule of Denmark and Sweden and finally achieved sovereignty only in 1905. Finland was effectively occupied by Russia as from 1808 and declared its independence in 1917. For both countries, the years before and after the turn of the century were years of struggling for their freedom and battling to establish their independence, all of which left a profound stamp upon the intellectual and cultural developments of the day.

The growing sense of patriotic identity prompted a new flowering of nationalistic ideas. For those countries which had not yet gained independence, it now became particularly important to raise their profile with a distinctive culture of their own. The huge World Expositions provided a welcome first forum for their efforts. Norway regularly took part in these international exhibitions, presenting brightly colored weavings, carved furniture, and glass cabinets formally inspired by stave churches and displaying bottles of aquavit (a grain- or potato-based spirit flavored with caraway seeds) and tins of herring in oil. The folkloric character of these entries, it must be said, did not make a major contribution to international cultural exchange. It was only with the emergence Europe-wide of the idea of a renewal of art that Norway and Finland began to

Oluf Tostrup
Lamp, before 1900
Enamelwork, 22.2 cm high
14.3 cm diameter
Kunstindustrimuseet, Oslo
Norway did not want to forgo the production of Art Nouveau "knick-knacks" altogether, and manufactured "curios" in the traditional enamel technique so popular around 1900.

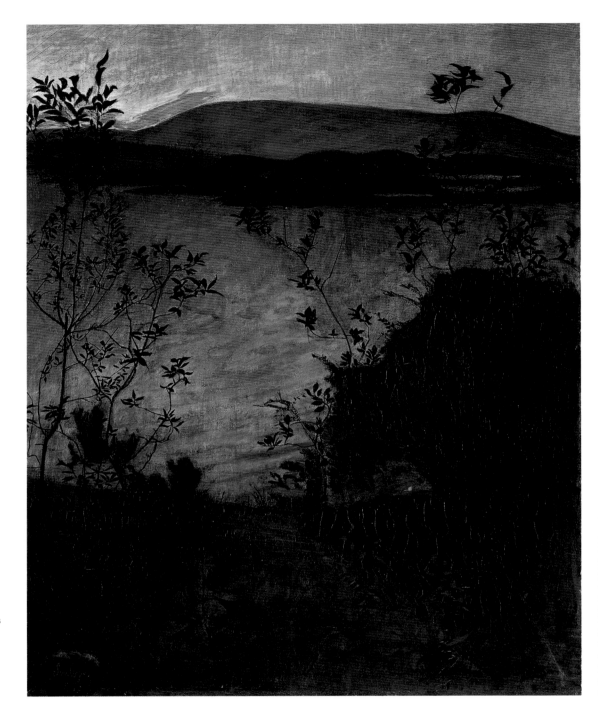

Harald Oskar Sohlberg
Night Glow, 1893
Oil on canvas, glaze technique,
79.5 x 62 cm
Nasjonalgalleriet, Oslo
Harald Oskar Sohlberg painted
magnificent examples of landscapes
as "vehicles of mood" using a
transparent glaze technique. He is
probably the most "Nordic" of all
the Norwegian painters in the
clarity of his light and his almost
surreal vision of nature.

Edvard Munch
Madonna, 1895–1902
Lithographic chalk, ink,
needle, 60.5 x 44.2 cm
Munch Museet, Oslo
Munch lent the portrayal of his
Madonna an expressive linearity and
a symbolic meaning. Seen through
his eyes, the relationship between the
sexes seems to be first and foremost
one of torment: "Woman in her
different nature is a mystery to
man." (see note 4). Woman as saint
and whore – this is the provocative
message of his *Madonna*.

look back to their artistic traditions and their genuine folk art. Art Nouveau acknowledged the artistic validity of folk art in its own right; as a result, it was no longer viewed in isolation as something separate from the rest of the arts. This also meant that certain stylistic characteristics of folk art could serve as an inspiration and a starting point for new works. Norway and Finland had no shortage of sources in this regard. Pronounced patriotic tendencies, which are found above all in politically suppressed regions, encourage people to reflect upon their origins.

Hence favorite themes tend to be the life of the people, myths, legends, and the native landscape. Although Art Nouveau was from the very start an international movement – something which usually implies a rejection of everything "local" – it nevertheless produced its most dazzling achievements in precisely those places where patriotism was one of the driving forces behind renewal – for example, in Nancy, Finland, and Norway. Norway's contribution largely concentrated upon painting.

Edvard Munch – Portraits of human emotion

These pictures, which currently still seem rather incomprehensible, will – I believe – be much easier to understand when taken all together. They deal with love and death.
Edvard Munch[2]

Thanks to his outstanding importance, the great Norwegian artist Edvard Munch is seen less as a Norwegian than as a sort of "international cultural asset", and certainly not as an Art Nouveau painter. And while we do not wish to dispute this last point, his person and his work are nevertheless proof that *no* artist at the turn of the century, not even Munch, was left untouched by the structural characteristics of Art Nouveau – the apotheosistic end of an era accompanied by the dawning of a new age – nor by its literary, intellectual, and sociological bases, which expressed themselves in various ways depending on nationality and disposition of the artist. Munch's oeuvre became the forum for a confrontation between Nordic spirit and French form, a confrontation which in turn became a new and vital component of Art Nouveau painting as a whole.

It was an era in which a definitive image was sought of the concept of "woman", far removed from genteel lady or even female individual. Themes such as the beautiful animal-woman, the sphinx, the vampire, the *femme fatale*, the seductive serpent and Salome were cultivated and stylized in the painting of Symbolism. Munch lent the portrayal of his *Madonna* an expressive linearity and a symbolic meaning (ill. p. 285). "This oral undulation is visibly amplified by the sexual dimension introduced by aspects of the male – sperm and fishes – whose presence wistfully implies the union between mother and son, the fulfillment of which is forbidden under the prohibition of sexual relations between mother and child. The scene dissolves into a quagmire under the pressure of social dictates."[3] Seen through Munch's eyes, the relationship between the sexes appears to be first and foremost one of torment: "Woman in her different nature is a mystery to man."[4] Woman as saint and whore – this was the provocative message of his *Madonna*. It is interesting to note that Thomas Mann, in his novella *Gladius Dei* (1902), interwove Munch's *Madonna* and Franz von Stuck's *Sin* (ill. p. 222) into a collage in order to create the ultimate "sinful" picture. Stuck's *Sin*, with its sumptuous, cool colors and gemlike brilliance within its opulent gold frame, also

Frida Hansen
The Milky Way, tapestry, 1898
Wool, silk and cotton,
transparent weaving technique,
260 x 330 cm
Museum für Kunst und Gewerbe, Hamburg
The technique of transparent weaving offers an artistic means of lending the pale figures and the veil a transparent, floating effect.

Gerhard Peter Munthe
The Horses of the Sea, tapestry, 1907 (design 1899)
Weaving, 172 x 69 cm
Nordenfjeldske
Kunstindustrimuseum, Trondheim
Munthe's tapestry designs were inspired by ancient Norwegian tradition and derived their subjects from mythology and the realm of fairytale. His illustrations to the *Heimskringla*, a history of the Norse kings by Snorri Sturluson (1179-1241), yielded some of the most beautiful designs, as for example *The Horses of the Sea*.

became famous. Munch and Stuck were born in the same year, 1863, and before the turn of the century held each other in the highest esteem. Whereas Stuck became a "gilt frame" painter, Munch's *Madonna* has nothing soft or luxurious about her, and is inescapably encircled by closed, wavelike lines, the "locks" of her own hair.

Landscape as a vehicle of mood

The Symbolist world view fermenting its way across the whole of Europe also reached the North and Munch. Alongside idyll, decadence, and earthly paradise, there also arose images of fear and despair, sorrow and melancholy – like the visions of D'Annunzio: "In vain our lives! Before us, shadowy, without a torch, death puts on its finery."[5] "A fear of life has accompanied me ever since I could think," wrote Munch in his diary[6], and he gave his pictures titles such as *Fear*, *The Scream* and *Death*. A favorite theme around the turn of the century was the three stages of womanhood. Amongst the many artists fascinated both by the subject and the formal possibilities of the motif was Jan Toorop in his *Three Brides* (ill. p. 165). Munch also drew upon the theme in his *Dance of Life* and *Girl on a Bridge*. "Now life reaches out its hand to death. The chain is complete. It links a thousand generations who have died to the thousand generations that are coming."[7] Munch interpreted landscape painting, a genre so important

for Art Nouveau and Scandinavia, in a similarly symbolic way: "Nature is the means, not the ends. If one can achieve something by altering nature, one should do so. A landscape will have a certain effect on someone who is in a good mood. By creating a landscape, one will arrive at a picture which corresponds to one's own mood. This mood is what counts. Nature is only the means. To what extent the picture looks like nature is not important."[8]

Magnificent examples of landscapes as "vehicles of mood" were created by Harald Oskar Sohlberg (1869–1935) using a transparent glaze technique. Sohlberg is probably the most "Nordic" of all the Norwegian painters in the clarity of his light and his almost surreal vision of nature. In 1894 Sohlberg's work received an important mark of recognition with the purchase of his *Night Glow* (ill. p. 284) by the Oslo National Gallery. Over the following years the National Gallery would become one of the most important patrons of new trends in art, thanks to its director Jens Thiis, a close friend of Munch and later his biographer.

Duplicity of nature and style – Tapestries

The fairytale demonstrates a tendency toward two-dimensional, even linear figures and objects. It is as if the characters of fairytale were paper figures from which you could snip off little pieces here and there without them changing in any fundamental way.
Max Lüthi[9]

Originally a landscape painter, Gerhard Peter Munthe (1849–1929) acquired his international reputation only from 1890 with tapestries woven to his designs – Norway's most important contribution to the decorative arts around the turn of the century. It was Jens Thiis who provided the stimulus for a revival of the traditional techniques of weaving. He set up a weaving studio in Trondheim and chose the motifs and colors of the works produced there himself. "My idea as regards the studio is to start up something similar to what has already started up (with Norwegian help) in Scherrebeck, in the south of Jutland. … And I don't see why Norwegian art weaving on Norwegian soil shouldn't earn just as much acclaim and prove just as rewarding as that on German soil. To create a model weaving studio is in my opinion the biggest and best thing we can do to give Norwegian weaving an artistic boost."[10] Thiis purchased numerous watercolors by Munthe, which formed the foundation of the weaving school's artistic production. Munthe's designs were inspired by ancient Norwegian tradition and derived their subjects from mythology and the realm of fairytale. His illustrations to the *Heimskringla*, a history of the Norse kings by Snorri Sturluson (1179–1241), yielded some of the most beautiful designs, for example *The Horses of the Sea* (ill. opposite page).

At Munthe's suggestion, the wool used in the tapestries was not dyed into subtle shades, but was blended during carding so as to preserve the clear Norwegian colors. In all other respects, however, Munthe harbored a certain mistrust toward weaving technology, and above all toward women weavers. On many an occasion he is supposed to have said: "I don't want to be woven by women."[11] However, the second leading figure in the art of tapestry weaving was precisely one such "weaving woman": Frida Hansen's large and impressive tapestries were acquired by all the major museums of Europe, although in her own country she was considered not national enough. For Thiis, at any rate, there was only one artist who would be able to reinvigorate the decorative arts in Norway – and that was Munthe. In fact, Munthe went so far as

Gerhard Peter Munthe
Blue Anemones, dinner service, 1892
Painted porcelain,
Serving dish: 23.8 diameter
Made by the Porsgrund Porcelain Factory
Kunstindustrimuseet, Oslo

Gerhard Peter Munthe
Chair, from the "Fairytale Room", Tourist Hotel, Holmenkollen, 1898
Painted wood, 124 cm high
Norsk Folkemuseum, Oslo

to refuse to exhibit alongside Frida Hansen. Like her "antipode", Frida Hansen (1855–1931) took traditional Norwegian weaving as her starting point, but was more international in her style. Much can be traced to Japanese influence, and her figural style also reveals links with the Glasgow group of artists. Frida Hansen achieved fame with the tapestry *The Milky Way* (ill. pp. 286–287), which she wove for the World Exposition of 1900. It depicts a biblical subject and employs a "transparent weaving" technique which lends the pale figures and the veil a transparent, floating effect.

Globalism and native tradition

We were familiar with the art of the Japanese. There was nothing to connect this art with the styles of the European past. It was the immediate and lively expression of an ancient, thousand-year culture which had developed independently of the West.
M. Osborne[12]

Like Frida Hansen, Hans Stoltenberg-Lerche (1867–1920) stood for "international" Art Nouveau in Norway. His work – stoneware, glass, metalwork – exercised a strong influence on Norwegian applied art. Born in Germany and active chiefly in Italy, he was never considered a

Right:
Akseli Gallen-Kallela
The Tree of Knowledge of Good and Evil, closet, 1899
Wood, carved relief ornament,
129 x 96 x 52 c
Gallen-Kallela Museum, Espoo

Akseli Gallen-Kallela
Aino Myth, 1891
Oil on canvas, original frame,
153 x 153 (central panel) and
153 x 77 cm (left and right-hand panels)
Ateneum, Helsinki
In this painting the artist wanted to create an allegory of Finland – from its landscape and mythology to its folk art and Karelianism.

particularly typical representative of his nation, a verdict which also reflected the widespread tendency to view Norway as limited to a "Nordic" form of Art Nouveau. Only in very recent times has attention begun to be paid to the lively and international exchange of ideas taking place in Norway around 1900. In his notebook of 1890, Munthe wrote: "The interest in Japanese art now spreading across Norway has arisen out of our previous neglect of the arts and crafts – an unintentional neglect, in contrast to Japan, which put all its efforts into the decorative arts."[13]

The Aesthetic Movement, originating from England, also gained a foothold in Norway under the same name, significantly assisted by the publication of the book *Japansk Malerkunst* (Japanese Painting) by the Dane Karl Madsen (b. 1855), the first work on the subject to appear in a Scandinavian language. A group of artists had already come together at Fleskum Farm in Dælivannet, near Christiania (present-day Oslo), in the 1880s. Its members had all studied either in Paris or Munich and together cultivated Neo-Romantism and Japonisme. Fleskum members Munthe and Christian Skredsvig (1854–1924) and art historian Marit Werenskiold played a major role in the development of the decorative arts in Norway. Skredsvig, a close friend of Madsen, followed progressive trends in Denmark with great enthusiasm and was responsible for establishing the highly significant link between Munthe and the great Danish "arts and crafts-man" Thorvald Bindesbøll (ill. p. 311). It is thanks to Munthe that, for all the outside influences which it absorbed, Norway remained "national" in the positive sense. It was able to appreciate not just the folkloristic "dragon" style of its ancient Viking ships, but also their perfection and formal accomplishment: "In their beauty and their exemplary design (material, technique, plan) they outstripped everything that had ever set sail before."[14]

An optimum design solution had thus already been found centuries earlier on Norwegian soil. Munthe processed the past into individual works of enduring effect (ill. p. 289). Norway did not want to forgo the production of Art Nouveau "knick-knacks" altogether, however, and manu-factured "curios" in the traditional enamel tech-nique so popular around 1900 (ill. p. 283).

Hugo Simberg
Frost, 1895
Watercolor, 27 x 18 cm
Ateneum, Helsinki
Encouraged by his teacher Gallen-Kallela, who recognized his talents as a watercolorist, Simberg transposed experiences of nature into often frightening figures which at times bear only a general resemblance to humankind. He proclaims the unity of creature and cosmos in his small-format works in impressive fashion. He refused to provide commentaries on his paintings, but hoped that "people, when looking at them, would weep and wail in their innermost heart of hearts" (see note 16).

Left:
Akseli Gallen-Kallela
Finland Awake, stained-glass window, 1896
26 x 37 cm
Gallen-Kallela Museum, Espoo
The fanning of emotions by means of pictorial subject or accompanying lines is Symbolist in origin; Gallen-Kallela, too, infused the mythological and mystical bases of his art with the yearning for a "symbol" felt by almost all the artists of his generation.

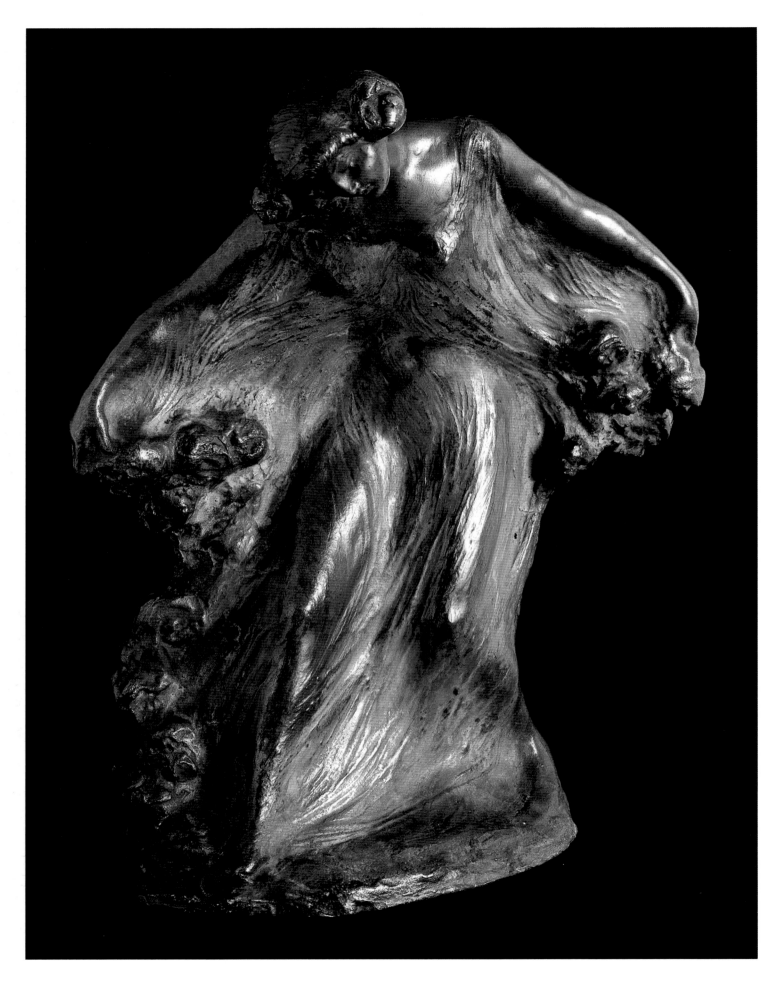

Ville Vallgren
Rose Dance, 1899
Bronze, 28.5 cm high
Ateneum, Helsinki
Ville Vallgren, the "Frenchman" amongst the Finns, was another who wanted his art to stir up emotions rather than simply provide aesthetic pleasure. His sculptures, unmistakably *femmes de l'Art Nouveau*, were nevertheless chiefly exercises in style: female dancers in the roundelays of the turn of the century. Vallgren's homage to woman fell fully in line with the spirit of the age; as he himself acknowledged: "Woman is my god and I her servant." (see note 17)

Arabia
Vases in the *Fennia* series, 1902–12
Stoneware, enamel painting,
8.5 cm to 34.5 cm high
Arabia Museum, Helsinki
In the *Fennia* series by Arabia, the
attempt to use traditional forms for
industrial manufacturing was
emphatically successful. The designs
were supplied by the architects
Saarinen and Lindgren – Gallen-
Kallela was probably involved, too –
and the series was hand-painted in
the factory. Form and decor are an
expression of the conscious striving
toward a national language of form
at an international level.

Akseli Gallen-Kallela – The Finnish soul

*... untouched wild nature, the tree-lined lake with berries
and moss. At the edge of the lake my small camp with its
open fire, a falcon calling into the pale evening, and a pine
transferring its needles carefully, one after the other, to the
forest floor.*
Akseli Gallen-Kallela[15]

Finnish art around 1900 has still received
relatively little attention. This is perhaps because
the stylistic designation "Art Nouveau" –
implying a decorative, vegetal formal vocabulary
– does not always characterize the essence of
Finnish painting, architecture and applied art
from around the turn of the century. Instead their
rather more naturalistic flavor was the product of
a different set of sociological circumstances. Art
in Finland was driven not, as in western Europe,
by positivism and industrial wealth, but by a
population which was largely rural in structure,
and which was struggling to achieve outer and
inner independence in difficult political circumstances and in a fringe geographical location.
Finnish art around 1900 also drew upon the past
– upon saga, myth, and the visual imagery of the
Kalevala, the Finnish national epic (published in
1849 by Elias Lönnrot). It did not, however,
sound the closing bars of the outgoing century.
The central figure in fine and applied art of *fin de
siècle* Finland was undoubtedly Akseli Gallen-
Kallela. Trained in Paris, he returned home shortly

Ville Vallgren
Door knocker, ca. 1894
Bronze, 51 x 18 cm
Ateneum, Helsinki
The stylized figure is typical of
Vallgren's combination of sculpture
and applied art.

Nuutajärvi Glassworks
Vase, ca. 1900
Hand-painted glass, 20 cm high
Taideteollisuusmuseo, Helsinki

Gesellius, Lindgren & Saarinen
Exterior view of Suur-Merijoki
Manor, Viipuri, Karelia, 1901–03
Watercolor by Eliel Saarinen, 1902
Suomen rakennustaiteen museo,
Helsinki
In 1903 Finland, too, was given its
"total work of art" – Suur-Merijoki,
a dramatic fortified manor house in a
forest setting, with heavy granite
foundations, imposing gateways, a
massive tower, an English hall with
a wide flight of stairs up to the
second story, a billiard room, a
boudoir, and a music room,
furnished in exquisite harmony and
adorned with wrought, woven,
crocheted, painted, plastered, and
sculpted ornament of firmly
established, beautiful simplicity.
Suur-Merijoki was finished from the
very start, so to speak, and its
occupants were required to add very
little of their own. On the contrary:
the house shaped the lifestyle of the
family.

after 1890 and became the impassioned artist of the "Finnish soul". His austere, animated stylization derives from the strength of its forms, without degenerating into a mere striving for effect (ill. p. 282). He perceived the heroes of the *Kalevala* and the *Kanteletar*, a collection of Finnish folk poetry (published by Elias Lönnrot in 1840), as the personification of the forces of nature which imbued the land which he loved and which he portrayed over and over again. His work is thus often labelled as "National Romanticism", a highly imprecise designation popularly applied to smaller outlying countries.

The term "National Romanticism" can be traced all the way to the first half of the 19th century and the development of ethnography and nationalistic thinking. In Norway, a country in many respects similar to Finland, this development proceeded in a more or less linear fashion up to and beyond the turn of the century. In Finland, however, National Romanticism in the sphere of the visual arts was strongly influenced by the spirit of resistance to Russia which characterized the years around 1900. This ultimately led it, in a somewhat ephemeral way, to seem more "genuine" than early National Romanticism. Thus, in Finland, the national need for self-expression, influenced by the ideas of the German philosopher Georg Wilhelm Friedrich Hegel, received a stylistic form which would come to be described as a "Golden Age".

Finland's "Golden Age" – The artist-designers

Gallen-Kallela's first National Romantic work based on the *Kalevala* was his *Aino Myth* (ill. p. 290). In this painting, the artist sought to create an allegory of Finland – from its landscape and mythology to its folk art and Karelianism. In practical line with his ideals, he withdrew to Karelia (the region between the Gulf of Finland and the White Sea in Finland and north-west Russia) and devoted himself more and more to the applied arts. His love of nature was nevertheless accompanied by a cosmopolitan outlook and international contacts. It was through Gallen-Kallela that the influences of *Pan* and Jugendstil reached Finland from Germany. He himself assimilated these influences into his handicraft works, but without losing his "nationality". His preferred material was thus that of his homeland, wood (ill. p. 290), while one of his stained-glass windows bears the title *Finland Awake* (ill. p. 291). The fanning of emotions by means of pictorial subject or accompanying lines is Symbolist in origin; Gallen-Kallela, too, infused the mythological and mystical bases of his art with the yearning for a "symbol" felt by almost all the artists of his generation. The Swedish theosophist Emanuel von Swedenborg (1688–1772) had prepared the ground in Scandinavia for the reception of spiritual and transcendental theories, and in Finland, too, it had become fashionable to read Baudelaire and enthuse about Richard Wagner.

One of Gallen-Kallela's pupils, Hugo Simberg (1873–1917), translated the "marginal experiences" of the Symbolist way of seeing into his pictures. He had little interest in folk art and National Romanticism; for him the original existed only in the imagination of the artist. Encouraged by his teacher, who recognized his talents as a watercolorist, Simberg transposed experiences of nature into often frightening figures which at times bear only a general resemblance to humankind. He proclaims the unity of creature and cosmos in his small-format works in impressive fashion (ill. p. 291). He refused to provide commentaries on his paintings, but hoped that "people, when looking at them, would weep and wail in their innermost heart of hearts"[16].

Ville Vallgren (1855–1940), the "Frenchman" amongst the Finns, also wanted his art to stir up emotions rather than simply provide aesthetic pleasure. His sculptures, unmistakably *femmes de l'Art Nouveau*, were nevertheless chiefly exercises in style: female dancers in the roundelays of the turn of the century (ills. pp. 292, 293).

Gesellius, Lindgren & Saarinen
Entrance lobby, Suur-Merijoki
Manor, Viipuri, Karelia, 1902
Design drawing, watercolor by Eliel
Saarinen, 1902, 14 x 20 cm
Suomen rakennustaiteen museo,
Helsinki

Vallgren's homage to woman fell fully in line with the spirit of the age; as he himself acknowledged: "Woman is my god and I her servant."[17] As one of the group around the Symbolists, he exhibited in Paris in their Salon de la Rose-Croix, to which only works of "noble spirit, beauty, and poetry" were admitted.

A pronouncedly French trend was not the only foreign influence to make itself felt in Finland; the impact of William Morris, too, can hardly be overestimated. The social criticism at the heart of Morris's thinking served to inspire many designers, who from now on saw handicraft as an honest alternative to mass production. In the *Fennia* series by Arabia (ill. p. 293), the attempt to use traditional forms for industrial manufacturing was emphatically successful. The designs were supplied by the architects Saarinen and Lindgren – Gallen-Kallela was probably involved, too – and the series was hand-painted in the factory. Form and decor are an expression of the conscious striving toward a national language of form at an international level. The most beautiful glassware of Finnish Art Nouveau issued from the Nuutajärvi factory: functional outlines fuse with a confident graphic decor (ill. p. 293).

Meanwhile, the English painter and ceramic artist Alfred William Finch (1854–1930), who spent a number of years working in Brussels, founded the more commercially oriented Iris workshops in Porvoo, Borgå. The pleasant linear style of its products met with an enthusiastic reception. Like Norway, Finland also saw a revival of its traditional weaving industry. Armas Eliel Lindgren (1874–1929), who worked with Saarinen, produced designs that were surprisingly Art Nouveau in style (ill. p. 298), while the works of Väimö Blomstedt (1971–1947) remained indebted to National Romanticism.

Finnish architecture

Absolutely the simplest and absolutely the most beautiful pavilion.
On the Finnish pavilion at the Paris World Exposition of 1900[18]

Finnish architecture, with Eriel Saarinen (1873–1950) as its most important representative, exerted a profound influence upon the development of modern architecture. The first built testaments to the departing century arose under the aegis of Karelianism. Like their painter colleagues, the architects in Karelia sought to incorporate the original and unspoilt elements of Finnish culture into their style. They dedicated

Opposite page and above:
Gesellius, Lindgren & Saarinen
The Finnish Pavilion at the Paris World Exposition, 1900, interior and exterior view, 1898–1900
Wood, walls hung with coccolith slabs and painted fabric
The pavilion, a "painted stone imitation", was a triumphant success. This recognition occurred at a time when the Russian empire was beginning to exert palpable pressure against Finland's autonomy. The architecture of a small country fearing for its very existence had earned international acclaim for the first time.

Eliel Saarinen
Chicago Tribune Tower, competition entry, second prize, 1922
Perspective drawing, contemporary reproduction
Suomen rakennustaiteen museo, Helsinki
On November 29, 1922 when the winners of the competition for the *Chicago Tribune* Tower had already been chosen, an entry arrived from Finland. The jury was so impressed by "the colossal beauty of this 11th-hour entry" (see note 21) that it awarded the design second prize. It was the work of Eliel Saarinen, whose son Eero would, in the 1950s and 1960s, become one of America's best architects.

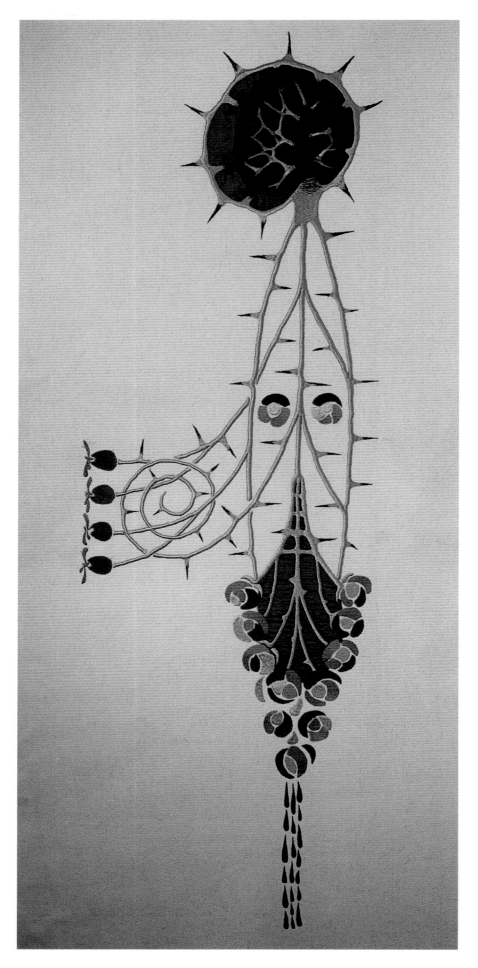

themselves to finding new and rational applications for the materials most abundantly available in their homeland, namely granite and wood. These materials had an important symbolic value: at the same time as forming the basis of indigenous architectural traditions, they were also suitable for use with modern building techniques. The almost primitive medieval castles and churches which in Finland greet the viewer at every step now became the source of both stylistic and technical stimuli for modern architecture. The sensible functionalism of vernacular architecture was thus adopted into the first buildings of Karelianism. Around the turn of the century, however, pure tradition was no longer enough for the projects of the young, ambitious generation of architects, who now turned for inspiration to the Arts and Crafts Movement in England – and above all to Baillie Scott, whose well-known watercolor illustrations of interiors in *The Studio* had a great impact in Finland – as well as on the Mathildenhöhe group in Darmstadt and on Art Nouveau in France and Belgium. Amidst these overlapping trends arose the architectural firm of Gesellius, Lindgren & Saarinen, known as GLS. The firm immediately secured itself a leading position by winning the competition for the Finnish Pavilion at the Paris World Exposition of 1900 (ills. pp. 296, 297). The pavilion, a

Gesellius, Lindgren & Saarinen
Hvittorp House, Kirkkonummi, exterior view, 1901–04
Watercolor by Eliel Saarinen, 1902
Reproduced from *Moderne Baukunst* [Modern Architecture], November 1905
Suomen rakennustaiteen museo, Helsinki

Gesellius & Saarinen
Bedroom, Remer House, Lake
Molchow, Brandenburg March,
1905–08
Watercolor by Eliel Saarinen, 1905,
22.5 x 22 cm
Suomen rakennustaiteen museo,
Helsinki
Another house approached as a total
work of art was the Remer House on
the shores of Lake Molchow north of
Berlin. This "international"
commission also assumed an
international shape, drawing upon
the economic, elegant style of
Wiener Werkstätte interiors and
reflecting the early influence of
Charles Rennie Mackintosh upon
the architects.

"painted stone imitation", was a triumphant success. This recognition occurred at a time when the Russian empire was beginning to exert palpable pressure against Finland's autonomy. The architecture of a small country fearing for its very existence had earned international acclaim for the first time. The new style was thereby firmly established, and even houses in the course of construction were altered correspondingly. Design was dominated by plasticity and a proximity to nature. It was an organic architecture of wood and granite; proximity to nature was achieved by steps and paths, terraces and balconies everywhere, oriels, turrets, and similar details. Interiors were designed in the same spirit: as caves and grottos, lofty halls with groined vaults, niches and inglenooks, stairs and floors at varying levels. Ornament, with its themes drawn chiefly from native flora and fauna, also signified proximity to nature, as did the fabrics, rye matting and furs which covered walls, sofas, and floors in coordinating color schemes (ill. p. 295).

Gesellius, Lindgren & Saarinen

We listen to the sounds, they rock themselves gently into our minds and we hear magical melodies in our dreams – we sense a new music – the music of the future ...
Whistler's spirit hovers over the waters: all the elemental forces come from the North or from America ...
Walter Leistikow[19]

In 1903 Finland, too, was given its "total work of art" – Suur-Merijoki (ill. p. 294), a dramatic fortified manor house with heavy granite foundations, imposing gateways, a massive tower, an English hall with a wide flight of stairs up to the second story, a billiard room, a boudoir, and a music room, furnished in exquisite harmony and adorned with wrought, woven, crocheted, painted, plastered, and sculpted ornament of firmly established, beautiful simplicity. Suur-Merijoki was finished from the very start, so to speak, and its occupants were required to add very little of their own. On the contrary: the house shaped the lifestyle of the family. It was

Eliel Saarinen
Chair for Hannes Saarinen, 1908
Varnished mahogany, ebony inlay;
Upholstery: imitation leather with
snakeskin pattern, ca. 90 cm high
Made by N. Boman's joinery
workshop, Kuoplo
Suomen rakennustaiteen museo,
Helsinki
Around 1907 Saarinen developed a
new, unmistakable style of furniture
design; as in his architecture, his
forms became sharper in focus and
more angled.

commissioned by the Wiborg manufacturer Neuscheller; the architects were GLS, and the site Viipuri, at that time the most important town on Finland's eastern border – something symbolic in itself. The house made a profound impression on all its visitors; today that experience is denied us. Suur-Merijoki was destroyed in the Second World War, and since 1944 its grounds have lain on the far side of the Russian border. Those in search of a concentrate of Finnish art around 1900 need look no further than Suur-Merijoki. It represented a synthesis of all the contemporary trends in architecture, the applied arts and painting.

Finnish architects right up to Alvar Aalto (1898–1976) continued to hold on, almost stubbornly, to the dream of the total work of art, in other words to the notion of the environment as a total work of art which, merely by dint of its existence, would be able to affect and influence all of society – a piece of Finnish National Romanticism, something with which Saarinen, the head of GLS, was also closely linked. The creation of the total work of art was his ideal, and went beyond the private house to embrace urban planning as a functioning environmental whole. This goal remained the thread running through his entire oeuvre. His style had its origins in Finland's "Golden Age", where the creation of a Finnish identity was being sought in all sectors of cultural life: in the music of Jean Sibelius (1865–1957), in the poetry of Eino Leino (1878–1926), and in the paintings of Gallen-Kallela. An early effort by the GLS triumvirate in this regard is the "fortified" Hvittorp House (ill. p. 298). Another house approached as a

total work of art was the Remer House on the shores of Lake Molchow north of Berlin. This "international" commission also assumed an international shape, drawing upon the economic, elegant style of Wiener Werkstätte interiors and reflecting the early influence upon GLS of Charles Rennie Mackintosh (ill. p. 299). Around 1907 Saarinen also developed a new, unmistakable style of furniture design; as in his architecture, his forms became clearer and more angled (ill. opposite page).

The evolution of architecture into the 20th century

And you too, my dear, could add warmth and feeling to your style by hanging up the academic dogma of the imitation of nature for good.
Richard Dehmel to Arno Holz[20]

In Finland, the discussion of constructivism and rationalism as design principles at the purely theoretical level was something which followed upon the meeting between the Finnish architect Sigurd Frosterus (1876–1956) and Henry van de Velde. Up till then, the two trends had appeared only in isolated, albeit confident practical experiments. Frosterus's own, noteworthy works went unappreciated, however. He was the only representative of an Art Nouveau trend in design and architecture which had long been discredited in Finland as "swan's neck curves" (ill. p. 301). Frosterus's "style" earned him the reputation of an arch rationalist, something for which his "Belgian connection" gave not the slightest grounds, however. Also fated to be an outsider

Sigurd Frosterus
Dining room on a steamship, 1907
Design drawing, 26.5 x 36 cm
Suomen rakennustaiteen museo,
Helsinki
Frosterus's noteworthy works went unappreciated. He was the sole representative of an Art Nouveau trend in design and architecture which had long been discredited in Finland as "swan's neck curves". Frosterus's "style" earned him the reputation of an arch rationalist, something for which his "Belgian connection" – a past stay with Henry van de Velde – gave not the slightest grounds, however.

Selim Avid Lindqvist
Suvilahti Power Station, Helsinki, 1908
Project drawing
Suomen rakennustaiteen museo,
Helsinki
Suvilahti Power Station marks the climax of Lindqvist's rich oeuvre. The building is worked in reinforced concrete, and its skeleton of twin pillars and steel girders also defines the exterior.

was the architect Selim Avid Lindqvist (1867–1939), who pursued his own linear evolution outside all debate and whose work was closely allied with Viennese Jugendstil, above all with Otto Wagner. Having begun his career still in the age of historicism, he later turned – like Victor Horta – to flexible skeleton buildings with cast-iron columns and pillar-and-glass facades. Suvilahti Power Station (ill. p. 301) marks the climax of Lindqvist's rich oeuvre. The building is worked in reinforced concrete, and its skeleton of twin pillars and steel girders also defines the exterior. This beautiful and logical building shows that even Lindqvist was not left unmoved by the emerging trend toward monumental architecture. Nevertheless, this new trend did not mean that the concept of the total work of art was dead; instead of the private home, however, it now found its realization in monumental buildings such as Saarinen's Helsinki Central Station

(ill. above). Here, the decor increasingly becomes one with the architecture and serves to heighten the effect of the construction. The language of form has crystallized and builds upon clear verticals. Nevertheless, ornament remains an inseparable part of the whole, whereby its task is to accentuate those components of the building of structural interest. Saarinen's decor from now on became almost sparing and abstract; the "bears" and "frogs" of his youth disappeared in favor of a preference for stylized human figures which, incorporated into the vertical structure, fuse with the actual building (ill. opposite page). A vital factor behind the design of the station's high vaulted roof was the introduction of concrete. Both Helsinki Central Station and Saarinen's subsequent works were built in this new material. The competition for the station was held in the spring of 1904, but the complex was not completed until 1914. Saarinen's use of

Eliel Saarinen
Helsinki Central Station, front view, 1904–14, 1919
Watercolor by Eliel Saarinen, 1910
Suomen rakennustaiteen museo, Helsinki
The concept of the total work of art found its realization no longer in the private home, but in monumental buildings such as the Central Station in Helsinki. Saarinen's language of form has here crystallized and builds upon clear verticals. Nevertheless, ornament remains an inseparable part of the whole, whereby its task is to accentuate those components of the building of structural interest. A vital factor behind the design of the high vaulted roof was the introduction of concrete. Both Helsinki Central Station and Saarinen's subsequent works were built in this new material.

verticals is emphatically restated in the soaring clocktower, a beacon signalling Saarinen's future. In 1922 the *Chicago Tribune* held a competition for the design of its new tower (ill. p. 297). Twelve works were initially selected, all of which "would be a credit to Chicago, Michigan Avenue, and the *Tribune*". They included all the eventual prizewinners, with the exception of one late entry, which arrived from Finland on November 29, when the winners had already been chosen. The jury was so impressed by "the colossal beauty of this 11th-hour entry"[21] that it awarded the design second prize. It was the work of Eliel Saarinen, whose son Eero would, in the 1950s and 1960s, become one of America's best architects. The elder Saarinen later built a highly influential school near Chicago. His *Chicago Tribune* design reveals a high degree of formal discipline, placing the former National Romantic in the phalanx of the great architects of the 20th century.

Eliel Saarinen
Helsinki Central Station, figures on the main entrance, 1904–14
Approx. 400 cm high
Saarinen's decor is here sparing and abstract; the "bears" and "frogs" of his youth have disappeared in favor of a preference for stylized human figures which, incorporated into the vertical structure, fuse with the actual building.

Denmark and Sweden

Handicraft is to Scandinavia what painting is to France, music to Germany and the mountains to Switzerland.
Ulf Hård af Segerstad[22]

From "sophisticated" handicraft to design

When the photographer Hjalmar Ekdal vowed, in Ibsen's *The Wild Duck*, to elevate the "crafts" to "art"[23], he underlined the dependence of the abstract will to art (to taste) upon the "lower" reality of handicraft. The crucial issue of the period around 1900 was thus one concerning the Norwegian dramatist, too: the possibility of a symbiosis of art and handicraft. This new unity, this new "being" still had two faces, but just one body: the applied arts. The "birth" of this new genre was vehemently pursued in all the countries dedicated to Art Nouveau, with the result that the child had a thousand different faces. Although Scandinavia around the turn of the century was not amongst the driving forces behind Art Nouveau, over the following years it would translate its ideas into works of

unsurpassed quality. After 1920, and even more so after the Second World War, Scandinavian applied art came to dominate the furnishing stores of Europe and was greeted by an enthusiastic public. "For Danes, Finns, Norwegians, and Swedes, the home is the hub of their existence to a particular degree … The inhabitants of Southern countries spend most of their time outdoors. The opposite is true in the North … and so it is only natural that the Scandinavian should perceive his home not simply as somewhere to eat and sleep, but as the setting for his family life."[24] The idea of making that setting as cultured as possible, even in the home of the average citizen, fitted perfectly with the doctrines of the champions of Art Nouveau, who wanted to bring art to the people and free it from the stigma of being something exclusively for the wealthy. It was a question of producing objects of everyday use which were both good and affordable. "In the South people get together in restaurants or bars, in the North in their own homes."[25] Hence it was also necessary to redesign and embellish the laid table with silverware and porcelain. The injection of new ideas into porcelain decoration was thus

Einar Nerman
Headpiece to Hans Christian Andersen, *The Swineherd*, ca. 1910
Halftone

Erik Nielsen
Fox, 1903
Porcelain, underglaze painting,
7.3 cm high
Made by Den Kongelige
Porcelainsfabrik, Copenhagen
Badisches Landesmuseum
Karlsruhe, Museum beim Markt –
Angewandte Kunst seit 1900

initiated not by the long-established factories of Meissen, Sèvres and Berlin, but by one which, albeit old, had never been amongst the leaders: the Kongelige Porcelainsfabrik (Royal Porcelain Factory) in Copenhagen. The Swedish Rörstrand porcelain works also played a major role for a while.

Den Kongelige Porcelainsfabrik – The Royal Danish Porcelain Factory

Who would like to predict how many new forms this same spirit has meanwhile taken, forms which pass amongst us still unrecognized, but all the more powerful for that?
Dolf Sternberger[26]

In 1972 the Neue Sammlung in Munich played host to an exhibition from Stockholm entitled "China and the North" (*Kina och Norden*), in which old Chinese and new Scandinavian ceramics were displayed together. Even without a commentary, it was clear to the viewer from which source the modern Scandinavian works were drawing their inspiration. At the end of the 19th century, following the discovery of Japanese pottery, Europe was engulfed by a wave of enthusiasm for the ceramic art of the Far East. The 18th century's love of chinoiserie gave way to a preference for the china of the T'ang and Sung dynasties and an appreciation of undecorated ware, simple forms and harmonious glazes. A description of *chien yao*, Japanese tea bowls produced in China, could be applied word for word to the porcelain produced by the Royal Danish Porcelain Factory in Copenhagen: "… Variations are to be found above all in the glazes, which recall hare skin, birds' feathers, tortoiseshell and splashes of oil. The colors employed are usually dark blue, brown, and green. Their effect is that of a bundle of rays radiating out from a central point, or of clouds. The glaze is applied in several layers which are fired several times, resulting in an ever-changing impression of color depending on the strength of the light falling upon the surface … Leaves and flowers are often drawn in calligraphic shorthand on larger bowls, vases, and jugs."[27] Knud Valdemar Engelhardt, head chemist at the factory, produced objects of the type just described (ill. p. 306). It was the color chemists, more than anyone, who were spurred on by the newly discovered beauty of Japanese and Chinese glazes to unlock the secrets of their production. The factory laboratories became testing grounds for the new "surfaces" which would determine the evolutionary course of

design. Engelhardt's specialities included his crystal glazes, whose craquelure created an "abstract" decor on the sides of the vessel and formed richly inventive patterns. The purchase of the Copenhagen factory by Philip Schou in 1882 marked the beginning of its rise to stardom. The Danish architect and painter Emil Arnold Krog (1856–1931), employed for the factory since 1884 and appointed its artistic director in 1891, created an entirely new type of porcelain decoration which was unmistakably influenced by Japanese color woodcuts. Krog was introduced to Hokusai, Utamaro, and Hiroshige in Samuel Bing's gallery in Paris in 1886. Bing also showed his Japanese collection in Copenhagen on the occasion of the "Nordic Exhibition" of 1888, and thereby made a profound impact upon artistic production both in the city and in Scandinavia as a whole. This encounter with Japan must have acted like a catalyst upon the "renewers" of art. Karl Madsen's book on Japanese painting[28] had already exerted a great influence on the Aesthetic Movement in the North. Madsen was also a dealer in Japanese art

Gotfred Rode
Vase, 1898
Porcelain, underglaze painting,
43 cm high
Made by Den Kongelige
Porcelainsfabrik, Copenhagen
Many of the decorative schemes employed on vases such as this one reflect Japanese influences in their stylization and their skillful distribution across the body of the vessel. Amongst the numerous designers working for the Royal Danish Porcelain Factory – truly the "king" of its field – was Gotfred Rode, whose designs pointed the way forward into the next century.

Carl Frederik Liisberg
Vase with cock-fight decor, 1888
Underglaze painting, gold,
13.5 cm high, 7.3 cm diameter
Made by Den Kongelige
Porcelainsfabrik, Copenhagen
Badisches Landesmuseum
Karlsruhe, Museum beim Markt –
Angewandte Kunst seit 1900

and possessed a profound understanding of the Japanese attitude towards applied and free art. "This is why they have succeeded in painting the same subjects in the same way both in their pictures proper and on faience and lacquer pieces. This is why, without offending good taste and breaking the eternal laws of decorating art, they have made bold use of all possible natural forms in their full free distinctiveness. ... The best painters have not considered themselves too good to give craftsmen model drawings for decorations. In fact, many of them have given important impulses to decorative art by working themselves in ivory, shaping and decorating faience ..."[29] Amongst the protagonists of Japonisme in Denmark were the members of the *Dekorationsforeningen* (Decoration Society), Thorvald Bindesbøll, Pietro Krohn, Joachim and Niels Skovgaard and Theoder Philipsen. Madsen supported their appearance at the "Nordic Exhibition".

The Kongelige Porcelainsfabrik celebrated its first international success at the World Exposition in Paris in 1889, where Krog's underglaze painting was enthusiastically received.

While the decoration he executed in this complicated technique was derived from Danish flora and fauna, its stylization and composition on the body of the object was Japanese in origin. Amongst the many designers working for the Royal Danish Porcelain Factory – truly the "king" of its field – was Gotfred Rode (1862–1937), whose designs pointed the way forward into the next century (ill. p. 305).

"Most porcelain is fashioned into ridiculous dolls"[30], said Winckelmann, in an implicit condemnation of "knick-knacks" way back in the 18th century. The turn of the century nevertheless became the era of the statuette in porcelain, too. These convenient "art works" offered an ideal means of embellishing the average home with art. Statuettes became the sculptures of the private sphere, sculptures which also found a place in the living room.

Once again, the Copenhagen factory assumed a leading position in the field of small porcelain sculpture (ill. p. 304). With its sophisticated technique of underglaze painting, its restrained palette and soft surfaces, it became clear that the factory was able to produce highly stylish

Above:
Aron Jerndahl
Lidded container (detail), 1903
Chased cast tin, relief decor modeled in the round,
17 cm high, 23.5 cm diameter
Water is rendered as undulating lines on the body of the container, which the figures encircle as if in a whirlpool, emerging and vanishing again back into the material. The rhythm established by the violin player extends in a linear direction across the surface. The motif is related to the Dance of Life, a theme explored in numerous variations by Edvard Munch as an existential symbol.

Emil Arnold Krog,
Knud Valdemar Engelhardt
Four vases, 1895-1910
Porcelain, multicolored underglaze, crystal glaze,
8.2 cm to 24 cm high
Made by Den Kongelige Porcelainsfabrik, Copenhagen.
It was the color chemists, more than anyone, who were spurred on by the newly discovered beauty of Japanese and Chinese glazes to unlock the secrets of their production. The factory laboratories became testing grounds for the new "surfaces" which would determine the evolutionary course of design. A particular speciality of head chemist Knud Valdemar Engelhardt were his crystal glazes, whose craquelure created an "abstract" decor on the sides of the vessel and formed richly inventive patterns.

Rörstrand, Aktie Bolag
Lidköping, near Stockholm
Vase with field poppy, ca. 1900
Porcelain, underglaze painting,
silver fitting, 25 cm high
Badisches Landesmuseum
Karlsruhe, Museum beim Markt –
Angewandte Kunst seit 1900

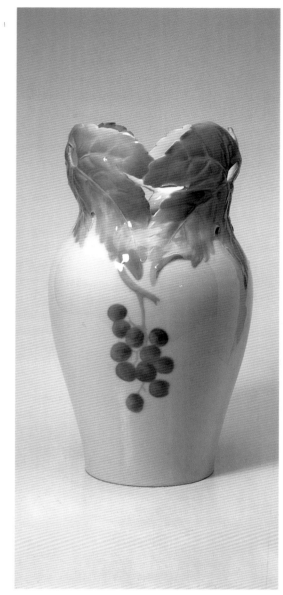

Below:
Gunnar G:son Wennerberg
Iris vase, ca. 1900
Etched and cut flashed glass,
33.9 cm high, 14.7 cm diameter
Made by Kosta Glasbruk
Smålands Museum, Växjö
In the figure of the glass artist
Gunnar G:son (= Gunnar's son)
Wennerberg we may recognize the
"dawn" of Swedish glass art.
Formally influenced by the works of
Emile Gallé, his cut and etched
glasses are of high technical quality
and represent Sweden's first "artist
glassware".

Nils Lunstrøm
Vase, ca. 1900
Porcelain, underglaze painting,
32 cm high, 13 cm diameter
Made by Rörstrand, Aktie Bolag
Lidköping, near Stockholm
Badisches Landesmuseum
Karlsruhe, Museum beim Markt –
Angewandte Kunst seit 1900
A typical feature of Rörstrand
porcelain were plant motifs in relief
which "grew" over the body of the
object and were usually decorated in
two shades of the same colour. The
Rörstrand dinner services and coffee
sets, with their flowers in relief or
leaves and tendrils in underglaze
painting, their economic stylization
and muted coloring, may be seen as
definitive examples of beautiful
tableware.

works even in this difficult area (ill. p. 305). The Danish manufacturers Bing & Grøndahl were also successful entrants, with their porcelain figures, in the competition for beautiful design.

The Swedish porcelain company of Rörstrand, based in Lidköping near Stockholm, was similarly successful with works modified from the Danish type. Characteristic of its decorative schemes were plant motifs in relief which "grew" over the body of the object and were usually decorated in two shades of the same color (ill. above). The Rörstrand dinner services and coffee sets, with their flowers in relief or leaves and tendrils in underglaze painting, their economic stylization and muted coloring, may be seen as definitive examples of beautiful tableware.

Mastery in silver – Georg Jensen

Ousting silver out of daily use, and employing it only for special items which are seldom used, is absurd.
Review of around 1900[31]

Georg Jensen (1866–1935), Scandinavia's most famous silversmith, was another who began as a ceramicist. He studied sculpture at the Copenhagen Academy, giving him a confident feel for plastic effect, and then worked in the studio of Mogens Ballin (1871–1914), one of Denmark's leading metalwork artists, who produced everyday utensils in powerful Art Nouveau forms. After an extended stay in France and Italy, Jensen joined forces with Joachim Petersen (b. 1870) to found a small porcelain studio – a venture which was not successful, however. After this "ceramic intermezzo", Jensen turned to his true forte, silver and goldsmithery.

In 1904 he opened his own studio and shop; still running, it is now a large-scale enterprise. His chased silverware is "crowned" by extravagant motifs, drawn primarily from the plant kingdom. Umbels and capsules, and the opium poppy so beloved of the Symbolists, adorn the handles and lids of his curvaceous services, whose highly original style of decoration makes them instantly recognizable as "Jensens" (ill. below). In his jewelry – most of it silver – he combines flower and insect motifs from Art Nouveau with traditional Nordic ornament; semiprecious stones and enamel add colorful accents (ill. opposite page). Just one year after setting up his business, Jensen exhibited his works in the Folkwang Museum in Hagen to great acclaim. The painter Johan Rohde (1856– 1935), Jensen's friend and business partner, had a hand in many of the designs, which explains the "painterly" quality of Jensen's jewelry, at times bordering on baroque. In 1918 Jensen moved his business into its own premises. Replicas of his Art Nouveau works are still on sale today.

Visions and "Northern Symbolism"

The "seen-in-a-dream" quality of the North, residing in the Scandinavian twilight and running like a thread through the literature and music of the turn of the century, was something that the Swedish artist Aron Jerndahl (1858–1936) strove to translate into three-dimensional form. Each of his works is unique in the sense of its artistic independence. Fashioned from simple tin, Jerndahl's pieces attempt to express a sense of alienation – an unusual starting-point for everyday objects such as a lidded container (ill. p. 306). Water is rendered as undulating lines on the body of the container, which the figures encircle as if in a whirlpool, emerging and vanishing again back into the material. The rhythm established by the violin player extends in a linear direction across the surface. The motif is related to the Dance of Life, a theme explored in numerous variations by Edvard Munch as an existential symbol.

Equally original and rich in nuance was the jewelry designed by the Danish artist Erik

Georg Jensen
Coffee and tea service, 1905
Chased silver, ivory
5.3 cm to 23 cm high
Jensen's chased silverware is "crowned" by extravagant motifs, primarily from the plant kingdom. Umbels and capsules, and the opium poppy so beloved of the Symbolists, adorn the handles and lids of his curvaceous services, whose highly original style of decoration makes them instantly recognizable as "Jensens".

Magnussen, (1884–1961), in which insects serve as a fantastical, eerie ornament which has severed all connection with the obligatory elegance of its French forerunners (ill. above).

From North to South

The supreme "all-rounder" in Danish art was Thorvald Bindesbøll (1846–1908), who contributed to the development of Danish art around 1900 in all areas. He was gifted with a flat, graphically excellent ornamental style which he employed in every sphere of applied art: ceramics, bookbinding, endpapers, illustration, silverwork, posters, jewelry, and architecture. Characteristic of Bindesbøll's style is his translation of vegetal forms into broad bands which condense into points at the ends. The manner, too, in which his decor expresses itself freely in the plane reflects his familiarity with Japanese art (ill. p. 311). His works are lent a distinctive note by his palette, which he concentrated by preference upon the contrast between black and yellow. In his architectural works, Bindesbøll represented the Nordic block-like style also practiced by the Swede Ragnar Östberg (1866–1945), with ornament incorporated into the body of the building (ill. right).

In Sweden, which in the 1920s would become famed around the world for its glass, the glassware produced in the Art Nouveau style was still somewhat eclectic. In the figure of the glass artist Gunnar G:son (= Gunnar's son) Wennerberg, however, we may recognize the "dawn" of Swedish glass art. Formally influenced by the works of Emile Gallé, his cut and etched glasses are of high technical quality and represent Sweden's first "artist glassware" (ill. p. 307). It is essential to note, however, that the exchanges taking place at the international level around 1900 were reciprocal, and did not just travel from the West and the South to the

North in a one-sided fashion. In the field of painting, illustration and poster design in particular, Scandinavian artists exerted an enduring influence upon the rest of Europe; an outstanding example is the Norwegian Olaf Gulbransson (1873–1958), who was active in Germany. As in the case of the Swede Einar Nerman (b. 1888) (ill. p. 304), Gulbransson's strength lay in his almost cartoon-like abbreviation of his pictorial components.

Danish art resembles Dutch art in its fundamental principles. It, too, is honest, serious, unpretentious, sincere, lost in reverie, technically sound, innerly Teutonic, albeit also trained more recently in the French school. It is remarkable just how important a role light has played in painting right from the very start, something which can perhaps be explained by the atmospheric quality of the air of this coastal land ... In the sphere of modern handicraft, the products of the Copenhagen Porcelain Factory are attracting particular attention. It is achieving outstanding results in its animated and naturalistic portrayals of animals and its wonderful shading and coloring. Amongst the Swedes, we must mention Anders Zorn in particular. ... As a sculptor, he is highly gifted in lending powerful expression to inner emotion. He has offered his own important contribution, in bronze, toward solving the problem of combining two naked and intertwined human figures, a man and a woman, into a three-dimensional group which has commonly become known as *The Kiss*. In contrast to the comfortable middle-class atmosphere exuded by Danish pictures and the French perfume which wafts out of many Swedish paintings, namely those from the elegant capital of Stockholm, the Paris of the North, the paintings of fresh snow and springtime yearning by the Norwegians are a breath of the delicious, bracing air in which fishermen and farmers grow up. Far and away the most brilliant of them all is Edvard Munch, highly artistic, multi-talented, tied to no single thematic area or technique, painter, lithographer, portrait artist, psychologist, satirist, landscape painter, and illustrator of his own fantasies. An artist in whose hands forms and contours seem to flow, even though in reality they are clearly defined and firmly fixed, ... a creator who points back to Rembrandt himself in his ability to infuse life into his creations, so that their mouths breathe and their eyes speak ... Occupying a particular place within Russian painting are, of course, the Finns ... Axel Gallen, who – in the fashion of a Jan Toorop – excels in the stylized narration of Norse fables.
Friedrich Haack, *Grundriss der Kunstgeschichte – Die Kunst des XIX. Jahrhunderts*, Esslingen am Neckar, 1904

Form follows function
New York and Chicago

Forms emerge from forms, and others arise or descend
from these. All are related, interwoven, intermeshed,
interconnected, interblended. They exosmose and
endosmose. They sway and swirl and mix and drift
interminably. They shape, they reform, they dissipate.
They respond, correspond, attract, repel, coalesce,
disappear, reappear, merge and emerge: slowly or swiftly,
gently or with cataclysmic force – from chaos into chaos ...
Louis Henry Sullivan[1]

Functional organism

The delicate balancing act between functionalism and the organic – a metaphor for art around
1900 – finds its most convincing resolution in the
"pure culture" and architecture of America.
Objects and buildings functionally tailored to the
organic outlasted the sensual delirium of the
turn of the century. Not only did they have a
permanence in themselves, but the principles of
their construction shaped architecture internationally. Purely superficial ornament, on the
other hand, faded away and became for many
years the object of posterity's derision. Sullivan's
effusive hymn to the power of form found early,
visionary expression in his Chicago buildings. At
around the same time, Louis Comfort Tiffany
was creating his glassware in New York – exotic
blooms grown in an organic hothouse in an
entirely different climate.

The land of unlimited opportunity! Although 19th-
century America was no longer a blank on the
map, its development and lifestyle were still
somehow "exotic" and were greeted in Europe –
in the milieu of decadence – with arrogance or
admiration, depending on mood. The picture of
North America held by most Europeans was
unreal and oscillated between the image of vast

prairies where life was simple and that of rapid
economic progress driven by technology straight
out of science fiction. "The forms of the Old
World, the inheritance of the 'Beaux Arts', the
old colonial style and the 'pure' Greek style all
have a place in this world, but not necessarily out
on the prairie. They may be right for Connecticut
or Virginia, the Boulevard Montparnasse or
Buckinghamshire, but they are not suitable for
the endless open spaces of the New World.
Criss-crossed by the great railroads of the
Midwest, with its new cities founded by hills
men, cattle ranchers, by men who can meat and
export corn, by men with heads full of inventions
and ideas, the country poses special new
challenges.

Whatever we may think about the men who have
made America what it is today, they nevertheless
represent a new phenomenon, and the time has
come to find new forms of expression for the
lives they are seeking to live. There is no
pettiness in their lives, and it is to this that the
sense of unity and expansiveness found in the
works of Frank Lloyd Wright may be attributed ...
To repeat, a style arises organically, and the style
of the 20th century would lack essence and
reality if it did not reflect the influences which
form the background against which the life of our
day is played out."[2] The reformer Charles Robert
Ashbee here offers a sensitive insight into the
background to American Art Nouveau. These
"formative conditions" apply not simply to Frank
Lloyd Wright, however, but also to Louis Comfort
Tiffany.

Louis Comfort Tiffany
View of Oyster Bay, stained-glass window, 1905
Lead glazing, 185 cm high
Tiffany drew his inspiration for this motif from the place he loved the best and where he built himself a house – Cold Spring Harbour on Oyster Bay in New York. The window was executed for William Skinner's New York home.

The American Dream – Louis Comfort Tiffany

It is all a question of upbringing and education; as long as people do not learn to distinguish between the beautiful and the ugly, they will not live with true works of art.
Louis Comfort Tiffany[3]

The history of the family of Louis Comfort Tiffany – alongside Emile Gallé, the most popular and most talented glass artist of Art Nouveau – is a tale of the "American Dream" come true. Tiffany's father, Charles Lewis Tiffany, later to become one of the richest men in America, was just 25 when, in 1838, he founded Tiffany & Young, a firm of silversmiths and jewelers, with minimal start-up capital and the collaboration of a schoolfriend. The young men initially concentrated upon importing jewelry from Europe, but in the 1850s, as their turnover grew, they started making their own. The firm's liquidity is impressively demonstrated by some of its acquisitions: in 1850 it purchased the diamonds formerly owned by Marie Antoinette, the queen of France beheaded in 1793; in 1887 it acquired part of the French crown jewels at a price of over two million (gold!) francs; and in 1889 it bought the

biggest yellow diamond in the world. The name Tiffany became a synonym for luxury, not just in America but all across the European continent, where the company had showrooms in Paris and London.

Louis Comfort Tiffany (1848–1933) was thus born with the proverbial golden spoon in his mouth, and into a golden age. There seemed to be no limits to growth; railroads crossed the country, trading posts became towns, towns cities, and cities like New York metropolises. With progress came – to borrow a term from Lewis Carroll, author of *Alice in Wonderland* – a high degree of "uglification", although this did not seem to bother most people, carried along as they were on the general tide. It was a development which disturbed and oppressed Louis Comfort, however, which in turn alarmed his family. The artistic leanings expressed by the young boy, designated to succeed his father as head of the growing firm, were a cause for concern. Despite much opposition, however, Louis Comfort began studying painting in New York under George Inness (1825–1894) and Samuel Colman (1832–1920), albeit in a rather casual fashion, since his definition of "beauty" went far beyond the merely academic sphere. In 1865, at the age of 17, he crossed the Atlantic to continue his training in Paris under the painter Leon Bailly (1826–after 1868), who cultivated the newly fashionable style of "Orientalism". Inspired by this, Tiffany traveled to the original arenas of such art, namely Africa, Spain, and Egypt. In what proved a key experience for him, he made an intensive study of the Early Christian mosaics in Ravenna in Italy and the 12th- and 13th-century stained-glass windows in Chartres cathedral in France. He was profoundly and enduringly impressed by the beauty and perfection with which the materials were worked, but also by their free, ornamental approach to composition. Tiffany joined numerous well-regarded artists' associations during his student years, but in 1878, after an exhibition of his landscape paintings, he abruptly switched *métier* and became a decorative – Art Nouveau – artist. Without a doubt, Tiffany's understanding of art was influenced by William Morris and the Arts and Crafts Movement in England and was further inspired by the enormous fund of "applied art" which he had acquired during his extended trips through Europe and Africa. Nevertheless, he always remained specifically "American". At the Paris World Exposition of 1900, he showed the dazzling stained-glass window *The Four Seasons*, whose message to the visitor was not simply

Louis Comfort Tiffany
Apple Blossom (detail), window, 1899–1928
Lead glazing, 75 x 75 cm high
"In Tiffany's glass panels, it was as if a piece of the sky, a bed of flowers or a collection of precious stones had been melted down and turned into glass."
(Hugh McKean, see note 5)

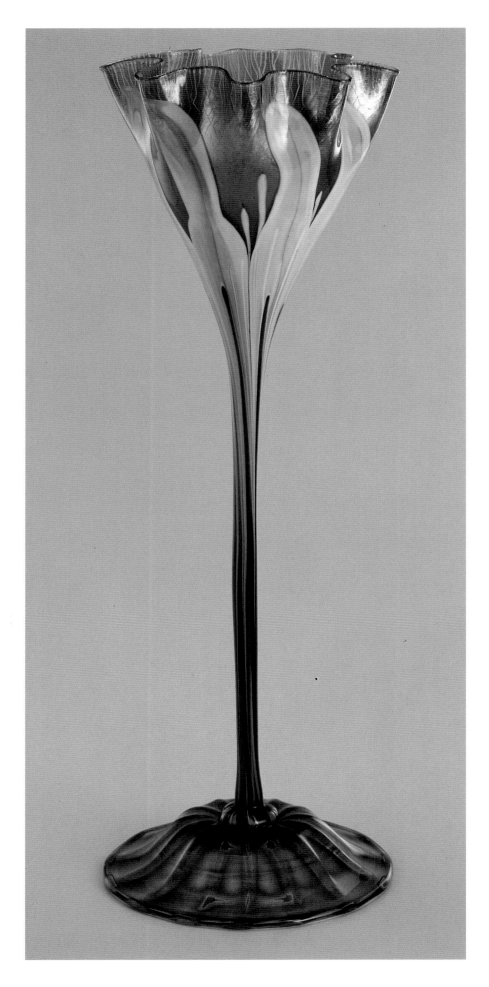

artistic: hovering above the entire scene is the American heraldic bird, a fearless sea eagle, who extends his wings protectively over an inscription which reads: "Wealth, Freedom and Prosperity".

Stained-glass windows – A luminous play of color

I was particularly fascinated by the old glass which was used for church windows in the 12th and 13th century; for me, these stained-glass windows have always been the ultimate in supreme beauty.
Louis Comfort Tiffany[4]

Back in New York, Tiffany became a sought-after interior designer amongst the members of high society. His interiors demonstrate a preference for exotic foreignness, but are designed with invariably surefooted taste. An essential component of these interiors were lead-glazed, colored-glass windows, which owed their origins to the chemical experiments with opalescent glass first conducted in 1876 by the Louis Heydt Factory in Brooklyn, in collaboration with the glass painter John La Farge (1835–1910). "In Tiffany's glass panels, it was as if a piece of the sky, a bed of flowers or a collection of precious stones had been melted down and turned into glass"[5] (ills. pp. 314, 315). Tiffany had found the material which, over the following years, he would make "sing". In 1879 he founded the firm of Louis Tiffany & Company Associated Artists, which employed chemists, designers, and glass experts. Leaving aside Tiffany's complex manufacturing techniques and patented processes, such as his antique-style opalescent glass, the quality of his glass was the result first and foremost of the lengthy and detailed consideration which he gave to its aesthetic appearance. Consequently, too, Tiffany's Chapel and Sullivan's Golden Gate for the Transportation Building – both exhibits at the World's Columbian Exposition in Chicago in 1893 – were spectacular but isolated phenomena within the historicizing "Roman classic" theme of the remaining architecture. The mosaics of Favrile glass, mother-of-pearl and semiprecious stones which adorned the Chapel were greeted as the creations of an original and independent spirit and earned Tiffany an international name. They also brought him into contact with Samuel Bing, so important as a "sponsor" of Art Nouveau.

Tiffany Studios, New York
Vase in the shape of a flower,
ca. 1900–05
Favrile glass, 28.6 cm high
Louis C. Tiffany Museum
Nagoya, Japan
In its essence, Favrile glass recalls mosaic glass painting – painting with glass. Pulverized metal or precious metal was coated over the body of the object in a thin layer, in the same manner as cased glass. Depending on the composition of the metal, the coating that resulted was either matt, lustrous or gloss. In the final stage of the process, vapors containing oxides deposited themselves on the outer walls to create a luster effect.

Louis Comfort Tiffany
Vase, 1909
Iridescent Favrile and Lava glass,
9.5 cm high
Tiffany looked back in his work
across the entire history of glassmaking: his so-called Cypriot and
Lava glasses reveal in their surface
structure the characteristics of the
glassware of antiquity – porous,
dotted with bubbles, and marbled
with pale bands of color.

"Favrile" – Invention and inventiveness in glass

His ability to look at a lump of white-hot glass and visualize precisely what the finished piece would look like once it was strewn with glass particles, blown, decorated, and cooled, was almost uncanny.
Hugh F. McKean[6]

On a trip to Europe in 1889, Tiffany met for the first time not only Venetian glass and the iridescent glassware of the Roman Empire, but also the works of Gallé, which excited him not so much by their design as for their underlying notion of "art for all". These encounters led to his decision to devote himself more intensively to "decorative glassware". He took to heart the words of Gallé (1846–1904), whose aim was to embellish the home of every Frenchman with beautiful art objects. Tiffany had worked for the Vanderbilts and the Rockefellers, but the American middle-class home was still as ugly as ever. In 1890 his response was to found the Storbridge Glass Company on Long Island. Here he sought to recreate the "rainbow" luster effect of antique glassware through chemical pro-cesses and to manufacture glassware on a larger scale. New methods were constantly being developed to these ends.

The number of stained-glass windows which Tiffany could sell was, by its very nature, limited. On the other hand, the *Belle Époque's* need for decoratively styled practical items such as lamps, vases, and toilet articles seemed almost limit-less. There was an economic factor in the equation, too: the manufacture of stained-glass windows accounted for only a relatively small proportion of the enamel glass, with its shimmering hues, available in large quantities. Tiffany therefore began producing decorative items of blown glass of a type which he called Favrile glass, a word derived from the early modern English word *fabrile*, meaning "relating to craft", "masterly" (ill. right). The material had already been employed in windows in the past. In essence, this luster glass recalls mosaic glass painting – painting with glass. Pulverized metal or precious metal was coated over the body of the object in a thin layer, in the same manner as cased glass. Depending on the composition of the metal, the coating that resulted was either matt, lustrous or gloss. In the final stage of the process, vapors containing oxides were de-posited on the outer wall to create a luster effect. Without the aid of a floral stencil, the decor thus "blossomed" out of a chemical but handcrafted process into a vegetal, linear design.

Louis Comfort Tiffany
Vase, 1897
Iridescent cased and threaded glass,
foot of silver-plated metal modeled in
the round, mounting studded with
pearls, precious stones on the base
and collar, 37 cm high
Foot made by Tiffany & Co.,
London
The number of stained-glass
windows which Tiffany could sell
was, by its very nature, limited. On
the other hand, the *Belle Époque's*
need for decoratively styled practical
items such as lamps, vases, and toilet
articles seemed almost limitless.
There was an economic factor in the
equation, too: the manufacture of
stained-glass windows accounted for
only a relatively small proportion of
the enamel glass, with its
shimmering hues, available in large
quantities. Tiffany therefore began
producing decorative items of blown
glass of a type which he called
Favrile glass.

Tiffany glass objects also drew conciously upon the plant kingdom for their overall form. Thus vases echo the shape of opened calyxes, while slender stems bear fragile cups which harden into glass as if by chance (ill. p. 316). Light, color, and movement flow "anarchically" one into the other in these exquisite flowers of the imagination. These "products of chance" were unquestionably the result of supreme artistic and technical skill. There is similarly no doubt that Tiffany had already seen lusterware by the Bohemian Loetz' Witwe company at Lobmeyr's, the famous Austrian glass manufacturer in Vienna.

Nevertheless, the secret of Tiffany's "blooms" lay in the "gardener's" enormous creativity and eagerness to experiment. The famous paperweights by the French firm of Baccarat provided Tiffany with the inspiration for another original group of works (ill. p. 313). These masterpieces owe their "floral" character to a mosaic glass technique which dates right back to the Ancient Egyptians. In this technique, different colored strands of glass were combined under heat into a bundle and then sliced into thin cross-sections whose cut surface bore the shape of a flower. The viscous bundles themselves could be made up of any combination of colors, placing almost no limits on the ornamental "flowers" that could be produced. In the final stage of the manufacturing process, these individual cross-sections were then fused by the glassblower into a single bloom.

Tiffany was also inspired by Monet's *Water Lilies* series. The outlines of his "flora" become blurred, and in place of the flowers themselves we see the light they reflect – glass impressions. Tiffany looked back in his work across the entire history of glass-making: his so-called Cypriot and Lava glasses reveal in their surface structure the characteristics of the glassware of antiquity – porous, dotted with bubbles and marbled with

Opposite page:
Louis Comfort Tiffany
Jack-in-the-pulpit vase,
experimental piece, ca. 1900
Favrile glass, lustered, with
craquelure, 40.3 cm high
Tiffany reached the pinnacle of his
"formal inspiration" in his *jack-in-
the-pulpit* models, exclusive,
exquisite vases so called after the
spathe of the American woodland
herb.

Louis Comfort Tiffany
Wisteria, lamp, ca. 1899–1925
Favrile glass, copper setting, bronze
foot, 42.5 cm high
The "stars" of Tiffany's enormous
product range were his lighting
appliances, an absolutely central
feature of the repertoire. In 1882
Tiffany had designed gas lighting for
the White House and other
important clients. Designing lights
allowed him to combine all his main
interests – his love of light effects of
all kinds, of the iridescent interplay
of colors, and of glass as a material.

Louis Comfort Tiffany
Loetz' Witwe
Necklace, 1896
Iridescent luster glass, gilt setting,
65 cm long, 25 cm wide
Made by Tiffany Glass and
Decorating Company, New York

Rookwood Pottery,
Cincinatti, Ohio
Jug with handle, 1895
Clay with colored pastes, slip
painting under transparent glaze,
silver casing, 27.5 cm high
Painting by Harriet E. Willox
Casing by Gorham, Manufacturing
Company, Providence, Rhode
Island
Badisches Landesmuseum
Karlsruhe, Museum beim Markt –
Angewandte Kunst seit 1900
The Rookwood Pottery was
particularly successful around 1900
with pieces combining a floral silver
casing over a base decorated in slip
painting in Japanese style.

pale bands of color (ill. p. 317). There are Tiffany glasses which have a deceptively metallic appearance and which seem to be made out of bronze or iron.

Persian perfume bottles were the starting point for his "goose-neck" vases, which bend their necks asymmetrically like Oriental vessels designed for sprinkling rosewater. The magician of glass reached a pinnacle of "formal inspiration" in his "jack-in-the-pulpit" models, exclusive, exquisite vases so called after the spathe of the American woodland herb.

The English art critic Cecilia Waern, writing in *The Studio* in 1898, succinctly described the secret of the unvarying quality of Tiffany glass, for all the extravagance of its ornament: "… the shapes are often capricious but with all the sheer waywardness of this exquisite material; they are almost invariably simpler, less slight, less tortured, and more classical in the deepest sense than the blown glass from Europe."[7]

Tiffany lamps – Glass pictures flooded with light

He concerned himself again and again with questions of interior design and lighting, was very interested in growing flowers and gardening and also dedicated himself with great enthusiasm to landscape architecture.
Hugh F. McKean[8]

The "stars" of Tiffany's enormous product range were his lighting appliances, an absolutely central feature of the repertoire. In 1882 Tiffany had designed gas lighting for the White House and other important clients. Designing lights allowed him to combine all his main interests – his love of light effects of all kinds, of the iridescent interplay of colors, and of glass as a material (ill. p. 318). It brought him great satisfaction, too, to know that Tiffany lampshades of stained glass and Favrile glass were bringing beauty into American living rooms – not to mention boosting the company's turnover at the same time. His ambitions for the firm were impressive: its operations included a department supplying complete interiors, furniture workshops, a "sacred art" division, a ceramics studio, a jewelry atelier, a metal workshop and much more. His holding company also produced less sophisticated objects for everyday use, which nevertheless always retained the flair of the one-off work of art (ill. p. 318). The number of Tiffany imitators is

Opposite page:
Steuben Glass Works,
Corning, New York
Dish, ca. 1914
Colorless glass, threaded decor,
iridescent
6.7 cm high, 12.8 cm diameter
Kunstmuseum im Ehrenhof,
Düsseldorf
Influenced by Tiffany, the Steuben
Glass Works produced decorative
glasses with a luster effect.

Frank Hazenplug
The Chap Book, before 1898
Color lithograph, 51.8 x 35.6 cm
American graphic art found its own
vocabulary entirely free from stylistic
reminiscences. *The Chap Book*,
which appeared from 1894, was
wholly devoted to this new style. It
was not just a forum for writers and
illustrators from Europe, but a
compendium of the graphic art being
created in the New World.

countless; many of his pupils set up business on their own, including Martin Bach and Thomas Johnson, producers of "quetzal" glass, so called after a Central American bird with shimmering plumage. Influenced by Tiffany, the Steuben Glass Works in Corning, New York, produced decorative glasses with a luster effect (ill. p. 321). Joseph Webb, working for the Phoenix Glass Company, was highly successful with his "pearl satin glass", which he later patented. In his elegant showrooms, Tiffany showed, alongside his own pieces, ceramics by the Rookwood Pottery in Cincinnati, Ohio, which was particularly successful with pieces combining a floral silver casing over a base decorated in slip painting in Japanese style (ill. p. 320).

Like a true Art Nouveau artist, Tiffany also produced his own total work of art. In his home on Oyster Bay, the "non-architect" translated all his knowledge of art into reality. The house was laid out like a seraglio with gardens, inner courtyards, fountains and an endless succession of stained glass: the *Arabian Nights* in New York (ill. p. 314). Even if the end of his life was overshadowed by the problems of the company conglomerate, a photo taken on his 80th birthday shows a vivacious grand seigneur and lover of beautiful cars dressed in a white suit in Miami Beach. Showered with honors, he was the most important American craftsman of his era.

Graphic art

If Rembrandt had known about lithography, who knows what he might have done with it?
From the catalogue to an exhibition of lithographs[9]

The 1893 Chicago exhibition turned the international spotlight not just on Sullivan and Tiffany, but on a third great American artist: William H. Bradley (1868–1962). In 1895 *The Studio* published an in-depth review of his work, emphasizing his talent and comparing him with Beardsley. The bold style of the great English artist had undoubtedly made an impact on Bradley, who trained as a draughtsman. However, it was an apprenticeship in printing that led him to develop his own poster-like style. His technical understanding of the printing process enabled him to translate his ornamental works, tending toward the abstract, precisely into print and to secure himself a leading place amongst the pioneers of change in the sphere of book illustration. Under the influence of Morris, he founded his own press and published the magazine *His Book*. He thereby relinquished the traditional border

Ethel Reed
In Childhood's Country, poster, ca. 1900
Color lithograph, 63 x 29 cm
Ethel Reed, one of the few women artists of Art Nouveau to achieve celebrity, produced illustrations based on sensitive portrait studies. In 1895 she made her career breakthrough with the advertisement for a book by Gertrude Smith. The poster-like style of that design proved a recipe for success, one which she went on to employ in numerous illustrations and posters.

In Childhood's Country By Louise Chandler Moulton Pictured by Ethel Reed

Boston: Copeland and Day Price $2.00

around every page, as employed by the Kelmscott Press, in favor of a new emphasis upon dynamic, whiplash line. Just how far Bradley was capable of escalating this characteristic feature of his style can be seen in a vignette of Loïe Fuller (ill. p. 312). "The American painter Bradley drew Loïe Fuller – the veil dancer who, also from America, had been taking all of Europe by storm since 1893 – vanishing into billows of flowing cloth, bathed in colored light, a pure wave of color and light. This alone is what concerns the artist and what has sparked his imagination. There is only a semi-ironic allusion to the actual presence of the dancer. The undulating waves of her veils are more real than she herself; they are true form, that which is present and believable, all that is visible – the object, the objectivity of art."[10] French echoes can be heard here both in the subject and in the "dancing" sweep of Bradley's line, reminiscent of Jules Chéret. American graphic art nevertheless found its own vocabulary entirely free from stylistic reminiscences. *The Chap Book*, which appeared from 1894, was wholly devoted to this new style (ill. p. 322). It was not just a forum for writers and illustrators from Europe, but a compendium of the graphic art being created in the New World. Ethel Reed (b. 1876), one of the few women

artists of Art Nouveau to achieve celebrity, produced illustrations based on sensitive portrait studies. In 1895 she made her career breakthrough with the advertisement for a book by Gertrude Smith. The poster-like style of that design proved a recipe for success, one which she went on to employ in numerous illustrations and posters (ill. p. 323).

Louis Henry Sullivan

Form follows function.
Louis Henry Sullivan[11]

The Eiffel Tower demonstrated the structural principle of the iron skeleton, as a symbol of technology in all its naked glory. In Victor Horta's Maison du Peuple we can identify an early example of a curtain wall, that is, the structure of the exterior already expresses that of the interior – the walls are, as it were, latched into the skeleton. In the case of Louis Henry Sullivan (1856–1924), "skin and bones" are brought into harmony; ornament is no longer understood as showy decoration, but as architectural stimulation lending emphasis to the details of the "joints" (ill. pp. 328–329). As Ruskin observed in 1849: "We have a bad habit of trying to disguise

Burnham & Root
Rookery Building, 109 South La Salle Street, Chicago, glass-roofed well, 1885–87
Daniel Hudson Burnham and John Wellborn Root opened their joint offices in Chicago in 1873 and provided an exemplary demonstration of steel-frame building in their Rookery Building. The fame of the building also rests on its groundplan, which offered an entirely new solution to the organization of space within a department store.

disagreeable necessities by some form of sudden decoration ..."[12]. Some 43 years later Sullivan warned: "I should say that it would be greatly for our aesthetic good if we should refrain entirely from the use of ornament for a period of years, in order that our thought might concentrate acutely upon the production of buildings well formed and comely in the nude."[13] As far as "teetotalism" in ornament was concerned, however, Sullivan never went as far as his pupil Frank Lloyd Wright (1869–1959), who remained entirely abstinent in this regard. *The Grammar of Ornament* by the Englishman Owen Jones (1809–74), published in London in 1856 and in the United States in 1880, was a bestseller. In his book, which became the Bible of modern-thinking American craftsmen, Jones beat the drum above all for a stylized pure form of ornament, for simplification. Surface decoration must remain planar, he argued. In other words, it must adapt itself to the geometric structure and understand ornament in grammatical terms. It is here that Sullivan's decorative principle has its origins. Sullivan had a revulsion, on the other hand, for the rehearsal of historical styles, something he had encountered during his time at the École des Beaux Arts in Paris. Meanwhile, he shared the enthusiasm for engineering and held up as his model a simple technician – himself – who, with no more than an ordinary education, had in 1868 erected a steel bridge across the Mississippi. In 1879 Sullivan went to Chicago, which in 1871 had been swept by a great fire, leaving over a third of the city in ruins. The urgent task of rebuilding the city even bigger and better than before was one which fired the imaginations of architects and engineers alike. It would inspire a building tradition whose first pinnacles were reached in the works by the principals of the Chicago School of Architecture.

The Chicago School of Architecture

Having spent many years over there, I still blush with shame when I think of the ridicule to which German arts and crafts were subjected.
Adolf Loos[14]

The Chicago School of Architecture produced prototypes of modern architecture. It was the School's maxim that a building's design had to fulfill the requirements of economy, function, and well-being, and at the same time accentuate rather than hide the organic function of the building. "[Sullivan] admittedly went far beyond Ruskin, who denied technology and fought

its machines. But his 'philosophy', and the Romantic pathos of his decoration and his prose, were to be the net with which technology could be tamed and if necessary trapped."[15] Sullivan is seen as the father of functionalism, and it was in this spirit that he interpreted the skyscrapers which he designed, as can be seen in the example of the Guaranty Building in Buffalo, New York (ill. p. 325). Sullivan believed that "it is of the very essence of every problem that it contains and suggests its own solution. This I believe to be natural law."[16] He nevertheless appears to have reversed his own "form follows function" formula into "function follows form" when

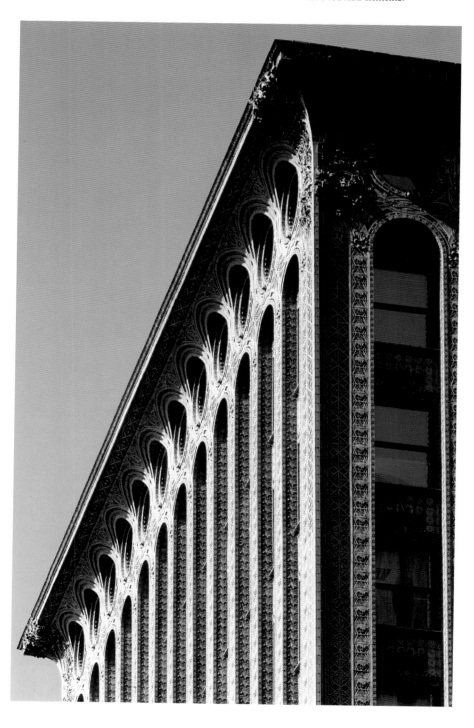

Louis Henry Sullivan
Guaranty Building, Buffalo, cornice (detail), 1895
Standing in apparent contradiction to Sullivan's "form follows function" is the highly individual ornament which he developed for his architecture: a sharply defined, complex composition of Gothic and Art Nouveau elements.

Frank Lloyd Wright
House and stables for William H.
Winslow, River Forest, Illinois,
entrance facade, 1893
The first building by Wright to bear
his unmistakable stamp was the
Winslow House of 1893. The
horizontal emphasis, an opening
inwards as well as outwards, the
unity with nature – all are to be
found here.

speaking of the artistic impact of a building: "It demands of us, what is the chief characteristic of the tall office building? And at once we answer, it is lofty. This loftiness is to the artist nature its thrilling aspect. It is the very open organ-tone in its appeal. It must be in turn the dominant chord in his expression of it, the true excitant of his imagination. It must be tall, every inch of it tall. The force and power of altitude must be in it, the glory and pride of exaltation must be in it."[17] Another apparent contradiction lies in the highly individual ornament which Sullivan developed for his architecture: a sharply defined, complex composition of Gothic and Art Nouveau elements.

Sullivan's "prototype", always cited as the fore-runner of modern architecture, is the Carson Pirie Scott Department Store in Chicago, whose con-struction is determined by a pragmatic empiri-cism. As if Sullivan wanted to compensate for the self-imposed asceticism of the upper storys, the first and second storys of the plinth zone are overlaid with a network of exquisite filigree ornament. Multiplicity, imagination, and animation not only offer an astonishingly agreeable contrast to the reflective smoothness of the store win-dows, but underline the independence of the decoration, whose validity is unaffected by the architect's fundamental rejection of built orna-ment. Sullivan's later buildings – such as the National Farmers' Bank in Owatonna, Minnesota and the Merchants' National Bank in Grinnell, Iowa – are less monumental than his early Chicago works, but they are particularly impressive demons-trations of his ability to make "architectural design" real. They are a three-dimensional translation of his own words: " ... They [the forms] sway and swirl and mix and drift interminably"[18] (ill. p.330).

Frank Lloyd Wright
Country house for Avery Coonley,
Riverside, Illinois, view of the
entrance facade from the drive, 1907
Although Wright designed big
projects, too, he preferred to work on
private houses. The free plan and the
human scale are the two main
principles underpinning his work,
whereby he also attached great
importance to "Nature". In his so-
called Prairie architecture, he fused
all these elements into elongated,
usually boldly composed buildings
with projecting roofs and open
groundplans.

Frank Lloyd Wright
Katsura Rikyu, Imperial Villa,
Kyoto, ca. 1590
The Katsura is not merely a
masterpiece of Japanese architecture,
but can be seen as a medium of
Japanese art *per se*. The German
architect Bruno Taut described the
villa – without false pathos – as one
of the "wonders of the world".

Following double page:
Louis Henry Sullivan
Stained-glass windows, side wall of
the Merchants' National Bank,
Grinnell, Iowa, 1914
Subdivided by pillars, lead-glazed
With Sullivan, "skin and bones" –
in other words the structure and
outer skin of the building – are
brought into harmony; ornament is
no longer understood as ornate
decoration, but as architectural
stimulation lending emphasis to the
details of the "joints".

Daniel Hudson Burnham (1846–1912) and John
Wellborn Root (1849–91) opened their joint offices
in Chicago in 1873 and provided an exemplary
demonstration of steel-frame building in their
Rookery Building. The fame of the building also
rests on its groundplan, which offered an entirely
new solution to the organization of space within
a department store (ill. p. 324). Burnham and
Root also contributed to the sphere of high-rise
architecture; their Monadnock Building demonstrates the sensitivity with which the two architects handled not just steel, but also brick: the
textured material is elegantly married with the
building's upthrusting momentum. The steps of
the Rookery Building were one of the first
commissions executed by Frank Lloyd Wright.

Frank Lloyd Wright

*Truly ordered simplicity in the hands of the great artist
may flower into a bewildering profusion, exquisitely
exuberant, and render all more clear than ever.*
Frank Lloyd Wright[19]

"Morris once said to me, speaking in favor of a
refined style of ornament: 'We do without it,
unless the building to which we are applying it is
itself refined.' Lloyd Wright's buildings fulfill this
demand."[20] Morris's theses, drawn upon by the
Art Nouveau generation of artists, thus also
found expression in the figure of Frank Lloyd
Wright. His designs aim at a tectonic rectangularity, but also take up the dynamic lines which
arise out of ornament; these are no longer
merely aesthetic "appliqués", however, but
place a deliberate emphasis upon structure. An
architectural "noble-mindedness" became Wright's
guideline: "Buildings like people must first be
sincere, must be true and then withal as gracious
and lovable as may be."[21]
Wright came out of the Chicago School, worked
on occasions with Burnham and called Sullivan
his "Lieber Meister" (dear master). While he
may have evolved far beyond his teacher in many
respects, Wright nevertheless matched the
image of the architect created by Sullivan,
namely one who expressed his talents not just
through building, but through his writings and
other forms of art. The European architects who
were training their eyes on America looked for
many years to Wright, and thereby to a very
specific form of American architecture which had
its roots in the experiences of the avant-garde in
Europe. The striking, simple forms of Wright's
buildings are clear and unmistakable. He didn't
invent them; they corresponded to the American

way of life. Whereas the English country-house architects had insisted that every room should be a world in itself, the open groundplan is an American concept, as is the placing of a massive fireplace in the middle of the house, off which the rooms radiate. Although Wright designed big projects, too, he preferred to work on private houses. The free plan and the human scale are the two main principles underpinning his work, whereby he also attached great importance to "Nature". In his so-called Prairie architecture, he fused all these elements into elongated, usually boldly composed buildings with projecting roofs

and open groundplans (ill. p. 327). The natural textures and colors which he retained in his building materials and decorative architectural components fuse tactically and harmoniously into their surroundings. "We European architects frequently look with hungry eyes at our more fortunate colleagues in the New World, with their magnificent sites, their broad expanses of uninhabited land and their cities awaiting artists, and at the munificence of their clients as regards the costs involved."[22]

Louis Henry Sullivan
National Farmers' Bank, Owatonna, Minnesota, banking hall with view of the main entrance, 1907–08.
Sullivan's later buildings – such as the National Farmers' Bank and the Merchants' National Bank – are less monumental than his early Chicago works. It is nevertheless these buildings in particular which demonstrate his special ability to make "architectural design" real and which embody his philosophy in three dimensions: " ... They [the forms] sway and swirl and mix and drift interminably." (Louis Henry Sullivan, see note 18)

Zen and Prairie

Architecture provokes moods in people. It is therefore the task of the architect to specify this mood.
Adolf Loos[23]

In addition to the vital factor of liberal-spending clients, the inimitable "Wright style" was made up of another, perhaps all-important, entirely un-American component. "It is frequently possible to identify Japanese influences; we see how he endeavors to match Japanese forms to American circumstances."[24] Wright expressed his concept of the open plan as the organic fusion of interior and exterior space. The principle of open wall elements replaces the window as a hole in the wall and thereby draws upon the traditions of Japanese domestic architecture (ill. p. 333). In the Katsura Rikyu, an imperial villa near Kyoto, Japan the building and its natural surroundings merge to form a perfect unity; the man-made complex is entirely natural in its shape, and the architecture is at the same time a model of utmost simplicity (ill. p. 327). The Katsura is not merely a masterpiece of Japanese architecture, but can be seen as a medium of Japanese art *per se*. The German architect Bruno Taut (1880–1938) described the villa – without false pathos – as one of the "wonders of the world". What European modernism saw as the yawning divide between calculation and spontaneity appears fully resolved in the tradition of Japanese Zen. Meditation creates an inner state of receptive emptiness, just like the disciplined, transparent, light, sliding, unmonumental outer spaces of Japanese architecture. One year after Wright had completed his last building in Chicago in 1915, he left America to design the Imperial Hotel in Tokyo.

The first building by Wright to bear his unmistakable stamp was the Winslow House of 1893. The horizontal emphasis, an opening inwards as well as outwards, the unity with nature are all to be found here (ill. p. 326). In the house which he designed for Frank Thomas in Oak Park, Illinois, the spacious country setting where he had already built himself a house in 1889 (something Walter Gropius would also do in 1938), we can recognize another of Wright's principles: the rhythm which he lends to the structure, and which here serves to underpin the architecture as a whole. The Coonley House in Riverside is a clear illustration of Wright's motto: "... in the nature of materials"[25]. All the materials are employed as appropriate to their nature, whereby the natural "material" of light is also impressively incorporated into the whole.

Frank Lloyd Wright
Composition in Light – Interpretation of the American flag, stained-glass window, for the country house for Avery Coonley, Riverside, Illinois, ca. 1912
Glass, zinc bars, painted wooden frame, 153.6 x 30.5 cm
The Coonley House is a clear illustration of Wright's motto: " ... in the nature of materials" (see note 25). All the materials are employed as appropriate to their nature, whereby the natural "material" of light is also impressively incorporated into the whole.

Page 333:
Frank Lloyd Wright
House for Frank Thomas, Oak Park, Illinois, view of the living room from the lobby, 1901
Wright expressed his concept of the open plan as the organic fusion of interior and exterior space. The principle of open wall elements replaces the window as a hole in the wall and thereby draws upon the traditions of Japanese domestic architecture.

Even though we may not see in Wright's work the characteristics of Art Nouveau as it is usually defined and understood, he nevertheless belongs in the canon of new trends around the turn of the century. *"Organic architecture.* This is the chief principle from which Wright derives all other principles ... 'Form follows function'; Wright on the other hand speaks of a relationship between form and function and the functions of a house. Organic is the name he gives to an architecture which is there for people and not for show, and not, either, for art."[26]

Buildings like people must first be sincere, must be true and then withal as gracious and lovable as may be. Above all, integrity. The machine is the normal tool of our civilization, give it work that it can do well – nothing is of greater importance. To do this will be to formulate new industrial ideals, sadly needed.

[...] An artist's limitations are his best friends. The machine is here to stay. It is the forerunner of the democracy that is our dearest hope. There is no more important work before the architect now that [sic] to use this normal tool of civilization to the best advantage instead of prostituting it as he has hitherto done in reproducing with murderous ubiquity forms born of other times and other conditions and which it can only serve to destroy.

[...] This is the modern opportunity – to make of a building, together with its equipment, appurtenances and environment, an entity which shall constitute a complete work of art, and a work of art more valuable to society as a whole than has before existed because discordant conditions endured for centuries are smoothed away.

Frank Lloyd Wright, "In the Cause of Architecture," in *Architectural Record,* 1908

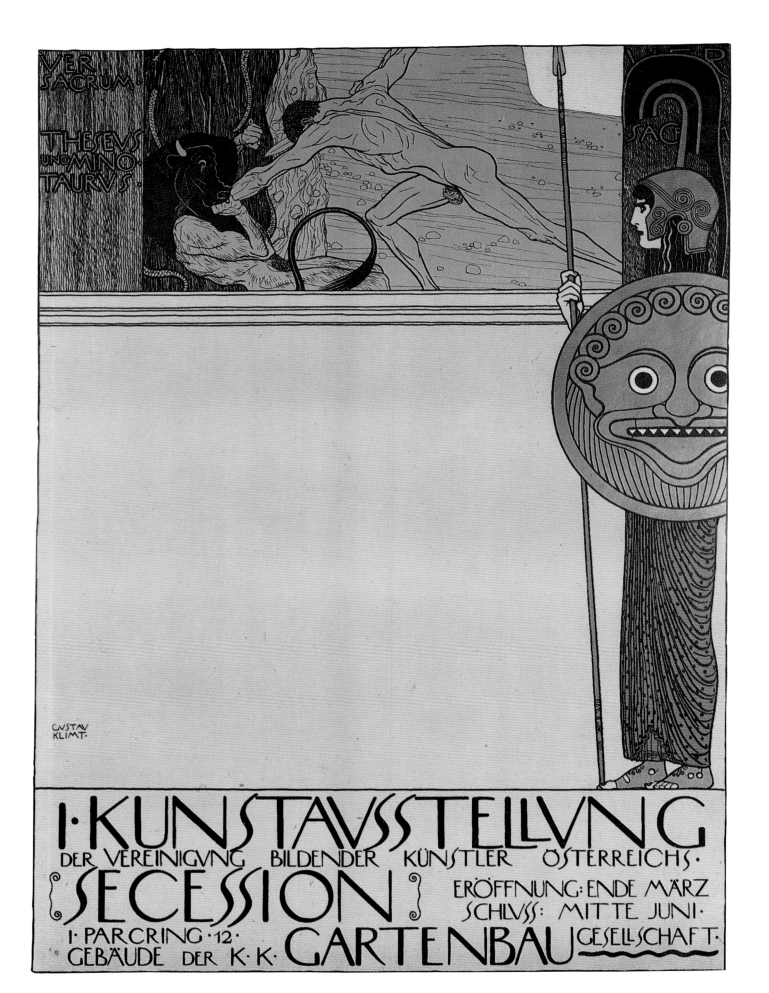

End of an era
Vienna

Gustav Klimt
Theseus and the Minotaur, poster for the first Secession Exhibition, 1898 (pre-censored state)
Color lithograph, 97 x 70 cm
Klimt's poster demonstrates that the introduction of the empty plane was the concern not only of architects, and that around the turn of the century everything had its own "causative agent". Sullivan and his comrades-in-arms – later Adolf Loos – were propagating the simple, smooth surface and were preparing the way for functionalism. In this poster, the empty plane also seems to be a sort of wall, as suggested by the cornice at the top. Contradictory elements are combined into a whole; in the tension which infuses the contrast between the empty plane and the figures, there lies an incredible modernity.

Let me remind you once again of how things were ten years ago, in the bleak period from 1880 to 1890, when we were cut off from the rest of Europe as far as the arts were concerned. In those days, if I mentioned Vienna in Paris, the reply was always the same: "Là-bas? C'est en Roumanie? n'est-ce pas?". We were an Asiatic province. And in Berlin people thought the Austrians were good only for vaudeville.
Things have changed.
Hermann Bahr[1]

Imperial Royal Vienna – Waltzing in bliss

In 1898 Hermann Bahr (1863–1934) – a man of letters intimately acquainted with every stylistic trend, discoverer of the young Hofmannsthal, champion of Expressionism and fearless defender of the artists of Viennese Jugendstil – issued the challenge that these last would make their own: "Swathe our people in Austrian beauty!"[2] Ten years later Adolf Loos (1870–1933) was raging against the tasteless swaddlings of everything from music to lifestyle: "Ornament is not only perpetrated by criminals, but is itself a crime."[3] Only the philistine "snaps after ornament like a dog after a sausage," mocked Karl Kraus (1847–1936), Vienna's often cynical vocal conscience, who also observed: "We haven't heard, so far at least, whether the implements used for the break-in were made in the Wiener Werkstätte."[4] Such were the "situation reports" from Vienna around 1900, from the growing metropolis in which art was surrounded by controversy like nowhere else. The abrupt juxtaposition of exquisite, undulating linearity, precious, symbol-laden ornament, and rigid rectangularity makes it impossible to categorize the turn of the century under any

hasty, ill-conceived heading (ills. pp. 336, 339). In truth, it is *fin de siècle*, the end of an era, the Decadent Movement grown weak and stylized, but also Art Nouveau, Jugendstil: a new departure and a mutation.

"An Austrian art! Each one of you knows what I mean ... when you see the sun shining on the railings of the Volksgarten, with the scent of lilacs in the air and little Viennese girls jumping over their skipping ropes, or when you hear a waltz floating out of a courtyard as you pass, then a strange feeling comes over you, and none can explain why he is so happy that he could cry, but can only smile: That's Vienna for you! This 'that's Vienna for you' is what you must paint."[5] But what was Vienna? The capital of the Austro-Hungarian Empire, whose decline is described by Robert Musil (1880–1942), in his novel *Mann ohne Eigenschaften* (Man without Qualities), published 1930–43, as the "particularly clear collapse of the modern world"?[6] Light-hearted Vienna, where no one took anything really seriously, and where playful elegance, coquettishness, and a sophisticated love of life held sway? Vienna the city of the "cult of femininity," full of living and artificial pictures of beautiful women, the city of the dashing officer? Home of the glittering waltzes of Johann Strauss and at the same time – thanks to Sigmund Freud – the birthplace of psychoanalysis! The magnificent buildings lining the Ringstrasse were a manifestation of upper middle-class culture which profoundly changed the face of the city, even as Socialism was brewing in the suburbs. The capital of a country embracing a wide diversity of peoples and cultures, Vienna was at the same time Grinzing, one of the little wine-growing villages on its outskirts. The definition of life

Koloman Moser
Sherry decanter, ca. 1900
Optic blown glass with "dimples", silverplated brass, 23.5 cm high
Distributed by E. Bakalowits & Söhne, Vienna

around the turn of the century was ambivalent, and embraced both beauty and horror; a yearning for death and a glorification of life formed a counterpoint to which few gave more polished expression than Hugo von Hofmannsthal (1874–1929). The same counterpoint was a characteristic feature of Art Nouveau and Jugendstil. The apparently incompatible simultaneity of reaction and modernism, of naive delight and emphatic seriousness, indeed the very pluralism of Vienna's languages, cultures and peoples, proved instead a fortunate coincidence which found its resolution in an artistic confrontation with complexity.

Coffeehouse culture – The Secession

To the Age its Art, to Art its Freedom
Joseph Maria Olbrich[7]

"The greatest success of the Secession is to have finally provoked Vienna, the ancient city of music, to get heated up – indeed, to 'échaufferize' – about the fine arts. Even the stir caused by Hans Makart in his early years does not compare with this, having been more local in character. Only the battle fought and won by the Wagnerians, in Vienna as everywhere else, measures up to the triumph of the Secession in all the capitals of the world. Within the narrow artistic confines of Vienna, the Secession was an act of audacious youthful idealism. In the spirit of sacrifice and with a willingness to work hard, the nineteen, who have today become seventy, plunged into a fight whose outcome was highly uncertain. How lucky that there are more artists than businessmen amongst them! Had they realized, for example, that the first exhibition would cost 40,000 florins, they would perhaps have lost heart. But they didn't know, and the Viennese public helped. Even this enormous outlay brought a net profit."[8] The year 1897 – the year of the foundation of the Vienna Secession, the sign of the dawn of a new era which was barely less dramatic than the transition from the Middle Ages to the Renaissance – represents the beginning of "modernism" in Austria. As in Munich and Berlin, it signified the drawing of a line under the illusionism and verism perpetuated by the art academies, and the establishment instead of an "interdisciplinary art". Jugendstil, today considered a historical phenomenon, was in its own day the first in a string of "anti-art movements", insofar as it ranked graphic art as well as handcrafted objects amongst the primary arts (ill. p. 352). The Vienna Secession – officially

Gustav Gurschner
Table lamp, ca. 1900
Patined bronze, *turbo marmoratus* shell (South Sea mussel), 53 cm high
In the growing metropolis of Vienna around 1900, art was surrounded by controversy like nowhere else. The abrupt juxtaposition of exquisite, undulating linearity, precious, symbol-laden ornament and rigid rectangularity makes it impossible to label the turn of the century under any hasty, ill-conceived heading.

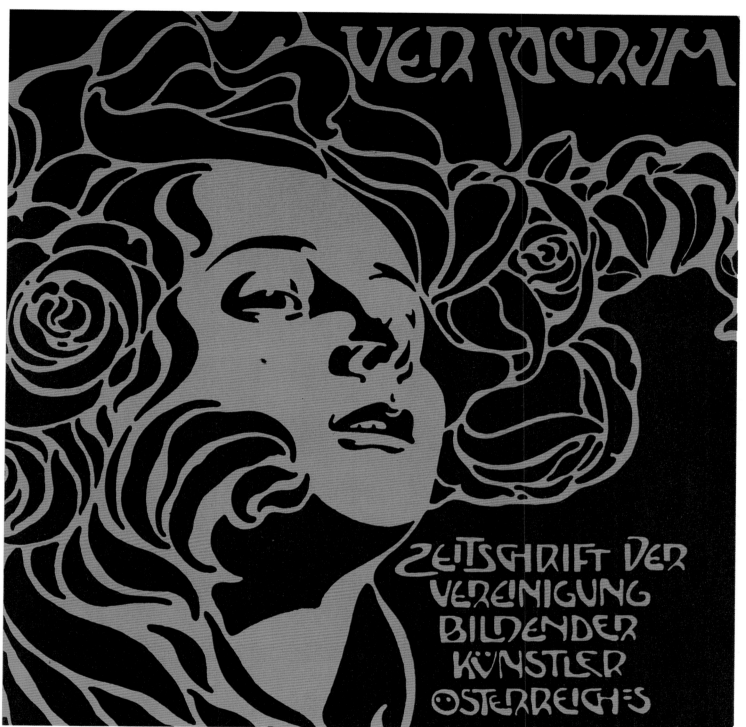

Koloman Moser
Cover for *Ver Sacrum*, II, no. 4, 1899
Color lithograph, 42.5 x 41.8 cm
The title of the art journal was taken from a poem by Ludwig Uhland (1787–1862): "You have heard what God wishes, / Go, prepare yourselves, silently obey! / You are the seed grain of a new world, /That is the sacred spring he desires." (see. note 11). *Ver Sacrum* is not just an informative and entertaining chronicle of the Secession, but – in the original illustrations which many artists contributed to its pages – an exact mirror of its age.

entitled the Austrian Association of Applied Artists (Verein Bildender Künstler Österreichs) – brought together the young and the dissatisfied amongst Austria's artists. Their aims were not revolutionary, but purely aesthetic: they were concerned only with finding the form, the "material" being already at hand – Vienna! It was only natural, therefore, that the Secession should have been founded in a coffeehouse, the second home of every Viennese citizen – in this case, the legendary Café Griensteidl. "Your boots are torn – Coffeehouse! You earn 400 crowns and you spend 500 – Coffeehouse! You can't find any girls you like – Coffeehouse! You're contemplating suicide – Coffeehouse! You hate and despise people but still can't do without them – Coffeehouse! No one will give you any more credit – Coffeehouse!"[9] wrote Peter Altenberg (1859–1919), one of the last European Bohemians, a Viennese François Villon of the turn of the century. Thus, too, the forerunner to the Secession, the Hagen Society (Hagengesellschaft) founded in 1876 (and which in 1900 became the Hagenbund), was named after the proprietor of the Zum blauen Freihaus restaurant, while the rendezvous for the Siebener Club was the Café Sperl. What finally prompted all of these artist groups to sever the umbilical cord with official-dom was the exhibition policy of the Vienna Künstlerhaus under its president Eugen Felix (1837–1906). Spokesman for the 50 founding members of the Secession was Gustav Klimt (1862–1918). Comparable to Franz von Stuck in Munich, Klimt was the leading figure in the Vienna art scene around the turn of the century, a genius of the Symbolistically decorated pictorial plane (ill. pp. 342–343), in whose shadow he

sketched highly erotic, sensitive nudes on paper. He protected and supported two young, provoc-ative insurgents: "chief rebel" Oskar Kokoschka (1886–1980) and "self-seer" Egon Schiele (1890–1918). Klimt's fellow combatants included Josef Hoffmann, Koloman Moser (1868–1918), Joseph Maria Olbrich, the painters Carl Moll (1861–1945) and Max Kurzweil (1867–1916), and the "architectural giant" Otto Wagner, as well as the "Parisian Czech" Alfons Maria Mucha (1860–1939). "Young rebels" were not the only ones to have a say in the Secession, however. At the head of a delegation which presented Emperor

Gustav Klimt
Music, 1895
Oil on canvas, 37 x 44.5 cm
Bayerische Staatsgemäldesammlungen, Neue Pinakothek, Munich.
In this painting Klimt creates an
"ideal plane" which asserts itself in
opposition to the modeling of the
body. In his works, gold and silver
grounds stand alongside zones of oil
painting. To a certain extent, Klimt
here anticipates the "collage"
employed, for example, by Antoni
Gaudí in his architecture. The
subtle, "textile" quality which Klimt
so magically lends the pictorial plane
has never been equalled.

Franz Joseph I (b. 1830; Emperor 1848–1916) with an invitation to the First Secession Exhibition was the association's 85-year-old honorary president, Rudolf von Alt (1812–1905). The 67-year-old emperor expressed his astonishment that the young artists were being headed by a man even older than he was himself. "I may indeed be rather old, your Majesty," replied von Alt, "but I still feel young enough to keep starting all over again."[10] The "adolescent" movement was granted recognition by the emperor's attendance at the exhibition, even if this was simply a gesture of good will. In order to verbalize the Secession's artistic activities — something generally obligatory around 1900 – it was decided to publish a monthly art journal: *Ver Sacrum* (Sacred Spring). The title was taken from a poem by Ludwig Uhland (1787–1862): "You have heard what God wishes, / Go, prepare yourselves, silently obey! / You are the seed grain of a new world, /That is the sacred spring he desires."[11] *Ver Sacrum* is not just an informative and entertaining chronicle of the Secession, but – in the original illustrations which many artists contributed to its pages – an exact mirror of its age (ill. p. 357). Virtually ignored was the fact that Adolf Loos, having initially been closely linked with the Secession, later severed his ties but continued to write numerous articles for *Ver Sacrum*.

Adolf Loos
Clock, 1900
Brass, glass, cut by hand, 30-day movement at the rear freely suspended in the housing, 48 x 21.5 x 26.5 cm

Gustav Klimt and the "empty plane"

... only when he rebels against Vienna and his art assumes its most personal expression does Gustav Klimt – following a fundamental law of genius – become the fullest embodiment of Viennese art.
Hans Tietz[12]

In line with the lifting of "class barriers" between the arts, Klimt too turned to graphic art and illustration. The poster which he designed for the First Secession Exhibition (ill. p. 334) provoked an immediate reaction: the censor demanded that trees should be printed over the body of Theseus to hide it. "... Theseus is naturally wearing the simple but pleasing garb of a hero, namely nothing at all ... the painter was compelled to conceal half his Theseus behind a number of tree trunks. We may now ask whether Canova's Theseus will also be taken back to his quiet temple dungeon

(the pavilion in the Burggarten), its doors locked and the key thrown into the Danube?"[13] Klimt was already at the zenith of his career and had left academicism behind him with his spandrels for the Kunsthistorisches Museum. Greek antiquity, personified by a young woman, becomes pure *fin de siècle* art in her pose. Curving linearity, undulating lines and the interpretation of woman as *femme fatale* all demonstrate the new "art of synthesis". In his painting *Music* of 1895 (ill. p. 338), Klimt creates an "ideal plane" which asserts itself in opposition to the modeling of the body. In his works, gold and silver grounds – almost Byzantine in character – stand alongside zones of oil painting. These are joined in his *Beethoven* and *Stoclet* friezes by an expansion into the third dimension in the ornamental shape of mosaics, metal, majolica, and semiprecious stones. To a certain extent, Klimt here anticipates the "collage" employed, for example, by Antoni Gaudí in his architecture. Klimt's luxurious cult of materials had its origins on the one hand in the painting and literature of Symbolism, and on the other in the French tradition of exquisite handicraft and in Charles Rennie Mackintosh. The subtle, "textile" quality which Klimt so magically lent his paintings has never been equalled.

The spectacular opening exhibition by the Secession made an impact upon Klimt's work, too. At the center of the foreign works on display were the cartoons by Pierre Cécile Puvis de Chavannes (1842–98), works by Arnold Böcklin (1827–1901), Auguste Rodin (1849–1917), Jan Toorop and Fernand Khnopff. Khnopff's images of dreamily somnabulent women (ill. p. 132), related to the Pre-Raphaelites, find their way into Klimt's inimitable portraits. "There is always a sensitive eye at work, seeking out the charms of womanhood in each individual. Some enchanting feature resides in every woman, reveals itself in every woman in some sign, and Klimt always discovers it – even in one less attractive. It might be an eye, which he makes shine in such a way that the whole picture seems to be all eye; or a dry, thirsty mouth, which he paints with such eloquence that all else vanishes besides this mouth, or it is the line of her body, the gesture of her hands, or her hair."[14] Klimt's magnificent female portraits, timelessly intuitive, nevertheless caused feelings to run high. It was presumed that Klimt had not just painted his models – immortalized wearing a relaxed smile in often daring poses – but had also become their lover. His ceiling paintings of the three secular faculties for the university, again employing female figures as allegories, caused a scandal; Klimt was deeply hurt by the reactions of his critics. "… the negative response by the majority of the Vienna press, even the feeble accusations of pornography, failed to upset Klimt's feelings. But when a number of university professors and members of parliament also added their voices to the outcry when the painting *Medicine*, destined for the university, went on show, he lost his patience … The Ministry, understanding and supportive of Klimt, nevertheless had to insist that he delivered the works he had been paid for. Klimt's testy reply: 'I'll not have my work insulted like this any more; if you send soldiers and they shoot, I'll have to surrender, since I can't shoot back.'"[15] While scandalized art philistines dwelled upon the possible obscenities in his pictures, Klimt himself took another, progressive direction in his work. His poster for the First Secession Exhibition (ill. p. 334) shows that the

introduction of the empty plane was the concern not only of architects, and that around the turn of the century everything had its own "causative agent". Sullivan and his comrades-in-arms – later Adolf Loos – were propagating the simple, smooth surface and were preparing the way for functionalism. In Klimt's poster, the empty plane also seems to be a sort of wall, as suggested by the cornice at the top. Contradictory elements are combined into a whole; in the tension which infuses the contrast between the empty plane and the figures, there lies an incredible modernity. "… But now I was puzzled. Klimt's earlier works had captivated me, and some of his murals in the Hofmuseum had reminded me of Giorgione, but in this drawing I was suddenly faced with something entirely new which had nothing to do with memories of other Masters. It was already in the distinctive Klimt style …"[16] Thus Koloman Moser recalled his first encounter with the "empty plane" in Klimt's work. Just how close Klimt the painter, apostrophized as the author of beautiful female portraits and powerful collages of color, came to the architect in his way of seeing can be deduced from Olbrich's commentary on his own Secession building: "It was to become walls, white and gleaming, sacred and chaste. Solemn dignity was to envelop all. Pure dignity of the kind that came over me and enthralled me when I stood alone in Segesta before the unfinished temple … I wanted to hear only my own emotions in its note, to see my warm feelings frozen into cold walls."[17] Olbrich's words conceal a palpable longing for "plain ornament"; only the fact that his language seems to date from an earlier era distinguishes it from Loos' thoughts on the same subject: "Superfluous ornament and affected additions stupefy the brain, make the senses go stale and squander the energy to work. They are an erotic substitute like graffiti on toilet walls, only less honest, puffed up, spruced up and frozen."[18] Olbrich's talent was recognized, appreciated and encouraged by his teacher Otto Wagner. While Olbrich's first design for the Secession exhibition building was still heavily indebted to Wagner, he ultimately arrived at a consummate and original solution in a building which is stunning even today (ills. opposite page and left). Ludwig Hevesi described the "magical impression" made by its gilded laurel cupola in euphoric terms: " … the small building is and will always be memorable in the history of Viennese architecture; the old breakers smashed against it, and it stood as a tangible sign of new possibilities."[19]

Opposite page and above:
Joseph Maria Olbrich
Vienna Secession exhibition building, view of the front and detail, Vienna, 1897–98
While Olbrich's first design for the Secession exhibition building was still heavily indebted to Wagner, he ultimately arrived at a consummate and original solution in a building which is stunning even today. Ludwig Hevesi described the "magical impression" made by its gilded laurel cupola in euphoric terms: "… the small building is and will always be memorable in the history of Viennese architecture; the old breakers smashed against it, and it stood as a tangible sign of new possibilities." (see note 19)

Georg-Anton Scheidt
Cigarette case, ca. 1900
Silverplated and embossed metal, cabochon stone, 9 x 9 cm
The universal triumph of the "made in Austria" label was "managed" by the Austrian Museum of Arts and Crafts and led to a modern-day style of mass production whose dangers were not recognized at the time.

Gustav Klimt
Let this kiss be for the whole world!, *Beethoven* frieze, 1902
Casein paint on plaster, secco technique, gold leaf, gilded
plaster, color gemstones, mother-of-pearl, charcoal, graphite
pencil and pastel crayon, 216 x 1378 cm
Österreichische Galerie im Belvedere, Vienna

"The arts transport us into that ideal realm where we can
alone find pure joy, pure happiness, pure love. Chorus of the
Paradise Angels. 'Freude, schöner Götterfunken' [Joy,
beautiful radiance of the Gods] . 'Diesen Kuß der ganzen
Welt' [Let this kiss be for the whole world!] "
(Commentary in the catalogue to the 14th Secession
Exhibition, Vienna 1902)

The Beethoven Exhibition – A scandal

... And in [Austria], furthermore, a genius was only ever held to be a lout, and never a lout to be a genius, as happened elsewhere ...
Robert Musil[20]

The Second Exhibition by the Secession took place in its own building, whose interiors by Olbrich, Moser, Hoffmann, and Wagner lent the exhibition an additional dimension, as it were. The Secession's subsequent exhibitions, too, were exemplary in their conception and design, whereby one stood out uniquely from all the rest: the 14th Secession Exhibition of 1902, which centered upon the Beethoven memorial by Max Klinger, "framed" by Klimt's *Beethoven Frieze* (ill. pp. 342–343). But Vienna would not have been Vienna if the singing and cheering had not been interspersed with excesses of bitter invective. An aristocratic art patron and collector who attended a preview became just this "excessive" at the sight of Klimt's frescos. "He shrieked the word in a high, shrill, cutting voice, as if someone had pinched him. It was like the crack of a pistol in the silence. He flung the word up at the walls like a stone: *monstrous*"[21].

Overshadowing all else in the exhibition, the *Beethoven* frieze signified a radical shift in Klimt's work, influenced by Toorop's monumental linear works and mystical understanding of com-

Else Unger, Emilio Zago
Writing desk, ca. 1900
Stained wood, carved relief, copper handles;
Footrest: buckskin,
171 x 101 x 53 cm
Awarded a gold medal at the 1900 World Exposition in Paris
The pliant and pleasing style practised by the artists who had banded together into the – unquestionably highly successful – Secession became a veritable box-office hit. And rightly so, since handicraft was thereby liberated from its narrow confines and allowed to form a synthesis with interior design and the liberal arts, a synthesis which brought with it a sense of "liberated" living. The attractiveness of the handicraft items issuing from Vienna was demonstrated at the World Exposition of 1900 in Paris, where public response to the objects on display was enthusiastic.

Koloman Moser
Writing desk (detail), 1902
Various wood veneers, inlay of elm,
jacaranda, ebony, mother-of-pearl
and ivory, silverplated fittings,
145 cm high

position. It marked the start of Klimt's "golden style," in which ornament asserted its independence alongside powerful allegorical figures traced in almost graphic outline. The Beethoven Exhibition marked a turning point in the development of many other artists as well as Klimt, and occupies a key position in the history of the Secession. "The yawning divide between the 'naturalists' and the 'stylists', which in 1905 would become one of the main reasons for the departure of the Klimt group, was already evident at the Beethoven Exhibition ... Viewed in an even wider context, the Beethoven Exhibition clearly documents the transition from the 'aesthetic-decorative' to the 'monumental' phase in which style generally found itself shortly after 1900 ... The Beethoven Exhibition exerted a decisive influence upon every genre in art, in particular the applied arts. The complementary nature of the exhibition paved the way for projects such as the Kunstschau exhibition, the Palais Stoclet and the Steinhof Church."[22]

Vienna Secession style

Even the convolutions of the Jugendstil man's brain are lost in ornament.
Karl Kraus[23]

The pliant and pleasing style practised by the artists who had banded together into the – unquestionably highly successful – Secession became a veritable box-office hit. And rightly so, since handicraft was thereby liberated from its narrow confines and allowed to form a synthesis with interior design and the liberal arts, a synthesis which brought with it a sense of "liberated" living. The attractiveness of the handicraft items issuing from Vienna was demonstrated at the World Exposition of 1900 in Paris, where public response to the objects on display was enthusiastic (ill. opposite page). These graceful objects and pieces of furniture were contemporary, free from historicist additives, yet without being avant-garde; neither in their shape nor their decor did they break new ground. They composed tasteful interiors for educated citizens who didn't want to overload themselves with too much art. It was only natural that the Viennese style would also prove a financial success. The universal triumph of the "made in Austria" label was "managed" by the Austrian Museum of Arts and Crafts (Österreichisches Museum für Kunst und Handwerk) and led to a modern-day style of mass production whose dangers were not recognized at the time (ill. p. 341). This form of

Koloman Moser
Cabinet, 1900
Jacaranda, precious wood inlay, sleeves of nickelplated copper and metal, embossed silverplated copper, luster glass, black paintwork, 193 cm high "Of the artists who founded the Vienna Secession, Kolo Moser was unabashedly the boldest, and one of those who caused Viennese philistines the most trouble in the early days of the Secession. Wherever there was something to reform in Viennese arts and crafts – and where wasn't that needed? – you could find Kolo Moser working away with perseverance, intrepidness, taste and astounding technical skill. ... Blessed with an extraordinarily fine instinct for the practical and aesthetic possibilities latent in the material, and with an innate understanding of how to bring them out through technical means, and at the same time master of what might be called an almost hypertrophic imagination as regards the inventiveness of his forms, Kolo Moser crafted decorative and practical utensils which rank amongst the very best that modernism has produced in this field up till now." (Arthur Roeßler, see note 24)

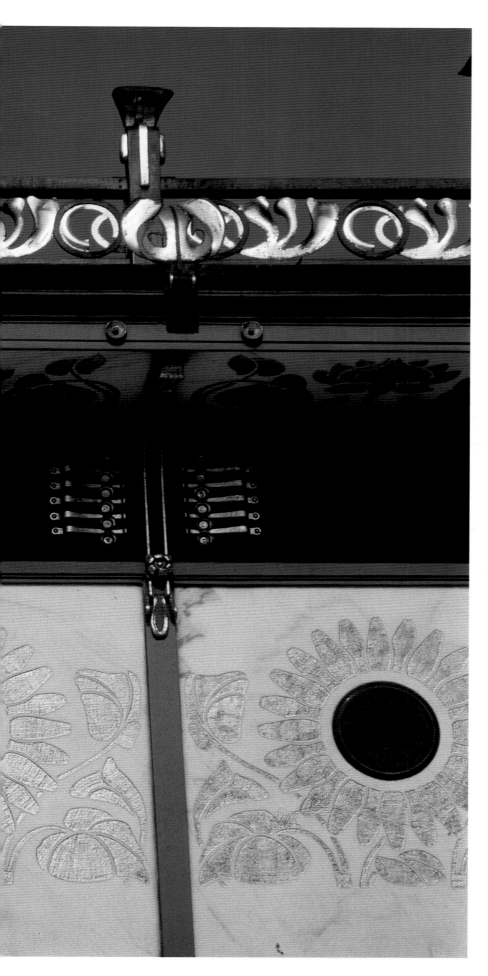

progress considerably displeased Hoffmann, Klimt and Moser, the leading voices of the Secession. "Of the artists who founded the Vienna Secession, Kolo Moser was unabashedly the boldest, and one of those who caused Viennese philistines the most trouble in the early days of the Secession. Wherever there was something to reform in Viennese arts and crafts – and where wasn't that needed? – you could find Kolo Moser working away with perseverance, intrepidness, taste and astounding technical skill. … Blessed with an extraordinarily fine instinct for the practical and aesthetic possibilities latent in the material, and with an innate understanding of how to bring them out through technical means, and at the same time master of what might be called an almost hypertrophic imagination as regards the inventiveness of his forms, Kolo Moser crafted decorative and practical utensils which rank amongst the very best that modernism has produced in this field up till now."[24] (ills. pp. 335, 345). When Moser, Hoffmann and Klimt quit the Secession, the "sacred spring" came to an end; those who remained behind proved unable to sustain the glittering series of Secession exhibitions, and "production" was overtaken by apathy.

Otto Wagner and modern architecture

The shift is so radical, however, that we cannot speak of a renaissance of the Renaissance. What has issued from this movement is a naissance.
Otto Wagner[25]

"In the face of Otto Wagner's genius, however, I strike my sails"[26] – thus the words of that ever-belligerent "architectural revolutionary" Adolf Loos. There could be no better summary of Wagner's outstanding personality. The teacher of Hoffmann, Olbrich, Loos, and Antonio Sant'Elia laid the "foundation stone" of modern architecture (ill. p. 359). "Entirely at odds with Wagner's 'dream' of being – amongst other things – the architect of the Ringstrasse, the consummation of imperial and upper middle-class notions of pomp and lifestyle, was the reality of Otto Wagner the artist of building, the first architect of modern Vienna."[27]

Otto Wagner (1841–1918) early on addressed urban requirements from both a practical and a theoretical angle – in his plans for the Vienna Stadtbahn metropolitan railway network, his Post Office Savings Bank and his essay *Moderne Architektur* (Modern Architecture) of 1895. In the opening years of his career he experienced

Otto Wagner
Karlsplatz station, Vienna Stadtbahn, Wiental line, Karlsplatz 2, Vienna, 1894–99
Karlsplatz station is lent its distinctive character by two pavilions facing each other on either side of the tracks. Unlike the other Stadtbahn stations, which were finished in plaster, these pavilions employ a steel skeleton clad on the exterior with slabs of marble, and on the interior with slabs of white plaster. The slabs bear a sunflower motif which also appears on the semicircular gable. Their Secessionist Jugendstil decor makes these two "functional" buildings appear almost luxurious.

Otto Wagner
Majolica House, detail of the facade, apartment block, Linke Wienzeile 40, District VI, Vienna, 1898–99
The two apartment blocks which Wagner built and rented out at Wienzeile 38 and 40 are milestones along the road to a decent standard of living for "ordinary people". The facades are Secessionist in style and caused a sensation with their splendid fronts, chosen by Wagner bearing in mind the magnificent boulevard which was planned for Wiental. Linke Wienzeile 38 featured gilt medallions and stucco by Moser, while Linke Wienzeile 40 was entirely faced with colorful ceramic tiles bearing a floral-vegetal decor – a forceful testament to the possibility of the successful marriage of ornament and architecture.

Otto Wagner
Front facade of the dispatch offices of *Die Zeit*, Kärntnerstrasse 39 / Annagasse, Vienna, 1902
Iron construction covered with sheet aluminum;
Lights: nickelplated sheet iron,
450 x 332 cm
In Wagner's entry facade for the dispatch offices of the daily newspaper *Die Zeit*, a new material took the spotlight: the iron construction of the entry was clad with sheet aluminum. This front facade is important in the history of architecture insofar as it gave a leading role, for the first time, to the "newborn" material of aluminum.

Vienna's metamorphosis into a metropolis, as the city was lent stature by the monumental buildings springing up along the Ringstrasse in particular. He was not yet involved himself, however; only with his plans for the Stadtbahn railway system in 1894 was he able to make his first contribution towards shaping the new face of the city. Wagner's early buildings were clothed in historicist style, with a pronounced emphasis upon classical architecture. The forms, details and groundplans of his early villas are based upon the Renaissance-style villas of the 19th century, but already demonstrate a clarity of organization and construction. Like Berlage and Behrens, Wagner made a close study of the works of Gottfried Semper; this historical "lesson" saved him and his pupils from abandoning the legacy of architecture and producing trivial or even merely harmless works.

Wagner was less interested in houses for private individuals, however, than in tenements – in other words, in solutions to the housing requirements of broad sections of a conforming urban population. The two apartment blocks which Wagner built and rented out on Wienzeile are milestones along the road to a decent standard of living for "ordinary people". The facades are Secessionist in style and caused a sensation with their splendid fronts, chosen by Wagner bearing in mind the magnificent boulevard which was planned for Wiental. The house Linke Wienzeile 38 featured gilt medallions and stucco by Moser,

while Linke Wienzeile 40 was entirely faced with colorful ceramic tiles bearing a floral-vegetal decor – a forceful testament to the possibility of the successful marriage of ornament and architecture (ill. above).

After protracted preliminary planning of its routing and countless discarded proposals, the construction of the Vienna Stadtbahn was commenced in 1893. In order that this modern mode of transport should be given a contemporary form, Otto Wagner was appointed artistic adviser to the Transport Commission in 1894. His brief was to produce stylish designs for everything from the Stadtbahn stations, bridges, and viaducts, etc., to the interior furnishings of the trains themselves. In order to meet this challenge on time, Wagner enlarged his studio – which already included Olbrich and Hoffmann – to 70 people: a germ cell of modern architecture. The fruits of the collaboration of this team of artists were overwhelming; but a hidebound city bureaucracy destroyed many of their achievements after the First World War. Karlsplatz station is lent its distinctive character by two pavilions facing each other on either side of the tracks. Unlike the other stations, which were finished in plaster, these pavilions employ a steel skeleton clad on the exterior with slabs of marble, and on the interior with slabs of white plaster. The slabs bear a sunflower motif which also appears on the semicircular gable. Their Secessionist Jugendstil decor makes these two "functional" buildings

appear almost luxurious (ill. pp. 346–347). "It can
be taken as proven that art and artist always
represent their own age."[28] With his Steinhof
Church, built in 1902, Wagner realized his
thoughts on modernism in sacred architecture;
for all its aestheticism, this sacred building is
again characterized by impressive functionality.

Naissance – The Austrian Post Office Savings Bank

That Wagner was a "functional Constructivist" is
evidenced by his most famous work, the Post
Office Savings Bank in Vienna (ill. p. 350) – both
in its details and in the design of its main space,
the banking hall (ill. below). "The roof of the
banking hall, an arched glass skin, is suspended
from the supports which can be seen criss-
crossing the hall ceiling. The principle of the
suspension bridge is thus here being applied to a
roof, probably for the first time. In this case, by
the way, it didn't work, because Wagner failed to

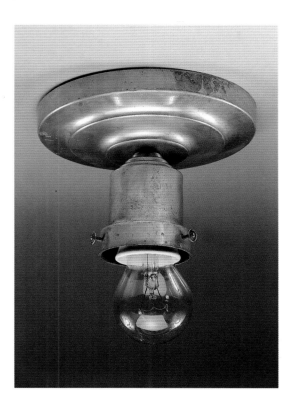

Otto Wagner
Ceiling light, main banking hall,
Austrian Post Office Savings Bank,
1904–06
Aluminum, 16 cm diameter

Otto Wagner
Austrian Post Office Savings Bank,
part of the facade, Georg-Coch-
Platz, District 1, Vienna, 1904–06

protect his glass skin with a second skin of glass
… If we understand Wagner correctly, the reason
why he didn't do so was because it would have
left the principle of the suspended construction
less visible to the eye … From the corridor in the
story above the hall roof, you could originally see
through the windows to the truss in the
courtyard; today you look out into the space
between the new roof and its suspended skin.
The hall is still an architectural sensation. The way
in which the supports crisscross the roof, apparently bearing no load at all, is a cause for astonishment, as is the light glass vault … Wagner the
classical architect has here created an entirely
unclassical space, for he has expressed – and put
into practice – the transformation of space as
previously understood by architecture *through
the construction*. In this respect, Wagner was
more modern than Loos; and it is of course no
coincidence that the works of his pupils between
1898 and 1910 should appear so extraordinarily
modern in their construction."[29] Wagner and his

team of architects also undertook the interior
design of the entire Austrian Post Office Savings
Bank (ill. p. 349).

Wagner announced his break with the past as
early as 1895. The concept of a "naissance" also
extended to the person of the architect himself,
who was now to be architect and engineer
in one. From now on, Wagner the "artist of
building" employed modern and unconventional
materials, such as aluminum, and clad his
facades with slim, contemporary marble slabs,
as in the case of Karlsplatz station. In his front
facade for the dispatch offices of the daily
newspaper *Die Zeit* (Time), a new material took
the spotlight: the iron construction of the entry
was clad with sheet aluminum. This front facade
is important in the history of architecture insofar
as it gave a leading role, for the first time, to the
"newborn" material of aluminum (ill. p. 348). On
the basis of various historical photographs we
know that the entry survived at the latest until
1908. Its location remained a focal point of

Opposite page:
Otto Wagner
Armchair for the dispatch offices of
Die Zeit, 1902
Bentwood, beech, aluminum sleeves
and edging, upholstered, 79 cm high
Made by Jacob & Josef Kohn,
Vienna
"The word *Baukunst* [architecture]
embraces two concepts. *Bau*
[building] = the static, regular.
Kunst [art] = free, plastic, artistic
design. What is true of architecture
is also true of furniture. We can find
principles of architecture, for
example, in the design of a chair,
which is also governed by the laws of
statics. Or we can put it the other
way round: like a chair on its four
legs, so today's skyscraper stands on
its supports. … Both, room and
furniture, form a unity … Going
beyond its mere function, furniture
should stand within the room like a
piece of free sculpture, but
nevertheless related to it by the task
which it is intended … to fulfill."
(Werner Blaser, see note 32)

modernism, however. Subsequent architectural exercises on the same site included a delicatessen with a white-lacquered entry, and the "Loos portal," while the "temple facade" of the Spitz jewelers' shop survived till the mid-1930s. "All modern creation must comply with the new materials and requirements of the present, if it is to be appropriate to modern humankind."[30] Thus the progressive tendency of Wagner's facade design for the offices of *Die Zeit* matched the character of the paper itself, which had evolved out of the weekly of the same name and which kept its sophisticated readership up to date with front-line developments in the arts and the latest "dispatches". Wagner had "vanquished" the Secession style.

Furniture as architecture

Architecture embraces the consideration of the whole physical setting of human life.
William Morris[31]

The armchair designed by Wagner for the *Die Zeit* dispatch offices and made by the Viennese firm of Jacob & Josef Kohn – bentwood with aluminum sleeves and edging – is an exemplary piece of "furniture as architecture" (ill. below). "The word *Baukunst* (architecture) embraces two concepts. *Bau* (building) = the static, regular. *Kunst* (art) = free, plastic, artistic design. What is true of architecture is also true of furniture. We can find principles of architecture, for example, in the design of a chair, which is also governed by the laws of statics. Or we can put it the other way round: like a chair on its four legs, so today's skyscraper stands on its supports. Skin and bones are as clearly distinguished in furniture as

Michael Thonet
Chair no. 14, 1859
Bentwood, 89 cm high
Die Neue Sammlung, Staatliches Museum für angewandte Kunst, Munich
Functionally efficient, organically conceived and in many cases folding, Thonet's chairs were a huge success. This bentwood design, also known as the "Viennese coffeehouse chair", is still manufactured today and has sold about 100 million. The secret of its enduring success lies in its social as well as technical serviceability, its low production costs and its competitive price.

Loetz' Witwe
Table lamp, ca. 1900
Luster glass, combed and drawn
waving lines, gilded bronze foot,
opalescent cabochon stones,
53 cm high
Jugendstil, today considered a
historical phenomenon, was in its
own day the first in a string of "anti-
art movements", insofar as it ranked
graphic art as well as handcrafted
objects amongst the primary arts,
and credited a lamp, for example,
with the same powers of artistic
expression as a painting.

they are in a building. A chair, too, is built … Does the architect design the furniture for the room or the room for the furniture? Both, room and furniture, form a unity, created on the basis of the same principles. Going beyond its mere function, furniture should stand within the room like a piece of free sculpture, but nevertheless related to its setting by the functional and intellectual task which it is intended to fulfill."[32]

Prior to the 19th century, the materials of building had been wood and brick, stone and mortar for as long as anyone could remember. Suddenly, however, new building materials appeared on the scene which would bring about nothing short of a revolution in architecture: iron and glass, and later, reinforced concrete. The Crystal Palace built in London in 1851 by Joseph Paxton (1801–56) was amongst the first outstanding examples of iron-and-glass construction. Ten years earlier, following continuous experimentation, Michael Thonet (1796–1871) had registered his first patents for bentwood furniture. In the following years he moved his workshop from Boppard on the Rhine to Vienna. Common to both the Crystal Palace and bentwood furniture is their construction principle on the basis of flexible, robust materials. Functionally efficient, organically conceived and in many cases folding, Thonet's chairs were a huge success (ill. p. 351). The famous "coffeehouse chair" is still manufactured today and had already sold 50 million by 1930. The secret of its enduring success lies in its social as well as technical serviceability, its low production costs and its competitive price.

Bentwood and Vienna are synonymous; alongside Thonet, the Kohn company was also producing legendary pieces of furniture, such as Josef Hoffmann's Fledermaus chair and furniture designed by Otto Wagner. Wagner's chair for the *Die Zeit* offices makes clear the correlation between detail and overall construction – a "total work of art" from both an intellectual and practical point of view.

Iridescent color from Bohemia

The ornament plague has been given official recognition and is being subsidized with public money.
Adolf Loos[33]

While the finest examples of the "grammar of ornament" are to be found in the works of the Wiener Werkstätte, ornament as a "universal language of artistic expression," that is, as a design medium *per se*, condensed itself into the glass creations of Austrian Jugendstil. In Loos' con-

Opposite page:
Loetz' Witwe
Vase, ca. 1900
Astralit glass, dichroic shimmer,
glass fragments fused into the body,
molded, iridescent, 16 cm high
Physical chemistry, which had
emerged as a new discipline around
1870, provided the true foundation
for the delicate luster and iridescent
glassware issuing from Loetz'
Witwe. The natural scientists
became artists, producing in their
laboratories the new and fascinating
color effects which lend the
amorphously curved glasses their
charm.

Loetz' Witwe
Peacock vase, before 1900
Luster glass, combed and drawn
waving lines, 16.8 cm high
Peacock feathers, butterfly wings,
and soap bubbles seem to take
concrete form. In 1898 Loetz'
Witwe was granted a patent for its
"luster glass technique". In Paris the
following year, the company showed
its *Papillon* glasses with their
luminous spots of iridescent color for
the first time, together with its latest
Phänomen: glassware incorporating
a decor of glass threads fused either
within or on top of the glass body,
combed, and in some cases
employing metallic colors.

Vilmos Zsolnay
Vase with landscape motif (detail),
ca. 1903
Faïence with eosin (metallic luster
glaze), painting, *pâte sur pâte*, 34.5
cm high
Pécs, Hungary

Haida Technical College
Bonbonnière, ca. 1910
Clear glass, painted enamel decor,
23.5 cm high
Made by Joh. Oertel & Co.

demnation of the criminal function of ornament, however logically argued, we may also recognize the philistinism criticized by Karl Kraus. Synesthesia, the goal of art around 1900, finds its expression in a diary entry by Robert Musil, in which he describes the fusion of impressions received simultaneously through his various senses into a *single* sensual impression: "Today, for the first time, I 'experience' my room – this hideous mixture of stylistic blasphemies – as something unified, as a totality of areas of color, organically fused with the icy night outside … "[34] In the broader sense, therefore, it is perfectly possible to be moved by the combination of multiple layers of design.

Glass as the architectural medium of transparency and weightlessness offered Art Nouveau a new discipline, one which extended into the sphere of small objects. Iridescent colors and vegetal modeling find more elegant and noble expression in glass than in other materials. In Bohemia, which boasted a long and glorious tradition of glassmaking, the flowering of handicraft around the turn of the century helped elevate Bohemian glass to new heights and international renown. Many factories produced pieces testifying to the happy alliance of ornamental style and glass (ill. left).

At the forefront of Austrian glassmaking was the Loetz' Witwe company (ills. pp. 352, 353). Physical chemistry, which had emerged as a new discipline around 1870, provided the true foundation for the delicate luster and iridescent glassware issuing from Loetz' Witwe. The natural scientists became artists, producing in their laboratories the new and fascinating color effects which lend the amorphously curved glasses their charm. Peacock feathers, butterfly wings, and soap bubbles seem to take concrete form. In 1898 the firm was granted exclusive production rights to its "luster glass technique". In Paris the following year, Loetz' Witwe showed for the first time its *Papillon* glasses with their luminous spots of iridescent color, together with its latest Phänomen glassware incorporating a decor of glass threads fused either within or on top of the glass body, combed, and in some cases employing metallic colors (ill. above left). Loetz' Witwe developed numerous types of glass, including *Pavonia* and *Persika,* colored glasses with a luster effect, *Calliope, Cynthius, Formosa* and *Orpheus*, which immortalized in glass the fleeting colors of the rainbow. These supremely artistic creations are anonymous and owe their uniqueness to the sensitivity and imagination of the glassmaker. From 1903 the Wiener Werkstätte also collaborated with Loetz' Witwe and the arabesque was joined by the "square". The "luster effect" was an Imperial Royal success and also inspired a specific type of pottery (ill. above).

Adolf Loos – Austerity on the attack

The art which afforded the old man his floor and vaulted the Christian's church is now deformed on tins and armbands. The times are worse than we think.
Johann Wolfgang von Goethe[35]

Loos cites Goethe's words in his writings to show that Goethe, too, was a modern man – something not to be disputed. Goethe also seems to have been a model for Loos as regards the all-important question of the "inhabitability" of architecture. After visiting Palladio's Rotonda – Palladio villas are pure architecture – the great German poet is supposed to have observed that it was "inhabitable but not homely".[36] Alexander Pope (1688–1744) went even further; when a member of the English aristocracy showed him

his Palladian villa, Pope recommended: "If I was you, my lord, I would build a small, comfortable brick house next door, through whose windows you could admire your magnificent villa." He expressed the same thoughts in verse: "My noble Lord, it is very fine, / But where will you sleep, and where will you dine?"[37] Which brings us directly to the wittiest lampoon that Loos ever directed at the Secession, *The Tale of a Poor Rich Man*,[38] in which Loos describes the "dream house" of a Jugendstil architect: "Each room composed a perfect symphony of color. Walls, furniture, and fabrics were coordinated in the most exquisite fashion. Each object had its designated place and was orchestrated with the rest into the most wonderful combinations … The architect meant very well. He had thought of everything. Even the tiniest box had its own place, specially made for it. The apartment was comfortable, but it was taxing on the brain. The architect therefore monitored how it was lived in for the first few weeks, to make sure no errors crept in. The rich man tried his very best, but it happened nevertheless that he put down a book and, sunk in thought, placed it in a drawer

Adolf Loos
Exterior view of the Villa Karma for Professor Dr. Theodor Beer, 171 Rue du Lac, Burier, Montreux-Clarens, 1903–06
Even Adolf Loos, the most audacious spirit in architecture, was a child of his time. Under the art that was to be rejected he understood the art of ornament. Beauty and harmony nevertheless remained law. He deprived ornament of its rights and replaced it with costly materials. At the end of the day, the concept of the *Raumplan* (plan of volumes) which he developed was also interior design. His first private house, the Villa Karma on Lake Geneva, was designed for the Swiss neurologist Theodor Beer. Loos took the existing house, thoroughly revamped and reorganized it, and lent it classical proportions. The arrangement of its stairways already looks forward to the free volumes of his famous *Raumplan* concept.

Adolf Loos
Commercial block for Goldmann &
Salatsch, Michaeler Platz, District
1, Vienna, stairs leading up to the
apartments, 1909–11
The most trenchant observation on
the Michaeler House stems from
none other than Otto Wagner: "We
have refrained from going to the
defense of the work under attack in
public, since we too do not consider it
altogether faultless. But there is one
thing that I can say: more artistic
blood flows through the veins of its
architect than through those of the
architect of many a palais which has
been left in peace because it has
absolutely nothing to say." (see
note 39)

intended for newspapers. Or that he knocked off the ash of his cigar into the hole in the table designed to receive the candlestick ... And sometimes the architect had to unroll the detailed drawings in order to re-establish the correct home for a box of matches." One day the rich man nevertheless decided to make himself a little comfortable and greeted the architect in slippers. The architect was shocked to the core: "'What on earth are those slippers you're wearing?', he ejaculated painfully. The master of the house looked down at his embroidered footwear. But then he sighed with relief. This time he felt entirely blameless. The slippers had in fact been worked to an original design by the architect himself. So he replied superciliously: 'But Mr Architect! Have you forgotten already? You designed the shoes yourself!' 'Indeed', thundered the architect, 'but for the bedroom. Here you are completely ruining the mood with those two impossible splashes of color. Can't you see that?'" Loos' delightful polemic against

interior design, against the total work of art, ends with the question: " ... and how does one die in such rooms?"
Loos, who was born in Brno, was one of the many major Viennese architects and personalities who originated from Bohemia and Moravia, including Olbrich from Troppau, Hoffmann from Pirnitz, and Kafka, Mahler, and Meyrink. The Austro-Hungarian Empire, a melting pot of peoples, was thus also a breeding ground for genius. Loos, the son of a stonemason, completed his architectural training at technical colleges before leaving Europe for two years to discover America. There he worked various jobs – including washing dishes – before returning to Vienna in 1896 to dedicate himself whole heartedly to architecture. Initially linked to the Secession, Loos soon angered the association with his essay on *Die Potemkin'sche Stadt* (The Potemkin City), which appeared in *Ver Sacrum* in 1898. A break with its leading architects was inevitable. Loos' "smooth architecture"

Page 359:
Egon Schiele
Otto Wagner, 1910
Pencil, watercolor, opaque white,
42.5 x 26 cm
Historiches Museum der Stadt
Wien
"In the face of Otto Wagner's
genius, however, I strike my sails" –
thus the words of that ever-
belligerent "architectural
revolutionary" Adolf Loos (see note
26). There could be no better
summary of Wagner's outstanding
personality. The teacher of
Hoffmann, Olbrich, Loos, and
Antonio Sant'Elia laid the
"foundation stone" of modern
architecture.

(ill. p. 355) led him more and more into isolation, and he was worn down, too, by the constant battle against public opinion. Increasing deafness would ultimately make him a complete outsider. Disillusioned, in 1923 he moved to France, where he exerted a profound influence upon modern French architecture, and above all upon Le Corbusier. In 1931 Bauhaus founder Walter Gropius said of the pugnacious Viennese architect: "Adolf Loos is a prophet". But as is so often the case, the prophet was without honor in his own land.

The liberation of beauty from ornament

Yet even Adolf Loos, the most audacious spirit in architecture, was a child of his time. Under the art that was to be rejected he understood the art of ornament. Beauty and harmony nevertheless remained law. He deprived ornament of its rights and replaced it with costly materials. At the end of the day, the concept of the *Raumplan* (plan of volumes) which he developed was also interior design (ill. p. 357). Loos took the ideas of the English, Belgians, French, Germans, and Americans, and those of Gaudí too, combined them with a new concept of living and expanded upon them. His first private house, the Villa Karma on Lake Geneva, was designed for the Swiss neurologist Theodor Beer. Loos took the existing house, thoroughly revamped and reorganized it, and lent it classical proportions. The arrangement of its stairways already looks forward to the free volumes of his famous *Raumplan* concept (ill. p. 355).

The Michaeler House, built in 1909–11, signified an attack by austerity on ornamental Viennese architecture (ill. p. 356). The commercial block was undoubtedly planned as an affront. The utter rejection which confronted Loos and his "classicism" was too much even for the uncompromising fighter, however, and he fell seriously ill. The most trenchant observation on the Michaeler House stems from none other than Otto Wagner: "We have refrained from going to the defense of the work under attack in public, since we too do not consider it altogether faultless. But there is one thing that I can say: more artistic blood flows through the veins of its architect than through those of the architect of many a palais which has been left in peace because it has absolutely nothing to say."[39]

That our turbulent second half of the nineteenth century should seek an expression, a form for its own unique understanding of art, is understandable. But events unfolded faster than art. It was only natural, therefore, that "art", in its haste to catch up with what it had missed, proceeded to seek and – so it believed – find the Grail everywhere, and that so many "artists", upon tapping into the vein of a past style, cried "Eureka" and sought and found enthusiastic followers of the camp they represented. The way that we have raced through every stylistic tendency over the past few decades has been the result of this trend ... Although it satisfied the large majority in the short term, while its products still recalled the good old works of the past, this artistic hangover could not last, since the "works of art" thus created revealed themselves as merely the fruits of archeological studies and lacked any creative value of their own.
THE TASK OF ART, INCLUDING MODERN ART, REMAINS THE SAME AS IT HAS ALWAYS BEEN, HOWEVER. THE ART OF OUR AGE MUST OFFER US MODERN FORMS CREATED BY OURSELVES AND APPROPRIATE TO OUR ABILITIES, TO WHAT WE DO AND DON'T DO ...
Our dress, our fashions are dictated and approved by the public at large, and in this regard rule out even a hint of error. Hence the disharmony is not to be sought here, but must lie by its very nature in the works of contemporary art.
And indeed, this is the case.
THINGS WHICH HAVE SPRUNG UP OUT OF MODERN ATTITUDES (whereby we mean, of course, only those which have actually ripened into artistic form) ACCORD PERFECTLY WITH OUR MODERN DAY; COPIES AND IMITATIONS OF EARLIER WORKS, NEVER.
A man in a modern railroad car, for example, will go very well with the station hall, the sleeping car, and indeed all our vehicles. But what would be our reaction if, for example, we saw a figure in Louis XV dress riding a bicycle?
Otto Wagner, *Die Baukunst unserer Zeit – Dem Baukunstjünger ein Führer auf diesem Kunstgebiete*, 4th edition, Vienna, 1914

The total work of art accomplished
The Wiener Werkstätte

Josef Hoffmann
Geometric design, ca. 1905
Pencil, ink, 29.5 x 21 cm
The early phase of Hoffmann's oeuvre might be called a "homage to the square"; the square dominated the first years of his career and earned him the nickname of "Quadratl-Hoffmann" (Little Square Hoffmann).

A white square on white squares, only alternating with black ones in the floor. Black is also white; it is simply the darkest shade of white, just as white is the lightest shade of black ... There is no sweetness about this white room. Snow is not sweet, either. Snow is bracing and cold, but rubbing yourself with it will make you warm.
(In the words of a snob)
Ludwig Hevesi[1]

Art and patronage

Josef Hoffmann, the same age as Adolf Loos and friends with Joseph Maria Olbrich, was indebted in his early work to the Secession style and to a luxuriantly curving, dynamic line, before switching almost radically to the square and to black and white. Alongside architecture, his gift for formal invention expressed itself above all in his designs for handicrafts and exhibition interiors and buildings. In view of these artistic talents, he was somehow destined to become the head of an enterprise such as the Wiener Werkstätte (Vienna Workshops), which specialized in the "total work of art" like no other Art Nouveau or Jugendstil group of artists. Like the poet and playwright Hugo von Hofmannsthal, Hoffmann too was driven by the desire to fuse the seemingly irreconcilable elements of his age into one. According to Hofmannsthal, the poet must "absorb within himself a wholly irrational degree of the unhomogeneous, ... which can become a torment to him ... [must] uncover the world of relationships between the fragmentary elements, the hidden forms through which the different parts of life are interlinked."[2] Like a figure from the Baroque era, Hofmannsthal called for a multi-lingual reality. Hoffmann's concept of the totality and harmony of divergent parts, an intellectual

cult of beauty, is also part of the legacy of the Baroque. He was the architect of the aristocratic upper middle classes, but also the architect of whom his pupil Josef Frank (b. 1889) wrote, on the occasion of his teacher's 60th birthday: "What modern architecture owes to Hoffmann is not just the fact that he turned away from historical ... forms ... but also that he simultaneously reclaimed the lightness and transparency which today appear to us as its most important characteristics."[3]

In the spring of 1905 a storm broke out within the Secession. Its cause was essentially trivial, but it brought into the open conflicts which had been smoldering beneath the surface for a while. Klimt, Hoffmann, Moser and a further eighteen of the prominent and dominant members of the Secession left the association. "The enormous stature of Klimt and the artists of the Wiener Werkstätte inevitably led to their dominating the Secession. The result was jealousy and consequently discontent."[4] For all that he regretted the split in the highly successful Secession, Hevesi observed perceptively: "Once again the Viennese won't go under, because that is one of the few things for which they have no talent ... "[5] Neither Vienna nor the Viennese artists went under; on the contrary, through the Wiener Werkstätte, its architectural achievements and its handicraft products, Vienna ultimately rose to international fame as a center of the new art. On May 19 1903 the firm "Wiener Werkstätte, Productivgenossenschaft von Kunsthandwerkern in registrierter Genossenschaft mit unbeschränkter Haftung" (Vienna Workshops, manufacturing cooperative of artist craftsmen in Vienna, cooperative with unlimited liability) was incorporated in the Vienna Trade Register. Its directors were Josef Hoffmann

Koloman Moser (attributed)
Plant stand, 1903
Painted beech, painted sheet iron,
92 x 40 cm
Moser effectively developed his plant stand out of the facade of the Purkersdorf Sanatorium: in its composition of sheet-iron boxes with black-and-white chequered sides, held by vertical beech supports rising from the cross-struts and frame of the square base, Moser's plant stand duplicates the chequered pattern of the tiling found on the outside of the building – furniture as architecture once more.

and Koloman Moser, both professors at the School of Arts and Crafts in Vienna, and its treasurer Fritz Waerndorfer, the Viennese manufacturer. In the figure of Waerndorfer we meet another of the generous patrons of art without whose help Art Nouveau, and in this case Jugendstil, could never have reached ultimate fruition. Waerndorfer's business activities – the young banker's son was a textiles buyer – frequently took him to England. In London he came into contact with the Aesthetic Movement and was introduced to the workshops founded as part of the Arts and Crafts Movement. He was impressed most profoundly of all, however, by the works of the Glasgow artists, which he encountered for the first time at their moderately successful show in London. Filled with curiosity, in 1900 Waerndorfer traveled to Glasgow and made the acquaintance of the Mackintoshes, whom he invited to take part in the Eighth

Secession Exhibition. The refined charm of the simple Scottish designs made an enduring impact in Vienna, and the 1902 issue no. 23 of *Ver Sacrum* was entirely devoted to the Glasgow School. That same year, Mackintosh designed a music salon for Waerndorfer, "the habitation of the souls of the six princesses" in the words of the Belgian poet Maurice Maeterlinck. "Hoffmann has undoubtedly received much fruitful inspiration from British and Scottish interior designers, who have already staged numerous successful exhibitions in Vienna. The brilliant Scottish artist Charles Rennie Mackintosh in particular has surely opened up many new and far-reaching possibilities for the younger Viennese."[6]

Waerndorfer – not an active artist himself, although indubitably artistic in nature – put up the entire capital for the Wiener Werkstätte, firmly convinced of the important contribution it had to make. In his memoirs, Leopold Wolfgang

Josef Hoffmann
Two elliptical vases with loop handles, 1906
Silver-colored metal, glass inserts, 25 cm high
Within the vast spectrum of materials employed by the Wiener Werkstätte – ranging from fabric to reinforced concrete – precious metals occupied a special place. Unlike Wiener Werkstätte ceramics and glassware, which were not produced in-house but were manufactured in other factories to designs by Wiener Werkstätte artists, the works in silver and metal were executed by the artists themselves. They lend convincing form to the Wiener Werkstätte's functional aesthetic.

Josef Hoffmann
Serving spoon, ca. 1905
Chased silver, mother-of-pearl,
moonstone, turquoise, coral, small
blue and black stones, 21 cm long
Made by Anton Pribil
"We start from the purpose in hand,
usefulness is our first requirement,
and our strength has to lie in good
proportions and materials well
handled. We will seek to decorate,
but without any compulsion to do
so, and certainly not at any cost.
We use many semi-precious stones,
especially in jewelry – they make up
in beauty of color and infinite variety
what they lack in intrinsic value by
comparison with diamonds. We love
silver for its sheen and gold for its
glitter. In artistic terms, we consider
copper to be just as valuable as
precious metals."
(Josef Hoffmann, Wiener
Werkstätte Work Program,
see note 9)

Josef Hoffmann
Clock, ca. 1904
Patinated copper, Alpaca
(nickel silver alloy),
hammered, 21 cm high
Made by Carl Kallert

Ludwig Heinrich Jungnickel
Wine glass, "Monkey frieze" decor,
ca. 1911
Frosted glass, black broncit,
18.6 cm high
Wiener Glasmuseum, Lobmeyr
Collection
In his frosted glasses with their black
broncit decor, Jungnickel combines
striking designs with original,
fairytale-like motifs.

Rochowanski[7] describes how, at a meeting in the Café Heinrich, the artists dissatisfied with the Secession obtained from Waerndorfer, without further ado, the 500 crowns they needed to start something new. A few days later the money was all gone, and the exhibition room in which they had already installed their works could not be used. So Waerndorfer approached his wealthy mother and subsequently placed 50,000 crowns at the artists' disposal. Above and beyond his permanent willingness to assist the Wiener Werkstätte, Waerndorfer maintained a lifelong friendship with Gustav Klimt, whom he accompanied on virtually all his trips abroad, since Klimt depended upon his skills as a linguist. The enthusiastic patron was not just a friend and sponsor, but also one of Klimt's and the Wiener Werkstätte's best customers. Depressingly, Waerndorfer's only reward for his exemplary support was to lose his entire fortune – a fate which also befell the industrialist Otto Primavesi. In 1914 Waerndorfer emigrated to America at the behest of his family. As a farmer, textile designer and painter, "Fred" Waerndorfer was homesick for Europe and was never happy in the New World, as his voluminous correspondence with his old friends reveals.

Although the Wiener Werkstätte started out as a commercial success, it – and with it, Waerndorfer – would ultimately founder financially on the conflict inherent in Jugendstil, whose ideology swung like a pendulum between aesthetic exclusivity and the demand that art should be the property of all. Thus the first issue of *Ver Sacrum* proclaimed its creed in 1898 – "We know no distinction between 'fine art' and 'handicraft', between art for the rich and art for the poor. Art is common property."[8] But even if the old distinctions were now erased in theory, in practice the masterly objects crafted by the Wiener Werkstätte remained expensive, the cheaper products of the Secession affordable but mass-produced.

The inspired *métier* of the artist craftsman

We are in no position to chase after daydreams. We stand with both feet firmly planted in reality and need tasks to carry out.
Josef Hoffmann[9]

In the periodical *Deutsche Kunst und Dekoration* (German Art and Decoration) of 1904/5, Josef August Lux (1871–1947) offered a lengthy description of the young Viennese firm: "An arts and crafts enterprise in the grand style has quietly taken shape in Vienna under the direction of its founders Professor Josef Hoffmann, Professor Koloman Moser and Fritz Waerndorfer. This consortium of artist-craftsmen has set up shop in a spacious new building in Neustiftgasse; the 'Wiener Werkstätte' is amply housed on three floors, with its own workshops for metalwork, gold and silverwork, bookbinding, leather, cabinet-making, and varnishing, as well as its own machine rooms, architectural offices, design rooms, and showroom. Here, in the midst of factory noise, artist-craftsmen pursue their quieter, inspired manual labors. For machinery is by no means absent; on the contrary, the 'Wiener Werkstätte' is fully equipped with all the technical innovations facilitating the production process. Here, however, the machine is not a ruler and a tyrant, but a willing servant and assistant. Thus products bear the stamp not of machine manufacture, but of the spirit of their artistic creators and the skill of practised hands. The characteristic principle of the Werkstätte, and one that must be instilled into every craftsman if he is to achieve the most perfect result possible, is that it is better to work for ten days on one item than to produce ten items in one day. Every object thus embodies the maximum of technical and artistic ability, and its artistic worth resides where it is so rarely found and where it should in truth be sought – not in decorative externals or formal trimmings, but in the seriousness and dignity of mental and manual labor. Every object carries the imprint of both: it is not only designed by the artist, but bears the mark of the maker, the craftsman, the worker who alone manufactured it. This is a further aspect of the socio-political insight of the founders, who aim, through these

and other measures, to increase and reinforce their craftsmen's sense of self-worth and the pleasure which they derive from their work. Raising the level of morale in this way has a beneficial effect upon performance. Other educational steps that have been taken include the banning of all bad language on Werkstätte premises, and on one occasion the dismissal of a member of the administrative staff who was foolish enough to utter a thoughtless remark to a worker.

Acting on the assumption that an intelligent worker would arrive with certain expectations as regards his workplace, the rooms have been furnished and equipped accordingly. Factory and workshop are words that usually prompt a slight shudder in civilized people, with their overtones of grime, unhappiness, and sad, faceless surroundings in which people work not for the love of it, but under the iron rod of financial necessity. Even though we may be told that the view of an industrial zone holds its own beauty, it remains all too true that the church spires of industry – as the towering stacks are sarcastically called – have never yet touched anyone's heart but that of the industrialist who calculates his profits according to the height of his chimneys. Upon entering the 'Wiener Werkstätte', however, one is pleasantly surprised to discover that the workshops are all optimally furnished even from an aesthetic point of view, and provide a happy

Eduard Klablena
Parrots, ca. 1911–12
Stoneware, underglaze painting, overglaze details, each approx. 10.6 high, approx. 27.5 cm long
Made by Langenzersdorfer Keramik

Josef Hoffmann
Purkersdorf Sanatorium,
east facade, perspective drawing,
1904
Ink, graphite
Galerie Metropol, Vienna
In 1904 Viktor Zuckerkandl,
brother-in-law of Wiener Werkstätte
admirer Berta Zuckerkandl,
commissioned Josef Hoffmann and
his colleagues to design a new
building for his Westend
Sanatorium in Purkersdorf near
Vienna. The building, the first major
commission for the Wiener
Werkstätte, has gone down in
architectural history as the
Purkersdorf Sanatorium. A close
relationship is established between
exterior and interior space through
the recurrent use of line, cube, and
plane as aesthetic statement both
within and without. This
relationship is reinforced by a
generous use of glass and transparent
partitions, a second theme running
through both the inside and the
outside of the Sanatorium.

setting for creative activity. Their striking beauty derives from the underlying principle of hygiene, whose case is argued with light, cleanliness, and fresh air. Walls and wood are painted white, iron is painted blue or red. The workshops are each dominated by one particular color, which is also employed for their respective entry books to avoid any confusion. It is easy to imagine that, for some of those on the long list of employees, the whole thing was so new that they felt quite intimidated to start with; none of them, certainly, had ever worked in such superb conditions. The first step was to accustom them to this sound and healthy working environment – not always an easy task, as in the case of teaching people to use the washbasins in the hygienic WCs, for example. Social concerns cease to exist in this enterprise; the 'Wiener Werkstätte' today boasts an elite of artist-craftsmen who feel a sense of solidarity with the firm and are fired by the praiseworthy ambition to do their best in their specialist field. The showroom, which one enters first, offers an overview of the whole. White is the dominant color. Fitted glass cabinets contain numerous art objects made of precious metal, wood, leather, glass and precious stones, together with jewelry and objects of everyday use, all strictly practical in design and honoring the nature of the materials employed ..."[10] (ill. p. 363). Lux's contemporary description, quoted here at length, is both informative and perceptive. In founding their workshops, Hoffmann

and Moser drew inspiration from William Morris and John Ruskin, as well as from Charles Robert Ashbee's Guild and School of Handicraft. As a "late flowering" of Jugendstil, the Wiener Werkstätte was able to fulfill both the social and artistic conditions stipulated decades earlier in England, but at the same time point to the future in its sensible integration of the machine into its working processes. Other factors that still seem "modern" today include the "people-centered" and "environmentally friendly" working environment, the use of a "logo" (ill. opposite page) and the encouragement of a "corporate identity" within each workshop, reflected in the use of a color-coding system. As the large number of workshops listed by Lux suggests, the Wiener Werkstätte also answered Henry van de Velde's call for a "synthesis of the arts". Art Nouveau was concerned at all times and in all places with "a true union of art and life". Figuratively speaking, the barriers between art and life were being broken down, inviting everyone and everything to begin a life in beauty. Architects addressing questions of purpose, use and practical demands thereby insisted upon hygiene and suitability, tested materials against requirements, and limited the range of materials employed so as to remain unostentatious and avoid wastage. But however rigorous the emphasis upon practicality in theory, in practice it was nevertheless subservient to the overall concept of homogeneous beauty. Thus the Wiener Werkstätte, too, stood at the disposal

Otto Prutscher
Plant stand, ca. 1905
Wood, painted white, zinc container,
88 cm high, 49.5 cm diameter

of "the swinish luxury of the rich" so despised by Morris. In this *casus belli*, the Wiener Werkstätte – like its English forebear – was denied the satisfaction of using beauty to tear down class barriers. The Wiener Werkstätte nevertheless crossed borders effortlessly: following international acclaim, it opened offices not just in Germany and Switzerland, but also in the USA, and there was not an international exhibition at which the Viennese did not steal the limelight.

Josef Hoffmann and Koloman Moser – Purkersdorf Sanatorium

Hoffmann never attempts to create the illusion of an organism where such a one does not already exist in itself. Julius Baum[11]

The Wiener Werkstätte achieved the fusion of hygiene, serviceability, and simplicity into a single "work of art" at the first attempt. In 1904 Viktor Zuckerkandl, brother-in-law of Wiener Werkstätte admirer Berta Zuckerkandl, commissioned Josef Hoffmann and his colleagues to design a new building for his Westend Sanatorium in Punkersdorf near Vienna. The building, the first major commission for the Wiener Werkstätte, has gone down in architectural history as the Purkersdorf Sanatorium. A close relationship is established between exterior and interior space through the recurrent use of line, cube, and plane as aesthetic statement both within and without. This relationship is reinforced by a generous use of glass and transparent partitions, a second theme running through both the inside and the outside of the Sanatorium (ill. opposite page). To complement the Sanatorium's rigorously cubist exterior, Koloman Moser designed furniture for the entrance hall, whose matt-varnished lathwork, in its geometric and down-to-earth austerity, reflects the structure of the whole house (ill. right).

The early phase of Hoffmann's oeuvre might be called a "homage to the square"; the square dominated the first years of his career and earned him the nickname of "Quadratl-Hoffmann" (Little Square Hoffmann) (ill. p. 360). His interiors for the Purkersdorf Sanatorium – like the other objects he designed during the same period, 1904–06 – still read as a textbook of early Wiener Werkstätte design even today.

The decorative principle of the cube employed in designs by Jutta Sika (1877–1964) (ill. opposite page), Otto Prutscher (ill. p. 366), Moser and Hoffmann turns our conventions of seeing upside down. In place of fanciful ornamental creations, decoration now consists of simple lines drawn

Wiener Werkstätte registered trademark, from the Work Program, 1905
Aspects of the Wiener Werkstätte that still seem "modern" today include its "people-centered" and "environmentally friendly" working environment, the use of a "logo" and the encouragement of a "corporate identity" within each workshop, reflected in the use of a color-coding system.

Koloman Moser (attributed)
Wardrobe, ca. 1903–05
Wood, painted white with rectangular decor, 190 cm high

Koloman Moser
Armchair for the Purkersdorf Sanatorium, 1903
Painted beech, painted cane seat, 72 x 66.5 x 66 cm
Made by Prag Rudniker
To complement the Sanatorium's rigorously cubist exterior, Moser – keeping the ideal of the total work of art always in his mind – designed furniture for the entrance hall, whose matt-varnished lathwork, in its geometric and down-to-earth austerity, reflects the structure of the whole house.

Jutta Sika
Vase, 1905
Opaque, bright red flashing over
colorless glass, three colorless
spherical feet, etched geometric
decor, 21.6 cm high
Made by Loetz' Witwe,
Klostermühle, Bohemia in 1905 for
E. Bakalowits & Söhne, Vienna
Torsten Bröhan Collection
The decorative principle of the cube
employed in designs by Jutta Sika,
Otto Prutscher, Moser and
Hoffmann turns our conventions of
seeing upside down. In place of
fanciful ornamental creations,
decoration now consists of simple
lines drawn with a ruler.

with a ruler. This linear structure cannot be summarized (and thereby simplified) as plain linearism, however. What we read as a single plane suddenly tranforms itself into a representation of several planes. Objects composed of straight lines initially present themselves to the viewer as homogeneous. The conflict between two-dimensional plane and three-dimensional space dramatically activates the viewer's attention. We undergo an experience which runs counter to our desire to fix a form. Here Hoffmann is concerned not with geometry alone, but with the artistic tension created by formal means reduced to their absolute essentials. The elongated grid structure of the Sanatorium with its flat roof (ill. p. 366) – most avant-garde for its day – is taken up in smaller-scale designs for household objects and furnishings. Thus the grid of the windows in the Sanatorium facade is elaborated in planters, tables and étagères. In one example, Koloman Moser effectively develops a plant stand out of the facade (ill. p. 361): in its composition of sheet-iron boxes with black-and-white checkered sides, held by vertical beech supports rising from the cross-struts and frame of the square base, Moser's plant stand duplicates the checkered pattern of the tiling found on the outside of the building – furniture as architecture once more. "It seems rather a pity that, in order to enjoy one of the wonderful white Purkersdorf cubicles, you have to be of somewhat unsound mind."[12]

Jutta Sika, Koloman Moser, Jutta Sika, Josef Hoffmann
Four jugs, ca. 1901–05
Porcelain, underglaze painting, 16.8 cm to 18.5 cm high
"… the services by Koloman Moser, Jutta Sika and Therese Trethahn, produced around 1900, were thereafter to be seen in *Das Interieur*, *The Studio* and other specialist magazines. With their highly individual, original forms, and decorative designs, they became 'classic' examples of their kind, inimitable in their simplicity and clarity." (Waltraud Neuwirth, see note 15)

"Ornamental madness" – Colored squares

And then there is Hoffmann, the man who is never ruffled by anything … I think he would have made an excellent surgeon. One look at Kolo Moser's face would be enough to reassure even the most fainthearted. If Hoffmann is calm, and Klimt confident of his strength, Moser is impish.
Ludwig Hevesi[13]

Presented with the exceedingly "total" nature of the Wiener Werkstätte's total works of art – even the fresh flower arrangements supplied to the Purkersdorf Sanatorium came under the "artistic direction" of the Wiener Werkstätte – satirical voices in Vienna were quick to be heard. In 1906 the Wiener Werkstätte staged an exhibition entitled "The Laid Table" (*Der gedeckte Tisch*), for which the creative genius Koloman Moser even designed specially shaped pastries – although it was with some difficulty that he found a baker who could actually make them. "The geometric element guides both of our artistic table-layers [Hoffmann and Moser] in their creations, and the new grace at mealtimes will surely have to be: 'Bless these lines which we are about to receive' … Two parallel strands of macaroni can only be bisected in infinite space … for which a theoretical grounding and practical tutorials are first necessary … To carve the beef with stylistic correctness, you need a ruler and dividers; the dumplings are hand-turned by a craftsman, and the only stylistically pure black-and-white

Josef Hoffmann
Brooch, ca. 1905
Silver, malachite, lapis lazuli, moonstone cabuchons, coral, 4.5 x 4.5 cm
"For whenever a new style makes its appearance, it is in architecture that its first indications are to be seen" – the hypothesis put forward by *The Studio* (see note 16) is particularly true of the Wiener Werkstätte's "architectural jewelry". Hoffmann's designs for jewelry, employing precise squares, circles, borders, symmetrical patterns of stylized leaves and standardized flower motifs, reveal the hand of the architect.

Josef Hoffmann
Tumbler from the "Var. B" set of
glasses, ca. 1910
Frosted glass, broncit decor,
10.4 cm high
Made via J. & J. Lobmeyr, Vienna
Wiener Glasmuseum,
Lobmeyr Collection

desserts are the poppy-seed puddings improved by Koloman Moser ... . here madness marries geometry."[14]

But if madness married geometry, so too did color, as illustrated by the beautiful flashed and cut glasses by Otto Prutscher (1880–1949), with their typical faceted and windowed stems (ill. above). Making bold use of contrast, the sparkling colors of these glasses embrace the whole spectrum from violet to turquoise, dissolved into checkerboard patterns and "little squares". The black-and-white decor so characteristic of the Wiener Werkstätte also found its way into glass, however (ill. left). In the broncit glassware by the Lobmeyr company, it was nevertheless "reconciled" with floral ornament; thus a delicate, vegetal decor flowers within a geometric framework out of the broncit coating which offered the artists of the Wiener Werkstätte a perfect vehicle for their design aesthetic (ill. opposite page). Up until 1910 the Wiener Werkstätte's glassware was "published" by Bakalowits & Söhne, after which Lobmeyr took over the leading role. Designs by the "disciples

Josef Hoffmann
Jardinière, 1914–15
Frosted glass, broncit decor,
9.3 cm high, 22.1 cm long
Made via J. & J. Lobmeyr, Vienna
To create the broncit decor, the glass
was first coated with a layer of
bronzite, the decorative design then
painted over the top in a protective
varnish, and the remainder of the
bronzite etched away.

Mela Köhler
Fashion designs; three Wiener
Werkstätte postcards, ca. 1907
The Wiener Werkstätte succeeded in
permeating every sphere of life by
artistic means. Dining tables, flower
arrangements and even fashion – as
with van de Velde, a statement of
reformist thinking – were all
integrated into an overall symmetry.

Koloman Moser,
Josef Hoffmann
Reception, Flöge fashion salon,
Mariahilferstrasse, Vienna, ca. 1903
Three young women from a well-to-
do middle-class background decided
to venture into business – an almost
revolutionary step around 1900. In
their fashion salon the Flöge sisters –
Emilie Flöge was Klimt's partner –
wanted to place modern dress in a
modern setting. The interior of the
salon's reception was designed by the
Wiener Werkstätte and conveyed to
customers, even before they had
bought anything, the "aesthetic
unison" of this progressive female
firm.

of the square" were also executed by Loetz'
Witze, however, and indeed by almost every
well-known glassworks in Austria (ill. p. 368).
The technical classes run by Hoffmann and
Moser at the Vienna School of Arts and Crafts
during the Secession years had already inspired
a "ceramics renaissance" (ill. p. 369). "… the
services by Koloman Moser, Jutta Sika and
Therese Trethahn, produced around 1900, were
thereafter to be seen in *Das Interieur*, *The Studio*
and other specialist magazines. With their highly
individual, original forms and decorative designs,
they became 'classic' examples of their kind,
inimitable in their simplicity and clarity."[15] Many
of the Austrian ceramic works focused on the
"re-birth" of stoneware, and there arose a wealth
of animated, stylistically assured works (ill. p. 365).
The Wiener Werkstätte succeeded in permeating every sphere of life by artistic means. Dining
tables, flower arrangements and even fashion –
as with van de Velde, a statement of reformist
thinking – were all integrated into an overall
symmetry (ill. p. 371). The flawlessness of its
architecture was taken up without a break in its

Josef von Divéky
Bar, Cabaret Fledermaus,
Kärtnerstrasse 33, Vienna, 1907
Wiener Werkstätte Postcard No. 75
Architect: Josef Hoffmann
Interior design: Wiener Werkstätte
Rupertinum – Salzburger
Landessammlungen, Salzburg
"In 1907 Fritz Waerndorfer, a
sophisticated gentleman with a great
deal of money and taste – two things
which, as everyone knows, almost
never go together –, decided to
commission the Wiener Werkstätte
to build a cabaret. Both the
colorfully tiled bar and the black-and-
white auditorium were jewels of
intimacy and noblesse." (Egon
Friedell, see note 17)

interiors and utensils. Its best results were always those where client and artist shared a similar vision, as in the case of the Flöge fashion salon, founded by three young women from a well-to-do middle-class background who decided to venture into business – an almost revolutionary step around 1900. In their fashion salon the Flöge sisters – Emilie Flöge was Klimt's partner – wanted to place modern dress in a modern setting. The interior of the salon's reception was designed by the Wiener Werkstätte and conveyed to customers, even before they had bought anything, the "aesthetic unison" of this progressive female firm. Hoffman was considerably influenced by Japanese art and this was particularly evident in the Flöge fashion salon. The

simple, Eastern flavour of the interior and the emphatically two-dimensional decor combined to make the room a perfect foil for its "three-dimensional" subject: the formal inventions of *couture* (ill. p. 371).

Within the vast spectrum of materials employed by the Wiener Wienerstätte – ranging from fabric to reinforced concrete – precious metals occupied a special place. Unlike Wiener Werkstätte ceramics and glassware, which were not produced in-house but were manufactured in other factories to designs by Wiener Werkstätte artists, the works in silver and metal were executed by the artists themselves. They lend convincing form to the Wiener Werkstätte's functional aesthetic (ills. pp. 362, 363, 364). The

Josef Hoffmann
Coffeehouse chair, ca. 1906
Painted bentwood, leather
upholstery, 74 cm high
Made by Jacob & Josef Kohn,
Vienna

same may be said of the Wiener Werkstätte's "architectural jewelry"– proof of the irrefutability of the hypothesis: "For whenever a new style makes its appearance, it is in architecture that its first indications are to be seen."[16] Hoffmann's designs for jewelry, employing precise squares, circles, borders, symmetrical patterns of stylized leaves, and standardized flower motifs, reveal the hand of the architect (ill. p. 369).

Cabaret Fledermaus – A "miracle of design"

"In 1907 Fritz Waerndorfer, a sophisticated gentleman with a great deal of money and taste – two things which, as everyone knows, almost never go together – decided to commission the Wiener Werkstätte to build a cabaret. Both the colorfully tiled bar and the black-and-white auditorium were jewels of intimacy and noblesse."[17] The "miracle of design" that was the Cabaret Fledermaus was executed "unimpeded by the interferings of a patron"[18] (ill. opposite page, left). Alongside furniture designers (ill. opposite page, right), ceramic artists, silversmiths, and designers for its lighting, tableware, and table decorations, the Cabaret Fledermaus offered graphic designers in particular a wide range of activities: posters, tickets, menus, programs, postcards, and even specially designed name-badges for the staff. The "imaginative stroke of decorative originality"[19] – as Hevesi described the colorful mosaic of majolica tiles cladding the Cabaret Fledermaus walls – is found condensed in Michael Powolny's *putti* with their Klimtesque cascades of fruits and flowers, which – executed in both black-and-white and colored versions – testify to the harmonious juxtaposition within the Cabaret Fledermaus of contradictory "design persuasions" (ill. p. 373). "From these rooms, imbued with an artistic sophistication of the highest degree, one can see how much is now possible in Vienna … [Here is] a confident, dignified, honest, almost chaste unfolding of

Michael Powolny
"Spring" (right) and "Autumn" *putti*, ca. 1907
Porcelain, colored underglaze painting; "Spring": 36 cm high; "Autumn": 38 cm high
The "imaginative stroke of decorative originality" – as Hevesi (see note 19) described the colorful mosaic of majolica tiles cladding the Cabaret Fledermaus walls – is found condensed in Michael Powolny's putti with their Klimtesque cascades of fruits and flowers, which – executed in both black-and-white and colored versions – testify to the harmonious juxtaposition within the Cabaret Fledermaus of contradictory "design persuasions".

Josef Hoffmann
Palais Stoclet, view of the street facade from the northwest, Brussels, 1905–11

The Palais Stoclet in Brussels is universal, complete, flawless, encyclopedic – a masterpiece of a thousand years of architectural history. From 1905–11, in the city of Victor Horta, Henry van de Velde and Paul Hankar, Hoffmann, Klimt and the Wiener Werkstätte crowned the entire Art Nouveau movement with their total work of art. The Utopia of Jugendstil is made reality in the Palais Stoclet. From the cutlery to the gardens, from the facade to the bathroom, coordination and harmony govern every facet of this artistic gem.

splendor, the harmony and power of the chromatic idiom, melodious design crystallized out of the purpose in hand,"[20] enthused Berta Zuckerkandl. Karl Kraus couldn't resist a reply: "There was a long debate about whether [the hygienic needs of the audience] would be better served by using the paper on which the art reviews of Ms Zuckerkandl were printed, or by a special dress for the lavatory lady which Professor Hoffmann was to design. In the end, however, it was agreed that the cistern was to be painted white and the beloved checkerboard pattern imprinted upon it."[21] The retort from Oskar Kokoschka: "Kraus has bitten the Fledermaus lavatory attendant in the leg because she's not wearing clothes from the Hoffmann collection."[22]

Palais Stoclet – *The* total work of art

And this is what our age owes to Josef Hoffmann: the universality of his artistic genius.
Peter Behrens[23]

The Palais Stoclet in Brussels is universal, complete, flawless, encyclopedic – a masterpiece of a thousand years of architectural history. From 1905–11, in the city of Victor Horta, Henry van de Velde and Paul Hankar, Hoffmann, Klimt and the Wiener Werkstätte crowned the entire Art Nouveau movement with their total work of art. The Utopia of Jugendstil is made reality in the Palais Stoclet (ill. below). From the cutlery to the gardens, from the facade to the bathroom, coordination and harmony govern every facet of this artistic gem.

Josef Hoffmann
Tower and figural group, Palais
Stoclet, Brussels, 1905–11
The "sculpture tower" points to the
symbiosis of all the arts – a theme
taken up again in the interior, where
the rooms form a sequence of
contrasting compositions.

Gustav Klimt
Fulfillment, cartoon for the Stoclet
Frieze in the dining room of the
Palais Stoclet, Brussels, ca.
1905–09
Watercolor, gouache, paper on
wood, 192 x 118 cm
Musée des Beaux-Arts – Palais
Rohan, Strasbourg
"Klimt's influence upon the Wiener
Werkstätte was palpable, as *vice
versa* was its influence upon the
middle phase of Klimt's oeuvre.
The common ground they shared
assumed its most beautiful
expression in the frescoes which
Klimt designed for the exhibition of
Klinger's 'Beethoven', and in his
wall frieze for the dining-room in the
Palais Stoclet in Brussels, that
monument to a Viennese cultural
epoch." (Carl Moll, see note 26).
Uncompromising in their decorative
two-dimensionality, Klimt's wall
mosaics are simultaneously a step
towards abstraction.

Josef Hoffmann
Dining room, Palais Stoclet,
Brussels, ca. 1905–11
Mosaics by Gustav Klimt, silver
tableware by Josef Hoffmann
The dining room may be seen as
typical of the interior design of the
Palais Stoclet as a whole. The
severity of the room, with its lavish
materials of different colored
marbles, precious woods and gold-
embossed leather, is echoed in the
silverware designed by Hoffmann.
At the same time, it finds both its
contrast and its completion in the
mosaics by Klimt adorning the
walls.

Adolphe Stoclet was the archetypal art patron of
the turn of the century: cosmopolitan, educated,
wealthy, and dedicated to the furtherance of the
arts, his relationship with the Wiener Werkstätte
architects was highly congenial. "His black beard
shot with silver, his manner – charming, with just a
hint of pomposity – and his distinguished appearance lent him a remarkable affinity in style with the
objects [of archaic and overseas art] in his collection, with which he seemed to have an almost
natural rapport. Indeed, the polished marble surfaces in the large entrance hall matched him just as
well as they matched his carvings … He was completely at home in such monumental company."[24]
The preciousness of its materials – marble,
bands of gilt metal – and its seductive air of

nobility rob the building of none of its modernity:
"The Palais Stoclet, now world-famous, belongs
equally to the history of 20th-century art as to the
history of 20th-century architecture."[25] Propor-
tioning and rhythm, skilful deployment of natural
and artifical light, color and surface treatment,
even iconographic characterization are the consistent hallmarks of the overall design.

The house is integrated into its surroundings in
exemplary fashion. Reflections of linear beauty
are mirrored in the waters of the artificial pond,
"organically" duplicating the elegant animation
of the architectural masses. The "sculpture
tower" points to the symbiosis of all the arts (ill.
p. 375) – a theme reiterated in the interior of the
Palais Stoclet, where the rooms form a sequence

Page 379:
Josef Urban
Design for the facade of the Max
Reinhardt Theatre, 50th and 51st
Street, New York, 1929
Watercolor, ink, 37.5 x 28.6 cm
Joseph Urban Archives, Rare Book
and Manuscript Library, Columbia
University, New York
The richly inventive architect Josef
Urban took the Wiener Werkstätte
style to America. In 1922 he put up
the capital for the foundation of the
Wiener Werkstätte of America, Inc.,
and designed the branch's showroom
on Fifth Avenue.

of contrasting compositions. The dining room (ill. p. 377) may be seen as typical of the whole: the severity of the room, with its lavish materials of different colored marbles, exclusive woods and gold-embossed leather, is echoed in the silverware designed by Hoffmann. At the same time, it finds both its contrast and its completion in the mosaics by Klimt adorning the walls (ill. p. 376). "Klimt's influence upon the Wiener Werkstätte was palpable, as *vice versa* was its influence upon the middle phase of Klimt's oeuvre. The common ground they shared assumed its most beautiful expression in the frescoes which Klimt designed for the exhibition of Klinger's 'Beethoven', and in his wall frieze for the dining room in the Palais Stoclet in Brussels, that monument to a Viennese cultural epoch."[26] Uncompromising in their decorative two-dimensionality, Klimt's wall mosaics are simultaneously a step towards abstraction. The 20th century is articulated throughout the Palais Stoclet with every clarity, even in its "secondary" rooms. The bathroom by Hoffmann is functional, the children's bedroom by Ludwig Jungnickel (1881–1965) "child-oriented" in the fairytale character of the animal frieze decorating the walls, a decorative scheme also taken up in other objects designed by the same artist (ill. p. 364).

Linearity, latticework, grid and "little square" would go on to conquer the New World, where Wiener Werkstätte member Josef Urban (1872–1933) translated the formal vocabulary of Hoffmann's early years into the architecture of the 1920s (ill. opposite page).

The immeasurable harm caused in the realm of arts and crafts by shoddy mass production on the one hand, and mindless imitation of old styles on the other, has swept through the entire world like a huge flood. We have lost touch with the culture of our forebears and are tossed about by a thousand contradictory whims and considerations. In most cases the machine has replaced the hand, and the businessman has taken the craftsman's place. It would be madness to swim against this current.

All this notwithstanding, we have founded our workshop. It exists to provide on native soil a point of repose amid the cheerful noise of craftsmanship at work, and to give comfort to all who accept the message of Ruskin and Morris. We make our appeal to all those who value culture in this sense, and we hope that even our inevitable mistakes will not deter our friends from promoting our ideas.

We wish to establish intimate contact between public, designer, and craftsman, and to produce good, simple domestic requisites. We start from the purpose in hand, usefulness is our first condition, and our strength has to lie in good proportions and materials well handled. We will seek to decorate, but without any compulsion to do so, and certainly not at any cost. We use many semiprecious stones, especially in jewelry – they make up in beauty of color and infinite variety what they lack in intrinsic value by comparison with diamonds. We love silver for its sheen and gold for its glitter. In artistic terms, we consider copper to be just as valuable as precious metals. We feel bound to admit that a silver ornament can be just as valuable as an object made of gold and precious stones. The worth of artistic work and of inspiration must be recognized and prized once again. The work of the artist craftsman is to be measured by the same yardstick as that of the painter and the sculptor ...

The substitutes provided by period reproductions are strictly for *parvenus*.

Josef Hoffmann, from the *Wiener Werkstätte Work Program*, Vienna 1905 (see note 9)

FACADE · OF · THE · PROPOSED · MAX · REINHARDT · THEATRE · IN · NEW · YORK · CITY

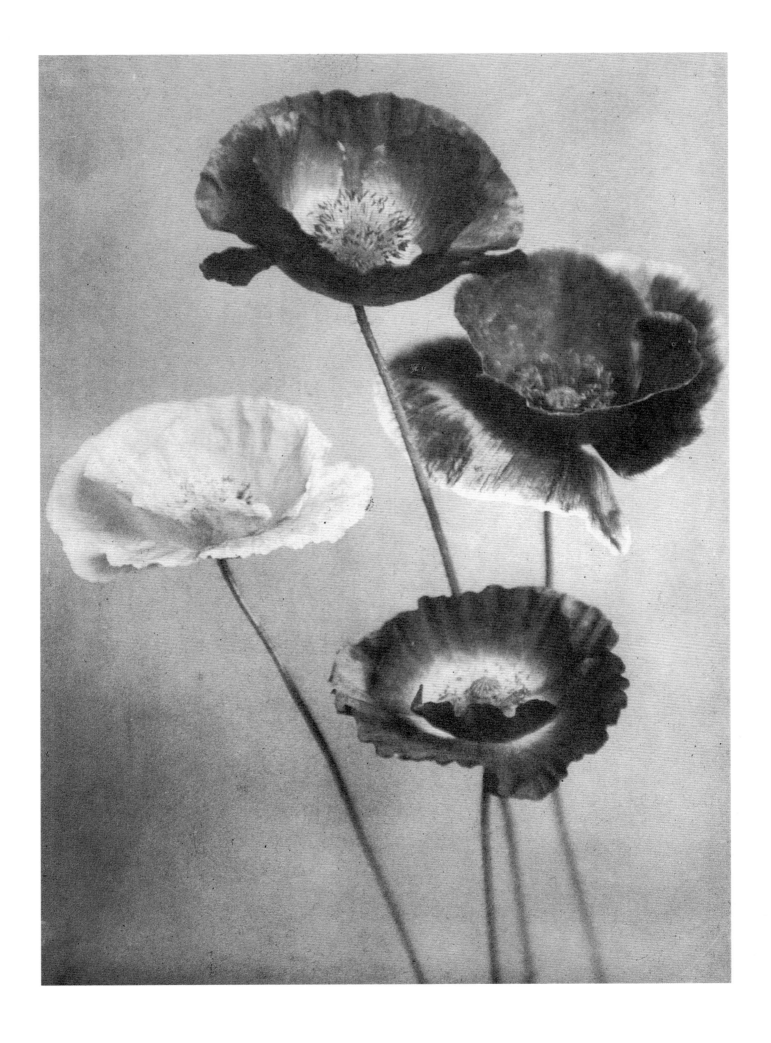

Bibliographic notes

Unless otherwise stated, all foreign language quotes have been rendered into English by the translators.

The final chord and a new beginning (p. 6–23)

1 Johann Wolfgang von Goethe, 1819. Quoted in *Maximen und Reflexionen*, Frankfurt/Main, 1840.
2 Erwin Panofsky. *Sinn und Deutung in der bildenden Kunst*. Cologne, 1975.
3 Dolf Sternberger. *Panorama des Jugendstils*. Quoted in *Ein Dokument Deutscher Kunst 1901–1976*, exhibition catalog, Vol. 1, Darmstadt, 1976.
4 Hans Sedymayr. *Die Revolution der modernen Kunst*. Cologne, 1985.
5 Quoted from Françoise Gilot, *Leben mit Picasso*, Munich, 1965.
6 Kaii Higashiyama. *Das Schöne in der japanischen Kunst*. Quoted in *Japan und der Westen*, edited by Constantin von Barloewen and Kai Werhahn-Mees, Vol. 3, Frankfurt/Main, 1986.
7 Julius Lessing. *Berichte von der Pariser Weltausstellung 1878*. N. p., 1878.
8 Atushi Tanigawa. *Art Nouveau als ein Phänomen der Arabeske*. Quoted in *Art Nouveau – Jugendstil*, exhibition catalog, Tokyo, 1990.
9 Thomas Zacharias. *Japonismus oder das Klatschen mit einer Hand*. Quoted in *Art Nouveau – Jugendstil*, exhibition catalog, Tokyo, 1990.
10 Josef Hoffmann. *Arbeitsprogramm der Wiener Werkstätte*. Vienna, 1905. Quoted from W. H. Schweiger, *Wiener Werkstätte, Design in Vienna 1903–1932*, translated by Alexander Lieven, London, 1984, p. 43.
11 See note 9.
12 Arno Holz. *Gedichtzeile*. Quoted in *Ver Sacrum*, Vol. 2, 1898.
13 Ernst Haeckel. *Kunstformen der Natur*. Quoted from Hermann Obrist in *Pan*, No. 1, 1895.
14 Dolf Sternberger. *Über den Jugendstil und andere Essays*. Hamburg, 1956.
15 See note 14.
16 Jean Moréas. *Le Symbolisme* [Symbolist Manifesto]. Quoted in *Figaro Littéraire*, September 18 1886 (original publication). Quoted from Fritz Heinmann, *Symbolische Kunst*, dissertation, Berlin, 1926.
17 Gustave Flaubert. *Salammbô*. Paris, 1862.
18 Charles Baudelaire. *Les Fleurs du mal*. Paris, 1857.
19 Charles Baudelaire. *Œuvres Posthumes*. Paris, 1908. Quoted in *Journaux Intimes*, edited by Adolphe van Bever, Paris, 1920.
20 Wolfram Waldschmidt. *Dante Gabriel Rossetti*. Jena-Leipzig, 1905.
21 Stefan George. *Teppich des Lebens*. 1900. Quoted in *Werke*, edited by Helmut Küpper, Vol. 1, Munich, 1958.
22 Georg Wilhelm Friedrich Hegel. *Vorlesungen über Ästhetik*. Heidelberg, 1827. Quoted from Hans Joachim Störig, *Kleine Weltgeschichte der Philosophie*, Vol. 2, Stuttgart, 1950.
23 Günther Metken. *Fest des Fortschritts*. Quoted in *Weltausstellungen im 19. Jahrhundert*, exhibition catalog, Munich, 1973.
24 Title of the exhibition catalogue *Traum und Wirklichkeit* [Dream and reality], Vienna 1870–1930. Vienna, 1985.
25 Oswald Spengler. *Der Untergang des Abendlandes – Umrisse einer Morphologie der Weltgeschichte*. Edited by Helmut Werner. Munich, 1959.
26 From the television program *Hans Hollein – Architekt und Künstler*, ORF2, March 1996.
27 See note 14.
28 Translation, quoted from André Maurois, *Engländer*, Munich, 1933.

England (p. 24–51)

1 Henry van de Velde. *Zum neuen Stil*. From his writings, selected and introduced by Hans Curjel, Munich, 1955.
2 Translation, quoted from André Maurois, *Engländer*, Munich, 1933.
3 Translation, quoted from Wolfram Waldschmidt, *Dante Gabriel Rossetti*, Jena-Leipzig, 1905.
4 Frédéric Boutet. *Seltsame Masken*. Munich, 1913.
5 D. Frey. *Englisches Wesen in der bildenden Kunst*. Stuttgart-Berlin, 1942.
6 Julius Posener. *William Morris und die Folgen – Vorlesung zur Geschichte der Neuen Architektur III*. Quoted in *59 Arch+*, Aachen, 1981.
7 See note 6.
8 Julius Posener. *William Morris und die Folgen – Vorlesung zur Geschichte der Neuen Architektur III*. Quoted in *59 Arch+*, Aachen, 1981. Quoted from Gabriele Fahr-Becker, *Wiener Werkstätte*, translated by Karen Williams, Cologne, 1995, p. 4.
9 Karl Friedrich Schinkel, 1830/40. *Aus Schinkels Nachlaß*. Edited by Alfred von Wolzogen. Berlin, 1862.
10 Aymer Vallance. *Mr Arthur H. Mackmurdo and the Century Guild*. Quoted in *The Studio*, Vol. 16, No. 73, London, 1899, p. 187.
11 Translation, c.f. Charles Robert Ashbee. *Craftsmanship in Competitive Industry*. London, 1908.
12 See note 11.
13 See note 6.
14 Translation, c.f. Richard William Lethaby. *Architecture and Modern Life*. Essay for the Royal Institute of British Architects, London, 1917. In this essay Lethaby ironically refers to William Morris's critics with whom he does not agree.
15 Henry van de Velde. *Déblaiement d'Art*. Lecture, Brussels, 1894. Quoted in *Zum neuen Stil*. From his writings, selected and introduced by Hans Curjel, Munich, 1955.
16 Translation, c.f. Walter Crane. *Line and Form*. London, 1900.
17 See note 16.
18 See note 16.
19 Friedrich Haack. *Grundriss der Kunstgeschichte – Die Kunst des XIX. Jahrhunderts*. Esslingen am Neckar, 1904.
20 Translation, quoted from André Maurois, *Engländer*, Munich, 1933.
21 Translation, quoted from André Maurois, *Engländer*, Munich, 1933.
22 Inscription on Aubrey Beardsley's grave chosen by Beardsley himself from a short text which accompanied his drawing *The Death of Pierrot* in *The Savoy*, October 6 1896, p. 32.
23 Haldane Macfall. *Aubrey Beardsley. The Man and his Work*. London, 1971, p.1.
24 Robert Schmutzler. *Art Nouveau – Jugendstil*. Stuttgart, 1962.
25 Hans Hermann Hofstätter. *Aubrey Beardsley – Zeichnungen*. Cologne, 1977.
26 Translation, quoted from Hans H. Hofstätter, *Aubrey Beardsley*, Zeichnungen, Cologne, 1977.
27 Translation, quoted from Sir John Rothenstein, introduction to Brian Reade's *Aubrey Beardsley*, Stuttgart, 1969.

Glasgow (p. 52–69)

1 Julius Posener. *Charles Rennie Mackintosh – Das englische Landhaus. Vorlesung zur Geschichte der Neuen Architektur III*. Quoted in *59 Arch+*, Aachen, 1981.
2 Quoted from a letter to Andrew McLaren Young, 1967, whilst preparing for the exhibition *Charles Rennie Mackintosh 1868–1928 – Architecture, Design and Painting*, Edinburgh, 1968.
3 See note 2.
4 See note 1.

5 Hermann Muthesius. *The English House*. Edited by Dennis Sharp and translated by Janet Seligmann. Oxford, 1979, p. 52.
6 Quoted in Charlotte and Peter Fiell, *Charles Rennie Mackintosh*, Cologne, 1995, p. 22. Quoted from Gabriele Fahr-Becker, *Wiener Werkstätte*, translated by Karen Williams, Cologne, 1995, p. 59.
7 Ovid. *Metamorphosen III, 509/10 – Narcissus in florem*. Quoted from Dolf Sternberger, *Über den Jugendstil und andere Essays*, Hamburg, 1956.
8 Dolf Sternberger. *Zauberbann*. Quoted in *Über den Jugendstil und andere Essays*, Hamburg, 1956. Quoted from Gabriele Fahr-Becker, *Wiener Werkstätte*, translated by Karen Williams, Cologne, 1995, p. 15.
9 Ludwig Hevesi. *Altkunst – Neukunst*. Vienna, 1909.
10 Wolfram Waldschmidt. *Dante Gabriel Rossetti*. Jena – Leipzig, 1905.
11 Julius Meier-Graefe. *Entwicklungsgeschichte der modernen Kunst – Vergleichende Betrachtung der bildenden Künste zu einer neuen Ästhetik*. Vol. 2. Stuttgart, 1904.
12 Nikolaus Pevsner. *Pioneers of Modern Design*. 1975. Quoted from Charlotte and Peter Fiell, *Charles Rennie Mackintosh*, Cologne, 1995, p. 56.
13 See note 11.
14 Hermann Muthesius. *The English House*. Edited by Dennis Sharp and translated by Janet Seligmann. Oxford, 1979, p. 52. Quoted from Gabriele Fahr-Becker, *Wiener Werkstätte*, translated by Karen Williams, Cologne, 1995, p. 59.
15 See note 9.
16 See note 9.
17 See note 1.

Paris (pp. 70–105)

1 (In slow metamorphosis,/ white marble into white flesh,/ rosy flowers into rosy lips,/ are re-fused in different bodies.) Théophile Gautier. *Affinités secrètes. Madrigar pantheiste*. From the cycle *Emaux et camées*.
2 (We need religion for religion's sake, morality for morality's sake, art for art's sake. The way of usefulness, or even beauty, cannot be via the good and the holy.) Victor Cousin. *Cours de philosophie*. Collected lectures, published in Paris from 1826.
3 Translated from Paul Verlaine, *Confessions*, Paris, 1895.
4 Contemporary account, 1871. Quoted from Günter Metken, *Fest des Fortschritts* [Festival of Progress]. Quoted in *Weltausstellungen im 19. Jahrhundert* [World expositions in the 19th century], exposition catalog, Munich, 1973.
5 See note 4.
6 Ernst Robert Curtius. *Französischer Geist im 20. Jahrhundert* [French spirit in the 20th century]. Marburg, 1952.
7 Quoted from Karl Marx, *Klassenkämpfe in Frankreich* [Class struggles in France]. Quoted in *Neue Rheinische Revue*, 1852.
8 (This piece of iron must be arranged with taste; it must be placed logically, with method, and it is only in this way that you will find true beauty.) Hector Guimard. *La Renaissance de l'Art dans l'Architecture moderne* [The renaissance of art in modern architecture]. Quoted in *Le Moniteur des Arts*, Paris, 1899.
9 Quoted from Hector Guimard. In *Architektur in Paris um 1900* [Architecture in Paris around 1900], exposition catalog, Munich, 1975.
10 Karl Boetticher. *Das Prinzip der Hellenischen und der Germanischen Bauweise hinsichtlich der Übertragung in die Bauweise unserer Tage* [The principle of Hellenic and Germanic building styles with regard to its transference into the building styles of the present day].

Quoted in Schinkel Memorial Speech, Berlin, March 13 1846.
11 Dolf Sternberger. *Zauberbann* [Magic spell]. Quoted in *Über den Jugendstil und andere Essays* [On Art Nouveau, and other essays], Hamburg, 1956.
12 Ludwig Hevesi, *Le Castel Béranger*. Quoted in *Acht Jahre Sezession (März 1897–Juni 1905) – Kritik, Polemik, Chronik* [Eight years of the secession movement, March 1897–June 1905 – A critique, polemic and chronicle], Vienna, 1906.
13 See note 12.
14 See note 12.
15 See note 12.
16 See note 12.
17 See note 12.
18 Sherban Cantancuzino. *Hector Guimard*. Quoted in *The Anti-Rationalists*, edited by James M. Richards and Nikolaus Pevsner, London, 1973.
19 (He said to me: I dreamt this night/ I had tresses round my neck/ I had your hair like a black necklace/ Around my nape and on my breast …) Pierre Louÿs. *La Chevelure*. From the poem cycle *Chansons de Bilitis*, 1895.
20 Hans Hermann Hofstätter. *Symbolismus und die Kunst der Jahrhundertwende* [Symbolism and fin-de-siècle art]. Cologne, 1978.
21 Quoted from *Sammlung Ian Woodner* [The Ian Woodner Collection], exhibition catalog, Munich, 1986.
22 Quoted from Atsushi Tanigawa, *Art Nouveau as a Phenomenon of the Arabesque* in *Art Nouveau*, exhibition catalog, Tokyo, 1990.
23 See note 22.
24 I saw the Devil the other night;/ And, underneath his skin,/ It was not easy to determine/ Whether to say of him She or He. Paul Jean Toulet (1867–1920). *Le Garno*. From the cycle *Le Contrerimes*.
25 Enrique Gómez Carillo, who has written a book called *Die Salome*, quoted from the Insel Almanac for the year 1906.
26 (Speak to me softly;/ speak without voice to my soul.) Marceline Desbordes-Valmore (1786–1859). *Elégies*.
27 No byline. In *Neues Wiener Journal*, 1900.
28 Albrecht Bangert. *Jugendstil–Art Deco, Schmuck und Metallarbeiten* [Art Nouveau–Art Deco, ornament and metalwork]. Munich, 1981.
29 Quoted from *René Lalique, Catalog of the Gulbenkian Collection*, Lisbon, 1982.
30 Samuel Bing. *Japanischer Formenschatz* [Treasury of Japanese forms]. Hamburg, 1989.
31 (These nymphs, I want to perpetuate them.) Stéphane Mallarmé. *Le Faune, Eglogue* [The faun, an eclogue]. From the cycle *L'Après-midi d'un faune*.
32 Quoted from *Alfons Mucha 1860–1939*, exhibition catalog, Darmstadt, 1980.
33 Translated from Eugène Samuel Grasset, *La Plante et ses applications ornementales* [Plants and their use as ornament], Paris, 1897–1899.
34 Alfons Mucha. *Three Statements on Life and Work*. Brno, 1936.
35 Quoted from Julius Meier-Graefe, *Die Doppelte Kurve – Essays* [The double curve – essays], Berlin, 1924.
36 Julian Marchlewski. *Sezession und Jugendstil – Kritiken um 1900* [Secession and Art Nouveau – critiques from around 1900]. Dresden, 1974.
37 Riichi Miyake. *Ein Streifzug durch den europäischen Jugendstil* [A brief survey of Art Nouveau in Europe]. Dortmund, 1991.
38 Quoted from Le Corbusier, *Vers une Architecture*, Paris, 1958, p. 165.
39 Friedrich Ahlers-Hestermann. *Stilwende – Aufbruch der Jugend um 1900* (A change of style – the emergence of youth around 1900). Berlin, 1941.
40 Loïe Fuller. *Quinze ans de ma vie* [Fifteen years of my life]. Paris, 1908.

41 Henri de Toulouse-Lautrec, 1881. Quoted and translated from Maurice Joyant, *Henri de Toulouse-Lautrec 1864–1901, Peintre* [Henri de Toulouse-Lautrec, 1864–1901, painter]. Paris, 1926.
42 Quoted from Armand Lanoux, *Amour 1900* [Love 1900], Hamburg, 1964.

Nancy (pp. 106–129)

1 (I gather mysterious flowers in secret.) Alfred de Musset (1810–1857). *Poésies nouvelles*.
2 (Come too close and you'll be pricked.)
3 (My roots are in the depths of the woods.) Émile Gallé. *Ecrits pour l'Art, 1884–1889*. Edited by Henriette Gallé-Grimm, Paris, 1909.
4 (The flora of Lorraine has provided us with models for our art.) *Programme de l'École de Nancy*, 1901. Published in the foreword of the exhibition catalog *Exposition lorraine des arts du décor*, Paris, 1903.
5 Henri Frantz, in *The Studio*, Vol. 28, 1903, p. 109.
6 Joris-Karl Huysmans, *A rebours*, Paris, 1884.
7 Roger Marx, *Émile Gallé – Pyschologie de l'artiste et synthèse de l'oeuvre* [Émile Gallé – psychology of the artist and synthesis of his work]. Quoted in *Bulletin des Sociétés Artistiques de l'Est*, Nancy, 1904.
8 (Let us bless the whim of fate in getting a Japanese born in Nancy.) Émile Gallé. *Le Décor symbolique* [Symbolic decoration]. Inaugural speech at the public session of the Académie de Stanislas, Nancy, May 17 1900. Gallé had been elected a member in 1891. Published in *Mémoires de l'Académie de Stanislas*, Vol. 17, 5th series.
9 Henri Frantz. "Art at Nancy, Émile Galle" in *The Magazine of Art*, March 1897, p. 249.
10 (All objects have outlines; but whence comes the form that moves us?) Émile Gallé, see note 3.
11 Translated from Émile Gallé, see note 3.
12 Philippe Garner. *Émile Gallé*. Munich, 1979.
13 Translated from Marcel Proust, *Le Côté de Guermantes*, in *À la recherche du temps perdu*, Paris 1913–27.
14 Translated from Marcel Proust, *A l'ombre des jeunes filles en fleurs*, in *À la recherche du temps perdu*, Paris 1913–1927.
15 (The decoration of modern furniture will have expression because the artist, in communion with nature, cannot remain insensitive to the nobility of living forms.) Émile Gallé. *Le Mobilier contemporaine orné d'après la nature*. Quoted in *Revue des Arts décoratifs*, Nov./Dec., 1900.
16 Roger Marx, see note 7.
17 Robert Schmutzler. *Art Nouveau – Jugendstil*. Stuttgart, 1962.
18 Translated from Émile Gallé, see note 3.
19 (This wealth of documentation, this warmth of poetic excitement necessary for decorative composition – the artist will never exhaust it in putting together line and color.) *Programme de l'École de Nancy*, 1901, see note 4.
20 Translated from Émile Gallé, see note 3.
21 Julian Marchlewski, see note 36, Paris.
22 Julius Meier-Graefe, see note 35, Paris.
23 Julius Meier-Graefe, *Die Weltaustellung in Paris 1900* [The World Exposition in Paris 1900]. Paris–Leipzig, 1900.
24 (To apply industrially the true principles of decorative art.) Henri Clouzot. *Daum verrerie d'art*. Nancy, 1930.
25 (Because we want more light and shade/ No colour, nothing but light and shade!) Paul Verlaine. *Jadis et naguère*. From the cycle *Art poétique*.
26 Max Bill. *Ich und die Stangenvasen* [Stem vases and I]. Quoted in *Nancy 1900 – Jugendstil in Lothringen* [Nancy 1900 – Art Nouveau in Lorraine], exhibition catalog, Munich–Mainz, 1980.
27 (We have sought to derive from natural documents the methods, components, and character needed to create a

modern style of ornamentation, a color or sculptural clothing suited to modern practice.) *Programme de l'ecole de Nancy*, 1901, see note 4.

Belgium (pp. 130–161)

1 (This spectacle has an indefinable magic, something supernatural, to ravish the mind and the senses.) Jean-Jacques Rousseau (1712–78). *Discours sur les sciences et les arts*. Paris, 1750.
2 Sar Mérodack Joséphin Péladan. *Rosicrucian manifesto, preface to the catalog of the 1st exhibition of the Salon de la Rose-Croix at Durand-Ruel*, Paris 1892. Quoted from Richard Muther, *Geschichte der Malerei im 19. Jahrhundert* [History of painting in the 19th century], Munich, 1893–94.
3 Dolf Sternberger. *Über den Jugendstil und andere Essays* [On Art Nouveau, and other essays). Hamburg, 1956.
4 (The flesh is sad, alas! and I have read all the books.) Stéphane Mallarmé. *Brise Marine*.
5 Jean Moréas. *Le Symbolisme* [Symbolist manifesto]. Quoted in *Figaro Littéraire*, September 18 1886 (first issue). Quoted from Fritz Heinmann, *Symbolische Kunst* [Symbolic art], Dissertation, Berlin, 1926.
6 Stéphane Mallarmé. Quoted from foreword to exhibition catalog of *Cinquantenaire du Symbolisme*, Paris, 1936.
7 Walter Leistikow. *Moderne Kunst in Paris* [Modern art in Paris]. No place or year.
8 Maurice Maeterlinck. Quoted from Dolf Sternberger, note 3.
9 Hermann Bahr. In *Ver Sacrum*, 1898.
10 Gottfried Semper. *Vorläufige Bemerkungen* [Provisional remarks]. N.P., 1834.
11 Eugène Emmanuel Viollet-le-Duc. *Dictionnaire raisonné de l'architecture française*. Paris, 1854–69.
12 Quoted from Dolf Sternberger, see note 3.
13 Dolf Sternberger, see note 3.
14 (A double-flight staircase of green marble echoed by a glass ceiling …) *Mémoires Horta*, archives inéditées [unedited papers]. Quoted from Horta exhibition catalog, Brussels, 1973.
15 Quoted from Dolf Sternberger, see note 3.
16 Gottfried Semper. *Wissenschaft, Industrie, Kunst* [Science, Industry, Art]. Mainz – Berlin, 1966.
17 No byline. In *Dekorative Kunst* [Decorative art], Vol. 4, 1899.
18 Adolf Loos. T*rotzdem 1900–1930. Sammlung der Dokumente des Kampfes* [Nevertheless 1900–1930. Collected documents of the struggle]. Innsbruck, 1930.
19 (Your eyes, where nothing is revealed,/ Either sweet or bitter,/ Are two cold gems in which mingle/ Gold and iron.) Charles Baudelaire (1821–67).
20 (Snowing white bouquets of perfumed stars.) Stéphane Mallarmé. *Apparition*.
21 Joris-Karl Huysmans. *Le dîner de denil* In *A rebours*, Paris, 1884.
22 Henry van de Velde, maiden speech at Royal Academy in Antwerp, 1893. Published in *L'Art Moderne*, 1893/94 and in *Prinzipielle Erklärungen*, from *Kunstgewerbliche Laienpredigten* [Statements of principle, from lay sermons of arts and crafts], Leipzig–Berlin, 1902.
23 Julius Posener. *Jugendstil* [Art Nouveau]. Lecture, in *59 Arch+*, Aachen, 1981.
24 The first model dates from 1896.
25 Kurt Bauch. *Einleitung* [Introduction]. Quoted in *Jugendstil – Der Weg ins 20. Jahrhundert* [Art Nouveau – the way to the 20th century]. Edited by Helmut Seling, Heidelberg – Munich, 1959.
26 Klaus-Jürgen Sembach. *Henry van de Velde*. In special issue of Zürich-based periodical *DU* on Art Nouveau in *Belgien* [Art Nouveau in Belgium], May, 1975.
27 Henry van de Velde. *De XX* [Les Vingt]. In *Van Nu en Straks*, 1893.

28 In *Le Précurseur*, May 10 1893. Quoted from *Henry van de Velde – Ein Europäischer Künstler seiner Zeit* [A European artist of his time], exhibition catalog, Hagen, 1992.
29 Henry van de Velde. *Kunstgewerbliche Laienpredigten* [Lay sermons of arts and crafts]. Leipzig–Berlin, 1902.
30 Julius Meier-Graefe. Quoted in *Dekorative Kunst* [Decorative art], Vol. 2, 1898.
31 Julius Meier-Graefe. Quoted in *Illustrierte Frauen-Zeitung* [Illustrated women's paper], May 1 1896.
32 Klaus-Jürgen Sembach, see note 26.

The Netherlands (pp.162–177)

1 Quoted from *Fernand Khnopff 1858–1921*, exhibition catalog, Tokyo, 1990.
2 Dolf Sternberger. *Zauberbann* [Magic spell]. Quoted in *Über den Jugendstil und andere Essays* [On Art Nouveau, and other essays], Hamburg, 1956.
3 (He hewed, filed down and sculpted a perverse ability, a science of parish, without light and without anguish.) Émile Verhaeren. *Le Menuisier*. From the cycle *Les Villages illusoires*.
4 Cornelius Gurlitt. *Im Bürgerhaus*. Dresden, 1887.
5 Quoted from Thomas Zacharias, *Blick der Moderne*, Munich/Zürich, 1984.
6 Hendrik Petrus Berlage. *Gedanken über den Stil in der Baukunst* [Thoughts on style in architecture]. Leipzig, 1905.
7 Julius Posener. *Berlage und Dudok*. Lecture in *48 Arch+*, Aachen, 1979.
8 Piet Mondrian. In *De Stijl*, 1919.
9 Quoted from Thomas Zacharias, see note 5.
10 Dolf Sternberger, see note 2.

Italy and Russia (pp. 178–193)

1 Gabriele D'Annunzio. *Il piacere* [Pleasure]. Milan, 1889.
2 Julian Marchlewski, *Sezession und Jugendstil – Kritiken um 1900* [Secession and Art Nouveau – critical essays around 1900]. Dresden, 1974.
3 (Oriental splendor spoke discreetly to the soul in its sweet native tongue.) Charles Baudelaire (1821–67). *Spleen et idéal, L'invitation au voyage*. From the cycle *Les Fleurs du mal*, Paris, 1857.
4 (… a uniform style that is nothing but Austro-German style.) Quoted from E. Godoli, *Polemiche sull'architettura dell'esposizione* [Critiques of exposition architecture], in *Torino 1902 – Le Arti Decorative Internazionali del Nuovo Secolo* [The international decorative arts of the new century], exhibition catalog, Turin, 1994.
5 F. T. Marinetti, *Establishment and Manifesto of Futurism*, 1909. Quoted from Umbro Apollonio, *Der Futurismus* [Futurism], Cologne, 1972.
6 Quoted from Ute Stempel's epilogue to German-language edition of Gabriele D'Annunzio's *Il piacere* [Pleasure]. Zürich, 1994.
7 See note 7.
8 See note 7.
9 See note 7.
10 Carlo Carrà. *Die Malerei der Töne, Geräusche und Gerüche* [Painting colors, sounds, and smells]. 1913. Quoted from Umbro Apollonio, see note 5.
11 (The renaissance of the decorative arts.)
12 Quoted from Italo Cremona, *Die Zeit des Jugendstils* [The Art Nouveau Era], Munich/Vienna, 1966.
13 Julian Marchlewski, see note 2.

Barcelona (pp. 194–211)

1 Joaquim Torres Garcia. *Mestre Antoni Gaudí – Universalismo constructivo*. Montevideo, 1929.

2 Julius Posener. *Jugendstil*. Lecture in *59 Arch+*, Aachen, 1981.
3 Quoted from Masayuki Irie, *Besuch des Professors Kenji Imai in Barcelona im Jahr 1926* [Professor Kenji Imai's visit to Barcelona in 1926]. Quoted in *Antoni Gaudí*, exhibition catalog, Barcelona–Munich, 1986.
4 Translation, c.f. Richard Ford. *Handbook for Travellers in Spain*. London, 1845.
5 See note 4.
6 *Vicens Vives*, Report on the session of the Unió Catalanista, in the town hall at Manresa, March 27 1892, quoted in *Antoni Gaudí*, exhibition catalog, Barcelona, 1986.
7 Quoted from Joseph Palau i Fabre, *Picasso – Kindheit und Jugend eines Genies, 1881–1907* [Picasso – childhood and youth of a genius, 1881–1907], Munich, 1981.
8 *La Illustración*, Josep Palau i Fabre, see note 7.
9 Roberto Pane. *Antoni Gaudi*. Milan, 1982.
10 Juan Bassegoda Nonell. *Der Mensch Gaudí*. Quoted in exhibition catalog, see note 3.
11 Quoted from César Martinelli, *Gaudí – His Life, His Theories, His Work*, Barcelona, 1975.
12 See note 11.
13 See note 11.
14 Juan Bassegoda Nonell. Introduction to exhibition catalog, see note 3.
15 Juan Bassegoda Nonell, *Mozart und Gaudí – Antoni Gaudí*, Barcelona, February 13 1984. Quoted in exhibition catalog, see note 3.
16 Quoted from Juan Bassegoda Nonell, *Das Religiöse und Mystische* [The religious and the mystic]. Quoted in exhibition catalog, see note 3.
17 *La Illustración*, Juan Bassegoda Nonell, see note 16.
18 Quoted from César Martinelli, see note 11.
19 (Friends, nature is going Psst! Psst! at us.) Le Corbusier. *Vers une architecture*. Paris, 1958.
20 Quoted from César Martinelli, see note 11.
21 James Hillman. *Der Mythos der Analyse*. Frankfurt am Main, 1972.
22 Quoted from Masayuki Irie, see note 3.

Munich (pp. 212–233)

1 Stefan George (1886–1968). *Der Dichter und sein Kreis*. Marbach, 1968.
2 Hans Rosenhagen. *Münchens Niedergang als Kunststadt*. Munich, 1902.
3 Thomas Mann. *Betrachtungen eines Unpolitischen*. Munich, 1918.
4 Thomas Mann. *Gladius Dei*. Munich, 1902.
5 See note 3.
6 August Endell. *Vom Sehen*. Quoted in *Die Neue Gesellschaft*, Vol. 1, 1905.
7 See note 3.
8 August Endell. *Um die Schönheit – Eine Paraphrase über die Münchner Kunstausstellung 1896*. Munich, 1896.
9 Quoted from *Leben und Meinungen des Bildhauers Josef Hartwig*. No single author, Frankfurt/Main, 1955.
10 Quoted from Jürgen Kolbe, *Heller Zauber – Thomas Mann in München 1894–1933*. Munich, 1987.
11 Hermann Obrist. *Nachlaßschriften*. Quoted from Siegfried Wichmann, *Hermann Obrist – Wegbereiter der Moderne*, exhibition catalog, Munich, 1968.
12 August Endell. Quoted in *Berliner Architekturwelt*, Vol. 4, 1902.
13 Hermann Obrist, see note 11.
14 Georg Fuchs. *Hermann Obrist*. In *Pan*, No. 1, Berlin, 1896.
15 See note 11.
16 Hermann Obrist, see note 11.
17 Friedrich Naumann. *Deutsche Gewerbekunst*. Berlin, 1908.

18 Paul Klee, 1898. Quoted in *Tagebücher 1898–1918*, No. 68, edited by Felix Klee, Cologne, 1957.
19 Otto Julius Bierbaum. *Stuck*. Bielefeld–Leipzig, 1899.
20 Quoted from Anton Sailer, *Franz von Stuck – Ein Lebensmärchen*, Munich, 1969.
21 Dolf Sternberger. *Das Reich der Schönheit*. Quoted in *Über den Jugendstil und andere Essays*, Hamburg, 1956.
22 BHStA MK 14 095 (Bavarian State Archives Department I and archive number). Quoted from Thomas Zacharias, *Akademie zur Prinzregentenzeit*. Quoted in *Franz von Stuck und seine Schüler*, exhibition catalog, Munich, 1989.
23 Michael Georg Conrad, Anna Crossant-Rust and Hans Brandenburg (eds.). *Otto Julius Bierbaum zum Gedächtnis*. Commemorative publication, Munich, 1912.
24 In *Jugend*, No. 3, 1896.
25 In *Kunst und Künstler*, 1903.
26 Max Halbe. *Jahrhundertwende*. Munich, 1926.
27 Quoted from Jürgen Kolbe, *Heller Zauber – Thomas Mann in München 1894–1933*, Munich, 1987.
28 Caption accompanying the caricature *Der Münchner Jugend-Brunnen* [The Munich fountain of youth] in: *Simplicissimus*, 1897.
29 Rudolf Alexander Schröder. *Aus Kindheit und Jugend*. Munich, 1934.
30 Walter Gropius in the Preface to the Programme of the State Bauhaus, Weimar, April 1919. Quoted from Hans M. Wingler, *Das Bauhaus*, Cologne–Bramsche, 1975.
31 Julius Posener. *Peter Behrens I – Vorlesungen zur Geschichte der Neuen Architektur III*. Quoted in *59 Arch+*, Aachen, 1981.
32 Georg Fuchs. *Angewandte Kunst in der Secession zu München 1899*. Quoted in *Deutsche Kunst und Dekoration*, Vol. 5, 1899/1900.
33 Dolf Sternberger. *Zauberbann*. Quoted in *Über den Jugendstil und andere Essays*, Hamburg, 1956.

Darmstadt (pp. 234–253)

1 Friedrich Ahlers-Hestermann. *Stilwende – Aufbruch der Jugend um 1900*. Berlin, 1941.
2 Letter from the banker Osthaus to his young son Karl Ernst, the later patron of Henry van de Velde and a great champion of Jugendstil. Quoted from Karl Ernst Osthaus, *Leben und Werk*, Recklinghausen, 1971.
3 Quoted from Golo Mann, *Der letzte Großherzog*, Darmstadt, 1977.
4 See note 3.
5 See note 3.
6 Joseph Maria Olbrich. *Ideen von Olbrich*. Vienna, 1900.
7 Quoted from Henry van de Velde, *Zum neuen Stil*. From his writings, selected and with an introduction by Hans Curjel, Munich, 1955.
8 Ludwig Hevesi. *Acht Jahre Secession (März 1897–Juni 1905) – Kritik, Polemik, Chronik*. Vienna, 1906.
9 See note 6.
10 Erich Mendelsohn. *Das Problem einer neuen Baukunst*. Berlin, 1919.
11 Henry Paris. *Einige Stunden bei Professor Olbrich*. Quoted in *Echo de Paris*, 1906, translated by Micheline Schöffler.
12 Julius Posener. *Peter Behrens I – Vorlesungen zur Geschichte der Neuen Architektur III*. Quoted in *59 Arch+*, Aachen, 1981.
13 Friedrich Nietzsche. *Thus spake Zarathustra*, III, *The Bedwarfing Virtue*. Translated by Thomas Common. London, 1967.
14 Hans Christiansen. In *Deutsche Kunst und Dekoration*, Vol. 2, 1898.
15 Hans Christiansen. In *Die Ausstellung der Künstler-Kolonie Darmstadt 1901 – Main catalogue: Die Ausstellungsbauten*, Darmstadt, 1901.

16 W. Stöffler. *Kunst und Industrie*. Quoted in *Zeitschrift für bildende Kunst*, 1907.
17 Quoted from *Darmstädter Tagblatt* of July 14 1901.
18 Quoted from Brigitte Rechberg, *Das Überdokument 1901 auf der Mathildenhöhe*. Quoted in *Ein Dokument Deutscher Kunst 1901–1976*, exhibition catalog, Vol. 5, Darmstadt, 1976.
19 Julius Meier-Graefe. *Darmstadt – Athen*. Quoted in *Die Zukunft*, Vol. 39, 1902.
20 Alfred Lichtwark. *Briefe an die Kommission für die Verwaltung der Kunsthalle*. Edited by Gustav Pauli. Hamburg, 1923.
21 Albin Müller. *Aus meinem Leben*. Typed manuscript. Darmstadt, undated (ca. 1940).
22 Paul Ferdinand Schmidt. Commemorative publication upon the 25th anniversary of the reign of his Royal Highness the Grand Duke Ernst Ludwig von Hessen und bei Rhein. Leipzig, 1917.

Berlin (pp. 254–281)

1 Quoted from Henry van de Velde. *Zum neuen Stil*. From his writings, selected and with an introduction by Hans Curjel, Munich, 1955.
2 Wilhelm II. Speech at the inauguration of the Siegesallee, Berlin, December 18 1901.
3 Quoted from Golo Mann, *Der letzte Großherzog*, Darmstadt, 1977.
4 Quoted from *Edvard Munch – Liebe, Angst, Tod*, exhibition catalog, Bielefeld, 1980.
5 Peter Behrens. *Walter Leistikow*. In *Dekorative Kunst*, Vol. 3, 1899.
6 Quoted from Henry F. Lenning, *Julius Meier-Graefe*, New York, 1942.
7 See note 6.
8 Julius Meier-Graefe. *Die doppelte Kurve – Essays*. Berlin, 1924.
9 Paul Wunderlich. *Der Stein und ich*. In *Die Zeit*, No. 37, 1980.
10 Henry van de Velde. *Zum Tode Otto Eckmanns*. In *Innendekoration*, Vol. 8, 1902.
11 G. Mourey. "The Salon of the Champ de Mars" in *The Studio*, vol. 8, 1896, p. 17.
12 Friedrich Nietzsche. *Sils-Maria*. 1884. Quoted from Robert Saitschik, *Dichter und Denker*, Zurich, 1949.
13 Hans Sedlmayr. *Die Revolution der modernen Kunst*. Cologne, 1985.
14 Rainer Maria Rilke. *Worpswede*. Bielefeld–Leipzig, 1903.
15 Walter Gropius. *Monumentale Kunst und Industrie*. Lecture given in Hagen on January 29 1911.
16 Ludwig Hevesi. *Altkunst – Neukunst*. Vienna, 1909.
17 Julius Posener. *Peter Behrens I – Vorlesungen zur Geschichte der Neuen Architektur III*. In *59 Arch+*, Aachen 1981.
18 Count Harry Kessler. *Aus den Tagebüchern* (diary entry of May 16 1926). Frankfurt/Main, 1965.
19 Rainer Maria Rilke. *Über Kunst*. 1898.

Scandinavia (pp. 282–311)

1 Bjørnstjerne Bjørnson. *Das Licht – eine Universitätskantate*. In *Pan*, No. 3, 1896.
2 Edvard Munch. *Diaries*. Quoted from *Edvard Munch 1863–1944*, exhibition catalog, Munich–Salzburg–Berlin, 1987.
3 Gert Reising. *Zur Psyche im Jugendstil*. Quoted in *Ein Dokument Deutscher Kunst 1901–1976*, exhibition catalog, Darmstadt, 1976.
4 See note 2.
5 Gabriele D'Annunzio. *In Vano – Poema paradisiaco*. Quoted from Dominik Jost, *Literarischer Jugendstil*, Stuttgart, 1980.
6 See note 2.

7 See note 2.
8 See note 2.
9 Max Lüthi. *Das europäische Volksmärchen*. Berne, 1947.
10 Jens Thiis. *Gerhard Munthe*. German translation by Jan Opstad. Trondheim, 1904.
11 Quoted from *Gerhard Munthe 1849–1929, Bildteppiche*. Exhibition catalog, Munich–Hamburg–Berlin, 1989.
12 Quoted from Hans Hermann Hofstätter, *Jugendstil – Druckkunst*, Baden-Baden, 1973.
13 See note 10.
14 See note 10.
15 Quoted and translated from *Antell Collection – Ateneum Guide*, Helsinki, 1987.
16 Hugo Simberg. Quoted and translated from *Antell Collection – Ateneum Guide*, Helsinki, 1987.
17 Ville Vallgren. Quoted and translated from *Antell Collection – Ateneum Guide*, Helsinki, 1987.
18 Contemporary review of the Finnish Pavilion at the World Exposition of 1900 in Paris. Quoted and translated from *Finskt 1900*, exhibition catalog, Stockholm, 1971.
19 Walter Leistikow. *Moderne Kunst in Paris*. N.p., n.d.
20 Richard Dehmel in a letter to Arno Holz. Quoted from Richard Dehmel, *Ausgewählte Briefe 1883–1902*, Berlin, 1923.
21 Quoted from *100 Jahre Architektur in Chicago*, exhibition catalog, Munich, 1973.
22 Ulf Hård af Segerstad. *Skandinavische Gebrauchskunst*. Stockholm–Frankfurt/Main, 1961.
23 Henrik Ibsen. *Die Wildente – Dramen*. Ottobrunn bei Munich, 1982.
24 See note 22.
25 See note 22.
26 Dolf Sternberger. *Jugendstil – Begriff und Physiognomik*. Quoted in *Neue Rundschau*, June 1934.
27 Bo Gyllensvärd. *Introduction*. Quoted in *Kina och Norden*, exhibition catalog, Stockholm–Munich, 1970; German edition by Gabriele Sterner.
28 Karl Madsen. *Japansk Malerkunst*. Copenhagen, 1885.
29 Gerhard Munthe and "The movement that from Japan is moving across Europe now" in *Scandinavian Journal of Design History*, no. 4, 1994.
30 Quoted from Erich Köllmann, *Porzellan*, in *Jugendstil – Der Weg ins 20. Jahrhundert*. Edited by Helmut Seling, Heidelberg–Munich, 1959.
31 Review of ca. 1900. Quoted from Helmut Seling, *Silber und Schmuck*, in *Jugendstil – Der Weg ins 20. Jahrhundert*, edited by Helmut Seling, Heidelberg–Munich, 1959.

New York and Chicago (pp. 312–333)

1 Louis Henry Sullivan, 1901. Quoted from *Kindergarten chats*, New York, 1947, p. 44.
2 Translation, c.f. Charles Robert Ashbee. *Frank Lloyd Wright – Eine Studie zu seiner Würdigung*. Berlin, 1911.
3 Translation, c.f. *The Lost Treasures of Louis Comfort Tiffany*, New York, 1980.
4 See note 3.
5 Quoted from Hugh F. McKean, *Louis Comfort Tiffany*, Weingarten, 1981,
6 See note 5.
7 Cecilia Waern. "The Tiffany or 'Favrile-Glass' – The Industrial Arts of America" in *The Studio*, June 1898.
8 See note 5.
9 Quoted from *Die Lithographie*, exhibition catalog, Bremen, 1976.
10 Kurt Bauch. *Introduction*. In *Jugendstil – Der Weg ins 20. Jahrhundert*, edited by Helmut Seling, Heidelberg–Munich, 1959.
11 Louis Henry Sullivan. *A System of Architectural Ornament According with a Philosophy of Man's Power*. New York, 1924.

12 John Ruskin. "The Lamp of Beauty" in *The seven lamps of architecture*. London, 1849, p. 122.
13 Louis Sullivan. 'The Auditorium and the High Rise 1886–95' in *Ornament in Architecture*, 1892, p. 51.
14 Adolf Loos. *Ins Leere gesprochen 1897–1900*. Innsbruck, 1931.
15 Peter C. von Seidlein. *Die erste Chicago School of Architecture*. Quoted in *100 Jahre Architektur in Chicago*, exhibition catalog, Die Neue Sammlung, Munich, 1973.
16 Louis Sullivan, "The Tall Building Artistically Considered", 1896.
17 See note 16.
18 Louis Henry Sullivan, 1901. Quoted from *Kindergarten chats*, New York, 1947, p. 44.
19 Frank Lloyd Wright. *An American Architect*. New York, 1955.
20 Translation, quoted from Charles Robert Ashbee, *Frank Lloyd Wright – Eine Studie zu seiner Würdigung*, Berlin, 1911.
21 Frank Lloyd Wright, "In the Cause of Architecture" (1908) in *Architectural Record*, New York, 1975, p. 55.
22 Translation, quoted from Charles Robert Ashbee, *Frank Lloyd Wright – Eine Studie zu seiner Würdigung*, Berlin, 1911.
23 Adolf Loos. *Trotzdem 1900–1930. Sammlung der Dokumente des Kampfes*. Innsbruck, 1931.
24 Translation, quoted from Charles Robert Ashbee, *Frank Lloyd Wright – Eine Studie zu seiner Würdigung*, Berlin, 1911.
25 See note 19.
26 Julius Posener. *Frank Lloyd Wright I – Vorlesungen zur Geschichte der Neuen Architektur*. Quoted in *48 Arch+*, special issue celebrating the 75th birthday of Julius Posener, Aachen, 1979.

Vienna (pp. 334–359)

1 Hermann Bahr. Speech on Klimt. Vienna, 1901.
2 Hermann Bahr. Quoted in *Ver Sacrum*, May/June 1898.
3 Adolf Loos. *Ornament und Verbrechen*. Vienna, 1908.
4 Karl Kraus. Quoted in *Die Fackel*, 1908/09.
5 See note 2.
6 Robert Musil. *Der Mann ohne Eigenschaften*. Hamburg, 1952.
7 Inscription on the front of the Secession building by Joseph Maria Olbrich in Vienna.
8 Ludwig Hevesi. *Zwei Jahre Secession*. In *Ver Sacrum*, September/October 1899.
9 Peter Altenberg (1862–1919), Vienna 1918. Quoted in *Peter Altenberg: Vita Ipsa*. Berlin, 1918.
10 Quoted from Christian M. Nebehay, *Gustav Klimt – Sein Leben nach zeitgenössischen Berichten und Quellen*, Munich, 1976.
11 Ludwig Uhland. *Gesammelte Werke*. Vol. 2. Edited by H. Fischer. Stuttgart, 1892.
12 Hans Tietze. *Gustav Klimts Persönlichkeit*. Vienna, 1919.

13 Ludwig Hevesi. *Acht Jahre Sezession (März 1897–Juni 1905) – Kritik, Polemik, Chronik*. Vienna, 1906.
14 Felix Salten. *Geister der Zeit – Erlebnisse*. Vienna–Leipzig, 1924.
15 Carl Moll. *Erinnerungen an Gustav Klimt*. In *Neues Wiener Tagblatt*, January 24 1943.
16 Handwritten note by Koloman Moser, archives of the Vienna City Library. Quoted from Michael Pabst, *Wiener Grafik um 1900*. Munich, 1984.
17 Joseph Olbrich. Quoted in *Der Architekt*, 1899. Quoted from Michael Pabst, *Wiener Grafik um 1900*, Munich, 1984.
18 See note 3.
19 Ludwig Hevesi. *Altkunst – Neukunst*. Vienna, 1909.
20 See note 6.
21 See note 14.
22 Marian Bisanz-Prakken. *Der Beethovenfries von Gustav Klimt in der XIV. Ausstellung der Wiener Secession (1902)*. Quoted in *Traum und Wirklichkeit, Wien 1870–1930*, exhibition catalog, Vienna, 1985.
23 Karl Kraus. Quoted in *Die Fackel*, 1902/03.
24 Arthur Roeßler. *Zu den Bildern von Koloman Moser*. In *Deutsche Kunst und Dekoration*, vol. 33, 1913/14.
25 Otto Wagner. *Die Baukunst unserer Zeit – Dem Baukunstjünger ein Führer auf diesem Kunstgebiete*. 4th edition, Vienna, 1914.
26 Adolf Loos. *Die alte und die neue Richtung in der Baukunst*. Quoted in *Der Architekt*, 1898.
27 Peter Haiko. *Otto Wagner 1904–1907*. Quoted in *Traum und Wirklichkeit, Wien 1870–1930*, exhibition catalog, Vienna, 1985.
28 See note 25.
29 Julius Posener. *Otto Wagner – Die Rolle Hans Poelzigs vor 1918. Vorlesungen zur Geschichte der Neuen Architektur II – Die Architektur der Reform (1900–1924)*. Quoted in *53 Arch+*, Aachen, 1980.
30 See note 25.
31 Translation, c.f. William Morris. *The Prospects of Architecture in Civilization*. Lecture. London, 1889.
32 Werner Blaser. *Furniture as Architecture – Architektur im Möbel*. Zurich, 1985.
33 Adolf Loos. *Trotzdem 1900–1930. Sammlung der Dokumente des Kampfes*. Innsbruck, 1931.
34 Robert Musil. [Diary Vol. 4] [?1899–1904 or later] *Blätter an dem Nachtbuche – des – monsieur le vivisecteur*. Quoted in *Tagebücher*, edited by Adolf Frisé, Reinbek bei Hamburg, 1976.
35 Adolf Loos. *Trotzdem 1900–1930. Sammlung der Dokumente des Kampfes*, Innsbruck, 1931.
36 Horst Viehoff. *Goethes Leben*. Vol. 1. Stuttgart, 1847–54.
37 Alexander Pope. *Miscellanies*. London, 1728.
38 Adolf Loos. *Das Andere*, 1903. In *Sämtliche Schriften*, edited by Franz Glück, Vienna–Munich, 1962.
39 Quoted from Burkhardt Rukschcio, 1909–1911, *Adolf Loos – Das Haus am Michaelerplatz*. Quoted in *Traum und Wirklichkeit, Wien 1870–1930*, exhibition catalog, Vienna, 1985.

Wiener Werkstätte (pp. 360–379)

1 Ludwig Hevesi. *Ein moderner Nachmittag*. Quoted in *Der kleine Salon*, edited by Hansjörg Graf, Stuttgart, 1970.
2 Quoted from Dominik Jost, *Literarischer Jugendstil*, Stuttgart, 1980.
3 Josef Frank. *Zu Josef Hoffmanns 60. Geburtstage*. Edited by the Österreichischer Werkbund, Vienna, 1930.
4 Carl Moll. *Erinnerungen an Gustav Klimt*. Quoted in *Neues Wiener Tagblatt*, January 24 1943.
5 Ludwig Hevesi. *Acht Jahre Sezession (März 1897 – Juni 1905) – Kritik, Polemik, Chronik*. Vienna, 1906.
6 (No single author) Quoted in *Innendekoration*, Vol. 8, 1902.
7 Leopold Wolfgang Rochowanski. *Josef Hoffmann*. Vienna, 1950.
8 In *Ver Sacrum*, Vol. 1, 1898.
9 Josef Hoffmann. *Arbeitsprogramm der Wiener Werkstätte* [Wiener Werkstätte work program]. Vienna 1905. Quoted from Werner J. Schweiger, *Wiener Werkstätte, Design in Vienna, 1903–1932*, London, 1984.
10 Josef August Lux. *Wiener Werkstätte – Josef Hoffmann und Koloman Moser*. Quoted in *Deutsche Kunst und Dekoration*, Vol. 15, 1904/05.
11 Julius Baum. *Wiener Werkstätte – Vienna*. Quoted in *Deutsche Kunst und Dekoration*, vol. 9, 1906/07.
12 Karl Marilaun. *Gespräche mit Josef Hoffmann*. In *Neues Wiener Journal*, 1918.
13 Ludwig Hevesi. *Altkunst – Neukunst*. Vienna, 1909.
14 Armin Friedmann. *Secessionistische Tafelfreuden*. Quoted in *Neues Wiener Tagblatt*, 1906.
15 Waltraud Neuwirth. *Österreichische Keramik des Jugendstils*. Vienna, 1974.
16 "The Art-Revival in Austria" in *The Studio*, 1906.
17 Egon Friedell. *Jubiläumsband zum 25jährigen Bestehen der WW*. Vienna, 1928.
18 Josef Hoffmann, unpublished manuscript from his estate. Quoted from Werner J. Schweiger, *Wiener Werkstätte – Kunst und Handwerk 1903–1932*, Vienna, 1982.
19 See note 13.
20 Berta Zuckerkandl. *Das Cabaret Fledermaus*. Quoted in *Wiener Allgemeine Zeitung*, 1907.
21 Karl Kraus. *Eine Kulturtat*. Quoted in *Die Fackel*, 1907/08.
22 Oskar Kokoschka. Letter to Erwin Lang. Quoted in *Agathon – Almanach auf das Jahr 48 des 20. Jhs*, edited by Leopold Wolfgang Rochowanski, Vienna, 1947.
23 Peter Behrens. *Josef Hoffmann*. Quoted in *Die Wiener Werkstätte 1903–1928, Modernes Kunstgewerbe und sein Weg*. Commemorative publication. edited by Mathilde Flögl. Vienna, 1929.
24 G. S. Salles. *Adolphe Stoclet Collection*. Brüssels, 1956.
25 Werner Hofmann. *Von der Nachahmung zur Erfindung der Wirklichkeit. Die schöpferische Befreiung der Kunst 1890–1917*. Cologne, 1970.
26 See note 4.

Glossary

à jour enamel
Abbreviated form of *plique à jour* enamel (q.v.).

amethyst
Type of quartz classified as a semiprecious stone and used in jewelry for its violet color.

amourette
Rare type of acacia tree belonging to the mimosa genus, used as a hardwood for inlay work.

androgyne
A creature that is physically and mentally a mixture of both sexes.

appliqué work
A sculptured lump of glass is fused on to the glass while still soft and worked after it cools down.

arabesque
A type of surface ornamentation derived from Islamic art. It consists of a pattern of lines and stylized plant motifs.

arborizing
Relating to sundry species of tree that grow in the open. Derived from *arboretum*, a garden planted with many kinds of trees growing in the open.

Astralit glass
Glass that after being cut appears almost black, but displays a red crystallization in direct sunlight.

baroque pearls
Pearls of irregular shape.

beaten
Sheet metal that has been hammered into shape with the aid of various chasing hammers or beak-irons and hand-hammers or molds.

bentwood
Wood shaped in steam at a temperature of 100–120°C. To prevent the wood cracking during the process, it is clamped and compressed between steel jaws. Straight-grained woods such as beech are particularly suitable.

broncit glass
The surface of the glass is covered with a black or brown, slightly metallic, lustrous coating. The ornamentation is then covered with lacquer and the uncovered undercoat is etched away with hydrofluoric acid so that the drawing is left black or brown on a matt glass surface.

bronze, gilt
The surface of the bronze is painted with a solution of mercury and gold and treated so that the mercury vaporizes and the gold sticks firmly to the undercoat. Also called ormolu.

bureau plat desk
A writing desk invented by the French ébéniste Charles Cressent (1685–1768). It has a rectangular writing surface, usually a leather top and stands on four feet.

buttress
Gothic wall support that is either solid against the wall or used as a prop (flying buttress), to counter the outward pressure from the roof.

cabochon
A precious stone with a dome-shaped cut.

cameo cut
Glass relief modeled on antique cameos.

candelabra
Candlestick with branches.

catenary arches
Arches superimposed on each other.

cantilevered
Having a projecting support carrying a higher part of the building (e.g. an arch).

carding
A process for napping material, in which the spinning material is passed through a card to clean it, remove knotted threads (burls) and expose the fibers. These are parallelized and arranged in a sliver or web as a connected pile. In the raising machine, the dried heads of fuller's teasels are used or any similar specially cultivated thistle-like plant.

caryatids
Pairs of sculptures in the shape of fully draped females acting as columns to support an entablature.

casein paint
Paint that includes casein as a binding agent. Casein is a constituent of lactoprotein, and lime paste or borax is used in its production.

chalcedony
A variety of quartz that takes its name from the ancient Greek city of Chalcedon on the Bosporus.

chamfered
Having a rectangular edge cut off or ground off diagonally.

champlevé enamel
Hollows are gouged or etched out of the metal base and filled with enamel.

chase
To work metal with a graver, chisel, file or similar tool in order to apply ornamentation.

chien yao
Shallow Japanese tea dishes that in earlier times were produced in China. Their glaze recalls rabbit fur, bird's feathers, turtle shells or oil spots. The predominant color tones of dark blue, brown, and green pan out from the center or form cloud-like patches. The glaze is applied in several layers which are fired several times. The result is that, as the light striking the surface varies, the color apparently keeps changing.

china grass
A species of nettle used to make matting.

chromolithic stoneware
Unglazed stoneware adorned with colored decor set in the still-moist body before firing.

chryselephantine
A combination of gold and ivory.

chrysoprase
Semiprecious stone resembling chrysoberyl, a green precious stone.

cire perdue
Bronze casting by means of 'lost wax': the sculpture is modeled in wax that was previously put on a clay core. A casting coat of fine sand or clay is then laid on the wax, hugging the shape of the wax. The wax is subsequently melted away and the bronze poured in the ensuing cavity. After casting, the mold is broken.

cloisonné enamel
Wires or stays are soldered on to the background to hold in the liquid enamel, but they remain visible. (Fr. *cloison* = partition)

Clutha glass
Green, turquoise-brown or even gray-colored glass which is mixed with copper crystals and finishes up shot with schlieren, streaks and bubbles. The name comes from the Anglo-Saxon word for the River Clyde in Scotland, whose cloudy waters are said to resemble the character of the glass.

coccolith slabs
Slabs cut from sedimentary rocks created by limestone algae deposits on the deep North Atlantic seabeds.

combing
Type of decoration obtained with a slate pencil or comb-like implement. The still-soft glass fibers are displaced to form wavy or feathered patterns.

cornice
A S-shape molding running horizontally along the top of a building; alternatively, the top of an entablature.

crackle glaze
Glaze containing deliberately produced fine cracks covering the surface like a web. The crackle arises from the different degrees of expansion between glaze and body.

crown glass
Flat glass for window panes produced by an ancient technique: the glassblower's pipe is revolved quickly to flatten the glass, which is subsequently drawn out by twisting the pontil. The pane that results is cut into semicircles. The thicker center part produces bull's-eye panes.

crystal glaze
Glaze in which crystals are deposited during cooling, more often dark than light but also in a different color.

curtain wall
In a building, an exterior wall with no load-bearing function. The wall components are latched to the frame.

cut glass
Glass finished by polishing or grinding.

Cymric
A range of silverware and jewelry sold by the London Art Nouveau firm Liberty & Co. The Celtic name was a tribute to the Welsh ancestors of Liberty director John Llewellyn.

De Stijl
A school of modern painting and applied art that limited itself to using only basic forms such as vertical and horizontal lines and primary colors. Such pure representation also had ethic objectives. The movement was set up by the Dutchman Theo van Doesburg, who from 1917 published a ideological monthly called *De Stijl*.

dichroic
Showing two colors in different directions.

Doric order
The most ancient of the three orders (Doric, Ionic, and Corinthian) used on Greek columns. The orders determined the shape and proportions of columns and entablature. In the Doric order (from c. 630 BC) the column has a shaft with no base but with vertical flutes, a rounded beveled capital and square cap.

earthenware
Unglazed, porous and usually darkish clayware, e.g. terracotta.

ébéniste
Cabinet-maker who specialized in veneered furniture, using ebony and other woods for inlays.

eggshell (or quasi) porcelain
A light, thin-walled frit porcelain with a glassy consistency and ivory coloring. Its composition is even today a trade secret of the porcelain manufacturer Haagsche Plateelbakkerij Rozenburg in The Hague.

églomisé see verre églomisé

electrolytic polishing
In glassmaking, a process that replaces mechanical polishing, during which unevennesses in the glass are removed with hydrofluoric acid.

émail see champlevé enamel, cloisonné enamel, mat velouté enamel, plique à jour enamel

émaux mattes
Matt and velvety enamels.

enamel paints
Enamel paints are mixed from pulverized glass and colored oxides. They are rubbed with turpentine and stand oil and applied to glass with an artist's brush. The paints are heated in a chamotte muffle away from steam and smoke until they melt and become shiny. Enamel paints are divided according to their translucency into translucent (i.e. the metal background shines through) and opaque enamels. In the case of translucent enamels, a distinction is made between transparent (like clear glass) and translucid enamels, which are slightly cloudy. Opacity is produced in the opaque paints by the addition of opacifiers, to render their effect independent of the metal background.

engraving
Cutting or etching patterns in wood or metal. *see* glass engraving, woodcuts, etching

eosin glaze
A product of the Hungarian porcelain manufactory of Zsolnay, in Pécs. The ruby-colored metallic luster glaze was developed by the firm in collaboration with Professor Vince Wartha (Gr. *eos* = dawn).

étagère
A popular item of Art Nouveau furniture consisting usually of three tiered shelves of different sizes and used for displaying small objects. The shelves are carried by slender supports. Also known as a 'whatnot'.

etched glass
Ornamental glass in which hydrofluoric acid is used either to produce an incised pattern or give a satin, rough or frosted finish. Parts that are not to be treated are protected by an acid-resistant layer or template. The strength of the fluoride mixture determines whether the glass finishes up polished or matt. The protective coat is subsequently washed off in cold, then warm water and finally with soap.

etching on metal
A graphic technique and form of engraving in which a copper plate is coated with acid-resistant, resinous matter called the resist. The image is then scored in it with the etching needle – a sharp steel needle – so deeply that the copper is laid bare. When the acid is then poured on, it eats into the bare areas, etching the pattern into the plate. The longer it is left, the deeper the etching. From the artist's point of view, etching is very like drawing on paper.

faience
Clay objects coated with tin glaze and subsequently cased with a transparent lead glaze.

Favrile glass
A luster glaze developed by Louis Comfort Tiffany reminiscent of mosaic window techniques. Pulverized (precious) metal was applied to the body of the object, in the same way as in flashed glass. Depending on the composition of the metal, the coating that resulted was either matt, lustrous or gloss. In the final stages of the process, vapors containing oxides left a deposit on the outer walls to create a luster effect. The decor thus 'blossomed' out of a chemical but hand-crafted process into a vegetal, linear design without requiring the use of a floral stencil.

Tiffany derived the word *favrile* from the 17th-century English adjective *fabrile*, meaning 'relating to craft' or 'masterly', which itself came from Latin *fabrilis*, i.e. to do with a *faber* or artificer. The term *follis fabrilis* (fire-worker) is found in Livy and Cicero, *follis* being a leather bag, particularly a bellows. The change from Latin *b* to English *v* is quite common, e.g. Latin *rabidus* (raging, crazy) is not only the source of *rabid* but also the verb *rave*.

feldspar
Collective term for a large group of rock minerals of different colors, alkaline or alkaline earth silicates of aluminum that are light in color and rich in water.

figura serpentina
Sculptural term for a design in which the figure develops upward from the plinth while twisting round the central axis. From Latin *serpentinatus* = serpentine.

filigree glass
Glass containing colored threads which constitute a pattern.

flambé glaze
Bright red or purple coloring produced by oxidizing copper in a ferrous glaze. The term is also used to denote an abstract decoration on stoneware which develops during firing by exposing the glaze to different temperatures. The glaze runs, forming blobs and dots or lines.

flashed glass
The glass body is dipped in a molten colored glass mass to be coated in one or more additional layers and then blown to its final shape. A distinction is made between external flashing (clear glass base, colored coating) and internal flashing (colored base, clear coating).

flint glass
Extremely pure lead glass – hollow glass with a high lead oxide content instead of calcium – first developed in 1675 at Ravenscroft in England and used mainly for optical equipment. The term 'flint glass' is inaccurate inasmuch as this originally referred to a glass in which pure silicon in the form of flint was added to the melt.

flowing glazes
The glazes mingle as a result of colored glazes being coated with a slightly fusible glaze containing boric acid. Firing involves oxidization.

flowing colorants
Colorants used for underglaze to which a high percentage of oxide has been added to make them run.

flux
An additive to glazes that melts at a low temperature and causes other components to melt as well.

folio
Book format not less than 11 inches in height.

frit porcelain
Porcelain with a frit coating or decoration, i.e. pulverized glass that is heated until it is soft so that the individual parts stick together superficially but do not melt, unlike in a glaze.

funicular model
An architectural model using weights suspended from a piece of string, to establish the most desirable shape of a structure from a loadbearing point of view.

Futurism
Italian movement in modern art and poetry, launched in 1909 with the publication of a Futurist manifesto by the poet Filippo Tommaso Marinetti (1876–1944). Futurism demanded a complete break with tradition. The painting of the future should represent simultaneity, i.e. fuse several temporally distinct situations in the real world and temporally discrete experiences.
The protagonists of the movement included Giacomo Balla (1871–1958), Umberto Boccioni (1882–1916), Carlo Carra (1881–1966), Luigi Russolo (1885–1947), and Gino Severini (1883–1966).

gilt bronze *see* bronze, gilt, also ormolu

glass engraving
Application of patterns on glass by using wheels attached to a flywheel instead of a grindstone. The grinding agent is a mixture of oil and emery powder. A distinction is made between 1. line engraving; 2. incising (deep-cut, i.e. the pattern is cut into the glass as a negative impression); and 3. cutting away (the pattern is left in relief by cutting away the unwanted areas).

glaze
Glass-like coating on earthenware, to seal porous bodies. All glazes consist of quartz and one or more metal components. Glazing is done mostly by dipping; other processes include pouring on, spraying, and the volatility process.

glaze technique
To varnish a picture with transparent colors.

gouache
Opaque paint using watercolors combined with binding agents and zinc white which after application dries to give a pastel-like effect.

graphite
Soft black material made of carbon.

grès
French term for stoneware.

guéridon
Pedestal table.

half-tones
Black and white photos for reproduction in a book.

hammered *see* repoussé

haute-lisse (high-warp) technique
Weaving method for tapestries and wall-hangings in which the warps are placed, 'high', i.e. vertically (Fr. *haute-lisse*), on the loom.

heliogravure
Manual photogravure process for reproducing a picture photomechanically. Slides and halftone negatives are copied onto pigment paper, as a result of which areas exposed to light harden. To reproduce halftones, asphalt powder is melted on to a polished copper plate, and the developed pigment paper is then pressed on to the plate and peeled off the backing paper. Finally, an etching process takes place in which the acid must circulate round the particles of powder. After repeated etching, the gelatine layer of the slide is washed off and the copper plate is ready for the press.

high-fire alkaline glazes
Glazes using fluxes such as feldspar, limestone, plaster or bone ash.

honeycomb glass
Glass with small air inclusions. These can be produced artificially by piercing the soft glass with a needle. After the needle is withdrawn, the outer skin quickly closes up again. If the glass is turned and extended immediately after being pierced, spiral threads of air can also be created.

hyperbola
Mathematical conic section. The hyperbola is the geometric location for all points that have a constant difference of distance from two focuses.

hyperbolic paraboloid
Mathematical concept describing the surface of a saddle, having a parabolic section crossways and a hyperbolic section lengthways.

incrustation
Colored decoration of surfaces by means of inlays of various materials.

intercalaire
Glass already flashed and ornamented is flashed again, mostly with transparent glass, and the transparent flashing is cut away or incised according to the artist's intentions.

iridescent
Having a lustrous surface in the colors of the rainbow. Iridescence is produced with metal oxide vapors from gentle heating in a melting furnace or by luster painting in which a thick coating of luster paint is applied to the finished glass and fired.

ironwood
Any hard, heavy wood such as teak growing mainly in the tropics or subtropics.

jack-in-the-pulpit
A species of arum native to North America (arisaema triphyllum), commonly called jack-in-the-pulpit but also known as Indian turnip. It is a plant with a single cotyledon and tuberous rhizome whose flower is enclosed in a spathe without any petals, a spathe being an upright leaf like a sac.

jardinière
A large flower stand for holding cut or indoor plants.

jet pearls
Gems made of jet, a hard bituminous coal.

Lava glass
Glass imitating obsidian, a silica-rich natural glass.

leaded glazing
A method of joining small panes of glass into windows, using lead cames of various sizes to make up composite fields.

line-etching
A process used in book printing to make printing plates for reproducing matter of a linear nature. In line-etching, the linear negative is copied photochemically on to a zinc plate which is etched after development. The parts protected by color which are to be printed are not eaten away and remain proud.

lithography
The oldest flatbed printing technique, invented by Alois Senefelder (1771–1834) about 1789. It is based on the discovery that grease repels water. The drawing is applied to the lithographic plate using a greasy chalk or brush. The plate is made of Jurassic limestone, the best type of which comes from Bavaria (Solenhofen stone). This is porous enough to suck up both grease and water. The plate is coated with acid and then treated with a solution of gum arabic. This has the effect of allowing parts of the plate not containing the drawing to absorb water. When greasy printing ink is rolled on, only the picture retains the color, the non-pictorial areas, previously treated with damp rollers, repelling it.

luster glaze
An extremely thin glaze in bright colors or with a metallic surface. Lustrous glazes are produced in two ways: one is to use silver chloride or nitrate, which leaves a metallic or pearly sheen, the other involves salts of cobalt, manganese, copper, iron, silver, and bismuth. The glaze is rubbed shiny with carbon black.

majolica
In the 19th century, majolica described all colored and especially multi-colored glazed earthenware not counted as porcelain.

marquetry/marqueterie
Inlay work in wood.

marqueterie de verre
Inlay work in glass. Colored or partially clear glass is pressed into the surface while it is still warm and bonded to the decor during the blowing process or shaping or cooling. Finishing is done with the engraving or grinding wheel.

mat velouté enamel
Glazing technique in which the glazing base is given a velvety texture by means of an etching process.

millefiori glass
Colored glass threads are melted together in a bundle and cut into disks. The cross-section displays a spiral or floral pattern of threads. The disks are subsequently embedded in lumps of hot, colorless glass which are then blown into shape. The end products are usually paperweights. (From Italian *millefiori* = 1000 flowers)

monism
A philosophical doctrine asserting that the multiplicity of reality can be reduced to a single ultimate principle. This can be of a spiritual or material nature, e.g. spirit, God, matter, activity, will or something else. The doctrine was systematized by the German philosopher Christian Wolff (1679–1754).

moonstone
Transparent to translucent feldspar in pale colors ranging from bluish-white to yellowy-brown.

mosaic glass
Hollow glass technique already known to the ancient Egyptians. Colored glass threads are melted into a bundle and drawn out into various shapes. The bundles are then cut across to produce little panes that display a floral-like pattern. The pieces are placed on an iron plate and the glass rolled up. On blowing and shaping the glass pieces bond with the hollow glass body.

mosaic window
"Painting with glass," in which glass painted and cut *en masse* is put together to make a painted window.

Murano technique
Murano is an island north of Venice that in medieval times was the center of Venetian glassmaking. "Venetian glass" is a generic concept for all glass that is distinguished for its

lightness and clarity of mass. Filigree and *millefiori* glass and elegant, sophisticated glassware in general are often described as Venetian or Murano glass.

mycologist
A botanist expert in mushrooms and related plants.

navette (shuttle) diamonds
Diamonds ground into the shape of navettes (shuttles on a loom).

nénuphar
The Egyptian waterlily.

nishiki-e
Polychrome printing used in Japanese woodcuts notable for its sophisticated coloring. A development of basic color printing, called *benizuri-e* in Japanese.

opal
Type of quartz valued as a gemstone for its shimmering, changing colors.

opalescent glass
Marbled glass obtained by founding, using a mixture of colored, frosted, and opal glass.

opal glass
Semitranslucent, whitish glass with opalescent luster produced by the addition of horn or bone ash, possibly also stannic oxide.

ormolu
Various methods of achieving a gold appearance on metal mounts on furniture, the most common being gilt bronze.

oxblood glaze
Glowing red glaze produced by reduced copper (i.e. the kiln contains less oxygen during certain stages of firing).

oxidation
Process combining metal with oxygen. Particles of metal are introduced into the glass which then oxidize to produce coloring in the wall of the vessel.

panneau décoratif
Decorative wall or surface panel.

Papillon glass
"Butterfly" glassware made by the firm Loetz' Witwe. It is an iridescent glass with mottled patterns.

parabola
Mathematical conic section. It is a symmetrical curve stretching to infinity, the points on which have the same distance from a fixed point and fixed straight line.

paraboloid
Mathematical term describing a parabolic curved surface.

pastel
Picture painted with pastel colors, which are a mixture of chalk and clay with added coloring and binding agents.

pâte decoration
Decoration in relief, applied *en masse*.

pâte de verre
Pulverized glass paste mixed with a binding agent and soft enough to work. Color can be added as required. The paste is pressed into a pre-prepared mold, built up from inside and often endowed with relief decoration on the inner or outer wall. Firing follows at a low temperature.

pâte sur pâte
A difficult technique used mainly on porcelain. Successive layers of clay slip are carefully applied with a brush on to the bare or pre-fired body, until a differentiated relief is produced.

patinated bronze
Bronze treated with chemicals to produce a light grey-green surface layer or patina.

pattern
Damp wooden or cast iron mold in which liquid glass is founded.

pewter
An alloy in which tin is the principle constituent, used for making utensils and decorative objects. Other constituents may be copper (best quality), antimony or lead (inferior quality).

plique à jour enamel
A process in which enamel windows – frame-like grids with no metal back – are filled with translucent (*plique à jour*) enamel on precious-metal surfaces. The background foil required for the process is subsequently etched away with nitric acid.
Abbreviated form: *à jour* enamel.

porcelain
Vitrified (i.e. baked) body made of kaolin (china clay), feldspar, and quartz. Porcelain is waterproof, impermeable, and translucent.

pot painting
Painting with metal oxides or clays. The mushy mass is poured from the founding vessel on to the clay and subsequently fired.

pressure curve
Structural engineering term for vaulting pressure, i.e. the pressure exerted by the vaulting on the supporting walls, piers or columns.

pulverized glass technique
A process in which the still-hot glass body is coated with a different color of pulverized glass in streaks, flocculent or mixed, then reheated until the powder bonds with the body. The glass is then flashed in a new coating.

putto (plural: putti)
Small naked boy figures with or without wings. Popular chiefly in Renaissance and Baroque art.

ramie fiber [cambric fiber]
Fiber from china grass, a kind of nettle plant.

Régence
The style of French art during the rule of Philippe of Orléans (1715–23). It emphasized decorative elements and the elegance and lightness of line.

repoussé work
Hammered surfaces.

resist (or reserve)
A protective paste applied in dyeing materials or etching materials according to the design, to prevent dye being absorbed or the metal being attacked by the etching acid.

salt glaze
A thin glaze produced by throwing common salt into the kiln once the fire reaches its maturing point. In the steam environment, the salt breaks down into sodium and hydrochloric acid. The sodium combines with the silicic acid of the body to make sodium silicate, which combines with the other components of the clay to make a real glass glazing.

schliere
Transparent streaks in the glass arising from an inadequate firing heat.

secco technique
Painting on dry plaster.

sharp-fire glaze
Underglaze or overglaze colorants that are subjected to a sharp fire, i.e. a fire at a very high temperature. The sharp fire produces motifs whose edges lack sharp, prominent outlines and the effect of which is to create a high degree of softness.

Shunga
A collection of erotic woodcuts (= "Spring pictures" in Japanese).

silver pewter
A lead-free alloy of tin with a silvery sheen.

sinkabe kozo
The interiors of Japanese houses are partitioned with wooden sliding doors. The spatial arrangement was brought to its final form in the Tokugawa period (1605–1867) with the use of paper-covered sliding doors which were frequently painted, as were the wooden pillars. The architecture became more stylish as sinkabe kozo, the tasteful arrangement of rooms, was consciously cultivated.

slip
Clay thinned to a creamy liquid and used for glazes. Slip glazes can be fired at low temperatures as the clay contains natural fluxes. Colors are mostly earthy.

slip painting
Painting in which the slip is applied in layers to the bare or pre-fired body.

stained-glass windows
Windows made of pieces of glass colored with metallic oxides, pigments or enamel. The pieces are joined together with lead fillets to make a design or picture.

stereotomy
A branch of geometry dealing with calculating the surfaces of spatial things, especially the cut stone of vaulted structures.

Stile Liberty
Italian generic term for Art Nouveau, named after the English Art Nouveau store Liberty, whose distribution system made the style popular throughout the world.

stoneware
Pale-colored firing clay mixed with quartz and feldspar. The body is likewise light in color, impermeable, and nontransparent.

Style Guimard
Term for French art circa 1900, named after its chief protagonist Hector Guimard, whose work is notable for its use of line and the interplay of light and contrasts.

Style Métro
A term for the characteristic floral, linear trend in *fin-de-siècle* art, as exemplified in Hector Guimard's structures for the Paris Métro.

Sung Dynasty
Chinese dynasty (961–1278 AD). Sung stoneware is notable for its inventive use of glazes.

Suprematism
School of modern painting established in Moscow in 1913 by the Russian artist Casimir Malevich (1878–1935). It

demanded a return to pure painting, i.e. sharply defined color surfaces such as right angles, squares and circles, on a white background.

symbiosis
Combining different qualities to their mutual benefit.

synesthesia
The blending of sensations from different senses (eyes, ears, smell, etc.), evoked by the excitement of one sense organ during the stimulation of another.

tempera
Paints with water, oil or resinous binding agents.

terracotta
A fired, unglazed article made of colored (white, yellow, brown or most commonly red) firing clay; also a term for a small figure made of alumina.

threaded decor
Liquid glass is dripped on to the glass body and then drawn out in the form of threads, which are then melted to the surface.

tiled panel
A recessed field filled with tiles that make up a pattern or picture.

tourmaline
A precious stone, whose colors vary from brown through red, green and black to colorless.

translucent enamel *see enamel plique à jour*

transparent weaving
Weaving in which the warp that goes through the weft yarn is not stretched taut, resulting in a transparent weave. The quality of yarn plays a decisive part. Whereas for tapestries wool or coarse yarn is used, in transparent weaving wool, silk, and cotton are used.

Tudric
A range of pewter ware sold by the London Art Nouveau store Liberty & Co. The Celtic name was chosen as a tribute to the Welsh ancestors of John Llewellyn, a director of Liberty.

ukiyo-e
Japanese color woodcuts (= "pictures of the floating world").

underglaze
Colored decoration applied to the vessel under the glaze. Contrasts with painting on to the glaze and then firing.

verre églomisé
Special type of back painting in glass developed by the Parisian art dealer Jean-Baptiste Glomy (d. 1786). The glass is coated with black lacquer, and ornaments and figures are left blank or scraped clear. The glass is then given a deposit of metal foil or gold bronze.

vignette
Decorative and margin ornamentation on the printed page. Alternatively, a picture with irregular edges and no frame, that shades away at the sides.

vitrification
External application of colored pulverized glass that is fired but not subsequently flashed again.

woodcut
The earliest form of wood engraving. A drawing is cut into a block of wood, leaving it proud of the background so that it can be used for printing. The finished printed picture is the woodcut.

Zen
Japanese version of Buddhism that seeks union with Buddha and the universe through meditation, an active life force, and great self-control.

zinc glazing
The same as leaded glazing of windows, except that the cames are made of zinc instead of lead.

Biographies

by Priska Schmückle

André, Émile

1871 Nancy – 1933 Nancy
French architect and craftsman
André studied architecture at the École des Beaux Arts in Nancy and embarked on study tours to Egypt, Italy, and Tunisia before finally settling in Nancy in 1901. Initially he collaborated with his father, the architect Charles André (1841–1921). Later, he partnered Eugène Vallin, with whom he worked out a number of basic principles for Art Nouveau architecture. At the École de Nancy, where he and Émile Gallé were the leading lights, André taught applied art and architecture, and he is considered its chief representative in the field of architecture.
As a craftsman, André designed furniture, while as an architect he built several residential houses in Nancy, the facades of which are notable for their highly ingenious compositions using many different materials. André stood apart from his colleagues in Nancy for his free application of Art Nouveau in architecture. He won a number of awards for his work.

Arabia O.Y.

Founded 1874 in Helsinki
Finnish porcelain and ceramics factory
The Arabia company was founded in Helsinki in 1874 as a subsidiary of the Swedish porcelain factory Rörstrands Porslinsfabriker, in order to supply the Finnish and Russian markets. In 1916 it became an independent concern and in 1948 was taken over by the Wärtsila company. Arabia's products represented an important contribution to Art Nouveau within Finnish applied art. In stylistic terms they were largely shaped by the Belgian artist Alfred William Finch (1854–1930), who had lived in Finland since 1897 and who in 1902 became professor of ceramics at the Central School of Arts and Crafts in Helsinki.

Ashbee, Charles Robert

17.5.1863 Isleworth – 23.5.1942 Godden Green, Kent
English architect, interior designer, silversmith, artist craftsman, art theoretician, and poet
After studying humanities at King's College, Cambridge, from 1882 to 1885, Ashbee trained with the architect G. F. Bodley, a specialist in church architecture. In 1888 he founded the School of Handicraft in London – a training workshop for architecture and interior design – which he affiliated with the Guild of Handicraft. In 1902 he moved the school to Chipping Campden in Gloucestershire. The school's work was exhibited in London, Düsseldorf, Munich and Vienna, and was so successful that the school's designs for silverware and furniture were copied by several London firms, especially Liberty's, who sold their versions for the same price but with a higher-quality finish. This brought financial difficulties to Ashbee's school, forcing it to close in 1907. In 1902 Ashbee was made an honorary member of the Munich Academy and in 1915 became professor of English literature in Cairo. He worked as an advisor for urban development in Jerusalem between 1918 and 1922 before returning to England in 1923.
As an architect, Ashbee built with a view to simplicity and function, concentrating mainly on the detached family house, where the building and its interior formed a homogeneous unit. He also restored numerous historical buildings and between 1897 and 1898 worked with Mackay Hugh Baillie Scott on designs for a number of rooms in the New Palace in Darmstadt. Inspired by William Morris, Ashbee took an interest in the problems of art in the industrial age, and published many books and essays on this subject.

Auchentaller, Josef Maria

2.8.1865 Vienna – 31.12.1949 Grado, Italy
Austrian painter, draftsman, and graphic artist
After studying at the Technische Hochschule in Vienna (1886–89), where he won three prizes (in 1886, 1888, and 1889), Auchentaller began studying with Franz Rumpler at the Academy in Vienna. He was professor in Munich from 1893 to 1895. In 1898 he joined the Vienna Secession and worked for the periodical *Ver Sacrum*. He eventually settled in Grado in Italy in 1901, where he later became port master.
Auchentaller's graphic work was heavily influenced by his contemporaries in England. He produced illustrations, etchings, and lithographs for *Ver Sacrum* and designed many posters, counted among the best Art Nouveau posters in Austria, and painted mainly atmospheric landscapes and genre scenes.

Auger, Georges

1864 Paris – 1935 Paris
French goldsmith and jewelry designer
In 1900 Georges Auger took over the company his father, Alphonse Auger (1837–1904), had founded in 1862 (La Maison Auger), renaming it simply 'Georges Auger'. Alongside the rival French firms Vever and Cartier, Auger produced some of the most famous jewelry of his day. Besides jewelry, Auger's company also made many gold-worked articles for the applied arts, such as decorative rapiers, book covers and presentation cups.

Baillie Scott, Mackay Hugh

1865 Douglas, Isle of Man – 1945 Bedfordshire
English architect, interior designer, and arts and crafts designer
After training with C. E. Davis, Bath's city architect, Baillie Scott worked for the architect F. Saunders on the Isle of Man, setting up his own business on the island in 1893. He received commissions from England, Poland, Russia, Germany, and Switzerland. In 1898 he was asked to join the colony of artists in Darmstadt, where he and Charles Robert Ashbee designed several interiors for the New Palace. In 1901 he won first prize in a German crafts competition and returned to England that same year.
Baillie Scott's style is similar to that of the Glasgow Four. He was not as popular and well-known in his native England as he was in the rest of Europe (especially in Germany), where through him English Art Nouveau was introduced to a wider audience.

Balat, Alphonse François Hubert

15.5.1818 Gochenée, Namur – 16.9.1895 Ixelles, near Brussels
Belgian architect
Balat studied architecture at the academies in Namur and Antwerp (1831–38) and after a brief period in Paris (1840–46) set himself up as an architect first in Namur and then in Brussels. In 1852 he was made architect to the Duke of Brabant, who was crowned King Leopold II of Belgium in 1865. Balat received commissions from the Belgian royal family (e.g. the Grand Winter Garden for the Royal Palace at Laeken, for public buildings (the Palais des Beaux-Arts in Brussels, 1875) and for rebuilding and restoration work on numerous palaces. He was also Victor Horta's teacher.

Basile, Ernesto

31.1.1857 Palermo – 26.8.1932 Palermo
Italian architect
The son of the architect Giovanni Battista Basile, Ernesto Basile studied architecture in Palermo until 1878. In 1881 he moved to Rome, where from 1883 he taught at the university as a visiting lecturer. In 1888, he was commissioned to plan the Avenida de Libertacoa in Rio. He returned in 1891 to Palermo, where a year later he was appointed to a chair in architecture. In 1902, he moved his architectural practice to Rome.
Initially his buildings were eclectic in style, but around 1900 he adopted the floral version of Art Nouveau. In later years, he returned to the classical style and was an opponent of 1920s' rationalism. At the Turin Exposition in 1902 he received an award for his architecture and interiors.

Beardsley, Aubrey Vincent
21.8.1872 Brighton – 16.3.1898 Mentone, Alpes-Maritimes
English draftsman, graphic artist, caricaturist, and illustrator
After working as a draftsman in an architect's office and as a clerk for the Guardian Insurance Office (1888–92), Beardsley acted on the advice of Edward Burne-Jones and Pierre Cécile Puvis de Chavannes and started working as a freelance artist in 1892. Beardsley was largely self-taught, but did attend evening classes at the Westminster School of Art for a short time at the suggestion of Burne-Jones. In 1892 he achieved success with his illustrations for Malory's *Morte d'Arthur* and in 1893 designed the first cover for the periodical *The Studio*. From 1894 he worked for *The Yellow Book*, a journal for art and literature, and after his dismissal in 1895 as a result of the Oscar Wilde scandal, became art editor of *The Savoy*. He died from tuberculosis at the age of 25 in 1898.
Beardsley produced book illustrations, complete with ornamental title pages, artistic initials, vignettes, and borders decorated with figures and ornaments, caricatures, designs for invitation cards, and ex libris prints. His work betrays the influence of the Pre-Raphaelites and the flat, surface artwork of Japanese woodcuts, of Greek vase painting and the French Rococo. Beardsley's style is an amalgamation of all of these elements, characterized by his use of strong, black-and-white contrast, and his sketched outlines. His style heavily influenced the further development of book illustration and Art Nouveau in Europe and in America. His main works include his illustrations for Oscar Wilde's *Salome* (1894), Ben Jonson's *Volpone* (1896) and Alexander Pope's *The Rape of the Lock* (1896).

Behrens, Peter
14.4.1868 Hamburg – 27.2.1940 Berlin
German architect, painter, graphic artist, industrial designer, applied artist, typeface designer, and book artist
Behrens, who studied painting in Karlsruhe, Düsseldorf, Munich, and with the *luministes* in the Netherlands from 1885 to 1892, was initially drawn to Impressionist painting. As from 1897, however, influenced by Justus Brinkmann's collection of Japanese prints, he turned to applied art and produced works in the ornate Munich Jugendstil style, before arriving at a simpler, rectilinear, and functional style around 1904. From 1899 to 1903 he was a member of the Darmstadt artists' colony, where he designed furniture and furnishings (wallpapers, textiles, decorative glass), as well as theater sets, and where he first turned his attention to architecture. In 1901 he built his own house on the Mathildenhöhe, designing its interiors in a style influenced by Henry van de Velde and Charles Rennie Mackintosh. From 1903 to 1907 he was head of the School of Arts and Crafts in Düsseldorf. His buildings from this period are characterized by simple cubic forms with a linear ornament. From 1907 to 1914 he was a member of the AEG artistic advisory committee in Berlin, in which capacity he designed – alongside all AEG's factories and office buildings – typefaces, advertising material, and electrical goods (including domestic appliances and lighting). In 1922 he was appointed professor of architecture at the Academy in Vienna and in 1936 took over as head of the Architecture Department at the Academy in Berlin.
Behrens' formal influence upon industrial design, architecture, and typography is not be underestimated. His major works include the AEG Turbine Hall in Berlin (1909), in which structural components were for the first time left undisguised as elements of the architecture, the Mannesmann offices in Düsseldorf (1911–12), the German Embassy in St. Petersburg (1911–12), the Hoechst Dyeworks in Frankfurt (1920–25), the Gutehoffnungshütte foundry in Oberhausen (1925) and the State Tobacco Factory in Linz (1933). In his graphic works, which reveal the strong influence of van de Velde, he fused classical motifs with abstract Jugendstil ornament. He also created two new typefaces: Behrens

Italic and Behrens Roman. Behrens was amongst the founders of the Munich Secession (1892), the Freie Vereinigung Münchner Künstler (Free Association of Munich Artists, 1893), the Vereinigte Werkstätten für Kunst im Handwerk (United Workshops for Art in Handicraft) in Munich (1897) and the Deutscher Werkbund (1907). Walter Gropius (1883–1969), Ludwig Mies van der Rohe (1886–1969) and Le Corbusier (1887–1965) all worked in Behrens' Neubabelsberg studio.

Beltrami, Giovanni
26.2.1860 Milan – 1.2.1926 Milan
Italian glass artist
Even during his studies of painting at the Accademia di Brera in Milan, Beltrami showed great interest in glass painting. In 1900 he founded the firm of G. Beltrami & Co. in Milan with three co-students as partners, namely the engineers Guido Zuccaro and Innocenti Cantinotti and the artist Giovanni Buffa. The factory focused its efforts on producing *objets d'art* in glass. In its field, it became the most important workshop in Italy. Its products were successfully exhibited at the Turin Exposition in 1902 and at the Venice Biennale in 1903 and 1905. After Beltrami's death in 1926, the firm slowly dwindled away.

Bergé, Henri
1870 Diarville – 1937 Nancy
French artist, porcelain and glass painter, sculptor
After being apprenticed to the sculptor François Raoul Larche, from 1897 to 1914 Bergé produced decorative designs for vases and *pâte de verre* for Daum Frères' glass factory in Nancy, whose artistic manager he became in 1900. After 1908 he turned to sculpture, making models for glass sculptures for the firms Daum Frères and Almaric Walter. As a member of the École de Nancy, he designed all its graphic items including posters, cards, and menus.

Hendrik Petrus Berlage
21.2.1856 Amsterdam – 12.8.1934 The Hague
Dutch architect, town planner, and designer of furniture and arts and crafts articles
After studying architecture at the polytechnic in Zürich (1875–78), where he was strongly influenced by the theories of Gottfried Semper (1803–79), Berlage was involved in the construction of the waxworks in Frankfurt am Main. He undertook several study tours to Italy, Austria, and Germany (1880–85) before returning to the Netherlands in the 1890s to set up an independent architectural practice. In 1900, together with Jacob van den Bosch and W. Hoeker, he set up the interior furnishings firm 't Binnenhuis Inrichting tot Meubileering en Versiering der Woning, which was awarded a gold medal for its furniture at the Turin Exposition in 1902. In 1911, he embarked on a tour of the U.S.A., where the buildings of Louis Henry Sullivan, Henry Hobson Richardson (1838–86), and Frank Lloyd Wright greatly impressed him. Berlage is one of the most important Dutch representatives of modern architecture. In his buildings, he cast off the shackles of historical imitation; his later buildings are noted for their objective functionality and structural transparency, in which the structural components are all visible. The same applies to his furniture: typically, they have a simple linearity, in which the ornamentation is formed from the structural elements and the appropriate use of materials. In his writings, he endeavored to promote a better understanding of the connections between architecture, art, and society. His principal works include the construction of the Amsterdam Bourse (1898–1903), Holland House in London (1914), a design for the Kröller-Müller Museum (1917), the Gemeente Museum in The Hague (completed 1935), and the town planning for Amsterdam South (1915, which was implemented

by the Wendingen group of architects). His work on style, *Thoughts on Style in Architecture* was published in 1905.

Berlepsch-Valendas, Hans Eduard von
(real name Hans Karl Eduard)
31.12.1849 St. Gallen – 17.8.1921 Planegg, near Munich
Swiss illustrator, designer, craftsman, and painter
After studying architecture at the Zurich Polytechnic (1868–91) and working for a building society in Frankfurt (1873–75), Berlepsch-Valendas attended the Academy in Munich (1875–79). In 1895 he turned away from painting and dedicated himself solely to design and applied art. That same year he joined the Munich Secession. From 1897 onwards he participated in numerous arts and crafts exhibitions, including at the Munich Glass Palace (1897, 1898, 1899), in Darmstadt and Berlin (1898), in Dresden and Vienna (1899), and in St. Louis (1904). He won prizes at both the World Exposition in Paris in 1900 and at the 1902 International Exhibition of Decorative Modern Art in Turin. At his home in Planegg he founded a small school of architecture and applied art.
For Berlepsch-Valendas, the primary task of art was to improve the quality of life. He was the first in Germany to call for a greater appreciation of the decorative arts, in line with the Arts and Crafts Movement with which he had come into contact on a trip to England. Many young artists were influenced by his writings.

Bernhard, Lucian
(real name Emil Kahn)
15.3.1883 Stuttgart – 29.5.1972 New York
German painter, graphic artist, book illustrator, architect, and interior designer
Bernhard studied painting at the Munich Academy. He was self-taught as a designer and architect. After working for the printers Hollerbaum and Schmidt in Berlin, in 1910 he became head of the Deutsche Werkstätte, for which he produced numerous furniture and furnishing designs (wallpapers, carpets, lights). From 1920 to 1923 he taught advertising art at the Berlin Academy of Art. He subsequently emigrated to the United States, where he opened a studio for commercial graphics and interior design in New York, and took up teaching posts at the Art Students League and at New York University. Around 1930 he turned to painting and sculpture.
Bernhard was a member of the Deutscher Werkbund while in Berlin, and in New York became a member of the American Institute of Graphic Arts, the Art Guild, and the Society of Illustrators. He was also joint founder and director of Contempora, an international company for graphics and design in New York.
During his Berlin years Bernhard was Germany's best-known poster artist and exerted a profound influence on the development of functional goods advertising, earning him the title of "father of the advert" (Julius Klinger). In 1905 he won first prize in a poster competition.
His wide-ranging oeuvre includes several typefaces named after him (including Bernhard Gothic, Bernhard Roman and Bernhard Italic), furniture designs, color lithographs and etchings, book designs, trademarks and packaging (including decaffeinated Haag coffee in 1908 and the Adler typewriter in 1909), as well as designs for office buildings, factories, and apartment houses, including their interiors (e.g. the Karl Henkell House in Wiesbaden).

Bilibin, Ivan Yakovlevich
4.(16.)8.1876 Tarkhovka – 7.2.1942 Leningrad (St. Petersburg)
Russian painter, illustrator, graphic artist, and set-designer
While studying law (1896–1900) at the St. Petersburg faculty, Bilibin also attended a drawing course at the Society for the Promotion of the Arts (1895–98). From 1898 to 1904, he studied with the painter Ilya Yefimovich Repin. During this

period, he was also a member of the Mir Iskustva group of artists. From 1907 to 1917 he taught at the Drawing School of the Society for the Promotion of the Arts, designed stage sets and did illustrations and graphics for books and periodicals. After a study tour to Italy and Switzerland, he went to France in 1919, and from there to Egypt (1920–25). In 1936, he returned to Leningrad, where until 1942 he taught at the College for Painting, Sculpture and Architecture of the All–Russian Academy of Arts.
Bilibin was known mainly for his book illustrations. The expressive coloring of his ornamental decorative style was strongly influenced by the folklore of his native land.

Bindesbøll, Thorvald
21.7.1846 Copenhagen – 27.8.1908 Copenhagen
Danish architect, graphic artist, and craftsman
At the same time as studying architecture at the Copenhagen Academy of Art (graduating in 1876), Bindesbøll also acquired a diploma in chemistry at the Polytechnical College (1874).
For Bindesbøll, ornament was of particular importance. Geometric in his earlier works, inspired by the floor mosaics and ceiling decorations of classical antiquity, it later became freer and more organic. In his chairs, he contrasted simple, disciplined forms with a rich ornamentation, while in his architecture he went so far as to subordinate structure to ornament. His oeuvre also includes new contributions to typography, designs for silverware, embroideries, and leather, metal, and ceramic works. In 1882 he won the ordinary gold medal from the Copenhagen Academy of Art, and at the 1900 Paris World Exposition he was awarded a gold medal for his furniture. His most important building was the Foundation for Postal and Telegraph Employees in Copenhagen (1901). His confident feeling for color, line, and context made him a leading designer in all areas of modern Danish art.

Blake, William
28.11.1757 London – 12.8.1827 London
English painter, poet and copper engraver
Blake began taking lessons with Henry Pars at the London School of Drawing at the age of 11. He started training with copper engraver James Basire in 1771 and completed his education with a brief period of study at the Royal Academy of Arts. Blake illustrated works by Edward Young, R. Blair and Dante, among others. Although he was friends with John Flaxman and Johann Heinrich Füssli, during his lifetime Blake remained an unknown, his work ignored. His artwork first received recognition during the mid-19th century, when the Pre-Raphaelites showed an interest in his mystical view of the world and honored him as their precursor.

Blérot, Ernest
1870 Brussels – 1957 Elzenwalle, France
Belgian architect
Blérot was educated at the Collège Saint-Louis and the Académie Saint-Luc in Brussels. In 1897 he made a name for himself as the architect of a residential building (demolished 1989) in the rue Washington in Brussels. From 1900, he worked on building complexes such as the houses in the rue Ernest Solvay, also in Brussels. Thereafter he devoted himself to conversions and interiors of existing residences and mansions. After the First World War he dedicated himself entirely to the reconstruction and restoration of his family seat of Elzenwalle in Voormezele near Ypres.

Blomstedt, Väinö
1.4.1871 Savonlinna – 2.2.1947 Helsinki
Finnish painter, draftsman, illustrator, and textile designer
After studying at the School of Drawing at the Finnish Association of Art in Helsinki (1888–91), Blomstedt went to

Paris, where he studied at the Académie Julian (1891), the Académie Colarossi (1893) and in Paul Gauguin's studio (1893–94), which strongly influenced his style. In 1900 he won a bronze medal at the Paris Salon d'Automne. During his long career as a teacher (1900–37) at various art colleges and Helsinki University, he also traveled to Denmark, Germany, England, the Netherlands, Italy, Spain, and above all France, to which he regularly returned.
Through his studies with Gauguin (1848–1903) in Paris, Blomstedt became interested in Symbolism. Back in Finland, however, he re-embraced his native traditions and subsequently became an enthusiastic supporter of the National Romantic movement. Around 1910 he discovered Impressionism and designed textiles in a tapestry style.

Blossfeldt, Karl
13.6.1865 Schielo, Harz – 9.12.1932 Berlin
German photographer
Following an apprenticeship as a modeler in Mädgesprung, Harz, Blossfeldt was awarded a grant in 1884 on the basis of his talent to study at the Unterrichtsanstalt des Königlichen Kunstgewerbemuseums in Berlin. In 1890 he started to work for Professor Moritz Meurer, helping him to develop teaching materials for plant drawing. His photographs from this period were reproduced in Meurer's publications. In 1896 he started his long career as a teacher at various art schools, his final post being at the Hochschule der Bildenden Künste in Berlin (1921–32). Magazines started printing his photos in 1925 and in 1928 his illustrated book, Urformen der Kunst, was published, earning him instant acclaim.
Blossfeldt's photographs show details of plants and organic forms, often enlarged many times and completely concentrated on the object. They depict shapes which were adopted as decorative elements in art and as ornamental forms and structures in architecture.

Boccioni, Umberto
19.10.1882 Reggio di Calabria – 17.8.1916 Verona
Italian painter, sculptor, graphic artist, and writer on art
From 1897 to 1899, Boccioni studied at the Accademia delle Belle Arti in Rome, where his acquaintance with Giacomo Balla (1871–1958) introduced him to Neo-Impressionism. After spells in Paris and Russia, he settled in Milan in 1909 and with Giacomo Balla and Gino Severini (1883–1966) joined the Futurist Movement of Filippo Tommaso Marinetti (1876–1944) and became its spokesman. Boccioni designed Symbolist compositions and vignettes in the Art Nouveau manner. In the development of 20th century art, he counts as a leading theoretician of Futurism, his works including inter alia the Technical Manifesto of Futurist Sculpture (1912) and Futurist Painting and Sculpture (1914).

Boldini, Giovanni
31.12.1842 Ferrara – 12.1.1931 Paris
Italian painter
After attending the Accademia delle Belle Arti in Florence (1864–69), Boldini studied English portrait painting in London from 1869, then in 1872 set up in Paris as a portrait painter. Though he also painted genre and landscape pictures, Boldini was known above all as a major and popular portrait artist for the upper classes, whose sophisticated elegance he captured on canvas most effectively.

Bonnard, Pierre
13.10.1867 Fontenay-aux-Roses – 23.1.1947 Le Cannet
French painter and graphic artist
Initially, Bonnard studied law, but from 1886 he also attended the Académie Julian in Paris and subsequently (from 1888) the École des Beaux-Arts. In 1889, he and his friends

Maurice Denis (1870–1943), Paul Sérusier (1864–1927), Ker–Xavier Roussel (1867–1944), and Edouard Vuillard (1868–1940) joined Paul Gauguin's Nabis group of artists, whose works are generally grouped under Symbolism. After his first great success as an artist (a poster for France Champagne in 1890), Bonnard gave up the law. From 1910, he lived alternately in various cities (mainly Paris) and rural regions of France (Dauphiné, Normandy), as the subject matter of his pictures shows.
In his painting, which comprises portraits, landscapes and still lifes, Bonnard went back to Impressionism, which he extended by constructing his pictures in a completely new way and adopting a different palette. As a member of the Nabis group, Bonnard designed sets, costumes, and program vignettes for sundry French theaters and did illustrations for several periodicals, including La Revue Blanche. His lithographical work, e.g. for Paul Verlaine's Parallèlement (1900) and Longus's Daphne et Chloé (1902), strongly influenced modern book graphics.

Bosch, Jacob van den
19.10.1868 Amsterdam – 27.8.1948 Haarlem
Dutch craft artist
Van den Bosch studied at the Arts and Crafts College in Amsterdam from 1885 to 1890. In 1900, he was a cofounder of 't Binnenhuis Inrichting tot Meubileering en Versiering der Woning along with W. Hoeker and Hendrik Berlage, who in their plain furniture laid great emphasis on the appropriate use of materials. Van den Bosch also designed tiles for the firm of Holland and did frescoes and decorative work.

Bosselt, Rudolf
29.6.1871 Perleburg – 2.1.1938 Berlin
German sculptor, medallist, and jewelry and metalware designer
After an apprenticeship as an engraver with the Otto Schulz company in Berlin, and after studying at the School of Arts and Crafts in Frankfurt and concurrently at the Städelschen Institute of Anatomy, also in Frankfurt, from 1897 to 1899 Bosselt attended the Académie Julian in Paris. In 1899 he was appointed to the Darmstadt artists' colony (until 1903), where he designed medals, plaques, decorative and practical bronze utensils, and ivory and tortoiseshell jewelry in a simple, rigorous style. From 1903 he collaborated with the Carl Poellath mint in Schrobenhausen and in 1904 was offered, through Peter Behrens, a post teaching sculpture at the Düsseldorf School of Arts and Crafts, where he devoted himself increasingly to monumental sculpture and tombstone art. After his departure in 1911 he headed the schools of arts and crafts in Magdeburg (1911–25) and Brunswick (1928–31). Bosselt was also one of the founders of the Sonderbund (1909) and took part in the World Expositions in Paris (1900) and St. Louis (1904), as well as in the major German exhibitions.

Bradley, William H.
10.7.1868 Boston, Massachusetts – 25.1.1962 La Mesa, California
American graphic artist
His interest in the graphic works of the English artists William Morris, Edward Burne-Jones, and Aubrey Beardsley, and also in French poster artists such as Jules Chéret, led Bradley, who had trained as a printer, to become a draftsman and illustrator. His works were first published in the English journal The Studio in 1895. That same year, he accepted an invitation from Samuel Bing to show his works in the first Galerie L'Art Nouveau exhibition in Paris. Also in 1895 he founded the Wayside Press in Springfield, Massachusetts, through which he published the small magazine His Book, concerned with the theory and practice of book printing as well as with art and literature in general, and illustrated with

Bradley's own woodcuts. Despite Bradley's personal success as an artist, the Wayside Press went bankrupt in 1897. Bradley subsequently worked as an art teacher and for the type foundry of the American Type Founders Company, for which he published the journal *The American Chap-Book*. Bradley, whose oeuvre consists above all of book illustrations and artistically designed toys, was one of the leading American printers of the first quarter of the 20th century and earned the title "Dean of American Typographers" in the latter years of his life. He may be considered the best representative of American Art Nouveau. Strongly influenced by William Morris, Walter Crane, and Edward Burne-Jones, he was stylistically very close to Aubrey Beardsley, whom for a while he imitated.

Braut, Albert
1874 Roye, Somme – 6.12.1912 Pau
French painter
Braut studied in Paris under Gustave Moreau among others, and became a painter of landscapes and genre pictures. He is best known for his pictures of Paris society. From 1905, he was a regular exhibitor at the Salon des Indépendants and the Salon d'Automne.

Brega, Giuseppe
1877 – 1929
Italian architect
Brega studied architecture at the academy in Urbino. He worked as both architect and designer in the experimental studio of the building ceramics firm Ceramica Ruggeri. He constructed the Villa Ruggeri in Pesaro in 1902, which is considered one of the most important works of the Italian *Stile Liberty*.

Bugatti, Carlo
6.12.1856 Milan – 1940 Molsheim, Alsace
Italian craft artist and painter
Bugatti came from an Italian artistic dynasty whose roots date to the 15th century – the Art Nouveau painter Giovanni Segantini (1858–99) was his brother-in-law. After studying painting at the Accademia di Brera in Milan, he turned to designing furniture, collaborating with the *ébéniste* Mentasi. Around 1890, he and G. Osio set up a furniture-making workshop in Milan and, at almost the same time, another in Paris, where Bugatti was attending the École des Beaux-Arts. In 1898 came the founding of the firm of Carlo Bugatti & Co., which exhibited at the major international expositions. In 1904, he gave up his furniture workshop and went to Paris, where he designed jewelry and everyday articles from silver and also worked as a painter.
Bugatti received several awards (London 1888, silver medal in Paris in 1900, *prix d'honneur* in Turin in 1902). His furniture, which was inspired by African culture, is characterized by functional connections between the design and the many different materials used. Cubic forms rather than ornamentation determined the design.

Bugatti, Rembrandt
16.10.1884 Milan – 8.1.1916 Paris
Italian sculptor and painter
Bugatti trained as a sculptor and painter. Like most Art Nouveau artists, he used nature as his model, studying it primarily in zoos. Whereas his elder brother Ettore Bugatti (1882–1947) constructed cars, Rembrandt Bugatti became known for his small-scale animal sculptures.

Burne-Jones, Sir Edward Coley
(original name Edward Coley Jones)
28.8.1833 Birmingham – 17.6.1898 London
English painter, graphic artist, and handicrafts designer

Burne-Jones's first course of study was theology at Oxford. During his studies, he attended lectures given by the art critic John Ruskin (1819–1900), visited exhibitions of Pre-Raphaelite art and met William Morris. In 1856 Burne-Jones met Dante Gabriel Rossetti; this meeting, combined with his above experiences, convinced him to abandon his theological studies and become an artist. Until 1870 Burne-Jones painted only watercolors and was also a member of the Society of Painters in Watercolors. Post-1870 Burne-Jones did graphic work and illustrations together with his friend William Morris for the Kelmscott Press (including illustrating the works of Geoffrey Chaucer in 1897). He concentrated on designing craft articles (carpets, decorations, stained glass, ceramics, mosaics, jewelry, and furniture) which were manufactured in Morris's factories. The first exhibition of his work was held in 1877 in the Grosvenor Gallery. He joined the Royal Academy in 1895 and received a baronetcy in 1894.
Burne-Jones's characteristic style, his decoratively flowing line, grew out of his studies of Florentine *quattrocento* art. This line, threading through all genres of his work, greatly influenced Art Nouveau and especially Jugendstil in Munich and Vienna. His most famous work is a series of wall hangings which depicts the legend of King Arthur and the Holy Grail.

Burnham & Root
Founded 1873 in Chicago
American firm of architects
Daniel Hudson Burnham (1846–1912) and John Wellborn Root (1849–91) founded the architectural firm of Burnham & Root in 1873. Burnham's organizational and business skills combined with Root's technical and artistic talents to create one of Chicago's most successful partnerships. The buildings they designed were considered masterpieces in their day. For this reason, they were commissioned with the planning of the World's Columbian Exposition of 1893. After Root's death in 1891, Dwight Perkins took his place. Around 1900 the firm turned to urban planning. Its 1909 plan for Chicago remains one of the most important early exercises in this field.
Burnham and Root were members of the Chicago School of Architecture, to which they made an important contribution, although they were harshly criticized by architects such as Louis Henry Sullivan and Frank Lloyd Wright for bringing their architecture into line with that of the East Coast and with broad public taste. Their major works include the Rookery Building (1885–87) and the Reliance Building (1890–94) in Chicago.

Cardeilhac, Ernest
1851 Paris – 1904 Paris
French gold and silversmith
After learning his craft under Harleux, Cardeilhac won a silver medal at the Paris World Exposition in 1889 with his first pieces. In 1900, he took over the management of the gold and silversmith business founded in 1802 by his grandfather Vital Antoine Cardeilhac. Under the artistic direction of Lucien Bonvallet, the firm supplied articles to Samuel Bing's Galerie L'Art Nouveau and for the 1900 World Exposition in Paris. Known for his naturalistic, simple decorative style, Cardeilhac varied his works by using ivory, wood, and various patinas. In 1951, the firm was bought by Christofle & Cie.

Carriès, Jean Joseph Marie
15.2.1855 Lyons – 1.7.1894 Paris
French sculptor and potter
Carriès served an apprenticeship with various sculptors and for a while attended the École des Beaux-Arts in Lyons (1868–74), but thereafter he was self-taught. Deeply impressed by Japanese pottery and other stoneware shown at the 1878 World Exposition in Paris, he set up a pottery

studio in Saint-Amand-en-Puisaye while still a young man. He later added a second workshop at Château Monriveau, Nièvre, which was taken over at his death by his friend Georges Hoentschel. Initially Carriès made superb bronze busts, but later he turned equally successfully to glazed clay sculptures and pots, including strongly *japoniste*, plain vases with fine glazes. His great influence and his success led to the development of an artists' colony in Saint-Amand-en-Puisaye from 1890.

Cartier
Established 1847 in Paris
French jewelry and goldsmith firm
Louis–François Cartier (1819–1904) established his jewelry business in Paris in 1847. There followed several moves before the business finally settled in its present premises in rue de la Paix. In 1871, Cartier attempted to gain a foothold in London, but had to close the branch after only two years. It reopened only in 1902, and since 1921 has been an independent business. In 1874, Alfred Cartier (1841–1925) took over the firm. When his son Louis became a partner in 1898, the company was renamed "Alfred Cartier et Fils". In 1910, Cartier finally achieved world status under the direction of the three brothers: Louis in Paris, Pierre in New York, and Jacques in London. Cartier's speciality was showy pieces of jewelry in the mainstream of 19th-century taste, especially diamonds in gold settings. Fashions of the day were ignored. By the beginning of the First World War, most members of the European royal and aristocratic houses were numbered among its clients.

Cauchie, Paul
7.1.1875 Ath – 1.9.1952 Etterbeek
Belgian painter and architect
Even before he completed his studies at the École des Arts Décoratifs of the Brussels Académie Royale des Beaux-Arts (1893–98), Cauchie had founded (in 1896) a successful fresco business. Though self-taught as an architect, he built himself a house in Brussels in 1905. This was followed in 1918 by the establishment of another business in La Haye making pre-fabricated (and therefore cheap) wooden houses.

Caussé, Julien
Dates unknown
French sculptor
Causse studied under the sculptor Alexandre Falguinere, among others. His sculptures (busts, statuettes, candlesticks) were mainly inspired by mythology and the age of symbolism, and from 1888 were regularly exhibited at the Salon d'Automne in Paris. His best known work is *La fée des glaces* [the Ice Fairy].

Cheret, Jules
31.5.1836 Paris – 23.9.1932 Nice
French painter and graphic artist
A self-taught artist, Chéret completed his apprenticeship at a Paris printing press before joining a London firm that did lithographic work. In 1866 he set up his own printing press in Paris. He sold out in 1891 and turned to arts and crafts, doing textile designs and wall decorations. In 1899 he was awarded the Légion d'Honneur.
Chéret's speciality was advertising posters, which he developed into an art form. He was one of the first, in the mid-1870s, to use color lithography for his poster art. He not only designed the poster, but also the drawing on the lithographic plate. In 1893, under the influence of Henri de Toulouse-Lautrec, he went over to a decorative surface style, and it was his output, together with that of Alfons Maria Mucha, that set the course for the development of Art

Nouveau poster art. Over his 40-year career he designed about 1,200 posters. Their lively, occasionally even frivolous style corresponded exactly to the taste of the Paris salons.

Chini, Galileo
2.12.1873 Florence – 19.2.1956 Florence
Italian painter, potter, and interior designer
Chini learnt his skills in his father's restoration and decoration business, followed by brief spells at various art schools in Florence. From 1897 to 1904 he was artistic director of the porcelain and ceramics business of Arte della Ceramica in Florence. When the firm was taken over in 1907 by the ceramics company of Chini & Co. (Manufatturi Fornaci S. Lorenzo, Mugella), which belonged to a relative of his, he resumed the artistic director's seat, remaining until 1927. He spent the years from 1911 to 1914 in Thailand, whose culture greatly impressed him. From 1896 to 1898, Chini did illustrations for the periodicals La Fiametta and Il Cavalier Cortese, and between 1901 and 1936 regularly took part in the Venice Biennale. In the 1920s, he did the ceramic decoration for various buildings, particularly projects of the architect U. Giusti.

Christiansen, Hans
6.3.1866 Flensburg – 5.1.1945 Wiesbaden
German painter, graphic artist, craftsman, and writer
After an apprenticeship with a decoration painter in Flensburg and studying at the Munich School of Arts and Crafts (1887–88), in 1889 Christiansen began working as a technical college teacher and a decoration painter in Hamburg. As a member of Oskar Schwindrazheim's Volkskunstverein (Association of Folk Art), he was introduced to Justus Brinkmann and his collection of Japanese prints, which inspired him to develop a new, two-dimensional ornamental style. He was so impressed by the Tiffany glass that he encountered at the 1893 World's Columbian Exhibition in Chicago that he subsequently produced designs for opalescent glassware, in collaboration with the art glazier Karl Engelbrecht. In 1895, while studying at the Académie Julian in Paris, he encountered the Art Nouveau style of Georges de Feure and Henri de Toulouse-Lautrec, which strongly influenced his work. From 1897 he worked for the magazine Jugend and turned increasingly towards applied art. In 1898 he was invited to take part in the Darmstadt Exhibition of Arts and Crafts and in 1899 became one of the founder members of the Darmstadt artists' colony. Although he left again in 1902, he continued to live in Darmstadt, spending the winter months in Paris. In 1911 he moved to Wiesbaden, where his philosophical and literary writings were published in 1915. After the First World War he became a successful portrait painter, until the National Socialists banned him from painting because his wife was Jewish.
Christiansen was an important representative of German Jugendstil. Bearing the pronounced stamp of French Art Nouveau, his best-known works include designs for fabrics and wallpapers, characterized by continuously self-repeating serpentine lines. He also designed silver jewelry, stained-glass windows, and delicate items of domestic glass, as well as graphic works and the "Christiansen rose" motif named after him. Even though Christiansen devoted himself chiefly to applied art during his years in Darmstadt, for the large part of his life he remained first and foremost a painter.

Cissarz, Johann Vincenz
22.1.1873 Danzig – 23.12.1942 Frankfurt
German painter, graphic artist, and glass designer
From 1895 to 1896 Cissarz was a master pupil of the Belgian history painter Ferdinand Pauwels (1830–1904) at the Academy in Dresden. After completing his studies, he won commissions for posters and book illustrations and from

1898 onwards was a designer at the Dresdner Werkstätten für Handwerkskunst (Dresden Workshops for Handicraft). In 1903 he was appointed to the artists' colony in Darmstadt, where he was active in the fields of interior design and applied art. After his departure in 1906 he took up a teaching post (as from 1909 a professorship) in book design at the Teaching and Experimental Workshops (Lehr- und Versuchswerkstätte) attached to the School of Arts and Crafts in Stuttgart, and from 1916 to 1940 ran the painting masterclass at the School of Arts and Crafts in Frankfurt. As from 1912 he was also a member of the Deutscher Werkbund. Cissarz was well-known as a poster designer and illustrated books for the Eugen-Diederichs-Verlag publishing house.

Colenbrander, Theodoros Christiaan Adriaan
31.10.1841 Doesburg – 28.5.1930 Keppel
Dutch architect, designer, and potter
After working for several years in his homeland as an architect, Colenbrander spent ten years (1870–80) in Parisian artist circles. He returned to take over the artistic direction of the porcelain factory Haagsche Plateelbakkerij Rozenburg in The Hague. The decoration of his pottery is very lively and often marked by fanciful or odd motifs. Around 1900, he began designing carpets, though he continued working as a designer of porcelain as well.

Combaz, Gisbert
23.9.1869 Antwerp – 18.1.1941 Brussels
Belgian painter and craft designer
Combaz abandoned his law studies to go to the Académie Royale des Beaux-Arts in Brussels. In 1895, he began his long teaching career at various Belgian schools and academies. In the 1930s, he, R. Grousset, H. Maspero and Paul Pelliot published several studies and other works on Oriental art. A highly educated artist, Combaz is considered one of the most important protagonists of Belgian Art Nouveau, for the sheer range of his work.

Cranach, Wilhelm Lucas von
27.9.1861 Stargardô Pomerania – 31.3.1918 Berlin
German painter, interior designer, and jewelry designer
After studying in Weimar and Paris, Cranach, a descendant of the famous painter Lucas Cranach the Elder (1472–1553), worked as from 1893 as a portrait and landscape painter in Berlin. He also designed interiors for several castles in eastern Germany, including Wartburg castle near Eisenach in Thuringia. Influenced by the Russian Joullovski, in the 1890s he turned to gold and silverware designs, which are distinguished by their skillful use of various precious metals and with which he won a gold medal (for a brooch) at the Paris World Exposition of 1900.

Crane, Walter
15.8.1845 Liverpool – 14.3.1915 Horsham, Sussex
English painter, graphic artist, illustrator, and arts and crafts designer
Crane, who studied under the art critic John Ruskin (1819–1900) and the painter William James Linton (1812–97), concentrated his output from 1864 onwards on book illustration. He joined the Art Worker's Guild in 1884 and became one of the leading figures of the Arts and Crafts Exhibitions Society in 1888. Between 1893 and 1899 he held several directorships in succession, first at the Manchester School of Art, then at Reading College and finally at the Royal College of Art in South Kensington. From 1894 onwards he also worked for William Morris's Kelmscott Press.
Crane's work is strongly influenced by the Pre-Raphaelites and also by Florentine quattrocento art, which he studied

intensively during his two journeys to Italy (in 1871 and 1888). He is famous for his book graphics, and especially his illustrations for fairy tales, which are reminiscent of Japanese color prints and which were widely publicized in Germany. For the arts-and-crafts trade he designed carpets, wallpaper, embroidery, and majolica tiles. He also made a major contribution to the stylistic development of Art Nouveau as a theoretician.

Dammouse, Albert-Louis
22.10.1848 Paris – 16.6.1926 Sèvres
French sculptor, painter, potter, and glass artist
As the son of a sculptor at the Manufacture de Sèvres, Dammouse grew up with the techniques of porcelain-making. He studied in Paris, initially at the École Nationale des Arts Décoratifs and from 1868 under the sculptor François Jouffroy at the École des Beaux-Arts. He went on from there to work with the potter Marc-Louis Solon (known as Milès) before setting up on his own as a potter in Sèvres in 1871. At the ceramics exhibition in Paris in 1898 he exhibited for the first time small articles made in pâte de verre, a technique he had refined and employed successfully for the production of decorative objects. More than most of his contemporaries, Dammouse was influenced by Japanese art. His products, the decoration of which consists largely of marine plants and stylized flowers in grey, green and brown, are noted for their extravagant glazes on pâte d'émail (a very fine, opaque type of glass). Dammouse exhibited at numerous exhibitions, and in 1889 was awarded a gold medal.

D'Aronco, Raimondo
31.8.1857 Gemona – 3.5.1932 San Remo
Italian architect
D'Aronco studied at the Accademia delle Belle Arti in Venice from 1877, and was a successful entrant in various competitions even in his younger years. As an architect he worked not only in Italy but also in Turkey, where among other things he restored Hagia Sophia and repaired the Grand Bazaar. At the Turin Exposition of Arts and Crafts in 1902, he was commissioned to design the main building and entrance pavilion.
D'Aronco's style manifests the influence of the Viennese school of Otto Wagner and the Darmstadt architectural style of Joseph Maria Olbrich. Along with Ernesto Basile and Giuseppe Sommaruga (1867–1917), he is the most significant representative of Art Nouveau in Italy.

Daum Frères
Established 1875 in Nancy
French glass factory
Established by Jean Daum (1825–1885) and continued by his sons Jean-Louis Auguste (1854–1909) and Jean-Antonin (1864–1930), throughout the 1880s the glassware factory produced mainly period glass and tableware. In 1891, however, impressed by the success of Émile Gallé, the brothers went over entirely to producing glassware in the Art Nouveau style, in the same year founding the Atelier d'Art à la Verrerie de Nancy with its own training workshop. During this period, Jean-Antonin Daum was responsible for artistic design. In 1900, Henri Bergé, who had worked for the factory since 1897, took over the design workshop. In the same year, the firm was awarded the Grand Prix at the World Exposition in Paris. From 1905 to 1930, Edgar Brandt and Louis Majorelle also worked for Daum, designing iron mountings for the glassware.
From 1902, the firm produced glass decorated with floral and abstract motifs and made with Gallé's techniques and style. In the 1920s, Daum stopped working in the Art Nouveau style, and began producing thick-sided glassware with geometric Art Deco patterns.

Dearle, John Henry
1860 – 1932
English arts and crafts designer
Dearle, who trained as a picture weaver in 1878, was William Morris's assistant and his successor as director of Merton Abbey, one of Morris's workshops founded in 1881 for wallpaper, carpets, tapestry, textiles, and glass. Morris and Dearle were the main producers of designs for these items, inspired by Jacobean textile patterns.

Décorchemont, François-Émile
26.5.1880 Conches – 19.2.1971 Conches
French potter and glass artist
Décorchemont studied at the École Nationale des Arts Décoratifs from 1893 to 1897, where his father taught. In 1902, he established a glassworks to turn out *pâte de verre* wares. His first works were small statues, masks, and bowls, produced by the *cire perdue* method. His translucent pots were decorated with animal and flower patterns. Though an Art Nouveau artist, he used thick glass and a new stylized ornamentation of a type later associated with Art Deco.

Delaherche, Auguste
27.12.1857 Goincourt, near Beauvais – 27.6.1940 Paris
French potter
After studying under the landscape painter Louvrier de Lajolais at the École Nationale des Arts Décoratifs in Paris (1877–82), Delaherche worked in various studios doing glass windows and gold work before taking up pottery in 1883. In 1886, the firm of Christofle & Cie took him on as head of the galvanoplastics department. From 1900, Delaherche concentrated on the production of porcelain and, together with Ernest Chaplet, from 1904 turned out stoneware of such high quality that he has come to be regarded as one of the leading French potters of the *fin-de-siècle*. Delaherche had a special preference for stoneware with variegated glazes, for which he developed several firing techniques. He also favored grooved and openwork decoration.

Den Kongelige Porcelainsfabrik
Founded 1760 near Copenhagen
Danish porcelain factory
The Royal Danish Porcelain Factory succeeded in manufacturing true porcelain only in 1773, through Franz Heinrich Müller. After going bankrupt, in 1799 the factory passed into the possession of the king, and was subsequently called Den Kongelige Porcelainsfabrik – the name by which it is still known today. In 1867 the factory passed into the hands of A. Falck and in 1882 merged with the faience factory Aluminia, whose director, Philipp Schou (1838–1922), also took over the running of the Royal Porcelain Factory. Under the artistic guidance of Emil Arnold Krog (1885–1916), the chemist Adolphe Clément (1860–1933) and his successor, Knud Valdemar Engelhardt, the factory created innovative decors influenced by naturalism and Japanese color woodcuts which, together with the crystal glazes developed by Engelhardt, brought the company international fame.

Divéky, Josef von
28.9.1887 Farmos – 1951 Sopron
Hungarian painter and graphic artist
Divéky, who studied at the Academy of Fine Art in Vienna and as from 1906 under Larisch, Löffler and Carl Otto Czeschka (1878–1960) at the School of Arts and Crafts in Vienna, worked from 1910–14 as a graphic artist in Brussels and Zurich, before settling in Behtlis, Switzerland in 1919. In 1941 he became a professor at the Budapest School of Arts and Crafts. Divéky's work consists chiefly of book illus-

trations, works for magazines and commercial graphics for the Wiener Werkstätte.

Doesburg, Theo van
(real name Christiaan Emil Marie Küpper)
30.8.1883 Utrecht – 7.3.1931 Davos
Dutch painter, architect, and writer on art
Van Doesburg studied painting, and from 1912 was a pupil of the painter Vassily Kandinsky (1866–1944). Along with the architects Jacobus Johannes Pieter Oud and Jan Wils and the painter Piet Mondrian, he was in 1917 a co-founder of the De Stijl group of artists, to which architects, painters, sculptors and poets belonged. Doesburg was the initiator of the group and editor of the eponymous periodical, which had a great influence on the development of abstract art. In 1922 he joined the Dadaists, whom he publicized in the Netherlands. Doesburg painted non-representational pictures, initially restricting himself to rectangular lattice forms, to which he added diagonals in 1924. In his architectural designs he attempted to put De Stijl principles into practice. However, his numerous theoretical writings were still more important, exercising great influence on German art and modern architecture (Bauhaus movement).

Domènech i Montaner, Lluís
1850 Barcelona – 1923
Spanish architect
Montaner took a degree in architecture in 1873 at the University of Madrid and quickly became well-known, thanks to successes in public competitions. In 1875 he began a long period of teaching at the architectural school in Barcelona, becoming director in 1910. He built the Grand Hotel and Café-Restaurant for the World Exposition in Barcelona in 1888, but his work outside that was mainly private houses. His style was imbued with Catalan Gothic architecture, which he varied with elements of Classicism, the Renaissance and Japanese art.

Dresser, Christopher
4.7.1834 Glasgow – 24.11.1904 Mulhouse, Alsace
English botanist, art theoretician, and handicrafts designer
Dresser studied at the Somerset House School of Design from 1847 to 1853 and taught botany there from 1854. He received an honorary doctorate from the University of Jena for his books on botany in 1860. In 1875 he began concentrating on arts and crafts, designing silver tableware and after 1879 also glass, furniture, textiles, and the first Art Nouveau ceramics made in England. After a trip to the Far East in 1876, Dresser became one of the main protagonists of Japonisme and opened a store for imported Japanese goods, Dresser and Holmes, in 1879.
Dresser's work is marked by its simple design and strong line. He was inspired by Asian and Pre-Columbian pottery, and by the vocabulary of forms of Islam, classical antiquity, India, China and the Celts. Dresser also issued many publications on questions concerning the justice of material and function, on the formal design of industrial products, and on botany and its use in arts and crafts.

Dubois, Fernand
28.10.1861 Renaix – 1939 Sosoye
Belgian sculptor, jeweler, and medal-maker
After a brief spell at the Free University of Brussels, Dubois became a pupil of the sculptor Charles van der Stappen. Besides teaching jewelry at the École Professionelle des Arts Appliqués, Dubois successfully exhibited his craft pieces at numerous exhibitions. They included not only jewelry but also sculptures, medals, and everyday articles. His artistic output came to an end in 1925.

Dudovich, Marcello
21.3.1878 Trieste – 1962 Milan
Italian graphic artist
In 1897, the firm of Ricordi took on Dudovich as an artist, where he translated the designs of Metlicovitz, Hohenstein, and Capiello on to lithographic plates. At the same time, he took classes at the Società Artistica e Patriottica. His talent was quickly recognized by the young Bolognese publisher Edmondo Chappuis, who commissioned posters from him. Dudovich developed into one of the most important and successful poster artists of Italian Art Nouveau, but he also did illustrations for various Italian periodicals (including *Italia Ride*) and the German periodical *Simplicissimus*. On top of this, he also worked – especially later in his life – as a painter and interior designer.

Durrio, Paco
(real name Francisco Durrio de Madron)
1875 Valladolid – 1940 Paris
Spanish jeweler and craft artist
From 1883, Durrio lived mainly in Paris, where he exhibited his jewelry with great success at the 1904 Salon d'Automne. Even though most of his life was spent in France, he is considered as a representative of Spanish Art Nouveau, as his work is strongly imbued with the culture of his homeland.

Eckmann, Otto
19.11.1865 Hamburg – 11.6.1902 Badenweiler
German painter, graphic artist, book illustrator, typeface designer, and craftsman
After an apprenticeship as a clerk, Eckmann studied at the schools of arts and crafts in Hamburg and Nuremberg, and as from 1885 at the Academy in Munich. Although successful as a painter, in 1894 he auctioned off all his paintings and dedicated himself exclusively to graphic art and applied art. He contributed to the magazines *Pan* (1895–97) and *Jugend* (1896–97) and from 1897 taught at the Berlin School of Arts and Crafts.
Eckmann is one of the most important representatives of floral Jugendstil. The symbolic image of the swan, which appears throughout his graphic works, illustrations, and textile designs, became the emblem of Jugendstil. Eckmann was influenced by Japanese prints, from which he adopted his free, naturalistic stylization of plants and animals, his renunciation of perspective in favor of a decorative two-dimensionality, his color woodcut techniques and his color mixes, which he developed himself. His oeuvre includes furniture designs, interior decors, works in metal, ceramics, jewelry, and textiles. For the Karl Klingspor printers in Offenbach, he also created the Eckmann Type which bears his name, and which became highly fashionable as *the* Jugendstil typeface.

Eiffel, Alexandre Gustave
15.12.1832 Dijon – 28.12.1923 Paris
French engineer
After graduating in engineering from the École des Arts et Manufacture, Eiffel specialized in the construction of railway bridges (including the Maria Pia bridge over the Douro near Porto 1877–78 and the Truyère Bridge near Garabit 1880–84) and halls. He also became involved in developing metal construction techniques – initially for constructing bridges and later for other structures, especially large glass roofs. His masterpiece is the Eiffel Tower, built for the Paris World Exposition in 1889 and named for him (1885–89). The Tower showed that functionality and structural logic can have an artistic effect of their own.

Eissenloeffel, Jan
10.1.1876 Amsterdam – 17.9.1957 Laren, near Amsterdam
Dutch silversmith, metal artist, and craft artist

After training in art in Amsterdam, in 1896 Eissenloeffel entered the Amsterdam silversmith firm of W. Hoeker, and in the same year took over the metals department of Hoeker's firm Amstelhoek. In 1900, he spent a year in Russia studying the work of Peter Carl Fabergé. In 1907 and 1908 he worked at the Vereinigten Werkstätten für Kunst im Handwerk [Associated Workshops for Art in Handicraft] in Munich, which won him a wide reputation in Germany. Eissenloeffel favored severe forms, which he adorned sparingly with geometric, abstract motifs. His metal work is distinguished for its emphasis on the metal structure. Besides everyday and luxury articles, he also undertook larger items such as wall fountains, fireplaces, and grandfather clocks. His pieces won awards at arts and crafts exhibitions in Turin (1902), Dresden (1904) and Munich (1908).

Endell, August
12.4.1871 Berlin – 15.4.1925 Berlin
German architect and applied art designer
Endell studied philosophy, mathematics, psychology, and aesthetics before turning in 1896 – under the influence of Hermann Obrist – to architecture and applied art. In Munich, he produced designs for handicraft objects and books as from 1897 and worked for the magazines *Pan* and *Dekorative Kunst*, amongst others. That same year he also designed his first architectural work, the Hof-Atelier Elvira, whose decoration made an enduring impact upon Jugendstil. From 1901, in addition to a theater, he also built numerous town houses and villas in Berlin and Potsdam. In 1904 he founded the School of Formal Art, which closed ten years later. In 1918 he became director of the Academy of Art and Applied Art in Breslau.
Particularly during his Munich years, Endell was of great importance for Jugendstil, both as an artist and as a theoretician. Although Obrist exerted a very strong influence upon him, he succeeded in developing an entirely new and individual formal style. His ornament was no longer oriented toward the forms of nature, but consisted of an impressive interplay of forms and colors. In his Berlin years, he moved on to a sober, functional language of form. His major works include the Hof-Atelier Elvira in Munich (1897–98, partially destroyed in 1944, demolished after 1945), the Sanatorium on Föhr (1898), stands for the Mariendorf trotting circuit (1913) and the Theater des Überbrettl in Berlin (1901). Amongst his most important writings are *Formschönheit und dekorative Kunst* [Formal Beauty and Decorative Art, 1898] and *Die Schönheit der Großstadt* [The Beauty of the Metropolis, 1906].

Engelhardt, Knud Valdemar
see Krog, Emil Arnold; Den Kongelige Porcelainsfabrik

Evenepoel, Henri Jacques Édouard
3.10.1872 Nice – 27.12.1899 Paris
Belgian painter and graphic artist
Evenepoel went to the academies of Saint-Josse-Noode and Brussels, then continued his studies from 1893 in Paris under the painter Gustave Moreau (1826–98). His pictures, successfully shown at several exhibitions in France and Belgium, are noted for their intense colors, his favorite subject matter being ordinary life in Paris and Algiers. At first he adopted the style of Édouard Manet (1832–83), Edgar Degas (1834–1917) and Henri de Toulouse-Lautrec, but after an prolonged stay in North Africa (1887–98) he turned to Fauvism. He died from typhoid fever when only 27.

Fabergé, Peter Carl
18.5.1846 St. Petersburg – 24.9.1920 Lausanne
Russian goldsmith and jeweler

Peter Carl Fabergé was the best-known and most inventive member of the Huguenot goldsmith family Fabergé, which first opened a jewelry shop in St. Petersburg in 1842. He joined the business in 1864 after completing his studies in Dresden, Frankfurt, and Paris, and took it over in 1872. Although he had worked for the Imperial Family and the aristocracy of the whole of Europe since the 1860s, it was not until the Paris World Exposition of 1900 that his work became known to a broad public. Up to the outbreak of the First World War, Fabergé's business continued to grow, establishing workshops and showrooms in Moscow, St. Petersburg, Kiev, and Odessa and a branch in London (1905–15). His workforce of 500 included his brothers and sons, who also worked as designers. The October Revolution forced the business to close in 1918, driving the family into emigration in Switzerland.
Besides his famed Easter eggs, Fabergé made icons, clocks, cases, mounted glassware, animal figures in cut gemstones and metal, sumptuous bowls, etc. as well as the biggest jewelry production of the *fin-de-siècle*. The things he made, employing a wide variety of materials, combine functional requirements with highly sophisticated techniques. From 1883 to 1900 Fabergé was a disciple of the Art Nouveau movement. The patterns he designed in this period consisted mainly of plant, insect, and animal designs. After 1900, he went over to more geometric, functional forms.

Feure, Georges de
(real name Georges van Sluijters)
6.9.1868 Paris – 26.11.1943 Paris
Dutch–French painter, graphic artist, set designer, and crafts artist
While apprenticed in the book trade in The Hague, Feure became acquainted with Symbolism. He came so strongly under the influence of Pierre Cécile Puvis de Chavannes that in 1890 he moved to Paris and became a pupil of Jules Chéret. His first commissions were stage sets and illustrations. At the suggestion of the art dealer Samuel Bing (1838–1905), he turned to arts and crafts, and with the architect Theodor Cossmann set up a workshop for arts and crafts in Paris. Feure was so successful at several exhibitions that Bing, whose pavilion he had fitted out for the 1900 Paris World Exhibition, took over the marketing of his products. Before the outbreak of the First World War he moved to England, where he worked mainly as a set designer. In 1928 he returned to Paris, where he was appointed professor at the École Nationale Supérieure des Beaux–Arts.
Feure worked in all fields of arts and crafts. He designed furniture, porcelain, jewelry, textiles, glass windows, glassware and posters, and did book illustrations. His work is notable for its filigree ornamentation, and has a pronounced feminine effect.

Fidus
(real name Hugo Höppener)
8.10.1868 Lübeck – 23.2.1948 Schönblick, near Woltersdorf
German draughtsman and book illustrator
Fidus studied at the technical high school in Lübeck and at the Academy in Munich. Up to 1889 he was a student under W. Diefenbach, who gave him the name "Fidus" and strongly influenced him. Fidus, who held mystical, theosophical beliefs, made a name for himself as a book illustrator and executed drawings for the magazines *Jugend*, *Pan* and *Sphinx*. In his works he combined realistic figures with abstract, stylized forms.

Fouquet, Georges
1862 Paris – 1957 Paris
French jewelry artist
In 1895, Fouquet took over his father's jewelry business, for

which he had already designed jewelry since 1885. He quickly developed into one of the best French Art Nouveau jewelry artists. For this reason, he was elected president of the jewelry body of the Exposition Internationale des Art Décoratifs et Modernes in Paris in 1925 and again for the international exposition in 1937.
Fouquet made jewelry based on designs by the Art Nouveau artists Eugène Samuel Grasset and Alfons Maria Mucha, among others. His work was inspired by Japanese, Oriental, and Egyptian art.

Frosterus, Sigurd
4.6.1876 Asikkalassa – 1.3.1956 Helsinki
Finnish architect and philosopher of art
Frosterus, who studied under Henry van de Velde, was an early supporter of functionalism. Amongst the principles he embraced were the most rational use of the material, minimum expenditure, and a restriction to constructional essentials. His major works include the Stokman Department Store (1924–31) in Helsinki.

Gaillard, Eugène
31.1.1862 Paris – 1933 Paris
French architect and craft designer
Gaillard was first and foremost a furniture designer. He, Georges de Feure and Edward Colonna (1862–1948) were responsible for the design of Samuel Bing's Art Nouveau pavilion at the Paris Exposition in 1900. In 1906, he published *A propos du mobilier* [On furniture]. As with many other artists of the period, nature was a source of inspiration. In his case, the plant or animal motifs in his decorations are transformed into fanciful patterns rather than used naturalistically.

Gaillard, Lucien
1861 – after 1945
Gaillard learnt his trade from his father, the jeweler Ernest Gaillard, and became known for his goldsmith work, which was based on Japanese models. His special interest was in the various techniques of metalworking, in which he soon became a virtuoso. His silver work was exhibited at the Paris World Expositions of 1889 (where he was awarded a gold medal) and 1900. Impressed by René Lalique, he set about using more fantastic patterns in his jewelry designs. From 1900, he employed Japanese jewelry artists, and tortoiseshell and ivory carvers in his workshop. He expanded his studio and produced costly artefacts from mixed materials which brought him rapid success and another gold medal at the salon of the Société des Artistes Français.

Gallé, Émile
4.5.1846 Nancy – 23.9.1904 Nancy
French glass artist, potter, and furniture designer
Following a period of training in his father's faience and glass factory, Gallé studied philosophy, zoology, and botany and from 1864 to 1866 went to a private art school in Weimar. In 1867, he completed his practical training at the glassworks in Meisenthal (north Lorraine) and worked as a designer at his father's workshops in Nancy, Saint-Clément, and Meisenthal. From 1871, some time studying in Paris and London, where he came into contact with Japanese art, which was to have a lasting influence on his work. In 1874, he took over the artistic direction of his father's business. Ten years later, in 1884, he set up a furniture workshop, which by 1886 had expanded into a furniture factory. At the World Expositions in Paris in 1878, 1889, and 1900, he exhibited ceramics, glassware, and furniture with great success, gaining major awards. In 1890, he became a member of the Académie de Stanislas in Nancy and in 1891 of the Société Nationale des Beaux-Arts in Paris. In

1894, he founded the Société Lorraine des Arts Décoratifs and in 1901 the École de Nancy, to which he devoted much effort. His last designs date from 1903, but Gallé glassware continued to be made until 1931. The firm itself closed in 1935.

Gallé is considered one of the most outstanding glassmakers of his time, who made an enormous contribution to the development of the art of glassmaking. Prompted by Chinese cutting techniques, he developed a process for the production of cut and incised flashed glass. In addition, he endeavored very successfully to enhance the brightness of his colors while retaining the transparency of the material. In his furniture, he abandoned the fashionable eclecticism of his time and attempted to develop forms and decoration from natural structures.

Gallen-Kallela, Akseli
26.5.1865 Pori, Björneborg – 7.3.1931 Stockholm
Finnish painter and graphic artist
Gallen-Kallela studied at the School of Art in Helsinki and from 1889 at the Académie Julian and Atelier Cormon in Paris, where the works of Jules Bastien-Lepages (1848–84) and Pierre Cécile Puvis de Chavannes made a profound impression upon him. Back in Finland, he started painting genre scenes of Finnish folk life in the naturalist style. Around 1900 he developed a monumental style close to Symbolism, characterized by strong outlines and flat areas of paint, which combined decorative elements with a powerful expressiveness. Gallen-Kallela, an outstanding portraitist and graphic artist, became the leader of a Romantic, nationalist art which drew its subjects from Nordic myth, and above all the *Kalevala* epic.

Gaudí, Antoni
(full name Antoni Gaudí i Cornet)
25.6.1852 Reus, near Tarragona – 10.6.1926 Barcelona
Spanish architect and craft artist
Gaudí was both devout and socially committed. In order to be able to translate his ideals into practice, he decided to become an architect, and from 1873 to 1878 went to the Escola Superior d'Architectura in Barcelona. Even while he was still a student he gained his first commissions. In 1883, he took over the site management of La Sagrada Familia church, which was financed entirely from offerings and donations, and this project remained closest to his heart to the end of his life. In the same year, he became acquainted with his patron and later friend, Count Eusebio Güell, for whom he built the Palacio Güell in 1885–90. In 1900, the Count commissioned him to build a garden suburb (now the Parc Güell), which reflects Gaudí's endeavors to design and build his structures so that they have the effect of being an organic part of nature.

Gaudí's architecture is different not only from anything that had gone before in Barcelona but also from the work of his contemporaries. His stylistic borrowings are mainly from Catalan Gothic. His efforts to improve Gothic structural systems statically, coupled with his love of experimentation and fantastic imagination, produced some unusual structural forms. His use of multi-colored mosaics in ornamentation and the play of light and space transform his buildings into monumental sculptures. His mosaics, furniture and other craft objects are likewise distinguished for their abstract forms and recreation of objects in unfamiliar guises.

Gesellius, Herman
1876 – 1916
Finnish architect
Together with Armas Eliel Lindgren and Eliel Saarinen, in 1896 Gesellius founded the architectural firm of Gesellius, Lindgren & Saarinen, known as GLS. The international fame of the three architects was based on the Finnish Pavilion which they designed for the Paris World Exposition of 1900. Their most important works included the Suur-Merijoki manor house in Viipuri (1901–03) and the "fortified" Hvittorp House in Kirkkonummi (1901–04). In conjunction with Saarinen, Gesellius built the Remer House near Berlin (1905). GLS was dissolved in 1907.

Gradl the Elder, Hermann
21.5.1869 Dillingen – 17.4.1934 Landsberg am Lech
German painter, sculptor, graphic artist, and craftsman
From 1890 Hermann Gradl studied at the School of Arts and Crafts in Munich, together with his brother Max Joseph (1873–1934). Both became landscape painters and made their first excursions into applied art in the wake of the Glass Palace exhibition of 1898. At the next exhibition in 1899, Hermann Gradl showed works made out of tin, for which he subsequently received commissions from various metalware factories. From 1900 to 1905 he was also engaged as a designer for the Nymphenburg Royal Bavarian Porcelain Factory, for whom he helped win new fame with his artistic stylization of floral motifs. Gradl took part in numerous exhibitions at home and abroad. No ceramic designs by him are known after 1906.

Grasset, Eugène Samuel
25.5.1841 Lausanne – 23.10.1917 Sceaux
Swiss French sculptor, architect, illustrator, painter, and craft artist
After studying architecture in Zurich, Grasset continued his studies from 1871 under Eugène Emmanuel Viollet-le-Duc. Even before the appearance of Art Nouveau, he had designed posters very successfully, which contributed materially to the fact that commissions for posters were subsequently given to artists at all. Unusually, his printing graphics featured a mixed technique of lithography and woodcuts. This combined style, which fitted in well with the Art Nouveau cult of materials, is found in other areas of his work, which besides posters and book illustrations comprised designs for carpets, materials, mosaics, ceramics, glass paintings, and, not least, jewelry. After 1900 he wrote a number of textbooks, and was appointed to a chair at the École normale d'Enseignement du Dessin in Paris.

Greiner, Daniel
27.10.1872 Pforzheim – 8.6.1943 Jugenheim
German sculptor, painter, and graphic artist
Greiner graduated from Giessen University in theology and philosophy and in 1897 became a pastor in the Protestant diocese of Schotten. In 1901, following a dispute with the church synod, he turned to art. After studying at the Academy in Paris and at the School of Sculpture in Berlin, in 1903 he was appointed to the artists' colony in Darmstadt, where he produced architectural and garden sculptures until his departure in 1906. He subsequently founded the Greiner and Guth Workshops for Tombstone Art in Jugenheim and in his latter years devoted himself increasingly to church painting. His political past as a Socialist meant that, as from 1933, his commissions dried up. But, despite his severely straitened circumstances, he nevertheless continued to work as a sculptor and painter.

Gris, Juan
(real name José Victoriano González Pérez)
23.3.1887 Madrid – 11.5.1927 Paris
Spanish painter and graphic artist
Gris abandoned his engineering studies in 1904 to go to the Arts and Crafts College in Madrid. In 1906, he moved to Paris, where he joined the circle around Pablo Picasso and took up "analytical" Cubism. Gris started out as a cartoonist, but he also did sets for the Russian Diaghilev Ballet in Monte Carlo and book illustrations. However, it was mostly still lifes, portraits, and figurative pictures that he painted.

Gris was the main representative of Cubism in France, which he developed independently after the First World War (synthetic Cubism). His considered and technically outstanding pictures count among the masterpieces of this style.

Gruber, Jacques
25.1.1870 Sundhausen, Alsace – 15.12.1936 Paris
French painter and craft designer
A scholarship from the city of Nancy enabled Gruber to study under Gustave Moreau (1826–98) at the École des Beaux-Arts in Paris. In 1894, Gruber returned to Nancy and produced decorative designs for vases for Daum Frères' glass factory, furniture for Louis Majorelle and book bindings for René Wiener. In 1897, he set up his own studio, and from 1900 went over almost entirely to glass mosaics and glass painting. At the same time he taught at the École des Beaux-Arts in Nancy and in 1901 was a cofounder of the École de Nancy.

Gruber was regularly represented at the Salon des Artistes Décorateurs from 1908 and at the Salon des Artistes Français from 1911. From 1920 to 1923 major honours were heaped on him, culminating in the Légion d'Honneur in 1924.

Guimard, Hector
10.3.1867 Lyons – 20.5.1942 New York
French architect, sculptor, and craft artist
Guimard studied in Paris from 1882 to 1885 at the École Nationale des Arts Décoratifs and subsequently at the École des Beaux-Arts. He received his first commission in 1887, to build a café-restaurant in Paris. This commission was succeeded by others. From 1894 to 1898 he taught at the École des Arts Décoratifs in Paris. After the First World War he was quickly forgotten, as Art Nouveau was no longer in fashion. In 1938, he finally emigrated to the United States.

The most important French representative of the organic, floral style of Art Nouveau, Guimard was initially strongly influenced by the Belgian architect Victor Horta, whom he had got to know in 1895. His own style (the "Guimard Style") is distinguished by its linearity and interplay of light and contrasts. As a furniture designer, he looked on furniture and the interior decoration of a house as parts of a total work of art. This led to very unusual designs for much of his furniture, some of which must be considered among French Art Nouveau's finest. His principal works include the Castel Béranger residential building (1894–99), which in 1899 was awarded a prize for the finest facade in Paris, and the station entrances of the Paris Métro (1899–1904).

Gulbransson, Olaf
26.5.1873 Christiania (today Oslo) – 18.9.1958 Schererhof (on Lake Tegern), Germany
Norwegian painter and graphic artist
Gulbransson, who studied at the School of Arts and Crafts in Oslo and was a pupil of Colarossi in Paris, held a permanent position from 1902 with the Munich magazine *Simplicissimus*. In 1929 he took up a teaching post at the Academy in Munich.

Gulbransson is one of the most important caricaturists of the 20th century. In his ironically naive, powerfully expressive drawings, he communicated the essential characteristics of his subject using only the most economic means, and later simply by use of outline. Alongside his work for *Simplicissimus*, he also illustrated books and published many of his caricatures in the Norwegian magazine *Tidens Tegn*. His major works include *Berühmte Zeitgenossen* [Famous contemporaries, 1905], *Aus meiner Schublade* [From my drawer, 1911] and his autobiography *Es war einmal* [Once upon a time, 1934].

Gurschner, Gustav
28.9.1873 Mühldorf – 1970 Vienna
Austrian sculptor and craftsman
Gurschner studied at the Vienna School of Arts and Crafts from 1888 to 1894 and in Munich in 1896, before moving to Paris in 1897 and attaching himself to the Art Nouveau artists Alexandre Charpentier (1856–1909), Jean-Auguste Dampt (1854–1946) and Ville Vallgren. Gurschner showed his works in numerous exhibitions; he took part regularly in the Salon du Champ de Mars in Paris and, after its foundation in 1897, in the exhibitions by the Vienna Secession. In 1900 he became a member of the Hagenbund, showing two marble sculptures in its opening exhibition, while at the 1902 Turin International Exhibition of Decorative Modern Art his works were to be seen in no less than three pavilions – the Austrian, the German, and the French. He subsequently restricted himself wholly to sculpture, in particular for tombs and monuments.

Haagsche Plateelbakkerij Rozenburg
Established in 1883 in The Hague
Dutch china manufacturer
The Haagsche Plateelbakkerij Rozenburg was established by a German, Wilhelm Wolff von Gudenberg, who himself prepared designs until Theodoros Christiaan Adriaan Colenbrander took artistic control. Under Colenbrander's management, the factory gradually went over to producing only Art Nouveau china. Models for the light-dark-contrast and vegetable patterns were taken from Javanese batik, but it was only under the direction of J. Jurriaan Kok (1894–1913) that the company developed a typical "Rozenburg Style". In 1899, in order to be able to produce objects in unusual designs, Kok and the chief chemist M. N. Engelden developed a very thin-sided body called quasi or eggshell porcelain, similar to frit porcelain. This enabled Kok to translate his unusual designs, an interaction of decoration and form, into reality.
Production at the factory was so uniformly arranged that it is not possible to distinguish the work of the various artists who worked there. They include Samuel Schellink (1876–1958), Jacobus Willem van Rossum (1881–1963), Roelof Sterken (1877–1943) and J. H. Hartgring (1876–1951).

Habich, Ludwig
2.4.1872 Darmstadt – 20.1.1949 Jugenheim
German sculptor and craftsman
Habich, a pupil of the Frankfurt sculptor Gustav Kaupert, was one of the founders of the Freie Vereinigung Darmstädter Künstler (Free Association of Darmstadt Artists) in 1898 and in 1899 was amongst the first seven to be appointed to the Darmstadt artists' colony. Alongside his work as an artist, Habich also taught sculpture at Adolph Beyer's art school in Darmstadt as from 1901. In 1906 he left the artists' colony and moved to Stuttgart, where from 1910 to 1937 he held a teaching post at the Academy of Art. In 1937 he returned to Darmstadt, but left the city again after his house was destroyed in the Second World War.
Habich created colossal figures, fountains, monuments and tomb art, small sculptures, and handicraft items. His bronze sculptures were shown at the World Expositions in Paris (1900) and St. Louis (1904). His major works include the oversized figural group Man and Woman (1900–06), the Goethe Temple and Bismarck Fountain, all in Darmstadt, and the War Memorial in Lauterbach.

Hamesse, Paul
1877 Brussels – 1956 Brussels
Belgian architect
Hamesse was a pupil and later a colleague of the architect Paul Hankar until Hankar's death in 1901. Around 1900, he began to enter competitions and built his first (private)

houses, mainly in Brussels. From 1903, he won numerous commissions for private houses, shops, and residential buildings, including the Hôtel Cohn-Donnay (today the Café-Restaurant Ultième Hallucinatie).

Hampel, Walter
17.7.1867 Vienna – 17.1.1949 Nussdorf am Attersee
Austrian painter and draughtsman
Hampel was a student at the State School of Handicraft and at the Vienna Academy under Eisenmenger, Angeli and L'Allemand. From 1900 to 1911 he was a member of the Hagenbund.

Hankar, Paul
11.12.1859 Framerie, Hainault – 17.1.1901 Brussels
Belgian architect and furniture designer
Hankar trained as a sculptor, but graduated from the Académie Royale des Beaux-Arts in Brussels as a pupil of the architect Henri Beyaert, for whom he did wrought-iron work. In 1888, he began his partnership with the interior designer Alphonse Crespin (1859–1944). In 1893, he built himself a house, which, along with the Hôtel Tassel by Victor Horta, is considered as the first Art Nouveau building in Brussels. While running his successful architectural practice, Hankar also designed furniture, and from 1894 he contributed to the periodical L'Emulation. For the Brussels World Exposition of 1897, he collaborated with Henry van de Velde, Gustave Serrurier-Bovy and Georges Hobé.
Paul Hankar and Victor Horta were the leading Art Nouveau architects in Brussels. Hankar was an enthusiastic proponent of the doctrines of Eugène Emmanuel Viollet-le-Duc and the English Arts and Crafts Movement, and looked on architecture as a synthesis of the arts.

Hansen, Frida
(real name Frederikke Bolette)
8.3.1855 Stavanger – 12.3.1931 Oslo
Norwegian textile designer
In the 1870s Hansen studied painting, winning a prize at the World's Columbian Exposition in Chicago in 1893 which enabled her to study textile design in Cologne in 1894, and in 1895 to study under Pierre Cécile Puvis de Chavannes in Paris. In 1900 she became a member of the Société Nationale des Beaux-Arts and was represented at the Paris World Exposition by her famous tapestry The Milky Way. Hansen perfected the technique of transparent weaving, which lends her figures an almost ghost-like quality. She was influenced both by Japonisme and the Pre-Raphaelites, and stood squarely within the Art Nouveau tradition in her thematic material.

Haustein, Paul
17.5.1880 Chemnitz – 6.9.1944 Stuttgart
German painter, graphic artist, and craftsman
Haustein, who studied painting at the Academy in Munich, worked for the magazine Jugend in 1898 and was a founder member of the Vereinigte Werkstätten für Kunst im Handwerk [Associated Workshops for Art in Handicraft] in Munich. He also produced designs for Jacob Julius Scharvogel's ceramics factory, the K. L. Seifert lighting factory in Dresden and the Bruckmann & Söhne silverware factory in Heilbronn. In 1900 he was invited to take over as head of the Meissen Royal Saxon Porcelain Factory, and was also offered a teaching post at the Magdeburg School of Arts and Crafts. He decided to remain in Munich, however, until being appointed to the artists' colony in Darmstadt in 1903. Here he developed his metalwork designs, influenced by the Arts and Crafts Movement, for which he won a prize at the World Exposition in St. Louis (1904). In 1905 he was offered,

via Bernhard Pankok, a teaching post in metal art at the Teaching and Experimental Workshops (Lehr- und Versuchswerkstätte) attached to the School of Arts and Crafts in Stuttgart, where he remained for 30 years. As a graphic artist, and above all as a book illustrator with a preference for stylized, vegetal ornament, Haustein ranked even in his own day amongst the most important artists of Jugendstil.

Hazenplug, Frank
1873 Dixon, Illinois – after 1908
American graphic artist
From 1894 Hazenplug worked with William H. Bradley, whose position with the Stone and Kimball company in Springfield he eventually took over, after a long and successful period of collaboration. Even though Hazenplug's works betray the strong influence of his elder colleague, in his palette and his use of perspective he nevertheless developed his own style – something visible above all in his posters.

Heine, Thomas Theodor
28.2.1867 Leipzig – 26.1.1948 Stockholm
German painter, graphic artist, and writer
Heine, who studied under Carl Janssen at the Academy in Düsseldorf (1885–88), started working as an illustrator for the magazines Jugend and Fliegende Blätter as from 1892. He attached himself to the young generation of artists around Lovis Corinth (1858–1925), Ludwig Dill (1848–1940) and Wilhelm Trübner (1851–1917) and from 1895 devoted himself to book illustrations and decoration. In 1896, together with Albrecht Langen and Ludwig Thoma (1867–1921), he founded the magazine Simplicissimus, on whose staff he remained, together with his colleagues Olaf Gulbransson, Bruno Paul, and Eduard Thöny (1866–1950), until the magazine was banned in 1933. He subsequently emigrated first to Prague, then Brno, Oslo, and finally in 1942 to Stockholm, where he became a Swedish national and was once again able to contribute to magazines.
Heine's graphic works represent a very important contribution to Munich Jugendstil. His animated line and his handling of areas of color recall the art of Japan and Henri de Toulouse-Lautrec. His surviving works include the portfolios Pictures of Family Life and Follies.

Hentschel, Julius Konrad
3.6.1872 Cölln, near Meissen – 9.7.1907 Meissen
German embosser and modeler
In 1889–90 Hentschel completed an apprenticeship as an embosser at the Meissen Royal Saxon Porcelain Factory, where his father, Julius Hentschel, was employed as a figure painter. The factory granted him a scholarship to study at the Academy in Munich from 1891 to 1893. From 1894 to 1897 he worked as an embosser and from 1897 as a modeler for the Meissen works. From 1899 to 1900 he studied at the Dresden Academy and in 1906 took part in the Third German Exhibition of Applied Arts in Dresden. Hentschel made a name for himself as a porcelain painter and designer of figures and tableware (e.g. his Crocus service of 1896) for the Meissen Porcelain Factory.

Hoentschel, Georges
1855 Paris – 8.2.1915 Paris
French architect, collector, and potter
Prompted by his friend Jean Carriès, architect and ceramics collector Georges Hoentschel designed pots in Carriès's style. After Carriès died in 1894, Hoentschel took over his workshop in Nièvre. Among the craftsmen who executed his designs were Émile Grittel, Paul Jeanneney, Nils Ivan Joakim de Barck, and E. Deschamps.

Hoentschel's Art Nouveau work, which includes furniture as well as pots, is notable for its light, Baroque sense of form. Later he went over to simpler forms, and, unlike his contemporaries, moved away from Japanese models.

Hoetger, Bernhard
4.5.1874 Hörde, Westphalia – 18.7.1949 Unterseen, Switzerland
German sculptor, painter, graphic artist, architect, and craftsman Hoetger, who trained as a stonemason and woodcarver, ran a church decoration workshop from 1895 to 1897 before becoming a master pupil of Carl Janssen at the Academy of Art in Düsseldorf in 1897. In 1911 he was appointed to the artists' colony in Darmstadt, where he created one of his major works, the plane-tree grove on the Mathildenhöhe, which he made into a total work of art with statues and reliefs. From 1924 to 1929 he was active as an architect in the artists' village of Worpswede, near Bremen. In 1943 he emigrated to Switzerland following the destruction of his home in Berlin during the war.
If Hoetger's work initially reflected the influence of Auguste Rodin (1840–1917), in whose atelier he worked from 1900 to 1907, it was Aristide Maillol (1861–1944) who later determined his style. As a result of his friendship with Théopile-Alexandre Steinlen (1859–1923), Hoetger turned to graphic art, and after a spell in Florence (1911–12) also started producing ceramic sculptures. His major works include the plane-tree grove on the Mathildenhöhe in Darmstadt (1912–14), the Brunnenhof in Worpswede (1921), the Café Worpswede (1925), the development of Böttcherstrasse in Bremen with the Paula Modersohn House (1926–30), and private houses in Worpswede (1928) and Berlin (1939–40).

Hoffmann, Josef
15.12.1870 Pirnitz, Moravia – 7.5.1956 Vienna
Austrian architect, graphic artist, and applied artist
After attending the State School of Applied Arts in Brno, Hoffmann studied achitecture at the Vienna Academy under Karl von Hasenauer and Otto Wagner. In 1897 he was one of the founders of the Vienna Secession, which he subsquently left in 1905 as part of the Klimt group. As a member of the Wiener Werkstätte, which he founded in 1903 with Koloman Moser, Fritz Waerndorfer, and Carl Otto Czeschka (1878–1960) and which he headed until 1931, his commissions included a new building for the Westend Sanatorium in Purkersdorf (1903–04), and the Palais Stoclet in Brussels (1905–11). In 1912 he founded the Austrian Werkbund and from 1920 was the head of the Viennese group within the German Werkbund. From 1899 to 1937 he taught at the Vienna School of Arts and Crafts and in 1920 became senior building surveyor to the City of Vienna.
Hoffmann numbered amongst the leading architects of Jugendstil and exerted, in particular through the Wiener Werkstätte, a profound stylistic influence upon the applied arts of his day. His oeuvre was determined by the concept of the total work of art, and he was correspondingly active in every sphere of applied art (furniture, metalwork, glass, leatherwork, jewelry, textiles). The principle of the repetition of identical elements, in particular the square, characterized his ornamental style. Individual components are thereby interchangeable, an innovative development in Jugendstil design.

Hofmann, Ludwig von
17.8.1861 Darmstadt – 23.8.1945 Pillnitz, near Dresden
German painter, graphic artist, and applied arts designer
After attending the academies in Dresden, Karlsruhe, and Munich (1883–89), Hofmann continued his training from 1889 to 1890 at the Académie Julian in Paris, where he became friends with Maurice Denis (1870–1943) and absorbed the influences of Pierre Cécile Puvis de Chavannes and Albert Besnard (1849–1934), whose wall paintings he copied. In 1890 he joined *Die Elf*, the group of artists formed at the instigation of Walter Leistikow, whose members also included Lovis Corinth (1858–1925), Max Klinger (1857–1920) and Max Liebermann (1847–1935). He painted and taught in Weimar from 1903 to 1908 and in Dresden from 1916 to 1918.
In his work, which also includes woodcuts for books and lithographs, Hofmann combines a traditional, academic style with Art Nouveau motifs. Using the stylistic means of contrast, he lends his pictures a coded meaning whose symbolism is nevertheless clearly recognizable.

Hokusai, Katsushika
21.10.1760 Edo (today Tokyo) – 10.5.1849 Edo
Japanese painter and master of colored woodcuts
Hokusai, a pupil of Katsukawa Shunsho and Shiba Kokan, produced numerous paintings and series of woodcuts and illustrated more than 500 books. He is one of the most versatile *ukiyo-e* artists and famous for his ingenious composition and drawing techniques. His colored woodcuts – the best-known is his series entitled *36 Views of Mount Fuji* – were much sought-after in the second half of the 19th century and had a lasting effect on the development of Art Nouveau.

Horta, Victor
6.1.1861 Ghent – 11.9.1947 Brussels
Belgian architect and designer of craft articles
Horta studied at the fine arts academies of Ghent and Brussels. He started work as an architect in Alphonse Balat's practice, which he took over after Balat died in 1895. In 1892, Horta turned away from historicism and in 1893 built his first Art Nouveau building, the Hôtel Tassel, which was followed by many others throughout Brussels. In 1912, he was appointed professor and in 1927 (to 1931) director of the Fine Arts Academy in Brussels. After a spell in the United States (1916–18), he became involved in the development of new building materials as well.
Horta and Paul Hankar were leading reformers of modern Belgian architecture. Horta's early houses – slender iron constructions – are notable for an unstinting use of glass and linear ornamentation, whereby the models for the lines were the stalks and stems of plants and not, as with other Art Nouveau artists, the blooms and the leaves. After his trip to the U.S.A., Horta turned away from Art Nouveau and went back to classicist forms, as for example on the Palais des Beaux-Arts. His main works include the Hôtel Tassel (1892–93), the Hôtel Solvay (1895–1900), the Maison du Peuple (1896–99) and the Palais des Beaux-Arts (1922–28), all of them in Brussels.

Huber, Patriz
19.3.1878 Stuttgart – 20.9.1902 Berlin
German architect, jewelry designer, and applied artist
Huber studied painting at the School of Arts and Crafts in Mainz and subsequently, from 1897, in Munich, where he soon developed an interest in applied art. While studying in Munich he designed typefaces for the Darmstadt publisher Alexander Koch and took part in competitions held by the magazines *Innendekoration* and *Deutsche Kunst und Dekoration*. From 1899 to 1902 he was a member of the artists' colony in Darmstadt, for which he designed interiors and furniture. In 1902 he took part in the Paris World Exposition and showed a kitchen installation at the "Modern Art of Living" exhibition at the Wertheim Department Store. That same year he opened his own studio in Berlin, working in collaboration with his brother, the architect Anton Huber, and Henry van de Velde. Together with his brother, he developed his so-called "skeleton style", in which struts, pillars, beams, and doors were incorporated into the decor.

Hyland, Fred
Dates unknown
English graphic artist
No biographical information is available for Hyland. He worked for the periodical *The Savoy* and seems to have been part of the circle of artists around Aubrey Beardsley.

Jensen, Georg
31.8.1866 Raavad – 2.9.1935 Copenhagen
Danish ceramicist, gold and silversmith
After an apprenticeship as a goldsmith in Copenhagen, in 1887 Jensen took lessons in sculpture at the Copenhagen Academy. He made his first ceramic pieces in 1899 in the workshop run by Mogens Ballin (1871–1914). After a study trip to Italy and France (1900), he joined forces with Joachim Petersen to found a small porcelain workshop, but the venture was unsuccessful. After this disappointment, Jensen turned back to goldsmithery and in 1904 opened his own studio and shop, making and selling jewelry and silverware. In 1905 his works were included in the International Exhibition in The Hague. In 1907 he entered into a lifelong partnership with the painter Johan Rohde (1856–1935), who supplied many of his designs up till 1935. By 1918 Jensen's studio had grown into a large company with a workforce of over 200. It has employed important artists such as Sigvard Bernadotte af Wisborg (b. 1907) and Harald Niesen.

Jerndahl, Aron
1.1.1858 Östervad, Möklinta – 2.9.1936 Stockholm
Swedish sculptor and painter
After studying at the Academy of Art in Copenhagen (1886–88), Jerndahl worked in the studio of the painter Peter Severin Krøyer (1851–1909). In 1891 he collaborated on the reliefs for the choir in Uppsala cathedral. In 1898 he attended the Technical Evening College in Stockholm and the school run by the Swedish Association of Artists. Jerndahl's works were featured in exhibitions by the Swedish Association of Artists and in exhibitions in Munich (1909) and Düsseldorf.

Jo, Léo
(real name Léontine Joris)
1870 Tournai – 1962 Brussels
Belgian graphic artist
Even as a child, Léo Jo showed a gift for drawing cartoons. She was supported by the sculptor Charles van der Stappen, but she did not want to give her regular lessons, for fear of destroying her natural talent. She did drawings for the periodicals *Samedi*, *Rire*, *Comica*, *Simplicissimus* and *Lustige Blätter*, and also illustrations for children's books and toys. From 1899, she exhibited her work at the Salon de la Libre Esthétique. In 1903, she was represented at the exhibition of the Société Nationale des Aquarellistes et Pastellistes de Belgique, and in 1912 took part in the Xth Venice Biennale.

Jourdain, Frantz
3.10.1847 Antwerp – 1935 Paris
Belgian-French architect, writer, and journalist
Jourdain studied at the École des Beaux-Arts in Paris from 1865 to 1870. In 1883, he was commissioned by E. Cognacq to build a store for Samaritaine. The building was completed in 1905, but extensions were undertaken in 1925 jointly with the architect Frédéric Henri Sauvage. In addition, Jourdain designed some pavilions for the Paris World Exposition in 1900, and took part in the restoration of a number of châteaux. He was a cofounder of a number of artists' organisations, including the Société du Nouveau Paris (1903) and the Salon d'Automne (1905).

Jungnickel, Ludwig Heinrich
22.7.1881 Wunsiedel, Upper Franconia – 14.2.1965 Vienna
German painter, graphic artist, and applied arts designer
Jungnickel, who attended both the School of Arts and Crafts and the Academy in Munich and the School of Arts and Crafts in Vienna, started working as a graphic artist in 1904. From 1911 he taught at the School of Arts and Crafts in Frankfurt. He was a member of the German and the Austrian Werkbund, and of the *Künstlerhaus* group. His main area of activity, however, was his work for the Wiener Werkstätte, for whom he designed the children's room in the Palais Stoclet in Brussels (1905–11). After a trip to Bosnia and Herzegovina (1913), he devoted himself increasingly to drawing. In 1938 he emigrated to Split and later to Abbazia. In 1952 he finally settled back in Austria.

Kayser & Sohn AG, Johann Peter
Founded 1862 in Krefeld-Bockum
German pewter foundry
In 1862 the Düsseldorf-based Kayser family, already in the tin industry, opened a new foundry in the Bockum district of Krefeld. The firm reached its maximum size in 1899 with a workforce of around 400. The Krefeld foundry run by Jean (Johann Peter) Kayser was devoted to mass production, whereby the designs originated from the Cologne studio of Engelbert Kayser. At the exhibitions in Paris (1900), Turin (1902), Düsseldorf and St. Louis (1904), the company enjoyed great success with its "Kayser pewter", a special lead-free alloy of tin and silver distinguished by its lasting gleam – success which it also owed to its outstanding designers: Hugo Leven, Karl Geyer, Hermann Pauser, Karl Berghoff, and Johann Christian Kröner. The decors they designed were inspired both by floral French Art Nouveau and by linear Jugendstil. It was the Kayser company's aim, through its use of the methods of mass production, to make artistically designed, contemporary objects of daily use accessible to a broad section of the public.

Khnopff, Fernand
12.8.1858 Grembergen – 12.11.1921 Brussels
Belgian painter and graphic artist
Having completed his law studies, in 1878 Khnopff began a painting course at the Académie des Beaux-Arts in Brussels, and subsequently became a pupil of Jules Lefebvre in Paris. He was a member of the Belgian artists' groups L'Essor, Les Vingt and La Libre Esthétique. An issue of the periodical *Ver Sacrum* was dedicated to him in 1898. In 1901, he collaborated with the Wiener Werkstätte on the Palais Stoclet in Brussels. Khnopff was the principal Belgian representative of Belgian Symbolism. Influenced by the English Pre-Raphaelites and Gustave Moreau (1826–98), he painted pictures with mystic and allegorical subject matter. His oeuvre includes landscapes, etchings, and book illustrations.

Klablena, Eduard
8.4.1881 Buscan – 6.11.1933 Langenzersdorf
Austrian sculptor and ceramicist
Klablena, who studied at the Vienna School of Arts and Crafts, was taken on by the KPM Royal Porcelain Factory in Berlin in view of his talents as a sculptor. In 1911 he founded his own ceramics studio in Langenzersdorf under the name of Langenzersdorfer Keramik. The studio specialized in representations of animals, generally described as "animal fantasies", and featured in all the major exhibitions at the Austrian Museum of Art and Industry. After 1912 Klablena sold his works through the Wiener Werkstätte.

Kleukens, Friedrich Wilhelm
7.5.1878 Achim, near Bremen – 22.8.1956 Nörtingen

German painter and graphic artist
Kleukens received his training as a draftsman in a silverware factory in Hemelingen and under E. Döpler at the School of Arts and Crafts in Berlin. In 1900, together with Fritz Helmut Ehmke (1878–1965) and G. Belwe, he founded the Steglitz Workshop for Applied Arts and Commercial Graphics, which two years later was affiliated to a printing college. From 1903 to 1906 he taught at the Academy of Graphic Art in Leipzig. In 1907 he became a member of the artists' colony in Darmstadt, where he taught decorative art at the Grand-Ducal Teaching Studio until 1911. In addition, he ran the newly founded Ernst Ludwig Press from 1907 to 1914. In 1919, together with L. C. Wittich, he founded the Ratio Press in Darmstadt, for which he worked until 1930.
Alongside graphic works and drawings inspired by William Morris, Kleuken's oeuvre includes mosaic pictures and ornamental designs which he produced for the 1914 exhibition by the Darmstadt artists' colony.

Klimt, Gustav
14.7.1862 Baumgarten, near Vienna – 6.2.1918 Vienna
Austrian painter and graphic artist
Klimt was just 14 when he won a scholarship to the School of Arts and Crafts in Vienna. Together with his brother Ernst Klimt and his fellow student Franz Matsch, between 1882 and 1892 he carried out a number of major commissions for wall and ceiling paintings. During this period he was also awarded the Golden Order of Merit and the Imperial Prize. In 1897 he was a joint founder of the journal *Ver Sacrum* and the Vienna Secession, which he left in 1905 with a number of his friends, including Josef Hoffmann and Otto Wagner, in order to found the Wiener Werkstätte. In 1917 he was made an honorary member of the Vienna and Munich academies.
Klimt ranks amongst the leading representatives of Viennese Jugendstil. While his early paintings still betrayed the influence of Hans Makart (1840–84), after the death of his brother he moved away from academic painting and developed his own two-dimensional style, in which representational elements are combined with ornament to achieve a decorative effect. Although this style caused several scandals in his own day (e.g. his ceiling paintings for Vienna University, 1900–03), it also made him a pioneer of modernism. His major works include the *Beethoven* frieze (1902), *Judith* (1905–08), *The Kiss* (1908) and his wall mosaics for the Palais Stoclet in Brussels (1909–11).

Knox, Archibald
1864 Isle of Man – 1933 Isle of Man
English silversmith and painter
Knox attended the Douglas School of Art on the Isle of Man from 1878 to 1884 and taught there until 1888. In the 1890s he moved to London, where first he worked for Christopher Dresser and later for Liberty & Co. (his main employer). Liberty's used Knox's designs for its Cymric silver series and after 1903 for the Tudric pewter series. The motifs Knox borrowed from Celtic art later became one of the trademarks of English Art Nouveau. Although Knox's name appears neither on Liberty objects nor in their catalogs (Liberty's did not issue the names of its designers with its goods), we know that Knox was responsible for over 400 Liberty designs. He stopped working for Liberty's in 1912 and resumed his teaching post on the Isle of Man in 1913.

Köhler (-Broman), Mela (Melanie Leopoldina)
18.11.1885 Vienna – 15.12.1960 Stockholm
Austrian graphic artist and craftswoman
Köhler studied at the Hohenberger School of Painting in Vienna and from 1905 to 1910 under Koloman Moser at the Vienna School of Arts and Crafts. In 1907, while still a student, her works were published in the English journal *The*

Studio. Her first exhibition took place in 1908 at the School of Arts and Crafts in London. Köhler illustrated fairytales for the Konegen publishing house and contributed to the Viennese fashion magazine *Wiener Mode*. She was also a member of the Austrian Werkbund and the Wiener Frauenkunst group of women artists. In 1934 she emigrated to Sweden.

Königlich-Sächsische Porzellan-Manufaktur Meissen
[Meissen Royal Saxon Porcelain Factory]
Founded 1710 in Meissen
German porcelain factory
The first European factory to make hard porcelain, the Königlich-Sächsische Porzellan-Manufaktur Meissen was founded in 1710 by the Saxon Elector August the Strong, initially under the name of Kursächsische Manufaktur [Electorate of Saxony Factory]. In 1918 it was renamed the Staatliche Porzellan-Manufaktur Meissen [Meissen State Porcelain Factory]. Around the turn of the century, the sculptor and modeler Emmerich Andersen (1843–1902) introduced the Art Nouveau style. Employing designs by major Jugendstil artists such as Henry van de Velde, Peter Behrens, Joseph Maria Olbrich, and Richard Riemerschmid, the factory produced a large number of dinner services, decorative figures, animal sculptures, and ornamental plates.

Koepping, Karl
24.6.1848 Dresden – 15.7.1914 Berlin
German painter, etcher, and glass artist
After obtaining a diploma in chemistry, from 1869 Koepping studied painting at the Academy in Munich and was subsequently apprenticed to the etcher A. Waltner in Paris. In 1890 he returned to Germany and headed the master studio for copper engraving and etching at the Academy in Berlin. In 1896 his works were reproduced in the magazine *Pan*, of which he was joint publisher. From 1895 Koepping experimented with glass and employed the technical assistance of Friedrich Zitzmann. Their collaboration lasted only a few months, however, after which Koepping's designs were patented and manufactured by the Saxon Technical College and Workshops for Glass Instrument Makers in Illmenau. Through his links with Samuel Bing (1838–1905), Koepping's works were shown at the 1897 Salon d'Automne in Paris.
Koepping, whose works are made of very fine glass, was the foremost glass designer of German Jugendstil. What was new about his glass creations was that, instead of superimposing ornament upon the material, the form itself became the ornament.

Kohn, Jacob & Josef
Vienna
Austrian furniture factory
The company run by the Kohn brothers produced bentwood furniture to designs by leading Wiener Werkstätte artists, using the process patented by Michael Thonet in 1869. At the Paris World Exposition of 1900 they won the Grand Prix for the exhibition room designed by G. Siegel (a pupil of Josef Hoffmann). In 1904 the company comprised four factories and a workforce of around 6,300.

Kok, J. Jurriaan
6.4.1861 Rotterdam – 19.6.1919 The Hague
Dutch architect, designer, and potter
Kok trained as an architect but turned more and more to matters of design, and from 1894 to 1913 became director of the porcelain makers Haagsche Plateelbakkerij Rozenburg in The Hague. Javanese art was his main interest, and he had a comprehensive collection. The fantastic landscapes of the tropical island empire were as much a stimulus to his creativity as the ancient traditions of Javanese crafts, the

decorative sculptures on temple buildings, *Wayang* (shadow theater), and highly developed batik techniques. In the Rozenburg firm, Kok found a porcelain factory that could translate his subtle technical and decorative ideas into reality. As traditional clay bodies were not flexible enough for his unusual designs, Kok and the firm's chief chemist M. N. Engelden embarked on a series of complicated experiments to find a body that would make his designs feasible. In 1899, they finally succeeded in producing a light, thin-sided frit porcelain (today known as quasi or eggshell porcelain) that was ivory in color and had a glass-like consistency.

In Kok's work, the contours of the porcelain coincide with the decoration, which makes use of the whole palette of flower mysticism. The pattern stands out on the sides like a silhouette.

Krog, Emil Arnold
18.3.1856 Frederiksvaert – 7.6.1931 Tilvilde
Danish architect, painter, graphic artist, craftsman, and ceramicist
After an apprenticeship as a mason, from 1874 Krog studied at the Copenhagen Academy of Art, where he passed his architectural exams in 1888. While still a student (1884), he started working for Den Kongelige Porcelainsfabrik in Copenhagen, becoming its artistic director just one year later, in 1885 (until 1916).
The underglaze painting, inspired by Japanese woodcut prints, which served as decoration brought Den Kongelige Porcelainsfabrik international fame. Krog also supplied the formal designs of many of the factory's porcelain wares. His colleagues included the chemist Adolphe Clément (1860–1933) and his successor, Knud Valdemar Engelhardt, who made a name for himself with his crystal glazes.

Kunimasa, Utagawa
1773 – 1810
Japanese woodcut master
Kunimasa, who nurtured a great love for the theater, attended the school run by Toyokuni, the famous interpreter of *kabuki* scenes. Kunimasa worked as a woodcut master after the great woodcut master Toshusai Sharaku suddenly ended his profession.
Kunimasa's artistic legacy includes many masterly portraits of actors, which on the basis of their use of line and color can be described as extremely modern.

Lachenal, Edmond
3.6.1855 Paris – 10.6.1948 Paris
French potter
Lachenal was apprenticed to the potter Joseph-Théodore Deck (1823–91), whose studio in Paris was a training ground for many Art Nouveau artists, from 1870. In 1884, Lachenal set up his own workshop in Malakoff (Paris) to make faience and glazed and unglazed stoneware. In 1887, the business moved to Châtillon-sous-Bagneux.
Lachenal is considered the inventor of the *émail mat velouté* process. From 1895, he also manufactured pots designed by outside designers, including models by Auguste Rodin (1840–1917). From 1900 he worked for the glassware factory of Daum Frères as well, for whom he produced enameled glass pieces. From 1900 to 1901, he designed faience ornamentation for application to furniture and faience vases, to be combined with gold and silver work as *metallo-céramiques*. Among his pupils was Émile Decœur, who later became a well-known Art Deco potter.

Laeuger, Max
30.9.1864 Lörrach – 12.12.1952 Lörrach
German painter, architect, ceramicist, and sculptor

Laeuger, who studied painting at the Académie Julian in Paris, taught himself pottery. From 1893 he executed lead-glazed ceramic works which were manufactured in the Armbruster workshops in Kandern in the Black Forest. From 1895 to 1913 he was artistic head of the pottery in Kandern and also turned his attention to architectural ceramics. In addition, he designed fabrics for the Engelhardt textiles company in Mannheim. He gained international recognition at the Paris World Exposition of 1900, where he won the Grand Prix. From 1897 to 1913 he taught landscape and interior design at the Technical College in Karlsruhe, where he eventually founded his own workshop in 1916.
Laeuger's works include faience and stoneware vessels distinguished by the simplicity of their form and color, decorative tiles with a sculptural decor, mosaic paintings and architectural ceramics. Many of the buildings which he executed as from 1908, such as the Varieté Köchlin in Basle (1908), and the Paradise Park in Baden-Baden (1925), are decorated with ceramic works.

Lalique, René
6.4.1860 L'Hay-les-Roses, Val de Marne – 1.5.1945 Paris
French goldsmith, jeweler, and glass artist
After training as a goldsmith and studying at the École Nationale des Art Décoratifs in Paris, Lalique went to Sydenham College in London, where he did nature studies. Back in Paris, he sold his jewelry designs to major jewelers, and then tried his hand as a sculptor of small-scale sculpture and designer of fans, textiles, and wallpapers. In 1885, he took over a Parisian jeweler's studio, and forged close ties with the art dealer Samuel Bing (1838–1905) and the poster artist Alfons Maria Mucha. From 1891 to 94 he made a whole series of jewelry items for the famous actress Sarah Bernhardt, and these made his name.
Besides precious stones, gemstones, and pearls, he used materials that had hitherto been uncommon in jewelry, such as enamel, ivory, tortoiseshell, and horn. Work of this kind brought him his first great success at the World Exposition in Paris in 1900. In 1901, he exhibited for the first time jewelry made of clear crystal glass, thus launching himself on a new career as a celebrated Art Deco glass artist. After 1908, he went over entirely to glass, his interest in the material dating to 1894.

Langenzersdorfer Keramik
see Klablena, Eduard

Larche, François-Raoul
22.10.1860 Bordeaux – 2.6.1912 Paris
Larche studied at the École des Beaux-Arts in Paris under the sculptors Alexandre Falguière (1831–1900) and François Jouffroy (1806–82), who had a lasting influence on his work. Larche was regularly represented at the Salon d'Automne in Paris from 1884 to 1991. In 1886 he was awarded the second Grand Prix de Rome, and in 1900 won a gold medal at the World Exposition in Paris. Larche is known for his monumental sculptures, especially the group *La Loire et ses affluents* [The Loire and its tributaries], commissioned by the French state. However, his most famous work is his bronze figure of the dancer Loïe Fuller, designed as a lampstand.

Lavirotte, Jules Aimé
25.3.1864 Paris – 1928 Paris
French architect
A one-time pupil of Antoni Gaudí, Lavirotte adorned his facades with decorative ceramics, his designs being executed by the ceramic artist Bigot. Around 1900, Lavirotte achieved great success with his architecture in Paris. In his two most famous buildings, the apartment block in the

avenue Rapp (1901) and the Céramique-Hôtel (1904), he made use of decorative Art Nouveau floral elements like no other Parisian architect. His decoration is strongly symbolic, and is based on the world of animals and plants.

Lechter, Melchior
2.10.1865 Münster – 8.10.1937 Raron, Valais
German painter, book illustrator, and applied artist
Lechter studied glass painting in Münster and from 1883 to 1895 attended the Academy of Art in Berlin. In 1895 he was introduced to Stefan George (1886–1968), who from now until 1907 commissioned him with the illustration of his books. In 1896 his first exhibition was staged at Gurlitt's gallery, and in 1899 he was commissioned to design the wall decorations for the Pallenberg Room in the Cologne Museum of Arts and Crafts (completed in 1902). In 1909 he founded the Einhorn [Unicorn] Press.
Lechter, whose work is influenced by William Morris and the Pre-Raphaelites, mixed Jugendstil elements with mysterious symbols from George's world. Alongside book illustrations and interior decors, he produced designs for glass paintings and executed drawings and pastels.

Le Comte, Adolf
30.8.1850 Geestburg – 3.1.1921 The Hague
Dutch potter
After completing polytechnic studies, Le Comte went to the arts and crafts schools at Karlsruhe and Nuremberg, followed in 1872 to 74 by a course at the studio for interior design in Paris. From 1877 to 1915 he was artistic director of the tile manufacturer De Porcelyne Fles in Delft. In his early years there, he borrowed patterns from the Renaissance, but his designs were rarely used by the old-fashioned company. In 1885, he developed a new kind of ceramic such as was already being produced at the Haagsche Plateelbakkerij Rozenburg. He took his inspiration from Persian ceramics. Later he did designs for building ceramics, including work at Hamburg Zoo.

Leistikow, Walter
25.10.1865 Bromberg (now Bydgoszcz) – 24.7.1908 Schlachtensee, near Berlin
German painter and graphic artist
Leistikow, who studied under Hermann Eschke from 1883 to 1885 and under Hans Gude from 1885 to 1887, taught at the School of Art in Berlin from 1890 to 1893. In 1892 he became a founding member of the artist's association *Die Elf*, and was also active as a writer. The rejection of his picture *Lake Grunewald* by the organizers of the Berlin exhibition of 1898 was one of the reasons behind the foundation of the Berlin Secession. In 1903 he was amongst the founders of the Deutscher Künstlerbund (German Federation of Artists).
Leistikow, who was inspired amongst others by Pierre Cécile Puvis de Chavannes and by Japanese prints, ranks amongst the great masters of Jugendstil. He developed a decorative linear style which simultaneously separates and emphasizes his forms. He was also active in the sphere of applied art, in particular designing posters, wallpapers, and carpets. His favorite motifs were water, trees, and low-flying birds. In his latter years he devoted himself to landscape painting and portrayed the lake district around Berlin in Impressionistic mood paintings.

Lethaby, William Richard
1857 London – 1931 London
English architect
In 1877 Lethaby started work as an assistant in his friend Norman Shaw's London office. Shaw was a successful architect and helped Lethaby when he set up his own

business in 1889. In an artistic sense, however, Lethaby had more in common with William Morris and Philip Webb than with his mentor. In 1894 he became director of the Central School of Arts and Crafts in London which was run according to the principles of William Morris. In the same year he published a specialist book with Swainson on the Hagia Sophia Basilica in Constantinople. Publications on medieval art and Westminster Abbey followed. His collection of essays, including *Form in Civilization* (1922) and *Architecture and Modern Life* (1917), promoted progressive ideas. His few buildings include Avon Tyrell in Hampshire (1891) and his imaginative Brockhampton Church in Herefordshire (1900–02).

Liberty, Sir Arthur Lasenby
31.8.1843 Chesham – 11.5.1917 The Lee, near Chesham
English merchant
Liberty was the oldest of eight children born to a cloth merchant in Chesham. After having left Nottingham's University School for financial reasons at the age of 16, he started an apprenticeship with a cloth merchant in London, where he devoted himself to his favorite passions, art and the theater. In 1862 he began working for the Farmer & Rogers department store in Regent Street. Farmer & Rogers also ran a store for Oriental goods, where Liberty developed an interest in art from the Far East. In 1875, after 12 years with Farmer & Rogers, Liberty was refused a partnership in the company despite his commercial success. He thus set up his own business in Regent Street, the East India House, which sold all kinds of paraphernalia from the Far East. His store was so successful that Liberty was able to expand continuously over the next few years. Fascinated by the Aesthetic Movement, Liberty set up the Furnishing and Decoration Studio in 1883. The materials and furniture sold there were designed by Modern Style artists and became a big London attraction. In the 1890s Liberty started his own line in silverware (Cymric) and pewter (Tudric). In all areas of handicrafts he concentrated on, Liberty worked with well-known designers who helped characterize the "Stile Liberty".
Liberty's influence on English craftmanship was enormous. His name was synonymous with English Art Nouveau from the early 1890s to the outbreak of the First World War. Despite his poor background, Liberty had become a respected member of society and lived the life of a country gentleman in Thee Manor. He died childless in 1917 and left his emporium to his nephew Ivor Stewart, who changed his name to Stewart-Liberty. Stewart's grandson is the present chairman of Liberty's in London.

Liisberg, Carl Frederik
1860 Aarhus – 1909 Copenhagen
Danish sculptor and porcelain painter
After training as a painter and sculptor, in 1885 Liisberg was engaged by Den Kongelige Porcelainsfabrik in Copenhagen. He was predestined by his artist background for a career as a modeler of animal figures. As a painter, he also introduced the *pâte sur pâte* technique to the Copenhagen porcelain factory. In 1892 he went to St. Petersburg, again introducing the *pâte sur pâte* technique in his position as teacher and trainer at the Imperial Porcelain Factory.

Lilien, Ephraim Mose
23.05.1874 Drohobycz, Galicia – 1925 Badenweiler
Polish painter, graphic artist, and illustrator
After an apprenticeship as a signpainter, Lilien studied under the history painter Jan Matejko (1838–93) at the Krakow School of Art. In 1894 he won an honorary diploma in a competition in his home town. His application to study at the Vienna Academy was rejected, however. In 1896 he started working for a Socialist newspaper in Munich and three years

later founded the Jüdischer Verlag [Jewish Press] in Berlin, for which he acted as editor, publisher, and illustrator. He also founded the Bezalel Society for the Introduction of Art and Industry into Palestine. After several trips to Jerusalem he embarked upon a series of illustrations to the Bible.
Lilien followed in the footsteps of English Art Nouveau, whereby the ornament in his illustrations is characterized by a simpler, tauter design. Over time he abandoned all trace of the lyrical in favor of a rigorous, iconic, symbolic language. Lilien is not just a representative of German Jugendstil, but also – and above all – one of the great Jewish artists.

Lindgren, Armas Eliel
28.11.1874 Tavastehus – 1929 Copenhagen
Finnish architect
Together with Herman Gesellius and Eliel Saarinen, in 1896 Lindgren founded the architectural firm of Gesellius, Lindgren & Saarinen, known as GLS. The international fame of the three architects was based on the Finnish Pavilion which they designed for the Paris World Exposition of 1900. In 1905 Lindgren left the firm to work with Wivi Lönn, one of Finland's first women architects. GLS was dissolved in 1907. Lindgren chiefly built private houses and churches. The works which he designed in collaboration with Gesellius and Saarinen include the Villa Suur-Merijoki in Viipuri (1903) and the "fortified" Hvittorp House in Kirkkonummi (1901–04).

Lindqvist, Selim Avid
19.5.1867 Helsinki – 1939 Helsinki
Finnish architect
Following his studies at the Polytechnical College in Helsinki (1884–88), in 1888 Lindqvist designed the facades for a department store-cum-apartment block built by Elia Heikel. Both here and in the case of the Lundqvist Department Store (1900), he developed an entirely modern Constructivism out of the existing building: a system of load-bearing columns and large shop windows.
Lindqvist, a pioneer of concrete architecture, and Heikel were the first to demonstrate the Chicago style in Finland. Lindqvist's works included office blocks and private houses in Helsinki, buildings for the metropolitan railway network, the Suvilahti Power Station (1908) and distribution stations.

Loetz, Witwe
Founded 1836 in Klostermühle, Bohemia
Austrian glass factory
The glass factory founded in 1836 was purchased in 1840 by Johann Loetz (1778–1848) and run after his death by his widow under the name of Loetz' Witwe [Loetz' Widow]. In the last third of the 19th century the factory developed a type of chemically treated glass, paving the way for its successful production of luxury glassware featuring luster and iridescent glass. In 1898 the company was granted a patent for its "luster glass technique". At the Paris World Exposition of 1900, Loetz' Witwe shared first prize with Tiffany, Gallé, and Daum. The firm ranked amongst the most important glassworks in Europe, and up to 1900 its Jugendstil glasses bore only the company signature, while the designer remained anonymous. From 1903 various Viennese artists worked for the company, in particular members of the Wiener Werkstätte. By 1910, however, the company found itself in increasing financial difficulties, and was converted first into a limited company and then, after the First World War, into an incorporated society. Finally, at the start of the Second World War, the company was dissolved.

Loos, Adolf
10.12.1870 Brno – 23.8.1933 Kalksburg, near Vienna
Austrian architect and applied arts designer
After studying at the Technical College in Dresden, Loos spent

the years 1893 to 96 in Philadelphia (U.S.A.) working various jobs, before finally returning to Vienna in 1896 to set himself up as an architect. The publication of his essay "Die Potemkin'sche Stadt" [The Potemkin city] in the journal *Ver Sacrum* in the summer of 1898 brought an end to the good relationship he had previously enjoyed with the architects of the Vienna Secession. His book *Ornament und Verbrechen* [Ornament and Crime], published in 1908, revealed him as the absolute opponent of ornament and would ultimately lead him into total isolation.
In 1912 he founded a school of architecture, which closed during the First World War. Following a period as chief architect in the Vienna Department of Municipal Housing (1920–22), Loos went to Paris, where he exerted a significant influence upon modern French architecture, and in particular Le Corbusier (1887–1965). In 1928 he returned to Vienna, where he continued to voice his views on an urbane, functional everyday culture, which would later strike a chord with Walter Gropius (1883–1969) and the Bauhaus.
Loos may be seen as the most important pioneer of modern architecture. His buildings are distinguished by their lack of ornament, their geometric simplicity, and their use of materials left in their "natural" state. His major works include the Café Museum in Vienna (1899), the Villa Karma in Clarens, Switzerland (1904–06), the Kärntner Bar in Vienna (1907), the epoch-making Steiner House in Vienna (1910), the commercial block on Michaeler Platz in Vienna (1910), the house for Tristan Tzara in Paris (1925), the Khuner House in Payerbach, Lower Austria (1930) and the Müller House in Prague (1930). He also published the theoretical writings *Ornament und Verbrechen* (1908), *Ins Leere gesprochen* ([Spoken into the void], collected essays 1897–1900; 1902), and *Trotzdem* ([Nevertheless], collected essays 1900–30; 1931).

Lundstrøm, Nils
1865 Stockholm – 1960 Stockholm
Swedish sculptor and modeler
From 1896 to 1936 Lundstrøm profoundly influenced the style of the products issuing from Sweden's leading porcelain factory, Rörstrand, Aktie Bolag Lidköping, near Stockholm. His works from around 1900 are characterized by a soft relief style. He illustrated magnificent floral motifs in delicate colors on vases and tableware.

Macdonald Mackintosh, Margaret
1865 Newcastle-under-Lyme – 17.1.1933 Chelsea
and
Macdonald MacNair, Frances
1874 – 1921
Scottish graphic artists, furniture and arts and crafts designers
The Macdonald sisters, Margaret and Frances, studied embroidery, metalwork, goldsmithery, and other crafts at the Glasgow School of Art at the end of the 1880s. They met their future husbands, Charles Rennie Mackintosh (1868–1928) and Herbert MacNair (1869–1945), at the School and with the two men formed the group The Four in 1893. In 1894 the sisters opened a studio for the applied arts; their husbands supplied designs for furniture which together with the sisters' ideas made up a convincing synthesis of form and decoration. The work of the Macdonald sisters – embroidery, textile designs, jewelry, painted wall panels, hammered metalwork – was inspired by Celtic art and the Pre-Raphaelites. In contrast to other Art Nouveau creations, the sisters' work is more linear and contains far fewer curves.
Margaret is especially well-known for her wall decorations which combined a diversity of materials, such as fabric, plaster, and bronze. On leaving Glasgow for London with her husband in 1915, she turned to painting with watercolors. She took part in 40 exhibitions between 1885 and 1924 and her work was regularly published in art journals such as *The Studio*.

Mackintosh, Charles Rennie
7.6.1868 Glasgow – 10.12.1928 London
Scottish architect, interior designer, artist craftsman, graphic artist, and painter
Mackintosh began an apprenticeship at John Hutchison's architects' office in 1884. He changed his apprenticeship to Honeyman & Keppie in 1899, where he met Herbert MacNair (1869–1945). He also attended evening classes at the Glasgow School of Art, where he met his future wife, Margaret Macdonald, and her sister Frances. In 1890 Mackintosh won several competitions and received his first commissions. The Alexander Thomson Traveling Scholarship he was awarded in 1891 enabled him to visit France, Italy, and Belgium. In 1894 The Four (Mackintosh, MacNair, and the Macdonald sisters) exhibited together for the first time. In 1896 they took part in an exhibition in London organized by the Arts and Crafts Society. At the same time, Mackintosh won an architectural competition with his design for the Glasgow School of Art. From 1896 onwards he and his wife Margaret designed interiors for several tea rooms in Glasgow. Mackintosh also received commissions for villa and house designs at home and abroad, including a music salon for Fritz Waerndorfer. The Mackintoshes moved to London in 1915 where, except for a brief period in Port-Vendres in France (1923–27), they spent the rest of their days, concentrating on graphics and book art.
Mackintosh is one of the main representatives of Art Nouveau and a pioneer with his designs for furniture and textiles. Like his contemporaries, he found great inspiration in Symbolism and Japanese art and developed his own individual, incomparable linear style of decoration. His decorative interiors were always restrained and complemented the design of the furniture. Mackintosh also studied the theoretical writings of William Richard Lethaby and John Ruskin (1819–1900). Mackintosh's main works include the Glasgow School of Art (1897–99; extension with the library 1907–09), Miss Cranston's various tea rooms in Glasgow (1897–1911) and Hill House in Helensburgh (1902).

Mackmurdo, Arthur Heygate
12.12.1851 London – 15.3.1942 Wickham Bishops, Essex
English architect, draftsman, and artist-craftsman
Mackmurdo, who studied in Oxford and was friends with the art critic John Ruskin (1819–1900), opened an architect's office in London in 1875. A year later he met William Morris, whose interests he shared. In 1882 Mackmurdo founded the Century Guild of Artists for designers, interior designers, and artists, and in 1884 began publishing the periodical *The Hobby Horse*. During the next 20 years Mackmurdo designed items in metal, textiles, wallpaper, and furniture for various companies, including Morris, Marshall, Faulkner & Company. He later became one of the founder members of the Society for the Protection of Ancient Buildings and from 1904 onwards concentrated his energies on economic and socio-political questions.
Mackmurdo was one of the main precursors of Art Nouveau and is counted among the pioneers of modern English architecture. His cover for *Wren's City Churches* (1883) is considered to be the first work with Art Nouveau character.

Magnussen, Erik
14.5.1884 Copenhagen – 24.2.1961 Los Angeles
Danish sculptor, draftsman, and craftsman
Magnussen, who studied under the sculptor Stephan Sinding (1846–1922), first worked in Copenhagen before later moving to Los Angeles. He made a name for himself with his ivory carvings for the Seville carnival and through his work for the film studios in Hollywood. He combined a variety of materials in his jewelry, preferably silver in conjunction with "exotic" materials.

Majorelle, Louis
27.9.1859 Toul – 15.1.1916 Nancy
French painter and craft designer
Majorelle studied at the École des Beaux-Arts in Paris, but after his father's untimely death in 1879 had to abandon his ambition to become a painter in order to take over the family business. At first, he continued the production of furniture and faience ware in neo-Baroque and period styles but, impressed by Emile Gallé and his great success at the World Exposition in Paris in 1889, he began to search for a new style of his own. His most important collaborators in this were Jacques Gruber and Camille Gauthier (1870–1963). While his furniture was initially in the Gallé manner, from around 1900 he gradually evolved a style of his own. Though wrought bronze and brass became the chief ornamentation of his furniture, he did large-scale metal work as well. Until the 1920s, he provided the glass factory of Daum Frères with designs for vase stands and lamp bases. Jointly with Gallé and Eugène Vallin, Majorelle was a board member of the École de Nancy, founded in 1901. In 1905, he carried out the refurbishing of Samuel Bing's Galerie L'Art Nouveau in Paris.

Margold, Emanuel Josef
4.5.1889 Vienna – 2.5.1962 Bratislava
Austrian architect, graphic artist, and applied arts designer
Margold was first a student under Anton Huber (Patriz Huber's father) at the Mainz School of Arts and Crafts and later, in the Department of Architecture at the Vienna Academy, a master pupil of Josef Hoffmann. After completing his studies, he joined Hoffmann in working for the Wiener Werkstätte. From 1911 to 1929 he was a member of the Darmstadt artists' colony, executing the buildings for its 1914 exhibition. In 1929 he set up as an architect in Berlin and devoted himself both at the practical and theoretical level to the Bauhaus style and the design of modern apartment housing. Margold was also a member of the Austrian and the German Werkbund. Alongside his career as an architect, he also designed furniture, wallpapers, glass, and porcelain. From 1912 he designed interiors, fabric patterns, and biscuit tins for the Bahlsen biscuit factory. He also designed the reception rooms for the International Exhibition of Architecture in Leipzig and for the Werkbund exhibition in Cologne.

Martin Brothers
Established in London in 1873
English ceramics workshop
The ceramics workshop was founded in 1873 by the four Martin brothers: Robert Wallace (1843–1923) was the modeler and designer, Walter Fraser (1859–1912) the pot-thrower, chemist, and kiln-maker, Edwin Bruce (1860–1915) designed the decoration and the company stamp, whereas Charles Douglas (1846–1910) was responsible for the management of the company. Their ceramic work in the Japanese style soon reaped success, enabling the brothers to open a studio and a store in Holborn in London in 1879. Art Nouveau began to exert its influence on their products in the 1890s: whereas their objects pre-1890 had been rather severe, they were now adorned with floral motifs and were often shaped like vegetables and became known as vegetable ware. Their vases boasted decoration in cut glass or other refined surface structures reminiscent of Japanese ceramics. It was, however, Robert Wallace's modeled masks and *objects d'art* in the form of grotesque birds and animals which earned the brothers their fame.

Masó i Valentí, Rafael Julio
1881 (or 1888) Gerona – 1935 Gerona
Spanish (Catalan) architect and designer
Masó studied architecture in Barcelona. Inspired by Charles Rennie Mackintosh and Josef Hoffmann, he developed a very modern style of his own that displays Catalan cultural influences. His principal works include Masramon House (1914) and S'Agarot (1929–35).

Massier, Clément
8.11.1844 Vallauris – 24.3.1917 Golfe-Juan, Alpes-Maritime
French potter
Massier was trained as a potter in his father's pottery in Vallauris, near Cannes, which he ran until 1883, when he set up on his own. From 1887 to 1896, he and the Symbolist painter Lucien Lévy-Dhurmer ran a pottery studio in Golfe-Juan, developing colored metal glazes inspired by Spanish and Moorish faience ware. From 1889, their work was exhibited at world expositions and the Paris Salon d'Automne.

Meissen Royal Saxon Porcelain Factory
see Königlich-Sächsische Porzellan-Manufaktur Meissen

Minne, Georges
30.8.1866 Ghent – 20.2.1941 Sint-Martens-Latem, near Ghent
Belgian sculptor and graphic artist
Minne studied architecture at the Académie des Beaux-Arts in Ghent from 1882 to 1884, and was later a pupil of Charles van der Stappen in Brussels. In 1895, he acquired a studio at the Brussels Academy, and in 1912 a chair in drawing at the Academy in Ghent. Minne is considered the principal figure of *fin-de-siècle* Belgian sculpture. Although his style is generally bracketed with naturalistic Symbolism, his slender, de-sensualized figures and his rhythmic compositions permit an Art Nouveau labeling as well. Besides sculptures, he illustrated the books of Emile Verhaeren and Maurice Maeterlinck. His main works include the *Fountain with Five Kneeling Boys* in Essen (designed 1898, executed 1906), and the Rodenbach memorial in Ghent.

Moll, Carl
23.4.1861 Vienna – 13.4.1945 Vienna
Austrian painter and graphic artist
Moll, who studied under Griepenkerl and Schindler at the Academy of Art in Vienna, was a member of the Künstlerhaus board in 1894 and one of the founders of the Vienna Secession in 1897. From 1898 to 1901 he worked for the journal *Ver Sacrum*, which published most of his woodcuts. In 1905 he left the Vienna Secession with the Klimt group and joined the Wiener Werkstätte, organizing its first exhibition.

Mondrian, Piet
(real name Pieter Cornelis Mondriaan)
7.3.1872 Amersfoort – 1.2.1944 New York
Dutch painter and art theoretician
In his early period, Mondrian adopted a near-Symbolist and Pointilliste approach, under the influence of Kees van Dongen and Jan Toorop. During his stay in Paris (1911–14), he became acquainted with Cubism, which had a long-term effect on his output. Mondrian began to depict his limited range of subjects in ever more advanced and finally geometric abstraction, until by 1915 his pictures consisted entirely of the rhythm of horizontal and vertical lines. These and the most simple basic colors formed the framework for his "neo-plastic" style, the principles of which were set out in his treatise *Le Néoplasticisme* published in 1920. Mondrian was, with Theo van Doesburg and Bart van der Leck, a cofounder of the De Stijl group of artists in 1917 and the eponymous periodical. In 1940, he emigrated to New York.

Morris, May
1862 – 1938
English arts and crafts designer
May Morris was William Morris's youngest daughter. She trained with her father and designed textiles, wallpaper, and jewelry for his company. She also did embroidery work. In 1888 she took over as manageress of the embroidery workshop in Merton Abbey and was a founder member of the Woman's Guild of Arts in 1907, later becoming its chairwoman. After the death of her father, she published his writings in 24 volumes which appeared between 1910 and 1924.

Morris, William
24.3.1834 Walthamstow, London – 3.10.1896 London
English painter, artist craftsman, designer, writer, and social reformer
Morris studied church history and medieval literature at Exeter College in Oxford, where he also formed a lifelong friendship with Edward Burne-Jones. He started an apprenticeship with the architect George Edmund Street in 1856 and also wrote for the *Oxford and Cambridge Magazine*. Under the influence of Dante Gabriel Rossetti and John Ruskin, he soon turned to painting and writing. In 1861 he set up a firm for the production of arts and crafts, called Morris, Marshall, Faulkner & Company, with Burne-Jones, Rossetti and Philip Webb among the partners. Morris wanted to offer an alternative to factory-made articles with the objects the company fashioned, namely furniture, glassware, woven items, wallpaper, embroidery, painted and stained glass and much more. All had the severe form and treatment of line characteristic of Gothic art. Morris, also a poet and lyricist, set up the Kelmscott Press in 1891, whose products were to be of great importance for the further development of book art. Morris, like his spiritual father John Ruskin, was highly critical of commercialism and turned to politics in the 1880s. In 1883 he joined the Democratic Federation; in 1884 he founded the Socialist League and began publishing the party magazine *Commonweal*. His ideas on social reform and his strict refusal to use machines in the manufacture of arts-and-crafts commodities made Morris the founder of the English Arts and Crafts Movement. He voiced his theories in speeches and in various books and essays, including *The Decorative Arts* (1878) and in his *Collected Works* (1915).

Moser, Koloman
30.3.1868 Vienna – 18.10.1918 Vienna
Austrian painter, graphic artist, and applied arts designer
From 1886 to 1892 Moser studied under Griepenkerl at the Academy in Vienna and from 1892 to 1895 under Franz Matsch at the School of Arts and Crafts in Vienna, where he held a teaching post himself from 1900 to 1918. In 1897 he was amongst the founding members of the Vienna Secession, which he left in 1905 with the Klimt group, and worked for the journal *Ver Sacrum*. Together with Josef Hoffmann, in 1903 he founded the Wiener Werkstätte, whose products were strongly influenced by his predominantly geometric style. As his artistic influence waned, he left the group in 1906 and concentrated exclusively on painting. He later became a member of the Austrian Werkbund founded in 1912.
Moser was active in every sphere of applied art, designing furniture, jewelry, glass, metalware, and book-bindings, together with posters, toys, theater sets, and interiors (e.g. the Westend Sanatorium in Purkersdorf, 1904). Moser was also one of the very few artists to design stamps in the Jugendstil style, including the first stamps for Liechtenstein (1912–18).

Mougin Frères
French ceramics manufacturer

The firm was founded in Paris by the brothers Joseph (sculptor and potter, 1876–1961) and Pierre (1879–1955) Mougin to make stoneware. Their output was exhibited at the Paris Salons from 1900, as a result of which it gained an international reputation and was later much sought-after by museums and collectors. Around 1904 the Mougins transferred the factory to their native city of Nancy, where they collaborated with the artists working there. Mougin Frères successfully continued making articles in the then fashionably modern Art Deco style. Joseph and his children Odile and François went on producing stoneware items until 1960, always in the latest designs.

Mucha, Alfons Maria
24.7.1860 Eibenschütz/Rosice, Moravia – 14.7.1939 Prague
After abandoning his singing studies in 1877 and fruitlessly attempting to gain a place at the Academy in Prague, Mucha went to Vienna, where he worked as a scene-painter. From 1883, he worked for Count Khuen-Belassi, who enabled him to go to the Academy in Munich to study. In 1888, he began a course at the Académie Julian in Paris, but switched to the Académie Colarossi the following year. While continuing his studies, he supported himself by working as an illustrator. In 1891 he made the acquaintance of Paul Gauguin (1848–1903) and began a collaboration with the publisher Armand Colin. In 1894, he had such success with his first poster for Sarah Bernhardt (1844–1923) that the actress signed an exclusive contract with him for six years, and Mucha gained numerous other commissions for posters, interior decorations, jewelry, fashions, and glass windows. Mucha participated in various exhibitions, and at the Paris World Exposition in 1900 he was awarded a silver medal for his furnishing of the pavilion of Bosnia-Herzegovina. In 1901, he was awarded the Légion d'Honneur. In 1906 he emigrated to the United States, where he taught in New York and Chicago and worked as an interior designer. In 1911 he finally settled in Prague, where he won major commissions and in his work became preoccupied above all with Slav sagas.
Mucha's style is reminiscent of Viennese Art Nouveau. It is characterized by artificial flower ornamentation and worldly elegance in the figures, combined with a strongly symmetrical treatment of surface and line and a dependence on color effects. Typically, a chic-looking young female face appears entwined in "hair ornamentation" or painted with mixed colors. The success of his posters enabled him to achieve an important objective, of making the man in the street aware of art.

Müller, Albin
13.12.1871 Dittersbach, Harz Mountains – 2.10.1941 Darmstadt
German painter, architect, and craftsman
After completing a joiner's apprenticeship, from 1893 to 1897 Müller worked as a furniture draftsman and interior designer, which enabled him to finance his studies at the schools of arts and crafts in Mainz and Dresden. He was self-taught as an architect. From 1900 he taught interior design at the Magdeburg School of Arts and Crafts. In 1902 he took part successfully in the International Exhibition of Modern Decorative Art in Turin and also showed works at the 1904 World Exposition in St. Louis and at other major exhibitions. In 1906 he went to Darmstadt, where he became a member of the artists' colony and was professor of interior design from 1907 to 1911. Following the death of Joseph Maria Olbrich in 1908, Müller became the leading architect at the Darmstadt colony. After the First World War he concentrated increasingly upon the development of wood houses, but turned to painting for lack of commissions.
Müller's major works include buildings and interiors for the exhibitions in Darmstadt (1908, 1910, 1914) and buildings and grounds for the German Theater Exhibition in Magdeburg

(1927). Müller was also an important writer on architecture. His publications include *Architektur und Raumkunst* [Architecture and interior design], 1909 and *Werke der Darmstädter Ausstellungen* [Works from the Darmstadt exhibitions], 1917.

Munch, Edvard
12.12.1863 Løten, near Hamar – 23.1.1944 Hof Ekely, near Oslo
Norwegian painter and graphic artist
Munch attended the School of Arts and Crafts in Oslo from 1882 to 1883 and subsequently continued his training alone. From 1885 he lived – with interruptions – in Paris, where he attended Léon Bonnat's art school and was influenced by the art of Paul Gauguin, Vincent van Gogh, Henri de Toulouse-Lautrec, Émile Bernard, and Maurice Denis. He also absorbed influences from the Symbolists and the writer August Strindberg (1849–1912). In 1892 his paintings caused a scandal in Berlin, leading a few years later to the foundation of the Berlin Secession. From 1902 he lived in Germany and in 1906 designed theater sets for Max Reinhardt. In 1908 he finally returned to Norway.
Munch, Norway's most important painter, was one of the forerunners of Expressionism, although his oeuvre also reveals the influences of Art Nouveau and Symbolism. His pictures consider the themes of love, death, fear, and the conflict between the sexes. Munch employed the interplay of line, color, and plane as his primary means of expressing moods and feelings. The motifs of his paintings frequently reappear in different forms in his outstanding graphic oeuvre, which embraces etchings, lithographs, and above all color woodcuts. His major works include *Madonna* (1894–95), *The Dance of Life* (1899–1900), *The Scream* (1893) and several versions of the *Frieze of Life* (started 1893).

Munthe, Gerhard Peter
19.7.1849 Elverum – 15.1.1929 Oslo
Norwegian painter, graphic artist, craftsman, and writer
Having begun his studies in Norway, in 1874 Munthe continued them in Düsseldorf and in 1877 in Munich, where he turned to landscape painting. In 1883 he returned to Norway and painted Early Impressionist-style landscapes. Around 1890 he developed a two-dimensional style influenced by Art Nouveau and at the same time expanded his subject matter to include Norwegian fairytales and sagas. His oeuvre includes numerous designs for tapestries (including *The Horses of the Sea*, 1907), in which he drew upon traditional Norwegian folk art, and woodcut illustrations. His major works include the interior decoration of the Håkonshalle in Bergen with wall paintings and furniture (1910–16, destroyed 1944).

Nerman, Einar
6.10.1888 Norrköping – unknown
Swedish painter and graphic artist
Nerman studied painting at the school attached to the Art Association in Stockholm and was a student under Carl Wilhelmson, before continuing his training in Paris. While still a student, he started working as a graphic artist for various newspapers, including *Søntagsnisse* and *Le Figaro*.
Nerman illustrated books, including Hans Christian Andersen's fairytales, and worked for the magazines *Die Dame* and *Pan*. He later emigrated to New York.

Nielsen, Erik
1857 Øksendrup – 1947 Tisvilde
Danish sculptor
After studying sculpture at the Academy in Copenhagen and working freelance, in 1887 Nielsen joined the artistic staff of Den Kongelige Porcelainsfabrik in Copenhagen. He worked

above all as a modeler of animal figures, whose plastic quality and exquisite painting reinforced the company's high standing in this sphere. He continued to work for the factory until 1926.

Nuutajärvi
Founded 1793 in Nuutajärvi
Finnish glass factory

The glass factory was founded in 1793 by Captain Jacob Wilhelm Depont and Harald Furuhjelm. The factory expanded under its subsequent owners and artistic directors and by the second half of the 19th century had become Finland's leading glass factory. In 1856 Nuutajärvi was already engaging outstanding glass designers and glassblowers from Germany and France. It conducted numerous experiments in glass and ceramics which, under the artistic direction of Carl Heitmann (1859–72) resulted in the product range being constantly expanded.

Around 1900, after a number of less successful years, a new company was founded, Costiander and Co., specializing in simple household glassware which nevertheless retained an artistic dimension. Competitions were held, and the first two were won by the architect Walter Jung and the designer Helena Wilenius with entries that were pure Art Nouveau. The factory may thus be seen as one of the pioneers of the marriage of art and mass production.

Social unrest in Finland and the First World War caused great problems for the factory up to 1920. After renewed success in the 1920s with its cut glass, the 1930s brought further decline. After the Second World War Nuutajärvi was bought up and run under the new name of Wärtsilä Group Ltd.

Obrist, Hermann
23.5.1863 Kilchberg – 26.2.1927 Munich
Swiss-German applied artist, draftsman, and sculptor

After breaking off his studies in natural science, in 1887 Obrist traveled to England and Scotland, where he encountered the Arts and Crafts Movement. He subsequently studied at the Karlsruhe School of Arts and Crafts and completed an apprenticeship as a potter. He rapidly went on to win gold medals for his ceramics and furniture at the 1889 World Exposition in Paris. From 1890 to 1891 he attended the Académie Julian in Paris and worked as an art critic in Berlin. In 1892 he founded an embroidery studio in Florence, transferring it to Munich in 1895. In 1896 he exhibited, for the first time, a number of embroideries designed by himself and executed by Berthe Ruchet, with great success. In 1897, together with his Munich friends, he founded the Vereinigte Werkstätten för Kunst im Handwerk [Associated Workshops for Art in Handicraft] and gave lectures throughout Germany on behalf of the Munich Association of Handicrafts. In 1902, together with Wilhelm von Debschitz (1871–1948), he founded the Studio for Applied and Free Art. In 1904, however, Obrist's deteriorating hearing obliged him to hand over the running of the studio to Debschitz. From this point onwards, his activities as an artist also began to diminish.

Obrist exerted a potent influence upon applied art in the 20th century, both as an artist and above all as a theoretician. He was a leading spokesman for Jugendstil, amongst other things through his essay *Neue Möglichkeiten in der bildenden Kunst* [New possibilities in the visual arts, 1903], and was an important forerunner of the Bauhaus. In line with his insistence that applied art must liberate itself from the pure reproduction of stylistic trends and the forms of nature, he arrived at sheer abstraction in some of his works. Alongside color embroideries, Obrist designed fountains, tombstones, tapestries, wallhangings, ceramics, metalwork, and much more.

Olbrich, Joseph Maria
22.10.1867 Troppau – 8.8.1908 Düsseldorf
Austrian architect and craftsman

In 1897 Olbrich, a student of the architects Karl von Hasenauer and Otto Wagner at the Academy in Vienna, was amongst the founding members of the Vienna Secession, whose exhibition building he went on to design. In 1899 he took up a post as architect and teacher at the Darmstadt artists' colony, where alongside his activities as an architect he also produced tinware designs and a number of graphic works. In 1907 he was a joint founder of the German Werkbund in Munich.

Olbrich was one of Jugendstil's most productive architects and a forerunner of Expressionist architecture, exerting a strong influence, for example, upon the architect Erich Mendelsohn (1884–1953) in the 1920s. He took part in numerous exhibitions, including the 1902 International Exhibition of Modern Decorative Art in Turin and the 1904 World Exposition in St. Louis. Olbrich's most important works were produced in Darmstadt: the development of the Mathildenhöhe (1900), the Ernst Ludwig House (1899–1901) and the Wedding Tower (1905–08). Other important buildings include the Secession building in Vienna (1897–98) and the Tietz Department Store in Düsseldorf (1907–09, today the Kaufhof Department Store). He published *Ideen* [Ideas], 1899, *Architektur* [Architecture], 1901–14, *Neue Gärten* [New Gardens], 1905 and *Der Frauenrosenhof*, 1907.

Östberg, Ragnar
14.7.1866 Stockholm – 5.2.1945 Stockholm
Swedish architect and designer

After studying in Stockholm, from 1893 to 1894 Östberg took extensive trips through Europe and America. From 1922 to 1932 he was a professor at the Academy of Art in Stockholm. Östberg primarily concentrated upon villas, although he also designed numerous public buildings in Stockholm. His most famous building is the Stockholm Town Hall (1911–23), which represents a major work of Swedish National Romanticism. He employed elements of Swedish Romanesque and Renaissance art and skillfully mediated between the architecture of the 19th and 20th century. The decorative details of his buildings reveal the influence of the English Arts and Crafts Movement, whereby Östberg in turn made a strong impact upon the English architecture of the 1920s.

Paczka-Wagner, Cornelia
9.8.1864 Göttingen – unknown
German painter and graphic artist

Paczka-Wagner, daughter of the famous political economist Adolf Wagner (1835–1917), studied at the Stauffersche Porträtklasse des Künstlerinnen-Vereins in Berlin and with Professor Ludwig Herterich at the Academy in Munich. At the age of 23 she went to Rome and studied copper engraving techniques. She obtained her diploma in Dresden in 1890. She spent some time in Madrid in 1894, where she copied paintings by Velázquez. In 1895 she moved to Berlin where she and her husband, the Hungarian Ferenc Paczka, set themselves up as painters, although she concentrated mainly on graphics. Paczka-Wagner did much work for *Pan* magazine and won a bronze medal at the World Exposition in Paris in 1900.

Pankok, Bernhard
16.5.1872 Münster – 5.4.1943 Baierbrunn, Upper Bavaria
German architect, painter, graphic artist, sculptor, and craftsman

After an apprenticeship as a restorer and decoration painter in Münster, from 1889 to 1891 Pankok studied painting at the academies in Düsseldorf and Berlin. From 1892 to 1902 he was based in Munich. As a portrait painter and graphic artist, he worked for the magazines *Pan* and *Jugend*. His friendship with Hans Eduard von Berlepsch-Valendas prompted him to turn his attention to applied art, and he showed his first efforts in this field at the Munich Glass Palace exhibition of 1897. That

same year he was also amongst the founders of the Vereinigte Werkstätten för Kunst im Handwerk [Associated Workshops for Art in Handicraft]. He was commissioned to produce the official catalog for the Paris World Exposition of 1900, which was admired as the most modern German book of its day. In 1902 he founded the Lehr- und Versuchswerkstätte [Teaching and Experimental Workshops] in Stuttgart and from 1913 to 1937 was director of the State School of Arts and Crafts. In 1908 he became a member of the German Werkbund.

Pankok is known above all for his interiors (including interiors for ships and Zeppelins) and handicraft designs employing fantastical ornamental Jugendstil forms. In contrast, his first buildings (around 1900) are more rigorously objective in conception. His contribution to German Art Deco lies in his use of cubic forms with a clear grid. His oeuvre also includes paintings (chiefly portraits), graphic works and stage sets (as from 1909). His major buildings include the registry office in Dessau (1900–02) and the Konrad Lange House in Tübingen (1900–01).

Partridge, Frederick James
1877 – 1942
English jewelry designer

Partridge studied at the Birmingham School of Art from 1899 to 1901 and in 1902 joined Charles Robert Ashbee's Guild of Handicraft, which moved from London to Chipping Campden in Gloucestershire that same year. Partridge opened a workshop in Soho in London where he designed jewelry for Liberty's. Between 1900 and 1908 he spent long periods working in Branscombe in Devon.

Partridge had much in common with the Arts and Crafts Society, yet his designs also incorporated the French style, his favorite material being horn. His colleague, the jewelry designer Ella Naper (1886–1972), was strongly influenced by Partridge.

Paul, Bruno
19.1.1874 Seifhennersdorf, Saxony – 17.08.1968 Berlin
German architect, painter, graphic artist, and craftsman

Paul studied at the Dresden School of Arts and Crafts and subsequently under W. Höker and Wilhelm von Diez at the Academy in Munich. While still a student, he supplied drawings to the magazines *Jugend* and *Simplicissimus*. In 1897 he was amongst the founders of the Vereinigte Werkstätten für Kunst im Handwerk [Associated Workshops for Art in Handicraft] in Munich. He won prizes for his interiors at the World Expositions in Paris (1900) and St. Louis (1904). Inspired by the Turin exhibition of 1902, he turned to machine-manufactured furniture. From 1907 he was based in Berlin, where he headed first the college attached to the Museum of Applied Art and from 1924 to 1932 the United State Schools for Free and Applied Art. After resigning his post in protest against National Socialism, in 1934 he moved to Düsseldorf and only returned to Berlin in 1954, where he was involved in rebuilding the city after the Second World War.

Paul was initially an adherent of Jugendstil. His works are distinguished by simple, clear stylistic elements combined with a contemporary functionalism. Although Paul was primarily active as an architect, his furniture designs were of greater significance, in particular his development of the first modular furniture (around 1906). As a draftsman he produced posters, signets, and illustrations. His major architectural works include the Feinhals House in Cologne (1908) and the Kathreiner highrise in Berlin (1927–28).

Picasso, Pablo
25.10.1881 Málaga – 8.4.1973 Mougins, near Cannes
Spanish painter, sculptor, graphic artist, and potter

Picasso studied at the Academy in Barcelona from 1895 to

1897, and set up independently as a painter in 1900. In 1901 his Blue Period began, which lasted until he moved to Paris in 1904. It was succeeded by the Pink Period (1905) and Cubism (1906). He soon won himself a place of honor in Parisian intellectual and artistic circles. In 1907 he became acquainted with Georges Braque (1882–1963), with whom he cooperated closely until 1914. They spent the summer of 1911 with Juan Gris in Céret at the sculptor Manolo's, and in summer 1913 Max Jacob joined the group. When the First World War broke out, the Cubist group fell apart and Picasso returned to Paris. In 1916 he got to know Sergei Pavlovich Diaghilev (1872–1929), for whose ballet company he designed costumes and sets until 1924. In 1917 he traveled with Jean Cocteau (1889–1963) to Rome and in 1919 with Diaghilev to London. From 1924 to 1930 he incorporated Surrealist elements in his work and in this period made wire sculptures. His work from 1936 to 1945 was strongly influenced by events in the Spanish Civil War and the Second World War. In 1947 he finally set up a pottery in Vallauris, near Cannes. From 1950, paintings by great Spanish artists served him as models. In the 1950s, Picasso became politically very active, having joined the French Communist Party in 1944, and this is visible in his art.

Picasso is considered the most important and versatile painter of the first half of the 20th century, who revolutionized artistic vision as a cofounder of Cubism. His work includes, in addition to the paintings, much graphic work (drawings, etchings, engravings and, after 1947, lithography), sculptures, and pottery.

Powell, Harry James
1853 – 1922
English glass artist

In 1873 Powell started work at the family glassworks, James Powell & Son, and became its manager several years later. Although the company was still deeply rooted in the English Stourbridge tradition, it was well-known for the modernity of its products. Harry Powell introduced the style and techniques of fine Venetian glass art to his company and experimented with it. The company was to become one of the forerunners of the Arts and Crafts Movement. Its products were printed in the magazine The Studio on a regular basis and were also shown at the international exhibition in Turin in 1902. Powell's company was one of the first to introduce Art Nouveau to glass art and in its day was heralded the best glassworks in England.

Powolny, Michael
18.9.1871 Judenburg, Styria – 4.1.1954 Vienna
Austrian sculptor and ceramicist

After an apprenticeship as a potter under his father, from 1894 to 1906 Powolny studied at the Pottery Industry College in Znaim and at the School of Arts and Crafts in Vienna, under Metzner and others. In 1897 he was amongst the founders of the Vienna Secession and in 1905/06, together with Berthold Löffler, cofounder of the Wiener Keramik company. From 1905 to 1910 he was employed on the interior design of the Palais Stoclet in Brussels. In 1912 his workshop merged with that of Franz Schleiß to form the Vereinigte Wiener und Gmundner Keramik [Associated Viennese and Gmunder Ceramic]. In his latter years he devoted himself increasingly to teaching. From 1909 to 1936 he taught a special ceramics course designed by himself at the School of Arts and Crafts in Vienna, and from 1932 a sculpture course. Powolny's work makes him one of the most important representatives of Viennese Jugendstil ceramic art.

Prouvé, Victor
13.8.1858 Nancy – 1943 Sétif, near Nancy
French painter, graphic artist, sculptor, potter, and craft artist

After studying drawing at the Civic Art School in Nancy from 1873 to 1876, and under the painter Alexandre Cabanel (1823–89) at the École des Beaux-Arts in Paris, Prouvé won a travel scholarship in 1888 and went to Tunisia. When he returned, he worked for Émile Gallé as a designer of furniture, jewelry, and glass. In 1890, he moved to Paris where, at the prompting of Pierre Cécile Puvis de Chavannes and Théophiles-Alexandre Steinlen (1859–1923), he took up sculpting. After his success at the Salon du Champ de Mars in 1894, he received commissions for monuments and decorative architectural sculptures on Art Nouveau buildings in Nancy. In 1901, he was a cofounder of the École de Nancy, which he directed from 1904 after the death of his friend Émile Gallé. In 1918, he took over the direction of the new École des Arts Appliqués in Nancy, where he taught until 1930.

Prutscher, Otto
7.4.1880 Bühl – 15.2.1949 Vienna
Austrian architect and craftsman

Prutscher, who studied architecture and applied art at the School of Arts and Crafts in Vienna and attended the Timber Industry College, was a pupil of Josef Hoffmann and Franz Matsch. In 1903 he became a member of the Wiener Werkstätte and taught at the Institute of Graphic Art. In 1909 he took up a teaching post at the School of Arts and Crafts in Vienna, and in 1918 became a vocational school inspector in Vienna. He was also a member of the Austrian and the German Werkbund, the Künstlerhaus and the Central Association of Austrian Architects.

Prutscher produced models for a number of Viennese ceramic and porcelain factories. Around 1900 he turned to glass and influenced artistic glass production in Austria up to the First World War. He worked for Lobmeyr, Bakalowits & Söhne, and Carl Schappel. He also designed jewelry, silverware, fabrics, wallpapers, and interiors.

Puvis de Chavannes, Pierre Cécile
14.12.1824 Lyons – 24.10.1898 Paris
French painter

After completing his studies as an engineer, Puvis de Chavannes taught himself to paint. He was influenced by Eugène Delacroix (1798–1863) and Théodore Chassériau (1819–56). The subjects of his paintings idealize an ancient world of figures. He produced fantastic murals in dim, cold colors, painted in oils on canvas in his studio and then affixed to the walls when finished. His main works include the panels entitled The Life of St. Geneviève (1874–77) and the murals in the Hôtel de Ville in Paris (1889–93). Puvis de Chavannes was one of the most significant Symbolist painters and thus a great source of inspiration for many Art Nouveau painters in France.

Quarti, Eugenio
1867 Villa d'Almé, Bergamo – 1929 Milan
Italian furniture designer and maker

After training in Paris and completing his practical apprenticeship with Carlo Bugatti, Quarti opened a small shop in Milan called Quarti-Casati. At the Antwerp World Exposition in 1894, he was awarded a silver medal as "a designer of fanciful furniture in an arborizing style." At the Turin exposition of 1898 he won the gold medal. As a successful furniture designer, he was able to expand his business in 1904, after which date he also took part in furnishing larger buildings. By 1905, Quarti-Casati had taken on the proportions of a small industrial business, with a rapidly expanding customer base. After Quarti's death in 1929, his son Mario took over the firm.

Ranson, Paul-Élie
29.3.1861 Limoges – 20.2.1909 Paris
French painter, graphic artist, and craft artist

Ranson was a student at the École des Beaux-Arts in Limoges from 1884, and from 1888 at the Académie Julian in Paris. In 1888, he teamed up with Paul Sérusier (1864–1927), Maurice Denis (1870–1943) and Pierre Bonnard (1867–1947) to form the Nabis group of artists. In 1908, he established the Académie Ranson in Paris, an art school where the leading artists in Paris taught.

As a member of the Nabis group, Ranson was among those who introduced Japonisme in painting and graphic art. His style, which is often notable for its monochromy and the bold use of outlines, made him an important force for promoting Art Nouveau. As a graphic artist, he was a contributor to La Revue Blanche and also illustrated books for publishers Mercure de France. In addition, he did sets for the Théâtre de l'Oeuvre.

Raspall i Mayol, Manuel
1877 Barcelona – 1937 Barcelona
Spanish architect and watercolorist

Raspall i Mayol gained his architectural diploma in Barcelona in 1905, and thereafter built mainly private houses. He was the city architect in Vallés, where he was responsible for restoration work. His buildings were very strongly influenced by the local culture there. He also painted watercolors, which were exhibited in Barcelona from 1896.

Redon, Odilon
(real name Bertrain-Jean Redon)
22.4.1840 Bordeaux – 6.7.1916 Paris
French painter and graphic artist

Redon was a pupil of the painter and sculptor Jean Léon Gérôme (1824–1904), the graphic artist Rodolphe Bresdin (1825–85) and the painter and graphic artist Henri Fantin-Latour (1836–1904). Influenced by Eugène Delacroix (1798–1863), Hieronymus Bosch (1450–1516) and Francisco de Goya (1746–1828), he depicted a phantasmagoric world of dreams and visions. From 1902, he devoted himself chiefly to painting in oil. His subjects are very rarely pure landscapes. They often contain fanciful and mythical elements as well as flowers. Redon counts as a representative of Symbolism, and was highly esteemed as a pioneer by the Nabis group of artists and later by the Surrealists.

Reed, Ethel
1876 Newburyport, Massachusetts – unknown
American painter and graphic artist

Reed, who received her training from the miniaturist Laura Hill, first made a name for herself aged just 18 with her book illustrations. The English magazine Punch commissioned numerous caricatures from her. In 1895 she made her breakthrough as a poster artist. Reed worked almost exclusively for the publishers Lamson, Wolfe & Company in Boston and New York.

Richard-Ginori, Società Ceramica
Established in Milan in 1896
Italian ceramics manufacturer

The Società Ceramica was created in 1896 by the merger of the firm Ginori in Doccia and Società Richard in Milan. Richard-Ginori was one of the most important Italian manufacturers of ceramics of the time. Its products were shown at various international exhibitions such as Turin in 1902 or Paris in 1925. They reveal the stylistic influence of Otto Wagner.

Ricketts, Charles
(real name Charles de Sousy)
2.10.1866 Geneva – 7.10.1931 London
English painter, graphic artist, and artist craftsman

Ricketts grew up in France and moved to England in 1879,

where he started an apprenticeship with a wood engraver and cutter in London. There he met William Morris and joined the Pre-Raphaelite circle. From 1889 to 1897 Ricketts and Charles Shannon (1863–1937) published the Art Nouveau periodical *The Dial*. In 1896 the two friends set up the Vale Press, a printing works that specialized in luxury book editions for which Ricketts did many of the illustrations. He also worked for the magazine *The Hobby Horse* and in 1922 became a member of the Royal Academy.

In his graphics Ricketts developed his own style, with generous curved lines akin to French Art Nouveau, although one can also clearly detect the influence of Aubrey Vincent Beardsley. Ricketts was also successful with his stage sets and metalwork.

Riegel, Ernst
12.9.1871 Münnerstadt – 14.2.1939 Cologne
German gold and silversmith, ceramicist
Riegel trained from 1887 to 1890 under the engraver Otto Pabst in Kempten and from 1895 to 1900 worked as engraver's assistant to the Munich goldsmith Fritz von Miller, who employed designs by major artists. In 1900 he won a gold medal at the Paris World Exposition, after which he founded his own workshop in Munich. In 1906 he was successfully represented at the Third German Exhibition of Arts and Crafts in Dresden and was subsequently appointed to the Darmstadt artists' colony, where he was given a workshop and a teaching post in applied art. From 1912 he taught at the School of Arts and Crafts in Cologne and from 1920 also headed the goldsmithery course at the Cologne Institute of Religious Art.

Riegel's oeuvre was multi-faceted: he worked both for private individuals and for museums, churches and state departments. His works were published in numerous journals of the day.

Riemerschmid, Richard
20.6.1868 Munich – 15.4.1957 Munich
German architect, craftsman, and painter
Riemerschmid, who studied painting at the Academy in Munich from 1888 to 1890, designed his first items of furniture in 1895, under the influence of the Arts and Crafts Movement, which he knew from the pages of the English magazine *The Studio*. In 1897 he was amongst the founding members of the Vereinigte Werkstätten für Kunst im Handwerk [Associated Workshops for Art in Handicraft] and showed furniture and paintings at the Glass Palace exhibition. He gained true recognition only at the 1899 German Exhibition of Art in Dresden, however. Together with Bruno Paul and Bernhard Pankok, he won a gold medal at the Paris World Exposition of 1900 for his *Room for an Art Lover*. From now on a successful artist, he was commissioned to build the Munich Schauspielhaus theater (1900–01) and worked as a designer for the Meissen Royal Saxon Porcelain Factory (1903–04) and for the Dresdner Werkstätten run by his brother-in-law Karl Schmid. From 1902 to 1905 he taught at the School of Art in Nuremberg. From 1913 to 1924 he was director of the Munich School of Arts and Crafts and from 1926 to 1931 headed the Industrial School in Cologne.

As a founder member of the German Werkbund (1907) and its president from 1921 to 1926, and through his activities as a teacher, association member, and author of numerous ideological essays on art, Riemerschmid was one of the leading figures in German Jugendstil. His oeuvre includes interiors, glassware, fabrics, and wallpapers, as well as numerous buildings, including the Munich Schauspielhaus (1900–01, today the Kammerspiele), the Garden City of Hellerau near Dresden (1907–08, development plan), the Deutsche Werkstätte factory building in Dresden (1909) and the Bavarian Radio building in Munich (1928–29).

Rietveld, Gerrit Thomas
24.6.1888 Utrecht – 26.6.1964 Utrecht
Dutch architect and craft artist
Rietveld completed an apprenticeship as a cabinet-maker, but was given his first job by a jeweler as a designer of jewelry. He subsequently set up a studio of his own in Utrecht. In 1918, he became acquainted with the De Stijl group of artists, remaining a member until the group broke up in 1931.
Rietveld designed villas (e.g. the Schröder house in Utrecht, 1924), terraced housing and exhibition pavilions (e.g. for the Biennale in Venice in 1954) which are noted for their great simplicity and elegance. In his interiors and furniture designs – his best-known piece is the Rood Blauwe Stoel [Red Blue Chair] of 1918 – he was fond of using primary colors, attempting to translate the geometric, functional ideal of the De Stijl movement into practice.

Rizzi, Antonio
18.1.1869 Cremona – 1941 Florence
Italian painter and graphic artist
Rizzi was professor of graphic art at the Academy in Perugia and a contributor to the Munich periodical *Jugend*. His work has a general resemblance to Munich Art Nouveau, in particular the work of Franz von Stuck. As a painter, he produced historical and genre paintings, portraits and sets.

Rode, Gotfred
3.12.1862 Torstedlund, near Aalberg – 14.9.1937 Frederiksvaert
Danish painter and porcelain painter
Rode studied at the Copenhagen Academy and from 1896 to 1933 was employed by Den Kongelige Porcelainsfabrik in Copenhagen as a porcelain painter and designer. From 1902 until his death he taught at the Copenhagen Academy. Rode was married to the well-known painter Ingelbert Kolling (1865–1932).

Rookwood Pottery
Founded 1880 in Cincinnati, Ohio
American pottery
Mary Louise Longworth Nichols founded the Rookwood Pottery in Cincinnati in 1880 and one year later set up an accompanying decorating studio, to which a metal workshop for fittings was also attached. Rookwood pottery reveals a Japanese influence in its ornament, although its decors derive their themes more from the North American culture and landscape. The pottery won a gold medal at the Paris World Exposition of 1889. Following the success of its dark-colored pottery with slip decors, around 1900 the company began producing architectural ceramics. In 1941 it was temporarily closed and the company changed ownership several times up to 1967.

Roosenboom, Albert
1871 Brussels – 1943 Brussels
Belgian architect
Rosenboom was born into an artist family of Dutch extraction, his father being a well-known genre painter in Belgium. After studying at the Académie Royale des Beaux-Arts in Brussels, he worked from 1896 as a draftsman in the architectural office of Victor Horta and Jules Barbier. Later he set up on his own, and in 1900 built himself a house in the rue Faider in Brussels. In the same year, he was appointed to a chair at the École des Arts Décoratifs d'Ixelles. In 1902, he constructed the Magasin de bière in Brussels, still in pure Art Nouveau architectural style. In subsequent years he went back to a historicising architectural approach, from 1905 building numerous buildings in a neo-Rococo style. In a letter to the periodical *Le Home* in 1910, he set out the reasons why he had abandoned Art Nouveau in favour of a historicising style.

Besides numerous building commissions in Brussels, Ypres, Leuven, and Bruly, he undertook restoration work, especially at the châteaux of Boisselles and Elverdinghe.

Rörstrands Porslinsfabriker A.B.
Founded 1726 in Lidköping, near Stockholm
Swedish faience and porcelain factory
The faience factory Rörstrands Porslinsfabriker, founded in 1726, was converted into an incorporated society in 1868. In 1850 it started producing porcelain and stoneware comparable to that of Den Kongelige Porcelainsfabrik in Copenhagen. It employed the techniques of underglaze painting, crystal glazes and, frequently, relief modeling. The designs originated from the artists Alf Wallander, artistic director from 1895 to 1914, Algot Erikson, E. H. Tryggelin, Nils Lundstrøm, and Waldemar and Karl Lindstrøm. In 1874 the company founded the subsidiary Arabia O.Y. in Helsinki, in order to supply the Finnish and Russian markets.

Rossetti, Dante Gabriel
12.5.1828 London – 9.4.1882 Birchington-on-Sea, Kent
English painter and poet
Apart from a period of study under the painter Ford Madox Brown (1821–93), Rossetti was largely self-taught. William Blake greatly influenced Rossetti in all spheres of his work. Rossetti, like John Everett Millais (1829–96) and William Holman Hunt (1827–1910), rejected academic historicism in painting. Together they formed the Pre-Raphaelite Brotherhood in 1848, which took as its models early Italian painting and nature. Rossetti's linear style, his mystical and sensuous depictions of women and his book illustrations were major contributory factors to the development of Art Nouveau in England. His works include *The Annunciation* (1850), *Beata Beatrix* (1863) and *Dante's Dream* (1870–71). Rossetti was also a poet of great significance.

Rousseau, François Eugène
17.3.1827 Paris – 12.6.1891 Paris
French potter and glass artist
Rousseau took over the ceramics and pottery business of his father in 1855. He worked with the artist Marc-Louis Solon (called Milès) designing decoration inspired by East Asian art. His ceramic work and thick-sided glass with colorations brought him success. In 1885, he sold his business to his pupil and colleague E. Leveillé, who continued trading under the name Rousseau-Leveillé until the 1890s.

Royal Doulton Potteries
Established in 1815 in Staffordshire
English manufacturers of ceramics and porcelain
In 1815 John Doulton founded a company for the manufacture of ceramics and porcelain in Staffordshire. In 1826 the company moved to Lambeth in London and was renamed Doulton & Watts on the basis of a newly formed partnership with John Watts. Henry Doulton took over production in 1835 and after the death of Watts in 1858 the company was again renamed, this time to Henry Doulton & Co. In the years to follow, the factory developed new techniques and production methods for porcelain and stoneware. The company's lines in production spanned all kinds of ceramic work, including terracotta tiling for walls. After initial success, the company's significance began to fade from 1899 onwards. In 1956 the plant was closed. Today the only branch which is still functioning is Doulton Fine China Ltd., Royal Doulton Potteries, Burslem.

Runge, Philipp Otto
23.7.1777 Wolgast, Pomerania – 2.12.1810 Hamburg
German painter, draftsman, writer, and art theoretician

Runge studied at the Copenhagen Academy from 1799 to 1801 where he was influenced by the figure ideals of John Flaxman (1755–1826) and William Blake. He continued his artistic education at the Dresden Academy in 1801. He was introduced to Romantic landscape painting by Caspar David Friedrich in 1802. It was at this time that he executed one of his most famous works, *The Times of the Day*. He started taking drawing lessons in Hamburg in 1803 and turned to portrait painting. He also explored the use of color, the results of which he published in a book in 1810.

Runge is said to have paved the way for Romantic art, not least through his theoretical writings, and to have helped free German painting from the clutches of academic classicism.

Rysselberghe, Octave van
22.7.1855 Minderhout – 30.3.1929 Nice
Belgian architect
Octave van Rysselberghe was a brother of the painter Theo van Rysselberghe (1862–1926). After completing his training at the Academy in Ghent, from 1871 he worked at the law courts in Poelaert. In 1874, he undertook a trip to Italy. He gained his first major architectural commission in 1879, for the Royal Observatory at Uccle. In 1882, he completed a palais for Count Goblet d'Alviella in Brussels, and the following year was runner-up in a competition for the Municipal Hall in Schaerbeek. In 1889, he retired to La Hulpe, where he threw himself with great enthusiasm but little success into growing grapes in hothouses, constructing a hothouse with a surface area of one hectare. The construction of a studio for his brother in 1893 brought him into contact with Paul Otlet, for whom he built a residence in 1894 in partnership with Henry van de Velde. This joint effort led to further cooperative commissions with van de Velde. In 1898, he was appointed professor at the Academy in Brussels without ever giving a lecture. In the following years, he won commissions mainly for houses and interior designs. Towards the end of his life, Rysselberghe retired to the South of France.

Saarinen, Eliel
20.8.1873 Rantasalmi – 1.7.1950 Bloomfield Hills, Michigan
Finnish architect, urban planner, designer, and painter
From 1893 to 1897 Saarinen studied painting at Helsinki University and architecture at Helsinki Polytechnic. He later painted only as a hobby. In 1896, while still a student, he founded the architectural firm of Gesellius, Lindgren & Saarinen, known as GLS, together with Herman Gesellius and Armas Eliel Lindgren. Alongside public buildings they also designed private villas, in which they realized the principle of the total work of work (e.g. Suur-Merijoki manor house in Viipuri, 1903). For this reason, from the 1890s onwards, Saarinen also designed furniture, which like his buildings drew upon Finnish tradition. In 1923 he emigrated to the United States, where he opened an office in Evanston, Illinois, transferring it to Ann Arbor, Michigan in 1924. He taught at the Michigan University of Chicago and from 1948 also headed the Graduate Department of Architecture and City Planning at the Cranbrook Academy of Art in Bloomfield Hills, Michigan.

Saarinen's first buildings were strongly influenced by the Finnish Gothic Revival and the English Arts and Crafts Movement. Their interiors, which frequently originated from the workshop of Akseli Gallen-Kallela, revealed predominantly Art Nouveau elements. In his later buildings, forms became more angular and more abstract. His most important work was Helsinki Central Station (designed 1904, built 1910–14).

Sant'Elia, Antonio
30.4.1888 Como – 10.10.1916 Monfalcone
Italian architect
Sant'Elia studied at the Technical Architectural School in Como, the Accademia di Brera in Milan and the Scuola di Belle Arti in Bologna. His first building was an Art Nouveau villa near Como (1911), which was influenced by the Italian Stile Liberty and the Viennese Secession. Later, his style, like that of Loos, was inspired by the architecture of the great American metropolises. In 1913, he drew up Utopian plans for cities, which made him a pioneer of modern Italian architecture. Sant'Elia was killed at the Front soon after Italy joined the First World War.

Scharvogel, Jacob Julius
3.4.1854 Mainz – 30.1.1938 Munich
German painter and ceramicist
After studying ceramics in London and Paris and experimenting in glass-making in the Bavarian Forest, Scharvogel worked for Villeroy & Boch. In 1897 he was a cofounder of the Vereinigte Werkstätten für Kunst im Handwerk [Associated Workshops for Art in Handicraft] in Munich, where one year later he founded his own workshop. From 1900 he collaborated with the painter Walter Magnussen (1869–1946), the graphic artist Paul Haustein, Theo Schmuz-Baudiss and Emmy von Egidy. At the Paris World Exposition of 1900 he won a gold medal for his stoneware. From 1904 to 1913 he headed the Grand-Ducal Potteries in Darmstadt, which took successful part in the Brussels exhibition of 1910. In 1907 he was amongst the founders of the German Werkbund. From 1915 to 1925 he taught architectural ceramics at the Technical College in Munich and acted as consultant on a project to set up a ceramics industry in Turkey.

Scharvogel may be seen as the first German ceramicist to develop sharp-fired stoneware featuring color glazes. This *grès flammé* was popularly used in Art Nouveau, especially in France. Around 1900 he turned away from decorative ceramics with a pronounced Japanese influence and instead toward the manufacture of functional ceramic items for interiors and architecture.

Schaudt, Johann Emil
14.8.1871 Stuttgart – unknown
German architect
Schaudt studied at the Technical College in Stuttgart and was a pupil of S. Neckelmann and Paul Wallot.

Schechtel, Fyodor Osipovich
1859 Moscow – 4.7.1926 Moscow
Russian architect
Schechtel was an assistant to the architect A. S. Kaminsky, who was a member of the Mir Iskustva artists' group and can be considered his most important teacher. In the 1880s, Schechtel set up his own architectural practice, and also worked with M. Lentovsky as a set designer. He employed the leading avant-garde Russian artists to do the decorative work of his buildings. His most important buildings are in Moscow, namely the Palais Rabushinsky (1902–06, now the Gorky Museum) and Jaroslav Station (1890–1910). In 1901, he was commissioned to build the Russian pavilion at the International Exhibition in Glasgow.

Scheidt, Georg-Anton
1900 Vienna – 1965 Huttar Heriberg
Austrian graphic artist and silversmith
Based in Vienna, Scheidt produced jewelry and silverware in a linear style to designs by Koloman Moser and others.

Schiele, Egon
12.6.1890 Tulln/Danube – 31.10.1918 Vienna
Austrian painter and draughtsman

Schiele studied at the Academy in Vienna from 1906 to 1909. In 1907 he met Gustav Klimt, who would become his spiritual mentor. Up till 1911 he worked in seclusion in his studio in Vienna, although he was a member of various artists' groups and the Federation of Austrian Artists. He exhibited at the Kunstschau in Vienna (1908), with the Sonderbund in Cologne (1912), in the Secessions in Berlin and Vienna (1915–16) and at the Kriegsschau [War Exhibition] in Vienna (1917). He found public recognition only shortly before his death, however.

Schiele initially adopted the ornamental graphic elements of Viennese Jugendstil, before developing, around 1902, the highly personal style that would make him one of the most important representatives of early Viennese Expressionism. His oeuvre includes landscapes, portraits, and above all nudes, which were considered scandalous in his day.

Schmithals, Hans
28.3.1878 Bad Kreuznach – 1964 Munich
German painter and craftsman
From 1902 Schmithals attended the Studio for Applied and Free Art in Munich founded by Hermann Obrist and Wilhelm von Debschitz, in which he later taught wallpaper printing. His first pictures and furniture designs were featured in the 1908 exhibition by the Verband für Raumkunst [Association for Interior Design]. In Munich, together with Wolfgang von Wersin, he founded the Austellungsverband für Raumkunst [Interior Design Exhibiting Society], which in 1913 showed many of his designs. After the First World War he designed the interiors of large buildings in Switzerland, Munich, and Berlin.

Schmithals, who borders on abstraction in his handicraft designs, and in particular in his tapestries, ranks amongst the pioneers of abstract art. The dynamic composition of his paintings is strongly influenced by Obrist.

Schmuz-Baudiss, Theo
4.8.1859 Herrnhut, Saxony – 20.6.1942 Garmisch
German painter and ceramicist
Schmuz-Baudiss studied at the Munich School of Arts and Crafts from 1879 to 1882 and at the Munich Academy up till 1890, before switching from painting to ceramics around 1896. His first vases were shown in the Munich Glass Palace exhibition of 1897. He worked with Jacob Julius Scharvogel and as a designer for the Thuringian firm of Swaine & Co. Schmuz-Baudiss became a member of the Vereinigte Werkstätten für Kunst im Handwerk [Associated Workshops for Art in Handicraft] in Munich in 1897 and took part in all the major exhibitions in Munich, Paris, Leipzig, Dresden, Berlin, and Turin between 1899 and 1902. In 1902 he was appointed to the KPM Royal Porcelain Factory in Berlin. Initially responsible for setting up the underglaze department, from 1908 to his retirement in 1925 he was head of the factory. The decorative techniques which Schmuz-Baudiss developed lent his stylized floral ornament echoes of Scandinavian porcelain. He also reintroduced the *sgraffito* technique. His porcelain was distinguished by its differentiated palette.

Schnellenbühel, Gertraud von
1878 Jena – 1959 Dresden
German craftswoman
Schnellenbühel studied painting under Frithjof Smith and from 1900 under Angelo Jank in Munich. In 1902 she switched to applied art and joined the metalwork course at Debschitz's school. She was supported in her work by Hermann Obrist and produced successful jewelry designs and silverware. At the 1906 Nuremberg Exhibition of Arts and Crafts she showed silver bowls. In 1911 she worked in the workshop of the silversmith and court employee

Adalbert Kinzinger. She took part in the Werkbund exhibition in Cologne in 1914, after which date no further works by her are known or have been published.

Seger, Hermann
26.12.1839 Posen – 30.10.1893 Berlin
German ceramicist
As director of the Chemical Institute at the KPM Royal Porcelain Factory in Berlin (1878–90), in 1880 Seger developed the "Seger porcelain" which bears his name. Seger porcelain is very well suited to carrying color metallic glazes, making it possible to achieve the quality of fine Chinese and Japanese chinaware. Seger pottery featuring oxblood glazes was shown at the 1884 exhibition in the Berlin Museum of Applied Art. Seger exerted a strong influence upon both KPM and the ceramic industry as a whole.

Serrurier-Bovy, Gustave
27.7.1858 Liège – 19.11.1910 Antwerp
Belgian architect and craft artist
Serrurier-Bovy studied at the Académie des Beaux-Arts in Liège in the 1870s. After becoming acquainted with the work of William Morris, he moved to London, where he worked as a designer of interior furnishings in the Modern Style. In 1884, he opened a shop for furniture and decorations in Liège, opening further branches in Brussels in 1897 and Paris in 1899. His own furniture designs display a certain plainness and severity. With his "Silex" range of birch furniture, he was a precursor of fold-up furniture. Serrurier-Bovy was a cofounder of the Brussels Salons de La Libre Esthétique in 1894, and the following year organised L'œuvre Artistique in Liège, an international exposition for applied art. In 1901, he established contact with the artists' colony in Darmstadt. Serrurier-Bovy was exhibited at several exhibitions in London and at the world expositions in Paris in 1900 and St. Louis in 1904. From 1896 to 1903, he was a regular participant at the Salon du Champ de Mars in Paris. His last designs were exhibited at the International Exposition for Arts and Crafts in Brussels in 1910.

Sika, Jutta
17.9.1877 Linz – 2.1.1964 Vienna
Austrian painter, graphic artist, and handicraft designer
Sika, who studied at the Institute of Graphic Art in Vienna from 1895 to 1897 and under Koloman Moser at the Vienna School of Arts and Crafts from 1897 to 1902, took part in numerous exhibitions, including "The Laid Table" in 1906 and at the world expositions in Paris in 1900 and St. Louis in 1904, where she won a bronze medal. From 1911 to 1933 she taught at vocational schools in Vienna. Sika was a cofounder of the Wiener Kunst im Hause [Viennese Art in the Home] association of interior designers, a member of the Austrian and German Werkbund and of the Vereinigung bildender Künstlerinnen Österreichs [Association of Austrian Women Visual Artists].

Silver, Rex
(Real name Reginald Silver)
1879 – 1965
English designer
In 1901 Silver took over his father's design studio for wallpaper and textiles founded in 1880, which supplied the biggest firms in Europe, especially Liberty & Co. in London. Silver also produced designs for the Liberty silver series, Cymric. His career was at its peak in the 1920s and 1930s. The Silver Studio was closed in 1963.

Simberg, Hugo
24.6.1873 Hamina – 11.7.1917 Ahtäri
Finnish painter and graphic artist
From 1895 to 1897 Simberg studied at Akseli Gallen-Kallela's school in Ruovesi, which served as a meeting point for the pioneers of Finnish Art Nouveau. Gallen-Kallela quickly discovered his pupil's remarkable talent and focused his training upon the techniques of graphic art. Together they formed the foundation of modern Finnish graphic art. As a painter, Simberg produced chiefly small-format watercolors and prints. His two favorite themes were the *Poor Devil* and *Death*. Simberg may be seen as one of the inspirational forces behind Finnish painting of the turn of the century.

Sohlberg, Harald Oskar
29.11.1869 Christiania (today Oslo) – 19.6.1935 Oslo
Norwegian painter
Sohlberg, who studied painting under W. Krogh at the Royal School of Drawing, spent the years 1895 to 1896 in Paris and 1897 in Weimar. From 1906 to 1911 he continued to attend evening classes with J. N. Nerbst. Sohlberg chiefly painted landscapes and views of architecture. His best-known work is *Winter's Night in the Mountains* (1914), which today hangs in the National Gallery in Oslo.

Stappen, Charles van der
19.12.1843 Sint-Josse-ten-Noode – 21.10.1910 Brussels
Belgian sculptor
Van der Stappen was a student at the Academy in Brussels from 1859 to 1868, spending 1864 in Paris, where he worked in a sculptor's studio while attending the École des Beaux-Arts. From 1877 to 1879 he lived in Rome, where he worked out the *cire perdue* technique. After his return, he established the Atelier Libre in Brussels, which soon became a favorite rendezvous for artists such as Constantin Meunier (1831–1905), Victor Horta and Octave Maus (1886–1919). In the 1890s, van der Stappen devoted himself to applied art, and was a cofounder of L'Art, a movement for "Art in Industry". Van der Stappen was exhibited at numerous exhibitions, including those of Les Vingt, the Salon de La Libre Esthétique and the Viennese Secession. His principal works include *Teaching Art* (1887), a bronze group at the Palais des Beaux-Arts in Brussels and another on the main steps of the City Hall in Brussels.

Steuben Glass Works
Founded 1903 in Corning, New York
American hollow glass works and decorative and domestic glass processing plant
The company, named after the district of Steuben, was founded in 1903 by Frederick Carder (1864–1963) and Thomas G. Hawkes. Under the direction of Carder, an English glass technician who had arrived in the United States in 1902, the company became highly successful. Its range of products was diverse and testified to the influence of René Lalique, Louis Comfort Tiffany, Émile Gallé and the glass styles of other countries. It also developed various techniques for decorating glass. During the First World War its operations were temporarily suspended. In 1918 the company was taken over by the neighboring Corning Glass Works, but Carder remained head of the firm until the 1930s.

Stoltenberg-Lerche, Hans
12.8.1867 Düsseldorf – 17.4.1920 Rome
Norwegian sculptor, graphic artist, ceramicist, and jewelry and glass artist
Stoltenberg-Lerche trained at the Düsseldorf Academy of Art, the Academy of Fine Arts in Florence and under Eugène Carrière and de Saint-Marceaux in Paris. He lived chiefly in Italy and opened a studio in Margellina, where he produced small terracotta figures. He also drew for the *Leipziger Illustrierte Zeitung* and designed interiors, jewelry, and ceramics. Stoltenberg-Lerche took part in numerous exhibitions, and was particularly successful in Paris: at the 1897 Paris Exposition Nationale de Céramique et des Arts du Feu he was awarded an honorary diploma, and he won a gold medal at the 1900 World Exposition. Together with Frida Hansen, he represented Norway at the Turin exhibition in 1902, and at the Venice Biennale of 1912 he showed glass works for the first time. His works were bought by collectors and museums around the world.

Strathmann, Carl
11.9.1866 Düsseldorf – 29.7.1939 Munich
German painter, graphic artist, and handicraft designer
Strathmann studied at the Academy in Düsseldorf from 1882 to 1886 and subsequently, until 1889, at the Weimar School of Art under Leopold Kalckreuth, whom he followed to Munich in 1890. There he joined the Bohemian set around Lovis Corinth (1858–1925). At an exhibition by the Munich Secession he was profoundly impressed by the mysticism of Jan Toorop and Fernand Khnopff. Although his own painting was strongly influenced by Dutch Symbolism, he published parodies of Symbolist art in the magazines *Jugend*, *Fliegende Blätter* and *Pan*. In 1894 he became a member of the Münchner Freie Vereinigung [Munich Free Association], a splinter group of the Munich Secession which included, amongst others, Peter Behrens, Lovis Corinth, Thomas Theodor Heine, and Otto Eckmann. Around 1900, in the studio which he had founded with A. Niemeyer, he turned increasing attention to applied art, designing fabrics, menus, wallpapers, and tapestries. He is also well-known for his gold medal jewelry, occasionally set with stones. Strathmann renounced traditional illusionistic techniques and emphasized the decorative character of his compositions. He thereby achieved the "fairytale atmosphere" so beloved of Munich Jugendstil.

Strauven, Gustave
1878 Schaerbeek – 1919 Faverge, France
Belgian architect and inventor
From 1896 to 1898, Strauven worked as a draftsman in the architectural office of Victor Horta, later joining the editorial staff of *La Gerbe*, a periodical for interior decoration and literature. Around 1900, he set up his own architectural practice, winning commissions for private houses, including that of the painter Saint-Cyr in Brussels (1903). After 1907, he devoted more and more time to inventing, and was hardly involved in architectural work.

Stuck, Franz von
(ennobled in 1906)
23.2.1863 Tettenweis, Lower Bavaria – 30.8.1928 Munich
German painter, sculptor, and craftsman
Stuck studied at the School of Arts and Crafts in Munich from 1878 to 1881 and until 1885 at the Academy under Wilhelm Lindenschmit (1829–1895) and Ludwig Löfftz (1845–1910). He rarely attended classes, however, working instead as a handicraft designer and contributing to the magazines *Jugend*, *Fliegende Blätter* and the Viennese journal *Allegorien und Embleme*. In 1888 he started painting in oils and in 1889 won the gold medal at the Munich annual exhibition. In 1892, together with Fritz von Uhde (1848–1911), Bruno Piglhein and Heinrich Zügel (1850–1941), he founded the Munich Secession. In 1895 he took over from Lindenschmit as professor at the Munich Academy. His pupils included Wassily Kandinsky (1866–1944), Paul Klee (1879–1940), Hans Purrmann (1880–1966) and Josef Albers (1888–1976). Between 1897 and 1898, with the assistance

of the architects Jakob Heilmann and Max Littmann, he created his total work of art: the Villa Stuck in Munich, his studio and home. A number of pieces of furniture designed by Stuck were shown at the Paris World Exposition of 1900. Stuck was a central figure in Munich Jugendstil who erased the boundary between fine and applied art. He painted chiefly allegorical, Symbolist nudes and mythical beasts. His major works include *The Twelve Months* (1887), *Sin* (1893), *War* (1894) and *Sphinx* (1895).

Sullivan, Louis Henry
3.9.1856 Boston, Massachusetts – 14.4.1924 Chicago
American architect
After studying briefly in Boston and working in the architectural offices of Frank Furness in Philadelphia and William Le Baron Jenney in Chicago, from 1874 Sullivan studied at the École des Beaux-Arts in Paris, where he explored historicist styles. In 1876 he returned to the United States and in 1881 founded his own architectural practice in Chicago with the German engineer Dankmar Adler. Between then and the ending of their partnership in 1895, the duo produced a number of successful, eclectic works. Although Sullivan won considerably fewer commissions after his split from Adler, the quality of his architecture improved. In 1899 he built his masterpiece: the Schlesinger and Mayer Department Store in Chicago.
Sullivan's oeuvre arose at a turning point in the development of architecture. As the chief representative of the Chicago School of Architecture, he designed the first functional steel-frame buildings in the United States and thereby ranks amongst the pioneers of modern constructivist building. In his own view, form arose from function. The decoration employed on his buildings is Art Nouveau in style. His major works include the Wainwright Building in St. Louis (1890–91), the Auditorium Building in Chicago (1886–88), the Guaranty Building in Chicago (1894–95) and the Schlesinger and Mayer (today the Carson Pirie Scott & Co.) Department Store in Chicago (1899–1904).

Thesmar, André-Fernand
2.3.1843 Châlon-sur-Saone – 5.4.1912 Neuilly-sur-Seine
French enamel artist
Thesmar was apprenticed in a textiles factory, and subsequently worked as a set designer in a studio for industrial design, then at Aubusson tapestries and subsequently in a foundry in Barbédienne. Around 1872, he set up independently in Neuilly, specializing in *émail cloisonné* work, which he later did on porcelain for the Manufacture de Sèvres. He won awards for his work as early as 1874, at an exhibition of the Union Centrale des Arts Décoratifs. At the World Exposition in Paris in 1878 the Japanese government, which had a high regard for his unusual techniques, acquired two of his exhibits. In 1888, he turned out his first artefacts in *plique à jour* enamel. He continued to develop enamel technology, eventually producing transparent enamel on metal. Thesmar's work represents a technically perfect, fragile, often dainty version of French Art Nouveau.

Thonet A. G., Gebrüder
Founded 1849 in Vienna
Austrian furniture factory
Michael Thonet (1796–1871), founder of the firm, was extraordinarily gifted as a craftsman, technician, and designer. After a number of years producing traditional furniture, from 1830 he developed new methods of laminating and bending wood. In 1845 production was transferred from Boppard on the Rhine to Vienna. The present-day Thonet company was founded in 1849 in the Gumpendorf district of Vienna under the name of Gebrüder Thonet [Thonet Brothers]. It was not until the last quarter of the 19th century, however, that the factory started to be truly successful with its serial manufacture of bentwood furniture, in particular its Chair No. 14, which is still produced today. The company also produced furniture to designs by major Jugendstil artists such as Otto Wagner, Adolf Loos and Josef Hoffmann, and thereby made an important contribution to the history of 20th-century furniture design.

Thorn-Prikker, Jan
5.6.1868 The Hague – 5.3.1932 Cologne
Dutch painter and graphic artist
Thorn-Prikker studied at the Academy of Art in The Hague, but in 1904 moved to Germany, where he worked as a church artist. He taught concurrently at art schools in Krefeld, Hagen, Munich, and Düsseldorf, and from 1923 to his death was a professor at the Arts and Crafts School in Cologne. Thorn-Prikker's work consists principally of frescoes and wall-paintings, but he also did painted glass windows, mosaics and *verre églomisé* work. His graphic work reveals similarities to that of the Macdonald sisters.

Tiffany, Louis Comfort
18.2.1848 New York – 17.1.1933 New York
American glass artist, painter, and craftsman
The son of the famous silversmith Charles Lewis Tiffany (1812–1902) studied painting under Georges Innes and Samuel Coleman in New York and under Leon Bailly in Paris. Originally a painter, by 1879 he had already developed an interest in the decorative arts and set up an interior design business in New York. His biggest commission was the renovation of the White House from 1882 to 83. His firm soon went under, however, and Tiffany devoted himself increasingly to glass. In 1885 he founded the Tiffany Glass Company, renamed the Tiffany Studio after 1900. He also founded a glass factory on Long Island in 1892, run by the Englishman Arthur Nash. The first glasses it produced were sent to Samuel Bing in Paris for inclusion in the opening exhibition of his Galerie L'Art Nouveau in 1895. From 1896 production expanded and became more commercial, as a result of which only a very few pieces of glass bore Tiffany's personal signature. From 1892 to 1905 the company also produced furniture, which was heavily decorated with wood mosaics, metal fittings, and glass spheres and was only loosely related to Art Nouveau. In 1902, after the death of his father, Tiffany took over the Tiffany & Co. jeweler's store in New York.
Tiffany became famous for his iridescent decorative glass-ware (known as Tiffany glass or Favrile glass) and is also well-known for his colorful, floral-shaped glass lampshades. From the Paris World Exposition of 1889 onwards, Tiffany took part in all the major exhibitions in Europe and became a model for many artists working in glass.

Toorop, Jan
(real names Johannes Theodor)
20.12.1858 Purovedyo, Java – 3.3.1928 The Hague
Dutch painter and graphic artist
Toorop's family returned from Java to the Netherlands in 1869, and Toorop studied at the academies in Amsterdam from 1880 to 1881 and in Brussels from 1882 to 1885. From 1886, he was a member of the *Cercle des Vingt* group of artists. He made several visits to London, returning to the Netherlands in 1889, where, under the influence of Georges Seurat (1859–91) and James Ensor (1860–1949), he turned out his first pointilliste paintings. Around 1890, impressed by the poetry of Maurice Maeterlinck (1862–1949) and Emile Verhaeren (1855–1916), he became a devotee of Symbolism. In 1905 he converted to Catholicism, and his pictures dealt increasingly with religious subject matter.
Toorop was the main representative of Symbolism in the Netherlands. His Art Nouveau work is characterized by a sweeping arabesque linearity bearing evidence of the influence of Beardsley.

Tostrup, Olaf
26.5.1842 Christiania (today Oslo) – 21.6.1882
Norwegian goldsmith
Tostrup, son of the engraver and goldsmith Jakob Ulrik Holfedt Tostrup, studied sculpture at the Royal College in Oslo from 1858 to 1862 and at the Academy in Berlin until 1864. He concluded his training with an apprenticeship under a Paris goldsmith (1864) and under Michelsen in Copenhagen (1865). After a number of study trips, including to Vienna (1873) and Paris (1878), he took over his father's workshop. While his works were initially traditional in style, from 1880 they became more modern.

Toulouse-Lautrec, Henri de
24.11.1864 Albi – 9.9.1901 Château Malromé, Gironde
French painter and graphic artist
Toulouse-Lautrec came from an old aristocratic family. Falls in his childhood left him a cripple. From 1880 he trained as a painter, his teachers being Jules Bastien-Lepage (1848–84) and Léon Bonnat (1833–1922). In 1886, he met Émile Bernard (1868–1941) and Vincent van Gogh (1853–90) in Paris for the first time, and he joined forces with them as the École du Petit Boulevard group of artists. Toulouse-Lautrec set himself up in a studio in Montmartre in Paris, where he had easy access to the world of cabaret. In 1889, he had his first shows in the Salon des Indépendants and the Cercle Volney, but his first important poster, the *Moulin Rouge*, came only two years later. In 1895, he became a regular contributor to *La Revue Blanche*, a literary and artistic periodical. On his travels, he became acquainted with Aubrey Beardsley and Oscar Wilde (1854–1900). He died at the early age of 37.
Influenced by Edgar Degas (1834–1917) and Paul Gauguin (1848–1903) and full of enthusiasm for Japanese color wood engravings, Toulouse-Lautrec developed a highly individual, expressive form of art using a very fluid line and flat color surfaces. He drew the maximum artistic effect from color lithography, and his posters had a great influence on poster art throughout Europe. He did over 500 paintings, more than 3,000 drawings and 368 lithographs. Among his principals works are the paintings *The Ball at the Moulin Rouge* (1890) and *In the Salon of the rue Moulin* (1892); the posters *Moulin Rouge* (1890) and *Ambassadeurs. Aristide Bruant dans son Cabaret* (1892); the lithographs *Le Café Concert* (11 prints, 1893), *Yvette Guilbert* (16 prints, 1894 and 1896) and *Mélodies de Désiré* (13 prints, 1895); and the drawings *Au Cirque* (22 prints, published 1905).

Unger (-Holzinger), Else
25.02.1873 Vienna – unknown
Austrian craftswoman and jewelry designer
Unger attended Josef Hoffmann's architecture course at the School of Arts and Crafts in Vienna and showed what was described as a "blue casket" at the 1900 Paris World Exposition as part of a display of exhibits submitted by the School. She also showed jewelry and enamelwork at the 1902 International Exhibition in Turin and the 1904 World Exposition in St. Louis. Unger was a member of the Wiener Kunst im Hause [Viennese Art in the Home] association of interior designers and produced chiefly silver jewelry.

Urania
Established in 1895 in Maastricht
Dutch pewter and metalwork factory
At the turn of the century, Urania was the sole manufacturer of pewter goods in the Netherlands. The models the

company produced were all designed by artists and were all originals. Urania's range of products included untreated, silver-plated and gold-plated metalware and pewterware. The forms of the items the factory produced were very Belgian; one can detect the influence of Victor Horta and Henry van de Velde. Urania's main sales area was Germany, where the company also had stocks of samples in Berlin and in Aachen.

Urban, Josef
25.2.1872 Vienna – 10.7.1933 New York
Austrian architect, craftsman, and stage designer
Urban, who studied under Karl von Hasenauer at the Academy in Vienna, was a founding member and later, from 1906 to 1908, president of the Hagenbund. In 1911 he emigrated to New York. Starting out as a stage designer, from 1918 to 1933 he was principal designer at the Metropolitan Opera. From 1920 he also designed for the movie industry and established close links with the newspaper magnate Randolph Hearst. He built a theater on Broadway for Ziegfeld's troupe, and opened the Wiener Werkstätte's New York offices and showroom on Fifth Avenue, where he also displayed his own designs.

Vallgren, Ville
15.12.1855 Borgå (today Porvoo) – 13.10.1940 Helsinki
Finnish sculptor
Vallgren was a student under Sjöstrand in Helsinki and from 1877 under Cavalier in Paris, where he lived and worked as an artist until 1913. He subsequently returned to Helsinki. His oeuvre includes bronze sculptures, statuettes of nudes in bronze, silver and china, monuments, portrait busts, and the *Havis Amanda* fountain in Helsinki (1904–07). His small, dancing bronze figures embody the *joie de vivre* so typical of Art Nouveau.

Vallin, Eugène
1856 Herbévillier – 1922 Nancy
French architect and *ébéniste*
Vallin trained at the École des Beaux-Arts in Nancy and his uncle's carpentry workshop, which specialised in church fittings. He took over the business in 1891, and at the Exposition des Art Décoratifs in Paris in 1894 was still exhibiting Gothic-style furniture. However, the influence of Émile Gallé changed all that in the following years, turning him into an Art Nouveau artist. His view was that the only adornment a piece of furniture needed was the harmonious interplay of its formal components. In 1896, he designed the great street gateway for Gallé's furniture workshops, and in 1905 he built the aquarium in the park of the present-day museum of the École de Nancy. In his architectural capacity, he pioneered the use of reinforced concrete. Vallin's sons Georges and Auguste (1881–1967) followed in their father's footsteps and became cabinet-makers.

Vallotton, Félix
28.12.1865 Lausanne – 29.12.1925 Paris
Swiss-French painter and graphic artist
Vallotton studied at the Académie Julian and the École des Beaux-Arts in Paris from 1882 to 1885 and initially concentrated on graphics. He illustrated books and worked for *La Revue Blanche* between 1894 and 1903. His woodcuts were also published in *Simplicissimus* from 1896 onwards. From 1900 he channeled his creative energies toward painting. He was friendly with the Nabis group of artists and was on the founding committee of the Salon d'Automne, together with Pierre Bonnard (1867–1947), Édouard Vuillard (1868–1940), Ker-Xavier Roussel (1867–1944) and Charles Cottet (1863–1925). He was offered a chair at the Académie Ranson in 1908. The First World War prompted his series of woodcuts entitled *C'est la Guerre* [This is war].

Vallotton's drawings and highly expressive woodcuts with their strong contrast of black and white are reminiscent of Aubrey Beardsley. Their popularity was rapidly spread through publication in various periodicals; they were later to exert a major influence on Expressionism in Germany.

Velde, Henry Clemens van de
3.4.1863 Antwerp – 25.10.1957 Zürich
Belgian architect, graphic artist, painter, craft artist, and writer
From 1881 to 1883, van de Velde studied painting at the Academy in Antwerp, and from 1883 to 1885 was a pupil of Durant in Paris. In 1885, he returned to Belgium and in 1889 joined the *Cercle des Vingt* group of artists. His acquaintance with William Finch (1854–1930) and Octave van Rysselberghe familiarized him with English arts and crafts and William Morris's reform movement. In 1890, he had a physical and mental breakdown, and decided to give up painting. Henceforth he devoted himself to the study of architecture and arts and crafts. In 1896, he was among those who fitted out Samuel Bing's Galerie L'Art Nouveau in Paris. His display of furniture at the Dresden Arts and Crafts Exhibition in 1897 was so successful that from 1898 to 1914 he gained many commissions from Germany. In 1898, he established workshops for applied art in Brussels, with a branch in Berlin (1899). In 1902, he was called to Weimar for the establishment of an arts and crafts school, which he directed from 1906 to 1914. In 1907, he was a founder member of the German Werkbund. After visits to Switzerland (from 1917) and the Netherlands (from 1921), he was recalled to Belgium in 1925 to set up the Institut supérieur des Arts décoratifs in Brussels, whose director he became in 1926. He held concurrently a chair at the University of Ghent. His last major commissions were the Belgian pavilions at the world expositions in 1937, 1939, and 1940. In 1947, he retired to Oberägeri in Switzerland.
Van de Velde was a leading personality in the development of Art Nouveau and things modern. He endeavored to create an individual but contemporary style in architecture and arts and crafts, and opposed the recreation of historical styles. A core principle of his was that form should be appropriate to the function and the material. The range of his work was vast: furniture, utensils, book bindings, graphics, ceramics, interior designs, architecture, and writing. The latter included *Renaissance in Arts and Crafts* (1901), *Lay Sermons on Arts and Crafts* (1902), *Les Formules d'une esthétique moderne* (1925) and the challenging *Le Nouveau Style* (1931). His own house in Uccle near Brussels (1895) is among his principal works, along with the interiors of the Folkwang Museum in Hagen (1900–02), the Werkbund theater in Cologne (1914, demolished 1920), the university library in Ghent (1935–40) and the Kröller-Müller Museum in Otterlo (1936–54).

Vereinte Kunstgewerbler Darmstadt
[Associated Applied Artists of Darmstadt]
Studio for applied art, architecture, painting, and sculpture
The association was formed in 1902 by Alfred Koch, C. F. Meier and Hans Günther Reinstein, all pupils of Peter Behrens. It was active in the spheres of furniture design, ceramics, metalwork, and book illustration.

Vever
Established in Metz in 1831
French jewelry firm
Established in 1831 in Metz by Pierre Vever, the business moved to Paris in 1871, and in 1881 was taken over by Pierre's grandsons Paul (1851–1915) and Henri (1854–1942). The artists that worked for the firm included the designers Eugène Samuel Grasset, Henri Vollet, Lucien Gautrait, the sculptors René Rozet, and the enamelist Étienne Tourette. Vever became – after Lalique – the leading jeweler in Paris, gaining numerous awards for its work and winning the brothers Paul

and Henri Vever the Légion d'Honneur. Henri was also an outstanding author, critic, and historian, publishing in 1908 the standard work on French 19th-century jewelry *La Bijouterie française au XIXe siècle*. The third volume of this contains biographical information on the leading Art Nouveau artists.

Viollet-le-Duc, Eugène Emmanuel
27.1.1814 Paris – 17.9.1879 Lausanne
French architect and writer on art
Viollet-le-Duc was self-taught as an architect, being driven by his enthusiasm for medieval architecture. He restored medieval buildings, including churches and especially great French cathedrals such as Notre Dame in Paris and Ste-Madeleine in Vézelay. This work did much to improve the care of historic monuments in the 19th century, and made Viollet-le-Duc a principle figure of the historicist style. In accordance with his view of a rationalist conception of architecture, he had later additions to the buildings torn down and replaced in the original Gothic form, as for example at Château Pierrefonds from 1859 to 70, an approach which attracted a storm of criticism. In his own, rather insignificant buildings, which were inspired by medieval art, he employed a floral ornamentation that anticipated Art Nouveau. As a theoretical writer, Viollet-le-Duc had a great influence on the development of modern architecture. His work *Dictionnaire raisonné de l'architecture du XIe au XVIe siècle* (10 vols., Paris 1854–) became a manual for the next generation of architects.

Vogeler, Heinrich
12.12.1872 Bremen – 14.6.1942 Kazakhstan
German painter, graphic artist, and craftsman
Vogeler, who studied painting at the Academy in Düsseldorf from 1890 to 1893, moved in 1894 to Worpswede, where he became a pupil of Fritz Mackensen (1866–1953) and Hans am Ende (1864–1918). On a trip to Florence in 1898 he met and became friends with the writer Rainer Maria Rilke (1875–1926) and subsequently received commissions for book illustrations. In 1908, together with his brother, he founded the Worpsweder Workshops, specializing in furniture and furnishings in Tarmstedt. After the First World War he became an adherent of Communism and founded a socialist college on an artistic basis in Worpswede. From 1922 to 1923 he produced his fresco cycle on the class struggle in Germany. In 1931 he emigrated to the Soviet Union, where he had received commissions for agitprop paintings, and produced pictures in the style of Social Realism.
Vogeler's drawings and etchings, together with his designs for book illustrations and applied art (mirrors, lights, cutlery), were influenced by the Pre-Raphaelites and fell within the sphere of Art Nouveau.

Voigt, Otto Eduard
12.3.1870 Dresden – 14.1.1949 Meissen
Modeler and painter
Voigt completed an apprenticeship at Villeroy & Boch in Dresden and from 1890 to 1895 worked as a painter for the KPM Royal Porcelain Factory in Berlin. In 1896 he became a flower painter for the Meissen Royal Saxon Porcelain Factory, where he carried blue painting to new heights and remained an important member of the artistic team until his departure in 1932. He produced large numbers of painterly designs (plants, animals and landscapes) as well as tableware designs.

Voysey, Charles Francis Annesley
28.5.1857 Hessle, Yorkshire – 12.2.1941 Winchester
English architect, graphic artist, and artist-craftsman
Voysey studied architecture with J. P. Seddon at Dulwich College. In 1882 he started working as a freelance architect

and erected country houses in the London area for which he also designed interior furnishings, such as the furniture, wallpaper, textiles, tiles, and various pieces of equipment. He became a member of the Art Workers Guild in 1884 and his work was first exhibited at the Arts and Crafts exhibitions in London in 1893. In 1936 he was given the title Royal Designer for Industry and in 1940 was awarded a gold medal by the Royal Institute of British Architects.

Voysey's simple houses were designed to blend in with their surroundings and display a greater independence from historical styles than most buildings constructed around 1900. This is also true of his other areas of work: his furniture has a stronger leaning toward geometrical form and his metalwork is plainer in design than was usual for his day. Voysey seemed to anticipate the style of the 1920s. His architecture and forms of decoration influenced Charles Rennie Mackintosh and were instrumental in the development of the Modern Style. Voysey's work was copied almost to excess between the two world wars in England.

Wagner, Otto
13.7.1841 Penzing, near Vienna – 11.4.1918 Vienna
Austrian architect
Wagner studied at the Technical College in Vienna from 1857 to 1860 and at the Royal Academy of Architecture in Berlin from 1860 to 1861, and from 1861 to 1863 attended the School of Architecture at the Vienna Academy, where he later himself became a teacher from 1904 to 1912. His first buildings were villas in the style of the Florentine Renaissance. From 1893 he turned away from historicism and called for a new style suited to the needs of the modern day. In other words, he called for a language of form based on considerations of function, material and construction – one of the principles of modern architecture of the 1920s. He expanded his ideas in his book *Moderne Architektur* [Modern architecture] of 1896. His most important buildings in this new style are those for the Vienna Stadtbahn metropolitan railway (1894–1901) and the Austrian Post Office Savings Bank (1904–06).

Wagner was of major significance for the development of architecture around 1900 and a pioneer of modern architecture. His pupils, who included Joseph Maria Olbrich and Josef Hoffmann, developed his ideas even further. Alongside his activities as an architect, Wagner also produced designs for applied art, particularly during his membership of the Vienna Secession (1899–1905), which he left with the Klimt group.

Webb, Philip
12.1.1831 Oxford – 17.4.1915 Worth, Sussex
English architect, interior designer, and artist-craftsman
After an initial period of training in an advertising agency, Webb was taken on by the architect George Edmund Street, where he met his future employer and friend William Morris. In 1856 he started freelance work as an architect in London and from 1859 to 1860 designed The Red House for Morris in Bexley Heath in Kent. In 1862 he became a partner of the newly-founded Morris, Marshall, Faulkner and Company, for whom he designed interior furnishings even after he left the company in 1875. He was later active in the preservation of historical buildings, developing a new technique to help hinder further decay to buildings by filling out the substance of old walls with new building materials.

Webb was a chief representative of the Domestic Revival in England. In his residential buildings and country houses he sought to effect a similarity with the late medieval style without resorting to historicism. He also designed furniture, embroidery, jewelry, glass, carpets, and interior furnishings. Morris owes many of his designs for wallpaper and textiles to Webb.

Weissemburger, Lucien
1860–1929
French architect
Weissemburger started practising as an architect in Nancy in the 1880s. He first attracted attention in 1900, with the building of the Royer printing press in the rue de la Salpétrière in Nancy. As a result of this, he was commissioned to build the Villa Majorelle in Nancy in 1901. Weissemburger worked mainly in Nancy, commissions including a joint contract with Victor Prouvé for the Anciens Magasins Réunis in 1907 and the Hôtel-Brasserie Excelsior in 1910, which was fitted out by Majorelle.

Wennerberg, Gunnar G:son
1863 – 1914
Swedish painter and glass artist
As the son of the well-known composer Gunnar Wennerberg, who arranged the celebrated University of Uppsala *gluntar* student songs in the 1840s, Gunnar G:son Wennerberg started his career as a portraitist and flower painter. However, it was the animated floral decors which he executed for the Gustavsberg potteries and for Kosta Glasbruk which made his name. In Paris he had encountered the cased glasses of the École de Nancy and hoped to become a Swedish Gallé. His wish was fulfilled. In 1898 he became a designer with Kosta Glasbruk and over the next five years produced numerous cut and etched glasses – stylistically the purest expression of Art Nouveau. In 1908 he went back to Kosta one last time to develop more stylized and ornamented glassware for the 1909 Stockholm exhibition. In 1909 he moved to Paris.

Wennerberg was the most important Swedish glass artist of the turn of the century and won international acclaim.

Whistler, James Abbott McNeill
10.7.1834 Lowel, Massachusetts – 17.7.1903 London
American painter and graphic artist
Whistler studied painting with Charles Gleyre (1806–74) in Paris and moved to London in 1859. He is considered to be the most important portraitist and landscape painter of his era, whereby his etchings and lithographs are also extremely significant. He was also one of the first 19th-century artists to discover colored Japanese woodcuts. He is heralded one of the precursors of Art Nouveau on the basis of his decoration of the Peacock Room for a private client in London (ca. 1876).

Wiener, René
1855 Nancy – 1940
French bookbinder
Wiener came from a bookbinding family, and trained as a printer and gilder. He took up bookbinding only in 1883, working to designs by Victor Prouvé and Camille Martin. His success was international, and he gained commissions from Art Nouveau artists from Nancy, Brussels, and Paris. Around 1900, at the time of the World Exposition in Paris, he suddenly retired, and two years later, after the death of his daughter, gave up his craft altogether.

WMF – Württembergische Metallwarenfabrik
[Württemberg Metalware Factory]
Founded 1853 in Geislingen
German glass, ceramics, and metalware factory
In 1853 Daniel Straub and the Schweitzer brothers founded the Geislingen plated metal factory, producing household utensils of silverplated sheet copper. Following the departure of the Schweitzer brothers, the company merged with the silvering plant A. Ritter & Sohn, before being converted in 1880 into an incorporated society under the name of Württembergische Metallwarenfabrik. In 1883 it opened a glass works in Württemberg and in 1889 also began producing silverplated cutlery services. Small bronze sculptures were added to the product range in 1894. Around 1907, under the influence of Albert Mayer, production shifted to floral Art Nouveau forms, without thereby relinquishing the historicist style. The company commissioned its designs from the best-known German artists of the day, making it a champion of the marriage of art and industry. Still operating successfully today, the company has regularly modernized itself.

Wolfers, Philippe
16.4.1858 Brussels – 13.12.1929 Brussels
Belgian sculptor, craft artist, glass designer, and jeweler
Wolfers studied sculpture under Isidore de Rudder at the Academy in Brussels before entering the workshops of his father, the goldsmith Louis Wolfers (1820–92) in 1875. From 1880, he designed silver work and jewelry in a neo-Rococo style. His work during the 1880s reveals the influence of naturalism and Japanese art. In 1897, he went over exclusively to jewelry work, and at the International Exposition in Brussels exhibited pieces in ivory, a material that no one had worked with before. Around 1900, he opened branches of his jewelry business in Antwerp, Liège, Ghent, Budapest, Düsseldorf, London, and Paris. After 1910, his style became much more geometric, a tendency that had become quite dominant by the time he came to design the Salon for the Paris Arts and Crafts Exhibition in 1925, where every detail was designed by him: furniture, curtains, carpets, porcelain, and equipment. This was the apogee and at the same time the finale of his artistic career.

Wolfers's success is comparable with that of Lalique, and was of great importance for the entire art of Art Nouveau jewelry. His gold work, which is imbued with Symbolism and uses expensive materials, displays a degree of luxury that mirrors the Decadent consciousness of his time. From 1897 to 1905, he made a whole series of pieces consisting of 109 individual items, and was represented at numerous international exhibitions during the period. Alongside his work as a crafter of jewelry, he did glassware designs, among others for the leading glass manufacturer in Belgium, Val-Saint-Lambert. After 1908, he became more interested in sculpture.

Wright, Frank Lloyd
8.6.1869 Richland Center, Wisconsin – 9.4.1959 Phoenix, Arizona
American architect and applied artist
After studying at the University of Wisconsin in Madison (1885–87), from 1888 Wright worked for the architects Adler & Sullivan in Chicago, where from 1890 he was responsible for all housing designs. In 1893 he left Adler & Sullivan and opened his own office in Chicago. The Japanese Pavilion at the World's Columbian Exposition in Chicago that same year aroused his admiration for Japanese architecture. He became a passionate collector of Japanese prints. In 1905 he made his first trip to Japan and in 1906 organized an exhibition of his Hiroshige prints at the Art Institute of Chicago.

In 1909 and 1910 he traveled to Berlin and collaborated on the book *Ausgeführte Bauten und Entwürfe* [Executed buildings and designs] published by Wasmuth. In 1913 he was back in Japan to finalize the contract for the Imperial Hotel. In 1915 he subsequently opened an office in Tokyo, where his extended stay proved a turning point in his work. After his return to Chicago, he published a number of essays, including "Modern Architecture" (1931), and gave lectures at the university. In 1931 an exhibition on his work was staged in New York, Amsterdam, Berlin, Frankfurt, Brussels, Milwaukee, Eugene, and Chicago. In 1932 he established the Taliesien community in Wisconsin, where he withdrew from the public eye. Up till 1940 he worked chiefly as a teacher and theoretician, after which he again accepted numerous commissions.

Wright was a student of Sullivan and, in line with the latter's thesis that "form follows function", built houses whose forms arise out of their function, material, construction and – not least – their natural setting. A good example of the close relationship established between his houses and their environment can be seen in his Prairie Houses, as they are known – low buildings with flat roofs, built of wood and stone, combined with sweeping terraces and gardens. Wright was very much an isolated phenomenon in his own day, but his influence upon the development of numerous movements in architecture was significant. Since 1910 his writings and buildings have formed a standard part of the curriculum for all modern architects. His major works include Prairie Houses such as the Winslow House in River Forest, Illinois (1893) and the W. R. Heath House in Buffalo (1905), the Imperial Hotel in Tokyo (1916–20), the administrative building for the Johnson Wax Co. in Racine, Wisconsin (1936–39), Falling Water House, built over a waterfall in Bear Run, Pennsylvania (1937–39), and the Guggenheim Museum in New York (1956–59, designed 1943).

Zitzmann, Friedrich
19.9.1840 Steinach, Thuringia – 20.2.1906 Wiesbaden
German glassmaker
Zitzmann spent a number of years working in the glass factories on Murano, near Venice. In the years around 1890, he produced ornamental glasses executed in the Murano technique in a historicist style, which were displayed primarily in the Bayerischer Kunstgewerbeverein [Bavarian Applied Arts Association] in Munich. As a consequence of his collaboration with Karl Koepping in Berlin (1895–96), he

refined his technique. Drawing without permission upon Koepping's designs, he produced and sold stylized glasses in vegetal forms, leading to a dispute with Koepping and to the end of their collaboration after just a few months. Koepping's influence was still evident in his work even after their split, however. In 1897 Zitzmann showed iridescent glassware at the Munich Glass Palace exhibition and became a member of the Bavarian Applied Arts Association. He also taught glass-blowing at various colleges.

Zsolnay
Founded 1862 in Pécs
Hungarian ceramics factory
In 1865 Vilmos Zsolnay (1828–1900) took over the ceramic works which his brother, Ignaz Zsolnay, had founded in 1862 in Pécs. The company developed new iridescent and luster techniques, and above all metallic lusterware in various shades. It was best-known for its large vases with a colorful luster effect, decorated with scenes from *Grimm's Fairy Tales*. Zsolnay was one of the best-known ceramics factories of the period around 1900, and won many prestigious awards. After the death of Vilmos Zsolnay in 1900, his son Miklos (1857–1922) took over the running of the firm, which continued to be successful into the 1920s. In 1949 it passed into state ownership and was renamed the Porzelángyár Pécs.

Zumbusch, Ludwig von
17.7.1861 Munich – 28.2.1927 Munich
German painter and graphic artist
Ludwig von Zumbusch, son of the sculptor Kaspar von Zumbusch, studied under Wilhelm von Lindenschmit

(1829–95) at the Academy in Munich and under Adolphe William Bouguereau (1825–1905) and Robert-Fleury at the École des Beaux-Arts in Paris. In Munich he worked as a graphic artist and was one of the first contributors to the magazine *Jugend*. His oeuvre consists chiefly of portraits, in particular of children, as well as scenes of children and delicate pastel landscapes.

Zwollo, Frans (senior)
4.4.1872 Amsterdam – 1945 Amsterdam
Dutch gold and silversmith
Zwollo was an apprentice at the firm of Bonebakker in Amsterdam, where his father was artistic director, but he also went to drawing classes at the local art school. He acquired further training as a goldsmith in Paris and Brussels. In 1897 he settled in Amsterdam as a goldsmith, initially designing articles in a Louis Quatorze style, mainly for Bonebakker. In time, he shook off these constraints and designed jewelry, lighting, and appliances with decorative elements in a floral Art Nouveau style. From 1910, his style was pervaded by straight lines, and his decoration became more geometric. He took part in sundry exhibitions from 1900, winning a gold medal in Turin in 1902. Production remained very homogeneous right up to the end of the Second World War, continuing to be influenced by Zwollo's earliest work.

Bibliographical references

Adriani Götz. *Toulouse-Lautrec – Das gesamte graphische Werk*. Cologne, 1976.

Agate, May. *Madame Sarah*. New York, 1969.

Ahlers-Hestermann, Friedrich. *Stilwende – Aufbruch der Jugend um 1900*. Berlin, 1941.

Ahlers-Hestermann, Friedrich. *Bruno Paul, oder: die Wucht des Komischen*. Berlin, 1960.

Alexandre, Arsène. *Jean Carriès – imagier et potier*. Paris, 1895.

Alexandre, Arsène. *Puvis de Chavannes*. London – New York, 1905.

Altenberg, Peter. *Vita Ipsa*. Berlin, 1918.

Amaya, Mario. *Art Nouveau*. London – New York, 1966.

Anscombe, I. and C. Gere. *Arts and Crafts in Britain and America*. London, 1978.

Apollonio, Umbro. *Der Futurismus* [Futurism]. Cologne, 1972.

Arnold, Matthias. *Edvard Munch*. Hamburg, 1986.

Ashbee, Charles Robert. *A Short History of the Guild and School of Handicraft*. London, 1890.

Ashbee, Charles Robert. *Craftsmanship in Competitive Industry*. London, 1908.

Ashbee, Charles Robert. *Frank Lloyd Wright – Eine Studie zu seiner Würdigung* [A study in his honor]. Berlin, 1911.

Bahr, Hermann. *Secession*. Vienna, 1900.

Bahr, Hermann. *Rede über Klimt*. Vienna, 1901.

Bairata, E. and D. Riva. *Giuseppe Sommaruga*. Milan, 1982.

Bajot, Edouard. *L'Art Nouveau – Décoration et Ameublement*. Paris, 1898.

Bangert, Albrecht. *Thonet-Möbel*. Munich, 1979.

Bangert, Albrecht. *Jugendstil – Art Déco, Schmuck und Metallarbeiten*. Munich, 1981.

Bangert, Albrecht and Gabriele Fahr-Becker. *Jugendstil – Möbel und Glas, Schmuck und Malerei*. Munich, 1992.

Bangert, Albrecht and Gabriele Sterner. *Jugendstil – Art Déco*. Munich, 1979.

Barati, E., R. Bossaglia, R. and M. Rosci. *L'Italia Liberty*. Milan, 1973.

Barloewen, Constantin von and Kai Werhahn-Mees (eds.). *Japan und der Westen*. 3 vols, Frankfurt/Main, 1986.

Barten, Sigrid. *René Lalique – Schmuck und Objets d'art*. Munich, 1978.

Bassegoda Nonell, Juan. *Domènech i Montaner*. Barcelona, 1981.

Baudelaire, Charles. *Les Fleurs du mal*. Paris, 1857.

Baudelaire, Charles. *Oeuvres Posthumes*. Paris, 1908. In *Journaux Intimes*. Edited by Adolphe van Bever. Paris, 1920.

Bauer, Roger (ed.). *Fin de siècle – Zur Literatur und Kunst der Jahrhundertwende*. Frankfurt/Main, 1977.

Bayard, Emile. *Le Style moderne – L'Art reconnaître les styles*. Paris, 1919.

Behrendt, Walter. *Der Kampf um den Stil in Kunstgewerbe und Architektur*. Berlin, 1920.

Behrens, Peter. *Feste des Lebens und der Kunst*. Jena, 1900.

Bell, Malcolm. *Sir Edward Burne-Jones – A Record and a Review*. London, 1892.

Benevolo, Leonardo. *Geschichte der Architektur des 19. und 20. Jahrhunderts* (History of 19th- and 20th-century Architecture). 2 vols, Munich, 1978.

Berlage, Hendrik Petrus. *Gedanken über den Stil in der Baukunst* [Thoughts on style in architecture]. Leipzig, 1905.

Bernard, Sacha. *A l'ombre de Marcel Proust*. Paris, 1978.

Bertsch, Georg C., Matthias Dietz and Barbara Friedrich. *Euro-Design-Guide*. Munich, 1991.

Bierbaum, Otto Julius. *Stuck*. Bielefeld – Leipzig, 1899.

Bing, Samuel. *Japanischer Formenschatz*. Hamburg, 1989.

Bjerke, Øivind Storm. *Harald Sohlberg – En Somhetens Maler*. Viborg, 1991.

Blaser, Werner. *Furniture as Architecture – Architektur im Möbel*. Zürich, 1985.

Blount, Berniece and Henry Blount. *French Cameo Glass*. Des Moines, 1967.

Boccioni, Umberto. *Bildnerischer Dynamismus* [Visual dynamism]. Milan, 1913.

Boccioni, Umberto. *Futuristische Malerei und Skulptur* [Futuristic painting and sculpture]. Milan, 1914.

Bohigas, Oriol. *Arquitectura modernista*. Barcelona, 1968.

Borisowa, Helena A. and Grigori J. Sternin. *Jugendstil in Rußland*. Stuttgart, 1988.

Borsi, Franco. *Bruxelles 1900*. Brussels, 1979.

Borsi, Franco and E. Godoli. *Paris 1900*. Brussels, 1976.

Borsi, Franco and Paolo Portoghesi. *Victor Horta*. Rome – Bari, 1982.

Bott, Gerhard. *Jugendstil in Darmstadt um 1900*. Darmstadt, 1962.

Bott, Gerhard (ed.). *Von Morris zum Bauhaus – Eine Kunst gegründet auf Einfachheit*. Hanau, 1977.

Bott, Gerhard (ed.). *The German Werkbund – The Politics of Reform in the Applied Arts*. Princeton, 1978.

Boutet, Frédéric. *Seltsame Masken* (Strange Masks). Munich, 1913.

Brandstätter, Christian. *Buchumschläge des Jugendstils*. Dortmund, 1981.

Brandy-Jones, John. *C. F. A. Voysey – Architect and Designer 1857–1941*. London, 1987.

Breicha, Otto and Gerhard Fritsch (eds.). *Finale und Auftakt, Wien 1898–1914*. Salzburg, 1964.

Bröhan, Torsten. *Glaskunst der Moderne*. Munich, 1992.

Brühl, Georg. *Jugendstil in Chemnitz – Die Villa Esche von Henry van de Velde*. Munich, 1991.

Brunhammer, Yvonne, K. Bussman, K. Koch and R. Koch. *Hector Guimard – Architektur in Paris um 1900*. Münster, 1975.

Buchanan, William (ed.). *Mackintosh's Masterwork – The Glasgow School of Art*. Glasgow, 1989.

Buchert, Josephe. *Fleurs de fantaisie*. Paris, n.d.

Buchheim, Lothar Günther. *Jugendstilplakate*. Feldafing, 1969.

Buddensieg, T. and H. Rogge. *Industrie Kultur – Peter Behrens und die AEG 1907–1914*. Berlin, 1979.

Carrigan, Kristine O. *Ruskin on Architecture – His Thought and Influence*. Madison, 1973.

Champigneulle, Bernard. *Art Nouveau*. New York, 1976.

Cirici Pellicer, A. *El Arte Modernista Catalan*. Barcelona, 1951.

Clouzot, Henri. *Daum verrerie d'art*. Nancy, 1930.

Conrad, Michael Georg, Anna Crossant-Rust and Hans Brandenburg (eds.). *Otto Julius Bierbaum zum Gedächtnis. Festschrift*. Munich, 1912.

Conrads, Ulrich. *Programme und Manifeste zur Architektur des 20. Jahrhunderts*. Berlin – Frankfurt/Main – Vienna, 1964.

Cook, Theodore A. *The Curves of Life*. New York, 1914.

Cousin, Victor. *Cours de philosophie*. Collected lectures, published in Paris from 1826.

Crane, Walter. *Linie und Form* [Line and Form]. Leipzig, 1901.

Cremona, Italo. *Die Zeit des Jugendstils* [The Art Nouveau era]. Munich – Vienna, 1966.

Curtius, Ernst Robert. *Französischer Geist im 20. Jahrhundert*. Marburg, 1952.

D'Annunzio, Gabriele. *Lust*. Zürich, 1994.

Dauberville, Jean and Henry Dauberville. *Bonnard – catalogue raisonné de l'oeuvre peint*. Paris, 1965.

Davey, Peter. *Architecture in the Arts and Crafts Movement*. New York, 1980.

Dehmel, Richard. *Ausgewählte Briefe 1883–1902*. Berlin, 1923.

Dewiel, Lydia. *Schmuck vom Klassizismus bis zum Art Déco*. Munich, 1979.

Dierkens-Aubry, Françoise. *Hortamuseum*. Tielt, 1990.

Dierkens-Aubry, Françoise and Jos Vandenbreeden. *Jugendstil in Belgien – Architektur und Interieurs* [Art Nouveau in Belgium]. Tielt, 1994.

Donelly, Marian C. *Architecture in the Scandinavian Countries*. London, 1922.

Dortu, M. G. *Toulouse-Lautrec et son oeuvre*. New York, 1971.

Drexler, Arthur. *The Architecture of Japan*. New York, 1955.

Duncan, Alastair. *Lampen Lüster Leuchter – Jugendstil Art Déco* [Lamps Chandeliers Lighting]. Munich, 1979.

Duncan, Alastair and Georges de Bartha. *Jugendstil und Art Déco – Bucheinbände*. Munich, 1989.

Eckmann, Otto. *Neue Formen – Dekorative Entwürfe für die Praxis*. Berlin, 1897.

Endell, August. *Um die Schönheit – Eine Paraphrase über die Münchener Kunstausstellung 1896*. Munich, 1896.

Engen, Luc de. *Le Verre en Belgique – Des origines à nos jours*. Antwerp, 1989.

Eschmann, Karl. *Jugendstil – Ursprünge, Folgen*. Herm, 1976.

Faber, Tobias. *Dansk Arkitektur*. Copenhagen, 1977.

Fahr-Becker, Gabriele. *Wiener Werkstätte 1903–1932* (English edition). Cologne, 1995.

Falk, Fritz. *Europäischer Schmuck vom Historismus biz zum Jugendstil*. Königsbach-Stein, 1985.

Fiell, Charlotte and Peter Fiell. *Charles Rennie Mackintosh*. Cologne, 1995.

Fierens, Paul. *La Tristesse contemporaine*. Paris, 1924.

Fischer, Wolfgang Georg. *Gustav Klimt und Emilie Flöge*. Vienna, 1987.

Flaubert, Gustave. *Salammbô*. Paris, 1862.

Fliedel, Gottfried. *Gustav Klimt*. Cologne, 1991.

Flögl, Mathilde (ed.). *Die Wiener Werkstätte 1903–1928, Modernes Kunstgewerbe und sein Weg*. Silver Jubilee issue, Vienna, 1929.

Fontainas, André. *Mes souvenirs du Symbolisme*. Paris, 1924.

Ford, Richard. *Handbook for Travellers in Spain*. London, 1845.

Fraipont, G. *La Fleur et ses applications décoratives*. Paris, n.d.

Frank, Josef. *Zu Josef Hoffmanns 60. Geburtstage*. Ed by Österreichischen Werkbund, Vienna, 1930.

Frey, D. *Englisches Wesen in der bildenden Kunst*. Stuttgart – Berlin, 1942.

Friedell, Egon. *Jubilee issue celebrating 25 years of the Wiener Werkstätte*. Vienna, 1928.

Frottier, Elisabeth. *Michael Powolny – Keramik und Glas aus Wien 1900–1950*. Vienna – Cologne, 1990.

Fuller, Loïe. *Quinze ans de ma vie*. Paris, 1908.

Gallé, Émile. *Notice sur la production du Verre*. Nancy, 1884.

Gallé, Émile. *Écrits pour l'Art, 1884–1889*. Edited by Henriette Gallé-Grimm, Paris, 1909.

Garner, Philippe. *Emile Gallé*. Munich, 1979.

Garner, Philippe. *Jugendstil-Glas*. Dortmund, 1981.

Gasser, Manuel. *München um 1900*. Berne, 1977.

George, Stefan. *Werke*. Ed. by Helmut Küpper, 2 vols, Munich, 1958.

George, Stefan. *Der Dichter und sein Kreis*. Marbach, 1968.

Geretsegger, H. and M. Peintner. *Otto Wagner*. Salzburg – Vienna, 1964.

Gide, André (ed.). *Anthologie de la Poésie Française*. Paris, 1949.

Gilot, Françoise. *Leben mit Picasso* [Life with Picasso]. Munich, 1965.

Goethe, Johann Wolfgang von. *Maximen und Reflexionen*. Frankfurt/Main, 1840.

Graf, Hansjörg (ed.). *Der kleine Salon*. Stuttgart, 1970.

Grasset, Eugène Samuel. *La Plante et ses applications ornementales*. Paris, 1897–99.

Graul, Richard. *Die Krisis im Kunstgewerbe*. Leipzig, 1901.

Gravagnuolo, Benedetto. *Adolf Loos – Theory and Works*. New York, 1982.

Gresleri, Giuliano. *Josef Hoffmann*. Bologna – New York, 1985.

Gropius, Tange, Ishimoto. *Katsura – Tradition and Creation in Japanese Architecture*. New Haven, 1960.

Grover, Ray and Lee Grover. *Art Glass Nouveau*. Rutland, Vermont, n.d.

Guerrand, Roger Henri. *L'Art Nouveau en Europe*. Paris, 1967.

Günther, Sonja. *Intérieurs um 1900*. Munich, 1971.

Günther, Sonja. *Josef Hoffman 1870–1956*. Karlsruhe, 1972.

Gurlitt, Cornelius. *Im Bürgerhaus*. Dresden, 1887.

Gysling-Billeter, Erika. *Objekte des Jugendstils*. Berne, 1975.

Haack, Friedrich. *Grundriss der Kunstgeschichte – Die Kunst des XIX. Jahrhunderts*. Esslingen am Neckar, 1904.

Haan, Hilde de and Ids Haagsma. *Architects in Competition – International Architectural Competitions of the last 200 Years*. London, 1988.

Haeckel, Ernst. *Kunstformen der Natur*. Leipzig – Vienna, 1899–1904.

Haftmann, Werner. *Malerei im 20. Jahrhundert*. Munich, 1954.

Hahn-Woernle, Birgit. *Bernhard Pankok*. Stuttgart, 1973.

Halbe, Max. *Jahrhundertwende*. Munich, 1926.

Hamann, Richard and Jost Hermand. *Stilkunst um 1900*. Berlin, 1967.

Hård af Segerstad, Ulf. *Skandinavische Gebrauchskunst*. Stockholm – Frankfurt/Main, 1961.

Harris, Margaret. *Loïe Fuller*. Richmond, 1979.

(Hartwig, Josef), no author. *Leben und Meinungen des Bildhauers Josef Hartwig*. Frankfurt/Main, 1955.

Hase, Ulrike von. *Schmuck in Deutschland und Österreich, 1895–1941*. Munich, 1977.

Hausen, Marika, Kirmo Mikkola, Anna-Lisa Amberg and Tyttii Vatto. *Eliel Saarinen – Projects 1896–1923*. Hamburg, 1990.

Heinmann, Fritz. *Symbolische Kunst*. Dissertation, Berlin, 1926.

Heise, Carl G. *Die Kunst des 20. Jahrhunderts – Malerei, Plastik, Raum, Gerät*. Munich, 1957.

Henderson, Philip. *William Morris – His Life, Work and Friends*. London, 1967.

Henning-Schefold, Monika. *Struktur und Dekoration*. Winterthur, 1969.

Hermand, Jost. *Jugendstil/Art Nouveau – research report 1918–1964*. Stuttgart, 1965.

Hevesi, Ludwig. *Acht Jahre Sezession (März 1897–Juni 1905) – Kritik, Polemik, Chronik*. Vienna, 1906.

Hevesi, Ludwig. *Altkunst – Neukunst*. Vienna, 1909.

Hillman, James. *Der Mythos der Analyse* [The myth of analysis]. Frankfurt/Main, 1972.

Himmelheber, Georg. *Die Kunst des deutschen Möbels. Vol. 3: Klassizismus – Historismus – Jugendstil*. Munich, 1973.

Hocke, Gustav René. *Die Welt als Labyrinth*. Reinbek, Hamburg, 1961.

Hoeber, Fritz. `Peter Behrens. Munich, 1913.

Hoffmann, Josef. *Arbeitsprogramm der Wiener Werkstätte*. Vienna, 1905.

Hofmann, Jacqueline and Werner Hofmann (eds.). *Wien*. Vienna – Munich, 1956.

Hofmann, Werner. *Von der Nachahmung zur Erfindung der Wirklichkeit – Die schöpferische Befreiung der Kunst 1890–1917*. Cologne, 1970.

Hofstätter, Hans Hermann. *Geschichte der europäischen Jugendstilmalerei*. Cologne, 1963.

Hofstätter, Hans Hermann. *Jugendstil – Druckkunst (printed art)*. Baden-Baden, 1973.

Hofstätter, Hans Hermann. *Aubrey Beardsley – Zeichnungen (drawings)*. Cologne, 1977.

Hofstätter, Hans Hermann. *Symbolismus und die Kunst der Jahrhundertwende*. Cologne, 1978.

Hollamby, Edward. *Red House – Architecture in Detail*. Harlow, 1991.

Hollander, Hans. *Musik und Jugendstil*. Zürich, 1975.

Howarth, Thomas. *Charles Rennie Mackintosh and the Modern Movement*. London, 1952.

Hutter, Heribert. *Jugendstil*. Vienna, 1965.

Huysmans, Joris-Karl. *A rebours*. Brussels, 1884. (Engl. edn?)

Jaffé, Hans. *Piet Mondrian*. Cologne, 1971.

Jencks, Charles. *Le Corbusier and the Tragic View of Architecture*. London, 1973.

Jones, Owen. *Grammar of Ornament*. London, 1918.

Jørgensen, Lisbet Balslev. *Danmarks Arkitektur*. Copenhagen, 1979.

Jost, Dominik. *Literarischer Jugendstil*. Stuttgart, 1980.

Joyant, Maurice. *Henri de Toulouse-Lautrec 1864–1901, Peintre*. Paris, 1926.

Juyot, Paul. *Louis Majorelle – Artiste Décorateur, Maître ébéniste*. Nancy, 1926.

Kemp, W. *John Ruskin – Leben und Werk* [Life and work]. Munich, 1983.

Kessler, Harry Graf. *Gesichter und Zeiten*. Berlin, 1935.

Kessler, Harry Graf. *Aus den Tagebüchern*. Frankfurt/Main, 1965.

Klee, Paul. *Tagebücher (diaries) 1889–1918*. Ed. by Felix Klee, Cologne, 1957.

Knipping, J. B. *Jan Toorop*. Amsterdam, 1947.

Koch, Robert. *Louis C. Tiffany – Rebel in Glass*. New York, 1964.

Kolbe, Jürgen. *Heller Zauber – Thomas Mann in München 1894–1933*. Munich, 1987.

Kornwolf, James D. *M. H. Baillie Scott and the Arts and Crafts Movement*. Baltimore, 1972.

Kubly, Vincent Frederick. *Thomas Theodor Heine 1867–1948, The Satirist as an Artist*. Dissertation, Wisconsin, 1969.

Kühnel, Ernst. *Die Arabeske*. Wiesbaden, 1949.

Kurrent, Friedrich. *Das Palais Stoclet*. Salzburg, 1991.

Lanoux, Armand. *Amour 1900*. Hamburg, 1964.

Le Corbusier. *Vers une architecture*. Paris, 1958.

Legrand, Francine-Claire. *Le Symbolisme en Europe*. Brussels, 1971.

Lehner, Margot. *Als München noch leuchtete*. Munich, 1978.

Leistikow, Walter. *Moderne Kunst in Paris*. N.p., n.d.

Lenning, Henry F. *Julius Meier-Graefe*. New York, 1942.

Lenning, Henry F. *Art Nouveau*. The Hague, 1951.

Lessing, Julius. *Berichte von der Pariser Weltausstellung 1878*. N.p., 1878.

Lichtwark, Alfred. *Briefe an die Kommission für die Verwaltung der Kunsthalle*. Ed. by Gustav Pauli, Hamburg, 1923.

Loos, Adolf. *Ornament und Verbrechen*. Vienna, 1908.

Loos, Adolf. *Ins Leere gesprochen 1897–1900*. Innsbruck, 1931.

Loos, Adolf. *Trotzdem 1900–1930*. Sammlung der Dokumente des Kampfes. Innsbruck, 1931.

Loos, Adolf. *Sämtliche Schriften* [collected works]. Edited by Franz Glück, 2 vols, Vienna – Munich, 1962.

Lüthi, Max. *Das europäische Volksmärchen*. Berne, 1947.

Lux, Joseph August. *Die moderne Wohnung und ihre Ausstattung*. Vienna, 1905.

Mackay, James. *Kunst und Kunsthandwerk der Jahrhundertwende* [Fin-de-siècle art & crafts]. Munich, 1975.

Madsen, Karl. *Japansk Malerkunst*. Copenhagen, 1885.

Madsen, Karl. *Thorvald Bindesbøll*. Copenhagen, 1943.

Madsen, Stephan Tschudi. *Sources of Art Nouveau*. Oslo, 1956.

Madsen, Stephan Tschudi. *Jugendstil – Europäische Kunst der Jahrhundertwende*. Munich, 1967.

Mann, Golo. *Der letzte Großherzog*. Darmstadt, 1977.

Mann, Thomas. *Gladius Dei*. Munich, 1902.

Mann, Thomas. *Betrachtungen eines Unpolitischen*. Munich, 1918.

Marchlewski, Julian. *Sezession und Jugendstil – Kritiken um 1900*. Dresden, 1974.

Martin, Timo and Douglas Sivén. *Akseli Gallen-Kallela*. Helsinki, 1984.

Martinell, César. *Gaudí – His Life, His Theories, His Work*. Barcelona, 1975.

Masini, Lara Vinca. *Art Nouveau*. Florence, 1976.

Maurois, André. *Engländer* (Les Anglais?). Munich, 1933.

McKean, Hugh F. *Louis Comfort Tiffany*. Weingarten, 1981.

Meier-Graefe, Julius. *Die Weltausstellung in Paris 1900*. Paris – Leipzig, 1900.

Meier-Graefe, Julius. *Entwicklungsgeschichte der modernen Kunst – Vergleichende Betrachtung der bildenden Künste zu einer neuen Ästhetik*. 3 vols, Stuttgart, 1904.

Meier-Graefe, Julius. *Die doppelte Kurve – Essays*. Berlin, 1924.

Mendelsohn, Erich. *Das Problem einer neuen Baukunst*. Berlin, 1919.

Miyake, Riichi. *Stile Liberty and Orientalism*. Tokyo, 1988.

Miyake, Riichi. *Ein Streifzug durch den europäischen Jugendstil*. Dortmund, 1991.

Moorhouse, Jonathan. *Helsinki Jugendstil Architecture 1895–1915*. Helsinki, 1987.

Morris, William and Sir Edward Burne-Jones. *Ornamentation and Illustrations from the Kelmscott Chaucer*. New York, 1973.

Mucha, Alfons. *Drei Äußerungen zum Leben und Werk* [Three statements on his life and work]. Brno, 1936.

Mucha, Jiri. *Alfons Mucha – His Life and Art*. London, 1966.

Müller, Albin. *Aus meinem Leben*. Manuscript (typed), Darmstadt, n.d. (ca. 1940).

Müller, Dorothee. *Klassiker des modernen Möbeldesign*. Munich, 1980.

Musil, Robert. *Der Mann ohne Eigenschaften* [The man without qualities]. Hamburg, 1952.

Musil, Robert. *Tagebücher (Diaries)*. Ed. by Adolf Frisé, Reinbek, Hamburg, 1976.

Muther, Richard. *Geschichte der Malerei im 19. Jahrhundert*. 3 vols, Munich, 1893–94.

Muthesius, Hermann. *Das Englische Haus*. Berlin, 1904.

Muthesius, Hermann. *Kunstgewerbe und Architektur*. Jena, 1907.

Naumann, Friedrich. *Deutsche Gewerbekunst*. Berlin, 1908.

Nebehay, Christian M. *Gustav Klimt – Sein Leben nach zeitgenössischen Berichten und Quellen*. Munich, 1976.

Nebehay, Christian M. *Egon Schiele – Von der Skizze zum Bild. Die Skizzenbücher* (The Sketchbooks). Vienna – Munich, 1989.

Neumeister, Erdman. *Thomas Mann*. Bonn, 1972.

Neuwirth, Waltraud. *Das Glas des Jugendstils – Sammlung des Österreichische Museums für angewandte Kunst, Wien*. Vienna, 1973.

Neuwirth, Waltraud. *Österreichische Keramik des Jugendstils*. Vienna, 1974.

Neuwirth, Waltraud. *Wiener Werkstätte – Avantgarde, Art Déco, Industrial Design*. Vienna, 1984.

Nietzsche, Friedrich. *Also sprach Zarathustra*. Ed. by Karl Schlechta, Munich, 1955.

Noever, Peter and Oswald Oberhuber (eds.). *Josef Hoffmann – Ornament zwischen Hoffnung und Verbrechen*. Vienna, 1987.

Obrist, Hermann. *Zweckmäßig oder Phantasievoll*. Munich, 1901.

Obrist, Hermann. *Neue Möglichkeiten in der bildenden Kunst*. Leipzig, 1903.

Oeser, Hermann. *Von Menschen, von Bildern und Büchern*. Heilbronn, 1922.

Olbrich, Joseph Maria. *Ideen von Olbrich*. Vienna, 1900.

Osthaus, Karl Ernst. *Leben und Werk*. Recklinghausen, 1971.

Ottomeyer, Hans. *Jugendstilmöbel – Möbelsammlung des Müncher*. Munich, 1988.

Pabst, Michael. *Wiener Grafik um 1900*. Munich, 1984.

Palau i Fabre, Josep. *Picasso – Kindheit und Jugend eines Genies, 1881–1907* [Childhood and youth of a genius]. Munich, 1981.

Paley, Morton O. *William Blake*. London, 1978.

Pane, Roberto. *Antoni Gaudi*. Milan, 1982.

Panofsky, Erwin. *Meaning in the Visual Arts*. New York, 1955.

Paret, P. *Die Berliner Secession – Moderne Kunst und ihre Feinde im Kaiserlichen Deutschland*. Berlin, 1981.

Pazaurek, Gustav Edmund. *Kunstgläser der Gegenwart*. Leipzig, 1925.

Pelichet, Edgar. *La Céramique Art Nouveau*. Lausanne, 1976.

Pevsner, Nikolaus. *Charles Rennie Mackintosh*. Milan, 1950.

Pevsner, Nikolaus. *Pioneers of Modern Design*. New York, 1949.

Polak, Ada. *Modern Glass*. London, 1962.

Polak, Bettina. *Het fin-de-siècle in de Nederlandse schilderkunst – de symbolistische beweging 1890–1900*. The Hague, 1955.

Pope, Alexander. *Miscellanies*. London, 1728.

Portoghesi, Paolo. *Hôtel van Eetvelde, Brussels 1894–1901*. Tokyo, 1977.

Posener, Julius. *Anfänge des Funktionalismus*. Berlin – Frankfurt/Main – Vienna, 1964.

Posener, Julius. *Berlage und Dudok*. Lecture in *48 Arch+*, Aachen, 1979.

Posener, Julius. *Frank Lloyd Wright I – Vorlesungen zur Geschichte der Neuen Architektur*. In *48 Arch+*, special issue on 75th birthday of Julius Posener, Aachen, 1979.

Posener, Julius. *Otto Wagner – Die Rolle Hans Poelzigs vor 1918. Vorlesungen zur Geschichte der Neuen Architektur II – Die Architektur der Reform (1900–1924)*. In *53 Arch+*, Aachen, 1980.

Posener, Julius. *Jugendstil*. Lecture in *59 Arch+*, Aachen, 1981.

Posener, Julius. *Vorlesungen zur Geschichte der Neuen Architektur III*. Includes *Peter Behrens I, Charles Rennie Mackintosh – Das englische Landhaus, William Morris und die Folgen*. In *59 Arch+*, Aachen, 1981.

Proust, Marcel. *A la recherche du temps perdu*. Paris, 1913–27.

Rathke, Ewald. *Jugendstil*. Frankfurt, 1958.

Reade, Brian. *Aubrey Beardsley*. Stuttgart, 1969.

Rheims, Maurice. *The Flowering of Art Nouveau*. New York, 1966.

Richards, James M. and Nikolaus Pevsner (eds.). *The Anti-Rationalists*. London, 1973.

Ridder, André de. *George Minne*. Antwerp, 1947.

Rief, Hans H. *Heinrich Vogeler – Das graphische Werk*. Bremen, 1974.

Rilke, Rainer Maria. *Über Kunst*. Munich, 1898.

Rilke, Rainer Maria. *Worpswede*. Bielefeld – Leipzig, 1903.

Rochowanski, Leopold Wolfgang. *Der Formwille der Zeit in der angewandten Kunst*. Vienna, 1922.

Rochowanski, Leopold Wolfgang (ed.). *Agathon – Almanach auf das Jahr 48 des 20. Jahrhunderts*. Vienna, 1947.

Rochowanski, Leopold Wolfgang. *Josef Hoffmann*. Vienna, 1950.

Rosenhagen, Hans. *Münchens Niedergang als Kunststadt*. Munich, 1902.

Rousseau, Jean-Jacques. *Discours sur les sciences et les arts*. Paris, 1750.

Ruskin, John. *The Seven Lamps of Architecture*. London, 1849.

Ruskin, John and Dante Gabriel Rossetti. *Pre-Raphaelism Papers 1854–1862*. New York – London, 1899.

Russel, Frank (ed.). *Art Nouveau Architecture*. London, 1979.

Rykwert, Joseph. *Ornament ist kein Verbrechen*. Cologne, 1983.

Sailer, Anton. *Franz von Stuck – Ein Lebensmärchen*. Munich, 1969.

Saitschik, Robert. *Dichter und Denker*. Zürich, 1949.

Salles, G. S. *Adolphe Stoclet Collection*. Brussels, 1956.

Salten, Felix. *Geister der Zeit – Erlebnisse*. Vienna – Leipzig, 1924.

Schinkel, Karl Friedrich. *Aus Schinkels Nachlaß* (unpublished papers). Ed. by Alfred von Wolzogen, Berlin, 1862.

Schmalenbach, Fritz. *Jugendstil – Ein Beitrag zur Geschichte der Flächenkunst*. Dissertation, Münster, 1934.

Schmidt, Paul Ferdinand. *Festschrift zum 25jährigen Regierungsjubiläum seiner Königlichen Hoheit des Großherzogs Ernst Ludwig von Hessen und bei Rhein* [Silver Jubilee Festschrift for Grand Duke Ernst Ludwig of Hesse]. Leipzig, 1917.

Schmutzler, Robert. *Art Nouveau – Jugendstil*. Stuttgart, 1962.

Schneede, Uwe M. *Umberto Boccioni*. Stuttgart, 1994.

Schotten, Frits. *Brieven tussen Jan Eissenloeffel en A. J. M. Gondriaan 1918–1929*. The Hague, 1989.

Schröder, Rudolf Alexander. *Aus Kindheit und Jugend*. Munich, 1934.

Schweiger, Werner J. *Wiener Werkstätte – Design in Vienna 1903–1932*. London, 1984.

Sedlmayr, Hans. *Die Revolution der modernen Kunst*. Cologne, 1985.

Sekler, Eduard F. *Josef Hoffmann – Das architektonische Werk*. Salzburg – Vienna, 1982.

Seling, Helmut (ed.). *Jugendstil – Der Weg ins 20. Jahrhundert*. Foreword by Kurt Bauch. Heidelberg – Munich, 1959.

Selle, Gert. *Jugendstil und Kunst-Industrie – Zur Ökonomie und Ästhetik des Kunstgewerbes um 1900*. Ravensburg, 1974.

Selle, Gert. *Die Geschichte des Design in Deutschland von 1870 bis heute*. Cologne, 1978.

Sembach, Klaus-Jürgen: *Jugendstil*. Cologne, 1978.

Semper, Gottfried. *Vorläufige Bemerkungen*. N.p., 1834.

Semper, Gottfried. *Wissenschaft – Industrie – Kunst*. Mainz – Berlin, 1866.

Service, Alastair (ed.) *London 1900*. London, 1979.

Sherman, Paul. *Louis H. Sullivan – Ein amerikanischer Architekt und Denker*. Berlin – Frankfurt/Main, 1963.

Simon, Hans Ulrich. *Sezessionismus*. Stuttgart, 1976.

Simon, V. (ed.). *Eberhard von Bodenhausen und Harry Graf Kessler – Ein Briefwechsel (letters) 1894–1918*. Marbach, 1978.

Singelenberg, Pieter. *H. P. Berlage – Idea and Style*. Utrecht, 1972.

Smith, John B. *The Golden Age of Finnish Art*. Helsinki, 1985.

Spencer, Robin. *Aesthetic Movement*. London, 1972.

Spengler, Oswald. *Der Untergang des Abendlandes – Umrisse einer Morphologie der Weltgeschichte*. Ed. by Helmut Werner, Munich, 1959.

Stempel, Ute. Postface to German edition of Gabriele D'Annunzio: *Lust (Il piacere)*. Zürich, 1994.

Sternberger, Dolf. *Über den Jugendstil und andere Essays*. Hamburg, 1956.

Sterner, Gabriele. *Jugendstil – Kunstformen zwischen Individualismus und Massengesellschaft*. Cologne, 1975.

Sterner, Gabriele. *Barcelona – Antoní Gaudí y Cornet, Architektur als Ereignis*. Cologne, 1979.

Sterner, Gabriele. *Oscar Wilde – Salome*. Dortmund, 1979.

Sterner, Gabriele. *Zinn vom Mittelalter bis zur Gegenwart*. Munich, 1979.

Sterner, Gabriele. *Jugendstil-Graphik*. Cologne, 1980.

Sterner, Gabriele. *Der Jugendstil – Lebens- und Kunstformen um 1900, Künstler, Zentren, Programme*. Düsseldorf, 1985.

Störig, Hans Joachim. *Kleine Weltgeschichte der Philosophie*. 2 vols, Stuttgart, 1950.

Straaten, Evert van. *Theo van Doesburg*. The Hague, 1983.

Sullivan, Louis Henry. *A System of Architectural Ornament According with a Philosophy of Man's Power*. New York, 1924??

Sutton, Denys. *James McNeill Whistler – Gemälde, Aquarelle, Pastelle und Radierungen* [Paintings, watercolors, pastel drawings and etchings]. Cologne, 1967.

Tahara, Keiichi. *Jugendstil – Aufbruch zu einer neuen Architektur*. Dortmund, 1991.

Taylor, J. R. *The Art Nouveau Book in Britain*. London, 1966.

Thamer, J. *Zwischen Historismus und Jugendstil – Zur Ausstattung der Zeitschrift "Pan" 1895–1900*. Frankfurt/Main, 1980.

Thiis, Jens. *Gerhard Munthe*. Trondheim, 1904.

Tietze, Hans. *Gustav Klimts Persönlichkeit*. Vienna, 1919.

Torres Garcia, Joaquim. *Mestre Antoni Gaudí – Universalismo constructivo*. Montevideo, 1962.

Traeger, Jörg. *Philipp Otto Runge und sein Werk*. Munich, 1975.

Uecker, Wolf. *Lampen und Leuchter – Art Nouveau und Art Déco*. Herrsching (Bavaria), 1978.

Uhland, Ludwig. *Gesammelte Werke (collected works)*. Ed. by H. Fischer, 6 vols, Stuttgart, 1892.

Vandenbreeden, Jos and Françoise Dierkens-Aubry. *De 19de Eeuw in België*. Tielt, 1995.

Velde, Henry van de. *Kunstgewerbliche Laienpredigten* [Lay sermons for arts & crafts]. Leipzig – Berlin, 1902.

Velde, Henry van de. *Zum neuen Stil* [On the new style]. Selected writings chosen and introduced by Hans Curjel, Munich, 1955.

Velde, Henry van de. *Geschichte meines Lebens.* [Story of my life]. Edited by Hans Curjel, Munich, 1962.

Verlaine, Paul. *Confessions*. Paris, 1895.

Verneuil, M. P. *L'Animal dans la décoration*. Paris, 1898.

Viehoff, Horst. *Goethes Leben*. 4 vols, Stuttgart, 1847–54.

Viollet-le-Duc, Eugène. *Dictionnaire raisonné de l'architecture française*. Paris, 1854–69.

Vogue, Emile de. *Remarques sur l'exposition de 1889*. Paris, 1889.

Wagner, Otto. *Die Baukunst unserer Zeit – Dem Baukunstjünger ein Führer auf diesem Kunstgebiete*. Vienna, 1914.

Wais, Kurt. *Mallarmé*. Munich, 1938.

Waldschmidt, Wolfram. *Dante Gabriel Rossetti*. Jena – Leipzig, 1905.

Waters, Bill and Martin Harrison. *Burne-Jones*. London, 1973.

Weintraub, Stanley. *Aubrey Beardsley – Imp of the Perverse*. The Pennsylvania State University Press, 1976.

Weisser, M. *Handbuch bekannter und unbekannter Künstler aus der Zeit des Jugendstils*. Frankfurt/Main, 1980.

Weisser, M. *Im Stil der 'Jugend'* (about influence of Münchner Illustrierte Wochenschrift on art). Frankfurt/Main, 1980.

Wersin, Wolfgang. *Vom Adel der Form zum reinen Raum*. Vienna, 1962.

Wichmann, Siegfried. *Jugendstil*. Herrsching (Bavaria), 1978.

Windsor, Alan. *Peter Behrens – Architect and Designer 1868–1940*. London, 1981.

Wingler, Hans M. *Das Bauhaus*. Cologne – Bramsche, 1975.

Wit, W. de (ed.). *Louis Sullivan – The Function of Ornament*. St. Louis, 1986.

Wright, Frank Lloyd. *An American Architect*. New York, 1955.

Zacharias, Thomas. *Blick der Moderne*. Munich – Zürich, 1984.

Zeitler, Rudolf. *Skandinavische Kunst um 1900*. Leipzig, 1990.

Zeller, Bernhard. *Wende der Buchkunst*. N.p., n.d.

Zuckerkandl, Berta. *Zeitkunst Wien 1901–1907*. Vienna, 1908.

Zukowsky, John (ed.). *Chicago Architecture*. Munich, 1987.

Periodicals

Apollo, London
Arch+, Aachen
Architectural Record, New York – London, 1891–
Art et Décoration, Paris, 1897–
Berliner Architekturwelt, Berlin
Bulletin des Sociétés Artistiques de l'Est, Nancy
Darmstädter Tagblatt, Darmstadt
De Stijl, Leiden, 1917–1932
Dekorative Kunst, München, 1897–1929
Der Architekt, Wien, 1895–
Deutsche Kunst und Dekoration, Darmstadt, 1897–1934
Die Fackel, Vienna
Die Insel, Berlin, 1899–1901; Leipzig, 1902
Die Neue Gesellschaft, Berlin
Die Welt, Berlin
Die Woche, Berlin, 1899–
Die Zeit, Hamburg
Die Zukunft, N.p.
DU, Zürich
Echo de Paris, Paris
Figaro Littéraire, Paris
G. A. Document, Tokyo
Gazette des Beaux-Arts, Paris
Illustrierte Frauen-Zeitung, Berlin, 1874–1911
Innendekoration, Darmstadt, 1890–1945
Insel-Almanach, Berlin
Jugend, München, 1896–1940
Kunst und Künstler, N.p., 1902–
La Illustracistler, N.p., 1902–
La Libre Esthétique, Brussels, 1894–1914
Le Moniteur des Arts, Paris
Le Précurser, Paris
Mémoires de l'Académie de Stanislas, Nancy
Mir Iskustva, St. Petersburg, 1899–1904
Neue Rheinische Revue, N.p.
Neue Rundschau, Frankfurt am Main
Neue Zürcher Zeitung, Zürich
Neues Wiener Journal, Vienna, 1893–
Neues Wiener Tagblatt, Vienna, 1866–
Pan, Berlin, 1895–1900
Revue Blanche, Paris, 1891–1903
Revue des Arts décoratifs, Paris, 1880–1902
Scandinavian Journal of Design History, Stockholm
Simplicissimus, Munich, 1896–1967
The Artist, London
The Chap Book, Chicago, 1894–98
The Dial, London, 1889–
The Hobby Horse, London, 1884–91
The Magazine of Art, London
The Savoy, London, 1896
The Studio, London, 1893–
The Yellow Book, London, 1894–97
Van Nu en Straks, Brussels and Antwerp, 1893–1901
Ver Sacrum, Vienna, 1898–1903
Wiener Allgemeine Zeitung, Vienna, 1879
Zeitschrift für bildende Kunst, Berlin

Exhibition catalogs (listed chronologically)

Exhibition of Artists' Colony, Darmstadt 1901. Darmstadt, 1901.
Exposition lorraine des arts du décor [Decorative arts of Lorraine]. Paris, 1903.
Cinquantenaire du Symbolisme [Golden Jubilee of Symbolism]. Paris, 1936.
München 1869–1958, Aufbruch zur Moderne [Emergence of Modern Art]. Munich, 1958.
Henry van de Velde. Zürich, 1958.
Art Nouveau – Art and Design at the Turn of the Century. New York, 1960.
Secession – Europäische Kunst um die Jahrhundertwende [Fin-de-siècle European art]. Munich, 1964.
L'Avanguardia – Jugendstil – Hans Schmithals. Milan, 1965.
Joseph Maria Olbrich 1867–1908. Darmstadt, 1967.
Charles Rennie Mackintosh 1868–1928, Architecture, Design and Painting. Edinburgh, 1968.
Art Nouveau in England und Schottland. Hagen, 1968.
Jugendstilsammlung Gerhard P. Woeckel [G. P. Woeckel's Art Nouveau collection]. Kassel, 1968.
Hermann Obrist – Wegbereiter der Moderne [Obrist – Forerunner of Modernity]. Munich, 1968.
L'Effort Moderne en Belgique 1890–1940 [Modernist endeavor in Belgium]. Brussels, 1969.
Jugendstilglas – Vorformen moderner Kunst [Art Nouveau glass]. Munich, 1969.
Jugendstil Illustration in München [Art Nouveau illustrations in Munich]. Munich, 1969.
Pankok, Riemerschmid, Paul – Interieurs Münchner Architekten [Interiors by Munich architects]. Munich, 1970.
Kina och Norden (China and The North). Stockholm – Munich, 1970.
Die verborgene Vernunft – Funktionale Gestaltung im 19. Jahrhundert [19th-century functional design]. Munich, 1971.
Loetz Austria – Irisierende Farbgläser des Jugendstils [Art Nouveau iridescent glass]. Munich, 1971.
Pionniers du XXe siècle [20th-century pioneers] – Guimard, Horta, van de Velde. Paris, 1971.
Finskt 1900 [Finnish Art 1900]. Stockholm, 1971.
Wiener Werkstätte. Graz, 1972.
Französische Keramik vom Ende des 19. Jahrhunderts [Hans-Jörgen Heuser Collection of fin-de-siècle French pottery]. Munich, 1972.
Hector Guimard – Architektur in Paris um 1900 [Guimard and architecture in Paris ca. 1900]. Munich, 1972.
Jugendstil aus Münchner Privatbesitz [Privately-owned Art Nouveau from Munich]. Munich, 1972.
Weltkulturen und moderne Kunst – Die Begegnung der europäischen Kunst und Musik im 19. und 20. Jahrhundert mit Asien, Afrika, Ozeanien, Afro- und Indo-Amerika [European art and its encounters with other cultures]. Munich, 1972.
Burne-Jones et l'influence des Préraphaelites. Paris, 1972.
Präraffaeliten [The Pre-Raphaelites]. Baden-Baden, 1973.
Horta. Brussels, 1973.
Bernhard Pankok 1872–1943. Stuttgart, 1973.
Hentrich Glass Collection – Jugendstil und 20er Jahre (Art Nouveau and the 1920s). Düsseldorf, 1973.
Finland 1900. Nuremberg, 1973.
World Expositions in the 19th Century. Munich, 1973.
100 Jahre Architektur in Chicago (100 Years of Architecture in Chicago). Munich, 1973.
Frida Hansen – Oeuvrefortegnelse og Biografisk. Oslo, 1973.
Futurismus 1909–1917. Düsseldorf, 1974.
Sir Edward Coley Burne-Jones – Studien, Zeichnungen und Bilder [Burne-Jones's studies, drawings and pictures]. Munich, 1974.
Liberty's 1875–1975. London, 1975.
Architektur in Paris um 1900 [Architecture in Paris ca. 1900]. Munich, 1975.

Morris & Co. Stanford, 1975.

Objekte des Jugendstils (Art Nouveau Articles). Zürich, 1975.

Symbolismus in Europa. Baden-Baden, 1976.

Grotesker Jugendstil (Grotesque Art Nouveau): Carl Strathmann 1866–1939. Bonn, 1976.

Die Lithographie. Bremen, 1976.

Japanese Influence on French Art 1854–1910. Cleveland, 1976.

Ein Dokument Deutscher Kunst [German art] 1901–76. Darmstadt, 1976.

Kunstindustrimuseet i Oslo [Oslo Museum of Applied Arts]. Oslo, 1976.

August Endell – Der Architekt des Photoateliers Elvira 1871–1925 [Endell and the Elvira Studio]. Munich, 1977.

Nancy Architecture 1900. Paris, 1977.

Henry van de Velde. Munich, 1977/78.

Simplicissimus (Munich-based satirical magazine Simplicissimus, 1896–1944). Munich, 1978.

Silber des Jugendstils (Art Nouveau silver). Munich, 1979.

Bestecke des Jugendstils (Art Nouveau cutlery). Solingen, 1979.

Edvard Munch – Liebe, Angst, Tod. Bielefeld, 1980.

Worpswede – Eine Deutsche Künstlerkolonie um 1900 (Worpswede Artists' Colony ca. 1900). Bremen, 1980.

Art Nouveau Belge (Belgian Art Nouveau). Brussels, 1980.

Alfons Mucha 1860–1939. Darmstadt, 1980.

Německá Secese (German Art Nouveau ca. 1900), Prague, 1980.

Peter Behrens und Nürnberg. Nuremberg, 1980.

Nancy 1900 [Art Nouveau in Lorraine]. Munich – Mainz, 1980.

Ernesto Basile – Architetto [The architect E. Basile]. Venice, 1980.

Das Wiener Kaffeehaus [Viennese cafés up to 1939]. Vienna, 1980.

Museum Künstkerkolonie Darmstadt [Darmstadt Artists' Colony Museum]. Darmstadt, 1981.

Christopher Dresser – A Victorian Designer 1843–1904. Cologne, 1981.

Kunsthandwerk im Grassimuseum (Arts and Crafts in the Grassi Museum). Leipzig, 1981.

Daum – Verrerie d'Art [Daum Glass ca. 1900]. Munich, 1981.

Auf den künstlerischen Spuren Emile Gallés [Gallé's glass]. Cologne, 1982.

René Lalique. Catalog of the Gulbenkian Collection. Lisbon, 1982.

D'Aronco – Architetto [The Architect R. D'Aronco]. Milan, 1982.

Franz von Stuck. Munich, 1982.

Adolf Loos. Munich, 1982.

Richard Riemerschmid – From Art Nouveau to the Werkbund. Munich, 1982.

Kandinsky in Munich 1896–1914. New York, 1982.

Scandinavian Modern Design 1880–1980. New York, 1982.

"Ver Sacrum" – Viennese Art Nouveau periodical 1898–1903. Vienna, 1982/83.

Adolf Loos 1870–1933 [Loos's room design and housebuilding]. Berlin, 1983.

Der Hang zum Gesamtkunstwerk – Europäische Utopien seit 1800 [The search for a synthesis of the arts]. Zürich, 1983.

Josef Hoffmann, Wien [Hoffmann, Art Nouveau and the 1920s]. Zürich, 1983.

Saarinen in Finland – Gesellius, Lindgren, Saarinen 1896–1907. Helsinki, 1984.

Saarinen – Suomessa in Finland. Helsinki, 1984.

Le Arte a Vienna [The arts in Vienna]. Milan, 1984.

Aubrey Beardsley in the "Yellow Nineties", 1891–1898. Munich, 1984.

Jugendstil Floral Funktional [Art Nouveau, floral and functional]. Munich, 1984.

Kunst um 1900 [Art ca. 1900 – Painting, graphic arts, crafts, sculpture]. Gera, 1985.

Traum und Wirklichkeit [Dream and reality, Vienna 1870–1930]. Vienna, 1985.

Emile Gallé. Paris, 1985/86.

Antoni Gaudí. Barcelona – Munich, 1986.

Hof-Atelier Elvira (Elvira Studio) 1887–1928. Munich, 1986.

Odilon Redon – Ian Woodner Collection. Munich, 1986.

Ian Woodner Collection. Munich, 1986.

Bernhard Pankok – Art Nouveau works. Münster, 1986.

Antell Collection – Ateneum Guide. Helsinki, 1987.

Licht des Nordens [Light of the North]. Düsseldorf, 1987.

Edvard Munch 1863–1944. Munich – Salzburg – Berlin, 1987.

Toulouse-Lautrec – All the graphic works from the Gerstenberg Collection. Munich, 1987.

Edvard Munch 1863–1944. Essen – Zürich, 1987/88.

Le Japonisme. Tokyo – Paris, 1988.

Walter Leistikow. Berlin, 1989.

Tsaarinajan Aarteet – 1000 Vuotta Venäläistä. Helsinki, 1989.

Die Meister des Münchner Jugendstils [Art Nouveau Artists of Munich]. Munich, 1989.

Franz von Stuck und seine Schüler [Stuck and his pupils]. Munich, 1989.

Gerhard Munthe 1849–1929, Tapestries. Munich – Hamburg – Berlin, 1989.

Pariser Schmuck [Parisian jewelry]. Munich, 1989.

Secessionismus und Abstraktion – Austrian Art 1900–1930. Vienna, 1989.

Franz von Stuck and the Munich Academy – From Kandinsky to Albers. Bolzano, 1990.

Finnish Art 1900–1990. Munich, 1990.

Art Nouveau. Tokyo, 1990.

Fernand Khnopff 1858–1921. Tokyo, 1990.

El Modernismo. Barcelona, 1990/91.

The Age of van Gogh. Glasgow, 1990/91.

Mingei – The Living Tradition in Japanese Arts. Glasgow, 1991.

Egon Schiele in the Leopold Wien Collection. Tokyo, 1991.

Henry van de Velde – A European Artist of His Time. Hagen, 1992.

Japanese Color Woodcuts from Three Centuries. Munich, 1992/93.

Mingei – Anonymous Craftwork in the Japanese Tradition. Munich, 1992/93.

Felix Vallotton – A Retrospective. Lausanne, 1993.

1893 – l'Europe des peintres [Painters' Europe]. Paris, 1993.

Schwarz-Gold – Bronzite Work by J. & L. Lobmeyr, Vienna. Vienna, 1993.

Il disegno del nostro secolo [20th-century design]. Milan, 1994.

Torino 1902 – Le Arti Decorative Internazionali del Nuovo Secolo [Turin Exposition 1902]. Turin, 1994.

Ludwig von Hofmann – Drawings, Pastels and Printed Graphics. Albstadt, 1995.

Autriche, Suède et Finlande – les nouvelles frontières du verre européen [Glass from Austria, Sweden and Finland]. Luxembourg, 1995.

Boccioni 1912 – Materia. Milan, 1995.

Loïe Fuller – Getanzter Jugendstil [Art Nouveau in dance]. Munich, 1995.

Georges de Feure. Saint-Germain-en-Laye, 1995.

Symbolism in Europe ca. 1900. Toronto, 1995.

Bauhaus Museum – Art Collections in Weimar. Weimar, 1995.

Acknowledgments

The present publication would not have been possible without the support and cooperation of numerous institutions, museums, libraries, and archives in many countries. My thanks go to all of them. For the cordial assistance of private collectors, especially Diana and Dr. Paul Tauchner of Munich, I owe a profound debt of gratitude. I should also like to express my deep esteem for the editor of this book, Christine Westphal of Cologne, who was always forthcoming with encouragement and, if necessary, critical advice. Her contribution to the success of my work was indispensable.

Picture credits

m = middle, l = left, r = right, t = top, b = bottom

AEG, company archives, Frankfurt/Main 270, 272, 273 l, 273 tr, 273 br
© Foto Agence photographique de la réunion des musées nationaux (RMN), Paris 13, 29 r, 32 r, 70, 81, 102, 112, 118, 126, 180 tl, 180 tr, 196 b
Albertina, Vienna (Graphische Sammlung) 356
Arabia Museum, Helsinki 293 t
Architekturmuseet (Architecture Museum), Stockholm 309 bl
Archiv Vereinigte Werkstätte, Amira AG, Munich 230 tr
Archive d'Architecture Moderne, Brussels 140 r, 147 b
Archivio fotografico dei Civici Musei d'Udine 180 b
Arothek Spezialarchiv für Gemäldefotografie, Peissenberg 18 r, 19 (photo by Joachim Blauel), 22 l, 44/5, 90 r, 132, 338, 342/3, 376
Ateneum, Helsinki and the Central Art Archives collection 290 b, 291 b, 292, 293
Author 53, 56, 106, 121 r, 121 l, 214 t, 214 b, 221 tl, 228 tl, 231 br, 257 b, 261 b, 324, 350, 367 l, 370 br, 371 tr, 371 tc, 371 tr, 371 b
Badisches Landesmuseum Karlsruhe, Museum beim Markt (Applied Art Since 1900 section) 37 t, 37 b, 166 r, 258 l, 304 b, 305 r, 307 tl, 307 tr, 320 r
Bangert, Dr Albrecht 114 r, 203 l
Bastin & Evrard, Brussels 20, 131, 134, 136 r, 137/138, 139, 140 b, 141 t, 142, 143 b, 144 tl, 144 tr, 145 l, 145 t, 145 bl, 145 br, 146 © De Ultième Hallucinatie, Brussels, 147 t, 149, 150 l, 151 l, 152 t, 157 l, 157 tl, 157 br, 161, 170 t, 188 r, 194, 200 l, 206, 278 r, 279, 281 (photo by Toma Babovici), 340, 341 l, 349 b, 375
Bauhaus Museum, Kunstsammlungen zu Weimar, Weimar 274 (photo by Dressler), 278 bl
Bavarian National Museum, Munich 101
Beer, Günter 197, 200 t, 201, 204, 205, 206, 207 t, 208
Bildarchiv Preussischer Kulturbesitz, State Museums, Berlin 259 (photo by Jürgen Liepe)
British Museum, London 33
Bröhan Museum, Provincial Museum for Art Nouveau, Art Deco and Functionalism (1889–1939), Berlin 159 (photo by Martin Adam), 229 t (photo by Hans Joachim Bartsch)
Bröhan Collection/Sammlung Torsten Bröhan, Düsseldorf 368
Cornacchi, Roberto 185
Danske Kunstindustrimuseum, Copenhagen 309 tl, 309 tm
DU, Vol. 26, No. 6, 1966, Zürich 115 l (photo by Franco Cianetti)
Dumont Archiv, Cologne 35 l, 49 tl
Frahm, Klaus, Hamburg 267/277
Franke, Roman, Munich 249
Futagawa, Y, Tokyo 64/65, 326, 327 t, 328/329, 330, 333
Galerie Peichert 129 (photo by Siegfried Layda)
Gallen-Kallela Museum, Espoo 282, 290 t, 291 t
Gastinger, Mario, Munich 6, 16 r, 17 l, 17 r, 18 l, 24, 26 l, 26 r, 35 r, 46, 49 tr, 49 br, 51, 52, 84 l, 87 tr, 87 b, 89, 91 r, 92 l, 93 l, 98 l, 99 tl, 99 bl, 100 l, 100 r, 103, 108, 109, 111, 113 l, 113 r, 116 l, 123 l, 123 tr, 123 br, 124/125, 127 l, 135 l, 168 r, 187 b, 191 r, 193, 195, 202, 215, 217 br, 218 r, 226, 227, 228 bl, 229 b, 231 tlm, 231 tr, 233, 236 l, 239, 250 r, 254, 255, 256, 258 r, 260, 261 t, 261 tr, 263 r, 268, 304 l, 320 l, 322, 323, 334, 337, 339, 353, 354 tl, 365, 367 tr, 369 b, 370 t, 373
Gnamm, Sophie Renate, Munich 9 b, 98 tr, 213, 223, 230 bl, 248 l, 248 t, 265 r, 275 tl, 305 l, 306 b
Grassimuseum, Leipzig 88 l (photo by Matthias Hildebrand)
Haags Gemeentemuseum (Municipal Museum), The Hague 166 l, 169, 170 b, 171, 174 tl, 175 b
Hartz, Jacques, Hamburg 25, 43 r, 122, 266 r, 306 r
Hiraki-Ukiyo-e Museum, Yokohama 11, 12, 15 r
Historisches Museum, Vienna 359
Iparművészeti Múzeum (Applied Arts Museum), Budapest 47 l

Jaulmes, Laurent Sully, Paris 71, 75, 78/79, 105
Joan Whitney Payson Gallery of Art, Westbrook College, Portland/Maine 14
Joseph Urban Archives, Rare Book and Manuscript Library, Columbia University, New York 379
Kargl, Georg, Vienna 366 t
Koch, Alexander Exhibition of Darmstadt Artists' Colony 241 r
Kröller-Müller Museum, Otterlo 157 l, 165
Kunstgewerbemuseum (Arts and Crafts Museum), Dresden 267 r (photo by H.-P. Klut, SKD)
Kunstindustrimuseet (Applied Arts Museum), Oslo 283 (photo by Teigens Fotoatelier, Oslo), 289 tr (photo by Teigens Fotoatelier, Oslo)
Kunstmuseum im Ehrenhof, Düsseldorf 263 l, 321
Lindo and A. Grassi, Maestri Vetrai, Milan 188 l
Louis C. Tiffany Museum, Nagoya 316
Mathildenhöhe Institute, Museum Künstlerkolonie Darmstadt 234, 237, 238 r, 240 tl, 240 bl, 240 tc, 240 c, 240 br, 241 l, 242, 243, 245 r, 245 c, 251, 253
Mingeikam – Japanese Folk Crafts Museum, Tokyo 9 r, 10 tl, 10 bl, 10 t, 11
Ministero per i Beni Culturali e Ambientali, Verona 187 t
Münchner Stadtmuseum (City Museum), Munich 217 tl, 217 t, 219 220 (photo by Wolfgang Pulfer), 221 bl, 230 br (photo by Wolfgang Pulfer)
Munch Museum, Oslo 278 tl, 285
Musée d'Archéologie et d'Arts décoratifs, Liège 152 b
Musée de l'École de Nancy, Nancy 110, 116 t (photo by Lucien Weissemburger), 120 (photo by Claude Phillipot)
Musée des Arts Décoratifs, Paris (photos by L. Sully Jaulmes) 74 l, 80, 85, 87 tl, 94 l, 98 b, 99 r
Musée d'Ixelles, Brussels 135 r
Musée d'Orsay, Paris 23 t (photo by H. Lewandowski), 32 r, 73 r, 119 l, 127 b (photo by R.-G. Ojeda)
Musée du Château, Boulogne-sur-Mer 115 r
Musée Horta, Brussels 136 l, 144 b
Musée National de l'Automobile, Schlumpf Collection, Mulhouse 182
Musées Royaux d'Arts et d'Histoire, Brussels 153
Museo delle Porcellane di Doccia Fiorentino 178
Museum Bellerive, Zürich (photos by Marlen Perez) 84 l, 156 t
Museum für Kunst u. Gewerbe, Hamburg 244, 286/287 (photo by Kiemer & Kiemer)
Museum Villa Stuck, Munich 221 br, 222
Museum voor Sierkunst (Decorative Arts Museum), Ghent 156 l
NAi Nederlands Architectuur Instituut, Rotterdam 175 t
Nasjonalgalleriet (National Gallery), Oslo 284
National Swedish Art Museum, Statens Kunstmuseer, Stockholm 311
Nordenfjeldske Kunstindustrimuseum, Trondheim 288
Norsk Folkemuseum, Oslo 289 br (photo by Teigens Fotoatelier, Oslo)
Oliver, Anthony, London 57
Parisini, Dr., Vienna 369 t
Philipps, Son & Neale, London 16 l, 69
Philipps-Universität, Forschungsinstitut für Kunstgeschichte (Bildarchiv Foto Marburg), Marburg endpaper, 133, 141 b, 216, 231 tl, 312, 374, 377
Pulfer, Wolfgang, Munich 42 l, 228 tr
R. C. S. Libri & Grande Opere SpA, Milan 47 r, 130
Rheingauer Verlagsgesellschaft mbH, Eltville 212
Richards, Louanne, London 23 r, 228 br, 230 ml, 238 l, 242 m, 245 l, 262, 265 m, 265 b
Rijksdienst Beeldende Kunst, The Hague 163, 167 t, 168 l (photo by RBK The Hague Tim Koster)
Robinson, Cervin, New York 325
Royal Academy of Fine Arts (Library), Architectural Drawings Collection, Stockholm 309 tr
Royal Photographic Society, Bath 380
Rühl & Borman, Werbefotografie 246/247
Rupertinum, Salzburger Landessammlungen, Salzburg 372 l
Santi Caleca SAS di Santi Caleca, Milan 186

Schlossmuseum, Darmstadt 236 t
Schlossmuseum, Kunstsammlungen zu Weimar, Weimar 224 (photo by Dressler)
Shinkenchiku-Sha, Dept. of Photography, Tokyo 327 b
Smålands Museum, Växjö 307 bl
Sotheby's, Amsterdam 162, 164, 174 tr, 174 r
Sotheby's, London 7, 8, 21 l, 27, 28, 29 l, 30, 32 l, 38, 39 t, 39 b, 40 l, 41, 42 tr, 42 br, 43 l, 54, 58 l, 59 t, 59 l, 60 l, 60 r, 61, 62, 63 l, 63 r, 66 t, 66 b, 67, 77, 82/83, 86, 90 l, 91 l, 93 l, 94 r, 95 r, 107, 114 l, 177, 181, 183, 203 r, 235, 264, 265 r, 271, 275 bl, 309 l, 313, 317 t, 317 b, 318 l, 318 b, 319, 335, 336, 341, 349 t, 351 l, 352, 354 tl, 354 bl, 354 tr, 357, 360, 361, 362, 363, 364 t, 366 bl, 367 r, 372 r
Sotheby's, Monaco 60 r, 60 l, 62, 88 r, 92 r, 95 l, 107, 148, 154/155, 156 b, 266 l, 308, 345 t, 345 b
Sotheby's, New York 127 r, 315, 331
Sotheby's, Rome 184 t, 184 b
Sotheby's Rome 184 t, 184 b
Staatliche Graphische Sammlung, Munich 225
Staatliches Museum für angewandte Kunst (Neue Sammlung), Munich 21 tr (photo by Mario Gastinger), 74 r (photo by Mario Gastinger), 158 (photo by Mario Gastinger), 171 (photo by Mario Gastinger), 218 l, 269 (photo by Sophie Renate Gnamm), 351 r
Studio Chevojon, Paris 73 l
Suomen rakennustaiteen museo, Helsinki 294, 295, 297 r, 298 r, 299, 300, 301 l, 301 r, 302, 303 b
Tahara, Keiichi, Paris 55, 96, 117, 172/173, 189, 190, 198, 199, 207 b, 346/7, 349 b, 355
Taideteollisuusmuseo, Helsinki 191 l (photo by Rauno Träskelin), 293 b, 298 l
Tate Gallery, London 22 b, 48
Ulmer Museum (loaned by Ministry for Family, Women, Further Education and Art, Badem-Württemberg), Ulm 211 (photo by Mario Gastinger)
Ver Sacrum, Vol. 1. No. 9, 1898, Vienna 3
Victoria & Albert Museum, London 36
© Viollet, Roger, Paris 72, 76 t, 76 l, 83 t, 97, 167 b, 296, 297 l
Verlag Josef Hannesschläger, Neusäss 314 (photo by Siegfried Layda)
Viennese Glass Museum, Lobmeyr Collection 16 t, 364 l, 370 l
Whitworth Art Gallery, University of Manchester 34
Wiesenhofer, Hans, Vienna 348 l
Wipperfürth, Olaf, Paris 2
Wood, Charlotte, London 31

Index

Chapter 3 Raising your IQ   45

Chapter 4 Mending and blending   95

Contents

Introduction

One of the problems with Adobe Photoshop is that the engineers always keep adding stuff to the program and as Photoshop has got bigger, there has been that much more to write about. This brand new addition to the *Photoshop for Photographers* series is intended as a companion to the main *Adobe Photoshop CS5 for Photographers* book. Rather than teach you all the basics of Photoshop, Camera Raw and Bridge, we wanted to concentrate more on what you can actually do with Photoshop. This book is therefore very much tutorial-based and packed with photographic examples shot by Martin Evening and Jeff Schewe. It is also unique in that it doesn't just show you how to use Photoshop, but explains the planning process leading up to the point where Photoshop is used and discusses some of the photographic techniques used, which are also illustrated throughout the book.

We have described this book as 'the ultimate workshop' and you will find that it has been broken down into thirteen different chapters, where each can be regarded as being like an individual workshop seminar program. Our aim has been to group the Photoshop techniques shown into this book into topic-related chapter sections. We hope this makes the book more easily accessible, as many of the chapters can easily be digested in a single reading session, just as if you were attending a real workshop event.

It's also rather ironic for this book to be co-authored by Jeff and Martin. Jeff was under contract to write a book tentatively titled *Photoshop for Photographers* back in the mid 1990s that for many reasons got scrapped. Martin had heard about Jeff's book project and had the good grace to ask permission to use the title – which Jeff gladly agreed to. Therein started a friendship between the two authors that now has them collaborating on this new *Photoshop for Photographers* title.

Acknowledgements

This book project began thanks to the support of Ben Denne, Marie Hooper, Hayley Salter and David Albon at Focal Press. Our thanks also go to the other people who helped directly with the production of the book: Rod Wynne-Powell for the tech editing, Charlotte Pover who took care of the proof-reading, Chris Murphy who supplied the press profiles, and Matt Wreford for doing the CMYK conversion work.

Quite a number of the photographs that appear in this book were shot in our London and Chicago studios. We would like to thank the following people for their assistance: our photographic assistants Harry Dutton and Mel Hill, Camilla Pascucci for makeup and hair, Harriet Cotterill for clothes styling, our models Courtney Hopper at Storm, Natasha DeRuyter, Alex Kordek and Lidia at MOT models, Stuart Weston, Neil Soni, plus Art Director, David Willett and Propabilities, Chicago, for supply of the studio props. We thank Kevin Raber of Phase One for the use of the P45+ digital back, Ben Rice for the loan of the HDR panoramic head equipment used in Chapter 9 and Imatest for the production of the lens test chart used in Chapter 3, along with Jon Tarrant and *What Digital Camera* magazine. We would also like to acknowledge the additional support in the early stages of the book production from Greg Gorman, Peter Krogh, Ian Lyons (the 'Leprish Iricon') and Marc Pawliger.

Thanks also go to all our friends at Adobe: Russell Brown, John Nack, Chris Cox, and co-architects Scott Byer and Russell Williams on Photoshop, and Thomas Knoll, Eric Chan, Zalman Stern and Tom Hogarty on Camera Raw. Obviously we owe a great debt of gratitude to Thomas and his brother John Knoll for authoring Photoshop in the first place and Adobe for having the brilliance to buy it. We also wish to thank Mark Hamburg for the years of 'useful' dialog (and for putting so many of our wishes into Photoshop).

Thanks also to the Pixel Genius crew: Mac Holbert, Mike Keppel, Seth Resnick and Andrew Rodney and our gone but not forgotten members Mike Skurski and Bruce Fraser. We miss them and so does the industry. We also give a nod to the Pixel Mafia, you know who you are…

Lastly, Martin would like to thank Camilla for all her love, support and understanding, and Jeff would like to thank his wife Becky and daughter Erica for their support and willingness to accept and love him (it isn't easy). And to Max, the dog who will be remembered.

We also wish to thank you, our reader, and hope you get what we are trying to do and enjoy the learning process – we do, and it never ends…

Photograph: Martin Evening.

Client: Altered Image | Model: Lydia @ MOT | Fuji GX 68 Mk II Camera | 110 mm | 100 ISO Ektachrome Film | Imacon 848 Scanner

Chapter 1

Before you shoot

Concepts and planning before you use Photoshop

T his book may be all about Photoshop and what you can do with the program, but we thought we would start by looking at where exactly Photoshop fits in to a photography workflow. While it is possible to do an enormous amount of work on the computer using Photoshop, just because you can doesn't mean you should. There is much to be said for taking a step back before you shoot an assignment and planning how you might end up using Photoshop, then shooting accordingly with that purpose in mind. Over the next few pages we have used a few studio shoot examples to illustrate this point.

Photo: © Martin Evening

Figure 1.1 Here is a simple example of where it makes more sense to extend the width of an image using Photoshop, rather than create the full-width scene 'in-camera'.

Identifying the authors

To tell which of us wrote which sections of the book, a clue lies in the banner icons at the top of each page. The sections written by Martin use the **Me** symbol and those written by Jeff use the **Js** symbol, and the sections where we collaborated together show both. You'll note the colors of these symbols are always designed to match in with the color of the chapter banners.

Before you shoot that picture!

In the days of film photography, we would often use a Polaroid™ as a way to test the lighting and show clients a preview of how the image would look. Photographers would often use the excuse that the quality of the Polaroid wasn't up to standard and that it would look OK once they saw the film (by which time it would be too late!). Now, in the age of digital photography, photographers are tempted to say 'we'll fix it in Photoshop'. Of course, Photoshop can be used to fix almost anything, but the trick to becoming a successful and productive photographer is to be able to work out when it is appropriate to use Photoshop and when it's better to get this right 'in-camera' first.

For commissioned shoots this is something that should be worked out before you pick up the camera, or earlier still at the layout stage. It all boils down to making the best use of your time. In Figure 1.1 you can see how Martin easily added extra width to a studio-shot picture using the content-aware scaling feature. It took a matter of a few seconds to do this in Photoshop, whereas it would have required extra space (and expense) in the studio to add extra width to the shot. For example, most seamless background rolls are only nine feet wide and Martin would have had to rent a studio with a wide enough cove and have it painted by hand to get the full backdrop width in camera.

Some people will call this cheating, while others will look at the economic necessities and conclude that using Photoshop in the post-production stage makes the most sense. These days a lot of movies and TV dramas are filmed on studio sets where many of the props and exterior details are missing and added in later. This kind of post-production work is so successfully done that you'll hardly be aware of the artifice that's involved.

Interpreting a brief

'Briefs' (normally called 'layouts' in the US) run the gamut from a highly detailed and exact rendering of what will be executed by the photographer, to a rough guide as simple as telling you whether the image is vertical or horizontal – and even that can sometimes evolve. Ideally, the relationship the photographer has with the art director or designer will determine how flexible the layout will be. The better art directors tend to be open to opportunities to improve the project with the input and creative ideas of the photographer.

It's incumbent on the creative team to know the limits and expectations of the ultimate client. The best photographers are always on the lookout for ways to enhance and extend the original concept and execution, while being diligent in maintaining the needs of the client.

All that said, it's not at all unusual for the layout to evolve (and hopefully improve) during the course of a project. When a layout is originally drawn, the reality of the final photograph is unknown – unless the layout has been created with stock photography, which can be a dual-edged sword. Ethically, a photographer should not merely copy another photographer's work and create a derivative work of the original. It's one thing to use another's work as inspiration, it's another thing entirely to infringe on the work of others.

Figure 1.2 is a prime example of a tight layout with room for flexibility in execution and evolution. Even the headline was changed after the photographic image was completed. The art director remained open to taking advantage of opportunities and the end client was not so rigid as to ignore the possibilities.

Figure 1.2 Here is a simple example of an evolution of a layout to final printed ad.

Shooting multiple elements – intelligently

There's no question that a really good photographer can create a compelling image in a single shot and not have to rely on Photoshop to make it great. But given the limitations of time and budget, it's often easier (and just as productive) to break down a final image into its essential parts before shooting anything; then shoot those parts and assemble them in Photoshop. This is a prime example of such a shot.

Photo: © Jeff Schewe

Figure 1.3 This is the final composite of two shots with retouching.

The shot of the Miller Lite bottle cap (Figure 1.3) was an assignment shot by me. Having experience of shooting liquid droplets, I knew that shooting the bottle cap with the droplets placed exactly correct would be tedious and involve lots of very detailed work up close. It would be a pain... So rather than even try to accomplish the final result in a single shot, I chose to shoot two shots: one with the bottle cap completely dry with the lighting finessed and the image optimized for the logo text, and a second shot where the water droplets were allowed to go where they wanted (Figure 1.4). I made no special effort to keep the background dry.

Figure 1.4 These are the two raw shots before layering and masking.

By planning in advance to shoot the assignment in two shots, I was able to simplify the individual shots to the point where the image assembly was quite simple. Also, by telling the art director that two shots would be better from the very start of the assignment, doing the two shots was not seen as a failure to 'get it' in one shot but a better way to accomplish the goals of the assignment. It also gave the art director the opportunity that art directors love so much: the chance to direct. But instead of looking through the ground glass of a view camera (whose image is upside down) and trying to direct the precise placement of water droplets, he could direct me sitting at the computer and add, delete or move them in Photoshop. To be honest, it didn't necessarily take less time but it was certainly less tedious dealing with a layer mask rather than the difficult task of placing the real water droplets. Using the separate elements approach was also much more efficient and precise, which led to a better result – the goal of both the art director and me.

Multi light blending technique

Shooting in the studio with controlled lighting can lead to
wonderfully lit still-life images. But you are often faced with the
realities of optics and physics, and the difficulties of getting light
exactly where you want it. As a result, I have become adept at
shooting subjects under varied lighting conditions and directions
and then compositing the resulting elements in Photoshop. Figure
1.5 shows the two original captures. The only real difference is that
the light was moved from the upper left to the lower right of the
image between shots. Both captures were processed in the same way
and were maintained in exact registration between the exposures.
The trick then was to 'paint with light' by using the second layer's
layer mask to determine the precise visibility of that layer.

This approach – locking the camera down and shooting
multiple exposures with different qualities of light (such as a Hard
Light mixed with a Soft Light) or, as in this example, with the
same light from different directions – is a creative approach that
marries the best of photography with the efficiency of Photoshop.
Sure, you could labor the long time it would take to finesse the
lighting using two separate light sources, but why when this
alternative is so simple (and easy)?

There are some caveats: you really should have a very stable
shooting platform and it's ideal to keep the lighting rather simple.
However, with Photoshop CS5's Auto-align function this has
become less mission critical. Ironically, for this book I did test

Figure 1.6 The Auto-align command
prompted this warning when trying to align the
two leaf layers.

Figure 1.5 The capture on the left was the starting position of the light. After capturing
and evaluating the first shot, the light was moved 180° and the second capture was made.

the Auto-align command on these layers and received the warning shown in Figure 1.6. It seems that the lighting was so different that the Auto-align logic was fooled. This wasn't a problem in this case since the registration was already excellent.

Figure 1.7 shows the final layer stack with the layer mask on the 'lower left' layer that modulated the visibility of that layer. Some areas were completely opaque while other areas were blended in partial opacity. The white areas of the layer mask allowed all of the lower left layer to show through. Figure 1.8 shows the final result 'painted by light'. There weren't a lot of tone and color adjustments made. The primary adjustment was a Hue and Saturation increase and a midtone contrast bump to pop some of the detail. More about those types of adjustments later in the book.

Figure 1.7 The final layer stack (with the adjustments grouped for brevity).

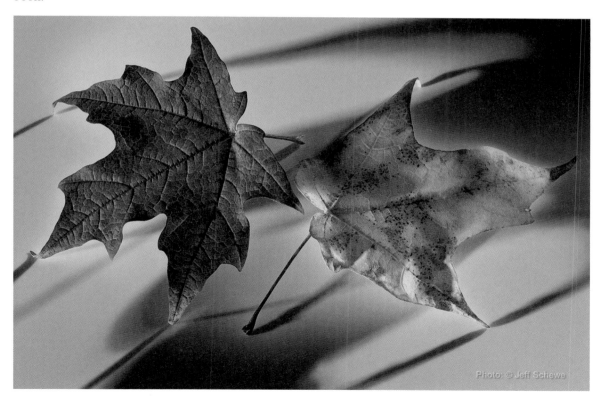

Figure 1.8 The final blended image.

Complex composite work

The previous examples were simple to composite because of the nature of the images. However, Figure 1.9 was not in the least bit easy to assemble. All of the individual elements had to be shot separately. However, the nature of the assembly dictated that each element shot had to have matching lighting that would enable the final assembly to look convincing. The element shots (see Figure 1.10) were set up so that the lighting would cast a shadow in the correct direction and provide realistic clues as to how to make the synthetic shadows that would be made in Photoshop. The additional challenge was to rig each shot so the model's action would be real. This required tieing off the pickaxe fellow's suit to make the action look more real. For the shot with the two people

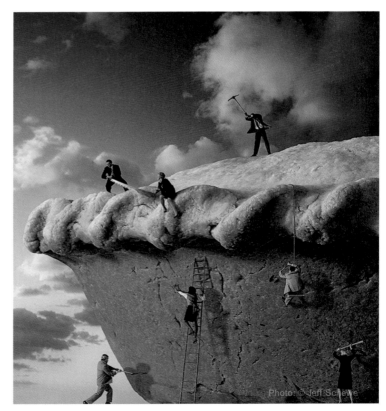

Figure 1.9 Left is the original layout provided by the client. Above is the final retouched composite.

Figure 1.10 The images above were shot with 120 mm color transparency in the studio. The two pie shots were done on 4 x 5 film. The sky background was studio stock. All of the element shots were outlined using the pen tool to create paths. Separate paths were made from the real shadows and then remade in Photoshop.

with the saw, they did actually have to engage with each other so their expressions would be real. The hatchet girl needed to be on a ladder and even though I rigged a line for the lady with the pickaxe (she couldn't actually hold it over her head), it was important that the lighting and the shadow were correct. Even the 70 year-old fellow with the shovel (I didn't know the gentleman was 70 at the time – but the model did actually have fun on the shoot) had to be suspended by real rope to look realistic.

The shot that actually dictated lighting direction and quality was the background image. Since the sunset had a low side light angle, the rest of the elements had to be shot to match. Try as he did, the food stylist couldn't get 'the perfect pie' so I took parts from two different pies for the final composite.

Figure 1.11 Knowing the end photograph will be edited in Photoshop does mean that one can take shots such as the one here, using an extreme wide-angle lens, and not have to worry if the model's head happens to overlap the edge of the backdrop. This kind of problem is easy to fix in Photoshop and you don't lose the shot.

Fashion and beauty retouching

Where would the fashion and beauty industry be without retouching? It's been used for many years now and has had quite an impact on the way fashion images look in magazines.

A Scottish hairdresser I worked with once told me how the clean hair lines and cuts shown in the photographs created for Vidal Sassoon in the sixties made a huge impression on other Scottish hairdressers and how as a result they refined their cutting techniques to match the precision in the photographs that they had seen. Little did they realize that the pictures had actually been retouched, but ever since Scottish hairdressing has became world famous for its technical precision!

One might argue that the ridiculous levels of retouching used on some photographs have become too much, but we reckon that good retouching work should be retouching that you don't notice. These days it is really easy to carry out effective skin retouching using tools such as the healing brush and now also the spot healing brush with the new content-aware healing mode. The best advice here is to always carry out your retouching on separate layers and when it comes to any work that is done to smooth the skin tones, such as a paint layer or skin blurring layer, then fade the opacity so that the effect is made more subtle. Figure 1.12 shows an image that is featured later in this book to demonstrate a Photoshop hair coloring technique. There have been several occasions where I have worked on a series of hair coloring shots to demonstrate a range of hair colors and it has been necessary to color a model's hair different shades of color (matching a sample color). You have to bear in mind here that to dye the hair for real, the models would be required to undertake a skin patch test to check for chemical sensitivity and the coloring process itself can take up to several hours to complete. So although doing it in Photoshop may not be so truthful, it is the only way many clients can afford to get the exact hair color look they are after and avoid paying high model fees.

I also believe one can now afford to be somewhat looser about the way you shoot. In the past, it was critical that the models kept within the bounds of the backdrop, whereas now it doesn't matter quite so much (as I have shown in Figure 1.11). I quite like having the freedom to shoot to capture movement and gesture knowing that Photoshop can be used to extend the backdrop if necessary.

Figure 1.12 Here is a before and after example of a photograph in which I carried out basic retouching to remove stray hairs, smooth the skin texture and adjust the color of the model's hair.

In this respect, Photoshop offers more ways to be creative because you have fewer restrictions.

When it comes to lighting for beauty and fashion photography, there is also more opportunity to shoot without limits. After a long career learning how to light precisely I certainly know how to control my lighting, yet I do now appreciate the freedom Photoshop gives me to break the rules and shoot without regard to the precise balance of lighting or optimal contrast. For example, I find that I now tend to light that much harder. I have always liked the drama that you get with strong, directional light, but at the same time been wary of the problems you get with strong harsh shadows on the face. However, it is now relatively easy to smooth these out in Photoshop and have the best of all worlds. Some might consider this a lazy approach to photography, but if Photoshop occasionally allows you to break the normal rules of lighting, why not allow yourself to experiment?

When not to use Photoshop

I recall that the client had originally contacted me because I was thought of as some sort of 'computer expert'. The idea was to create an image of a melted phone on the computer (Figure 1.13). I quickly realized that the client was both overestimating the ease of doing something like that in CGI and vastly underestimating what the costs would be. It would be far better and less costly if I just put a phone in the oven and melted the darn thing.

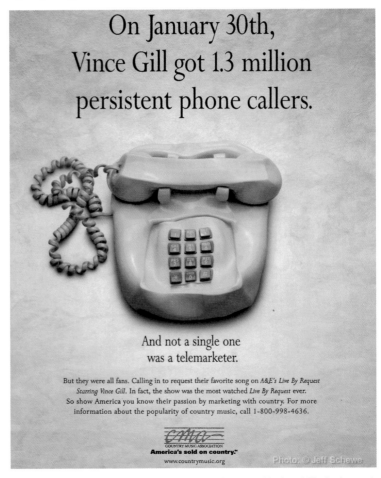

Figure 1.13 This figure shows the final image as it appeared in the ad. The background was shot separately and the layered phone (with shadows) dropped on top.

Figure 1.14 The melted phone on the left was shot on a medium gray background to minimize the reflections in the plastic. The image on the right is the retouched and layered phone with synthetic shadows.

The first test melt wasn't a huge success. The resulting mass of bubbling and blackened plastic looked like a biological experiment run amuck. But subsequent tests led to the technique of a longer time in the oven at a lower heat.

The key was to remove as much metal as possible and simply let gravity do its work. The longer time in lower heat also enabled me to prod certain areas and angle the base (a cookie sheet) while still in the oven. Clearly, as shown in Figure 1.14, there would be the need for some pretty heavy retouching after the melted phone was cooled. But the amount of work was minimal compared with trying to melt the phone in Photoshop.

Which really is the thrust of the main point we are trying to get across in this first chapter. There are things you can do very easily in front of the camera that would be very difficult after the fact in Photoshop. Yet knowing how to shoot for digital imaging can greatly ease the post-production burden and substantially improve the final result. If you have skills as a photographer and skills as a digital imaging artist, you can improve the final result (and make your life easier) by carefully choosing when to do what and by which means: photographic or Photoshop.

Photograph: Jeff Schewe.
Canon EOS 10D Camera | 17–35 mm lens at 23 mm | 1600 ISO

Chapter 2

Camera Raw workflow

Getting things right in Camera Raw first

With this chapter we wanted to show you some of the key benefits of using Camera Raw to carry out the initial image processing. You see, if you shoot using the raw mode on your camera, almost everything you want to do to an image can be done using Camera Raw first. And if you are using Lightroom, you can use the exact same controls that can be found in the Develop module to prepare a raw image. Our late colleague, Bruce Fraser, used to joke that Photoshop makes an excellent plug-in for Camera Raw. We don't think Bruce was completely joking when he said this. You really should use Camera Raw as your first port of call when editing your photos.

Camera Raw's history

Thomas Knoll, the co-author of Photoshop, is the founder and principal engineer of Camera Raw. Camera Raw 1.0 was released as a stand-alone product for Photoshop 7 and sold for $99. Camera Raw 2 was bundled with Photoshop CS, which was released in October 2003. Contributing engineers are Zalman Stern and Eric Chan. Mark Hamburg has also contributed to the Camera Raw processing pipeline and was the founder of Adobe Photoshop Lightroom, which built upon and added to Camera Raw's processing.

Optimizing images

Camera Raw or Photoshop?

When Adobe launched Camera Raw it was designed as a raw file format import plug-in that allowed Photoshop to access raw digital captures. It can now be argued that Camera Raw has been turned into its own editing domain called 'parametric editing' and, in some ways, challenges Photoshop for image editing of digital photographs. But don't lose sight of the fact that Camera Raw's main role is still to open images into Photoshop.

Inevitably, there will be a degree of confusion about what to do to images in which domain: parametric or pixel editing. The answer is really rather simple – use the best tool for the task at hand. Using Camera Raw is optimal for raw capture tone curve adjustments because you are working with the entire linear tone range of the raw capture. Waiting to do that in Photoshop would mean leaving image quality on the table. The same holds true for adjusting the

Figure 2.1 Camera Raw version 1.0 in Photoshop 7, released February 19th, 2003.

white balance of a raw capture. Nothing in Photoshop can rival the accuracy and efficiency of Camera Raw's white balance tool. If your camera sensor has a dust spot, you can use the spot removal tool in Camera Raw to remove a spot on one or one hundred captures. Therefore, doing these tasks in Camera Raw is more efficient than in Photoshop. Yet for all of its strengths, Camera Raw is not a pixel editor (the adjustment brush and gradient filter notwithstanding). When you need pixel-accurate masks or image composites, you need Photoshop.

The best approach is to devise a strategy and employ the correct tactics to achieve it. The strategy we like to use is the 80–20 rule (also called the Pareto principle) where the majority of the work can be done with the least amount of effort. So, Camera Raw is tactically employed to make mass adjustments accurately, quickly and efficiently while Photoshop is tactically employed on only a few select images that are truly worthy of the extra effort.

Figure 2.2 Camera Raw version 6.1 in Photoshop CS5, released June 1st, 2010.

Figure 2.3 The Camera Raw Camera Calibration panel showing the Process Version drop-down menu.

Figure 2.4 The Process 2003 badge which also behaves like a button.

Process 2003 Rendering

While the engineers tried very hard to maintain the older Process 2003 rendering capability, Process 2003 is still slightly different and not an exact match to previous renderings. Since the noise reduction was removed from the demosiacing engine in Camera Raw 6, Process 2003's rendering is slightly noisier than previous versions' rendering. If you need to match the noise signature of previous renderings, we suggest adding 15–20% to the Process 2003 Luminance Noise Reduction settings. This will make up for the removal of the previous versions' built-in noise reduction.

Process Versions in Camera Raw

Camera Raw has changed considerably since it was first released. However, it wasn't until Camera Raw 6 in Photoshop CS5 that the engineers had to consider the consequences of substantially changing the basic rendering in Camera Raw.

For version 6, the Camera Raw team made fundamental changes to the demosaicing and noise reduction as well as more gentle changes to the Recovery, Fill Light and Sharpening controls. These changes, while universally deemed improvements, did necessitate the introduction of a concept called 'Process Versions' to allow users to retain the rendering of previous versions. Figure 2.3 shows the Process Version drop-down menu found in the Camera Calibration panel. By default, raw images that have not had their settings modified beyond the Camera Raw 'default' will open in Camera Raw 6 already set to Process 2010 (Current). Images that have user-modified settings of any kind will by default open in Camera Raw 6 as Process 2003. Figure 2.4 shows the Process 2003 warning badge that appears in the lower right corner of the Camera Raw 6 preview window. The badge also doubles as a button to change from Process 2003 to Process 2010. In addition to clicking on the badge you can switch between versions via the Camera Calibration panel (Figure 2.3). Camera Raw 6.2 added the ability to create presets using the Process Version as a subset of a Camera Raw preset. This allows you to create a Process Version preset that can be applied in Bridge before even opening an image in Camera Raw.

Figure 2.5 Comparisons of the Camera Raw Detail panel showing the Noise Reduction differences between Process 2003 (left) and Process 2010 (right).

The biggest and most obvious difference is found in the Camera Raw Detail panel's Noise Reduction settings as shown in Figure 2.5. Process 2003 only allows older single Luminance and Color noise reduction settings. Process 2010 offers the addition of Luminance Detail and Contrast as well as Color Detail. The Luminance Detail slider controls the noise threshold for determining what is noise and what is image detail. Sliding to the right preserves more image detail. Dragging to the left increases image smoothing but at the risk of losing image detail. Luminance Detail allows you to preserve image contrast which might be lowered when using high luminance amounts. Both of these adjustments are really only obvious when working on high ISO images. The Color Detail slider allows adjustment of the detail of the color edges. Lower numbers may cause loss of color saturation with thin edges while too high a number may result in color blobs.

The best way to get the hang of using the Process Version renderings and the new noise reduction controls is to practice using them. You'll be better able to see the results by zooming in to 200–400% zooms and the improvement in noise reduction is more obvious with high ISO captures. Figure 2.6 shows the full image that is shown at 400% zoom in the detail images in Figure 2.7 below.

Figure 2.6 The full frame of the image captured with a Canon EOS 10D at ISO 1600. The area of the detail image is circled.

Figure 2.7 Comparisons of the Camera Raw Detail panel showing default rendering differences between Process 2003 (left) and Process 2010 (middle). On the right is the image optimized with the noise reduction settings shown in Figure 2.5.

Figure 2.8 The Camera Raw Camera Calibration panel showing the drop-down menu of available profiles.

Figure 2.9 A synthetic ColorChecker card made in ProPhoto RGB.

Camera Profiles in Camera Raw

When Camera Raw was first introduced, one of the more controversial aspects of image quality was the Camera Raw default color rendering. Many thought the color was inaccurate (or at least didn't match the color produced by the camera JPEG or camera software). Adobe took heed and introduced the DNG Profile addition to the DNG specification with DNG version 1.2.

Whether you were in the camp that thought Camera Raw's color rendering was fine or the camp that thought it sucked is moot – the DNG Profiles have now changed the Camera Raw rendering. If you want the same color rendering as your camera JPEG, you can pretty much match it. Figure 2.8 shows the Camera Calibration panel of Camera Raw 6. The default color profile is the Adobe Standard profile. This profile is designed to be colorimetrically accurate and an improvement on the previous table-based profiles (shown as ACR 4.4 and 4.3). The profiles starting with the name 'Camera' are designed to emulate the in-camera settings available as designed by the camera maker (although the actual names will vary). The drop-down menu in Figure 2.8 is for a Canon EOS1DS Mk III, while other cameras will have names that align with their own camera 'looks'.

For comparison, Figure 2.9 shows a synthetic Macbeth ColorChecker card. The bottom figure shows shots of a mini ColorChecker card that has been shot in daylight. The far left image of Figure 2.10 was rendered using the Adobe Standard DNG Profile. The middle image was rendered using the Camera Standard profile and the image on the right was a camera JPEG with the

Figure 2.10 Comparisons of the Adobe Standard profile (left), the Camera Standard profile (middle) and a camera-produced JPEG file (right).

camera set to sRGB. As you can see, the Camera Standard and JPEG are a close match. However, in terms of accuracy, the Adobe Standard rendering is a closer match to what the ColorChecker colors are supposed to produce. What does this prove? That color rendering from raw files is open for interpretation – there really is no single 'right' answer but there may be more accurate answers.

It doesn't really end here either. Adobe has released a free software utility called DNG Profile Editor which enables users to create their own DNG Profiles through manual editing or by using shots of ColorChecker charts. The documentation available is extensive, so if you are interested we suggest you download the DNG Profile Editor from http://labs.adobe.com and try it yourself (be sure to read the documentation). For real-world examples of the different renderings using the vender matching profiles, see Figure 2.11 below.

Color accuracy

Whether you spell it color or colour, photographers often think accurate is best. Not really. However, one of the most successful film launches ever was Fuji Velvia, which was anything but accurate. What photographers usually want is pleasing color and Camera Raw has 40 controls dedicated to color adjustments (not including the adjustment brush). But try to think of the DNG Profiles not as color correction tools but more as a color rendering tool that offers options for the start of your color editing needs.

| Adobe Standard | Camera Faithful | Camera Landscape |
| Camera Neutral | Camera Portrait | Camera Standard |

Figure 2.11 This shows comparisons of the DNG Profile rendering. Note, the naming convention will vary by camera manufacturer and not all cameras will have all variations.

Highlight checking

In Camera Raw there are several ways you can check that the important highlight information is preserved. One way is to click the highlight clipping warning in the Camera Raw histogram (circled in Figure 2.12). Alternatively, if you hold down the ⌥ alt key as you drag the Exposure or Recovery sliders, you will see the preview image change to show a threshold mode display, in which the clipped areas will appear colored (indicating which colors are clipped) or white (to indicate that all colors are clipped). You can use this as a guide to make sure important detail isn't clipped. Lastly, you can move the cursor over the highlight areas of the image and check the RGB values to see if these fall within an acceptable range for print output. Here, you usually want to make sure that the brightest areas of highlight detail don't go lighter than, say, 245,245,245.

Figure 2.12 The Camera Raw histogram.

Optimizing the image tones

This section deals with a few of the ways you can fine-tune images in Photoshop to improve their appearance. If you want to learn more about the basics of Photoshop image editing, then we reckon you'll find the Image editing essentials chapter in the main *Adobe Photoshop CS5 for Photographers* book a useful guide to working in Photoshop. To start with though, we thought it worth making a few points about how to optimize the shadows and highlights and dispel a few myths.

Optimizing an image in Camera Raw

A lot of people have got confused about how you are supposed to set the shadow and highlight points in Camera Raw and Lightroom, and why you don't have the same type of Levels controls as you do in Photoshop. Basically, you will sometimes read that the black point output levels should be set to an RGB value like 12, 12, 12, and the white output levels should be set to, say, 245, 245, 245. There are sound, historical reasons for such advice, because you don't want the blacks to clip to 0, 0, 0, when you send a file to be printed, since any blacks that are darker than a certain value will all clip to black. Likewise, you need to ensure that essential highlight information doesn't all burn out to paper white when printed. Yet in Camera Raw there are no output levels settings options. This is because they are not needed when editing images for RGB output and we'll explain why here.

When it comes to optimizing the highlights, you only need to worry about the non-specular highlights, which are basically the brightest whites that contain important tonal detail. With specular, or shiny whites, you can safely let these clip. So although you do have to be careful not to clip the highlights when adjusting the Exposure slider, in practice most pictures do contain some specular highlights. So, if you set the highlight clipping to clip these the important detail highlight information will usually be safely preserved within a margin of safety. Where there are bright areas in a picture that contain important detail, we first make sure that the threshold clipping display confirms that these areas are not significantly clipped and then use the Recovery slider in Camera Raw where it is necessary to make absolutely sure the highlight detail is preserved in these areas.

Optimizing the highlights

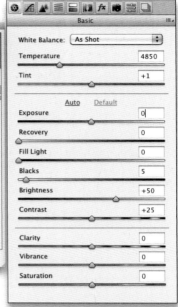

1 Here you can see a photograph opened in Camera Raw with the default Camera Raw settings. Although the photograph appears rather bright, I would say that it has been captured at an optimum exposure from which to process a tone-corrected image.

2 This shows the tone-corrected version in which I adjusted the Exposure, Recovery, Fill Light, Blacks, Brightness and Contrast sliders to apply the best combination of settings to achieve a nice level of contrast without blowing out the highlights. The important thing to note here is that I was extremely careful to make sure that the highlight detail in the white statue was well within range to print OK.

Figure 2.13 This shows, from top to bottom, the histogram for a Camera Raw processed RGB image, a conversion to CMYK, a conversion to a glossy inkjet paper profile and a conversion to a matte inkjet paper profile.

Optimizing the blacks

When it comes to adjusting the Blacks slider, the choice is simple: where are the blackest blacks and how much do you wish to clip them? Just as there is no one CMYK space that fits all, there is no one setting for the black point that will correctly set the blacks for every type of print output. Where you read advice to set the blacks lighter than 0, 0, 0, this dates back to the time before Photoshop 5, when there was no other way to ensure that the blacks in a photograph would print correctly without clipping. Some people have expressed concern that Camera Raw only allows you to adjust the input clipping levels values and that there is no control available for setting the output levels to something higher than 0, 0, 0. In actual fact, an output levels control is not really necessary these days, since the profile conversion can take care of all this for you and does everything automatically. With the advent of ICC-based color management now being built into Photoshop, this preparation step is no longer required and it is fairly easy to prove why. For example, in Figure 2.13 I opened a Camera Raw processed photograph in Photoshop (where the shadows has been deliberately clipped to go to solid black) and set the histogram display in the Photoshop Histogram panel to 'Luminosity'. The top histogram shows the Photoshop histogram for a Camera Raw processed RGB master image. Below that you can see the luminosity histogram for a CMYK converted version and below that a conversion to a glossy inkjet profile, followed by a matte inkjet paper profile. In these screen shots of the output-converted histograms you can see that the black point is automatically indented. This demonstrates how the profile conversion takes the guesswork out of setting the blacks, as well as how the amount of black point compensation actually varies for each different type of print output. This is because an ICC profile is able to work this out precisely, according to each type of print output.

The photograph shown on the page opposite was shot at Arches National Park near Moab, Utah. In the accompanying steps I show how I adjusted the settings in Camera Raw to deliberately clip the blacks so that the foreground shadow appeared completely black in the final Camera Raw-edited version of the picture. Another typical example would be a photograph of an object shot against a black backdrop, where you might also want to force any remaining shadow detail in the backdrop to go to a solid black tone.

1 Here is a photograph shot of an arch formation close to sunset with a strong dark shadow in the foreground. I began by applying an Auto setting in the Basic panel. As you can see, I also applied a black and white conversion and a sepia split toning effect.

2 In this version you can see that I adjusted the Basic panel settings to achieve a more contrasty result, where I mainly increased the Blacks slider amount until I had successfully clipped all of the shadow detail in the foreground shadow area. This is a good example of an image where it is not always important that you preserve all of the shadow detail.

25

Optimizing both the highlights and blacks

1 To complete this section on optimizing images in Camera Raw I have selected here a photograph where, as in the previous example, the blacks needed to be clipped, but it was also OK to clip the highlights as well.

2 In this adjusted version, I raised the amount for the Blacks slider to ensure the shadows were sufficiently clipped. In this particular image it was not necessary to preserve the extreme highlights, since I wanted to allow the bright reflections coming off the water to clip, and burn out to white. You'll notice here how I also raised the Exposure slider setting slightly.

Essential image editing steps

With so many tools and ways to edit photographs, it is easy to get confused when working out what is the best way to edit an image in Photoshop. This book offers advice and tips on how to improve the look of your pictures, but we find that 90% of the photographs we take can mostly be improved by applying the following editing steps: lens corrections, crop, color, tone, finesse, capture sharpen, noise reduction and spotting. We do this all in Camera Raw when processing our raw photos, because we find it to be the most efficient workflow available. We know some people have been put off shooting raw because they think it makes things complicated, but when you study the Basic controls in Camera Raw and Lightroom, they really aren't that difficult to master. In fact it seems to us quite odd that people are happy to shoot JPEG because it's 'simpler', yet they then end up jumping through all sorts of complicated hoops in Photoshop to perfect their images.

Camera Raw allows you to work both smarter and faster so you can spend more time taking pictures rather than getting bogged down in making endless photo adjustments. Plus you don't just save time editing single photographs. Get one photograph to look right and it's easy to synchronize all the adjustments across other images that have been taken in the same sequence. Essentially, our message is this: Why make things more difficult for yourself? The controls in Camera Raw are expressly designed to make the photo editing process easier to understand, while offering the ultimate in image quality as well as flexibility. Simple doesn't mean you have to compromise on quality. Adobe has devoted the best part of seven years to enhancing the Camera Raw editing process because in this day and age it makes more sense to carry out the color and tone editing working from the raw capture data. As Camera Raw has got better we have ended up doing all our major tone and color corrections in Camera Raw or Lightroom, leaving Photoshop as the program we use for the major retouching work.

As we say, nine times out of ten we can edit a photograph completely in Camera Raw using the following steps. For the remaining 10% of images either we make fuller use of the other Camera Raw tools such as the Tone Curve, HSL and Effects panels, or we use special techniques in Photoshop such as the Midtone contrast enhancing technique that is described in Chapter 3.

To help explain our approach, I thought I would show all the steps that were used to edit a single image in Camera Raw. Figure 2.14 shows the starting point for this series of steps. This isn't a particularly special photograph, as I deliberately chose a fairly typical image that would allow me to show how a few small adjustments here and there can help improve the look of a photo. You can access this image from the DVD, but you should be able to apply the steps shown here to almost any raw photograph you choose to edit in Camera Raw. The sequence of steps I applied to this particular photo are typical of how both of us approach our Camera Raw/Lightroom editing. Looking at the final version that's shown in Figure 2.29, there isn't really anything more that would be needed to be done to this photo in Photoshop other than to print it.

Figure 2.14 This shows the uncropped before version using the default Basic panel settings.

Auto Lens corrections

This is a new CS5 feature that is only available providing you have installed the free Camera Raw 6.1 update. Once installed you will find that most popular camera lenses for digital SLR camera systems are supported. Simply checking the Enable Lens Profile Correction option applies an instant auto lens correction to the image. In Figure 2.15 I began by applying an auto lens correction to the photo I was about to edit. In this instance the lens data was recognized and the default setting corrected the geometric distortion, chromatic aberration and lens vignetting. This is a useful correction to apply to all photos you are about to edit since it optimizes the capture data to give you the most optically correct image possible. Having said that, the default lens profile corrections may not always provide the best match for your lens, so follow the advice in the sidebar for customizing this adjustment.

Customizing Lens Profile corrections

A default Lens Profile correction may not always apply an optimum correction adjustment. This is because all lenses can vary slightly. Therefore, you can use the sliders at the bottom to fine-tune the Lens Profile correction to match the characteristics of your lens and then go to the Setup menu and choose Save New Lens Profile Defaults. This will now be the new default setting that's applied the next time this lens is recognized.

Figure 2.15 Applying an Auto Lens correction to the photo.

29

Crop

When you work in Camera Raw, there is no particular order that you must follow. That's the beauty of Camera Raw, it's a non-destructive process and you can undo and redo the adjustments as many times as you like. You can start with the tone and color editing and end with a crop, although I reckon it is always best to carry out the tone and color editing first before you decide how to capture sharpen. I simply suggest you crop the photograph first because once you have cropped an image you get a better feel for how the final image can look before you make the tone and color adjustments. It doesn't matter if you crop last, but generally you'll find the crop can sometimes change the whole feel of an image and you may end up having to revise your earlier adjustment settings.

In Figure 2.16 I cropped the photograph more tightly to remove a blurred object in the bottom left corner (but preserved the same 2:3 aspect ratio) and rotated the crop slightly so the cropped photo was more level with the horizon.

Figure 2.16 Cropping the image.

Color

Next, we come to the color adjustment stage. The white balance
controls are placed first at the top of the list of Basic controls, so
we'll start here. This photograph was shot with the camera using
an auto white balance setting. The As Shot white balance didn't
look too bad, but by dragging the Temperature slider to the right
I was able to apply a warmer white balance setting for the whole
photograph (see Figure 2.17). That's just one way you can do this.
Other methods include selecting a preset white balance setting
from the Color Temperature menu, or choosing the Auto option to
let Camera Raw work out the optimum setting. Usually, once you
have got the white balance right, most of the other colors in the
scene will fall into place.

Figure 2.17 Setting the white balance.

Tone

I was now ready to tone adjust the image. There are four main sliders that you can use here: Exposure, Recovery, Fill Light and Blacks.

Exposure

I recommend that you start with the Exposure slider and use this to gauge how much you wish to lighten or darken the picture. The one rule we would apply here is to always adjust the Exposure before you adjust the Brightness (which I'll come onto shortly). In Figure 2.18 you can see an Exposure adjustment being applied. As you adjust the Exposure you can also use the Histogram to be your guide to make sure that you don't push the Exposure slider so far that you clip the highlights. You can also use the highlight clip warning here, or hold down the ⎇ *alt* key as you drag the Exposure slider and check the appearance of the Threshold preview shown on the screen.

Figure 2.18 Setting the overall Exposure and highlight clipping point.

Recovery

The next step is to make sure that there is no significant clipping in important areas of highlight detail. This is something that was touched on earlier in the Optimizing the image tones section. When it comes to making Camera Raw adjustments the best advice is to use the Exposure slider first to adjust the overall brightness. As you do so, you will want to check the appearance of the extreme highlight detail as well as the RGB numbers to make sure these don't go too high. Quite often you'll find that as you set the Exposure, you can get both the brightness and highlight clipping right in one go. However, you shouldn't have to restrict an Exposure adjustment, because the Recovery slider can be used to preserve detail in the highlights, but without altering the effect of the Exposure adjustment (see Figure 2.19). So basically, you should adjust Exposure to expand the tones, making the image brighter or darker. Where you see signs of highlight detail clipping, you can use the Recovery slider to bring back more highlight detail.

Figure 2.19 Adjusting the Recovery slider to protect highlight details from clipping.

Blacks

I'll skip the Fill Light slider and look at setting the Blacks next. If you refer to the section earlier on setting the black clipping point, you will recall how we advise you to simply clip the blackest blacks in the picture as you see fit. There is no need to concern yourself with setting the output levels for the black point, since this can all be handled automatically in Photoshop when you send a file to print or make a CMYK conversion.

Because of the way Camera Raw calculates its tone adjustments, small incremental Blacks adjustments produce a much more noticeable shift in tone adjustment compared to corresponding Exposure adjustments. The default Blacks setting in Camera Raw is 5, which is usually about right for a lot of photographs, and our advice is to not take the Blacks slider any lower than 2 or 3. Or, you can increase the Blacks clipping if you feel it would be useful to hide some of the shadow detail and make these tones all clip to solid black. In the Figure 2.20 example, I raised the Blacks clipping point to 10.

Figure 2.20 Setting the Blacks clipping point.

Fill Light

It is usually best to add Fill Light after having set the Blacks. Fill Light can be used to lighten the shadows and reveal more detail. As with Recovery, it's not necessary for every picture, but for this example I added +25 Fill Light.

Brightness

As I mentioned earlier, you should always adjust the Exposure before you adjust the Brightness. In the steps shown so far, I used the Exposure and Recovery to expand the tones in the photograph and fine-tune to avoid clipping. In the Figure 2.21 step you'll notice how the Brightness adjustment was applied last to adjust the 'relative brightness' of the photograph. In this instance, the Brightness adjustment had little effect on the highlight clipping, but essentially it made the midtones darker. You can therefore think of the Brightness slider as behaving just like the Gamma slider in the Photoshop Levels image adjustment.

Don't overdo Fill Light

The Fill Light adjustment can work wonders at lightening the shadow areas while preserving the black clipping point. Take care not to overdo things with the Fill Light adjustment, because if you add too much Fill Light you can get unnatural looking shadows (it is worth checking these in close-up when adding a lot of Fill Light). If you need to dramatically lighten the shadows, it is better to use Tone Curve adjustments in conjunction with Fill Light. Having said this, I should point out that the Fill Light algorithm in Camera Raw 6 is much improved, such that extreme Fill Light adjustments will produce much better looking results.

Figure 2.21 Setting the Fill Light and Brightness.

Contrast

The steps applied so far all affect the image's global contrast and the Exposure and Blacks sliders in particular have the greatest effect here. The Contrast slider in the Basic panel can therefore be used at this stage to further modify the contrast. Basically, after you have set the highlights and blacks and adjusted the brightness, what do you think of the image? Does it look too flat at this stage or too contrasty? The Contrast slider provides a simple, yet effective means to adjust the global contrast. In the Figure 2.22 example I reckoned the photograph could have done with some added contrast. The default setting is +25, but here I chose to raise this to +50.

Of course, you can also go to the Camera Raw Tone Curve panel and adjust the contrast. While we both like using the Tone Curve there is a lot to be said for the simplicity of the Contrast slider. You don't have to switch panels to carry on editing the image and a simple slider adjustment is often all you need to get the contrast looking right at this stage.

Figure 2.22 Setting the Contrast.

Finesse

This step is about adding polish to the image. It's not obligatory, but something that we both do to quite a number of our images. You could include in this step things like HSL panel adjustments to selectively lighten or darken certain colors. Here, I wanted to keep this section simple, so we'll focus on just the Clarity and Vibrance sliders in the Basic panel.

Clarity

The Clarity slider provides a nice, easy to use adjustment for adding midtone contrast to an image. A little later on in this book in Chapter 3 we'll be showing two different Photoshop techniques that can be used to add variable midtone contrast. The Clarity slider combines a bit of both of these techniques and is an effective tool for enhancing detail contrast (as opposed to sharpness) in areas of flat tone. Most photographs can benefit from adding at least +10 Clarity; in the Figure 2.23 example I set the Clarity to +15.

Figure 2.23 The Clarity adjustment step.

Vibrance

Just below Clarity we have the Vibrance and Saturation sliders. Saturation has been around since version 1 of Camera Raw and provides a basic method for boosting saturation in a photograph as it applies a 'linear' type saturation adjustment to the image. This means that it boosts the saturation of all colors evenly, including those colors that are already quite saturated. The downside of this is that it is very easy to clip some of the already saturated colors when applying even a modest saturation boost. The Vibrance control, on the other hand, applies a non-linear saturation adjustment in which the least saturated colors get the biggest boost, while the already saturated colors receive less of a boost. Vibrance also tends to filter out skin tone colors so that these are more protected as you increase the Vibrance. In Figure 2.24 I applied a +30 Vibrance. This enriched the colors in the scene, but without clipping the richer colors.

Figure 2.24 The Vibrance adjustment step.

Capture sharpening

Finally, we come to the capture sharpening step, where I went to the Detail panel in Camera Raw and fine-tuned the four Sharpening sliders according to the sharpening needs of the image. When you first go to the Detail panel you'll see default settings of 25 Amount, 1.0 Radius, 25 Detail and 0 Masking. These offer a reasonable starting point for most images, so even if you do nothing here, Camera Raw still applies some capture sharpening.

Amount and Radius

The Amount and Radius need to be adjusted in tandem. The Amount determines how much sharpening is applied, while the Radius lets you decide how wide you want the halo edges to be. Basically, a Radius of 1.0 works well for most edges. Fine detailed subjects will benefit from a smaller Radius setting and soft detailed subjects such as portraits can do with using a wider radius of, say, 1.1–1.3. In the Figure 2.25 example I applied an Amount of 39 combined with a low Radius setting of 0.8 pixels.

Figure 2.25 The Amount and Radius sharpening step.

Sharpen for content

It is important to adjust the capture sharpening for the needs of the individual image. Once you have got the capture sharpening tailored to the requirements of each photo, the output sharpening that is applied at the end will be the same for every image.

Maximum detail

If Detail is set at 100, the sharpening effect is similar to that achieved when using the Unsharp Mask filter in Photoshop.

Detail and Masking

The Detail and Masking sliders act like suppression controls for the sharpening. Setting the Detail slider to an amount lower than 100 allows you to suppress the halo artifacts. With soft detailed subjects (such as portrait photographs) it is preferable to use a low Detail setting. With detailed photographs such as this, it was OK to increase the Detail setting and not suppress the halos quite so much, which allowed me to apply a stronger sharpening effect. The Masking slider can be used to apply a mask based on the image content that filters the capture sharpening effect. With detailed subjects we leave the Masking set to zero, but for other types of image it is worth raising the masking, as this can help protect some of the soft detailed areas from being over-sharpened. In Figure 2.26 I applied a Detail of 35 and set the Masking to 15.

Noise reduction

The noise reduction can now be applied using the three Luminance sliders (Luminance, Luminance Detail and Luminance Contrast) to

Figure 2.26 The Detail sharpening step.

suppress the grain-like effects of camera noise. The Color and Color Detail slider can be used to suppress the color speckle artifacts that are also a consequence of high ISO capture with some digital cameras. For most low to medium ISO captures I tend to stick with the default settings, but for high ISO captures, where more noise is usually visible, I tend to adjust the Color sliders first to remove the color speckles and then see if it is necessary to adjust the Luminance sliders to smooth out noise artifacts. We'll be looking at the new noise reduction controls in more detail in Chapter 3.

Localized adjustments

Next, I applied a few localized adjustments (see Figure 2.27). As you can see here, I selected the graduated filter tool and added a couple of graduated adjustments. I applied a darkening adjustment to the water and then added a further darkening adjustment to the sky, where I also applied a light blue color to make the sky appear slightly more blue.

Figure 2.27 Applying localized adjustments.

Spotting

The spotting can be done using the spot removal tool (as shown in Figure 2.28). Of course, you can apply this step at any time, but it is something that I usually prefer to do last. The reason for this is that all the preceding steps can be applied quickly and the settings easily shared across multiple images. I generally only want to go to the bother of spotting an image if I am really sure that I want to use it. While it is possible to share spot removal settings across multiple selected photos you have to be careful to make sure that the shared spot removal settings work OK on each individual image. Another thing to bear in mind is that some blemish sensor marks will only show up after you have adjusted all the tone settings, so you can see the problem more clearly if you do the spotting at the end rather than at the beginning.

Figure 2.28 This shows an example of the spot removal tool being used to spot the image. It so happened with this image that there were no sensor marks that needed to be removed. So here I used the spot removal tool to remove a bird from the roof of the building instead.

An overview of the Camera Raw workflow

The purpose of this chapter is to put the Camera Raw workflow into perspective and show how most of the image editing work can be done at the Camera Raw editing stage. While it is possible to repeat much of what is shown here using Photoshop image adjustment tools like Levels, Curves and Shadows/Highlights, why would you want to do that? Camera Raw allows you do just about everything you want, including the all-important capture sharpening and noise reduction non-destructively, before you take your photos into Photoshop. Figure 2.29 below compares the finished photograph with the version we started out with.

Figure 2.29 Here you can compare the before version (top) and the edited version below.

Chapter 3

Raising your IQ

How to improve your image quality

We naturally all want our photographs to look their very best when they are printed on the page. In this chapter we wanted to start by looking at some of the ways you can help guarantee getting the best digital results from your camera. We have therefore chosen to concentrate here on how to get the best from your camera lens optics, some shooting techniques to improve image quality as well as post-processing tricks that can be done in Photoshop.

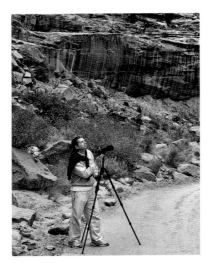

Figure 3.1 Martin on location in Capitol Reef National Park using a tripod to maximize image quality.

Improving camera capture sharpness

It is all very well using image sharpening to improve image detail, but it's also important to ensure that the images you capture are as sharp as they can be – before processing the images in software.

Choice of camera lens

The most obvious factor that affects sharpness will be the quality of the image optics used on the camera. In the past, camera lenses were designed to meet the specific needs of film. This is not to say that film-designed lenses are no longer any good. Many of the classic lenses are indeed well suited for digital photography, but there are certain limitations you need to be aware of. First of all, the lenses for 35 mm film cameras were designed to resolve well enough so as to capture a sharp image on a 24 mm $\times$ 36 mm area of film emulsion. Even when using the finest grain film emulsion processed under ideal conditions, the ultimate resolving power of 35 mm film cannot even begin to compare to the amount of detail that can be captured by the sensors found in some of today's digital SLR cameras. So, lenses that might have been great or OK 10 years ago are not going to allow you to get the most out of the resolving power of, say, a 16 or 22 megapixel camera. Even if you use a good quality zoom lens, there may not be any point capturing anything more than 16 megapixels of data. However, if you use a modern prime lens, you should certainly see a definite improvement in capture sharpness. At the end of the day, 11 megapixels of data captured on an average zoom lens is plenty of pixels for most reproduction quality work, but if you need extra detail, and want to make the most of what the sensor can offer, then you do need to think carefully about the lenses you shoot with.

Another consideration is the fact that film lenses were designed to resolve a color image to three separate (red, green and blue sensitive) film emulsion layers which overlaid each other. Consequently, film lenses were designed to focus the red, green and blue wavelengths at fractionally different distances and at even further distances apart towards the corner edges of the film emulsion area. Since the red, green and blue photosites are all in the same plane of focus on a digital sensor, lenses that are specifically designed for digital capture should now focus the red, green and blue wavelengths to a single plane of focus.

Shooting with a tripod vs. hand-held

There are some obvious benefits to shooting with the camera fixed to a tripod, especially when shooting in low light conditions where you would otherwise be forced to use a slower shutter speed or higher ISO setting. Figure 3.1 shows Martin using a tripod on location in Utah. One thing you do have to be careful of is to not use image stabilization when shooting on a tripod since with some older lenses, the image stabilization can actually end up destabilizing the image.

Improved sharpness using mirror-up mode

The action of the mirror flipping up on a digital SLR or medium format camera causes a small amount of internal vibration. This can be a problem when shooting with continuous light and where the time duration in which the camera body vibrates slightly makes up a significant proportion of the overall exposure. We therefore reckon this is more of an issue when using shutter speeds of around, say, 1/15th to 1/125th of a second and when photographing close-up subjects, as opposed to landscape scenes shot with a wide-angle lens (see Figures 3.2 and 3.3). We reached this conclusion after conducting tests on a series of shots, including the examples shown in Figure 3.3, where we found that the mirror vibration effect was most noticeable at around 1/60th of a second. Ironically, the problem can be made worse when the camera is mounted on a tripod. This is because the vibration movement originates within the camera itself and when the camera is supported on a free-standing tripod, such vibrations are unconstrained. When you hand-hold a camera the mirror vibration can be absorbed through your hands. You could say that the photographer holding the camera is acting like a giant shock absorber!

When we shoot non-moving exterior shots on a tripod or studio subjects lit with continuous lighting, we often use the camera in mirror-up mode when shooting close-up details. This can be tricky with some cameras, as it is often a custom user setting that is buried deep in the camera settings menus. One of the nice features of the latest Canon EOS cameras is that it is now much easier to set up the mirror-up mode as a favorite camera setting that can be accessed more easily when you are out shooting on location.

Image stabilizing lenses

Image stabilization can be achieved in two main ways. Image stabilizing lenses use gyroscopic motors to move the lens elements in an effort to keep the image steady. If you look through the camera and move the lens about quickly, you'll hear the motors whirring as they compensate for camera shake type movement and you'll sometimes notice how the image jumps every now and then as you do so. Some cameras can stabilize the image by using motors to move the sensor instead and the advantage of this is that you are not limited to working with specific image stabilizing lenses only. In either case, image stabilization can help you shoot sharp pictures at slower shutter speeds and this can effectively buy you a couple stops of exposure, where without image stabilization you would be forced to shoot at a higher ISO setting in order to get sharp pictures.

Figure 3.2 This shows a close-up view of a detailed subject where the top picture was shot with the mirror-up option switched off and the bottom picture was shot with the mirror-up option switched on. Canon EOS 1Ds MkIII with a Canon EF 100 mm f2.8 Macro lens, shot at 1/60th, f 7.1, 200 ISO.

Tripod: 70–200 f2.8 lens, mirror-up mode

Hand-held: 70–200 f2.8 lens, image stabilization on

Hand-held: 70–200 f2.8 lens, image stabilization off

Tripod: 28–135 lens, Normal mode

Figure 3.3 This shows the same subject that was shot in Figure 3.2, this time showing the difference between four methods of shooting, using the Canon EOS 1Ds MkIII at a 200 ISO setting with an exposure of 1/60th second at f7.1. The top left example was shot on a tripod using an EF 70–200 mm lens in mirror-up mode. Next to it, on the right, is a hand-held version shot with the lens image stabilization switched on and, bottom left, a shot taken with the image stabilization switched off. The bottom right picture shows the same subject photographed on a tripod, but with a less expensive Canon zoom lens.

Megapixel limits

Each year we see the bar raised as to the number of megapixels digital cameras can capture. There is, of course, a strong marketing drive for manufacturers to claim that their cameras can capture more megapixels than the competition, as this still remains a strong influencing factor in most digital camera purchase decisions. After all, having more megapixels must mean bigger, better pictures, right? Or does it?

How far can we keep going?

Many people have assumed that digital cameras will just keep having more megapixels. But surely there comes a point where it isn't possible to squeeze any more photosites onto a sensor? The main limitation here is that as the photosites on a sensor are made smaller, the physical number of photons that can hit each photosite diminishes accordingly. With a 21–24 megapixel full-frame 35 mm sensor, the number of photons resolved per pixel can be calculated as being as low as 6 for the darkest shadows. Photon detection is also random and the signal to noise ratio increases as there are fewer photons to record. This highlights another physical constraint and that is how well a sensor can resolve shadow detail as you attempt to squeeze more photosites into the same fixed frame size. In a paper by David B. Goldstein, *Physical Limits in Digital Photography,* published on the Northlight Images website (http://tinyurl.com/kqbett), Goldstein has taken into account the limits of shadow detail recording with small-sized photosites as well as the limits of current lens optics. He has suggested that in the case of full-frame digital SLRs, 25–35 megapixels is the current practical limit. This is based on research using the best quality lenses at an optimum lens aperture of f/10. Until there is some breakthrough in lens design that offers better performance at wider apertures, then this will be the physical limit.

The limits of lens optics

It should be self-evident that the image you capture can only be as good as the optics used to focus the image in the first place. It is no good having a 22 megapixel full-frame sensor unless the glass on the front of the camera is capable of resolving a picture that is sharp enough to make full use of those extra megapixels. Not only that, but you have to bear in mind that the optimum resolving power of a lens used with a full-frame digital SLR camera is probably somewhere around f/8. At the widest apertures you are more likely to experience a lens performance drop-off towards the edges of the frame. At lens apertures that are wider than, say, f/5.6 or f/8, the lens performance usually diminishes due to the limits of the lens optics' ability to resolve a fully sharp image evenly from the center to the edges of the frame. Obviously, there are some ultra-wide aperture prime lenses which can be expected to outpace other lenses at the widest aperture settings, but these too tend to perform better as the lens aperture is stopped down more.

All lenses will have an optimum aperture setting at which the lens performs at its best, and as you stop down and make the aperture smaller these benefits are limited by the effects of diffraction, which diminishes the effective sharpness of a lens. Basically, as the aperture is made smaller this causes the light waves to diffract and this leads to a softer contrast image containing less detail. The effects of diffraction are also linked to the physical size of the sensor. The diffraction limit for lenses used with full-frame digital SLR cameras is around f/10. With smaller compact digital SLR cameras, because the sensor is that much smaller, the diffraction effects start to become more noticeable at lens apertures of around f/7 or f/8.

We should also consider the implications for smaller format, compact digital cameras. According to Goldstein, with consumer digital cameras, the size of the sensor is so small that the diffraction effects can become noticeable at around f/2.4, and he points out that there is so far only one compact camera that allows you to shoot at an aperture as wide as that. As you stop the lens down the resolving capability at the smallest aperture decreases to just a few megapixels. So, with one of the latest 12 MP compact cameras, you are probably only going to be able to fully appreciate the benefit of all those megapixels if you can shoot using the widest lens aperture available. Therefore, in the case of compact digital cameras we have probably already reached the limit at 12 megapixels.

To sum up: the main limiting factors for lens optics performance are the ability to focus an image evenly from the center of the field to the edges, at the widest aperture, and the effects of diffraction at the smaller apertures. The optimum lens aperture therefore lies between these two extremes and the effects of diffraction are also affected by

Lens diffraction

As you stop down a lens and use a smaller lens aperture, you gain the benefit of increasing the depth of field, thereby improving the apparent sharpness of an image. However, as the lens aperture becomes smaller in size you need also to be aware of the effects of lens diffraction. This is due to the way light, which normally travels in straight lines through air, disperses when it travels through a small hole, such as the aperture of a lens. This effect is barely noticeable at the wider lens apertures but becomes more noticeable as the lens aperture is made smaller.

the ultimate resolving power of a camera's sensor at a given frame size. Figures 3.4 shows an example of a lens test report for a Canon 28–135 mm zoom lens shot using a Canon EOS 40D and Figure 3.5 below it shows actual examples of lens performance using this same lens, shot at the widest, optimum and minimum apertures, but using the Canon EOS 1Ds MkIII. As you can see, the photographs bear out the results shown in Figure 3.4. The widest aperture version is not as optically sharp as the f/5.6 example and the smallest aperture version suffers from fuzziness and a lack of contrast.

We are close approaching the limits imposed by the laws of physics as to how many megapixels can be achieved from full-frame digital SLR cameras or smaller. It seems to us that the only way forward now if you wish to achieve better image quality is to invest in a larger format camera system. It is therefore interesting to note that digital camera systems such as the Hasselblad H series, or the Phase One P65, that Jeff shoots with, are actually not that much bulkier than a full-frame Canon or Nikon digital SLR, but can offer better image quality through recording a higher number of megapixels from a sensor that is physically bigger than a standard 24 mm $\times$ 36 mm full-frame digital SLR. The same holds true for the latest Leica S2 system, which uses a 30 mm $\times$ 45 mm sensor. However, Goldstein points out that with bigger format camera systems you often need to stop down more to achieve a comparable depth of field to that of a smaller format camera system. So if matching depth of field capability is important, the trade-off is that you don't necessarily gain as much extra resolving power as you might expect.

One photographer's viewpoint

Based on my own experience, once digital SLRs were able to capture more than 10 megapixels, I found this was plenty of pixels to work with for most purposes. I have large A1-size framed landscape prints on the walls in my house that were shot using the Canon EOS 1Ds MkI, which was my first proper 11 megapixel digital SLR camera (see Figure 3.6). The fact that more recent versions of this camera are able to capture more megapixels is great. However, in order to fully appreciate the benefits of such high pixel capture resolutions it has been necessary for me to shoot using better quality optics, such as prime lenses and at optimum lens aperture settings.

Canon EF 28-135mm f/3.5-5.6 IS USM on Canon EOS 40D body

Variation of MTF50 with Aperture Setting

Figure 3.4 This lens test chart shows a typical lens response from the widest to the smallest lens aperture. As you can see, the peak lens performance for this lens is achieved at the midpoint aperture setting of f/5.6 at the minimum focal length and f/8 at other focal lengths. This graph was created with data obtained using Imatest software (www.imatest.com).

The graph shown here was supplied by Jon Tarrant and was taken from one of his *What Digital Camera* (www.whatdigitalcamera.com) lens tests.

Figure 3.5 This shows a comparison of a close-up detail shot using the Canon 28–135 mm lens featured in Figure 3.4 at the 28 mm zoom setting. Seen here are details from the widest aperture (left), the optimum aperture (middle) and smallest aperture (right). A layered image is also available on the DVD.

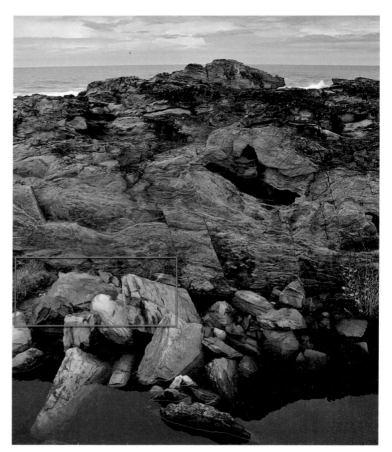

Figure 3.6 Here is a landscape photo that was shot in South Africa using the Canon EOS 1Ds MkI (11 megapixel) camera with an EF 24–70 mm Canon lens.

Figure 3.7 Here is a close-up view of the above photograph. As you can see, this 11 megapixel photo still has plenty enough detail to produce a large poster print.

Fine-tuning the auto focus alignment

Here is a subject that I have to say only recently caught my attention when Jeff pointed out to me that some of the latest high-end digital SLR cameras allow you to make micro focus calibration adjustments. This is something that had never occurred to me before since I had always assumed both the manual and automatic focusing to be fairly accurate on such cameras. However, as I was about to find out, this isn't necessarily always the case.

There are two issues at stake here: one is the accuracy of the auto focus detection mechanism in estimating the exact, correct focusing distance to produce a perfectly sharp image on the sensor. The other issue is to do with the accuracy of the focus screen used for manual focusing and whether the light path distance to the glass screen is exactly the same as that to the sensor. I am reminded here of what happened to a photographer's assistant who accidentally broke the ground glass screen of his boss's 5 × 4 plate camera. Not wanting to incur the wrath of the photographer (who was known to have a nasty temper), he set about finding a replacement screen and fixed it himself. The only problem was he put it in the wrong way round with the ground glass facing outwards and was caught out anyway.

Anyway, I digress. If there is even just the slightest amount of deviation in the physical distance for the screen, the sensor or the lens itself, this can result in minor fluctuations in focusing from the assumed factory standard. The main variable here is the lens itself and it is interesting, if not shocking, to discover just how much variance there might be between an individual lens and the 'assumed' lens focusing behavior.

Enter the LensAlign® system (www.lensalign.com), a calibration tool designed by Michael Tapes that provides a method for calibrating the lens focusing in those digital SLR cameras that provide a custom auto focus calibration setting control. These include the latest Canon EOS 1D MkIII, 1Ds MkIII, 5D MkII, the Nikon D3, D3X, D300 and D700, plus several more. Now I admit I do happen to know Michael, but my purchase of LensAlign came from a genuine desire (and need) to calibrate the lenses I shoot with and I have to say I'm glad I did, because it has revealed significant focusing errors with a couple of the lenses I use regularly.

Figure 3.8 The LensAlign Pro calibration tool.

Stored calibration settings

Providing you make the focus calibration adjustments on a per lens basis, the camera stores this information in its internal memory and automatically knows in future just how much correction to apply to the auto focus for whichever lens you choose to shoot with.

Here is how it works. The LensAlign calibration tool comes in two versions: Lite and Pro. Both offer the same degree of accuracy, but the Pro version is larger, more robustly built and can be adapted to take a long lens ruler adapter (Figure 3.8). Basically, you begin by setting up the LensAlign assembly so that it is aligned straight-on to the camera and at an optimal distance from the chart of ×25 the focal length of the lens to be tested. There are instructional videos on the website that show you how to do this and the tool is cleverly designed to allow you to check the alignment by spying through a tiny aperture at the back as well as when looking through the camera lens itself. Once aligned for the camera body and lens combination you wish to test, you set the lens aperture to its widest setting and simply let the auto focus system of your camera focus on the main target and take a picture. Now, because the ruler scale is positioned at an angle to the camera, when you examine the captured image in close-up, you can use the numbers on the ruler scale to help determine whether the focusing system of your camera is focusing correctly or not (i.e. when the sharpest detail on the ruler scale is at the zero point).

If it turns out that the camera and lens combination is not focusing correctly, you can now work out if the error is due to front or back focusing. Armed with this information, you then need to locate the Auto Focus calibration setting from the camera menu and try making a calibration adjustment for the lens you are currently shooting with. Shoot another test and see if this improves the focus accuracy. Once you have worked out the appropriate level of correction that's it, you can move on to test other lenses.

As I say, I was both impressed and shocked by what I found. One of my lenses required the maximum amount of front focusing correction available in order to achieve optimum sharpness (see Figures 3.9 and 3.10). The difference between the before and after is quite staggering. Bear in mind here that this test is designed to show up the focus accuracy at the widest lens aperture. When shooting normally it very often won't matter if the focusing is slightly out since at least some points in the photo will be at maximum sharpness and at smaller apertures the depth of field will increase to compensate and bring more points into apparent sharp focus. However, it is reassuring to know that for those times when pin-sharp focusing is required at wide apertures, there is now a way to ensure the focusing is as spot on as possible.

Figure 3.9 Here you can see a close-up view of an initial lens test in which the auto focus mechanism was clearly off target and front focusing.

Figure 3.10 In this example you can see how the LensAlign target was captured after I had applied an auto focus calibration adjustment via the camera.

Using Lens Corrections to improve IQ

Even if you use a great lens properly focused to make a shake-free exposure, the odds are that the capture will have issues due to lens defects. Lens designers try hard to design out as many lens defects as possible but even great lenses will show signs of distortion, chromatic aberration and lens vignetting. In Photoshop CS5 and Camera Raw 6 photographers can correct for these defects after the fact, computationally. Figure 3.11 shows an image I shot in Trafalgar Square with a Canon EF-S 10–22 mm lens that needed lens perspective correction.

Figure 3.11 The image on the left is before any lens correction. The image on the right is after basic lens profile corrections, but not perspective corrections, in Camera Raw.

In examining the differences shown above, the obvious change was to lighten the corners of the image to remove lens vignetting. You may also be able to see a reduction in the barrel distortion, which bows out without the correction (pincushion distortion bows in). What you can't see at this size is the lateral chromatic aberration, which is the inability of a lens to focus all colors of light at the same size. This results in color fringing, which is particularly noticeable in the corners of a wide-angle lens shot. You may also note that both of the above images are crooked. Normally, I would correct the rotation of an image to level it early in a processing session (I really hate it when images are 'slightly off'). However, with the addition of the manual transform controls in the Lens Correction panel, I find it useful to do a rotation correction there along with keystone corrections rather than using the leveling function of the crop tool.

Figure 3.12 The Profile tab of the Lens Corrections panel in Camera Raw allows you to automatically select a lens profile for supported lenses. Above left is the panel with the Enable button unchecked. The second panel shows Camera Raw automatically selecting the profile for the Canon EF-S 10–22 mm lens. The third panel shows what happens when a lens can't be found in the lens database. The final panel on the right shows the current list of lens manufacturers whose lenses may have been profiled. Not all lens have yet – it's an ongoing process.

Figure 3.12 above shows a series of displays you'll see in the Profile tab of the Lens Corrections panel. The panel is similar to the Lens Corrections feature of Photoshop CS5. Both use the same potential set of lens profiles (there are different profiles for raw and JPEG images). Also, while Photoshop can actually search online for new profiles (as shown in Figure 3.13), Camera Raw can't yet. This initiative by Adobe to offer automatic lens profile based corrections has been a massive effort. Unfortunately, not every lens has been profiled yet. So Adobe is enlisting the help of the user community to add custom lens profiles made by users and submitted to the lens profile database. You can download the free Adobe Lens Profile Creator from the Labs.Adobe.com website. The process is to print out a specially designed target, shoot it in the prescribed manner and run the images through the Lens Profile Creator application. Making a simple one-shot profile for a fixed focal length lens at a single f-stop is pretty easy. But shooting a series of focal lengths of a zoom lens and adding additional subject distances and f-stops is a serious task. Figure 3.13 shows the result of a profile search in Photoshop.

Figure 3.13 This shows a detail of the Lens Corrections feature in Photoshop CS5. The Search Online button can be used to search the Adobe lens profile database for newly added Adobe or user-made profiles. The dialog is showing the results of a search for a Canon EF 50 mm f/1.2 lens. There are two, both made by me. I suggest you select the second one since I kinda screwed up the first profile (but I couldn't unload it from the lens database).

Impact of the lens corrections

Like any interpolation algorithm, the lens profile and manual transforms will result in a softening of the image. The better the original image quality you have, the less noticeable the interpolation will be on your image. For this reason you should always double check and adjust your image sharpening settings after you've made the lens and manual transform adjustments.

Figure 3.14 On the left are the Correction Amount sliders that allow you to tweak the amount settings. On the right, the Setup drop-down menu is showing the ability to Save New Lens Profile Defaults. Once you do that, whenever Camera Raw detects the lens it will apply the profile plus your custom amount tweaks.

The Correction Amount sliders allow you to override the default correction amounts. Figure 3.14 shows how I adjusted the Chromatic Aberration amount up to 130. I've found that while the original Chromatic Aberration corrections are good, I usually need to run the amount up to 120 to 130 for most of my lenses.

The Lens Corrections panel also includes a Manual tab that offers manual transforms above and beyond the profile-based corrections. Figure 3.15 shows the panel as well as the image with transform adjustments being made. You'll note I turned on the grid overlay by pressing the **V** key. I zoomed into the image and tried to align important image detail such as building edges to the grid

Figure 3.15 The Manual tab of the Lens Corrections panel allows for manual transforms (left). The image on the right shows the grid overlay and the added gray area.

to make the adjustments of the perspective corrections and rotation more accurate. I also find it is useful to target a transform field and use the up and down arrow keys for more precise adjustment settings. Adjusting the perspective corrections always requires very accurate rotational corrections – sometimes the interaction is tricky.

Figure 3.15 also shows what happens when the transform has run out of real image data and how it adds a filler area of gray. You can choose to render the image with the added gray area or crop it out. If the gray area is a simple texture that Content Aware Fill will easily handle, I tend to keep it. In this example, however, I had shot the image loose enough that I chose to crop the gray area out. Figure 3.16 shows the Crop tool option that allows you to constrain or not constrain the crop to the actual image area. The final image seen in Figure 3.17 shows the result of the original lens profile correction, the additional Chromatic Aberration amount tweak as well as the transforms that were applied in Figure 3.15.

Figure 3.16 Above is the Crop tool menu showing the ability to select or deselect the option to constrain the crop to the actual image area only.

Figure 3.17 The final results of the Lens Correction panel adjustments.

PhotoKit Sharpener

PhotoKit Sharpener's sharpening workflow has proven to be successful – so much so that Adobe wanted Bruce Fraser to work with Thomas Knoll to incorporate the capture sharpening principles into Camera Raw and, later, output sharpening directly into both Camera Raw (5.2 and above) and Adobe Photoshop Lightroom. Unfortunately, Bruce passed away before seeing the results of the collaboration but I filled in for Bruce and helped complete the project. We're sure he would have been pleased.

Capture sharpening workflow

Even if you employ technical excellence in the capture of your image, you will still need to use image sharpening in Camera Raw or Photoshop. Why? Because the very process of digitizing an image softens the resulting image pixels. The problem then becomes when and how to sharpen your image. Bruce Fraser made a conceptual breakthrough when he devised the 'sharpening workflow' approach. The scheme was to break down the sharpening into three phases: 'Capture Sharpening' upon first opening an image, 'Creative Sharpening' for addressing local sharpening or smoothing, and 'Output Sharpening' at the last stage when the final size and resolution of an image are known. We'll cover capture sharpening here because it has such an impact on IQ.

Capture sharpening depends on both the source of the image and the image content. The content part of the equation is critical. For optimum sharpening, you need to adjust for the edge frequency – a higher radius for low frequency and a lower radius for high frequency edges. Figure 3.18 is an example of a low edge frequency image and shows the Detail settings used. While setting the Radius correctly is the first big step, it's really using the

Figure 3.18 With the image at a 100% zoom, the aim is to adjust the image until it looks 'good' at that zoom. The Radius was set to 1.5, which is appropriate for a portrait containing low edge frequency.

Figure 3.19 The image on the left is with no sharpening applied. The image on the right is with sharpening turned on. Both images are at 200% zoom, so the sharpened image will look slightly over-sharpened.

Determining edge frequency

An easy way to determine an image's edge frequency is to imagine a horizontal line across the image. Images with low frequency tend to have fewer alternating strong lights and darks, such as this portrait. Landscape images often have high frequency edges and need a lower radius setting. Of course, sometimes an image has a mix and for that you need to take some extra steps.

Masking that allows proper sharpening to be applied to those areas that need it, such as the eyes, lips and hair. Figure 3.20 shows the result of the masking preview. The white areas represent the edges which we want to sharpen and the black areas the surface areas which we don't. Setting the Radius and Masking properly allows us to use a more aggressive amount, which will optimize the detail in the image.

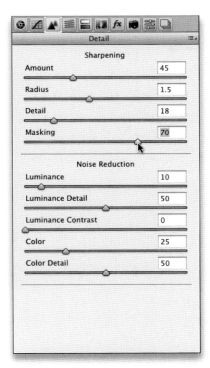

Figure 3.20 This shows the Figure 3.18 image with the Masking preview (hold down the ⌥ (alt) key while moving the slider) showing the edges and surfaces of the image. The Masking slider is set here to 70, which is a common setting for portraits.

For a portrait, it's also useful to lower the Detail slider to kick in the halo suppression it provides while reducing the emphasis on high frequency detail (the other thing the Detail slider does). The higher the Detail settings the more the sharpening concentrates on detail and allows stronger halos – which are not 'bad' as long as they are invisible when zoomed to 100%. The other thing to pay attention to is while there are four sliders called Sharpening, there's really a fifth slider that comes into play and needs to be set properly: Luminance Noise Reduction. Most images need at least some slight noise reduction even though it's off by default, and with the Figure 3.18 portrait image I found adding a Luminance setting of 10 to be sufficient.

For images with higher frequency edges – which are common for landscapes – the Radius should be lowered and often the Detail slider increased. Figure 3.21 shows the result of aggressive Detail and Amount settings with the Radius setting reduced from the default of 1 pixel to a setting of 0.7 pixels. The image is sharp, but without halos at a 100% zoom that would interfere with subsequent sharpening rounds in later phases (although the odds of needing creative sharpening are not high here).

Figure 3.21 This shows an example of an image with high frequency edges – lots of alternating lights and darks and small detail. Here the Radius was lowered to 0.7 and the Detail slider set to 40. Notice the Masking was still being used at a low setting and Luminance Noise Reduction had been applied.

Figure 3.22 This shows the Figure 3.21 image with the Radius preview (hold down the ⌥ *alt* key while moving the slider) showing the Radius setting at 0.7. The image is shown here at a zoom of 200%.

Figure 3.22 shows the Radius setting being reduced to 0.7 with the preview visible. Previewing the Radius (as well as the Detail slider) allows you to more accurately arrive at optimal settings. The image, shot on a Canon EOS 1Ds MII at ISO 200, benefited by adding noise reduction. Increasing the noise reduction setting also allows you to increase the strength of the Detail slider.

Figure 3.23 This shows the Figure 3.21 image at a screen zoom of 200%. The image on the left is shown here with no sharpening and the image on the right has the sharpening settings shown in Figure 3.21 applied to it.

So, that's all well and good if your image falls neatly into one of these two categories, but what about an image that has a mix of frequencies that puts it squarely in between? Well, you could compromise and adjust the settings to the middle ground, but that's not really optimal. For special cases where capture sharpening needs a blend of two types of sharpening – high and low frequencies – the best option is to optimize for both and composite the results in a single file. Creating two differently capture-sharpened copies of the raw file as Smart Objects allows you to blend between them.

Using Smart Objects with Camera Raw allows you to combine the benefits of working parametrically inside Photoshop. This is because a Camera Raw Smart Object remains editable inside a Photoshop file. To have Camera Raw open a raw image as a Smart Object, click on the Workflow Options info button and check the option to open as a Smart Object in Photoshop as shown in Step 1. Note, this setting will remain sticky until you uncheck it.

ProPhoto RGB: 16 bit; 5616 by 3744 (21.0MP); 300 ppi

The Camera Raw Workflow info button

1 By checking the option for Open in Photoshop as Smart Object, the raw file was embedded in the Photoshop document and retained its editability until it was flattened.

2 The image was opened in Photoshop as a Smart Object (as shown in the Layers panel view on the left). The Layers panel view on the right shows how the bottom layer had been duplicated using Layer ⇨ Smart Objects ⇨ New Smart Object via Copy and a layer mask applied so the copy layer would only be blended in the center. To edit a Smart Object layer, all you have to do is to double-click the image icon.

3 Within each Smart Object, different Sharpening settings were used to deal with low frequency detail (as shown on the left, and placed at the bottom of the layer stack), and high frequency (finer) detail on the right, and placed above. Note that with the low frequency image, the Radius was higher and the Detail slider made lower, with the Masking set to 30. Also note that the Luminance noise reduction was set to 40, which killed all the noise in the sky and water. These settings remained editable in Camera Raw so that I could still fine-tune each of the Smart Objects.

Photo: © Jeff Schewe

4 This shows the final result of the Smart Object capture sharpen blend. The original image was shot at dusk with a Canon EOS 1Ds MII with a 24–70 mm F2.8 lens.

Is it noise or image detail?

One of the issues in determining whether or not noise is going to be a problem in the final reproduction is that we currently can't accurately judge noise and image detail on a computer display. Even the best displays are only capable of about 110 pixels per inch (PPI). If you will be outputting your image at 300–360 PPI then your display is only about 1/3 of your image's resolution. If you zoom into the image to view at 100%, the problem is then that the image is about 3x as large as the print size. Ironically, one of the best ways of reducing the visual effect of grain is to downsample the image. Downsampling to 50% of the original size essentially makes the noise 1/4 less apparent. So, before you turn yourself inside out with anguish about image noise, be sure to see what the real visibility will be in the final reproduction.

Noise reduction

Noise is something that affects all digital images. If you shoot at the optimum ISO rating and proper exposure, the chances are you won't even see any noise. But as you increase the ISO rating the noise will soon become noticeable and perhaps objectionable.

The presence of noise, the 'noise signature' of a sensor, is actually determined by the sensor at the sensor's base ISO setting. Noise is there even at the lowest ISO, but it's just not really perceptible. When you increase the ISO setting, this increases the gain sensitivity of the sensor (which, bear in mind, is actually an analog device). The amplification of the signal coming from the sensor increases its sensitivity (and therefore its ISO rating), but it also amplifies the pseudo-random noise. The noise may seem random but there is actually a sequence that produces a pattern over time, so it's not really totally random. Note that increasing the ISO doesn't capture more actual photons, it only increases the sensitivity and this reduced photon count. Increased gain is where we start to perceive more noise in our captures.

There are two problems to address here; one is the color speckles caused primarily by demosiacing a Bayer array sensor and the other is luminance noise or the grain-like pattern that you see when you inspect an image in close-up. Figure 3.24 shows the two basic types of problem noise that can be reduced by image processing algorithms.

Inside Photoshop proper, you have a somewhat limited set of tools for noise reduction. The essential function is to blur the noise

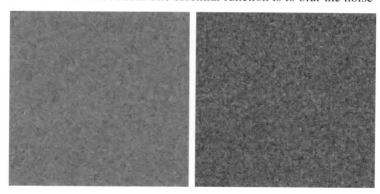

Figure 3.24 On the left is a typical example of color noise. On the right is pseudo-random noise that is primarily luminance-based noise. Both images are from a very noisy Canon EOS 10D (that I keep for noise demos) at 3200 ISO with a Photoshop zoom of 400%.

Figure 3.25 Filter ⇨ Noise ⇨ Reduce Noise (left) and Filter ⇨ Blur ⇨ Surface Blur (right) are two of the tools Photoshop provides for noise reduction.

in the surface areas (non-edges) while preserving the actual image edge detail. The Reduce Noise filter offers a lot of functionality, as shown in Figure 3.25. However, Surface Blur is a simplified blurring tool which can be set to use a threshold to preserve edges. But, to preserve the edge detail I use a 'surface mask' to apply the noise reduction only to the surfaces. Figure 3.26 shows the image I'll use to show how to make a surface mask. The outlined area in the main image is shown in the detail view at 400% zoom.

Figure 3.26 The image above was shot at ISO 1600 with a Canon Rebel XTi. The full image would reproduce 13" x 8.75" at 300 PPI. The detail image on the right is using the default Camera Raw sharpening but with no noise reduction.

Creating a surface mask in Photoshop

In order to create a mask to protect edges and apply the noise reduction primarily to the surfaces, a series of steps is required to create the mask from the data within the image itself. This makes the mask adaptive to the details and edges in the image.

1 The first step was to load the image's luminosity as a selection and then save it as a channel. I tend to use the simple method of ⌘ _ctrl_ clicking on the composite RGB thumbnail. Once saved as a channel you'll have the luminance data of the image, which can have a variety of uses.

2 The next step was to extract the edge data. To do so, I applied Filter ⇨ Stylize ⇨ Find Edges. This filter does a pretty good job of finding the edges but the results usually need a bit of additional processing in order to produce a useful surface mask.

3 To reduce the amount of scatter noise in the mask, I used a Levels command to increase the overall contrast and clip a lot of the white data. I set the white clip to 225. There really isn't a precise number to the toning that needs to be done. This will vary image by image and will depend more on the nature of the image edges and the noise signature.

4 The final step in the additional processing to create an edge mask was to use the Filter ⇨ Blur ⇨ Gaussian Blur. In this example, I used a radius of 4. This setting is also image dependent and will need to be adjusted. It should be noted that up to the blur amount the steps taken so far are the exact same steps I used for creating an edge mask for image sharpening. The primary differences are the amount of the blur and a final step to invert the channel so the edges would be white and the surfaces black. Edge masks tend to need a bit less Gaussian Blur than surface masks.

5 After creating the surface mask channel, I went back to the RGB image data. I duplicated the Background layer and applied a 'medium strength' Reduce Noise filter without any Preserve Details settings because I could control surfaces and edge preservation with the surface mask.

6 I loaded the surface channel as a selection and used the selection to make a layer mask for the Reduce Noise layer. I also changed the blending mode to Luminosity and reduced the opacity to 75% to cut back on the over-smoothing.

If you compare the image detail of step 6 with the noise shown in the original in Figure 3.26, you'll see that the process did indeed reduce the amount of noise visible in the image. Was it worth the effort? Well, yes. But I would be inclined to do this in an action rather than manually producing the surface mask each time.

The real question is: are the results optimal for a digital capture? I would say no. Rather than working through the steps in Photoshop, my natural inclination now is to do everything in Camera Raw 6. The new noise reduction capabilities in Camera Raw 6.x and the Process 2010 version mean that I've started to do pretty much all of my noise reduction within the raw processing pipeline. The advantage of this is that the image sharpening and noise reduction processing are interconnected and controllable within one panel in Camera Raw.

Figure 3.27 shows the results of doing both the image sharpening and noise reduction in Camera Raw. It should be noted that the higher the capture ISO the more Camera Raw 6's noise reduction shines, as Martin will show next.

Figure 3.27 The image above, at 400% zoom inside Camera Raw, shows better noise reduction and image detail than the results produced using the Reduce Noise filter.

73

Third-party noise reduction

There are several third-party plug-ins for reducing noise, such as Noiseware™ by Imagenomic® and Noise Ninja™ by PictureCode®. Most of our experience has been with using Noiseware, which is very good at reducing film grain from scanned images.

Adding noise

As well as removing noise you sometimes need to actually add noise instead. When you use Photoshop to retouch a photograph you may at times find yourself painting with what might be called 'pure pixels'. If you are cloning pieces from one part of the picture to another then you are probably not going to run into too many problems, but if you use the paint brush tool and apply gradients or blurs to parts of a photograph, there can be a mismatch. This is where the smoothness of the pixels painted using Photoshop does not match the inherent texture of the rest of the image. This is particularly true if editing a scanned film image that contains a certain amount of grain. You should therefore consider selectively adding noise whenever you add a gradient or paint with Photoshop. You can do this by using the Noise ⇨ Add Noise filter via the Filter menu. Note that 'add noise' options are already included in a lot of Photoshop features such as the Brush options, Gradient Fill layers and the Lens Blur filter.

Camera Raw noise reduction

So far we have looked at how to use the Detail panel in Camera Raw to handle noise reduction. Now that we have the new improved noise reduction in Camera Raw 6 for Photoshop CS5, we believe it makes most sense to carry out the noise reduction in Camera Raw. As has already been mentioned, one of the key benefits of this approach is that once you have optimized the settings to remove the noise from one image you can then share these settings across multiple photos.

The new improved Camera Raw noise reduction now makes noise reduction in Photoshop almost completely redundant. I say 'almost', because there are still times where it may be helpful to use Photoshop to reduce the noise in tricky images. There is of course the Reduce Noise filter which has been around in Photoshop for a few years now. Personally, I don't think this filter has anything special to offer now that you can carry out the noise reduction in Camera Raw. However, there are also a number of third-party noise reduction filters for Photoshop. These do arguably have some role to play still, especially if the aim is to reduce film grain in scanned images. I have used Noiseware™ by Imagenomic® for several years now and will probably continue to do so when treating scans from grainy film images.

As I say, if you are editing raw images, then the Camera Raw controls should be all you need and I reckon the Camera Raw Detail panel is the more appropriate tool to use as your first port of call. However, there are some situations where even the new improved noise reduction in Camera Raw 6 can do with a little extra help from Photoshop. I have found a few examples where the Camera Raw noise reduction is unable to remove all the noise completely and have found it necessary to use some further Photoshop image processing to improve the look of such photographs. In the example that's shown over the following pages a number of outlying pixels stubbornly remained in the image (these are the white speckles you can see in the Step 2 close-up view). No matter how I tried to remove them using the Luminance slider controls, I just couldn't get rid of them completely in Camera Raw. Here is how I went about editing this particular photo in Camera Raw and Photoshop in order to get the smoothest result possible.

1 This photograph was mainly illuminated by candle light and was shot using a 3200 ISO setting. As you can see the image is very noisy.

2 The first step was to enlarge the preview to a 100% view and go to the Detail panel. Shown here are the default noise reduction settings.

3 In this step I adjusted all three Luminance noise reduction sliders to remove the noise and at the same time retain as much image detail as possible.

4 I also adjusted the Color and Color Detail sliders to remove the color noise.

5 Here we can see the Camera Raw processed image opened in Photoshop (top). Camera Raw did a pretty good job of removing most of the noise, but there were still a lot of what we call 'outlying' pixels, which are the white speckles you can see here. To remove these, I went to the Filter ⇨ Noise menu and selected the Dust & Scratches filter. A 1 pixel Radius amount was all that was needed to eradicate the speckles, but I didn't want this filter step to soften the image too much, so I raised the Threshold slider to 10 levels. Basically, the Threshold slider acts here like a dampening control on the Dust & Scratches effect. As the Threshold is increased there has to be a greater pixel value difference between one pixel and a neighboring pixel before the Dust & Scratches filter comes into effect.

Figure 3.28 This image of a penguin chick was shot with a Canon EOS 1Ds MIII with a 70–200 mm F/2.8 lens at 200 mm and a shutter speed of 1/1000 of a second. The box shows the small area of the image that was used to show the results in the remaining figures on this page.

Grain addition

After telling you how to sharpen and then reduce the noise in images, it might seem a bit curious that I would turn around and tell you to consider actually adding grain. Since Camera Raw can now add grain, there must be a reason Thomas Knoll wanted it in Camera Raw. There is. It seems that after proper sharpening and noise reduction is done, images may have a 'synthetic' smoothness that can be eliminated by adding small grain back into the image. The key is to add smaller grain than the noise you started with.

In the example shown on these pages, getting a sharp image at capture was more important that shooting with a lower ISO. At ISO 400, I was able to shoot 2 stops faster and thereby get a sharp image. Figure 3.28 shows the full-frame view of the photo.

At the default Camera Raw sharpening settings, the close-up detail of the chick was technically sharp but was not yet fully optimized. Figure 3.29 shows the default sharpening settings (left) as well as the much stronger sharpening settings (right). As you can see, the image details were considerably sharper but so was the noise in the image. At this stage, the obvious answer was to add noise reduction. I could also cut down on the high detail setting of 42, but that would have reduced the non-noise image detail. This is always the struggle between sharpening image detail and reducing noise.

Figure 3.29 The image on the left is at the Camera Raw default sharpening settings. The image on the right has substantially increased settings of Amount: 76, Radius: 0.7, Detail: 42 and Masking: 15.

Figure 3.30 The image above has had fairly strong noise reduction added to reduce the increased noise.

Figure 3.30 shows the result of adding Luminance noise reduction as well as increasing the Luminance Detail. The results were reduced noise but with an introduced softness in micro-detail. That's where the grain addition can reduce the overall softness while increasing the appearance of greater micro-detail. The result is a more natural 'photographic' look that allows for a substantial increase in image sharpness while reducing the noise. The key to using the grain addition is to use a small Size combined with a fairly small Amount setting, as shown in Figure 3.31.

Figure 3.31 The image above has the grain addition shown on the right. The Roughness settings of 85 makes for a simulation of the clumps found in film grain.

Smart Object limitations

You'll notice here that rather than convert the Background layer to a Smart Object directly, I had to make a duplicate of the Background layer and convert the copy layer into a Smart Object. It shouldn't always be necessary to do this in order to use Smart Filter layers, but in this instance I had to because the Smart Filter options don't yet include Blend If sliders (although I wish they did).

Improving midtone contrast

Normal image contrast adjustments affect the image globally, but if you wish to improve the contrast in the midtone areas you can use the following two techniques in Photoshop to add more presence to your images.

The first one is designed to specifically target the midtone areas by applying a small, soft halo edge to the midtones only. The second technique allows you to apply a wider, softer halo edge, which can help improve the contrast in areas that have soft detail. The Clarity slider in Camera Raw basically offers a hybrid of these two types of adjustment. By showing here the individual Photoshop methods that make up Clarity, you can learn how to apply more controlled Clarity type enhancements to your photographs. So instead of having just one slider to improve clarity, you can effectively have three slider controls at your disposal. We don't suggest you need to do this with every image, but you may find with subjects such as softly lit landscape subjects that these steps give you added control to help make the detail stand out more.

1 Here I wanted to demonstrate how the medium contrast technique could be applied to a photograph as a Smart Filter. To begin with, I dragged the Background layer to the New layer button in the Layers panel. I then went to the Filter menu and chose Convert for Smart Filters.

2 With the Background copy layer selected (which is now a Smart Object), I went to the Filter menu and chose Other ⇨ High Pass. It does not matter too much at this stage what value was used here since I was able to re-edit this setting later in Step 4.

3 Now that I had applied the High Pass filter, I needed to change the layer blend mode setting to Overlay. To do this I double-clicked on the Background copy layer, targeting the blank space area (this is the area within the orange box in the Layers panel and not the thumbnail or the layer name itself). I set the blend mode to Overlay and at the same time, went to the Blend If options at the bottom and adjusted the 'This Layer' sliders so that they were split as shown above: 50/100 150/200 (to set the sliders like this you have to hold down the ⌥ *alt* key to initially split them apart).

4 The layer blend changes made in Step 3 meant that the halo effect created in Step 2 was applied to the midtone areas only. At this stage you might want to double-click the High Pass filter layer in the Layers panel (circled) to reopen the High Pass filter dialog and fine-tune the Radius setting.

5 Here you can see a close-up view showing how the photograph looked after it had been processed using this technique, compared with how it looked before. The difference is quite subtle, but you should be able to see how it has enhanced the contrast in the midtone areas. Note how the ripples in the water are also better defined in the right half of the picture.

High Radius Unsharp Mask technique

We know from experience that if we add contrast to a photograph this can make an image stand out more. Bumping up the contrast by adding an 'S'-shaped curve can certainly help improve the 'global' appearance of a photograph. However, if you add too much contrast, this can all too easily destroy the delicate tonal balance and ruin a perfectly good picture. The technique described here is another type of midtone contrast enhancing technique that allows you to add more contrast to a photo, but at a localized level.

It so happens that the human eye is more attuned to localized changes than to global changes in contrast and it was knowledge of this phenomenon that led Thomas Knoll at Adobe to propose a localized contrast enhancement technique based around the formula of using a high Radius and low Amount setting in the Unsharp Mask filter dialog. This in turn led Thomas to devise the new Clarity control for Adobe Camera Raw 4.1 and Lightroom 1.1 (incidentally, Michael Reichmann has written an excellent article outlining this technique, plus Thomas Knoll's thinking behind it, on the Luminous-Landscape.com website). As was mentioned earlier, on page 80, the Clarity adjustment combines the technique shown here with the midtone contrast technique described on pages 80–82. Even so, the 'high Radius/low Amount' technique is so effective when it's applied on its own that I thought it would be useful to share here. While this particular method of enhancing the midtone contrast is similar to using the Clarity adjustment in Camera Raw, when applying this technique in Photoshop you have the ability to selectively apply the effect. For example, following the steps shown on page 84 you could adapt this by first converting the background image layer into a Smart Object and applying the Unsharp Mask filter adjustment as a Smart Filter. You could then use the Smart Filter layer mask to selectively hide or show the filter effect.

In the example that's shown over the page, I chose a photograph where the atmospheric haze had softened the detail in the hillside in the distance. Here, you will notice how the low Amount setting combined with a high Radius created a soft shadow halo around the edges of the picture and this in turn helped remove a lot of the haze.

1 The first step was to choose Filter ⇨ Sharpen ⇨ Unsharp Mask and set the Radius to a really high value, such as between 30 and 70. This is a much higher Radius value than you would use normally and the trick is to keep the Amount slider to a low setting so that you don't end up applying too strong an effect.

2 This shows a 100% view, where you can see on the left the before version and on the right how the photograph looked after I had applied the Unsharp Mask filter. The difference can be quite dramatic. In this particular example the end result was like lifting a veil from in front of the lens.

Sculpting photos

Photography has always sought to represent three-dimensional scenes and objects in a two-dimensional medium. The most successful images tend to have an enhanced sense of shape and volume but mother nature doesn't always cooperate and provide the perfect light. Then it's up to the photographer to bring out the shape and volume using Photoshop. There are a lot of tools in Photoshop to help with that task, but sometimes it's best to use an alternative approach. Mac Holbert has perfected this technique (although others have used variations) to bring out the three-dimensional shape in images he prints for customers. It does employ a certain degree of brush work by hand (which always makes me nervous since I can't draw) but if I can do it, pretty much anybody can. You're always able to use Photoshop's extensive array of selection techniques to help in the painting.

The sculpting technique uses a layer set to an Overlay blend mode and filled with a 50% gray to start. Since overlay is a procedural blend, it screens when above 50% gray and multiplies below 50% gray. This lightens the lights and darkens the darks. The starting gray layer does nothing until you paint with black or white. By adding white to the gray layer, the area becomes lighter. The addition of black to the gray darkens the area. The key is to do so very gently in order to enhance the natural shape and forms already in the image. See Figure 3.32 for a before and after. The steps start on the following page.

Nash Editions

Nash Editions was a California company founded in 1990 by Mac Holbert and Graham Nash to provide a specialist fine-art digital printing service. They were the original pioneers of fine-art inkjet printing. Mac used this technique to bring out the depth and give more shape to many of the images he printed for customers. Mac is also the newest member of Pixel Genius and is currently working on a revision to PhotoKit Sharpener.

Figure 3.32 The image on the left is prior to sculpting. The image on the right is the result. The result of sculpting cannot be exactly duplicated using adjustment layers – it's really a unique solution for adding shape and volume to an image.

1 To begin with, I made a new empty layer on top of the Smart Object layer. The fact that the raw image was a Smart Object meant that I would always be free to go back to the raw image to tweak it (although I didn't need to here). The empty layer was filled with a 50% gray and the blend mode was set to Overlay. Thereafter, when I painted with white into the Overlay layer it would lighten by screening and darken when painting with black by multiplying the image data underneath.

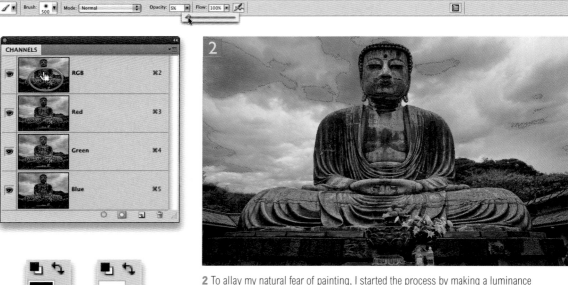

Figure 3.33 Setting the foreground color to black will darken the image while white will lighten. To toggle back and forth between the colors be sure to reset the colors then simply press the **X** key to toggle back and forth.

2 To allay my natural fear of painting, I started the process by making a luminance selection of the darker areas I wanted to enhance (to load the luminance as a selection hold the **⌘** **ctrl** key and click on the RGB channel). Since the 50% gray layer was set to 100% opacity, I needed to work gently and set the brush flow to only 5%. Much of the subsequent work was actually done with the flow set to 1–3%. I started painting into the selection using white as the foreground color. I also inverted this selection and painted with black to increase the separation between the areas. I used the **X** key to toggle back and forth between painting with black or white as shown in Figure 3.33. Lightening an area tends to visually make it move closer while darkening makes it recede. Thus by lightening and darkening adjacent areas I could increase the appearance of dimensionality.

3 In this step I zoomed into the image and painted white into the chin area and black under the lips to give a greater sense of depth and separation. As long as you work with a very low flow and build up the strokes, you don't need to worry about being too accurate with each stroke.

4 Not everything I needed to do could be done with a synthetic selection or by freehand painting. In this step I created a path to outline the Buddha and then made a selection from the path. The 1.2 feather radius was used to approximate the resolution of the edges in the image. If the selection was too sharp it would look like a cut-out and if too soft it would bleed the effects. A 1.2 feather radius matched the sharpness of the natural edge. By inverting the selection I could work on the sky or, by inverting again, work on the Buddha.

5 In the top figure I had inverted the selection to paint black to darken the sky beyond the Buddha's head. In the bottom figure I had reinverted the selection (to reselect the Buddha) and painted with white to lighten the shoulder.

6 One of the inherent problems with using an Overlay blend mode to sculpt an image is that when increasing the contrast of an image, you may also get a boost in the color saturation. To control that I created a merged layer set to Color blend inside a layer group. I deselected the Overlay layer and held the ⌥ alt key when selecting the Merge Visible option in the Layers panel. Placing the Color Control layer above the Overlay layer essentially removed the color saturation boost. I didn't bother with a layer mask for the Sculpting layer because it was really easy to get rid of the black and white in the layer by changing the foreground color to a 50% gray and painting or filling to reduce the effect of the layer.

7 This step shows the result of painting white and black in the various areas to alter the dimensionality of the final image. You'll see that the effect of adding black and white to the Sculpting layer is fairly subtle – as it should be.

8 Here is the final result. The original image of the Diabusu Buddha in Kamakura, Japan, was shot with a Canon EOS 1Ds with a 16–35 mm F2.8 lens.

Photomerge quality

Of course, all this is assuming that Photomerge in Photoshop is any good. When Photomerge first appeared in Photoshop CS, a lot of us got quite excited by this new feature, although truth be told, to achieve successful results you needed to shoot really carefully and not use too wide a lens. Photoshop CS4 saw a major improvement in Photomerge functionality, allowing you to merge wide angle and even fisheye lens images. Photoshop CS5 has seen a further fine-tuning of the Photomerge processing to the extent that Photomerge will work well with most types of lens as long as you provide sufficient overlap between each capture image.

Photomerging images to improve quality

Unless you are willing to carry a complete series of camera lenses with you wherever you go, you are often going to find yourself in situations where you are missing the right lens. This isn't such a problem if you need a long focal length lens, since you can always crop the image more tightly. However, if it is a wide-angle lens you want, your only option is to use a stitching technique such as the method shown here in Figure 3.34, where Photomerge was used to blend a series of shots together to create a wide-angle type view.

Although it is a time-consuming and cumbersome process to capture and stitch a handful of photos together in this way there can be a payoff in doing so, as you may end up with a better quality image than if you had originally shot the photo using a wide-angle lens. To start with, if you shoot, say, six or more overlapping photos, you will most likely end up with a merged image where the pixel resolution is higher than the native resolution of the camera that was used to take the photos. Secondly, by splitting the captured image area into sections you avoid the problems of image detail falloff towards the edges of the picture. You see, with any lens the image quality will always be at its sharpest in the center and less sharp towards the corners. If you are shooting with a good quality lens this shouldn't be much of an issue, but with other lenses it can be. I say it can be, because this does also depend on how important it is to see perfectly sharp detail in the extreme corners of an image. The point I am making here is if you are forced (or choose) to create a wide-angle view through combining a series of captures using Photomerge to produce such a view, there may be some benefits in taking this approach.

In the Figure 3.34 example, I was on a forest trek where I had hoped to photograph the wildlife, but instead came across this bilbao tree and its amazing, above-ground root structure. The widest lens I had was a 70 mm on the 70–200 zoom, attached to the Canon 400D camera. I photographed it using a series of 12 shots and stitched the images together using Photomerge to produce the wide-angle view seen here. The combined image had a resolution of 6600 × 4800 pixels compared to the 3888 × 2592 native resolution of the 400D. As you can see in the close-up view, the detail in the top left corner was sharper than one would expect from an enlarged single photo shot using a wide-angle lens.

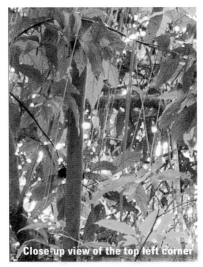

Close-up view of the top left corner

Figure 3.34 This shows the segmented view (top) of a Photomerge image and below, the final image.

Improving the shadows with Merge to HDR Pro

The Merge to HDR Pro feature is explained in more detail in Chapter 9, plus there is also a PDF extract on the DVD taken from the *Adobe Photoshop CS5 for Photographers* book that is all about working with the merge to HDR Pro feature. I briefly mention HDR imaging here because merging bracketed exposure images together to create a high dynamic range master is a useful thing to do since a low dynamic range image that is rendered from an HDR master will allow you to obtain improved shadow detail with smoother tones and without banding (see Figures 3.35 and 3.36).

Figure 3.35 Here you can see an example of a raw image that was processed using Camera Raw 6 and Process Version 2010 to produce the best image quality and tone balance possible from a single raw image. The close-up view has been lightened in order to reveal how there is image noise and banding visible in the extreme shadow areas.

Figure 3.36 In this example I used three bracketed raw images shot at +2 and −2 EV around the image exposure shown in Figure 3.35 and used these as the source files to create the Merge to HDR Pro image shown above. The aim here was to produce as close a result as possible to the Figure 3.35 version. As you can see in the lightened close-up view shown here, there is no noticeable noise or banding visible in the shadow areas of the Merge to HDR Pro image version.

Overexposing the shadows

This technique works because the Merge to HDR Pro image makes use of the overexposed bracketed exposure to define the darkest shadows. You may already be aware that there can be a significant drop-off in quality in the shadow areas of a normal exposed image relative to the brighter areas and this is one reason why the experts are inclined to advocate 'exposing to the right'. With HDR images you should have many more levels of tone detail information to work with in the shadows and this is why the shadows look better.

Chapter 4

Mending and blending

Photoshop repair work

Most people tend to think of Photoshop as a program for retouching photographs. Of course, Photoshop can do a lot more than that these days, but retouching is what the program is best known for. In this chapter we wanted to focus on a few of our favorite retouching techniques. Some of these are quite involved and require a certain level of expertise, while others are actually quite simple and provide some interesting shortcuts for correcting photos.

Healing brush modes

The healing brush offers a choice of blending modes. The Replace mode is identical to the clone stamp tool, except it allows you to merge film grain more reliably and smoothly around the edges of your brush strokes. The other healing brush blending modes can produce different results but in my opinion they won't actually improve upon the ability of the healing brush in Normal mode, since the healing brush is already utilizing a special form of image blending to perform its magic.

General retouching

Healing brush strategies

Those of you who have not used versions of Photoshop prior to version 7 must forgive us for thinking that the healing brush is a magical wonder, but it can't do everything. The clone stamp tool still has its uses, as does copying and pasting pixels. When to use what can be tricky – healing is best done away from strong contrast perimeters and where texture needs to be preserved (or added to). It's best used at full opacity and with a hard brush (just about the opposite of the clone stamp tool). Sometimes you need to seed an area with pixels before the healing brush can be made to work, other times it's better to use the patch tool where you can make an accurate selection prior to using the tool. Sometimes it is easier to simply grab pixels from some other source and blend them in. Figure 4.1 shows my Harley shot in the studio. There are issues: too narrow a background, wrinkles and a foreshortened foreground due to needing a front fill card. Figure 4.2 shows how the healing brush as well as the patch tool were used to fix these background issues. The Layers panel shows the addition of a pasted layer from a separate image shot on the same background. There are additional layers for tone adjustment and a fix for the Harley logo. The final retouched image is shown in Figure 4.3.

Figure 4.1 This is the before shot of my FLSTS Harley (I've sold that and ride a BMW now). You can see that the muslin background didn't cover the full width and is short in the foreground due to a required fill card. You can also see seams that need removal.

Figure 4.2 On the left, the healing brush was used to eliminate background seams — a function perfect for this tool. On the near right the patch tool made quick work of extending the background. On the far right is the final layer stack showing a foreground addition added from a separate shot to cover up the fill reflector card.

Figure 4.3 The final retouched image.

Adding lens flare

The Lens Flare filter is ideal for adding realistic-looking lens flare effects to photographs or computer rendered images, as this filter allows you to apply the ghosting type patterns that are normally associated with camera lens flare. Now that we have Smart Filters it makes sense to convert an image to a Smart Object layer first before you apply the filter. This way you have the ability to re-edit the filter settings and precisely reposition the source point for the lens flare effect.

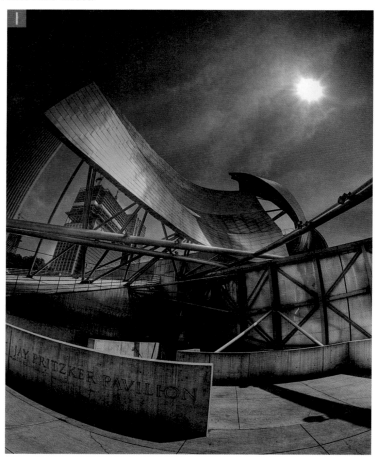

1 Here is a before version of a photograph, shot into the sun using a series of bracketed exposures and blended together using Photomatix Pro. The first step was to select the Background layer, go to the Filter menu and choose Convert to Smart Filter. This converted the layer to a Smart Object – you can see the Smart Object badge circled in the Layers panel.

Photo: © Martin Evening

2 I then went to the Filter menu and chose Render ➭ Lens Flare… This opened the dialog shown top right, where you will notice there are several different types of lens flare patterns that you can choose from. Since this photograph was originally shot using a 15 mm fisheye lens, I selected the 35 mm Prime option. I then clicked on the sun in the small dialog preview to set this as the flare center point. One can then adjust the Brightness slider to create a weak or strong lens flare effect. Since I was applying the effect as a Smart Filter I chose to set the brightness quite high at 150%. This allowed me to later edit the Lens Flare Smart Filter settings by double-clicking on the options icon (circled in yellow) next to the Lens Flare effect to open the Blending Options dialog shown here, where I could quickly fade the filter effect strength. The other advantage of applying as a Smart Filter is that I could double-click the Lens Flare effect (circled in red) to reopen the Lens Flare dialog and re-edit the filter settings (this is true for any filter that you are able to apply as a Smart Filter).

Alien Skin™ Exposure®

If you are after a good range of film simulation effects for digitally shot images, then check out the following link: www. alienskin.com/exposure/ This Photoshop plug-in can be used to apply film grain effects that match a variety of traditional film emulsions.

Simulating film grain

Most Photoshop users will be aware that you can use the Add Noise filter to get images to look more grainy, but the Add Noise filter will always tend to look rather 'electronic' if it's applied as a single filter. The following steps show one way you can modify the Add Noise filter effect to achieve a result that looks more like real film grain. For example, this technique might be used to simulate a grainy film look or to disguise retouching work that's been carried out on a scanned grainy film image.

1 The first step was to ⌥ *alt* click the Add New Layer button in the Layers panel (circled). This popped the New Layer dialog shown here where I set the blend mode to Overlay and checked the 'Fill with Soft-Light-neutral color (50% gray)' box.

2 With this new layer selected, I went to the Filter menu and chose Noise ⇨ Add Noise. Here, I selected the Gaussian mode, checked the Monochromatic box and applied an Amount of 45%. I followed this by going to the Filter menu again, selected Blur ⇨ Gaussian Blur and applied a 1.5 pixel Radius Blur.

3 I then applied a further dose of the Add Noise filter but this time added a lesser Amount of 10%, using the Uniform option, but still in Monochromatic mode. Lastly, I chose Filter ⇨ Sharpen ⇨ Unsharp Mask using the settings shown here.

4 In this final step you can see on the left the untreated image and on the right the same image with the film grain layer active. As you can see, the film grain steps described here can produce a very pronounced film grain effect, which can be made softer by either reducing the opacity of the film grain effect layer or modifying the filter settings that were applied in the previous steps.

Knowing how much grain to add

Remember, what you see on screen has little bearing on how the image looks when seen in print. The applied grain will therefore need to be quite strong for any apparent effect to be noticed in the printed image. To this end it may be worth printing out a series of differing amounts, possibly in the form of a test strip across the intended area to discover which settings work most effectively in print.

Matching grain

Digital artists who are accustomed to creating multi-image composites know that combining images from different formats or ISO settings can be problematic because of mismatched grain (or noise). Reducing the grain or noise in a capture or scan will often only partially mitigate the issue. You may also need to add a touch of grain to the image that is too smooth. While there are third party plug-ins and Photoshop tricks to add grain, perhaps the most efficient method to use now is Camera Raw's Grain tool in the Effects panel. The two images in Figure 4.4 show examples of mismatched formats and ISO. Figure 4.5 shows the final composite.

Figure 4.4 On the left is a digital capture from a Canon EOS Rebel XTi at ISO of 800 (accidentally left high) and on the right a capture from a Phase One P 65+ medium format camera back at ISO 100. In order to composite the two convincingly, I had to add grain to the medium format digital capture.

1 The first step was to actually create a composite of the two images. The Layers panel (far left) shows the Phase One capture added as a Camera Raw Smart Object with a layer mask. The image above left shows the original shot's blue sky and the noise contained in the Rebel capture. The image on the right shows the new sky composite in place. The detail images are shown here at a 300% zoom setting in Photoshop.

2 With the Phase One Smart Object layer targeted, I double-clicked the Smart Object icon to open up the Camera Raw Smart Object window. The advantage of using a Smart Object is that one can make parameter changes without having to commit to those changes until flattening. The Grain settings I applied here were able to replicate the noise of the Rebel capture rather well. Generally, I prefer to use a low Amount, a relatively small Size and high Roughness to better simulate film grain. While primarily designed for raw captures, the Grain effects can also work for scanned TIFF images.

Figure 4.5 The final composite can't show the accuracy of the grain matching because of the small repro size, but take my word for it, the two images blended well.

Displacement maps

The Displace filter requires a separate displacement map image that it can reference when calculating the displacement. Black (0) will produce the maximum negative displacement shift and white (255) will produce the maximum positive shift, while gray (128) produces no displacement. A displacement map must be saved as a grayscale image using the native Photoshop file format, but if you add a second channel the first channel determines the horizontal displacement and the second channel controls the vertical displacement.

Merging objects with displace distortion

The Displace filter is not the most intuitive of filters but is still quite invaluable if you need to distort a layer so that it appears to match the shape or texture of the underlying layers. The effect works well where the displacement map you use has been softened beforehand, plus you will find a large number of displacement maps are contained on the Adobe Photoshop disk and these can be loaded to create other types of texture displacements.

1 Here you can see the graffiti graphic and a brick wall image. To begin with I used ⌘ C ctrl C to copy the graffiti logo pixels. I then went to the brick wall image, created a new channel and pasted the logo into the channel (⌘ V ctrl V). I duplicated the new channel and edited them both so that I ended up with the 'Elvis Rules' and 'Tiny' alpha channels.

2 The next job was to create a displacement map image for the Displace filter step. To do this, I went to the Image menu, chose Duplicate and converted the duplicated image to Grayscale mode. I then applied a 4 pixel Gaussian Blur filter and saved this image to the desktop (where it would be easy to locate later). It is important to note that when you create a displace filter map the image must be in grayscale mode and saved using the native Photoshop (PSD) file format. It is also very important to delete the two additional alpha mask channels seen in Step 1 before saving.

3 I was now ready to blend the two elements together. Here I created a new layer group and added two solid color fill layers inside it. One used black as the fill color, where I set the layer blend mode to Multiply at a 50% Opacity. I used a dark brown for the other color layer and set the layer blend mode to Overlay and the Opacity to 85%. Next, I ⌘ *ctrl*-clicked on the Elvis Rules alpha channel in the Channels panel (see Step 1) to load this as a selection. I then selected the layer group shown here and clicked on the Add layer mask button at the bottom of the Layers panel (circled) to convert this to a pixel layer mask for the layer group. As you can see, I now had a single layer mask that masked the two Solid Color fill layers The graffiti didn't look particularly realistic yet, but I was about to work on that in the next step.

4 To get the lettering to look more graffiti-like, I needed to edit the Blending options for one or more of the Solid Color fill layers. For this particular image, I selected the black Solid Color fill layer that's highlighted in the Layers panel and double-clicked the layer, targeting the area you see circled here. This opened the Layer Style dialog, where I adjusted the underlying layer Blend If sliders (circled) to allow some of the mid to highlight tones to show through from below.

5 This shows how the graffiti design looked after I had modified the layer blending sliders for the underlying layer in Step 4. All I needed to do now was to distort the lettering so that it appeared to merge more realistically with the Background layer.

6 I selected the layer mask for the layer group and made sure it was correctly targeted. I then went to the Filter menu and chose Distort ⇒ Displace... The Displace dialog allowed me to set the displacement amount for the horizontal and vertical axes. You don't always want to enter too high amounts here. Start off with 10 and try redoing the displacement again using higher or lower values. In this instance the Displacement Map settings didn't make any difference because the pixel dimensions of the map I was about to use matched the image exactly. After I clicked OK in the Displace dialog, I was asked to locate a displacement map image file. This is where the saved grayscale image came in. I located the grayscale map that had been saved earlier to the desktop and clicked Open to use this as the displacement source image.

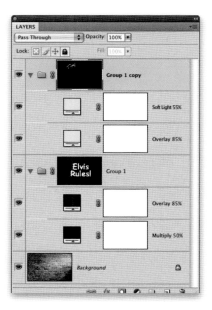

7 Here is the finished result, where the Elvis Rules logo was now distorted to match the shape and texture of the wall. You'll also notice how I added two yellow solid color fill layers and placed these in a new group, masked by the 'Tiny' alpha channel mask. I set one color fill layer to Overlay at 85% and the other to Soft Light at 55%, and applied the same Displace filter settings and displacement map to this layer mask.

How to create a spotlight effect

As we pointed out at the beginning of this book, although there is a lot you can do in Photoshop to retouch pictures and generate realistic-looking effects, it can still be useful to do extra work in-camera before you take the photographs into Photoshop. In the example that's shown here, I anticipated needing to light the wall in two different ways so that I could later combine these two captures to create a dramatic spotlight effect. The following steps show how I added a final twist to the 'Tiny Elvis Rules' image.

1 Shown here is the wall image lit with a spotlight (top), which was used as the backdrop image for the previous steps (as well as to create the displacement map image), and below that another shot taken of the same wall, but lit using soft diffuse lights that were filtered with blue gels to produce a soft shadow lighting look.

2 I dragged the soft lit wall image across to the layered master image, with the *Shift* key held down, so as to place it in register with the spot lit layer below. I then added a layer mask and painted with black on the mask to create a focused spotlight effect. I also added a darkening Curves adjustment which was clipped to the soft lit wall layer.

3 Here, I've made all the other layers visible to show the completed image, where you'll notice I also added an extra logo layer in the bottom right corner (this offers a small clue as to Tiny Elvis's true identity!)

109

How to create a sparkle brush shape

If you click on the Brush Presets item in the Brushes panel or view the Brushes panel in a non-expanded view (shown in Figure 4.6), you'll usually see a small thumbnail list of the different brush preset shapes that are available for use with the brush and other painting tools in Photoshop. You will also find even more brush presets can be loaded via the panel fly-out menu. However, if you want to, you can create your own custom brush preset designs by following the instructions shown here for creating a highlight sparkle brush preset. Once you name a brush preset, it will become appended to the current brush presets, but to make sure that the brush shape is saved permanently I suggest you choose Edit ➪ Preset Manager, select the brush or brushes you have just created and then choose Save Set…

Figure 4.6 This shows the non-expanded, list view for the Brushes panel.

1 The first step was to go to the Options bar for the brush tool and select a small (10 pixel) soft-edged brush. I then went to the Brush panel and checked the Shape Dynamics, where I set the Control options to Fade and I also set the Minimum diameter to 4%. Having done that, I checked the brush preview shown at the bottom of the panel and returned to the Control options, where I adjusted the number of fade levels so that the brush preview smoothly tapered from a full size brush (on the left) to a minimum size brush (on the right).

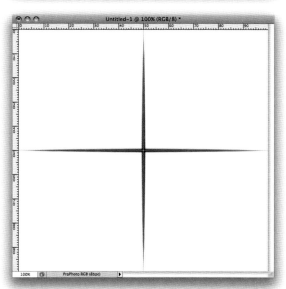

2 I was now ready to create a new custom brush shape. To begin with, I created a new image document that was 600 x 600 pixels in size. I chose View ⇨ Rulers, double-clicked the ruler guides to set the units to Percent and added two guides at 50% on the horizontal and vertical axes. I then selected the brush tool (using the settings shown in Step 1), clicked on the center point, held down the *Shift* key and clicked at the top of the image. This drew the first line. I then repeated this step to produce the initial sparkle shape shown here.

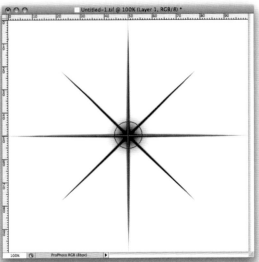

3 I then copied the Background layer (⌘ J ctrl J), set the new layer blend mode to Multiply, went to the Edit menu and chose Free Transform. I rotated the layer 45°, scaled the transform to make the layer smaller and clicked Enter. I then increased the brush diameter to 70 pixels and clicked once on the center point using 100% opacity and 100% flow in the Tool options for the brush tool.

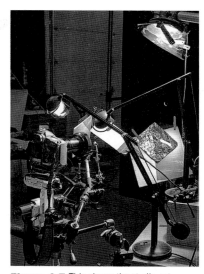

4 To create a new brush preset I first made sure that the guides had been cleared or were hidden. This is important, because you won't be able to create a new brush if the guides are visible. I went to the Edit menu and chose 'Define Brush Preset'. This opened the dialog shown here, where I gave the new brush a name and clicked OK. On the right you can see the brush cursor for the new 'Sparkle 1' brush preset.

Figure 4.7 This shows the studio set that was used to photograph the diamond ring shown in Step 5. You will notice that the camera was mounted on a view camera support. This made it easier for Jeff to adjust the focus, because he could keep the ring and focus setting on the lens static and smoothly adjust the camera distance relative to the ring.

5 Here is an example of the new brush preset in use, where I added a new layer to this shot of a diamond ring, and set the blend mode to Screen and the opacity to 62%. (Figure 4.7 shows the lighting set that was used for this particular shot.)

113

Sloping angles

With Vanishing Point you can also drag off new planes using a custom angle. So long as you get the initial plane description completely accurate, you should find that the consecutive planes will match the remaining perspective planes in the scene.

Vanishing Point

The Vanishing Point filter provides a modal dialog in which you can define the perspective planes in an image and then use the tools available in Vanishing Point to carry out basic retouching work that matches the perspective of the picture. You can make a selection within the Vanishing Point preview area and clone the selection contents within one or more predefined plane areas. You can paste the contents of a selection and align it in perspective with the target image, plus you can apply the stamp tool in Healing or Non-healing modes, or paint with the paint brush in perspective.

1 The picture on the left shows the original tower block photograph, where I used the ⌘ J *ctrl* J keyboard shortcut to copy the top section of the tower as a new layer and used a combination of the clone stamp and patch tool to remove the cranes from the top of the building.

2 I was now ready to complete the construction work to the tower using Vanishing Point in Photoshop. To start with, I added a new empty layer and named this 'Vanishing point layer'. I then went to the Filter menu and chose Vanishing Point…, which opened the dialog shown here where I used the create plane tool (circled) to define the first plane of perspective on the tower. To do this, I clicked on the edge of the front face of the building and then placed the cursor on the other side, and then at the top, and used the perspective lines of the building to guide me to match the first perspective plane shown here. You may find it helps to hold down the **X** key as you do this, since this will temporarily enlarge the preview to twice the current magnification.

3 After I had defined the initial perspective plane I used the edit plane tool (circled) to fine-tune the placement of the plane handles. I find that in most cases it is necessary to edit the plane corners in order to match the perspective; this is especially important since how you define the first plane can have a significant impact on the other planes you create relative to the first. For example, in this screen shot I held down the ⌘ ctrl key as I dragged on the middle handle (circled in red) and dragged a new plane out from the first. Vanishing Point always understands how to create further planes based on the first plane that you draw. Once you drag a new plane out in the way that I describe here, it may not always match the second plane perspective exactly – in which case you can always edit the corner handles as necessary. However, if the second plane definition exceeds certain limits, the plane outline will first turn yellow and then red, and this will act as a kind of warning.

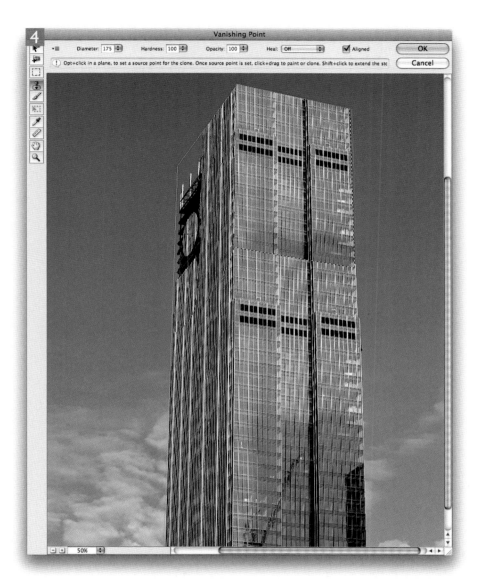

4 This screen shot shows the Vanishing Point retouching in progress. Here, I used the marquee selection tool in Vanishing Point to select the front side of the building and ⌥ *alt*-dragged to move a cloned copy of the selection further up the front of the building (matching the perspective). I then selected the stamp tool, adjusted the brush settings to get a hard-edged brush and, with the Heal mode switched to 'Off', I cloned sections of the building to cover up the crane scaffold and the unbuilt sections of the tower. The stamp tool works exactly the same as the clone stamp and healing brush in Photoshop itself: you use the ⌥ *alt* key to sample where to clone from, and as you can see, the stamp tool always shows an overlay preview.

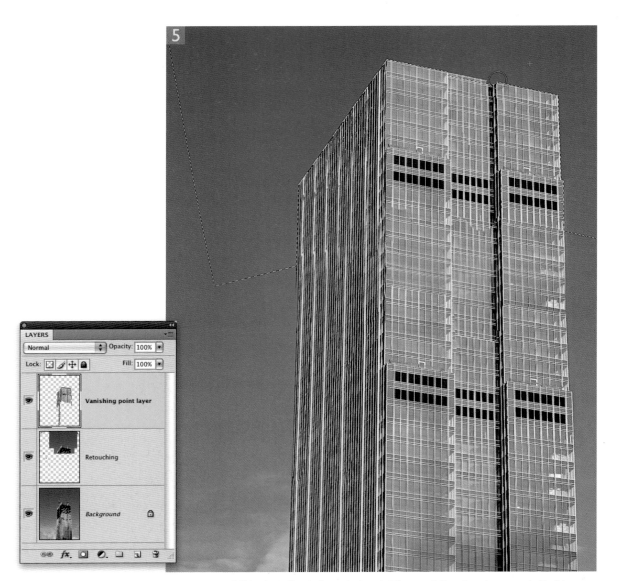

5 This shows the photograph almost at the completion stage. I now needed to tidy up some of the outer edges. To do this, I used the pen tool to define a path outline for the outside area at the top of the building and then used the stamp tool to copy from parts of the sky to produce a clean outline.

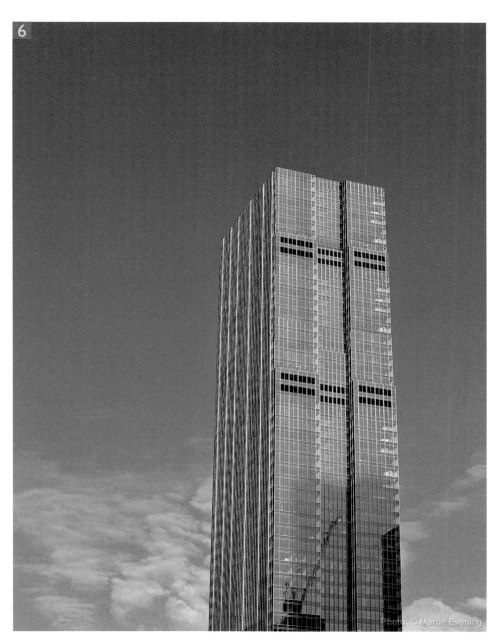

6 Here is the completed photograph, where I took the image into Vanishing Point one more time in order to clean up the joins on some areas of the building. To do this, I used a smaller sized stamp tool brush, which was again applied with the Heal options switched off.

Rendering options

People have long asked for angled guides in Photoshop. With Vanishing Point, you can now create an empty new layer, launch Vanishing Point, use the create plane tool to create a perspective plane and go to the Vanishing Point options menu (circled in Step 2) and choose 'Render Grids to Photoshop'. This will draw the guides shown in the preview on the empty layer. Likewise, you can use the Render Measurements option to do the same with the recorded measurements.

Vanishing Point planes and measurements

The following steps show a further example of how Vanishing Point can be used to edit a photo based on defined planes of perspective that have been first created using the create plane tool. If you happen to have the extended version of Photoshop, you can make a calibration measurement along a line on one of the planes and from this make further measurements of objects on associated planes. So for example, in Step 2 I was able to create a calibration measurement based on the known height of a room, and from that work out the distances and sizes of other objects in the room, such as the width of the door frame (see Step 3). Of course, the accuracy of the Vanishing Point planes and any subsequent measurements made is very much dependent on the degree of geometric distortion in the original photo. However, in Photoshop CS5 it is possible to correct for geometric distortion using the new improved Lens Corrections filter. Better still, if you are using Camera Raw 6.1 or later you can do so at the raw processing stage (see pages 58–61).

1 With Vanishing Point you can, as in the previous example, use the create plane tool to define the perspective planes for a photograph such as the room interior shown here. In this example I held down the ⌘ *ctrl* key as I dragged on the middle handle to create new planes that matched the perspective of the ceiling, floor and other wall.

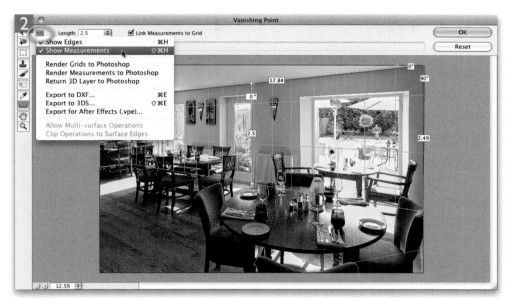

2 The measurement tool in Vanishing Point can be used to make comparative measurements in a perspective plane. Since I knew the height from the floor to the ceiling, I was able to select the measure tool and draw a measurement line along the vertical axis and enter a unit value (2.5 m) that corresponded with the known height of the room.

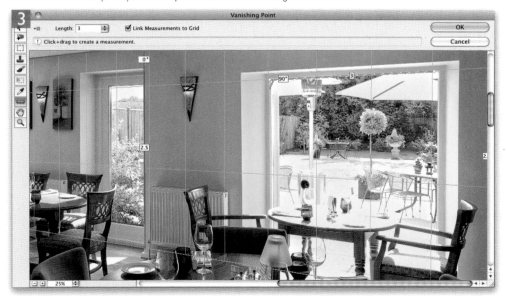

3 Once I had done that I could use the measurement tool to calculate other measurements relative to the first measurement (such as the width of the door frame).

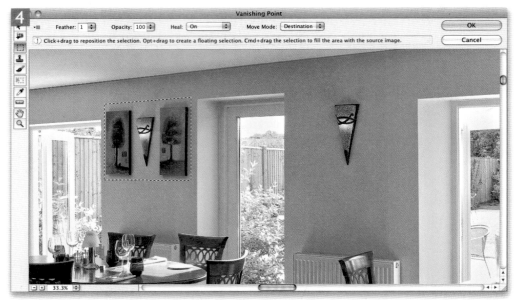

4 With the perspective planes defined, I was able to use the marquee tool to make a selection of an area that I wished to clone in the image, while maintaining the correct perspective.

5 With the Heal option set to Luminance, I held down the ⌥ *alt* key plus the *Shift* key and dragged the selected area to the right. Once I had the copied picture frames and lamp in position, I released the keys to place the cloned selection and clicked OK to apply these Vanishing Point edits.

6 Working in Photoshop, I created a mask outline of the rear wall that excluded the wall lamps, picture frames and foreground elements. I then loaded this mask as a selection.

7 Meanwhile, I opened an image of a brick wall texture. I used ⌘ A / ctrl A to select all, followed by ⌘ C / ctrl C to copy the selected contents. I then closed this image and returned to the main interior image and added a new layer so that the following Vanishing Point editing work would be added to this layer.

8 I opened Vanishing Point again and used ⌘ V *ctrl* V to paste the copied brickwork image contents into the image. As I dragged the pasted selection, the contents aligned to the perspective planes defined in Vanishing Point. Here, I found it necessary to press T so that I could access the Vanishing Point transform tool and scale the pasted selection.

9 To extend the wall, I held down the ⌥ *alt* key plus the *Shift* key and dragged the selection several times until the whole of the rear wall had been filled with the brick wall pattern.

10 To create the final version shown here, I set the layer blend mode to Multiply so that the brickwork layer blended more realistically with the shading on the wall, plus I also reduced the layer opacity to 70%.

Editing objects in 3D

Those of you who have been using Photoshop for a long time may recall a Photoshop plug-in called the 3D Transform. It was introduced in Photoshop 5 and basically it allowed you to define objects (preferably cube-shaped objects) and transform them in three dimensions. It was a rather crude tool, but considered quite a progressive feature at the time. More recently it has been possible to edit photographs in perspective using Vanishing Point, but one of the little things that you may not have been aware of is the fact that you can export the planes that have been defined in Vanishing Point as 3D layers.

This tutorial shows how you can now use Vanishing Point to prepare an image as a 3D object before fine-tuning its position in another photograph. The perspective shift in this example is quite extreme yet, with some careful adjustment of the 3D controls and post-placement retouching, it is possible to achieve a fairly convincing finished result.

1 The object of the steps shown here was to take this scene of an empty room interior and add the cabinet image (shown on the left), which had been shot in a separate location, and overcome the problem of how to match the perspective of the cabinet with that of the room interior.

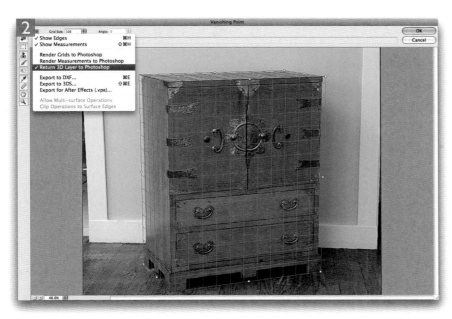

2 The first step was to select the photograph of the cabinet, go to Filter ⇨ Vanishing
Point and define the planes of perspective. Once I had done this for the three planes,
I went to the Vanishing Point options and checked 'Return 3D Layer to Photoshop'.
I then clicked OK to process the selected planes as a 3D layer.

3 Here is the new 3D layer that has been added to the layer stack. The important thing
to note here is that the planes defined in the previous step needed to be dragged far
enough to include all of the cabinet. Also, when one of the 3D tools is selected in the
tools panel, such as the 3D rotate tool, you'll see the 3D navigation widget shown here.

4 Next, I selected the move tool to drag and drop the 3D layer across to the photograph of the room interior.

5 I was now able to maneuver the 3D layer of the cabinet into position. Initially, I used the move tool to roughly position the cabinet against the wall and then selected one of the 3D tools from the Tools panel so that this switched on the 3D navigation widget shown here. If you look closely you will see a small magnifier icon. You can drag on this to scale the navigator to make it bigger (as shown here in the screen shot). Now comes the tricky bit of aligning the perspective of the cabinet with the room interior scene. Here I could have used the various 3D tools to select a specific 3D plane to manipulate. The other option was to click on the 3D navigator widget control, which allowed me to manipulate the scale, rotation and panning in each of the three planes.

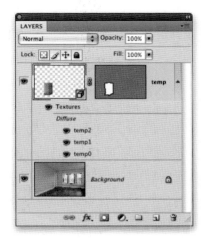

6 This shows the cabinet after I had fine-tuned the 3D controls to get it placed as accurately as possible against the wall. Once it was in place I used the pen tool to draw a vector path around the outline and then clicked on the Add vector mask button in the Masks panel to convert this to a mask.

7 In this final version I did a few extra things to make the new placement of the cabinet look more convincing. To start with, I added a new layer beneath the 3D cabinet layer, set the blend mode to Multiply and painted with dark sampled colors to add shadows below and behind the cabinet. I then added a darkening Curves adjustment layer above the 3D cabinet layer to darken the left side panel. I also used the vector mask created in Step 6 to clip the adjustment to the cabinet layer and painted on the pixel layer mask with black to prevent the Curves adjustment from affecting the front of the cabinet.

Chapter 5

Now you see it, now you don't

Some easy ways to retouch your photographs

For as long as there has been the means to retouch photographs (with or without the use of a computer), photographers have been interested in finding ways to manipulate their photographs. While Photoshop is a very complex program, this chapter has been designed to show you a number of handy retouching tricks that don't require you to be an accomplished retouch artist. The tutorials contained in this chapter are all fairly easy to follow and show a number of ways you can remove objects from an image quickly and easily without needing to use standard retouching tools such as the clone stamp or healing brush.

Removing objects

Removing foreground objects

Don't you hate it when street signs or overhead cables get in the way of a great view? Here is an easy way to get rid of offending foreground objects, although to use this technique you will need to shoot several frames of your subject and step slightly to the left or right between each exposure. You don't need to shoot using a tripod, just try to keep the background subject more or less in the same position in the frame. To process these photographs in Photoshop, all you have to do is choose the two best frames where there is enough displacement between the two shots to achieve a clear view of the main subject behind whatever objects are in front of it.

1 Here are two photographs shot of the same subject, but captured from two slightly different angles. In this example, I shot the frieze on this wall from across the street and sidestepped just a few feet to the right to capture the second exposure. The view of the frieze was more or less consistent, but this slight shift of camera perspective was enough to displace the street sign in both photographs.

2 I opened the two photographs shown in Step 1 and used the move tool to drag one on top of the other as a new layer. I held down the Shift key as I did this so that the second image was placed above the other, keeping the frame positions in exact registration.

3 To align the picture content, I needed to hold down the Shift key to select both layers and choose Edit ➪ Auto-Align Layers… This opened the dialog shown here, where I clicked on the Auto option to automatically align the two layers.

4 The retouching part was really simple. For this final step, I selected the uppermost layer and clicked on the Add layer mask button to add a new empty layer mask. I then selected the brush tool and used black as the foreground color to paint over the street sign. This technique worked well here because the auto-alignment in Photoshop had done a near perfect job of aligning the two layers.

Photo: © Martin Evening

133

Leaf blower technique

There are many ways that the new Content-Aware fill command can prove useful and here is one I have just discovered – it makes an excellent leaf blower. Real-life leaf blowers are a nuisance and, I gather, banned in certain parts of California, but the digital leaf blower offers a nice, eco-friendly alternative.

1 First of all we have here a photo taken of a lawn where we can see a lot of blossom petals have fallen on the grass. What I am going to do here is show how to remove these quickly from the picture, but without having to laboriously use the clone stamp tool or healing brush.

2 I went to the Select menu and chose Color Range… I used the eyedropper tool to select the petal leaf colors and also clicked on the 'add to selection' eyedropper tool to add more colors to the Color Range selection. I adjusted the Range and Tolerance sliders to perfect the initial selection and used Select ⇨ Modify ⇨ Smooth, entering the Sample Radius value shown here to smooth the selection.

3 I went to the Select menu again, chose Modify ⇨ Expand and entered a value of 1 pixel.
More may be needed sometimes, but in this instance, 1 pixel seemed to work best.

4 I then hid the selection and hit the *Delete* key. This popped the Fill dialog shown here,
where I left the options to the default setting with Content-Aware selected. The end result
was that the Content-Aware fill calculated how best to fill the selected area and produce the
result shown here, where the petals have all magically vanished.

Content-Aware filling

The Content-Aware fill is a major new tool in Photoshop CS5 and it has lots of different applications, a few of which are shown in this book. In the example shown opposite I switched to Quick Mask mode in Photoshop so that I could use the brush tool to simply paint over the areas I wished to remove, just as if I were marking up a proof image to indicate which bits needed altering. The difference here is that it is really easy to turn such brush strokes into a selection and from there invoke the Content-Aware fill command and automatically fill the selected areas. You'll notice in step 1 that I changed the quick mask overlay color from red to green. The reason I did this was in order to let the green overlay stand out more from the red rock in the photograph.

Multiple Content-Aware fills

The main thing to understand about Content-Aware filling is that it is a dumb process that mostly manages to do a pretty good job of knowing how to fill a selected area. It does this by sampling detail from outside the selection area and automatically works out how best to reconstruct the sampled data when reconstructing the area inside the selection. As automated processes go it's quite amazing the way it does this, but it's still a dumb process and you can't expect to see it work flawlessly every time you use it. I suppose part of the problem is that writers such as ourselves have carefully chosen just the right types of images to show the Content-Aware feature working at its best and this in turn may lead to false expectations. Our experience is that this is a tool you sometimes need to coax into producing the best results. One thing to watch out for is that you first make the most appropriate selection of the area you wish to fill. It is important here to make sure all the area you wish to remove is adequately selected and that the edge of the selected area doesn't intersect any detailed edges if possible. If the Content-Aware fill doesn't do a completely successful job the first time you fill a selected area (which is often the case), then you may find it helps to repeat applying the Content-Aware fill a second or even a third time. You see, each time you apply a Content-Aware fill you can often get better, smoother results. Another tip is to concentrate on just those areas where a Content-Aware fill hasn't done a perfect job, reselect these areas only and apply the Content-Aware fill again, but to the newly selected areas.

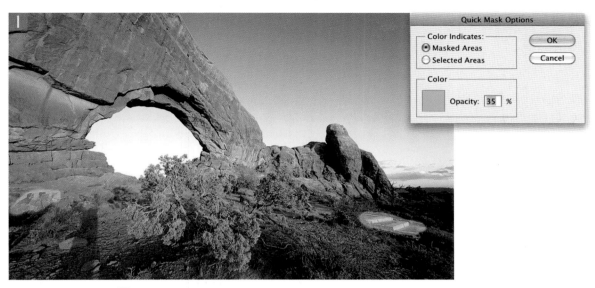

1 In this example I clicked **Q** to switch to quick mask mode using the Quick Mask Options settings shown here. I then selected the brush tool and simply painted over the areas I wished to apply the Content-Aware fill to.

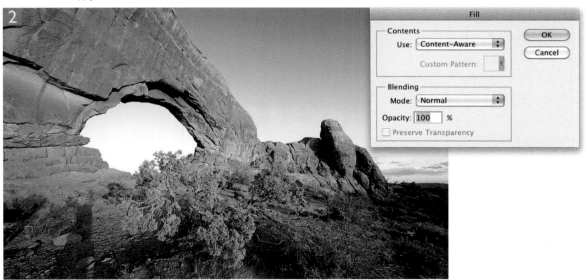

2 I then clicked **Q** again to switch back to selection mode and chose Select ⇨ Inverse to invert the selection. I then chose View ⇨ Hide Extras to hide the marching ants and clicked the *Delete* key to open the Fill dialog shown here with the Content-Aware fill option automatically selected. As you can see, the areas I had painted over in step 1 were now successfully filled using the surrounding image area detail.

Specialist applications

There are various types of specialist users who will find the Stacks rendering feature useful. Scientists can use this as a tool for detecting small differences between images. Forensics users can use certain types of Stacks renderings to amplify minute changes in a series of images, while astronomers can use the Mean rendering to remove extraneous noise when combining a series of astronomy photographs. Some of us have argued that the Median rendering method should be made accessible in the standard version of Photoshop as well but, for now at least, this technique is only going to be available to those Photoshop users who have the extended version of Photoshop CS3 or later.

Layer blending to remove tourists

The Stacks feature lets you use special formulae to determine how layered images are blended together. To summarize how this works, you can take a multi-layered image, select two or more layers, convert these to a Smart Object and apply a Stacks rendering. This feature was really designed as a tool for analytical work in areas such as forensics, medical imaging and astronomy photography (see sidebar). It is because of these rather specialist applications that the Stacks feature has so far been limited to the Extended version only of Photoshop, which is a shame really because the Median Stacks rendering mode can also be applied to creative tasks such as removing tourists from a busy location scene (or can be an effective way to reduce noise from a series of hand-held shots, as shown in Chapter 8).

Median rendering

Of all the different rendering methods you can apply to a series of layers in a Smart Object, the Median rendering is probably the most interesting. This is because it works by analyzing each and every pixel location in a stack of images and selects whatever is the most common pixel value to all the layers at a given point. A Median rendering can therefore be used to smooth out the differences found between individual exposures in a stack and is most useful for processing a sequence of photographs that have been shot from the same angle. This technique will allow you, as shown here, to remove people who have been captured moving through the scene in front of the camera. The following technique will therefore work best for photographs that have been taken using a tripod. Having said that, on the day we shot this a young photographer approached us; we got chatting and explained the technique. Later on that day he emailed us with the result he had got from hand-holding the camera using just half a dozen frames that had been shot over a much shorter period of time. The picture he created was actually pretty good for what was a quick, first experiment using this technique. Basically, you can make this work hand-holding the camera, but for best results we suggest you use a tripod.

1 This shows just a few of the photographs that we shot of a sculpture in Chicago that is popularly known as the Bean. We took these pictures early afternoon over a period of an hour, at a time when a large number of people were visiting. The most crowded area was right underneath the Bean itself, which was why Jeff and I took it in turns to capture well over a hundred frames. This ensured that we had enough pictures so that a Median Stacks rendering would allow us to remove all of the people from this scene.

Figure 5.1 The Median Stacks rendering technique works best if you do what we did here and shoot the pictures using a tripod with a cable release.

2 The first step was to go to the File ⇨ Scripts menu and choose Load Files into Stack. This opened the dialog shown here, where we clicked on the Browse... button to locate the folder containing all the images that had been shot that afternoon. We also checked the Create Smart Object after Loading Layers option (although you could do this separately in Photoshop afterwards). If these shots had been taken hand-held, we would also have checked the Attempt to Automatically Align Source Images option, but since these had all been shot using a tripod (see Figure 5.1) there was no need to do so. We clicked OK to start loading the layers.

3 It may take a while for Photoshop to open all the images, add them as layers and create a Smart Object. 128 images were added here and, as you might expect, the time this takes will all depend on the size of the individual images and how many there are. What we ended up with was a new document with a Smart Object layer that contained all the selected image documents grouped as layers within a Smart Object. When we double-clicked the Smart Object layer we were able to see the full expanded list of layers contained in the Smart Object.

4 Now for the clever part. First we needed to make sure that the Smart Object (that we showed open in Step 3) was closed, so that the Layers panel looked like the example shown here, showing a single Smart Object layer. We went to the Layer menu and choose Smart Objects ⇨ Stack Mode ⇨ Median. Again, the Stacks rendering took a little while to complete, but once it was finished the Median rendering managed to blend the layers such that nearly all of the people in the merged picture had disappeared completely.

5 Although the Image Stack Median rendering did a pretty good job of removing the people from the scene, it ended up smoothing out the sky to the point where we lost any cloud detail. We selected one of the original images where there were some interesting clouds, added this as a new layer and applied a linear gradient to the layer mask to replace the top half of the photograph.

Tidying hair against a busy backdrop

Here is an interesting challenge that I was presented with recently. I shot the model shown on these pages for an advertising job and was asked by the client to make sure that the skin tone and nails looked flawless. After they had seen the initial retouch work they also asked if I could clean up the hair outline. At first it looked like this would be impossible to achieve. After all, how on earth can one use the clone stamp or healing brush to tidy up the fine hair strands against a background which consisted of a busy wallpaper pattern? As it turned out, the solution to this problem was staring me in the face!

1 Here is a beauty photograph where I had retouched for the skin, eyes and nails, but the client requested that I tidy the hair outline more. As you can see, there were a lot of loose stray hairs that overlapped the wallpaper backdrop.

2 In search of an answer, I went to Bridge and checked out some of the other shots that I had taken during the shoot. Fortunately, I had not discarded the original test shots that were taken at the beginning of the shoot and found a photograph of the wallpaper without the model in front of it. The moral here is that you never know when a shot may prove useful, which is why we recommend you never delete anything.

3 I opened the two images that I had selected in Bridge and dragged the wallpaper image across to the main model photograph image to add this as a new layer.

143

Difference blend mode registration

As you can see here, the Difference blend mode is invaluable when it comes to positioning layers in register with each other. You can also use the Difference blend mode to carry out analysis work, such as when you wish to highlight minute differences between the way an image has been processed. For example, you can use this technique to compare the results from using JPEG compression settings.

4 The next thing was to align the backdrop layer with the main image below. I set the wallpaper layer blend mode to Difference, which made it easier to see when the wallpaper layer was in pin register (see sidebar) as I used the move tool.

5 As you can see in Step 4, I was first able to roughly align the two layers. The problem here though was that the wallpaper in the model image was blurred and the wallpaper in Layer 1 was sharp. In order to get the two layers to match, I kept the Layer 1 wallpaper layer in Difference mode and applied a Gaussian Blur filter until the Difference blend mode showed that the two layers matched more closely.

6 I returned the wallpaper layer blend mode to Normal again and ⌥ *alt*-clicked the Add new layer mask button in the Layers panel (circled) to add a layer mask to the layer, filled with black. I then used a hard-edged paint brush to paint with white on the layer mask. This allowed me to paint on the photograph from the wallpaper layer and clean up some of the stray hairs.

Photo: © Martin Evening

7 Here is the finished version where you can see a close-up view of the hair outline. If I hadn't taken a picture of the backdrop on its own, I could always have sampled bits of backdrop detail in other shots from the same sequence, but in this instance having access to the out-take backdrop image made my life a lot easier.

Coloring hair roots

As a beauty photographer who specializes in hair work, I often get asked to lighten the hair roots so that the hair looks like it has a more even color. Here is a fairly simple two-step process that can be used to help lighten the dark roots.

With this technique I basically add two empty layers and set one to Soft Light blend mode and the other to Color. Painting on the Soft Light layer then allows me to selectively add a fill light to the dark areas of the hair, while painting on the Color layer allows me to colorize the hair to make the hair color look more even. When I paint with the brush tool, I use the ⎇ *alt* key to switch to eyedropper mode and sample a new lighter hair color from the image and use this as the foreground color to paint with. The trick here is to use a low-opacity, soft-edged brush and to keep resampling new colors as you paint. The Soft Light mode worked well here at lightening the hair, but you may want to use the Overlay blend mode instead when retouching some hair shots.

1 To disguise the hair roots that were showing in this photograph I added a new empty layer, set this to the Soft Light blend mode and placed this layer inside a layer group.

2 I selected the brush tool and held down the ⌥ *alt* key to sample a color from the lighter hair color area and gently painted over the dark hair areas where the roots were showing most. This step colorized the hair yet also lightened the darker areas, but without destroying the detail in the shadows. This was kind of like a 'filling in the shadow areas' step.

3 I added a new layer within the layer group and set the blending mode to Color. I then used the brush tool to sample more colors (holding down the ⌥ *alt* key) to paint on the Color layer. I found when editing both this and the Soft light layer that it helped to use the eraser tool (rather than add a layer mask) to remove paint from these two layers. I was therefore able to work quite quickly by toggling between the brush tool and the eraser.

Photo: © Martin Evening

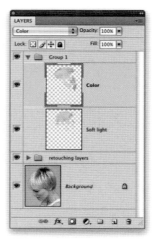

147

The History of History

The History feature was added to Photoshop 5 by Mark Hamburg, who had been tasked to add multiple undo. Mark had been influenced by seeing a demo I had done of Globe Hands and used it as inspiration for the History feature. Mark got a patent in his name and was named Silicon Valley Software Inventor of the Year (in 1999). I got a Photoshop feature designed just for him. A fair trade, in my opinion.

Snapshot painting

A different way of compositing

It's often said that those who forget history are doomed to repeat it. I'll alter that a bit and say that those who forget History are doomed to use layers. The History feature of Photoshop is a powerful and severely under-utilized tool and can radically alter the way digital imaging is done.

The proof that using History can be radical is the fact that the Globe Hands image was done in 1994 using Photoshop version 2.5 – well before Photoshop even had layers. The way of working is very different but the results cannot be duplicated using layers. To understand how to use History requires a bit of learning and practice, but once learned, it can be deployed for a range of imaging needs – as long as you don't forget History is there.

The Globe Hands image (Figure 5.3) is a composite of two original scans from 4 x 5 film (Figure 5.2) as well as substantial retouching for the globe and image warping for the hands. But before I get too far into the technique, I'll need to point out that this image was done back when computers could only hold megabytes of RAM, not gigs. As a result of the early computer limitations, I used a process where I selected a smaller portion of the image and sliced it out to do the heavy work, and only replaced the subsection after the imaging was completed.

Figure 5.2 The original hand scan, the original globe scan and the retouched globe layer.

Figure 5.3 The final image after compositing, retouching, final tone and color adjustments and the addition of a rough-edged frame.

Remembering the old times

In the past, Photoshop's primary limiting speed factor has been RAM access. Photoshop CS5 when run as a 64-bit application can access whatever the motherboard can address. But when I first started using Photoshop, it was a struggle to use a paltry 64 megabytes of RAM. Hence the use of techniques to minimize the size of the images being loaded into Photoshop.

Slicing an image

Photoshop used to have a plug-in called Quick Edit that would allow you to specify a subsection of an image to open and then save the manipulated subimage back into the full image file. What follows is the manual way of carrying out that same type of function, but with some added benefits. Note that this does take practice and attention to detail so that you can put things back together correctly in the end. But the technique still offers benefits.

The fist step is to decide what section of an image you wish to use as the subsection image. Create a marquee selection (Step 1) and then convert that into a path. Be sure to save the path in the full image before proceeding. For the Globe Hands image, the CENTER-DETAIL path would be turned back into a selection before cropping to the selection and then saving the cropped file as CENTER-DETAIL (Step 2). This new file would then be used for all the warping and snapshot painting.

Image warping

Prior to beginning the snapshot painting, I altered the shape of the two hands (see Steps 3 and 4). Even though I had the fellows wrap their hands around a cue ball that was mounted on a long rod running through the background, their hand shapes weren't round enough. To round out the hands I used Liquify.

After duplicating the background to a new layer and renaming it, I added a new layer named 'circle' that was the size and shape I wished to warp the hand to match (Step 2). I warped the hands using Liquify and allowed the circle layer to show as a guide, which is shown in Step 3 on the following page. I used the Show Backdrop option set to show the Circle layer.

Using the forward warp tool shown in Step 4, I gently pushed sections in or out to get a more rounded shape. I lowered the Brush Pressure to 24 and set the Brush Density to 100. I needed to do the work of warping them carefully. The hands didn't need to be perfectly round – that would have actually looked odd. The aim was to make them rounder without making it look like I had done anything to them. That's one of the keys to image manipulation – doing something so that the end results don't look like you did anything!

The image on the left had a marquee selection drawn in the center of the image that defined the area to be used for the main image manipulation. In the Paths panel I clicked on the Make work path from selection button. I suggest naming paths with a consistent and descriptive name so you'll remember what the path is intended to do.

2 After I had saved the cropped image, I named it HAND-DETAIL and duplicated the Background layer and renamed it Hands-unwarped. It didn't really matter what the name was, I was going to rename it anyway, but it was important to have a descriptive name so in drop-down menus (such as in Liquify) I could be assured of knowing what layer was doing what.

3 The first step was to go to the Filter menu and choose Liquify and activate the circle layer so it showed as a visible guide for where the hands needed warping.

4 The rest of the warping was done using various sized brushes to gently push and prod the shape of the hands into a more rounded shape. One of the keys to successfully warping images in Liquify is to first have a high enough resolution image to work with and secondly not to try to do too much. In this case, the amount of warp was sufficient to round out the hands to receive the globe image.

History basics

Before you can really make full use of History as a creative tool, you need to understand some of the fundamentals and how the different options work. In this particular example, I also had to do some preparatory work prior to actually doing the snapshot painting. I suppose the first thing to realize is that there is a relationship between layers and how those layers are used when creating snapshots. For the Globe Hands image, I prepped the HAND-DETAIL image so as to have the proper layers in place before making snapshots (see Figure 5.4).

First though is an explanation of the different options found in the History Options – they have an important role in using History successfully. To access the History Options, select the menu item from the fly-out menu.

Allow Non-Linear History allows you to go back in time, to use a History event without wiping out things you've already done (see Figure 5.6). If you are a sci-fi fan and understand the 'grandfather paradox' this means you can go back in time, kill your grandfather and you won't cease to exist. If you don't understand this, you can leave this unchecked (but I like to use it and so should you). The next check box makes sure that when you click on the Create new snapshot button, you'll get the full New Snapshot dialog (which is really important).

You can choose to have a new snapshot created when saving (I consider this marginal in usefulness). This option will do a full document snapshot when you save. The last option, Make Layer Visibility Changes Undoable, I actually find confusing so I don't use it.

Figure 5.4 The HANDS-DETAIL image (a subsection of the main image) had three layers: the Background image of the warped hands, the warped hands outlined as a separate layer and the globe layer sized and positioned for placement.

Figure 5.5 In the History panel, I selected the fly-out menu for the History Options which brought up a dialog box allowing the selection of various options.

Figure 5.7 Unless you check the Show New Snapshot Dialog by Default option, clicking this button simply makes a new snapshot of the Full Document, which is not useful for our purposes.

Figure 5.6 By default, the check box for automatically creating the first snapshot is checked. I suggest checking the additional check boxes shown above. I don't bother with creating a snapshot when saving – I save a lot so it would clutter the History panel. I also don't bother checking the layer visibility as part of the changes. That complicates the History steps and makes toggling a layer to see before and after part of the History.

Figure 5.8 When properly prepared, there would be a snapshot named Globe that had all layers merged into one and a separate snapshot named Hands which was a snapshot of only the hands floating on their own layer. The snapshot that will be used for any History function is selected by clicking in the active snapshot column. In this figure, the Globe snapshot was set as the History source (inside the circle) and would be used for filling and painting from History.

Making snapshots

In order to use snapshots, you first must make them and be sure of what is contained in the snapshot. Not all snapshots are created equal (nor are they all useful for snapshot painting). There are three flavors of snapshot: Full Document, Merged Layers and Current Layer. Of these, I'll only use the Merged Layers and Current Layer flavors. They do substantially different things and offer very different results. The Current Layer option (Figure 5.9) only stores the currently targeted Photoshop layer. This is useful when you want to be able to fill or paint using History to return to the state of that layer when you made the snapshot.

However, for creative purposes, the Merged Layers flavor (Figure 5.10) is far more useful – this is the only version that allows you to paint or fill from different layers. You'll note that on the preceding page, all three layers were currently visible (Figure 5.4). So, when I did a Merged Layers snapshot, I was able to take the image data from the Globe layer and blend it into the warped Hands layer. If you've never used this snapshot option, you may have never discovered this important feature – blending the results of multiple merged layers into the targeted layer using History.

Figure 5.9 For the Hands snapshot, I needed to make sure the warped hands layer was the current target. This snapshot would be of the hands before I did any blending.

Figure 5.10 For the Globe snapshot, I needed to create the snapshot using the Merged Layers option. It didn't matter what layer was the current target, all visible layers would be included in this snapshot.

The channels

I won't dwell on how I made the actual selections and turned them into channels to be used later. Figure 5.11 shows the Channels panel and the variety of channels created prior to starting the snapshot painting. Obviously, I needed an area to fill into, and that's what the Globe paste channel provided. I also would need to treat the highlights and the shadows of the hands image differently.

The Globe paste channel was made by combining the Hands Outline channel with a circular marquee selection. The Hands Highlights and Hands Shadows were made using Color Range selections on the hands layer. The Finger Details selection was made using the pen tool and drawing around the fingers and then inverting the resulting channel after turning the path into a selection.

Snapshot painting is fundamentally different from layers in that you don't use a layer mask, you use a selection to constrain where the snapshot painting is blended. So preparing the selections accurately before you start the blending is critical. On the other hand, you do have infinite flexibility when snapshot painting in that you can always return to where you started by simply using the prepared snapshots. But clearly defining where the fill or painting occurs is the job of really good masks.

Figure 5.11 The above channels were created using a variety of techniques. The Globe paste and Hands Outline channels were made with paths. The Hands Highlights and Hands Shadows were made using Color Range. The Finger Details were also made with paths and then inverted.

Figure 5.12 For this example, I used the Load Selection dialog box. I usually just ⌘ *ctrl*-click directly on the channel icon to load the selection. In this figure, I loaded the main channel (the Globe paste channel) as a selection. This was the active selection for the first few snapshot painting steps.

Contents Use: drop-down menu

Blending Mode: drop-down menu

Figure 5.13 The Fill commands will be set to use History as the content and a variety of blending modes will be used.

The blending

If you've never tried this process before, it can seem rather intimidating and complicated. But take heart, it's really not that hard once you grasp the functions of the snapshots and how to use History. It's important to remember that if you've properly created your snapshots of Merged and Current layers, you can interactively blend back and forth to achieve the results you wish. So, it's not like you'll really ruin anything if you make a mistake because you can always start afresh by using the correct History snapshot to get back.

To start the process, the targeted layer is the warped hands layer and the globe layer is no longer visible. It really has served its purpose once the Merged Layers snapshot has been created but it's still useful to keep in the event you need to remake a snapshot. The first steps will use the Fill command found under the Edit menu, although you can also use the keyboard command of *Shift* *Delete* to directly access the Fill command. Only after the fill series of adjustments is done will we start using the History brush to paint with.

The crucial setting in the Fill command is to make sure that the Contents drop-down menu is set to use History as shown in Figure 5.13. All of the blending will be done using the History option in the Fill dialog or using the history brush when doing actual brush-based painting.

The other thing to keep in mind is that there will be a variety of blending modes (shown in Figure 5.13) used while working towards the final look. The primary modes are Color, Multiply, Screen, Overlay and Luminosity. When needing to return to a previous state, the Normal mode is used. Creatively, the Multiply, Screen and the combo Overlay are used the most. Multiply blend adds to the existing image data by darkening based on the fill content. Screen lightens the image by the fill content. Overlay is a procedural blend hybrid of both in that it lightens the fill content above level 127 and darkens below level 127. So, it lightens the lights and darkens the darks.

You'll also note that the opacities are almost always on the low side, with nothing ever done at 100% opacity. Subtlety is important in the blending. I prefer to build up gradually to create the effect I'm looking for rather than going over the top and having to try to get back.

1 With the selection active, I used the Fill command and filled using a Color blend mode. Here I chose a 50% Opacity.

2 This shows the image after applying the Color blend fill. Next, I used Multiply with a 33% Opacity. The numbers for opacity are not an exact science. Much of the blending is based on a feeling (which takes time to develop). Remember you have multiple undo (the whole reason for the History feature) and you can always reblend from the other snapshot.

157

3 By using the Multiply mode, the whole Globe paste area had grown darker (which was to be expected). To bring back lightness, I used the Overlay blend mode, which screens above level 127 and multiplies below level 127. This lightened the lights and darkened the darks.

4 At this stage, the color and texture were growing towards the effect I wanted, but the luminosity had continued to get darker. To regain the original luminosity, I changed the History source to be the Hands snapshot and filled at 33% Opacity with Luminosity.

5 After filling in from the Hands snapshot, the History source was changed back to the Globe snapshot after loading the Hands Highlites channel as a selection.

6 After loading the Hands Highlites selection, I filled from the Globe snapshot using Screen (to lighten) again with a 33% Opacity.

7 Here, the Hands Shadow selection had been loaded and the blending mode had been changed to Multiply to darken the shadow area by filling in from the Globe snapshot.

8 The overall look was starting to get finalized, but there was an area on both wrists that required special attention. Prior to working on these areas, it was useful to grab the state of the image blend as it existed at this moment. So, it was time to take another snapshot of the Current Layer which would add a fourth snapshot in the History panel. This snapshot was used to reblend the current state in the event that the next step removed too much detail.

9 The time had come to do some brush work. The Finger Detail selection had been loaded and the history brush tool selected using a Normal blend and 25% Opacity. To return the original skin color and blend in the outer circumference of the Globe blend, the Hands snapshot had been set as the source for History. The Finger Detail selection would therefore only allow snapshot painting in the areas away from the fingers.

10 In this step, the Combo snapshot was selected as the History source and I painted back in some of the area I over-painted using the Hands snapshot. This is the interactive nature of snapshot painting that allows going back and forth between blend states by using the various snapshots as the source. While the whole image was looking pretty good, the last step was to zoom in and do some detail work to bring up the contrast and small textural detail in the image.

11 In these last stages, it's typical to bounce back and forth between the snapshots and blend out the final look of the color and texture. Selecting the Hands snapshot will return the area more towards the Hands snapshot while setting the Globe snapshot will bring more globe back into the image. If either produces undesirable results, you can regain the stage of the image where you made the Combo snapshot. In the final two figures you see the progression of the small detail being brought out. You should be warned that this process can be, well, addictive. At some point you need to call a halt and decide that enough is enough.

The wrap-up

As you can tell from the preceding steps, this process is not for the faint at heart. However, the creative potential is simply too strong to ignore. There are some limitations to using History and snapshots; for example, History and snapshots are live only while your image is open in Photoshop. Once you save and close the image, all History steps and snapshots are lost. You can re-create them if you need (as long as you have the requisite elements saved as layers). You can also save out snapshots as discrete image files that can be reopened and added back into the final file as temporary layers to remake snapshots as needed. The final step in the HAND-DETAIL image is to return the results back into the main image.

12 After saving the HAND-DETAIL image the original full image was reopened and the CENTER DETAIL path was loaded as a selection (⌘ *ctrl*-clicking loaded the path as a selection). The final HAND-DETAIL image was flattened (and closed without saving to preserve the layered image file) and with the selection active, I chose Edit ⇨ Copy and pasted the clipboard contents into the selection. By default, Photoshop's behavior is to paste into the exact center of an active selection. So as long as the pasted content and the selection were identical in size, I would have made a seamless assembly.

13 Pasting in the HAND-DETAIL image resulted in an exact pixel for pixel match. At this stage some final image adjustments were made to punch up the overall color and contrast and add the rough-edged frame around the final image. The end result is the appearance that the globe is painted onto the hands.

The Photoshop diet

You know how it's said that the camera adds ten pounds? Well, this is an easy weight-loss program courtesy of Photoshop (and you don't even have to go on a diet).

1 The first step is so easy, you'll kick yourself for not thinking of it yourself: non-proportional resizing. Simply uncheck the Constrain Proportions option (shown in the circle) in Image Size and enter in a reduced percent in the Width. This has the very simple ability to slim without any visible clue (as long as you keep to 4–8% maximum).

2 If the first step isn't enough, you can go to further lengths (or widths). The key thing here is to know that unlike most plug-in filters, Spherize actually works well even when a selection is feathered. In this step, an elliptical selection was made around the dancer's tummy and I chose Select ⇨ Modify ⇨ Feather and feathered the selection by 50 pixels.

3

This shows the result of a single pass of Spherize.

3 With the feathered selection active, I chose Filter ⇨ Distort ⇨ Spherize, entered a −10 amount and constrained the effect to the horizontal axis only. You can try to do a normal Spherize but this will sometimes draw the effect somewhat too strongly, giving a pinched look. Moderation is the key here (similar to your actual diet).

4 At this stage, both the non-proportional resize and two passes of −10 horizontal spherize had been applied (I added a second pass by using the ⌘ F ctrl F keyboard shortcut). However, I really must caution against overuse of this effect. You can too easily move from subtle to a cinched waist look that would be outlandish.

Portrait of Photoshop co-author Thomas Knoll by Jeff Schewe.
Hasselblad 500 ELX | 150 mm | 120 Ektachrome 100 | Imacon Flextight scan

Chapter 6

Retouching people

Tips for retouching portraits

This chapter is all about how to retouch portrait photographs and shows some of the retouching tips we both use when working in Photoshop. The key to good retouching is to do so in a way that it isn't noticed in the final image. Here, we have shown examples of ways to disguise your retouching to make the work that's done less noticeable, plus one example that isn't quite so subtle!

Fashion and beauty retouching

Adding lightness and contrast to the eyes

If you lighten the eyes too much they will look unnatural. Worse still, if you make them too white, the whites of the eyes will appear without any detail on the page and print as paper white. I use a fairly simple method for lightening the eyes, which is shown here. Of course, you could just select the whites of the eyes and lighten these areas on their own. That works too, but I find that by applying a Curves adjustment to the whole of the eye area, I can use the curve to anchor the brightness of the iris and tweak the curve to make the whites of the eyes lighter. This is just as effective as selecting the whites only but I find I have simultaneous control over the lightness of the pupils as well as the whites of the eyes.

1 To add more contrast to the eyes in this photograph, I selected the lasso tool and drew a selection around the outline of the left eye. I then held down the *Shift* key to draw around the right eye and added this to the lasso selection.

2 I was then able to apply a direct Curves adjustment (or add a Curves adjustment layer) and draw a lightening curve to add lightness to the eyes but keep the tone in the dark areas of the pupils the same. If you look at the curve shown here you can see how I placed an anchor point near the bottom of the curve to anchor the brightness for the pupils and then added extra points to lighten the pupils and whites of the eyes. Once I had done this I needed to feather the selection area, which I did by going to the Masks panel and setting the Feather amount to 2 pixels.

Repair work using a copied selection

We typically use the clone stamp and healing brush to carry out most repair work but there is another approach you can use, which is to copy a selection of pixels that have been sampled from another part of the picture (or a separate image even). Back in the mists of time before there were layers in Photoshop, you could duplicate a selection to make it a temporary layer by ⌥ alt -dragging inside a selection with the move tool. Well, you can still do this in Photoshop, but you will usually find it more practical to copy the selection contents as a new layer. To do this make a selection and then use Layer ➪ New ➪ Layer via Copy, or use the keyboard shortcut ⌘ J ctrl J. This will copy the selection contents as a new layer. Once you have duplicated the selection contents as a new layer you can use the copied layer to cover up another portion of the image by dragging it across with the move tool and transforming the layer as necessary.

In the step-by-step example shown here, I wanted to cover up the burst blood vessels that could be seen in the model's right eye. To do this I made a simple rectangular selection over the good eye, copied the contents to a new layer and transformed the new layer by flipping it horizontally. The add layer mask step is important because when you add a layer mask and fill or paint with black, you are not deleting the image data but merely hiding the layer contents. In this example the layer mask allowed me to initially hide all of the copied layer and (with white as the foreground color) selectively paint back the bits that I wanted to reveal. This allowed me to paint with the brush tool to replace the bloodshot areas of the eye with the copied selection from the good eye. One of the things you have to be careful of when retouching the eyes in this way is to make sure that you preserve the catch light reflections in the eyes, because if you were to flip the catch lights as well your subject could end up looking cross-eyed!

Registration is important too. One way to achieve this is to temporarily take the layer opacity down while you are moving a layer into position. The other thing you can do is to switch the layer blend mode to Difference. The effect this has is to cancel out any areas that are identical and display them as black. The Difference blend mode is therefore ideal when exact pin-registration is required when moving a layer.

1 In this close-up view you can see that the model's right eye has some burst blood vessels. Fortunately the model is looking straight to camera and I was easily able to make a repair by copying across pixel data from the good eye.

2 I made a selection of the other eye and used the ⌘ J ctrl J shortcut to copy as a new layer, and then used Edit ⇨ Transform ⇨ Flip Horizontal to match it to the other eye (with the opacity temporarily lowered to 70%).

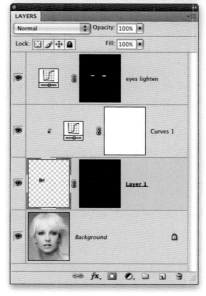

3 I then ⌥ alt -clicked the Add Layer Mask button to add a filled layer mask to 'hide all' on the layer. I selected the paint brush and with white as the foreground color gradually painted back in the good eye layer to repair the bloodshot area. Finally, I added an eye lightening Curves layer as described on pages 168–169.

Locking brush attributes

If you click on the lock icons in the Brush panel next to the brush attributes such as Shape Dynamics, you can lock these brush attribute settings so that these stay fixed whenever you choose a new brush preset.

Removing stray hairs

When I shoot for fashion and beauty clients I do all I can to make sure the hair is looking good at the capture stage. Even so, there will always be some stray hairs that need tidying later in Photoshop. The healing brush is great for most retouching tasks, but is not ideal when painting up against areas where there is a sudden change in tone. Therefore, in most instances I find it preferable to retouch loose hairs using the clone stamp or brush tool. Having said that, you can now in Photoshop CS5 make use of the spot healing brush in Content-Aware mode to more effectively remove stray hairs that cross over other hairs. The thing is, this feature doesn't really know which hairs you want to get rid of and which you want to keep, so while it is now a more effective tool to use, you can't rely on it completely, without helping guide the tool as you paint.

I always use a Wacom pen stylus and use a custom brush setting where the brush size is a round brush with a size of around 10 pixels, with the brush size and brush opacity linked to the amount of pressure that's applied. I have found this to be a useful brush setting for cloning hair strands and painting new strands of hair (see Figure 6.1). The brush size can then be modified and made larger or smaller using the square bracket keys on the keyboard. Using the clone stamp or brush tool in this way I can clone out cross-hairs, remove intricate strands of hair and paint new strands that match the texture and color of the existing hair.

If you are retouching fine strands of hair, pay careful attention to where the strands of hair originate, the direction they are flowing in and where they meet up with or cross over other strands of hair. A clumsy retoucher may simply lop off loose strands and such retouching always stands out as looking retouched (see Figure 6.2). When I am asked to tidy up fluffy loose hairs, I usually approach this type of task in gradual stages – gradually thinning out the hair rather than cutting it all off at once. This is because it would look unnatural to see a soft textured hairstyle suddenly change into a perfectly smooth outline. To keep the hair looking real I'll often leave some stray hairs in the picture. Sometimes I will begin by erasing the loose hairs around the hair outline and actually paint in some loose stray hairs afterwards (using the clone stamp tool configuration shown in Figure 6.1). Doing so enables me to achieve a more natural look to the hair.

Figure 6.1 When using the clone stamp tool to retouch hair strands, I use a special preset setting. The brush size is set to 10 pixels and the Shape Dynamics and Transfer (Opacity) are linked to the pen pressure of the Wacom pen. I then save this combination of settings for both the clone stamp and the brush tool as a 'hair retouch' brush setting.

Figure 6.2 On the left here we have the original unretouched image and in the middle a crudely retouched version where all I did was to clean up the outer edge of the hairline. The version on the right shows the result of a more detailed hair retouch where I carefully removed every loose strand of hair and filled in some of the gaps, all using the brush and clone stamp tool and the settings shown in Figure 6.1.

Pressure-sensitive pen and pad

I do much of my beauty retouching using the brush tool on this copied layer. I prefer to use a pressure-sensitive stylus and pad such as the Wacom™ Intuos™, because this allows me a much finer degree of control than I can get with a normal mouse. Whenever you select any of the painting tools you can select from a number of options from the Brush panel that will enable you to determine what aspects of the brush behavior will be governed by the way you use the pressure-sensitive stylus. Photoshop will not just be aware of the amount of pressure you apply with the stylus. If you are using the Wacom™ Intuos™, Photoshop is able to respond to input information such as the barrel rotation of the stylus, the angle of tilt or the movement of the thumb wheel (if you have one).

Beauty skin retouching

There are many different types of skin and the skin texture varies a lot on different parts of the body. For example, the skin under the eyes will usually have a coarse goosebump texture and the cheeks may be slightly more pitted than the rest of the face skin and have larger pores. With younger subjects the skin on the forehead will generally be quite smooth, but with minute horizontal lines, and the smoothest skin texture of all will be on the temples and sides of the nose. As you move down towards the neck area the texture of the skin changes to become coarser still. In addition to this you may notice a very fine downy hair on the face, especially just above the lips. I mention this because it is important to pay close attention to these changes in skin texture as you retouch a beauty image. When you use the clone stamp or healing brush tools you need to carefully choose the source point you sample from when cloning skin texture from one part of the face or body to another.

Disguise your retouching

The basic rule when retouching is to disguise your work so that whatever corrections you make to a photograph, it is not immediately apparent that the picture has been retouched. If you are working for a fashion client they will usually be looking for image perfection. Although I may sometimes employ a lot of Photoshop wizardry in order to satisfy the client, I feel it is important to fade out the retouching so that I let some of the original blemishes and underlying skin texture show through still. My preferred approach is to retouch the skin using the clone stamp and healing brush tools to clean up all the blemishes. I then add a painting layer in which I use a large brush to paint over the skin to soften the details and unwanted shadows. As you will see in the beauty retouching example that's coming up, I always reduce the opacity of the layer that contains the brush paint retouching work to let much of the original, unpainted skin texture show through from below. The net result, I feel, is a more natural-looking finish, where the model's skin looks perfect, but without looking too artificial.

Brush blending modes

The painting and other brush-type tools can be applied using a variety of blending modes and these are the same ones as are available in the Layers panel, Apply Image and Calculations dialogs. Of the numerous blend modes available, I reckon that the following modes are probably the most useful when used with the brush or gradient tools.

The Screen blend mode can be used to lighten and I often use this as a brush blend mode to lighten areas such as the eyes, or add highlight sparkles, as shown on pages 110–113. The Multiply blend mode basically darkens and this can be used to selectively darken specific features, sampling colors from the photograph as I paint. For example, I sometimes use a large, soft-edged brush set to a low opacity in order to gently build up more density in the eyebrows.

As an assistant, I used to work for a photographer called James Wedge who was well known at the time for his hand-colored black and white photography. He produced some rather beautiful work in which he would carefully mask areas of a picture and paint directly on the print using translucent colored inks. If you are working in Photoshop, the Color blend mode can be used to achieve similar types of results. More often, I find the Color blend mode is ideal for color correcting small color casts. For example, I sometimes use the brush tool in Color mode to get the skin tones to match the colors on other areas of the face or body, or to balance out the color seen in an uneven tan. Sometimes I find that caucasian skin tones can appear too red/magenta in the darker areas and clients will often ask me to make these match the skin color of the rest of the body. Again, this is another situation where the Color blend mode comes in useful.

The Overlay and Hard Light blend modes can be used to paint in contrast, while the Soft Light blend mode can be used (as was shown in the 'Coloring hair roots' example on pages 146–147) to paint in a soft contrast effect. In Chapter 7 I will be showing how the brush tool can be used in Overlay blend mode to clean up a silhouette mask while preserving important edge detail.

As you will see in the beauty retouching steps on the following pages, I also use the Lighten and Darken blend modes whenever I use the brush tool to smooth out the skin tones on a beauty photograph.

Beauty/fashion retouching

Fashion and beauty retouching is usually driven by the commercial requirements of clients, who in today's market will normally want every photograph that appears in print to have some level of retouching done to it. Photoshop has played a huge role in giving photographers the digital tools they need to retouch their own pictures. Yet, in the wrong hands this can lead to some truly dreadful photography! Over the next few pages I have shown all the steps I would use in a typical retouching session, where the objective was to clean up all the stray hairs and blemishes yet leave the model still looking human at the end of the process.

1 This shows the before version image without any retouching. As you can see, there were a lot of stray hairs to tidy, some spotting required on the black outfit and the skin tones needed to be made smoother.

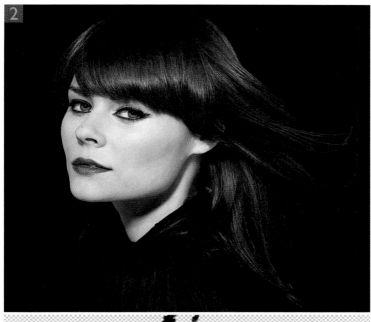

2 Before carrying out any retouching I added an empty new layer above the Background layer and set the tool options for the clone stamp and healing brush tools to Current Layer & Below. I was then able to carry out all the main spotting work on a separate layer. This meant that should I need to undo any of the retouching it would be easy enough to erase the bits that I didn't want included. There is also another benefit to doing this: you can ⌥ alt -click on the spotting layer eyeball icon to reveal the retouching layer only and use this to show how much spotting work had to be done (see the bottom screen shot example where the spotting is revealed against a transparent backdrop). This might be handy if the client starts asking why you have charged so much to work on a picture!

3 Next I wanted to concentrate on retouching the face. To do this I made a marquee selection of the face and neck and used the ⌘ ⌥ Shift E ctrl alt Shift E shortcut to create a new merged duplicate layer above the spotting layer. I then inverted the selection (⌘ Shift I ctrl Shift I) and hit the Delete key to delete the selected area. This left a merged copy of the selected area as a new layer, which I named 'Face retouching'.

4 I now used the brush tool to paint over the pixels on the Face retouching layer. For example, I began by painting with the brush tool in Lighten mode with a low-opacity brush (or ideally a pressure-sensitive pad and pen). I sampled a light flesh tone color by ⌥ alt-clicking on the image and then brushed lightly over the darker areas of the face such as underneath the eyes (when using Lighten mode only the pixels that are darker than the sampled color will be replaced). I also switched to Darken mode, which allowed me to sample a flesh tone color to paint the lighter colored pixels darker (it is a good idea to always keep resampling new colors as you paint). It doesn't matter that I overdid the retouching at this stage, as the next step could be used to moderate the level of retouching. The main goal here was to smooth the skin tones and, if necessary, remodel the light and shade on the face.

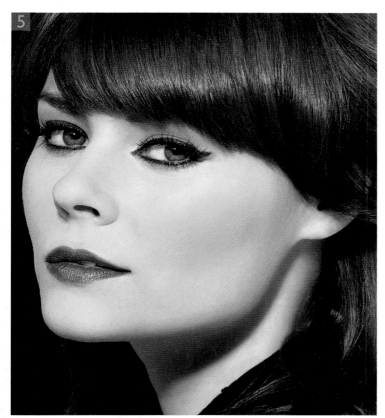

5 Some fashion photographers like the super-retouched look. Others argue that this makes models look more like plastic dolls than real women. It is up to you, but I usually prefer to fade the opacity of the retouched layer. In this instance I reduced the layer opacity to 60%. Doing this allowed more of the original skin texture to show through from the layers below so that the final retouched result looked more convincing. You will notice that I also added a layer mask to the layer and painted with black to hide the areas where the brush strokes overlapped important facial features (but don't forget to change the brush blend mode back to Normal).

6 I next wanted to tidy up the lips. Here I used the same technique as in step 3, where I made a rough marquee selection of the lips area and used the ⌘ ⌥ Shift E ctrl alt Shift E shortcut to create a new merged duplicate layer above the Face retouching layer. I inverted the selection ⌘ Shift I ctrl Shift I and hit Delete to delete the selected area (this screen shot shows the Lips layer viewed on its own). I then used the pen tool to draw a path outline of the lips.

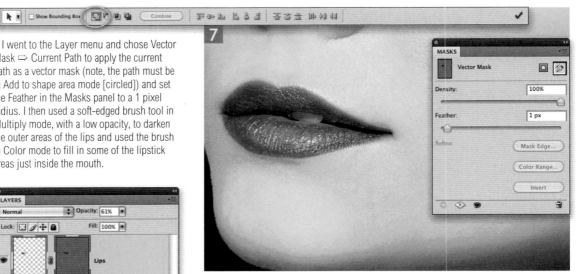

7 I went to the Layer menu and chose Vector Mask ⇨ Current Path to apply the current path as a vector mask (note, the path must be in Add to shape area mode [circled]) and set the Feather in the Masks panel to a 1 pixel radius. I then used a soft-edged brush tool in Multiply mode, with a low opacity, to darken the outer areas of the lips and used the brush in Color mode to fill in some of the lipstick areas just inside the mouth.

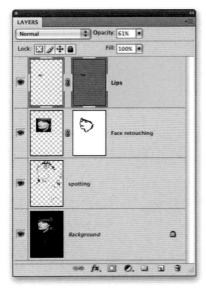

8 Once again I used the marquee tool to select the face area and used the ⌘ ⌥ Shift E ctrl alt Shift E shortcut to create a new merged duplicate layer above the Lips layer, inverted the selection and hit Delete. I then ⌘ ctrl-clicked on the new layer (which I named 'Liquify work') and chose Liquify... from the Filter menu. As you can see here, I used a few gentle brush strokes with the warp tool to make the eyes slightly bigger, made the lips a little more symmetrical and straightened the fringe.

9 Here is the final version showing the results of the Liquify work that was applied in Step 8. I also made a lasso selection of the pupils and added a Curves adjustment to add more contrast and lightness to the pupils only. As you can see, I added a 2 pixel feather in the Masks panel to soften the mask selection edge. The important points to note here are that although the face has been retouched, the skin tones still show the texture of real skin and the layered structure of the master image allowed me to re-edit certain portions of the image as necessary. The Background layer at the bottom remained untouched throughout.

Retouching portraits

Beauty retouching is about enhancing the makeup and the smoothness of the lighting on the face. Portrait retouching requires a fairly similar approach for getting rid of the blemishes and enhancing the skin texture of the subject. However, overall, I find that portrait retouching requires a more subtle approach, as you don't always want to reduce the lines and wrinkles quite so much when retouching portrait photographs. Not all blemishes should necessarily be removed. Take the case of the model Cindy Crawford. In the early years of her modeling career, a lot of magazines wanted a mole on her face to be retouched out. Later on, as she became more famous, nobody would dream of removing it because the pictures would no longer be recognizable as being Cindy!

It is interesting how there has been quite a backlash in recent years, with many celebrities reacting against pictures where their faces (as well as their bodies) have been retouched out of all recognition. Our friend Greg Gorman is a well-known celebrity photographer and he tells us that he has made a deliberate effort in recent years to reduce the amount of retouching that is carried out on the portraits he shoots. Having said that, Greg reckons there are many celebrities who quite like seeing themselves retouched and are happy to believe that's how they really look. Plus many of the magazines simply won't publish photographs that feature models or celebrities unless they have had at least a moderate level of retouching done to the images. When Photoshop first came out we saw lots of magazine images where the eyes and teeth were the same white as the paper stock. As a fashion photographer I see lots of examples of badly retouched testing photographs in models' portfolios. My gut feeling is that the magazine editors as well as the general public are becoming tired of the over-retouched look and in recent years we have seen magazines tone down the amount of retouching used, or they are at least now using better retouchers to do the work. Over the next few pages I have shown an example of a classic portrait where the retouching is more restrained, which if anything requires even more skill to get right compared with the beauty retouching example I showed you earlier.

1 This is a portrait of Alex, one of the models used on our Photoshop book shoot, taken by Jeff. Here I wanted to show you the kind of steps that I would typically use to retouch a portrait. These steps are slightly different to the beauty retouching method described earlier because the main objective here was to make the retouching look as completely natural as possible.

Photo: © Jeff Schewe

2 I began by adding a new empty layer with which to carry out all the initial spotting work using the clone stamp and healing brush tools. If you compare this version with the one above you will notice that I was careful to retouch all the small blemishes and tidy up things like the stray eyebrow hairs and stubble. I didn't remove the mole on Alex's cheek, but I did remove many of the other spots that I felt needed to be retouched.

3 Next, I wanted to tackle the bags under the eyes. Even though a fill reflector was used to bounce some light into Alex's face, I felt it would be a good idea to knock these back a little further. To do this, I carried out the Merge copy layer step that was used in the previous retouching example. I used the rectangular marquee tool to select the eyes only and used the ⌘ ⌥ Shift E (ctrl alt Shift E) shortcut to create a new merged duplicate layer above the Spotting layer, inverted the selection (⌘ Shift I ctrl Shift I) and hit Delete. I now had a merged copy layer of the eyes at the top of the layer stack. I selected the healing brush and used it to carefully remove the crease line. The trick here is to be very careful choosing where you sample from. In this example I had to make sure that the heal cloned texture correctly matched the surrounding skin texture. Once I had completed the healing brush work, I faded the layer opacity to 70% in order to let some of the bags and crease line show through. This avoided letting Alex look like his face had been pumped full of Botox.

4 I now wanted to open the eyes slightly. If you look closely you can see a reflection of the fill light reflector that was used to bounce more light into Alex's face. The downside of doing this is that his eyes were slightly squinted. To counteract this I repeated the Merge copy layer step, where once again I made a marquee selection of the eyes and used the ⌘ ⌥ Shift E / ctrl alt Shift E shortcut to create a new merged duplicate layer above the 'beneath eyes' layer, inverted the selection and hit Delete . I then went to the Filter menu and chose Liquify... In the Liquify dialog shown here I used the warp tool with a low Brush Pressure setting to gently push the lower eyelids open a little more. It was a rather subtle adjustment, but all that was needed to make the eyes look more natural.

5 I now wanted to make Alex's right eye slightly sharper. To do this I used a technique first devised by Bruce Fraser to create a depth of field sharpening layer. The first step was to create a new merged copy layer using the ⌘ ⌥ Shift E ctrl alt Shift E keyboard shortcut. I then double-clicked on an empty space in the layer (circled), to open the Layer Style dialog shown here, where I set the layer opacity to 50%, the blend mode to Overlay and adjusted the Blend If sliders as shown here.

6 I went to the Filter ⇨ Sharpen menu and applied the Unsharp Mask filter to the merged copy layer using the settings shown here, followed by the Filter ⇨ Other ⇨ High Pass filter using a 25 pixels Radius.

7 Here is the completed photograph. You will notice that I added a Curves adjustment layer to lighten the eye pupils. I added the adjustment layer first, filled the layer mask with black to hide the effect and then painted on the mask with white to reveal the adjustment in the pupils only. As I did this I was careful not to make the catch light reflection any lighter. If you compare this version with the original you'll see quite a transformation compared to what we started out with. Yet I still managed to preserve the skin texture and keep the portrait looking fairly natural.

Figure 6.3 Here you can see the lighting setup used to capture the photograph shown on this page.

1 This photograph was shot using a standard beauty light setup (see Figure 6.3), and shows the model with her normal hair color. In the following sequence of steps I want to show you how I was able to change her hair color using a precisely measured sample hair color swatch as guidance.

Hand coloring a photograph

One way you can colorize a photograph is to set the brush tool to the Color blend mode and set the foreground color to the color you wish to paint with. But here is a hand coloring technique that was originally devised by Jim Divitale as an ultra-flexible way to paint items a specific color. The way this works is that you pick a foreground color and then add three color fill layers of this same color, but using three different blend modes: Color, Overlay and Multiply. Color essentially colorizes the image, the Overlay blend mode applies color to the image as well, but also adds contrast, and lastly the Multiply blend mode adds color depth by adding color and darkening at the same time.

2 For this first step I used an X-Rite Eye-One spectrophotometer to take a series of measurements from selected hair color swatches in a hair color guide book.

3 I used the X-Rite Eye Share software to record the measurements made with the Eye-One device. I took several measurements of the desired hair color sample and clicked on the resulting sample swatch colors in the Eye Share interface to calculate the best average color reading (the color readouts were given in Lab values [circled below]).

4 I then opened the Color Picker in Photoshop and entered the (rounded up) Lab Color values in the Lab coordinates boxes (circled). It isn't absolutely necessary that you go through the pre-step of measuring the color swatch values with a spectrophotometer. The following steps will work just as well if you simply resort to guessing the color here. Once I was happy with the settings, I clicked OK to make this the new foreground color.

5 Next, I went to the Swatches panel and rolled the cursor down to the bottom of the list, where you'll notice how the icon changed to a paint bucket icon. I clicked here to add the foreground color as a Swatch preset, where I named it using the color reference from the hair swatch book in Step 2. Saving special colors like this in the Swatches panel can save you time if you need to reference such colors again.

6 At this particular point, you might find it helpful to record the following steps as a Photoshop action. This way you'll find it quicker to set up all the layers in future without having to do so manually. The first step here was to click on the Add adjustment/fill button in the Layers panel (circled) and add a new Color Fill layer using the current foreground color.

7 I then dragged the Color Fill layer to the New Layer button in the Layers panel to make a copy and dragged again to make a second copy. I set the uppermost Color Fill copy layer to Color mode using 50% Opacity. I clicked on the middle layer and set the blend to Overlay mode using 25% Opacity and lastly, I went to the original layer at the bottom and set the blend mode to Multiply using 10% Opacity. In the screen shot shown here, you'll notice that I renamed the layers, indicating the layer blend mode and opacity percentage. It is by no means essential that you do this, but if you are recording these steps in an action it may help if you identify the layers in this way.

8 | *Shift*-clicked to select all three Color fill layers and chose New Group from Layers… from the Layers panel fly-out menu (or use the ⌘ *G* *ctrl* *G* shortcut). I then ⌥ *alt*-clicked on the Add Layer Mask button in the Layers panel to add a pixel layer mask filled with black, which hid the layer group contents (if you have been recording these steps as an action, you can now press the Stop button to end the recording). After I had completed these steps I was able to paint with white on the layer group's layer mask to simultaneously reveal all three layers in the group.

9 Here you can see the finished result after I had finished painting on the pixel layer mask to define the outline of the hair. The blend and opacity modes I suggested using for the three layers are a good starting point. When you try this method out on your own photographs you may well want to adjust the opacity settings for the subject you are coloring.

Photo: © Martin Evening

Working with Liquify

Liquify is Photoshop's answer to warping and distortion of photographic images. It's a free-form tool that takes some practice to become proficient but the results really can't be accomplished in any other manner. Martin tends to use the tool in very subtle ways, whereas I like to use Liquify to really make a difference. Figure 6.4 shows the result of before and after a Liquify session.

Figure 6.4 On the left is the original scan from a 120 mm transparency. The image on the right shows the final Liquify warp and crop.

1 The first step was to take the *Background* layer and duplicate it so that the Liquify warp would be on its own layer. Then I opened the copy layer in Liquify. I used the forward warp Tool to start pushing parts of the image around. You'll note that I accidentally warped the briefcase. To fix that, I used the reconstruct tool in the next step.

2 To fix the unintended warp, I used the reconstruct tool to literally paint back the unwarped image. To avoid unintended warping of the briefcase later, I created a mask in the next step to constrain the warping.

3 I used the freeze mask tool to paint a mask over the briefcase which would then allow me to make sure that regardless of the subsequent warping, the briefcase would remain unwarped. I chose the option to show the mask while I was painting it in. I also chose the Mask Color to be red for easy identification. Just underneath the freeze mask tool is the thaw mask tool (really, I don't make this stuff up) which allows erasing of the mask. The easier alternative is to simply keep the freeze mask tool selected and use the ⌥ *alt* key to toggle to the thaw mask tool while painting.

4 I then zoomed into the image to work on specific details. I used the forward warp tool (left) to smooth out areas of the guy's jacket and used the bloat tool (right) to make his eyes bigger. The intend was to add a degree of cartoonish character while still maintaining a believable appearance.

5 The final step before clicking the OK button was to save the warp mesh as a separate file. This would allow me to reopen Liquify and modify the warp down the road (always a good idea when working with art directors). So, did I go too far?

How to remove reflections from glasses

When you photograph people who are wearing glasses you often have to be careful to watch out for reflections. This isn't always such a bad thing as the reflections can sometimes add to the look of a portrait, but they are usually less desirable when they show a reflection of the studio lighting or are in other ways distracting. In the step-by-step example shown here the reflections aren't at all unpleasant, but I thought it would be useful to show you how one could go about dulling these down in Photoshop. Using the technique described here, it was possible to fade the adjustments made and find the right balance between the uncorrected and corrected versions.

1 Here is a photograph, shot by Jeff, of Rod Wynne-Powell, who is the technical editor for this book. I began by adding a new empty layer and used this to carry out all the main spotting work. I then selected the pen tool in Path mode and used it to define the outline of the reflections, which you can see have been saved as a path in the Paths panel.

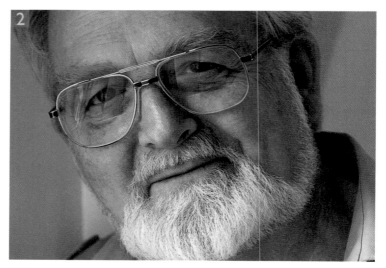

2 I then applied a darkening Curves adjustment layer and, with the path still active, clicked on the Vector path button in the Masks panel (circled). This applied a vector mask to the Curves adjustment mask using the path I created in Step 1 (if the vector mask appears inverted, follow the steps shown on page 180 to set the path mode to 'Add'). With the vector mask selected, I also applied a 2 pixel feather via the Masks panel to soften the mask outline. I then clicked on the pixel layer mask and used the brush tool to paint with black. This allowed me to further fine-tune the Curves adjustment masking.

3 The previous step left the eyes looking rather shaded. To address this, I added a further Curves adjustment – this time one that lightened the image. I filled the pixel layer mask with black and used the brush tool with white as the foreground color to paint on the layer mask and effectively dodge the areas inside the glasses to make them lighter.

4 Step 3 improved the photograph, but the eyes did now lack contrast. To complete the image, I added another Curves adjustment layer – this time a lightening adjustment that brightened the eyes. I filled the layer mask with black and used the brush tool with white as the foreground color to paint on the layer mask. My aim here was to mainly lighten the whites of the eyes, while preserving the darkness in the pupils.

Chapter 7

Masking and compositing

How to combine images and solve tricky problems

I n this chapter we wanted to look at some of the various masking and compositing techniques that we have both utilized over the years. This is one of those areas where Photoshop has evolved to provide a useful array of tools that can help you to produce convincing blends in your composite images. Of course, it is not all down to Photoshop. It often matters that you get the photography right to begin with. The techniques shown here should provide you with ideas and inspiration for how to become a master retoucher using Photoshop.

Figure 7.1 The two top shots were done on location at the Case dealer. The sign was done in Photoshop and the sunset was from studio stock.

Compositing work

Creating a realistic composite

In a perfect world where sunsets appear on cue and clients really do read (and send) memos, you don't need to worry about putting together a complicated production shot – it all falls magically into place. But in the real world, that rarely happens. This is an example of how the best laid plans indeed go awry and how you can use Photoshop to construct the image you need in spite of client miscommunications and weather that doesn't play nice.

In this instance, the art director promised me that he had seen the scouting shots of the Case IH dealer and it would work well as a nice dusk shot – and the building exterior even had shrubs (for some reason, he really liked those shrubs). However, the dealer did not get the memo for clearing out *that* particular bay of the building. The bay with the attractive shrubs had a Case IH Combine that was in about a thousand pieces. So, we were forced to shoot the big machine around the back of the building while we set up the exterior shot for dusk at the front side with the shrubs. Oh, and the sign, it seems that hadn't been manufactured yet so I wouldn't be able to shoot it, could I just make the sign in Photoshop? Sure…

This ended up being a far more complex composite than was originally planned. Figure 7.1 shows the two original shots and the synthetic sign element created from scratch in Photoshop. The key was to shoot both the interior and exterior shots from the exact same camera angle and camera height – even taking the steps of measuring the distance and the angles to be accurate.

The exterior dusk shot was done first with the timing aimed to get the right dusk light. The art director had hoped for a nice sunset (yeah, like that would happen). The sunset was visually uninteresting so the art director agreed we would need to use a stock shot. I had shot a bunch of really nice sunset photos in Montana earlier in the year while on assignment for Case. While they didn't use the sunset shot for that assignment, they did license the sunset for this one. The inside of the bay on the back side of the building was lit while waiting for the outside light to get right and shot later at night – it was a long night too!

Paths panel showing building outline

1 The first step was to use the pen tool to draw an accurate path around the building exterior that would be loaded as a selection, saved as a channel and then into a layer mask for the sky layer. When the sky layer was brought in I resized it to fit the full width of the image. You'll note in the Background layer, I had to add more canvas to the top in order to fit the layout. The sky covers that addition.

Layers showing sky and layer mask

2 To avoid working with the entire document when doing the center detail work, I used a process described on pages 150–151 and worked on this section of the image separately. Even after careful measurements when shooting I still needed to do a bit of Free Transform work to get the interior shot sized and positioned. Rather than apply a layer mask to this layer I made a duplicate of the Background layer and moved it to the top of the layer stack and masked it (as you'll see in the following step).

Layers showing detail of the two layers

Door outline channel

Layers showing Door overlay layer

3 It may seem backwards, but I often prefer to overlay a layer on top of something and then use a layer mask to reveal what's underneath. I find it more expedient to work this way. The layer mask was done using the pen tool to create an outline of the door opening with some softening done in the foreground to allow some of the warm light to spill out. Not enough in this case, which leads to the next step.

4 In order to get more warm light extending out of the doorway, I added a layer copied from the background and lightened it and added a warmer color balance.

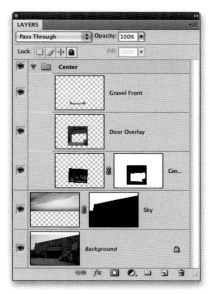

5 Going back to the main image, I dragged and dropped the three sub-layers (I didn't bother with the Background layer) and added them to a layer group named 'Center'. Since I had added a new sky to the photo and the original reflection in the tractor's glass window was of the 'as shot' sky, I needed to fix that.

6 I copied the far upper left portion of the sky and made it into a new layer. I then used Edit ⇨ Transform ⇨ Flip Horizontal (since the reflection was a 'mirror image' from that portion of the sky). For the window glass channel, I used the pen tool to create an accurate outline of the glass in the window and loaded the channel as a selection to create the layer mask. You'll note a second reflection was added – since the shiny parts of the cab also reflected the original sky I repeated the process by duplicating the flipped sky and used a different layer mask created using Color Range.

Layers showing Reflections group of 2 layers

The window glass channel

203

Case logo in Illustrator

Photoshop's Paste options for paths

The three channels

7 This is where it started to get complicated. The art director gave me an Illustrator file with the Case logo. In Illustrator, I selected the paths and copied them. Back in Photoshop I pasted as paths (see the Paste options). I transformed the paths to fit on the sign background I had previously made (based on a loose 'description' by the client). Then I loaded the paths as a selection and created a mask channel. Well, three channels to be precise: one for the text, one for the colored bar and a third that I blurred to create an outline glow to make the sign look like it was lit from behind. You'll note that I cut the Case logo into two separate channels because the logo had different fill colors.

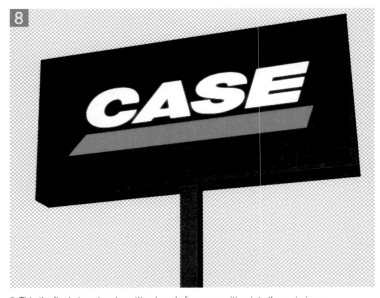

8 This the final sign already outlined ready for compositing into the main image.

9

9 Before I could position and size the sign, I had to know what sort of perspective I would need. I accomplished that by creating two-point perspective lines using the building as a guide for the vanishing points. I created the perspective lines using the pen tool (which can go outside the boundaries of the canvas) while the image was zoomed way out. Theoretically, I could have done a vertical set of perspective lines as well. But I had built the original sign with a keystone built in and would make that final adjustment by eye.

10

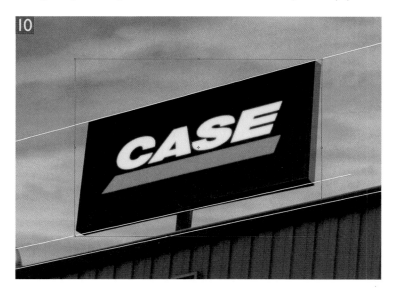

10 I used the Stroke path with brush to paint white lines on a separate layer to use as a guide for sizing and positioning. I then targeted the Sign layer and used Edit ⇨ Transform ⇨ Free Transform to size and position the sign.

Sign layer targeted with the perspective lines layer also visible.

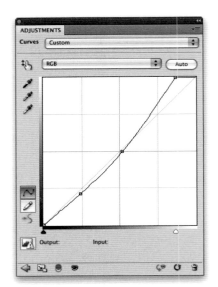

11 I needed three Adjustment layers to make final tone and color corrections to the composite. The first adjustment was to tone down the overhead door which appeared lighter than the side of the building. I used a Curves adjustment to darken just the door.

12 The second adjustment was to lighten the front of the building as well as the tractor. I used a layer mask to keep the adjustment off the sky and painted the area of the gravel out as well. In addition to the tone adjustment (above left) I also targeted the blue channel to reduce blue and warm up the color balance. Since the building was shot with basically a white sky, the building had looked too cool.

13 The last adjustment was to darken the sky using a gradient from the upper left. Very little of the sky needed to be darkened and I only darkened it slightly by shifting the Levels gamma slider to 0.9.

14 This was the final composite: eight pixel layers, three adjustment layers and a final overall midtone contrast boost. The final imaging took about three days' work including scanning the original film (35 mm), building the sign, searching for the stock sky and compositing the various layers. The art director was pleased (and a bit amazed). The only thing I haven't mentioned was the job was actually for two versions of the final image. You see, the job was to do the exact same image with the Case Construction (shown above) as well as the regular Case Tractors. That meant two signs, two exterior shots and two interior shots. Two times the work and two times the billing (even though it wasn't two times the hours since I could reuse pieces).

Third-party plug-ins

Most serious composite work is usually carried out against a plain backdrop. For example, the Ultimatte AdvantEdge software (www.ultimatte-software.com) requires that you shoot your subject against a blue or green backdrop. However, Vertus Fluid Mask (www.vertustech.com) is different in that it can do a very good job of cutting out images from busy background scenery.

Masking hair

If you are a people photographer and use Photoshop to create montage images, you will appreciate how difficult it is to successfully mask hair. There is always a lot of discussion on the various Internet forums about this particular subject, so I know it is something that will interest photographers and Photoshop artists. The problem most people have is how to get rid of the trace pixels around the edges of the hair, as these are always a sure giveaway that a picture has been composited badly. What follows on pages 210–216 is a hair masking technique that has served me well over the years, which you can apply using Photoshop without the need for any extra plug-ins.

The first thing I should point out here is that for this method to work, your model or subject must be photographed against a white or light colored backdrop. Now I know a lot of people come up to me at seminars and ask how they can adapt this technique to work with ordinary images shot against busy backgrounds. Well, it won't always work so well with such images and if this is your goal, then you'd be better off using the technique shown later on pages 217–220, or use a third-party plug-in such as Vertus Fluid Mask (see sidebar). The point here is that if you know you are about to create a cut-out composite image, then you must shoot your subject with this in mind. Some plug-ins, such as Ultimatte AdvantEdge, require that you shoot the subject that's to be cut out against a blue or green screen. Similarly, this Photoshop technique works best if you shoot against a white backdrop. As I say, it can work with backdrops that aren't pure white, but you'll just be making the task a lot harder for yourself.

How it works

This method revolves around making use of the existing color channel contents and copying the information which is already there in the image and modifying it to produce a new mask channel. So, instead of attempting to trace every single strand of hair on a mask with a fine-tipped brush tool, you can save yourself a lot of time if you make use of the information that's already contained in the color channels and use this to define the finely detailed edges. However, you may still find that the pen tool is useful for completing the outline around the smooth broad outline of the neck, shoulders and arms of the model's body. I've not shown how to do this here because I didn't want to make the following steps too complicated. If you do need to use the pen tool you can do so to define the areas that need to be included in the mask, then convert the vector path to a selection and fill with black.

The main message I want to convey here is that it is always worth exploiting the channel content as much as you can as a shortcut for building an accurate mask that is based on the actual image. As I show in the following tutorial, the tools I find useful here are the Apply Image command for building the initial contrast by blending a channel with itself, or with a second channel. Another great tip is to change the paint brush blend mode to Overlay blend mode when editing a black and white mask channel. In recent years, I have even found that the Shadows/Highlights adjustment, and in particular the Brightness and Contrast sliders therein, can be used to further improve the mask contrast.

Getting the different elements to match

This should go without saying, but in order to create a successful composite, you do need to make sure that the photographs you are about to combine all match in terms of camera angle and height, the focal length of the lens and, above all, lighting. It doesn't matter how good you are at Photoshop, if you can't get these things right from the start, you'll never be able to produce a realistic-looking composite. The camera angle and focal length matter most when you are working with wide-angle shots. If you are combining photographs that have been shot with a longer focal length lens there is a much greater margin of error. The lighting doesn't always have to be exact, but if you wish to merge a photograph taken in the studio with an outdoor scene, you will probably need to use a lot of top light and possibly include a direct spot to simulate sunlight. See also the sidebar on the Matchlight software solution for helping photographers calculate the optimum lighting setup.

Keep the mask edges soft

Retouched photographs won't look right if they have 'pixel-sharp' edges. A mask that's derived from a vector path will always be too crisp, even if it is anti-aliased. To create a more natural-looking result you should always use soft-edged masks. This is where the Refine Mask dialog comes in handy because it allows you to use the Radius, Contrast and Feather sliders to control the softness/hardness of the mask edges.

Matchlight software

Professional studio photographers may be interested in looking at the Matchlight system, where you can place a special disk in a location scene and the software will be able to interpret the camera angle and lighting you need to use in the studio to match the outdoor location. For more information go to: www.gomatchlight.com/products.html

1 The following steps describe how I would go about photographing a model with a view to adding a new backdrop later. I normally plan my shoots so that I always photograph the subject that is to be cut out against a white background, as this is the best way to mask the fine hair detail. In this example the background was not completely white, but there was certainly enough contrast between the hair and the backdrop for me to use the following technique to create a cut-out of the model and place her against a new backdrop image.

2 I began by looking at the individual color channels and duplicated the one that contained the most contrast; in this case I decided that the blue channel had the most contrast between the hair and the background.
I duplicated the blue channel by dragging it to the New Channel button in the Channels panel. This created the new Blue copy channel, which is the one shown active here.

3 To increase the contrast in the Blue copy channel I went to the Image menu and chose Apply Image... Here, I let the Blue copy channel blend with itself using the Multiply blend mode, which effectively darkened the channel. You could just as easily use a curves adjustment at this stage instead, but the main reason why I prefer to use Apply Image here is because you can sometimes choose to blend other color channels with the copy channel. For example, you might like to try blending the Green channel with a Blue copy channel. As well as using Multiply, you might like to experiment with using the Overlay blend mode here.

Black & White adjustments tip

I recently picked up a great tip from Photoshop engineer Gregg Wilensky, who suggests making a duplicate copy of a layer and applying the Black & White adjustment to increase and/or decrease the tone contrast where required in order to prepare a mask based on the color image content. Once you have done this you can copy the layer contents and paste this into a new channel.

211

4 I now wanted to increase the contrast to create a silhouette mask. To do this I used the brush tool set to Overlay mode and toggled between using black and white as the foreground color. When using the Overlay blend mode, as you paint with white, paint is only applied to the light colored pixels and as you paint with black, paint is only applied to the dark colored pixels.

5 The Overlay blend mode is therefore useful when painting on a mask because you can paint quite freely using a large pixel brush to gradually build up mask density around the outline of the subject, but without accidentally painting over the light areas. I continued to paint, taking care not to build up too much density on the outer hair strands (one can switch to Normal blend mode to finish the mask). I also prefer to paint using a pressure-sensitive Wacom™ pen and tablet, with the pen pressure sensitivity for Opacity switched on in the Brush panel Transfer options. Finally, I applied a direct Levels adjustment to boost the contrast slightly.

6 It was now time to add a backdrop photo. I opened up a new photograph of an outdoor scene, selected the move tool and dragged the backdrop image across to the model image window. This added the outdoor image as a new layer. I kept Layer 1 active, chose Edit ⇨ Free Transform and dragged the handles to scale the new layer so that it filled the bounds of the underlying layer. When I was happy with the scale transform I clicked OK.

7 I dragged the Blue copy channel to the Load Selection button in the Channels panel and then clicked on the Add layer mask button (circled) in the Layers panel to convert the active selection to a pixel layer mask.

8 This last step applied a layer mask to the salon backdrop layer, which basically punched a hole through Layer 1 and allowed the photograph of the model to show through from below.

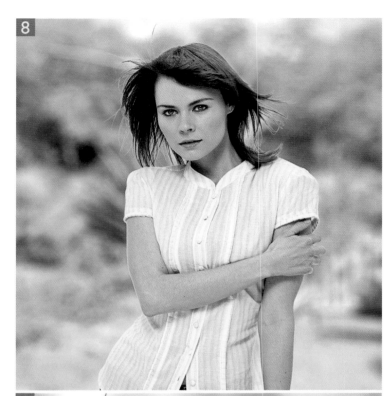

9 For this next step I set the layer blend mode to Multiply, which effectively 'projected' Layer 1 on top of the Background layer. As you can see, it is not a bad mask, but there are still some areas where we have white edges showing around the outline of the hair. The initial layer mask had worked reasonably well, but could still benefit from some fine-tuning.

10 Next, I made sure that the layer mask (not the layer image thumbnail) was selected and clicked on the Mask Edge... button in the Masks panel, to open the Refine Mask dialog shown here, where I selected the On Layers view in order to show the transparency of the mask. Here, I began by setting the Shift Edge slider to +40%, which effectively choked the mask. I know this sounds back to front, but remember that the mask that's used here was hiding the selected layer and I therefore needed to 'expand' the mask in order to shrink the size of the hole. Basically, you simply drag the Shift Edge slider left or right to see which setting works best. In this instance, using CS5, I didn't want to adjust the Radius option, but I did adjust the Feather slider to help keep the mask edge looking soft and raised the Contrast of the edge slightly to +15.

At this stage you can see how the edges of the mask looked more convincing and I was now getting a more convincing blend for the loose strands of hair against the outdoor image.

Refine Edge/Refine Mask/Mask Edge...

At this stage you might find all the above terms rather confusing. Essentially they all mean the same thing. Whenever you have a selection active the Select menu says 'Refine Edge...' and this allows you to use the dialog shown here to refine a selection prior to doing anything with it. This isn't particularly useful, since most of the time you want to adjust the controls with the selection already converted to and applied as a mask so that you can visualize the effect the controls have with the layer mask in place. When you have an active layer mask selected the Select menu says 'Refine Mask...'. The Mask Edge... item in the Masks panel opens the 'Refine Mask...' dialog and should really be labeled as such.

11 Here is the completed image in which you can see a full-length view of the model against the new image backdrop, and with just a few further modifications made to the picture. For example, I carried out some basic beauty retouching on the face and added a lightening curves adjustment that was clipped to the background.

   In the photograph you see here, I used one pass of the Refine Mask to achieve the best modification of the mask. Overall, I reckon the mask looked pretty good, but there were a few areas along the lower half of the model's left arm where I would probably want to improve the mask.

   If I wanted to be really precise here I could refine the mask edges with two applications of Refine Mask. To do this, I would go to the History panel and create a Snapshot of the current Refine Mask state. I would then undo the last Refine Mask step and reapply Refine Mask, but this time adjust the settings for say, the edges of the arm, then take another snapshot. Having done that, I would select the history brush and sample from either of the two snapshot history states to paint along the edge of the subject. As I say, it shouldn't always be necessary to go to such lengths, but it is possible to blend two different Refine Mask treatments should you need to.

Hair masking using Refine Mask

Photoshop CS5 now allows you to make use of the Refine Mask command to mask complex objects, such as hair, more easily.

1 To start with I placed the same backdrop layer, as was used in the previous step examples, directly below the layer shown here of a model photographed against a painted backdrop. The aim here was to show how it is possible to use a combination of a quick selection combined with the Refine Mask to successfully isolate the hair outline. So the first step here was to select the quick selection tool and drag to make the selection shown active here.

2 I then went to the Layers panel and clicked on the Add layer mask button (circled) to convert the selection into a layer mask that masked the outline of the model against the backdrop image on the layer below. As you can see here, this selection-based mask is OK around the outline of the model's body, but the hair outline so far has a blunt edge.

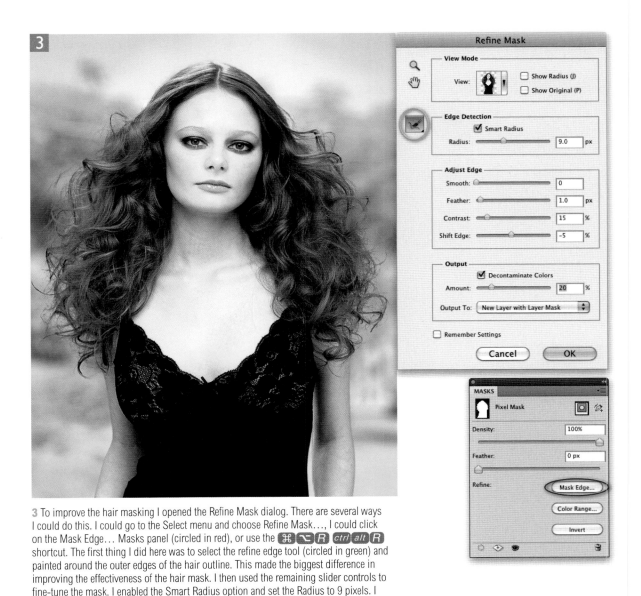

3 To improve the hair masking I opened the Refine Mask dialog. There are several ways I could do this. I could go to the Select menu and choose Refine Mask…, I could click on the Mask Edge… Masks panel (circled in red), or use the ⌘ ⌥ R ctrl alt R shortcut. The first thing I did here was to select the refine edge tool (circled in green) and painted around the outer edges of the hair outline. This made the biggest difference in improving the effectiveness of the hair mask. I then used the remaining slider controls to fine-tune the mask. I enabled the Smart Radius option and set the Radius to 9 pixels. I applied a Feather amount of 1 pixel and raised the Contrast to +15. I tightened the mask slightly by setting the Shift Edge slider to −5% and lastly, I checked the Decontaminate Colors option and set the amount here to 20%. Once I was happy with the settings applied here I clicked OK to apply the Refine Mask edit.

Client: Mack Hairdressing
Model: Ruth Bright

4 If you look in the Refine Mask options in Step 3, you will notice that the Output section in the Output To menu was set to generate a New Layer with Layer Mask. The thing to bear in mind here is that Refine Mask editing is a one-way process that changes the layer mask permanently. For this reason it is a good idea to have the Refine Mask edit process generate a duplicate layer with the revised layer mask made active.

Refine Mask controls

The controls in Refine Mask dialog include everything you need to modify a layer mask edge. You can open the Refine Mask dialog any time a layer mask is selected by going to the Select menu and choosing Refine Mask..., clicking on the Mask Edge... button in the Masks panel (Figure 7.2), or using the ⌘ ⌥ R ctrl alt R shortcut. The initial default preview may confuse you because it uses the On White view mode. Why this should be the default I don't know, but if you click on the button that's circled in Figure 7.3, this reveals all the View mode options. Here, I suggest you select the On Layers mode (L), then check the Remember Settings box at the bottom and click OK to save this as the new default.

The Refine Mask/Refine Edge dialog has been updated in CS5. The main thing to point out is that the Smart Radius option can be used to auto-calculate the optimum radius based on an analysis of the edge width detail in an image. Where there are narrow areas of contrast (such as along the arms of the model in the previous example), it applies a narrow radius. Where there are soft edges (such as a hair outline), the Smart Radius applies a wider radius. There is a PDF on the DVD that explains this and the other new Refine Mask features. These are also summarized over the next few pages, where I show how a mask was applied to the image shown in Figure 7.4 and edited using Refine Mask.

Figure 7.2 This shows the Masks panel with the Mask Edge... button highlighted.

Figure 7.3 The Refine Mask dialog showing the different view mode options.

Figure 7.4 This shows the image used in the following Refine Mask steps.

1 Here you can see the photograph shown in Figure 7.4 with a layer mask applied that was based on a simple quick selection. The steps used to create this were the same as those shown on pages 217–218.

2 The first thing I did was to use the ⌘ ⌥ R ctrl alt R shortcut to open the Refine Mask dialog. I then selected the refine edge tool (circled) and used this tool to paint around the ears and the chin to add the fine hairs to the mask edge. I then checked the Smart Radius option and set the Radius to 4 pixels. I had to be careful not to set the radius too high, otherwise too much of the background in the original photo would show through.

3 The Smooth slider can be used to help smooth out jagged selection edges. Normally you don't want to set the Smooth setting too high, but if you do so for whatever reason, increasing the Radius can help restore some of the edge detail. In this example I raised the Smooth value to 30 in order to exaggerate the effect.

4 Increasing the Feather amount uniformly softens the edges and can help produce a softer edged mask. You can sometimes use the Feather slider in conjunction with the Contrast slider to fine-tune the mask edge appearance.

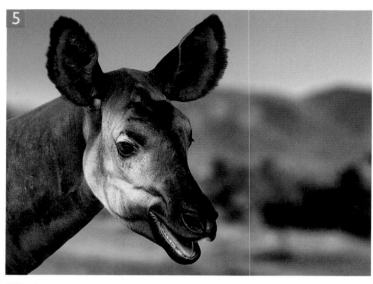

5 The Contrast slider can be used to make soft mask edges crisper as well as help remove artifacts along the edges of a selection. In this example, I applied a 50% Contrast adjustment in order to harden the feathered edge that was created in Step 4.

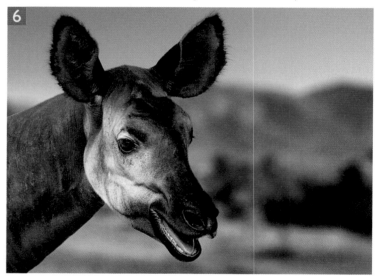

6 For this step I set the Feather to 1 pixel and reset the Contrast slider to zero. The Shift Edge slider acts like a choke control for the mask and shrinks or expands the mask. In the example shown here, I set the Shift Edge slider to −50% so that it masked the layer more tightly.

7 In this next example I set the Shift Edge slider to +50% so that it expanded the mask and didn't mask the edges quite so tightly. Very often you will find it useful to adjust the Shift Edge slider first, before you adjust the other sliders.

8 For this final step I adjusted all the sliders to achieve an optimum mask edge. I set the Feather slider to 0.5 pixels, the Contrast to 10% and the Shift Edge to −5%. Lastly, I checked the Decontaminate Colors option and set the Amount to 60%. This slider can be used to remove fringe traces of color in the original image background so that the image blends better with the colors in the image layer below.

Cheating a mask

Do you really need to spend ages creating a mask in Photoshop? If you are a still-life studio photographer, the answer may be staring you in the face. I wanted to give you here one example of a situation where a table-top studio setup can allow you to cheat at creating a mask by simply turning off the foreground lights, making an additional exposure with a digital camera and using the silhouette image this creates as the basis for a mask. As long as you are using a digital camera to capture the two exposures and the camera is mounted on a tripod, the mask created here will be completely pixel accurate. And believe me, as much as I am a fan of the pen tool, the thought of using it to outline something like this would keep me awake at night.

1 This shows the raw files of the fan opened in Camera Raw. In order to maintain the exact pixel for pixel relationship of these two shots, it was super-critical to make sure the crop for all the processed images was exactly the same. In this step I've got both images selected and clicked on the Synchronize button. In the resulting dialog, I selected the Crop option only to synchronize with and then clicked OK.

2

2 Here you can see the image with the front light off and the back light on opened and converted to grayscale. Since I was only working with this image in order to create a channel, there was no reason for me to work in color here. I did need to do a Curves adjustment to lighten up the background but without lightening the shadows too much.

3

3 I then zoomed in a bit and loaded the grayscale channel of the image itself as a selection, then painted around the fan to improve on the mask and eliminate as much tone as possible in the white areas. You'll note that prior to loading the selection I had already painted out the upper right corner that had the fill reflector card showing. Since that was a broad area far enough from the fan itself, I didn't need to worry about working with a selection. You'll also note that inside the fan's circular cage, the base still had some tones that would need to be knocked out. Rather than trying to paint these out by hand, I needed to fix that in the next step.

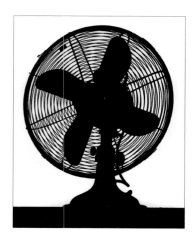

4 In order to accurately fix the base, I created a path that followed the contour of the base exactly. That path was turned into a channel (above left) and the original channel loaded as a selection. I then loaded the Base Outline channel, inverted it and set it to Intersect with Selection. This bit of 'Channel Chops' work resulted in the figure on the upper right. I also used the Base outline to clear the horizon line and outline the fan base. The next step shows how I copied the edited channel into the main RGB image of the fan.

5 Using the move tool, I dragged and dropped from the grayscale image (on the right) to the RGB image (on the left). It was important to hold down the *Shift* key once I had started the drag. Adding the *Shift* key while dragging instructs Photoshop to do a pin registered drop so the pixels will line up exactly. The Channels panel on the far left shows how the Fan outline channel had been added to the color image in registered position. Before using it as a layer mask, it was necessary to invert the channel mask using the *⌘* *I* *ctrl* *I* keyboard shortcut.

6 In this step I zoomed in (after inverting the channel) to work on some of the residual areas that needed fixing. This often happens with 'shiny things' that catch a bit of reflection, but it still beats using the pen tool!

7 For this final composite, you can see the main fan layer used the fan outline as a layer mask (after the base had been added to the channel). I also added a second fan layer in the composite – the original back-lit image (in color) that I made the mask from. This second fan image added a bit of tonality at the very base of the fan. The rest of the layers included image adjustments, shadows and a color tint layer to colorize the background.

Masking an object with a path

Martin and I both wish there was some sort of magic tool that could be used to make beautiful masks at the snap of a finger, but we've tried them all and when something must be very accurate we usually fall back on the pen tool to create a path. Because the pen tool has sub-pixel accuracy, no pixel-based selection can ever be as accurate. So, we both are very good at making paths in Photoshop. It's kind of the mark of a true craftsman if you are good at this, and pretty much guarantees a mask will end up 'perfect'.

The following combination was a job I wished I didn't have to do as a composite with a studio shot – February in Chicago would be a real nice time to go down and do a shoot on a cruise ship. Alas, there wasn't enough budget to do that, so I did research on exactly what the shot would look like if done for real, and Figure 7.5 is what I came up with.

Figure 7.5 The sky image was a personal stock image (which I charged stock rates for the client to use) and the image on the right was shot in the studio (in February) and lit to make it appear to be outside. I did try real hard to make a blue-screen attempt at knocking out the blue background but it didn't work.

Set to Paths mode

Pen Options

Figure 7.6 For me, it's important to work with the Pen Options set to Rubber Band mode. This means that once you place a point, the next point you will place will have a line behind the cursor that shows you where the path will be drawn, before it's actually drawn by placing the next point. This gives you the ability to predict what the resulting path will look like before dropping that next point. The other thing you need to be sure of is that the pen tool is in Paths mode. This will result in a path being drawn instead of a Shapes layer.

Figure 7.7 Using the direct select tool (shown top) I clicked on the path. Note that you can use the keyboard shortcut of ⌘ ctrl with the pen tool selected to get the direct select tool. I then clicked on the path (bottom) where I could move the point ever so slightly to improve the outline of the final path. It is also worth noting here that you can nudge the selected anchor point using the arrow keys.

1 The first step was to create a new path and then zoom way in. I prefer to draw paths when zoomed in to at least 200% to get a very accurate view of where the path will end up. I was also able to decide what would end up in or out of the final outline. Here, I started at the drink in the man's hand and began placing points. The cross-hair shows where the point will be placed and the line behind is the Rubber Band option showing where the path will be placed once I clicked (see Figure 7.6).

Figure 7.8 These are the two paths created. The main outline path was for creating an eventual layer mask and the Focus path was created to modify the final outline mask to add an apparent falloff in the depth of field to the Guy in Chair layer mask shown in Step 4.

2 Fast forward to the end and I was ready to make the last point and complete the path. While completed, the path may still need some fine-tuning in some places. Figure 7.7 shows zooming in and adjusting the path. The pen tool offers extremely accurate placement of what will eventually become a channel and then be converted to a selection for use as a layer mask. Those steps come next, including the use of the Focus path shown in Figure 7.8.

3 Here, I activated the main outline path (above left) and in the Paths panel flyout menu chose 'Make Selection…'. In the Make Selection dialog I used a 0.8 radius for the Feather Radius. I've learned that while you can always soften up a channel, it's very difficult to accurately harden the feather. So, I always tend towards a sharper feather and adjust it afterwards as I did in the next step.

4 After doing the main outline path, I created a new path that would give me areas where I could apply additional blurring. This was needed to give the feeling of depth of field falloff. I turned the Focus path – which included all of the areas behind the guy in the chair – into a selection and used a 2 pixel radius Gaussian Blur to slightly soften the channel.

5 After turning the final channel into a selection and making the section into a layer mask, I dragged the Guy in Chair layer onto the sky *Background* layer and positioned and resized it to fit.

Lens Flare applied to background layer

6 While the composite in Step 5 was close to being complete, it needed something atmospheric to help integrate the foreground and background. Since there was already a bit of lens flare I decided to do more. I created a new layer filled with black and set to a Screen blend mode. I wanted to put the lens flare on its own layer and using the Screen blend mode meant that it would lighten the composite only in those areas that were lighter than black. However, the Lens Flare filter has a problem when previewing a black layer – you can't see the layers underneath. So I use a trick. I apply the filter first on a layer where the preview will be able to guide me, apply it, then immediately undo it. Then I retarget the layer in which I want to apply it and use ⌘ F ctrl F to reapply the last used filter. There you have it, lens flare on a black layer (which is set here to 50% Opacity).

Lens Flare reapplied to the black layer

Smart Objects

Smart Objects can be made from pixels (as this example will demonstrate), vector art an even a Camera Raw image opened as a Smart Object. Any 'object' that needs the ability to adjust size and rotation without the normal limitations of layered images is an excellent candidate for Smart Objects.

Working with Smart Objects

It should be noted that some of my best friends are art directors, so don't take it as a slam that I mention one of the more frustrating aspects of dealing with them is they have this annoying habit of changing their minds. For digital imaging, that can cause real problems. When doing a traditional multi-layer composite, the resizing and rotation of a layer can cause image degradation. Positioning and sizing an object has to be a precise operation because if you use Free Transform to make a layer smaller and then find out you actually need it back at the original size (or bigger) you basically have to start over. The way to deal with this situation when doing a complex composite is to make those layers into Smart Objects. Smart Objects are embedded image objects that allow resizing, rotation and other select editing without actually changing the pixels in the object. The image layers are actually treated as a separate file embedded within the master file. You can't do all editing on the Smart Object, but you can open the original layers as a temporary file and do pixel-level editing there, then save the changes back into the Smart Object. The changes auto-update in the image in which the objects are embedded. It's easier to show than explain, so let's see an example of what I mean. In Figure 7.9 you can see a series of shots of electronic widgets (I really don't know what they are, I just shot them) that were outlined and put on a colored, textured background.

Figure 7.9 The original shots were done on 4 x 5 color film and scanned. Care was taken to finesse the lighting individually – hence the reason for shooting them separately. The background image was of a plaster cast of texture airbrushed to achieve the color and with cast shadows and light highlights.

1 The first step in this process was to prep the image for both outlining and adding cast shadows. The image above had been retouched at least as far as spotting and cloning was concerned. The overall color (of the object) was good. You'll note that the crop was wide enough to provide a hint of a natural shadow. This was important as the real shadow would be the basis of the made shadow. I used a path to create an outline and turned the path into a selection and used ⌘ J ctrl J to make it into a new layer.

2 The next step, after using the pen tool to create a path of the natural shadows, was to turn the path into a selection. After making the selection, I added a new layer under the object as shown in the Layers panel on the right.

3 I wanted the Lens Blur for the initial blur to be gradated. After filling the selection with black, I added a gradient in Quick Mask to add a mask for blurring. This Quick Mask was then turned into a selection and saved as a new channel.

4 The main thing I did then was to apply the Lens Blur filter to the shadow alpha channel and run the Radius all the way up to 100. Meanwhile, I selected the above gradient as the Depth Map. This allowed the filter to be applied in a way to help simulate a more natural blur to the cast shadow, using the gradient to map the falloff of the blur.

5 The falloff of the gradation needed an additional tweak. For this I used Motion Blur filter to make sure the slightly less than perfect drawn path's shadows were softened even more. The angle was selected to mimic the natural lighting direction and the Distance amount adjusted to provide a directional blur. After applying the blur, I reduced the opacity to 50%.

6 A new layer was added and, using the main shadow's opacity loaded as a selection (to keep any painting within the blurred main shadow), I added a second shadow layer to paint in a 'close shadow' that would help ground the object and keep it from looking like it was floating.

7 I selected the object layer and two shadow layers. I then went to the Layers panel and chose Convert to Smart Object (as seen in the upper Layers panel view). This created a single Smart Object layer. I then selected the object and dragged and dropped it into the background image (as seen in the lower Layers panel view, which I was in the process of renaming). As you can see, the scale was incorrect. However, because this was a Smart Object, I could resize, rotate and reposition it anyway I (or the art director) wished. To resize, I just selected the Smart Object and applied a Free Transform command. However the object was transformed, it didn't alter the object's pixels.

8 This is what the final composite looked like after adding all six of the objects onto the background. The layer stack with the named layers as Smart Objects is shown on the right. In a perfect world, this would be the finished piece but, don't you know, the art director decided that the upper right widget needed work. Smart Objects to the rescue! I just double-clicked the upper right object to edit it.

9 When you open a Smart Object for editing, you are presented with this dialog shown above. Read it and understand it before proceeding. What it basically means is that Photoshop will open the embedded object in a new window and allow you to do whatever edits you need to do. Once that is finished, you must save the document without doing a Save As, otherwise the link will be broken (which is really bad).

10 With the combined image still open, the upper right Smart Object was opened as a separate file showing its own layers and allowing a tone tweak to the widget. I used the object's transparency mask to create a layer mask for the Levels adjustment. Once the tweak was done, I saved the file without doing a Save As. Once saved, the adjusted image showed up in the main image with the updates displayed.

11 After saving the modified Smart Object, the edits were updated in the main image. After working on all the Smart Objects, I also did some overall adjustments. I added Vibrance and Hue/Saturation adjustment layers as well as a pair of graduated Curves adjustments. The other layers I added were some tone adjustments just above the Background layer to lighten and darken areas in a streaked pattern. In order to create them, I created a new channel, chose Filter ⇨ Render ⇨ Clouds, adjusted the density and ran a Blur ⇨ Motion Blur filter. I loaded the channel as a selection and filled with white for the lightening layer, and then inverted the selection and filled with black for the shadowing layer.

Adding atmospherics

I used to shoot a lot of tractors for Case (I never shot for Deere but I did shoot a Deere on this assignment). The ad was to promote a head to head shoot-out between Case and John Deere tractors. The company was doing various events around the country and I was assigned an event in Arizona to shoot while both tractors with drivers would be available. The events were being videotaped and made available to smaller dealers and tractor buyers – hence the ad for the video.

We had arranged to have the tractors and drivers very early in the morning, not long after sunrise. We had equipped the drivers with radios so the art director and I could give the drivers instructions about position and speed. I don't know if you've ever driven a tractor (I have), but they don't turn on a dime and they don't go very fast. They're like slow lumbering beasts, but the intent of the ad (note in Figure 7.10 the headline changed) was to imply a race with the Case tractor the winner. Try as we might, we just couldn't get both tractors in the right place at the right speed with the right amount of dust flying. This was clearly a job for Photoshop (something the art director and I both presumed we would need to do anyway).

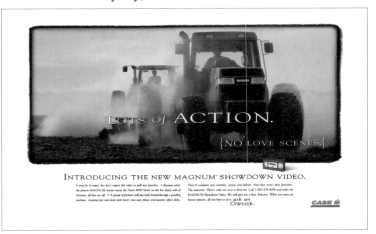

Figure 7.10 Top left is a scan of the actual layout. Below that are the two component shots that were chosen from several hundred frames of 35 mm film shot and above is the final image as used in the ad.

Figure 7.11 This figure shows the composite with and without the dust added. The dust added a sense of 'atmospherics' that helped integrate the two images.

1 The first step was to actually study what the real dust looked like in the shot where the tractor was stirring up lots of dust. This is an important step because before you can add something you need to really understand what it is you are adding. The dust has a sense of motion to it and reacts to its surroundings. So, just painting in with an airbrush would have made it look more like smoke, rather than dust caused by the tractor. Close study actually gave me the clue as to which tool to use: the Clouds filter. So, rather than try to point with a custom brush, I would point through a selection.

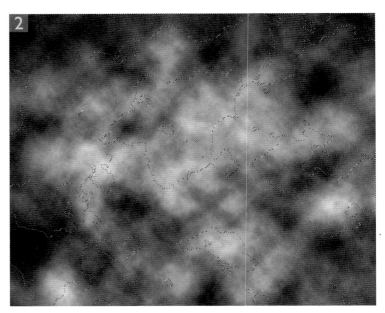

2 I created a new grayscale document, added a new channel named dust and used Filter ⇒ Render ⇒ Clouds to produce a random 'cloud' pattern. But, in reality, I duplicated the dust layer and reran the filter to get a second iteration of the Cloud filter (no two are ever the same) and used the Cloud copy, loaded as a selection, to modify the first dust channel. This allowed me to lighten or darken certain areas, but through the effects of a Cloud-based selection.

3 I needed to make further modifications. I used Filter ⇒ Noise ⇒ Add Noise to break up the pattern and then ran a very gentle Gaussian Blur to soften the noise.

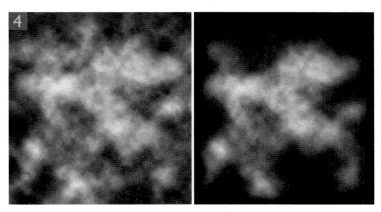

4 Prior to bringing the dust channel into the main image, I needed to modify the perimeter of the channel to make sure there would be no hard cut lines when painting through the mask. I painted all around the edges and selectively darkened some areas to give more of a feeling of tendrils of dust.

5 I copied the dust channel to a new channel in the two-tractor combo image and clicked to make it visible as well as the RGB image's Green channel. That way I could see the dust channel over the image for position and size. I rotated and sized the dust area of the channel where I needed to add the most dust in the composite.

6 With the dust channel loaded as a selection, I started painting with a lowered opacity. It's OK to play when you are doing this – the feeling of the atmospherics needs to build up as a process. I could always use the eraser tool to lighten up the effect.

7 In this step, I selected the marquee tool to take the active selection and move it to a different region. Once moved, I did more painting to build up more dust in different areas.

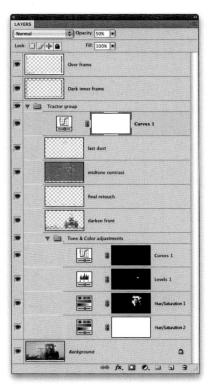

8 The next step was to select the eraser tool to reduce some of the areas where the dust effect got too strong. I could also have used a layer mask and painted into the mask with black to remove the excess dust. Also remember that a dust mask can be useful for erasures — you don't need to only use it for painting through.

9 This shows the final composite with tone, color and retouching as well as the addition of the 'cut-out negative carrier' look as a border around the image. Also note the addition of a midtone contrast layer to punch up the tractor contrast.

Simulating the effect of motion

Still photography is often called upon to give a sense of motion and aside from actually shooting something flying through space, the effects that imply motion usually require some pretty substantial work in Photoshop. In this example, actually shooting the glass flying wasn't really an option. In Figure 7.12 you can see the two original shots and the final result – glass flying as though a sledgehammer has broken the glass. Yes, I did have to break some glass to create this effect, but rather than trying to shoot it, I imaged the effect of motion.

The background image was shot with a static hammer showing through a broken pieces of glass with frosted type placed prior to breaking it. The glass was held in place in a wooden frame. Pieces of glass from the same break (and a few extras – I had lots of broken glass to choose from) were suspended on wire via hot-glue and shot under the same lighting as the main shot. The ability to shoot element shots under the same lighting conditions is critical to having a convincing final composite.

The original background shot.   The pieces of glass shot.   The final composite image shot.

Figure 7.12 The original shots were done on 4 x 5 color film and scanned. The main shot was done first and the glass pieces were positioned so the final assembly would match the lighting of the main shot.

Embossing the word

Prior to doing the motion effects, the first job in the imaging was to emboss the word CIPROFLOXACIN onto the hammer's front face. I have no idea what the word means, that's not my job. The image was done for a pharmaceutical firm so I guess it's the name of a drug. The letters were imported as paths into Photoshop and positioned over the face of the hammer, then a selection was made and turned into a channel. Then channel operations (chops) were used to offset multiple channels and create the effects of the emboss.

Emboss vs. Deboss

Note that the following steps are being used to show how to do an emboss. The exact same steps can be used to make a deboss, the primary difference being the direction of the offset and reversing the lighting directions. This series shows an 'innie' but the 'outie' is pretty much the opposite.

1 Step 1 was to create a base channel from which the resulting chop will be used to create offset selections. Several selections were used to build up the final emboss. The Channels panel shows the position relative to the hammer's front face. All of the chops were done by duplicating this main channel, offsetting it and then using the Load Selection dialog and picking the correct channel source and operation. It's important that all the chops were done on duplicate channels, not on this main channel, because I would always need this channel to constrain the other channels against.

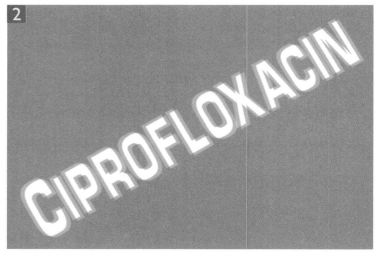

2 Next, I duplicated the main channel and (with the move tool selected) offset it using the arrow keys to nudge it into position. It's useful to click the display eyeball for both channels so you can see the relative positions. The copy channel was offset down and to the right and would become the cast shadow of the emboss.

3 I retargeted the main channel and loaded it as the selection. Then, using the Load Selection dialog (cropped for clarity), I set the selection load to be the main letters copy channel, selected the Invert option (because I needed the selection inverted prior to the operation) and set the Operation option to be Intersect with Selection.

4 This is the result of the preceding step, where you can see the result of the offset selection intersecting with the original main channel. This was the critical result of the channel operations. Once I got the correct result (which depended entirely on correctly setting the Load Selection dialog) I saved it as a new channel.

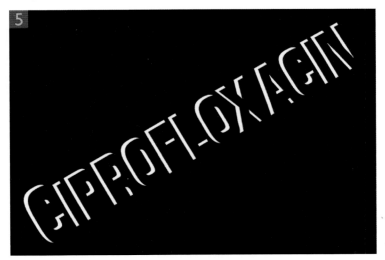

5 This is the saved channel that would be used to create the shadow that gave the emboss its shape. Variations on this operation could be a slight blur on the copy channel to give the impression of softer light or varying the offset to indicate a deeper or more shallow emboss. The main channel would be used to give a sense of overall darkness, the shadow channel used to indicate depth and the final touches would be highlights used to add realism and light. The steps used to create the highlights channels were the same as those shown here but with the channel offset up and to the left.

6 I loaded the main type channel as a selection and added a Levels adjustment to darken the area of the hammer face as the base for the type and also darkened the output levels. Since the brushed pattern of the metal was pretty consistent, I had no need to do an offset of the pattern. If the texture had had a discernible pattern I would have copy/pasted an offset of the pattern to help indicate depth.

7 I then loaded the Type shadow channel as a selection and applied another tone adjustment to make the shadow area even darker. The amounts you do something are a matter of taste and experience. There really are no absolute numbers here, just a 'feeling' that makes it 'look' right.

8 Rather than apply another adjustment layer, I added a new layer set to Screen blend mode then loaded one of the highlight channels as a selection and filled it with white. I had now made two separate highlight channels with slightly different softness edges to get a feeling of both a softer light and a harder light hitting the face of the hammer. I actually used the lighting on the hammer itself as a guide to how to create the highlight channels.

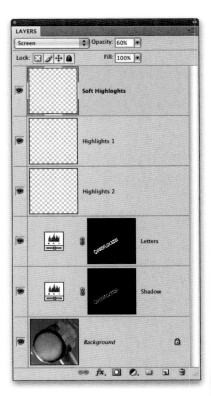

9 You can now see the results of the previous highlights having been added. But the last step needed some hand work. Using a new layer (also set to the Screen blend mode), I zoomed way in and lightly applied soft brush strokes at the corners where highlights would naturally concentrate. This hand work was needed because the emboss needed a sense of reality that chops often fail to introduce. It's the hand work that gives spontaneity and a more believable result. The Layers panel view shows the stack created for the emboss.

Adding motion

To do this final composite, the shot of the broken glass had to be outlined to create individual pieces. And, yes, that was a chore. The best solution (although not the fastest) was using the pen tool to create individual paths that were then turned into a selection. I've saved you from those gory details!

The key to giving a sense of motion in a still image is to use a step and repeat process to give the feeling of movement and then add speed lines (highlight giving a clue to the direction of the movement). It's not hard but is tedious, so try not to be in a hurry.

1 I selected a piece of glass to work on from the outlined glass image and copy/pasted it as a new layer to the main image. I used a layer mask to remove the solid portion of the blue interior of the glass so the background could show through. Without the mask, you would not see the background of the letter showing through and the glass piece would appear opaque. After positioning the glass, I created paths to give myself a direction for the movement and for scaling. Ultimately I would also use the paths to paint the speed lines with.

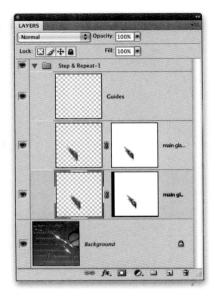

2 I duplicated the glass piece layer and moved it underneath the original layer. I then used Edit ⇨ Free Transform to both move and resize the layer smaller. I used the guidelines for position and size. I knew that once I got all of the step and repeat layers combined, I would always need to go back and fiddle with the exact positioning, but the guidelines gave me a good starting point.

3 After the sizing and repositioning, I needed to readjust the layer mask to keep the second layer from showing through the original layer. Here you can see I had partly painted away the offending parts on the second layer's mask.

Unlinking the layer mask.

4 At this stage, I had followed the previous steps to add five additional copies of the original layer. I wanted to start making position adjustments but rather then have to go to the Layers panel, I used the keyboard command to select the target layer. With the move tool selected, a **ctrl** (Mac) or right-mouse click on the area showed a context menu of the current layers with data under the cursor. It was then a simple task to select which layer to target.

5 To aid in giving a sense of movement, I gave each of the layers a small dose of Motion Blur. But there's a problem: if a layer has a linked layer mask, for some reason the ability to fade the filter is disabled. (Don't ya just hate that?) To work around this limitation I unlinked the pixel layer from the layer's mask so I could run the filter and then fade the results. I used a 15 pixel distance Motion Blur with an angle to match the layer's direction of movement. After running Motion Blur I set the Fade Opacity to 40%. I then continued the blurring and fading on the remaining four copy layers.

6 Prior to painting in the speed lines, I adjusted each of the step and repeat layers' opacity to go down as the layer got further away. The second layer's opacity was set to 80% and the last layer's opacity was set to 40%. This gave the layers a feeling of disappearing and aided in the sense of the main layer coming forward.

7 Next, I needed to paint the speed lines, which required some preparation. I wanted the brush size to fall off as the line was painted. That required changing the Brush Tip Shape Dynamics. I adjusted the brush's Shape Dynamics Size Jitter to Fade to a maximum of 27% of the starting size. Then I adjusted the Transfer Opacity Jitter also to Fade at 25% for the starting opacity. I then adjusted the overall Brush Opacity to just 10% so I could build the effect gradually. The last stage was to select the correct path to use to stroke along. I'm a poor 'painter' so, wherever possible, I use a path to make sure I paint straight lines.

8 The process of painting the guide lines really was a buildup of multiple low-opacity strokes performed by starting with a larger brush size, stroking, reducing the size and stroking again. I started large and adjusted the size smaller as I built up the effect. Since I was using a 10% starting opacity and I had got the brush size and opacity set to fade, it took multiple strokes to build up the effect.

9 The final step in this process was to do the same series of steps on the center speed line and then apply a layer mask to adjust the overall falloff of the lines. And yes, this entire series of steps was repeated for each and every single piece of glass (a total of 18 pieces). Hey, that's why we make the big bucks – the willingness to do what it takes to do a convincing and realistic image manipulation (and bill by the hour for it).

10 The final composite required umpteen hours of work (I really don't know how long it took but the invoice was for 12 hours of imaging) and almost 90 layers (counting the embossing).

Enabling Lens Blur as a Smart Filter

Smart Filters are mainly intended for use with value-based filters only and are not intended for use with filters such as Lens Blur. However, it is still possible to enable Smart Filters to work with the Lens Blur filter. Go to the File ⇨ Scripts menu in Photoshop CS5 and choose Browse… This opens a system navigation window and from there you will want to use the following directory path: Adobe Photoshop CS5 folder/Scripting/ Sample Scripts/Javascript and select: EnableAllPluginsforSmartFilters.jsx. Once you have located this script, you can click Open or double-click to run it, which will then show a Script Alert dialog. If you wish to proceed, click 'Yes'. The Lens Blur, as well as all other filters, will now be accessible for use as Smart Filters.

1 Here you can see the photograph that we started with, where we had so far added a few retouching layers to improve the appearance of the image.

Adding lens blur

One of the disadvantages of using smaller format digital cameras is that you often end up with a much greater depth of field than you would get when using a large format plate camera such as a 5 x 4 Sinar. We know a lot of still-life photographers rather like this large format look, so in the technique steps shown here, we wanted to show how you could use the Lens Blur filter to simulate a shallow depth of field effect, in which only the main subject appeared to be in a plane of sharp focus.

The Lens Blur filter is really useful should you wish to add convincing-looking blur effects to your photographs. What's different about the Lens Blur filter is that rather than simply blurring the pixels (which is what the Gaussian Blur filter does), it applies an adaptable iris-shaped blur and also allows you to control the way the highlights burn out.

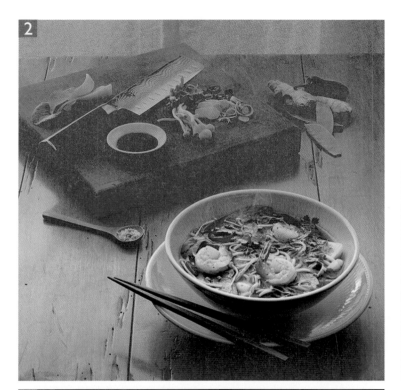

2 In this step we added a new Alpha 1 channel via the Channels panel, switched on the channel visibility and selected the gradient tool in reflected gradient mode. With white as the foreground color, we clicked roughly on the center of the soup bowl and dragged with the gradient tool down to the bottom of the photograph. This added the reflected gradient mask shown here as a red channel mask overlay.

3 We then used the pen tool to draw a pen path outline of the soup bowl and chopsticks (note: when drawing with the pen tool, we did so in the Add Path mode). Once the work path was complete, we converted this to a new path and then dragged the path to the Load path as a selection button (circled). We then selected the Alpha 1 channel to make it active and chose Edit ⇨ Fill, to fill the selected area with white. The only other thing we did at this stage was to deselect the selection and lighten the mask slightly using a Curves image adjustment.

4 We were now almost ready to apply the Lens Blur effect, but first, we selected all the layers in the Layers panel and chose Filter ⇨ Convert for Smart Filters. This converted the multi-layered image into a Smart Object, showing a single layer with a Smart Object icon in the bottom right corner of the thumbnail. There are a lot of slider controls in the Lens Blur filter dialog, but the ones that matter most are the Radius slider (which controls the amount of lens blur) and the Specular Highlights sliders, which determine how the highlights blow out in the brightest parts of the photograph. We also wanted to make use of the mask that was created in Steps 2 and 3, so we selected the Alpha 1 channel as the Depth Map source (circled green) and left the Blur Focal Distance at the zero setting. This is how we achieved the shallow depth of focus effect you see here in the preview window. We also inverted the mask (see check box circled in red) so that the white portions of the Alpha 1 mask now protected the image from becoming blurred, while the black portions of the mask became the most blurred and the gray mask tones allowed varying degrees of blur across the photograph.

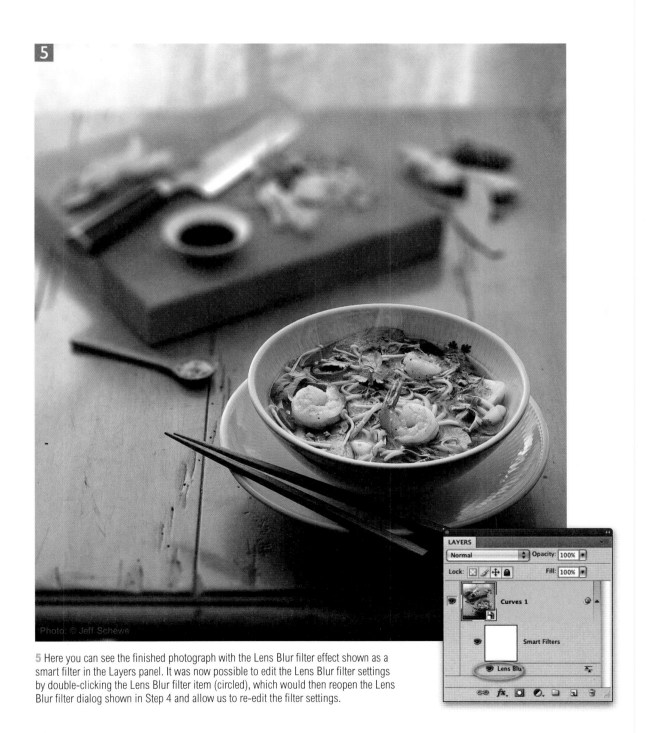

Photo: © Jeff Schewe

5 Here you can see the finished photograph with the Lens Blur filter effect shown as a smart filter in the Layers panel. It was now possible to edit the Lens Blur filter settings by double-clicking the Lens Blur filter item (circled), which would then reopen the Lens Blur filter dialog shown in Step 4 and allow us to re-edit the filter settings.

Scheimpflug principle

Named after Austrian army Captain Theodor Scheimpflug, it's a geometric rule describing the plane of focus where the lens plane and the film plane are intentionally altered out of parallel using camera movement to achieve an optimum plane of focus for the subject.

Extending the depth of field

Photographers have always faced the problem of a limited depth of field. You can stop down the lens, but then you need either more light or a slower shutter speed. You can use a view camera and try to use the Scheimpflug principle, or you can use Photoshop CS5's improved stacking to assemble multiple captures and blend them to achieve photographically impossible depth of field. Focus stacking, cool huh?

1 The digital captures shown above were all shot with a 100 mm macro lens at f/2.8 on a Canon EOS 1Ds MkIII while locked down on a tripod. They were brought into Camera Raw to optimize the settings – primarily to lighten the midtones and preserve highlight detail with Recovery. After syncing all the settings, I clicked the Done button. Back in Bridge, with the same images still selected, I went to the Tools ⇒ Photoshop menu in Bridge and chose Load Files into Photoshop Layers.

2 After Photoshop has loaded all the raw files as individual layers in Photoshop, some initial alignment had to be done prior to blending the layers. In the Layers panel I selected all of the layers.

3 With all of the layers selected, I went to the Edit menu in Photoshop and chose Auto-Align Layers. Since the images were shot with varying planes of focus, this changed the watch size slightly on each capture layer. The Auto-Align command resized the images and aligned them based on the content of the individual images. This step was required prior to blending them together for focus stacking.

4 The Layers panel on the left shows the result of the Auto-Align processing. You can see the top images were resized down and have transparency around the edges. Once aligned, the next step was to use the Auto-Blend Layers command (also found in Photoshop's Edit menu). This brought up the dialog box shown above. The Blend Method chosen for focus stacking is Stack Images and I also needed to check the Seamless Tones and Colors option. This kicked in the command's logic to try to achieve an optimal blending. It does a pretty good job overall, but will usually need a bit of help after the blend.

5 After Auto-Blend had done its business, the results were quite good. The processing produced layer masks that selected the sharpest portions of the layered images. There are usually a couple of things wrong. First, since the layers had been resized, one would typically see uneven blends at the edges. This can be fixed by cropping, but the other problem takes some hand work (see next step).

6 To manually fix the out-of-focus issue shown above (the other common problem), I copied the bottom layer, moved it to the top and repainted the layer mask to soften the transition. The final image below had minor spot healing to retouch some of the watch imperfections (I left some because it's a nice patina) and I applied a touch of midtone contrast increase.

Photo: © Jeff Schewe

Figure 7.13 This shows a studio shot view of the wine pour setup, snapped at the same moment as the main wine pour shot used here.

Merging studio exposures

Martin asked me whether I knew how to do a pour shot. I laughed and said, yes (it's what I used to do for a living). So when Martin visited Chicago for some shooting for this book, we decided to do a wine shot that would be composited to create an 'impossible shot'. We shot it using a Phase One P45+ back on a Sinar 4 × 5 view camera using high-speed ProPhoto electronic flash to freeze the motion (Figure 7.13). The flash duration was about 1/10,000th of a second. We used a laser trigger release so the wine being poured would trigger the flash.

The 'impossible' aspect of the final image is that wine being poured out of a bottle doesn't end nicely. It sort of dribbles out to nothing. As a result, the challenge was to get not only a great pour but enough element shots so the final composite could be pieced together from multiple components. Figure 7.14 on page 273 shows the final composite with all 13 layers.

1 I opened the ranked captures from Bridge in Camera Raw filmstrip mode to adjust the basic parameters of the raw files. I used Camera Raw's Batch Save to process the raw images saved out as PSD files. This is an important consideration because the Phase One raw format saves raws with a .tif extension. So, if you open a Phase One raw and resave it as a TIFF, you will save over the raw file if it's saved to the same folder. Normally I use TIFF files, but for this project I figured it would be safer to use PSD. Note that I also saved the files out to a folder named 'Processed' so the raws would remain separate (just in case).

2 After opening the base image, I expanded the canvas and added the image of the full glass cropped to only a portion of the image. The base had to be shot separately because I needed to be able to clamp the pour glass into a fixed place — which of course was not very photogenic.

3 I added a second pour shot because the original had an odd thin area inside the glass. Rather than try to retouch it, I just used a second pour. I used a Difference blend mode so I could see the position of both layers while I transformed the second pour shot. On the right is the layer with a layer mask.

4 I picked an earlier shot that had no wine coming through the bottle (a mistake actually that was nevertheless useful) and positioned it to cover the bottle in the base image that had wine coming through.

5 If you look back at the Bridge view of all of the images, you'll see I had shot some various trigger delays giving me both early and later shots of pours. Originally I wanted to get an 'ending' pour where the wine ended in mid-air, but that's not the way pours end. So, I took an early shot where the wine was just coming out of the bottle and rotated and repositioned it to look like a pour end. I also used a Difference blend mode to aid in the positioning.

6 I needed three separate layers for the various retouching steps. At the bottom of the retouching stack was a retouching layer specific for the bottle replacement. I used a separate layer for all the other wine- and glass-related retouching. Some were done with the healing brush and some with the clone stamp tool. In both cases, I chose to use the Current & Below option (from the Tool Options bar) for the sampling. The last part of the retouching was to paint in the background fix. This was done using an outline mask to keep the painting off the glass and bottle. To create the outline mask, the pen tool was used to create a path of the wine, glass and bottle. This outline was also used for the layer masks on the adjustment layers.

7 Using an inverted glass and bottle outline selection, I added a Hue/Saturation adjustment layer to eliminate any color cast in the background. Using a minus saturation adjustment was far easier than trying to neutralize the cast using Levels or Curves. The Levels adjustment shown here was used to lighten the center based on a circular gradient added to the layer mask.

8 The next adjustment was done to pin the black to a good black. When I processed the original images through Camera Raw, I didn't know how the images would end up blending together. So, I processed them a bit flat knowing I could punch things back up in Photoshop later. Here, I used Color Range choosing the Shadows selection option to create the mask.

9 The last step was to adjust both the color and density of the wine. I'll be honest, we didn't pour the 'good stuff'. The wine we poured was actually a mix of several bottles purchased for about $4/bottle and was recycled between pours. I used noted wine expert Greg Gorman to help me adjust the color to be a good color for a pinot noir, which was appropriate for the glass we shot.

Figure 7.14 The final composite of six different shots, three retouching layers and four adjustment layers. The final image was 19″ x 29″ @ 300 PPI. The layered file was 1.29 GB while the flattened TIFF was 378 MB. This large final size was without any upsampling and suitable for a large print or poster.

Figure 7.15 When you change the size of an image, the Layer Styles will not adjust proportionally. If it is important to retain the exact scaling, choose Layer ⇨ Layer Style ⇨ Scale Effects and enter a scale percentage that most closely matches the percentage change in image size.

Figure 7.16 Many Layer Styles (but not all) can be deconstructed into a series of layers. Choose Layer ⇨ Layer Style ⇨ Create Layers. Here is an example of how the layer style applied on page 279 would look if it were broken down into constituent pixel layers.

Layer Styles

With Layer Styles you can link various sorts of layer effects to any of the following kinds of layer: a type layer, an image layer, or a filled layer masked by a vector mask or layer mask. A Layer Style can be made up of individual layer effects and these effects can be accessed via the Layer menu or by clicking on the Add a layer style button at the bottom of the Layers panel. Layer styles can be applied individually or as a combination of effects to create a layer style and these can be saved by clicking in the empty space area of the Styles panel. As with adjustment layers, layer styles always remain fully editable.

When you add a new layer style, the Layer Style dialog opens to let you adjust the settings and create the desired layer effect. After you add a layer style, an italicized *fx* symbol will appear in the layer caption area and next to that a disclosure triangle. When you click on this disclosure triangle, an indented style effects layer will appear below containing an itemized list of the individual layer styles that have been used to create the master layer style. This allows you to control the visibility of the individual effects.

Layer styles are not directly scalable. So, if you resize an image the layer effect settings will not alter to fit the new image size; they will remain constant. However, if you go to the Layer menu and choose Layer Style ⇨ Scale Effects, you'll find you have the ability to scale the effects up or down in size (see Figure 7.15).

If you need to work with real layers, you can rasterize a layer style by going to the Layer menu and choosing Layer Style ⇨ Create Layers. This action will deconstruct a layer style into its separate components, placing the newly created layers in a clipping mask above the target layer (see Figure 7.16). You can deconstruct most layer style effects in this way, but be warned that with some layer style effects the rasterized layers won't always produce an identical-looking effect.

Over the next few pages we'll show how we went about using a 'water drops' layer style to add extra water droplets to a still-life photograph of a glass. If you are interested you can see in Figure 7.17 some of the behind the scenes photos of how this photograph was shot.

How to add extra water drops to a glass

Here is an example of a photograph where we wished to add some extra droplets of water that matched those already on the glass. To do this, we added a new empty layer with the Layer Style settings shown over the next two pages applied to the layer and set the Fill opacity to zero. The Layer Style settings used here were originally outlined by Greg Vander Houwen, but you may want to do what we did here and adjust some of the following Layer Style settings to suit the requirements of each individual shot.

Figure 7.17 This shows the studio setup for the glass shot shown here. You'll notice that we used a monorail camera setup with a Phase One back to capture the main image. Shown also here is the airbrush that was used to add some of the original water drops to the glass.

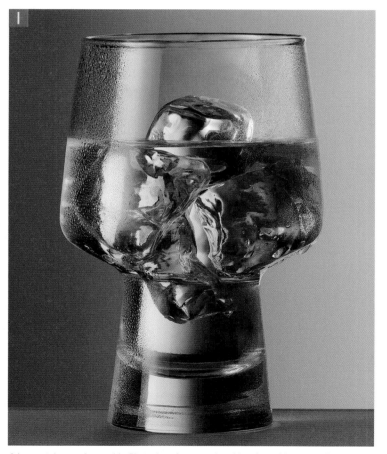

1 Layer styles can be used in Photoshop (among other things) to add texture effects to a picture. You will find the 'water drops' layer style used here on the DVD. To load this style on your system, simply double-click the layer style and Photoshop will automatically add this layer style to the Styles panel (see Figure 7.18).

Figure 7.18 The Styles panel.

2 The first step was to create the water drops layer style effect. We began by adding a new empty layer where the Fill was set to 0% and then went to the Layer Style menu to add a Drop Shadow layer. First we set the drop shadow opacity to 50% with a Distance of 1 pixel, a Spread of 4 pixels and a Size of 1 pixel. We applied a global light angle of 130° and selected a Cone contour for the Drop Shadow edge.

3 We next clicked on the Inner Shadow style, set the blend mode to Color Burn at 15%, using a Distance of 7 pixels a 0% Choke and 11 pixels Size.

Setting user Layer Style defaults

In Photoshop CS5 it is now possible to set your own default settings in the different Layer Style dialog subsections. If you happen to not like the Photoshop default setting, you can create one that suits your needs better and then click on the Make Default button at the bottom in order to set this as the new default for that particular section of the Layer Style dialog. Once you have done this, clicking on the Reset to Default button that's next to the Make Default button will reset the settings for that section to the Make Default or factory-set value (whichever applies). If you ever need to carry out a global reset, you will need to reset the Photoshop preferences when launching the program.

4 We then clicked on the Inner Glow style, kept the blend mode set to Screen, raised the Opacity to 82% and clicked on the color swatch to change the Inner Glow color to white. In the Elements section we selected the Softer option, using the Edge method, with a 0% Choke and a 5 pixel Size. In the Quality section we created a custom contour shape like the one shown here and set the Range to 68% and Jitter to 0%.

5 Lastly, we clicked on the Bevel and Emboss style. Here we selected the Inner Bevel style with a Chisel Soft technique, using a depth of 500%. We used the Up direction with a Size of 3 pixels and 4 pixels Soften. For the Shading we used the default Gloss Contour shape and blend modes, but set the Highlight Opacity to 100% and the Shadow Opacity to 70%.

6 Here is how the Layers panel looked after all the layer style options had been added. To save this style, we clicked on the Create new style button in the Styles panel and named it 'Water drops'.

7 After we had created the layer style we needed to create a custom brush setting to paint the water droplets with. Here we selected a small standard, round brush shape with a hard edge. We then went to the Brush panel and clicked on the Shape Dynamics section, linked the pen pressure with the size of the brush and raised the Size Jitter (the randomness of the brush size) to 80%. We clicked on the Scattering option and set the Scatter and Count Jitter to the maximum settings allowed. We chose this combination of settings in order to produce a random droplet effect when painting with the brush.

8

Photo: © Jeff Schewe

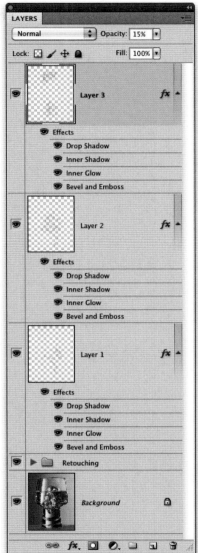

8 We were now ready to start painting on the empty new layer. As we painted with the brush tool, we were effectively able to paint using the layer style effect and produce the fine droplets of water that you see added here. The layer opacity had to be adjusted to fine-tune the density of the water droplets. You will note that in Step 2 we reduced the layer opacity to 60%, which was done to produce softer looking water drops. To create variable density droplets, we added two further layers, one at 40% and the other at 15% opacity, and painted on these separately, thereby creating a more realistic buildup of water droplets.

Editing layer styles

Double-clicking the layer or anywhere in the layer style list reopens the Layer Style dialog.

Layer what?

The Photoshop User Guide and Help menu sometimes describe the individual layer styles as layer effects, even though the Layer menu, Layers panel and Layer Style dialog refer to them as layer styles. It is unfortunate that Photoshop uses mixed terminology and naturally, this can lead to confusion, but basically, layer styles and layer effects are one and the same thing.

Copying layer styles

Layer styles can be shared with other layers or files. Select a layer that already has a style applied to it, go to the Layer ⇨ Layer Styles submenu and choose Copy Layer Style, then select a different layer and choose Paste Layer Style from the same submenu. Alternatively, you can ⌥ *alt* drag on the *fx* icon to copy the entire layer style from one layer to another. If you don't wish to copy the complete layer style, you can just ⌥ *alt* drag to copy just a single style effect from one layer to another layer in the same image.

How to remove edge flare

Layer styles are mostly used to create special effects for logos and type, but in the following steps I thought I would show you a photographic application for the Inner Shadow layer style. Here I wanted to show how you can compensate for edge flare on an object that's been isolated from the backdrop. Just bear in mind that the subject will need to be cut out from the backdrop first, before you apply the layer style.

1 A layer style can be applied to an image, shape or type layer by mousing down on the Add a layer style button in the Layers panel. When you add a new layer effect an italicized *fx* icon appears next to the layer name in the Layers panel.

2 In this example I added an Inner Shadow layer style in order to counteract the lens flare that was visible around the edges of the photograph. First I set the Angle to 90° (in order to match the direction of the overhead lighting used in this photograph). I then set the Multiply Blend Mode Opacity to 50% and set the Distance to 30 pixels, the Choke to 10% and the Size to 70 pixels.

Photo: © Martin Evening

3 This combination of settings proved sufficient to reduce most of the edge flare in the photograph. You will notice in the Layers panel below how the layer style appears indented in the Effects list associated with the current layer. To re-edit the settings, all you have to do is double-click the layer style in the list. You can also toggle, showing and hiding individual effects by clicking on the eyeball icon next to each effect.

Figure 7.19 This shows our model, Daniel, in the process of having white body makeup applied in preparation for the cover shot.

Figure 7.20 This shows our model, Daniel, being photographed by Martin in London, using a fairly simple lighting setup and plain backdrop.

How we created the cover image

With any book it is important to have a cover image that entices the reader and conveys something about the book's contents. In this instance, because the book is subtitled 'The Ultimate Workshop', we wanted the cover to illustrate this concept by photographing a model to look like a porcelain bust with the map of the brain of a well-educated Photoshop user. The idea for this came from looking at classic phrenology head busts, which typically feature a map of the brain that is meant to illustrate how the personality traits of a person can be derived from the shape of their skull. In the 19th century phrenology was quite influential in neuroscience and psychology, though even back then it was still regarded by many as a pseudo-science. However, it seemed like a good idea to take this as an inspiration for creating a Photoshop-user's head. Maybe we could even describe this as the science of 'Photoshopology'?

As you may be aware by now, Martin is based in London, England, and Jeff in Chicago, Illinois, and much of the communication that's required for the production of this book is handled via the Internet, with us both making use of Skype® and iChat®. One of the neat things about Apple's iChat service is that it now offers a 'screen sharing' feature whereby an iChat user can allow other iChat users to share their desktop screen views. Obviously, this is something that you only want to do with people you can trust, because it is just like offering someone a seat at your computer and giving them the ability to access anything they want from a remote distance. OK, so we trusted each other enough that this wasn't a problem. The big advantage of being able to share our computer screens was that Jeff could watch the shoot Martin was doing in London and see the photos download into Lightroom in almost real time and have the chance to 'art direct' (which was something Jeff rather enjoyed doing for a change).

Martin began by casting for a suitable model with a good-looking bald head. We chose Daniel, who you can see pictured in Figure 7.19 having his makeup applied by Martin's wife, Camilla. Daniel needed to look like a porcelain bust, so several layers of white body paint were applied, especially where it was necessary to cover up the tattoos on his chest and shoulders. For the lighting, Martin wanted to have a light gray backdrop with a soft sidelight coming from the right, to which a couple of blue-filtered lights were added on both the left and right to kick in a subtle hint of color on the sides of the head and the shoulders. The initial tests were pretty close to what we wanted, although as you can see in Step 3, in the Photoshop retouched version, Martin needed to add more blue color to the body to balance this with the color of the head. As you read through the following steps you will see how Jeff was able to monitor the shoot's progress via iChat and comment on the best images to select for the final retouch. Also, when Jeff was later to shoot the porcelain head in his studio in Chicago, Martin was able to watch this taking place via his office in London and likewise comment on the way the photo was looking. All that remained was to assemble the elements and here Jeff enlisted the help of David Willett, an art director he had worked with on many shoots in the past, to help advise on which would be the best fonts to use to create the new lettering. We wanted this to match as closely as possible the original lettering on the bust and also be easy to read.

Figure 7.21 During the shoot, Martin was able to communicate live with Jeff in Chicago via an Apple iChat screen sharing connection.

1 This shoot began in London, with Martin taking the initial photographs of our model, Daniel (see Figure 7.20), and using the new tethered shooting feature in Lightroom 3 to do this. Meanwhile, Jeff, who was in Chicago, was able to watch the photos as they downloaded via an Apple iChat screen sharing setup.

283

2 Once the shoot was complete, both Martin and Jeff were able to look through the photos together in Lightroom and select the two images shown here in the Survey view mode. It was felt that the shot on the left had the best body shape, while the one on the right offered the best head position.

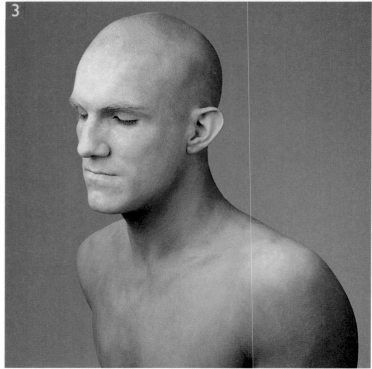

3 The next step was to take the two photos that had been selected in Step 2 and merge the head with the body. Martin then added further layers to tidy up the body makeup and balance out the color between the head and the rest of the model's body.

Figure 7.22 Here you can see Jeff photographing the phrenology head at his studio in Chicago. Jeff shot the head tethered to his P 65+ back on a Phase One 6 x 4.5 camera.

4 As was mentioned earlier, Jeff had been able to observe the shoot that took place in London and had already sourced a porcelain phrenology head from a local prop house. Now that the retouching of the Daniel shot was underway, Jeff knew the exact angle required for the shot he was going to do of the phrenology head (see Figure 7.22). During this shoot Jeff and Martin set up a further iChat screen share so that Martin could observe what Jeff was shooting and comment on the angle and lighting used to create this photo (see Figure 7.23).

Figure 7.23 Here you can see Jeff's computer screen being shared with Martin in London. The head is shown on the left in Capture One software. The shot of Daniel is in Lightroom on the right.

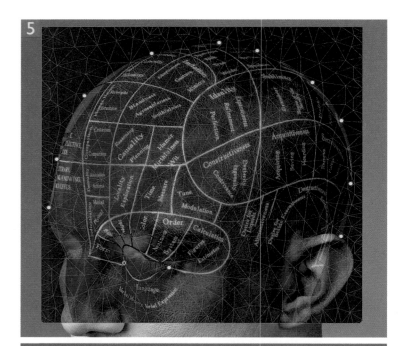

5 Now came the tricky bit of getting the phrenology head image to align with the photo of Daniel. To start with, Martin placed the phrenology head shot as a new layer and scaled it roughly to the same size as the model's head. This layer was then set to the Difference blend mode at 80%, which allowed Martin to see more clearly where this new image layer matched the outline of the layers below. Martin then went to the Edit menu and chose Puppet Warp. This added the mesh you can see here and Martin set about adding pins to the outline of the head.

6 Once a number of pins had been added, Martin was able to click and drag individual pins to fine-tune the shape of the phrenology head layer so that it matched as close as possible the layers in the master image. While the new Puppet Warp is quite powerful, this was admittedly quite a tricky step to carry out, as the Puppet Warp processing has a tendency to be quite processor-intensive. Once Martin was happy with the new puppet warped shape for the layer, he clicked *Enter* to apply the warp.

7 Martin then reset the phrenology head layer to the Normal blend mode at 100% Opacity and double-clicked the layer to open the Layer Style dialog shown. Here, he adjusted the This Layer Blend If sliders as shown on the left.

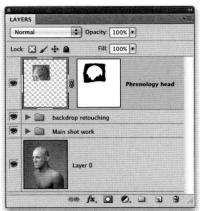

8 The edit adjustment described in Step 7 had the effect of fading out the highlight areas in the phrenology head layer and made the lettering appear to be merged with the photo of Daniel. At this stage the blend between these two images was beginning to work well. Originally, we had, at this stage, intended to make use of this result to draw pen paths that matched the outline of the lines seen here. In the end, we decided to make use of the real lines since they looked more interesting.

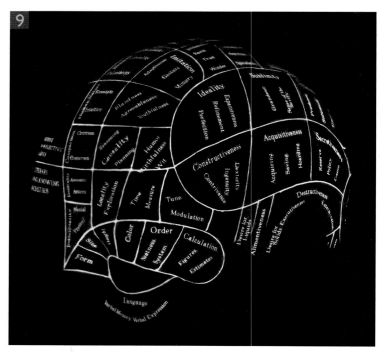

9 Martin created a new alpha channel based on the image view seen in Step 8 and edited the channel to create a high contrast mask. Then, after loading the channel shown above, he created a new layer and filled the selection with black. At this point, Martin handed over the file to Jeff for the addition of the new text and additional digital imaging.

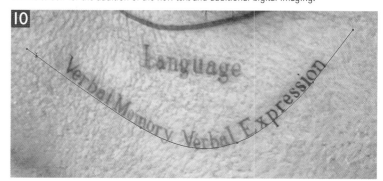

10 Martin, David Willett and Jeff had an email exchange regarding which font would match the original in look, feel and weight while retaining readability. David suggested Lucida Bright, which was one of the extended family of Lucida typefaces developed by Charles Bigelow and Kris Holmes, and first used in *Scientific American* magazine. Jeff decided to place the text using text along a path. As you can see above, he had already drawn a path along the same arc as the original words on the head.

11 As Jeff typed the words, they appeared along the path and using the type along the path allowed for very accurate placement. Jeff was also able to modify the path using the direct selection tool in Photoshop's tool bar. To keep all of the words and text layers organized, Jeff placed the individual text areas of the head in layer groups. On the right you can see the first layer group of words that were all located around the eye.

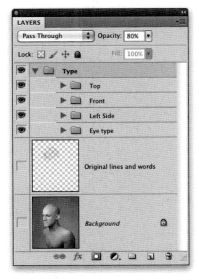

12 As you can see above, Jeff placed a lot of words — a total of 89 layers. All the text remained editable so Jeff and Martin could collaborate on which words were used where. Some of the words are features or tools and others are names. The common thread throughout was Photoshop.

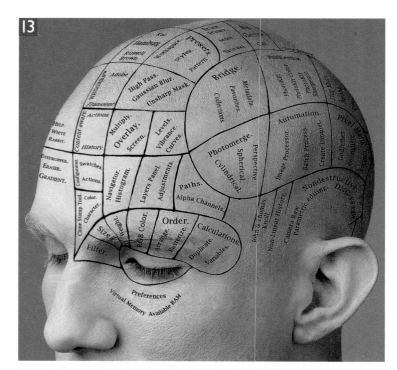

13 After the new words had all been placed, Jeff used a modified channel with the original words blacked out so only the lines showed to load as a selection. After he had created a new layer set to a Multiply blend, he filled the selection with black. He also created yet another layer group called Type & Lines so the treatment of these could be matched up.

14 Jeff found a slight complication with the sharpness of the vector type when compared to the more photographic nature of the lines. To deal with this he needed to create a softened version of the type layers. He duplicated the Type layer group and used the Merge Group command from the Layers panel fly-out menu.

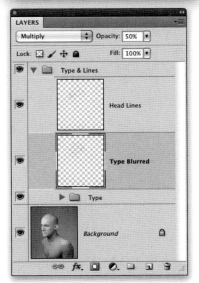

15 Jeff used a Filter ⇨ Blur ⇨ Gaussian Blur filter radius of 1 pixel to add a touch of softness to the text. The Type Blurred layer was changed to a Multiply blend using a 50% Opacity to reduce the strength of the effect. Adding the blur also had the effect of improving the readability of the text.

16 Jeff wanted to add a bit of texture to Daniel's white skin to make it look more like the craquelure that was in the glaze of the ceramic head. To sample the texture, he went back and shot the head from the side to get a large area of the head's texture. He was then able to expand on the size of the area of the texture using the new Content-Aware Fill feature. The detail image above right shows a close-up of the full texture image Jeff created.

17 Jeff copied and pasted the craquelure texture as a layer and used the Free Transform command from the Edit menu to both scale the texture image down and add a perspective that was consistent with the body image. He then used Filter ⇨ Liquify to warp the texture to wrap around the body. Note, Jeff used the Show Background option with the image of Daniel (the *Background* layer) set to be visible behind the texture image, which was set to 70% Opacity.

18 After zooming into the image Jeff warped the texture image to loosely follow the contour of the body. He used a combination of the forward warp, the pucker and the bloat tool. Don't laugh, that's what the engineers decided to call the various tools. Jeff then clicked *Enter* to apply the Liquify warp.

19

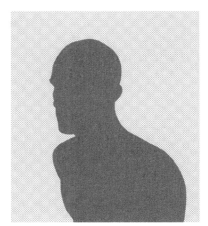

19 After the texture image had been warped with Liquify, the next step was to use a path drawn as an outline of the body to create a vector mask. This mask was used to clip the texture to the body outline only. Rather than use a regular pixel-based layer mask, Jeff chose to use a vector mask so he could also add a layer mask as the next step.

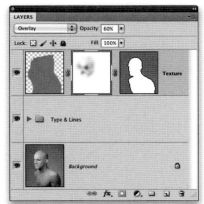

20 The vector mask took care of clipping the texture to the torso but Martin wanted Jeff to reduce the opacity of the texture around Daniel's face. So, Jeff lightly painted black into the layer mask around the eyes, the cheeks and the lips to reduce the opacity of the texture. At this point you might think the image was done but, alas, no. Jeff felt he needed to do additional work on the way the lines and words were layered over the face.

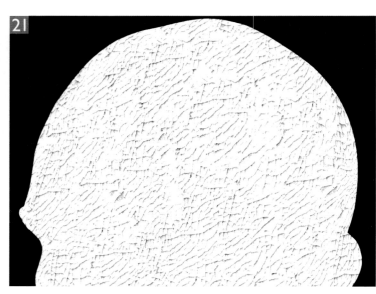

21 To apply the same craquelure to the type and the lines, Jeff copied the texture to a new channel (left) and used Image ⇨ Adjustments ⇨ Levels to substantially lighten the channel so that just the dark lines remained. Where the areas were light, all of the type and lines would show through. Where the texture was dark, the type and lines would be broken up.

22 To further modify the opacity of the type and lines, Jeff used the Filter ⇨ Noise ⇨ Add Noise filter to break up the larger areas in the channel mask. He then loaded the channel as a selection and used this selection to make a layer mask that would be applied to the Type & Lines layer group.

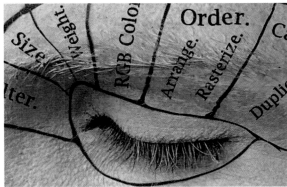

23 In addition to the texture and noise, Jeff painted directly on the Type & Lines layer mask to allow the underlying texture of the eyebrows to show through.

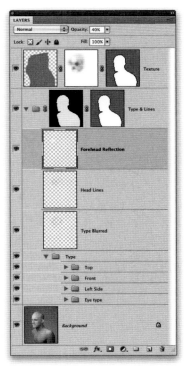

24 The very last step (we promise) was to add another layer at 40% Opacity inside the Type & Lines layer group and very gently paint a lightening effect using white. This was done to re-create the highlights that were seen on the original ceramic head.

Photograph: Martin Evening.
Canon EOS 1Ds Mk III | Sigma 12–24 mm lens: 12 mm | 200 ISO | f5.6 @ 36 minutes

Chapter 8

Photoshop after dark

Using Photoshop to process photos taken at night

Digital photography may be great for a lot of things, but working with photos that have been shot under low light conditions presents special problems that can be resolved either by choosing the right equipment to shoot with, or using Photoshop. This chapter explores some of the ways you can help improve the quality of photos shot in low light, as well as some of the special effects you can achieve when using Photoshop.

More about Stacks

Stacks is one of my favorite features for photographers. Unfortunately, it is only available as part of the extended version of Photoshop. Check out the tutorial on pages 138–141 in which we demonstrate how to remove tourists from a busy scene.

Combining images

Removing noise using multiple exposures

Here is a technique for reducing noise that makes use of the Stacks feature in Photoshop, where you can blend a series of identically shot photographs to produce a single image in which all the noise artifacts are smoothed out. This technique works very well for those situations where you are shooting pictures of still-life subjects in low light conditions but don't have access to a tripod. However, you can only use the following technique if you have the extended version of Photoshop CS3 or later. Here's how it works. Once you have aligned the photos using the auto-align method described here, the Median Stacks rendering method averages out the pixels at each point in the image. What you end up with is an image that not only will be noise-free, but may well appear smoother and sharper than the individual captures. This is because the rendering process also smooths out those shots where there was a slight amount of blur. There was also another Stacks processing technique described on pages 138–141, but this too can only work if you are using the extended version of Photoshop.

1 To begin with, I made a selection of nine photographs in Bridge that I wished to process as a stacked layer image. These pictures were all shot at night where I had simply hand-held the camera and fired off a short sequence of captures.

2 The first step was to open these photographs up in Camera Raw (using ⌘ R / ctrl R). I adjusted the White Balance plus other basic panel adjustments and synchronized these settings with the other selected photos by choosing Select All in the Camera Raw dialog, before clicking on the Synchronize... button. I then clicked the Done button to close the Camera Raw dialog and apply the settings.

3 I then went to the Tools menu in Bridge and chose Photoshop ⇨ Load files into Photoshop Layers... This opened the selected photos in Photoshop and added them as layers to a single image document. How the images were opened would depend on the workflow settings I had set in Step 2 (circled). In this instance the photographs were all processed at their native resolution using ProPhoto RGB at 16-bits per channel.

4 Since the photographs had all been captured using the camera hand-held, it was important to make sure that the layers were aligned correctly. I selected all the layers in the Layers panel, went to the Edit menu and chose Auto-Align Layers… This opened the dialog shown here, where I selected the Auto option and clicked OK.

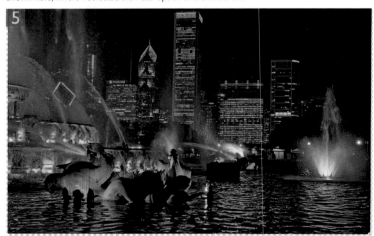

5 Here you can see the auto-aligned image. I now needed to go to the Layer menu and choose Smart Objects ⇨ Convert to Smart Object. This created the single Smart Object layer you can see here in the Layers panel on the left, but if I were to double-click the layer thumbnail I would see all the original layers that the Smart Object was comprised of.

I then went to the Layer menu again and chose Smart Objects ⇨ Stack Mode ⇨ Median. If you try this out for yourself, you may find the Stacks rendering will take a while to complete. How long it takes to apply the processing will depend, of course, on the size and number of layers, plus the bit depth of the images.

Single image   Stacks processed version

Photo: © Martin Evening

6 Once the processing was complete, you will notice how the Smart Object layer had a Stacks icon (circled) indicating that the Smart Object had been rendered using the Stacks feature. Here is a close-up view that shows a single exposure on the left and the stacks rendered version on the right where the nine separate exposures were merged to produce a smoother, noise-free image. The Median rendering was used here because it analyzed the pixel values from the lowest to the highest that occurred at any one point and picked the middle value, thereby eliminating nearly all of the noisy pixels that were present on each of the separate layers.

For non-extended users

As with the tourist removal and layer stack noise removal techniques, this is another Photoshop technique that is only available to customers who have the extended version of Photoshop CS3 or later. However, if you don't have the extended version you can reproduce a Maximum stacks rendering effect by manually setting each layer to the Lighten blend mode.

Combining photographs of fireworks

There are a number of traditional photographic shooting techniques that rely on the use of multiple exposures to produce a single blended exposure image. For example, a lot of still-life studio work is created via multiple exposures and architectural photographers may use such techniques to blend one shot of a building at dusk and another taken at night when the lights are all switched on in the building. In most cases you can successfully blend photos using the Normal or Screen blending modes. However, there are some assignments where you may like to try using the method described here, in which I used the Maximum stacks blend mode to add together 10 separate exposures of a firework display, but without losing the contrast and definition of the original single exposure shots. The Maximum stacks blend mode happened to work well when blending this particular series of images, but you may also wish to try the Range blend mode, which preserves slightly more detail in the extreme highlights.

1 This Bridge window view shows an edited selection of photos that I wished to blend together to create a single, merged firework photograph. First I selected all of the images displayed here, went to the Tools menu and chose Photoshop ⇨ Load Files into Photoshop Layers...

2 Step 1 created a single image document, in which all the selected photographs were all placed as individual layers in a layer stack. Here, we can see the topmost layer visible. In this instance there was no need to align these layers as they had all been shot using a tripod. What I needed to do now was to convert this layer stack into a Smart Object. To do this, I first used ⌘ ⌥ A ctrl alt A to select all of the layers.

3 I then went to the Layer menu and chose Smart Objects ⇨ Convert to Smart Object. This step created a single Smart Object layer.

Me **Martin Evening & Jeff Schewe**
Adobe Photoshop CS5 for Photographers: The Ultimate Workshop

4 Now that I had converted the layered image to a smart object, I went to the Layer menu again and chose Smart Objects ⇨ Stack Mode ⇨ Maximum.

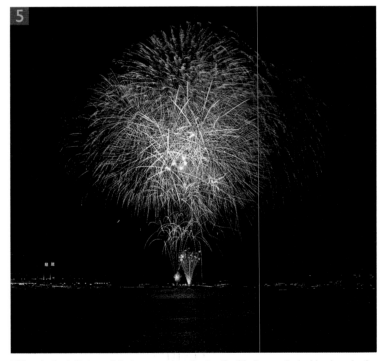

5 Here is the initial result that was produced using the Maximum stacks blend mode. As you can see, this blend method produced a merged composite image.

Photo: © Martin Evening

6 I thought that the water in the previous step looked a little dark, so I selected a couple more of the original firework shot layers and placed these inside a layer group above the Smart Object layer. I blended the top layer with the one below using the Screen blend mode. I then also set the layer group blend mode to Screen mode. This step lightened and added more detail to the reflections in the water, but didn't look so good over the sky area. To address this I added a pixel layer mask to the layer group and applied a black to white gradient which hid the top half of the layer group.

Photographing star trails

Star trail photographs are photographs taken of the night sky that record the rotation of the earth around its axis relative to the sky. To do this the camera must be firmly fixed on a tripod, pointing up at the sky and shot using a long time exposure. However, this is one of those techniques where it is actually more difficult to successfully shoot a subject like this digitally compared to shooting film. Let's begin by looking at the general problems associated with shooting star trail photos.

To start with you need to find a location that offers a good view of the night sky and is remote enough to avoid the effects of light pollution. If you live in a town or city you will rarely get the chance to view the night sky free of the light pollution that obscures the fainter stars and the Milky Way. For a city person like me, it is only when venturing out to the remote countryside that I have a chance to see the night sky in all its glory. You also need to make sure that the area of the sky you are photographing doesn't include a flight path, or the passage of the moon. Next, you need to choose an evening where there is likely to be a perfectly clear sky and you will ideally want to shoot in dry atmospheric conditions. If the air is moist, there is a good chance that the camera lens may get covered in condensation. Over the last few years, I have tried at various times to shoot star trail images, but it has usually only been possible for me to do so when staying somewhere that's remote enough and where the atmospheric conditions have been just right. Of course, I have also needed to find locations to shoot from that have included suitably interesting foreground elements. On a recent holiday trip to Mallorca I made the most of the remote villa location where we were staying to create the photo that's shown in the following steps.

Now you'll often hear people like me say how digital is better and easier to work with than film. But for this type of photography, digital presents a unique set of problems and it is in some ways more tricky to photograph star trails digitally than when shooting film. So here are a number of tips to bear in mind when shooting a star trail image at night using a digital camera. To start with you will need to capture a total exposure time of at least half an hour, or maybe as long as a couple of hours in order to record a decent star trail image. When I began shooting star trails I tried doing this using a single exposure. The problem with this approach was that when the shutter was left open for long periods of time, the sensor tended to generate a lot of random background noise which would accumulate throughout the exposure period and be most apparent in the darker areas of the image. When shooting film, noise would only be a problem in terms of film grain and if you were using, say, a 100 ISO or 200 ISO film emulsion, you could capture a perfectly smooth star trail image at any exposure duration. With digital, the random noise generation can be a real problem. In the early days of digital cameras even an exposure time of just a few seconds was enough to tip the balance and cause a serious deterioration in the quality of the image capture. These days it is possible to record much longer time exposures before seeing any adverse affects. When it comes to shooting really long exposures though, the best approach with current digital camera technology is to limit the maximum exposure time to around 2 minutes per exposure and then combine a sequence of exposures that have been captured one after another. I demonstrate how to do this in the tutorial that is coming up. Essentially, you can usually use the software that comes with the camera to shoot in tethered mode and configure the software to shoot a set number of shots in a continuous sequence. Or you may find there is an option in the camera menu itself that allows you to do this. Many digital cameras have an optimum ISO setting that is slightly faster than the lowest ISO speed setting. The pictures you see here were shot in raw mode using the Canon EOS 1Ds MkIII camera set to 200 ISO and with a lens aperture of f/5.6.

The other problem to watch out for is battery life. For as long as the shutter is open, the camera battery is going to be used to power the camera's sensor. CCD sensors can consume a lot of power, whereas the modern CMOS sensors are much more power efficient since they draw less charge. If you are about to shoot a sequence of long exposures, you will need to make sure you are using a fully charged battery. Some photographers overcome this limitation by using a power supply lead connected to an external power source such as a domestic power supply or a car battery. If shooting, as I did here, with the camera tethered to a laptop computer, it also important to make sure the computer itself has a sufficient amount of battery charge to last throughout the total series of time exposures.

For non-extended users

The technique is described over the following pages is another one of those that is only available to customers who have the extended version of Photoshop CS3 or later. However, as with the fireworks composite described at the beginning of this chapter, you can reproduce a Maximum Stacks rendering effect by manually setting each layer to the Lighten blend mode. The main reasons why I advocate using the Stacks rendering method here are a) it is quicker and b) you can also try using the Range Stacks rendering method which will produce a slightly different result (that can't be simulated using layer blending modes). The Range Stacks rendering produces a more contrasty and darker effect. It didn't work so well with the image example I used here, but it may be useful for other types of star trail images, especially if the cumulative exposures are looking too light.

Lighting the foreground

It is a good idea to frame your picture using foreground features such as buildings or trees, but you don't want these to appear in silhouette and they will therefore need to be lit.

As mentioned in the main text, you can use a torch light or a flashgun to do this. Since the technique shown here relies on the use of a sequence of photographs being taken I strongly suggest you create these additional shots either at the very beginning or at the end. This will leave you with the option to experiment and select which foreground exposures work best.

To shoot the night-time sky, choose a location during daylight hours, set your camera up on a sturdy tripod and compose the scene so that it includes something in the foreground. You don't want to shoot just the sky on its own, so look for interesting trees or buildings to include in the picture. Make a note of the camera field of view so that you can plan in advance how to expose the night scene later when it is dark, using either a torch light or a portable flashgun (see sidebar).

Figure 8.1 This shows the typical setup I use to shoot star trail photographs, where the camera is controlled via a laptop computer running the tethered capture software that comes with the camera.

1 To begin with, I set up the camera on a tripod during daylight hours (see Figure 8.1), selecting the ideal camera angle viewpoint to shoot from. In this instance, because I was shooting with a Canon EOS camera, I configured the EOS Utility software to shoot a sequence of photographs. Here, I adjusted the camera settings and made sure the shooting mode was set to Bulb. I then clicked on the Timer shooting button to open the dialog shown top right, where I set the Exposure time to 2 minutes (in which case, the Shooting Interval has to be at least 2 minutes 5 seconds) and configured the dialog to shoot 20 exposures. When I then clicked the Start button, the Timer Shooting Status dialog appeared to indicate how the shoot sequence was progressing.

2 Once I had finished shooting I was able to open the photos in Bridge and prepare to edit them in Photoshop. What I did here was to make a selection of all the shots and choose Tools ⇨ Photoshop ⇨ Load Files into Photoshop Layers…

3 At this stage I had an opened image in Photoshop that consisted of 18 stacked layers. I used ⌘ ⌥ A ctrl alt A to select all the layers and then went to the Layer menu and selected Smart Objects ⇨ Convert to Smart Object.

4 Once I had created the Smart Object layer I went to the Layer ⇨ Smart Objects ⇨ Stack Mode menu and selected the Maximum rendering method. In a stroke this processed all the images to reveal the cumulative star trail image seen here. The result looked pretty good and when applying this step you should end up with a decent finished image. However, in hindsight I should have made allowance for the fact that the lights on the building were likely to burn out the detail on the house.

5 What I should have done was to take a briefer exposure of the scene just prior to shooting the main exposure sequence. As it happens, I did make an exposure a little earlier during daylight hours, which was just as well, since I could use this to recover some of the lost image detail. What I did was to take the photo seen here, add this as a new layer above the star trail processed image and set the layer blending mode to Darken. I then added a layer mask filled with black and carefully painted on the mask with white to repair the burnt-out areas.

6 Here you can see the finished result. There were still a few more things I needed to do to get this photograph looking perfect. First, I added an empty new layer set to Color mode and used sampled paint colors to work with the paint brush and tidy up some of the areas, such as where there were uneven colors on the building and signs of some lens flare in the lower middle portion of the sky. You know what I said earlier about avoiding overhead flight paths? This was such a good angle to shoot from and although I was pointing the camera away from the main flight path, I still ended up recording a few light trails from overhead aircraft (you should be able to see some of these in Step 4). When I shot this picture I was using Photoshop CS4 and it was particularly tricky to remove these using the healing brush. Now with Photoshop CS5 I was able to use the spot healing brush in Content-Aware mode to effortlessly remove these completely.

Preserving the pixels

This technique also teaches an important lesson about the use of the Color blend mode to blend coloring adjustment layers such as the blue curves coloring layer I applied in Step 5 on page 315. Doing this produced a cleaner histogram compared to leaving the coloring adjustment layer set to Normal blend mode.

Demo Action

 The steps shown here are available as an action: CS5 Nocturnal, which is available from the DVD.

Nocturnal effect

There is a film by the French film director Francois Truffaut called *La Nuit Américaine* (known in the English-speaking world as *Night for Day*), where the title of the movie is based around the use of a photographic filter designed to make daylight footage resemble a moonlit night scene. In all my photographic career I never did manage to work out the elusive combination of filters used to pull off this trick, but I was recently inspired to see if a similar type of effect could be achieved directly in Photoshop.

In creating a simulation effect such as this, I needed to work out what exactly makes a scene look like it has been shot at night as opposed to day. There was certainly more to this than dimming down the exposure. First of all you have to take into account the way our human vision is compromised in low light conditions. Our eyes are less able to gauge colors and we therefore perceive everything as being more monochrome. We tend to think of moonlight as being blue in color, but the color temperature of moonlight is actually around 4125 K, which although slightly cooler than a tungsten halogen light is still warmer than normal daylight. The reason why we perceive moonlight to be blue is because of Purkinje's phenomenon, which describes how in low level lighting conditions red/yellow colors appear to become less luminous and green/blue colors appear to become brighter. It is these shifts in our human visual response combined with the dimmer lighting conditions that contribute to the way we perceive night-lit scenes differently compared to a daylight scene.

ProPhoto RGB editing

For any technique that involves using tone and color adjustments, the RGB space of the source image will always have a bearing on the final outcome. Such differences may often be so slight as to be unnoticeable, but not so when big changes are made to the image. This particular technique was devised for use with the ProPhoto RGB space, because only ProPhoto RGB was able to handle the huge color shifts applied in Step 2 before converting these into the tamer luminosity tone adjustment shown in Step 3. If you were to use sRGB or Adobe RGB, Step 2 would cause a lot of the color information to be clipped early on. You could modify the settings used here to achieve a similar result when working with smaller gamut RGB spaces, but for best results I suggest you use ProPhoto RGB throughout.

1 I started here with a normal color photograph in ProPhoto RGB and began by adding a Channel Mixer layer. Any photograph will do, but not all pictures will look convincing as a nocturnal image. Ideally, I suggest you begin with an image that is in 16-bits per channel mode since this technique involves a fair amount of pixel stretching.

2 In the Channel Mixer settings I set the channels as follows. In the Red channel I set Red to 0, Green to +100 and Blue to 0. In the Green channel I set Red to 0, Green to +200 and Blue to −100. In the Blue channel I set Red to 0, Green to 0 and Blue to 200. This combination of settings produced the false-color look seen here.

3 The Channel Mixer adjustment step was designed to boost the green luminance in the scene. The coloring effect was interesting, but not exactly the look I was after here, so I set the blend mode of the Channel Mixer layer to Luminosity. Next, I added a curves adjustment layer in Normal mode that darkened the scene to make the photograph look more night-like.

4 The next step was to knock back the yellow saturation. I added a Hue/Saturation adjustment layer, set the Yellows Saturation to −60 and the layer blend mode to Color. I then held down the *Shift* key, clicked on the Channel Mixer layer to select all three adjustment layers and chose Layer ⇨ Group Layers (⌘ G ctrl G).

5 Finally, I added a Curves adjustment layer to the top of the layer stack (above the Layer Group) and adjusted the red and blue curves (as shown here) to create a blue/cyan cast. I set the blend mode of this layer to Color and reduced the layer opacity to 50%. The reason I did this was because it gave me the freedom to tweak the coloring effect strength. You probably won't see much difference in the appearance of the image, but you'll see why this is important in the following step.

6 A series of adjustment layers can cumulatively stretch the pixels in the base image and create spikes and gaps in the image histogram. However, there are ways that you can mitigate such losses. On the left is a layer stack in which I followed all the stages up to Step 5 and left the final Curves layer in Normal blend mode. As you can see, the 8-bits per channel image histogram is quite choppy. On the right, I set the layer blend mode to Color, overlaid the histogram from using this blend mode over the Normal mode histogram and highlighted the difference in green. Note how the Color mode histogram has fewer spikes. If you apply these steps to a photo that is in 16-bit mode, you will see even fewer spikes and gaps in the final histogram.

Darkening bright colors

This technique worked well with the image used here. However, for shots that contain bright colors, such as say, a bright yellow taxi or red bus, you may need to add a further adjustment to tone such colors down to make such colors appear less saturated.

Preserving colors with ProPhoto RGB

Over the last 10 years, the advice on which is the best RGB color edit space to use has shifted. Initially, most experts suggested you use Adobe RGB, but in recent years opinion has changed and we now advocate you use the ProPhoto RGB as your edit workspace.

There are two main reasons for this. Firstly, many inkjet printers now have color gamuts that are typically wider than the Adobe RGB space. Therefore, by choosing ProPhoto RGB as your edit space you can make full use of the gamut of the printer, especially when it comes to reproducing shadow colors on glossy printing paper. Secondly, because ProPhoto is a wider gamut space, it is better suited for carrying out pixel calculations where the calculated pixel values may end up extending beyond the boundaries of a smaller gamut color space. Using the last tutorial image as an example, we can see how the ProPhoto RGB space offers extra headroom with which to make some big pixel shifts, whereas a smaller gamut space will simply clip the pixels that extend beyond the gamut limits.

ProPhoto RGB   Adobe RGB

1 These 3D diagrams allow us to compare the use of the ProPhoto RGB and Adobe RGB edit spaces. The pixels in the photograph on the left are shown here plotted to their RGB coordinate positions in each color space. You will notice that the ProPhoto RGB space does not constrain the pixels in any way and that the pixel colors in the ProPhoto RGB master image extend beyond the gamut limits of the Adobe RGB space, which is represented here (for comparison purposes) as a wireframe diagram within the ProPhoto RGB space gamut.

ProPhoto RGB   Adobe RGB

2 One of the early steps in the Nocturnal effect (described on page 313) involved applying an extreme Channel Mixer adjustment. This image adjustment really stretched the pixel values to the limits. It is therefore just as well that the huge color gamut of the ProPhoto RGB space was capable of containing this kind of adjustment and preserved the color and tonal relationships between all the individual pixels. If the Adobe RGB color space had been used to edit the image, the Channel Mixer adjustment would clip most of the colors because the gamut was simply not big enough to allow Photoshop to calculate such an extreme adjustment.

ProPhoto RGB   Adobe RGB

3 Although the Nocturnal effect applied an extreme color adjustment at the beginning, the pixel values were later squeezed back again to produce a more muted-color look in the finished image. You can't see the differences too clearly in these 2D representations of the 3D gamut shapes, but there was a substantial blue hue shift in the Adobe RGB edited version. What mattered most, of course, was which version would print better? For this last step I switched the color gamut profiles to wire frames and overlaid the color gamut of a glossy paper print profile as a solid shape. In the ProPhoto RGB example you will notice that although some blues are beyond the gamut of the printer, more color detail is preserved in the shadows.

317

Zion Park, Utah, USA. Photograph: Martin Evening.
Canon EOS 1Ds Mk III | Sigma 12–24 mm lens:13 mm | 200 ISO | f11.0 @ 1/25th–1/400th

Photomerges

Blending images together in Photoshop

As has been pointed out elsewhere in this book, working with Photoshop can often cause you to rethink the way you go about shooting certain subjects. This chapter focuses on the use of two key features in Photoshop: the Merge to HDR Pro and Photomerge. Using these tools you can use multiple captures to compress the dynamic range of the subject you are photographing, extend the camera viewpoint, or combine these techniques together to achieve both.

HDR toning

When you apply an HDR Toning image adjustment to a standard image, it is converted on-the-fly to 32-bits per channel, thereby allowing you to achieve a fake HDR to LDR conversion. Even though this isn't a real HDR image conversion, it does provide an interesting alternative to Shadows/Highlights image adjustments.

Merge to HDR Pro

The Merge to HDR Pro feature has been updated in Photoshop CS5 to provide improved merging of bracketed exposures to create merged 32-bit high dynamic range (HDR) images and better tone mapping conversions to 16-bit or 8-bit low dynamic range (LDR), incorporating better ghost removal and more extensive tone mapping controls. If you want to you can now reproduce the classic 'HDR look' using Photoshop, but you can also create more subtle HDR to LDR conversions. If you already own the *Adobe Photoshop CS5 for Photographers* book, there is a full account of the new Merge to HDR Pro controls in Chapter 7. If not, you can access this chapter in PDF form on the DVD that comes with this book.

There are several reasons why the Merge to HDR Pro feature can be considered useful. You can use the HDR toning controls to produce the obvious HDR look that fans of HDR photography seem to like. HDR toning can be applied when converting a 32-bit Merge to HDR Pro image to 16-bits or 8-bits per channel, or can even be applied as an image adjustment via the Image Adjustments menu to standard images. The main reason for using Merge to HDR Pro is to merge a bracketed sequence of exposures into a single 32-bit master image and thereby record the extended tonal range of a captured scene within a single image. From here you can use the tone mapping controls provided in the Merge to HDR Pro dialog (shown opposite) to map these to a low dynamic range 16-bit or 8-bit version. This is one approach, although personally I prefer to use Merge to HDR Pro to create a 32-bit image, save this as a master and then use the Image ⇨ Mode menu to convert to 16-bit or 8-bit as a discrete separate step. This way one can preserve a master version and use the Image ⇨ Mode step to spawn different renderings, while preserving the master 32-bit version. Whichever approach is used it is best to always create Merge to HDR Pro images from raw files rather than rendered images (even if these are in 16-bit per channel mode). Even then I find HDR toning can lead to some colors not looking quite right. The steps on the following pages show how adding an additional Color blend mode layer can help improve the image appearance. A further benefit of using Merge to HDR Pro is that even when you aim to produce a fairly normal-looking conversion (as shown here), the shadow detail will usually end up being much smoother. There is a good explanation of the reasons for this in the PDF extract that's on the DVD.

1 To use the Merge to HDR Pro feature it is best to do so from raw originals. Here you can see three raw files selected where the default develop settings had all been synchronized.

2 I then went to the Tools menu in Bridge and selected Merge to HDR Pro… This opened the above dialog, where I applied the settings shown here. I clicked OK to create a new Merge to HDR Pro image.

3 I returned to Bridge, opened the medium exposed image and adjusted the develop settings to obtain a close match to the Merge to HDR Pro version.

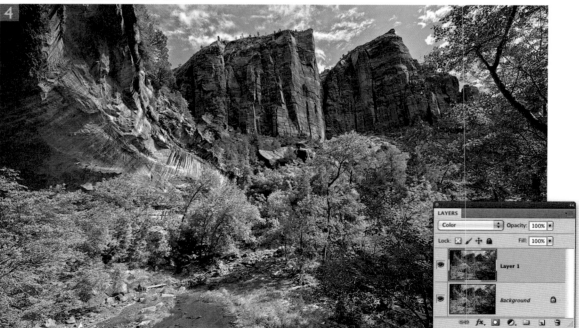

4 I opened this as a new image and dragged with the move tool (and the *Shift* key held down) to place this as a new layer above the Merge to HDR Pro layer, and set the blend mode to Color.

5 The reason for adding this extra step is because I find it can help you achieve smoother, more natural-looking colors in a Merge to HDR processed image. For example, with this image there was an unnatural saturation boost in the sky. Adding the Color blend mode layer improved the look of the sky by making the sky look less saturated and the clouds look less blue. The rocks by the stream had a pale yellow cast in the highlights. The Color blend mode layer was also able to get rid of this and, again, apply a more natural-looking color.

Camera settings

Before you shoot a set of panorama photographs, I suggest you set the exposure setting to manual so that the exposures are all consistent, the aperture remains the same throughout and the white balance setting is also consistent (although if you shoot raw, you can apply a single white balance in the Camera Raw processing later).

Blend Images Together

When the Blend Images Together option is selected, Photomerge looks for the optimal borders between each image layer, color matches these layers and applies a layer mask. When Blend Images Together is turned off, an alignment match only is performed. This allows you to edit the layers individually before you apply the Edit ⇨ Auto-Blend Layers… command.

Photomerge

Photomerge can mainly be used to stitch photographs together to create panoramic compositions. There are other programs that can do this with varying degrees of success, but I would say that the Photomerge feature in Photoshop has now evolved to become one of the best panorama stitchers out there. The complex interactive layout dialog option from the old Photomerge has been removed and, instead, you are offered a simple choice of layout options, of which Auto is usually the best one to choose.

There are four main ways to use Photomerge. You can go to the File ⇨ Automate menu in Photoshop, and click on the Browse… button in the Photomerge dialog (circled in Figure 9.1) and select a folder of images, or browse through the folders on your computer to add specific photos. Or, if the images you wish to merge are already open in Photoshop, select the Open Files option. The easiest way though is to select the images you wish to merge via Bridge and then choose Tools ⇨ Photoshop ⇨ Photomerge. This also pops the same Photomerge dialog as shown in Figure 9.1,

Figure 9.1 You can use the File ⇨ Automate ⇨ Photomerge… command in Photoshop, or choose Tools ⇨ Photoshop ⇨ Photomerge… in Bridge, to see the Photomerge dialog shown here.

where you can select the appropriate layout and blending options to create a Photomerge composite in one single step.

Alternatively, in Photoshop you can choose File ⇨ Scripts ⇨ Load Files into Stack… This opens the Load Layers dialog shown in Figure 9.2, where you can again manually select the photos you wish to process. When you click OK, this creates a single image in which all the selected photos are added as layers. Or, if you are in Bridge, you can simply to go to the Tools menu and choose Photoshop ⇨ Load Files into Photoshop Layers… This too creates a single layered image, but without having to show the Load Layers dialog. Whichever method you choose, once the layered image is opened in Photoshop, you can then choose the Edit ⇨ Auto-Align Layers… option to select the desired layout blend method (see Figure 9.3) followed by the Edit ⇨ Auto-blend Layers… option to carry out the blending step. By breaking the Photomerge process down into discrete steps, this allows you to experiment more easily with the different layout and alignment options before you choose to blend the layers.

Photomerge photography tips

For optimum results, you should aim for a 25–40% overlap between each photo. The focal length and focus should remain constant; do not attempt to zoom in or out as you are taking photographs. As you take your series of pictures rotate the camera in gradual steps, aiming to pivot the rotation around the center of the lens, and try to prevent the camera lens axis shifting too much. You can do this by hand-holding the camera but, to get the best results, you could consider using a tripod head like the Pan head from Manfrotto™ which, when used with the angle bracket clamp, will let you center the rotation accurately around the center of the lens axis. The captured photos should then align more easily in Photomerge.

Figure 9.2 If you choose File ⇨ Scripts ⇨ Load Files into Stack… in Photoshop, or choose ⇨ Photoshop ⇨ Load Files into Photoshop Layers in Bridge, you will see the Load Layers dialog shown here. Select the files that you wish to load as layers and click OK. With this dialog you also have the option to automatically align the source photos, but if you are going down this route, it makes more sense to apply the Photoshop Edit ⇨ Auto-Align Layers option separately.

Lens Correction options

The Lens Correction options will in most cases help you achieve better panoramic images. The Vignette Removal applies exposure compensation to the edges of any images that have darkened corners. This is a common problem with certain wide-angle lenses, although you can also correct for this in Camera Raw directly before you carry out a Photomerge or an auto-alignment. Geometric Distortion Correction can compensate for barrel or pincushion lens distortion, but will add significantly to the Photomerge processing. If you are blending images that were shot with a 'recognized' fisheye lens, Photomerge switches on the Geometric Distortion option automatically.

Basically, if you know which Photomerge layout mode and Lens Correction options you need to use, it is always easier and quicker to apply Photomerge directly as shown in Figure 9.1. If you are unsure as to which settings would work best it can be advantageous to use the indirect Load Files into Stack (also referred to as Load Files into Photoshop Layers in Bridge) method, since this allows you to open the images first before you decide which Auto-Align method to use. For example, you can use the Photoshop or Bridge method to open a selected number of files as Photoshop layers in a single image. In Photoshop you can then choose Edit ⇨ Auto-Align Layers (Figure 9.3), and select a layout and lens correction option to see what kind of panorama alignment this produces. If you're not pleased with the outcome you can simply undo the Auto-Align step, select Auto-Align Layers again and choose a different one instead. Once you feel you are on the right track you can then select the Edit ⇨ Auto-Blend Layers option (also shown in Figure 9.3) to apply the Panorama blend method. This allows you to complete the Photomerge alignment and blending.

Figure 9.3 If you want to align the layers in a layered image you can do so by choosing Edit ⇨ Auto-Align Layers. This opens the dialog shown here on the left, where the Projection/Layout and Lens Correction options are identical to those found in the Photomerge dialog seen in Figure 9.1. You can choose a combination of settings and click OK to apply the desired alignment. Afterwards, you can choose the Edit ⇨ Auto-Blend Layers option and select the Panorama blend method.

Resizing the source images

When you create a panorama image you will end up with a photograph that is considerably bigger in size than the individual photographs used to build the panorama. This was not such a concern when digital cameras could only capture small sized pictures anyway, but these days we often find it necessary to scale the individual source images down in size so that the resulting panorama doesn't end up being too big. If you are working from raw file originals, one way to do this is to go to the Workflow options in Camera Raw (Figure 9.4), change the file opening size and click 'Done' to apply the new size setting to the selected photos. Do this and the individual photos will open as smaller images and as a consequence of this the Photomerge processing can be much faster. Doing a test merge with images already downsampled in Camera Raw will also be a lot faster, particularly if you are working from 60 MP original captures as shown below in Figure 9.4.

Auto-Blend Layers

Auto-Blend Layers analyzes all the selected layers and masks the layers such that each area of the final composite is defined by a single portion from each individual layer. The layers themselves are cut out using a jagged outline that masks the edges of each layer element. This will usually produce a composite free of overlapping picture elements and fuzzy sections. We always keep the Seamless Tones and Colors option checked (see Figure 9.3) as this helps improve the blend smoothness between the layers.

Figure 9.4 The Camera Raw Workflow Options can be found at the bottom of the Camera Raw dialog. Click on the blue, underlined text to open the Workflow Options dialog and change the Size settings to apply a smaller or bigger file opening size. Remember to click on the Done button in Camera Raw when you are finished to apply this new setting to the selected photos.

File size limitations

If you find the Photomerge process stalls during the processing, this is probably because the individual files are too big and are preventing Photomerge from working successfully. You need to either install more RAM or work with smaller files. It may also be because you have the Geometric Distortion Correction option checked, which can make big demands on the file processing.

A simple, one-step Photomerge

I thought I would start with a simple example of how to create a Photomerge image. The Auto layout option is usually the best choice to select here, as it analyzes the source images first and tries to work out in advance which layout method (Perspective, Cylindrical or Spherical) will produce the best-looking panorama image. Although the Auto option gets it right most of the time, it doesn't always manage to guess correctly. So here's a tip. If you are combining a series of images to produce a landscape panorama, the Cylindrical layout method will usually keep the horizon line level in the picture (although not always straight). This is the layout method I select when I know it's the best one to use.

1 I began by opening Bridge and made a selection of the photographs that I wished to merge into a panorama. If you are working from raw files, you may at this stage want to open these pictures up in Camera Raw and make sure that the Camera Raw settings are synchronized across all the images. In addition to this, it can be a good idea to check the Workflow Options (mentioned on page 327), to set the file opening size of each image to an appropriate individual size (if you attempt to merge a series of full-size digital captures, you can end up with a really huge panorama image file). Once I had done that, I went to the Tools menu in Bridge and chose Photoshop ⇨ Photomerge…

2 Here is the Photomerge dialog, showing the photos selected in Bridge as the source files for the Photomerge. I selected the Cylindrical layout option and checked all the options at the bottom: Blend Images Together, Vignette Removal and Geometric Distortion Correction, then clicked OK to build the panorama. The resulting layers and layer masks can be seen in the Layers panel shown on the right.

3 Here is the completed panorama in which the selected images had all been merged together but not yet corrected using the Free Transform command.

4 The image seen previously in Step 3 showed some distortion in the resulting merge. The sky was too wide and the foreground too narrow. After merging the layers (shown in the Layers panel on the left) I used the Free Transform tool from the Edit menu (⌘T ctrl T). By holding down the ⌘ ⌥ ctrl alt keys (plus the Shift key to constrain to horizontal), I was able to drag the upper corners in and the lower corners out Fortunately, the horizon was nice and straight (a function of using Cylindrical vs. Auto in the Photomerge dialog).

5 Even with the corrections made in Free Transform, the upper left and right corners of the image had fully transparent areas that needed filling in. In days gone by, this was always a real pain. Trying to get the natural gradation and detail such as clouds to look real using even using the clone stamp or the healing tools was a chore. Well, the star of Photoshop CS5 has to be the Content-Aware Fill feature, and it did the trick in this image. I used the magic wand tool (yes, I'm willing to admit I do have a use for the magic wand) to select the transparent areas. To be sure the selection was big enough for Content-Aware Fill to gradation and blend, I used the Expand Selection command found under the Select ⇨ Modify submenu. I entered a 6 pixel expansion and clicked OK.

6 After expanding the selection, I used the Edit ⇨ Fill command and selected the Content-Aware option from the Contents drop-down menu and used a Normal blend mode. The result is shown above and the final image after cropping is shown below in Figure 9.5.

Figure 9.5 The original five images were captured hand-held with a Phase One 6 x 4.5 camera with a 45 mm lens and P 65+ back. The final image size was 67″ x 36″ at 300 PPI and was 1.24 GB in size when flattened.

A three-step Photomerge

The Photomerge command (from within Bridge) works very well almost every time. The Photomerge command is essentially carrying out a three-step process in which the first step is to add all the images as layers in a Photoshop document then auto-align the individual layers. The final step is to carry out an Auto-Blend operation in which the layers are aggressively layer masked.

The following tutorial shows an alternative approach in which the Load Layers, Auto-Align and Auto-Blend Layers steps are carried out separately, one step at a time. By breaking the Photomerge process down into separate steps, you can have more control (if you need it) over how the images are merged together.

1 The first step involved opening a series of images inside Camera Raw hosted by Photoshop. All eight of the images were selected and ready to open in Photoshop. While the Auto-Align command I used later controlled both the vignetting and optical distortion, the one thing this can't fix is chromatic aberrations. You therefore need to fix those inside Camera Raw. Here, I made the corrections needed and also added a Defringe: Highlight Edges setting.

Carry out a low-res test first

If you have a large selection of medium or large sized images, these can take a quite while to process. If you want to see a quick preview of how such a Photomerge will look, we suggest you run the Photomerge command with the Camera Raw Workflow Options set to the smallest size possible. Once you are satisfied with the way the panorama is looking, repeat the command, but at the larger pixel size.

2 After making the required image adjustments for the eight images in Camera Raw, I clicked on the Workflow Options button to change the settings. Prior to doing the full resolution merge, I had tested the images at a lower resolution (the 7.1 MP setting, which is checked above). Since I now wanted to do the final merge, I selected the full 60 MP resolution as well as selecting Pro Photo RGB and 16-bit for the bit depth. I clicked OK to open all eight images into Photoshop.

3 Once I had the eight images opened in Photoshop, I used the Load Layers function from the File ⇨ Scripts ⇨ Load Files into Stack... menu. The Load Layers dialog shown above allowed me to select all of the open images. At this point I decided not to attempt to align the source images nor to create a Smart Object. Eventually I would do both steps, but in the early stages I wanted to maintain the maximum flexibility. The Layers panel on the right shows the resulting layer stack that had yet to be aligned and blended.

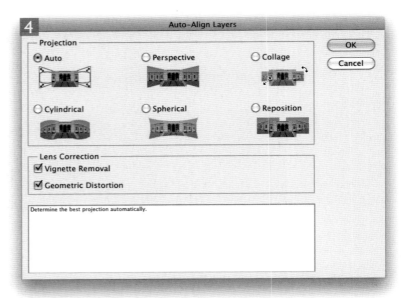

4 Once the images were loaded as layers in Photoshop (and after selecting all the layers as shown in Step 3) I used the Auto-Align Layers command found under the Edit menu. Since I had already corrected the Chromatic Aberration but not the lens distortion or vignetting, I made sure to check those options. I also chose the Auto projection option (even though my tests and natural inclination would be to choose Cylindrical). However, the problem I've found with Auto is that the resulting merge tends to lift up the sides (as you'll see in Step 5). This series of images was shot from a leveled tripod (for image quality reasons) and while I had been pretty careful, as is often the case when doing wide panoramas, the result needed correcting.

5 The Auto-Align command from Step 4 resulted in all of the image layers being transformed into position. The result was a pretty good alignment (although with an arc that would need correcting). The next step would deal with the blending, but not the distortion correction just yet. With all eight layers selected, I chose the Auto-Blend Layers command from the Edit menu.

6 The Auto-Blend Layers command is the third manual step of the three-step Photomerge. Here, I chose the Panorama Blend Method and made sure to check the box for the Seamless Tones and Colors (which is really a fancy phrase for 'to blend really well'). The result was layer masks on each of the eight layers that resulted in an excellent blend of the images. Since the overall images had an upward arc that needed correction, rather than merging the layers I wanted to take the eight layers with their masks and turn them into a Smart Object, retaining the individual layers and masks while allowing me the ability to treat all eight images as a single image. I made sure all eight layers were selected and selected the Convert to Smart Objects command from the Layers ⇨ Smart Objects menu. The resulting Layers panel with the layers turned into a Smart Object is shown above on the right.

7 While you can't do a perspective transform on a Smart Object (without rendering the object), you can use the Warp command found under the Edit ⇨ Transform menu. As shown above, I grabbed the warp transform handles and moved the center up while moving the ends of the image down. The Warp command was able to essentially remove the arc induced by the Auto-Align Layers command. Converting the Layers to Smart Objects maintained full layer and mask editability.

8 After doing the Warp transform, I wanted to confirm the final size of the assembled panorama. The original images were all shot just before sunset in Monument Valley, Utah, with a Phase One 6 x 4.5 camera and a 45 mm lens with a P 65+ 60 MP camera back. In Step 2, I had chosen a resolution of 300 PPI, but I had no idea what the final dimension of the merged image would be. I used the Image Size command from Image menu to alter the dimensions of the image. I deselected the Resample Image option because I didn't want to actually interpolate the image. I set the width to 93″ (the maximum length that the Epson driver can print to on Mac). Since the Resample Image was unchecked, the Resolution changed to 315.075 PPI and the Height ended up as 30.18″.

9 Once the image was sized, I needed to do a few tone and color tweaks for the final image. In the Layers panel on the right, you'll see how I added four graduated adjustment layers. I also added a graduated color blend layer to cool down the top of the sky. The final adjustment was to add a MidTone Contrast layer on top with a mask to keep the midtone contrast boost from affecting the towers' edges. The final assembly is shown below. The image above is at a 100% zoom showing people (who I did see when I shot) watching the sunset. You can just make out the camper off the road in the full shot below.

Photo: © Jeff Schewe

Viewpoint selection

It can, of course, be hard to predict the final outcome of a spherical photomerge, especially if you intend producing an equirectangular projection such as the one shown on page 349. The thing to watch out for is foreground objects appearing too big, unless you intend to make this happen. When shooting an interior it can therefore help to keep the camera viewpoint high to help avoid foreground objects appearing too enlarged.

Figure 9.6 This shows the Absolute 360 Precision head in use.

Figure 9.7 A leveling device is essential for ensuring that the tripod head is as level as possible before you shoot.

Stitching a spherical 360° panorama

When Photomerge was updated for Photoshop CS4, one of the objectives was to improve the ability to stitch together photographs that had been shot using certain fisheye lenses such as the Canon 15 mm lens. With the advent of Photoshop CS5, it is now possible to create successful photomerges with almost any lens. If there is no lens profile available for a particular lens, then it is fairly easy to build one using the Adobe Lens Profile Creator utility. Another thing that has changed is that in Photoshop CS5 you can now achieve more successful photomerges when blending fisheye lens photos that have been shot in 'portrait' mode. I mention all this is as a precursor to the following technique in which I show how you can create a spherical 360° panorama using Photoshop. Now, it has to be said that there are other ways of doing this. In particular, there is a program called PTGui (www.ptgui.com) that most professionals would prefer to use when creating such panoramic images. What I have done here though is to show how you can achieve similar results by using Photoshop CS5 only, based on a technique that was first demonstrated by Russell Brown.

Panorama shooting tips

As you might expect, there are a number of things you need to be aware of when shooting photos to build a panorama. Firstly, you need to use a special tripod head such as the Absolute 360 Precision head, which I used to take these photos (Figure 9.6). This particular head was calibrated for the Canon EOS 1Ds Mk III body plus Canon 15 mm lens so that the central axis position of the lens was centered correctly when rotating the camera in any direction. With a camera lens combination such as this it was necessary to shoot six frames at the precisely marked 60° click stop positions in order to capture the main 360° panoramic view. With this head I was also able to tilt the camera precisely upwards and directly downwards to capture the zenith and nadir viewpoints. With an interior like the one I photographed here I thought it useful to bracket the exposures as well so that I could use Merge to HDR Pro to prepare optimum images for the following Photomerge steps. It is essential that the tripod head is kept absolutely level so that the horizon line will eventually align correctly at either end of the Photomerged result. To this end it is helpful to use a leveling device such as the one seen in Figures 9.6 and 9.7) to make sure that the camera is perfectly level before shooting.

1 This shows a series of photographs that were shot of a church interior at 60° intervals using a Canon EOS 1Ds Mk III camera plus Canon 15 mm fisheye lens, mounted on the Absolute 360 Precision head. I also took one shot pointing upwards and three shots directly downwards, to record the zenith and nadir viewpoints. To create the spherical panorama it was important that I selected only the main panorama shots first.

2 With the above shots selected I chose Tools ⇨ Photoshop ⇨ Photomerge…, which opened the Photomerge dialog shown here, where I selected the Auto Layout option. I also checked the Blend Images Together, Vignette Removal and Geometric Distortion Correction options and clicked OK.

339

3 Since I was processing the shots that were selected in Step 1 at their native size, it took a while for Photoshop to generate the Photomerge panorama. Here you can see how the panorama image is made up of the six auto-blended layers and how it also includes a complete panorama view of the church interior with a fair degree of overlap at either end. At this stage there was no need to worry about the relative positions of the elements in the composition just yet. With this technique you have complete flexibility to centralize the image composition later (see Step 9).

4 I next went to the Layer menu and chose Flatten Image. I now needed to crop the panorama in order to achieve nice, clean edges on the left and right sides. You can do this using the crop tool and, if necessary, select the Image ⇨ Trim… command to make sure the image is trimmed as tightly as possible.

5 I now needed to prepare the image so that it could wrap around on itself. To do this, I first went to the Filter menu and chose Other ⇨ Offset... This allowed me to offset the horizontal axis which, as you can see, highlighted the fact that the left and right edges didn't perfectly match up yet. The main thing to point out here is that it is the Horizontal axis only that needs to be shifted; the Wrap Around option must be selected at the bottom and it doesn't really matter how much you enter here, as long as you offset the image sufficiently to work on correcting the extent of the overlap.

6 Next, I used the ⌘ R / ctrl R shortcut to reveal the rulers and dragged out a guide to align precisely with the point where the overlap occurred. I made a rectangular marquee selection of the right-hand portion of the image up to the guide. I then went to the Layer menu and chose New ⇨ Layer via Copy to make a copy of the selected area. I could now move this copy layer horizontally using the move tool or by selecting the move tool and nudging the layer using the arrow keys.

341

7 The idea here was to position the copy layer so that it aligned perfectly with the opposite edge of the blended panorama image. It is essential that you only nudge the layer left or right. If you remembered to level the tripod head perfectly at the time the photos were taken, the opposite ends should align perfectly. If not, you may want to include an extra step where you drag with the ruler tool across the image to define the correct angle of straightness, then after doing this, click on the Straighten button in the tool Options bar.

8 Once I had done this, I added a layer mask to the copy layer and applied a linear, black to white gradient on the mask in order to fade the edge where the two ends joined. I then cropped the panorama to the outer edge of the copy layer and again flattened the image to produce the version shown here.

9 I now had a perfect 360° Photomerged panorama that would indeed wrap around on itself. I was able to test this by going to the Filter menu and choosing Other ➪ Offset… again. If the end goal is a 2D image rather than a Quicktime® spherical panorama, the second Offset filter Step is crucial here for determining how the panorama looks. For example, here I felt it was important for the altar to be positioned centered in the photograph.

10 I now needed the image to have an exact 2:1 aspect ratio. To do this, I first went to the Image menu, chose Image Size… and entered an even integer value for the image width (and unchecked the Resample Image option to allow the pixel resolution to auto-adjust). I then went to the Image menu again and this time chose Canvas Size… Here, I entered a Height value that was exactly half that of the image's width.

11 OK, we now had a panorama image in which the canvas size had been adjusted to the correct 2:1 aspect ratio, from which one could generate a spherical panorama. At this stage it looked like there was a lot missing from this scene, but if you refer to Step 14, you can see how the equirectangular projection actually exaggerates these missing sections of the panorama.

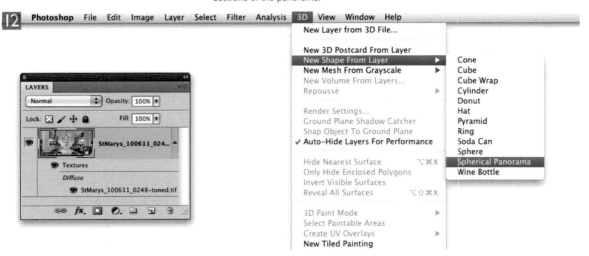

12 At this point I was ready to test the effectiveness of the spherical panorama image I had just created. To do this, I went to the 3D menu, chose New Shape From Layer and selected the Spherical Panorama option.

13 I could now use the 3D zoom tool to zoom out a little and use the 3D rotate tool to navigate the image in Photoshop as a 3D spherical panorama.

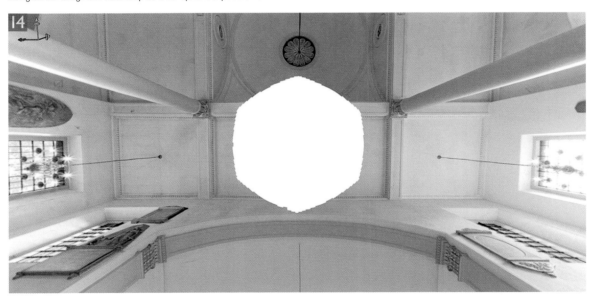

14 There still remained the question of how to fill the ceiling and floor sections of the image. As you can see in this ceiling view, the missing area wasn't so big, but this is where it was important that I had also shot the zenith and nadir viewpoints in order to make the spherical panorama complete.

15 If you refer back to the Bridge folder view shown in Step 1, you'll see that I had shot a zenith view of the ceiling of the church interior. The important thing to point out here is that while this shot was also taken with a fisheye lens, I knew that in order to place it within the 3D view, I would need to remove the geometric distortion. Therefore, the shot you see here was processed in Camera Raw using the new auto lens corrections feature to remove the distortion. I chose Select ⇨ All to select the entire image and then chose Edit ⇨ Copy to copy the selected area.

16 I then used the Edit ⇨ Paste command to paste the selection as a new layer in the 3D Spherical panorama view. However, even though the source image was of the same resolution as all the other photos used in this panorama assembly, it was necessary to use the Edit ⇨ Transform ⇨ Scale command to scale this image up by around 250%. I then carefully nudged the position of this pasted layer so that it matched the remaining image.

17 With this layer scaled and positioned correctly, I added a layer mask filled with black and then used the brush tool with white as the foreground color to paint over the layer mask to gradually reveal the contents. The problem now was that the pasted layer was brighter than the background, so I added a Levels adjustment and clicked the dividing line between the layer and the Levels adjustment to form a clipping group. I then adjusted the Levels gamma slider to make the layer darker (note that I used the Luminosity blend mode to preserve the saturation). I then went to the Layers panel fly-out menu and chose Merge Down, which merged the layer, in this case, rendering it as a 3D object.

18 All I had to do now was to repeat the same steps for the floor view or nadir viewpoint. You are normally advised to make three exposures when photographing the nadir view. You can take one with the camera pointing downwards and then another with the head swung around to the other side. Lastly, it is a good idea to memorize the position of the camera when pointing downwards, remove it from the tripod and make a further hand-held shot as best you can. With these three (auto-lens corrected) photographs it should be possible to create a view with the tripod, tripod head and photographer removed from the scene.

19 I placed the three photographs shown in Step 18 as layers, selected all the layers (⌘ A ctrl A), chose Edit ➪ Auto-Align Layers... and clicked OK to the Panorama option. This aligned the layers precisely. I then applied layer masks to the upper two layers so that I could end up with the image you see here, where the tripod legs and head had successfully been removed. I then flattened the image, made a selection of the floor area and chose Edit ➪ Copy to copy the selection contents. To be honest, when it comes to editing a photo like this in Photoshop, the hand-held shot would have sufficed. However, if you are using a program like PTGui to build the panorama, it is advisable to carry out these extra steps.

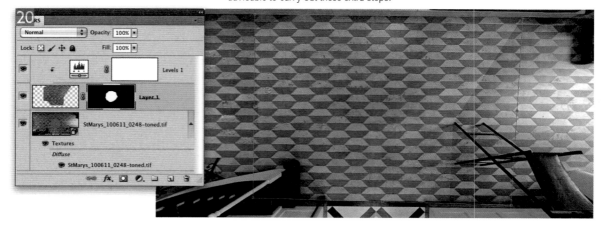

20 I then repeated Steps 16 and 17, pasting the floor selection as a new layer in the 3D spherical panorama view. Again, I scaled and rotated the pasted layer so that the floor pattern matched and applied a layer mask to reveal the layer over the center portion of the image only. When I was happy with the placement I adjusted the brightness of the pasted layer using Levels. Then, I went to the Layers panel fly-out menu and chose Merge Down.

21 I now had a complete 3D spherical panorama image that had been created entirely within Photoshop. Lastly, I double-clicked on the background in the Layers panel (circled) to reopen the 2D version of the image. The top view shows the image previewed as a complete panorama. Here you can see how the floor and ceiling sections have been added top and bottom, but you'll also notice the zig-zag edge Photoshop leaves top and bottom. In terms of how this image can function as an exported spherical panorama Quicktime movie, it's not such a big problem, but still not as neat a result as, say, a PTGui export. If, on the other hand, you wish to present a 2D flat view, then I reckon it is usually best to crop such images top and bottom anyway.

Quicktime® exports

To prepare for an export as a Quicktime VR or Flash movie, you'll need to edit the 3D view version by applying a fixed pixel value crop. There is also a Flash version of this image available to view on the DVD (with help from Rod Wynne-Powell).

349

How to create an aerial fisheye lens effect

Music fans of a certain age (especially those who liked progressive rock) may remember the band Yes, whose cover artwork would often feature the imaginary planet worlds of Roger Dean. This shows a simple way you can transform a panoramic photograph into an aerial fisheye view of a scene. I would definitely regard this as a novelty effect, but it is nonetheless a fun experiment to carry out and you never know when a client will ask you to come up with a quirky approach to a brief. For example, I have seen this technique being used in a recent UK ad campaign.

1 I began by selecting a group of photographs in Bridge which when merged together using Photomerge would produce a 360° panoramic image. To do this, I went to the Tools menu in Bridge and chose Photoshop ⇨ Photomerge… I then blended the layered photos together using the methods described earlier in this chapter to produce the flattened panorama shown below.

2 I flattened the image, cropped the skyline tightly and used the Image Size dialog to stretch the photograph and make it into a square image (note the Constrain Proportions box was left unchecked). I then went to the Image menu and chose Rotate Canvas ⇨ 180°. This prepared the image for the final step.

3 I went to the Filter menu, where I chose Distort ⇨ Polar Cooordinates and clicked on the Rectangular to Polar option. This produced the finished result shown here, where all I did was to crop the photograph slightly and use the healing brush and clone stamp tools to retouch out the single join line that ran from the top to the center of the photograph.

Photo: © Martin Evening

351

Chapter 10

Cooking with Photoshop

Taking your Photoshop skills to the next level

We are now ready to show you what you can do in Photoshop to push the boundaries a little and become a true Photoshop expert. As with some of the earlier techniques, it is not just about what you can do in Photoshop to enhance your photos – some of what we describe here, such as the Photomerge techniques, requires some planned shooting beforehand. The main message in this chapter is to show you just a few of the ways you can use Photoshop as your digital darkroom.

Moral rights

UK copyright law allows the copyright owner to assert what is known as their 'moral rights'. These include the right to be identified as the author of a work (although this must be asserted and is not automatic), plus the right to object to the derogatory treatment of a work. USA copyright law doesn't include this clause, but the 1990 Visual Artists Rights Act, 17 USC § 106A does give authors 'rights of integrity' which amounts to the same kind of protection against prejudicial distortion of a work.

1 Here you can see the original photograph shot of a harbor entrance. To prepare this photograph for content-aware scaling, I first needed to choose Select ⇨ All (⌘ A ctrl A) to prepare the image for a content-aware scale transform. It doesn't matter if the image is flattened and has a Background layer or, as in this case, has a single normal layer.

Content-aware scaling

The Content-Aware Scale feature was arguably one of the more interesting, and some might say, controversial new features that was first added in Photoshop CS4. As you can see here, you can use content-aware scaling to radically adjust the aspect ratio of some photographs, but without squashing or stretching important subject matter within the picture. Yes, this may be a contentious tool if used inappropriately and without permission of the copyright holder, but we feel it may prove very useful to design and advertising photographers. For example, most ads and design layouts are required to fit several different aspect ratios such as posters, magazine layouts and web banners. This tool allows you to easily modify a single photograph to fit various aspect ratio layouts.

2 I then went to the Edit menu and chose Content-Aware Scale (or I could have used the ⌘ ⌥ Shift C ctrl alt Shift C keyboard shortcut). This applied a bounding box to the image and allowed me to drag the right-hand side handle inwards to compress the picture horizontally. You'll notice in this screen shot how the content-aware scaling feature cleverly compressed all the soft areas of detail such as the harbor wall and the sea, while preserving the detailed subjects such as the lighthouse and boats.

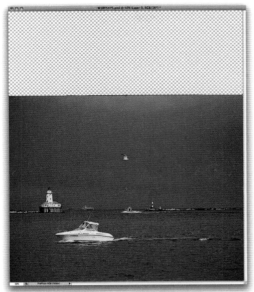

3 After I had applied the first content-aware scale transform I selected the crop tool to apply a crop to the photograph where I dragged the top handle of the crop bounding box upwards and clicked OK, in order to add more canvas area to the top of the picture. I once more chose Edit ⇨ Content-Aware Scale so that I could apply a second transform to the photograph.

4 Here you can see the result of the second content-aware scale transform, in which I dragged the top handle of the transform bounding box upwards to make the image fill the full height of the picture. What is interesting about this feature is the way that the content-aware scale transform appears to automatically recognize objects where the shape needs to be preserved, while compressing or stretching the areas that are of less importance. You'll also notice in this example how the content-aware scale transform preserved the position of the horizon and stretched the sky only.

Content-aware scaling – another use

Even without resorting to masking, the Content-Aware Scale feature can do remarkable transforms. However, it can also be used to remove things (or people) from a scene. In the example below a horizontal image has been transformed into a strong vertical proportion. In the third step a mask is used to eliminate the model.

1 To prepare this photograph for content-aware scaling, I first selected all of the layer contents on the Background layer (⌘ A ctrl A) to target the image for transforming. I then went to the Edit menu and chose Content-Aware Scale (⌘ ⌥ Shift C ctrl alt Shift C). I applied a normal content-aware scaling and was able to make the horizontal image into a vertical. I then tried making a wider image. That also worked well. These are both are examples of extreme scaling.

356

2 I wondered how the Protect skin tones option for protection would work on this image. I clicked on the option and as is often the case for full-length images, Protect skin tones did indeed protect the skin of the model, but not so much her body. The protected skin (above left) was clearly better than the unprotected skin tone option (above right).

3 Going back to the original image, I entered Quick Mask mode and created a rough outline using a hard-edged brush. This mask could be used to trigger content-aware scaling to squeeze this portion to remove it (more or less). So, after going to the Edit menu and choosing Content-Aware Scale, I selected the Quick Mask from the tool Options bar drop-down menu before applying the transform.

4 I dragged the transform handle on both the left and the right towards the middle. As is often the case when removing objects, a tiny remnant remained that required fixing. Now with Photoshop CS5's Content-Aware Fill, fixing such artifacts is less of a chore.

5 I used the marquee tool to select the area that needed the Content-Aware Fill. I then used the Fill command found in the Edit menu and selected Content-Aware from the drop-down menu.

6 When I zoomed in; I noticed a few things that Content-Aware Fill hadn't handled too well (above left). So, I used a combination of the healing brush and clone stamp to get rid of some of the duplicated shapes and other artifacts.

7 The last step was to crop off the building on the right because I found it distracting (personally, I actually like the shot with the model better, but this was a useful demo).

Digital darkroom effects

Advanced black and white conversion

Given the advances in the abilities of Camera Raw and Photoshop to do excellent black and white conversions, you might think that doing a manual conversion would be an anachronism. But there are times when a global conversion from color to black and white is less than optimal and this technique may prove effective. In order to understand the following approach it's important to understand that red, green and blue (RGB) images are, in fact, three flavors of black and white combined into a single composite image. The Red channel is the equivalent to being filtered by a Kodak Wratten 29 tri-color separation filter. The Green channel is a 61 while the blue is a 47. So with every RGB color image you already have three potential black and white conversions (the basis of this is what Photoshop's Black and White adjustment is based on). With a simple color to Lab conversion you can also access the Lightness channel, which brings the total to four (see Figure 10.1).

Figure 10.1 Above is the original RGB color image. Below are the Red, Green, Blue and Lightness channels that can be used for a black and white conversion.

The Red channel

The Green channel

The Blue channel

The Lightness channel

1 In this step I targeted the Red channel of the original color document (above left) and chose Select ⇨ Select All (⌘ A ctrl A). I then copied the channel to the clipboard (⌘ C ctrl C). In order to get the color channel information into a grayscale document I duplicated the original image (on the left) and converted the copy (on the right) to grayscale using the Image ⇨ Mode ⇨ Grayscale command.

2 Next, I targeted the grayscale copy image and pasted from the clipboard (⌘ V ctrl V). This took what was the Red channel and pasted it as a grayscale layer. I named this the 'red' layer (so I could keep track of which channel the layer was from). I added a Hide All layer mask by holding the ⌥ alt key and clicking on the new layer mask icon. I repeated the process for each subsequent channel/layer pairing including the Lightness channel. To get the Lightness channel I converted the RGB image to Lab using the Image ⇨ Mode ⇨ Lab Color command. From this point, it was merely a matter of deciding which layer had the best black and white image data on it and painting into the layer mask with white to make it visible. The layer stack shows the current Background layer, which is the Photoshop default grayscale conversion. For those interested, Photoshop's default conversion is a calculation based upon blending approximately 30% of the Red channel, 60% of the Green channel and 10% of the Blue channel. Using that as a basis, I could decide what percent of which channel would end up giving the optimal conversion – and the advantage is that I could do so locally with layer masks. But wait… there's more!

3 The image above had the final layer blending via layer masks shown in the layer stack. The one area where the layer blending failed to provide an optimum conversion was in the numbers on the door. Since I still had the color image open, I could use Select ⇨ Color Range to select the color of the numbers.

4 Using Color Range on the color image, I selected the door numbers. I used a high fuzziness setting and also used the Localized Color Clusters option (which first appeared in Photoshop CS4). With the selection active (left figure) I selected the marquee tool and started to drag the selection. Once I started the drag, I held down the **Shift** key before dropping the selection on the grayscale image (on the right). Holding down the **Shift** key instructs Photoshop to pin register the selection. Since the color and grayscale images had the exact same pixel dimensions, the selection was dropped exactly in the grayscale image where it started in the color image.

5 Using the selection of the numbers I added a Levels adjustment layer to darken the numbers in the image. As far as the color to black and white conversion is concerned I was done. However, the thing about black and white in the darkroom is that black and white wasn't really all about black and white, there was often color toning done to the silver gelatin print. The next and final step is done after reconverting the image from grayscale back to RGB to add color.

6 This is the final result. I added a Hue/Saturation adjustment layer set to the Colorize option and a hue of 49 (amber) and a Saturation of only 5. The top Color Balance adjustment was used to give the color a split toned look. Using the Highlights tone I adjusted the yellow/blue slider to −7 (warming) then used the Shadows tone to move the yellow/blue slider to +7 (cooling). This split tone is similar to the old sepia tone from the chemical darkroom.

Cross-processing

The cross-processing technique has long been popular among fashion and portrait photographers for distorting the colors in a picture and bleaching out the skin tone detail. There are two basic cross-processing methods: E-6 transparency film processed in C-41 chemicals and C-41 negative film processed in E-6 chemicals.

You can simulate cross-processing effects quite easily in Photoshop and do so without the risk of 'overdoing' the effect or losing important image detail. One simple way to cross-process an image is to use the Split Toning panel sliders found in Camera Raw working with a raw, a JPEG or a flattened TIFF image (see Figure 10.2). This is a fast and effective method and the Balance slider gives you that extra level of control whereby you can adjust the bias between the shadow and highlight coloring effects.

The technique that's shown over the next two pages aims to replicate the cross-curve effect you typically get when using a

Figure 10.2 Here you can see an example of how to use the Split Toning sliders in Camera Raw to apply a color cross-processing effect to a raw or flattened TIFF image.

C-41 film processed in E-6. In this example you'll notice how I managed to make the shadows bluer and gave the highlights a yellow/red cast. This is a technique that I have adapted over the years so as to make it more flexible. As with all the other coloring effects described in this chapter, the main coloring adjustments are applied as adjustment layers using the Color blend mode. This helps preserve the original luminosity, but if you want to simulate the high contrast cross-processed look, then use the Normal blend mode instead. In addition to this, you might want to consider deliberately increasing the contrast in the RGB composite channel (this also boosts the color saturation). You may also wish to experiment with using different color fills and layer opacities.

1 Here are the steps used to create a cross-processing effect that simulates C-41 film processed in E-6 chemicals. You can adapt this technique by using different channel Curve adjustments and different fill colors.

Luminance blending tip

One way to preserve the luminosity in an image is to always set the 'coloring' adjustment layer to the Color blend mode. Some techniques described in this chapter involve a series of extreme image adjustments or multiple adjustment layers. Therefore, if you are not careful, you may lose important highlight and shadow detail. One solution to this is to make a copy of the original Background layer and place it at the top of the layer stack, and set the layer blending mode to Luminosity. This will produce the same result as setting a single adjustment layer to Color mode, but by adjusting the layer opacity of the duplicate layer in Luminosity mode you can restore varying amounts of the original image luminance.

Double-click in this area
of the layer to open the
Layer Style dialog.

4 I then double-clicked the Color fill layer and adjusted the Underlying Layer blend
options. I ⟲ alt-clicked on the Underlying Layer shadow point triangle slider and
dragged to separate the dividers, splitting them in two, and dragged the right-hand
shadows slider (circled) across to the right.

5 Here you can see the finished result in which
I had created a transitional blend between the
underlying layers and the yellow Color fill
layer above.

Lab Color effects

Here is another type of Photoshop cross-processing effect which involves making use of the Lab Color mode to distort the colors in a photograph. This is not a cross-processing effect per se, but this technique can certainly allow you to mess with the colors in your images in some pretty interesting ways. I would suggest that this effect is best applied to medium or high resolution images and that the source image should be fairly free of artifacts. As you will see at the end of this tutorial in Step 7, I found that you can also create some interesting variations if you invert the layers that are used to create the coloring effect.

1 To start with I opened an RGB image and created a duplicate copy by choosing Image ⇨ Duplicate... I then converted the duplicate image to Lab Color mode by choosing Image ⇨ Mode ⇨ Lab Color. The Lab Color image contained a Lightness channel plus **a** and **b** color channels. I went to the Channels panel and selected the **a** channel first.

2 I then chose Image ⇨ Adjustments ⇨ Equalize, which expanded the channel contrast of the **a** channel. Next, I clicked on the Lab composite channel in the Channels panel (it is essential you remember to do this so that all three channels are selected again) and copied the enhanced image across to the original image as a new layer. You can do this by choosing Select ⇨ All, then copy and pasting the image contents. Or, you can select the move tool and drag the Lab image across to the original RGB version image. Make sure that you hold down the *Shift* key as you do so, as this ensures that the layer is centered when you let go of the mouse (there is no need to worry about the color mode mismatch: Photoshop automatically converts the image data back to RGB mode again as you copy it across). I set the blend mode for the Lab copied layer to Color and set the layer opacity to 30%.

3 This Lab coloring technique can sometimes generate ugly pixel artifacts, so I chose Filter ⇨ Blur ⇨ Surface Blur and applied a 5 pixel Radius blur using a Threshold of 100 levels. This blur filter treatment softened the image, of course, but because the new layer was added using the Color blend mode, the blur simply smoothed the color information on this layer and this had no adverse effect on the detail, since it did not alter the luminance.

4 I returned to the Lab copy image and went back one step in the History panel to the point where I had just converted the duplicate image to Lab mode. I now selected the **b** channel and once again applied an equalize image adjustment and copied the newly enhanced composite Lab image across to the original RGB version of the image.

5 The new layer appeared as Layer 2 in the layer stack and I once more set the blend mode to Color and the opacity to 30%, and applied the same Surface Blur filter treatment to the newly added image layer.

6 Here is the finished result. As you can see, when using the Lab Color cross-process method you end up with two brightly colored, semi-transparent layers. The fun starts when you adjust the relative opacity of each of these two layers to obtain different coloring effects.

7 In a further twist, I applied an Image ⇨ Adjustments ⇨ Invert adjustment to both of the coloring layers. This allowed me to produce an interesting color variation.

Photo: © Martin Evening

Black and white infrared film

Black and white infrared film emulsions are predominantly sensitive to infrared radiation. Vegetation in particular reflects a lot of infrared light, which is beyond the scope of human vision. Hence, green foliage will appear very bright and almost iridescent when captured on black and white infrared film.

Simulating the black and white infrared look

I first invented the black and white infrared technique some 10 years ago when I was asked to come up with different ways to convert a color image to black and white. I initially started out with a Photoshop method, which relied on the use of a Channel Mixer adjustment to boost the Green channel in the grayscale mix. Since then I have had the opportunity to make various improvements and more recently I have found that the Lightroom and Camera Raw approach now offers the best approach when creating the black and white infrared look. This is especially true now that you can apply a negative Clarity adjustment, which simulates the soft glow look that is so typical of black and white infrared photography. The following steps were all carried out using a raw capture file. To get the best results I suggest you work with a raw original, but you could use the same steps described here to process a JPEG or flattened TIFF image.

1 I chose this particular photograph to work with because it contained a lot of green foliage and was therefore an ideal subject for the black and white infrared treatment.

2 I began by adjusting the White Balance. Here, you can see that I adjusted the Temperature slider by taking it all the way to the right to make the image warmer and dragged the Tint slider all the way to the left in order to exaggerate the greens.

3 I then went to the HSL/Grayscale panel and checked the Convert to Grayscale box. I applied a manual Grayscale Mix adjustment, where I raised the Yellows and Greens to +100 and set the Aquas to +75. This lightened the green, yellow and aqua colors.

4 I now needed to go back to the Basic panel and make some corrective adjustments to the Exposure, Recovery, Fill Light, Blacks, Brightness and Contrast sliders. More importantly, I applied a negative Clarity adjustment, which created the soft glow effect that is so typical of black and white infrared photographs.

5 I then went to the Tone Curve panel and applied the parametric curve shape shown here, where I steepened the curve shape in the highlights to increase the highlight contrast.

6 I then went to the Split Toning panel to apply a color toning effect. Lastly, I added a grainy infrared film look, using the Grain sliders in the Effects panel.

7 This shows the final photograph, which was cropped slightly in Photoshop.

Origins of solarization

In this original photographic darkroom technique, associated with the artist Man Ray, the print paper is briefly fogged towards the end of its development.

Black and white solarization

Here is another Photoshop technique that has evolved into one that can now be done using Camera Raw. Ideally, you should use this method to edit raw originals, but it can also be made to work with JPEGs or flattened TIFFs.

The original Photoshop method was quite simple: you applied a Curves adjustment, clicked on the pencil button to switch to draw mode and created an inverted V-shaped curve. The Camera Raw method is similar. In the example shown here, I went to the Point curve editor in the Tone Curve panel, added three points to the curve and dragged the top right point down to the bottom right corner. This allowed me to create the inverted 'V' shape shown in Step 4. The best thing about using Camera Raw to solarize an image is that when you revisit the Basic panel you can readjust the main sliders there and this allows you to further modify the solarization effect. You will notice here that I opened the Camera Raw processed image as a Smart Object, which allowed me to create two versions of the original master and then blend the two together using a pixel layer mask.

1 As with the previous example, this technique was carried out on a raw original photograph, although you could get this to work equally well using a JPEG or flattened TIFF image.

2 I began by converting the photograph to black and white and adjusted the HSL/ Grayscale and Basic panel settings to achieve an optimum grayscale image from the color original. When I was happy with these settings I held down the *Shift* key to change the Open Image button to Open Object and clicked to open the photo as a Smart Object in Photoshop.

3 On the left is a Layers panel view of the Camera Raw Smart Object layer. I made a copy of this layer by going to the Layer menu and choosing Smart Objects ➪ New Smart Object via Copy. Note that you can also access this menu item by right-mouse clicking on the Smart Object layer and selecting New Smart Object via Copy from the contextual menu (Mac users who don't have a two-button mouse will have to hold down the *ctrl* key to access this menu). I made sure that the copy Smart Object layer was now selected so that the following steps were applied to this layer only.

4 I went to the Tone Curve panel, selected the Point curve editor option and made the inverted 'V' curve shape you see here to create the solarized look.

5 I then switched to the Basic panel and adjusted the tone controls to further modify the effect. This is where using the Camera Raw controls really gives you the edge, as adjusting the Exposure, Recovery and Fill Light sliders can make an enormous difference to the solarized effect. Note also that the behavior of these sliders is different in CS5.

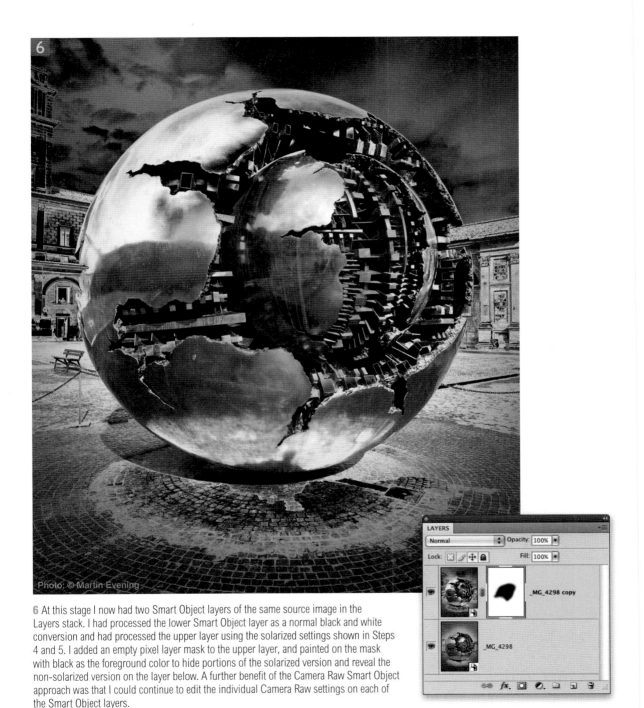

6

Photo: © Martin Evening

6 At this stage I now had two Smart Object layers of the same source image in the Layers stack. I had processed the lower Smart Object layer as a normal black and white conversion and had processed the upper layer using the solarized settings shown in Steps 4 and 5. I added an empty pixel layer mask to the upper layer, and painted on the mask with black as the foreground color to hide portions of the solarized version and reveal the non-solarized version on the layer below. A further benefit of the Camera Raw Smart Object approach was that I could continue to edit the individual Camera Raw settings on each of the Smart Object layers.

Coloring an object

It's not at all unusual for the color of things to be wrong even when the overall color is fine. So, the ability to alter or add color to an object is useful. In this case the image was prepared for a paper company that wanted to promote themselves as 'chameleons' in the paper biz (hey, we don't get to control the ad concepts). So the mandate was to use examples of their paper: fine writing paper, cardboard and even brown wrapping paper, and a chameleon. So, I hired a chameleon wrangler, made a model with paper and did the shots to combine. When working with animals, I've found it's a really good idea to want the animal to do what it does naturally (it's real hard to keep it from what it wants to do). For this assignment I shot the chameleon first, made the image pick and built the set around where the chameleon would be placed, as shown in Figure 10.3. The coloring on the lizard would be done in Photoshop.

Figure 10.3 These are the scans of the original 4 x 5 film shots. The chameleon's name was Fred and when placed on the set naturally he assumed the color of the cardboard (which was a good thing because he was green when he was first removed from his box and that would have been more work to fix). The figure on the right shows the set that was built after picking the main image. The 'leaves' were placed strategically to allow putting Fred on the 'branch'.

1 The first step was to composite the lizard (Fred) in place. Well, actually there were a lot of steps prior to getting to this stage such as creating a path around Fred and various retouching done on the two scans. But this is where we're starting from here. The layer stack shows the three layers that made up the shadows plus Fred.

2 The next step was to create the channels. The path of the chameleon was turned into a selection and saved to make the channel on the left. The channel was duplicated and the channel on the right was hand painted to reveal only the areas where the color would be added later.

3 The Lizard color mask channel was loaded as a selection using Select ⇨ Load Selection and the eyedropper tool was selected to choose the color to fill. The client wanted to use a color close to the writing paper so I sampled an area to arrive at the color. I then added a Solid Color fill layer from the layers panel icon using the foreground color that had just been selected.

4 The color fill layer's blending mode needed to be set to Color to only alter the color of the underlying image. The color blend mode contains both the hue and the saturation information (it's actually a combination of both) but not luminance. Filling (or painting) using a color blend is the trick to changing the color of an object. You can do it radically as in this example or you can paint or fill it in with a low opacity for more subtle effects.

5 Here the color fill had been accomplished. A slight Levels adjustment layer was put on top to tweak the color of the fill. This step shows a trick I use when dealing with art directors who have a habit of changing their minds (and sometimes the layout): non-destructive cropping. Rather than actually crop the image pixels (until the last moment), I used a channel with the channel options set to a Color of white and an 80% Opacity (sometimes it's at 100%). The advantage is you can see the whole image and the live area but only crop at the end. You can even transform the size and the location (don't rotate – that doesn't work) then simply load the crop channel as a selection and choose Image ⇨ Crop.

6 This shows the final composite, coloring, crop and butt fix. Fred had an 'issue' that had to be addressed by retouching on a separate layer.

Coloring effects using Match Color

The Match Color adjustment is available from the Image Adjustments menu and is mainly designed to allow you to match the colors in one image with those in a source image. For example, if you have two separate shots of an important product where the colors need to match, you can use Match Color to get these to match exactly. However, you can also use the Match Color adjustment in a creative way to sample colors from a source image, and apply these to other, completely different photos. This technique can produce interesting and sometimes unusual-looking results.

In Step 2 you will notice that I used the Equalize command to balance out the Match Color sample image before I saved the statistics. This can help you achieve a statistics file that can be used as a colorize adjustment, but without disrupting the tonal balance of the destination images. However, you may still need to make further adjustments in the Image Options section, using the Luminance, Color Intensity and Fade sliders.

If you are interested in using this technique then you might perhaps consider creating a library of Match Color statistics settings. Open up a bunch of images and save out different Match Color settings which you can then use on other images.

1 To demonstrate the following technique, I opened a photograph where the colors in the original scene were fairly muted.

blue–yellow cobbles.sta

2 Next, I needed to create a Match Color settings file. To do this, I opened the sample image shown on the right and chose Image ⇨ Adjustments ⇨ Equalize. This step was done to ensure that the tones ended up more evenly distributed. You don't have to apply this step, but it can help you produce a better Match Color statistics file. I then chose Image ⇨ Adjustments ⇨ Match Color and clicked on the Save Statistics… button (circled) to save this as a Match Color statistics setting.

3 I opened the image shown in Step 1, chose Image ⇨ Adjustments ⇨ Match Color again, then clicked on the Load Statistics… button and selected the previously saved Match Color setting. I then fine-tuned the Match Color settings. I set the Luminance to 70%, the Color Intensity to 75% and the Fade to 70% and clicked OK to apply the adjustment.

Match Color auto adjustments

The Match Color image adjustment can also function as an auto color correction tool for images that have a heavy color cast.

In the following tutorial you'll see how Match Color can be very effective at removing a deep blue/cyan cast from an underwater photograph. You can always try using the Image ⇨ Adjustments ⇨ Auto Color adjustment in Photoshop to remove such casts, but Match Color's ability to neutralize tricky subjects is usually more impressive. It's not just the fact that a Match Color neutralize is generally more effective, you also have the ability to use the Image Options sliders to moderate a Match Color neutralize adjustment. For example, if you use Match Color to auto-correct images with heavy casts this can result in images that have less overall saturation. You may therefore sometimes want to adjust the Color Intensity in the Match Color Image Options section in order to compensate for the lost saturation. In addition to this you can adjust the luminance of the image and fade the overall adjustment.

1 The Match Color image adjustment is a useful image correction tool in its own right. In this extreme example, I used the Match Color adjustment to remove the strong blue/cyan cast seen in this photograph taken by Jeff in his scuba diving days!

2 To do this, I went to the Image menu, chose Adjustments ⇨ Match Color and checked the Neutralize option (circled). This helped remove most of the color cast in the photograph.

3 Step 2 did quite an impressive job of removing most of the deep blue color. However, I felt that it would be useful to moderate the adjustment slightly. First of all, I raised the Luminance to +150%, which essentially lightened the photo. Since the photograph had now been neutralized, there wasn't an awful lot of color saturation left in the image, so for this reason I raised the Color Intensity to +200%. Lastly, I moved the Fade slider slightly to the right in order to fade the neutralize adjustment and restore a little more of the original color. The final result is a picture that still looks like an underwater photograph, but with more of a neutral color feel and perhaps a little closer to how Jeff perceived the original scene when he shot this picture.

Using Camera Calibration to distort colors

The Camera Calibration panel in Camera Raw is really intended for fine-tuning the color calibration of a camera and getting the Camera Raw processed colors to match as closely as possible to the colors in the original scene. However, one of the interesting things you can also do with the Camera Calibration panel is to deliberately mess up the colors in an image to create unusual color effects.

To achieve the result you see here I mostly adjusted the Hue and Saturation sliders in the Camera Calibration panel, taking the sliders to their extremes. If you want, you can link these adjustments with further modifications to the Temperature and Tint white balance sliders in the Basic panel, not to mention the Split Tone panel controls as well. Once you find a calibrate setting that you are happy with and would like to reuse on other images, it is a good idea to save this as a custom setting.

1 This shows a normal version of a raw image that had been opened up in Camera Raw, where all I had done so far was to set a custom white balance in order to achieve neutral-looking colors and had adjusted the other settings to achieve a corrected tone balance.

2 In this version I went to the Camera Calibration panel and adjusted the sliders as shown here to produce a color infrared type look.

3 Once I was happy with the Camera Calibration adjustment I clicked on the Presets panel and then clicked on the New Preset button (circled) to save the setting as a Camera Calibration only preset, which could be accessed again in the future.

Softening the focus

Fog effect

You can use the technique described here to create soft focus effects. Because this method makes use of Smart Filters you can reduce the Smart Filters opacity as necessary to restore more of the original image sharpness and thereby fade the effect. Alternatively, if you paint on the Smart Filters layer mask, you can fill or add paint to the mask and apply the soft focus effect selectively.

1 Here is a woodland forest scene that is in fact an HDR blend, converted to a low dynamic range image. The first step was to go to the Filter menu and choose Convert for Smart Filters. This changed the Background layer into a Layer 0 layer with a Smart Object icon in the bottom right corner.

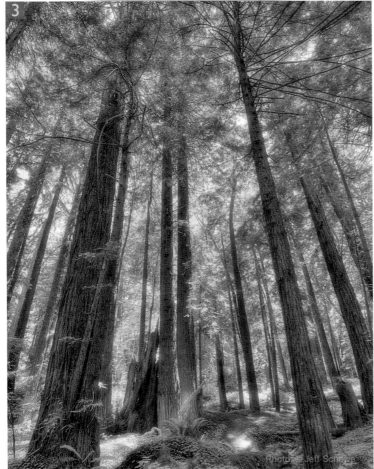

2 I then went to the Filter menu again, chose Blur ⇨ Gaussian Blur and selected an 8 pixel Radius. It didn't matter too much which setting I applied here, since a Smart Object layer will allow you the flexibility to re-edit the filter settings any time you want.

3 Here you can see the Layers panel with the Gaussian Blur Smart Filter layer applied to the image layer. To produce the soft focus lens effect seen here, I double-clicked on the Gaussian Blur filter blending options (circled), changed the Mode to Screen and reduced the Opacity to 70%. The Screen blend mode is ideal if you want the blow-out soft focus look. Otherwise, I suggest you try using the Lighten mode instead.

Figure 10.4 Here you can see the lighting setup that was used to capture the photograph shown here.

1 To demonstrate this technique, I started with a black and white studio portrait (see Figure 10.4). I went to the Filter menu and chose Convert for Smart Filters to convert the Background layer to a Smart Object layer.

2 I then went to the Filter menu and chose Blur ⇨ Gaussian Blur. I entered a 20 Radius blur here, but again, the amount doesn't really matter as with this technique you can re-edit the blur setting at any time.

Diffused printing effect

Here is a variation of the previous technique that can be used to simulate a traditional darkroom diffuse printing effect. As I mention at the end, for optimum quality it is best to do this with an image that starts out in 16-bits per channel mode.

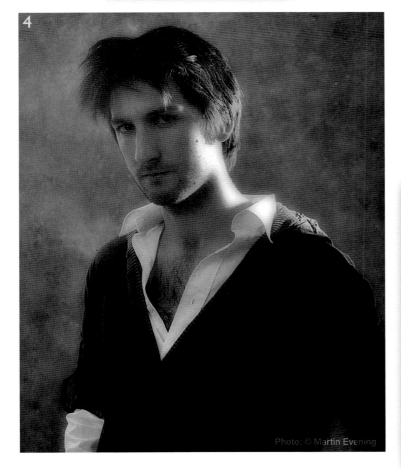

Photo: © Martin Evening

3 I followed this by double-clicking the Blending options icon (circled in Step 2) and set the Mode to Multiply. As you can see, choosing Multiply really darkened the image. You could try lowering the Opacity so that the image doesn't end up quite so dark, or you could try using the Darken blend mode at around 50%, which will also produce a gentler effect.

4 In this example, I left the Opacity at 100%, then went to the Image menu and chose Adjustments ➪ Shadows/Highlights using the settings shown below. Now the Multiply blend mode plus the Shadows/Highlights adjustment are in some ways canceling each other out here, but if the image you are editing has started out in 16-bits per channel, you should still end up with a smooth histogram.

Adding progressive blurs

Sometimes an overall blur isn't what's called for in an image. I like to add multiple blur layers and use a layer mask to paint in or out the blur effect. It's quick and easy to do, as in this example. Here I shot Martin's daughter Angelica with her grandmother Hannah in the background. The shot is nice but the visual complexity of Martin's office is a distraction.

1 This shows the original shot of Angelica with the camera lying on the floor.

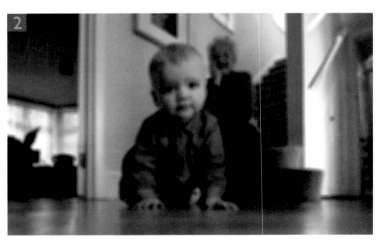

2 I duplicated the background layer and used Filter ➪ Blur ➪ Box Blur at a radius of 15 pixels. I then made a Hide all layer mask by holding the ⌥ alt key and clicked on the Add layer mask button. This way I could paint the blur in, not out.

3 Using a very large brush while zoomed out, I painted with white into the layer mask. I did a little touch-up work in the center area by painting with a smaller brush set to black to remove some excess blur effect. I then repeated the entire process of duplicating the background layer and adding another blur layer with a Box Blur of 30 this time. I prefer the Box Blur to regular Gaussian Blur because I like the bokeh (the out of focus look) it produces. It's also a lot quicker than using the Lens Blur (and simpler; I like simple).

4 This is the result with the multiple blurs added. Note that the second blur layer's mask cuts down on the opacity of the second blur. The blur 1 layer mask also shows the close work done to keep the blur effect off Angelica and Hannah. The final version here is slightly cropped to hide the bathroom door on the right and a bit more of Martin's messy office (even if it is blurred down).

Image border effects

Adding a border to an image

Here is a simple two-step technique for adding a new border to an image in Photoshop. For the following steps I used a scan of a black and white photograph that had a typical Polaroid™ border.

For those who don't know, the Polaroid company used to make black and white instant print film such as Type 55 or Type 665. The tear-off portion contained a usable negative which, when stripped from the positive print after processing, needed a bath of 18% sodium sulfite to remove the black coating on the back and other gunk. The border picture below shows the characteristic edges that you would get when making a darkroom print from such a Polaroid negative. I mention all this in case you feel like creating your own 'real' border images. Polaroid no longer manufactures the instant print films that they were once famous for, but if you hunt around you may still be able to get hold of old supplies of this material. Otherwise, feel free to use the sample image that is supplied on the DVD, or you could try using any other type of border such as the Clouds filter border effect demonstrated on pages 400–401.

1 I began here with the photo on the left, which was the picture I wanted to apply the border effect to, plus a second photograph which was a scan made from a print of a Polaroid™ processed border.

2 To prepare the Polaroid border image, I selected the rectangular marquee tool and carefully dragged inside the border area to define the inside area and, with white as the foreground color, used `⌥ Delete` `alt Delete` to fill the selection area with white. This cleared the inside area of the border frame and prepared it for use later in Step 4.

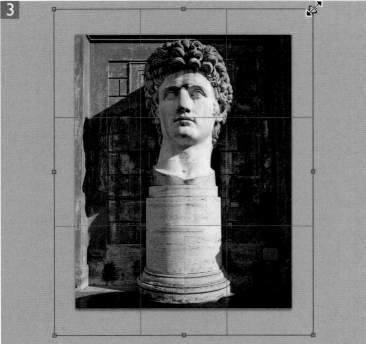

3 I now selected the main photograph and set the foreground/background color to the default setting so that white was the background color. I expanded the window size to show more of the canvas surrounding area. I then selected the crop tool and dragged to first select the whole of the image. I then held down the `⌥` `alt` key as I dragged on a corner handle to expand the crop size. This is a quick way to expand the canvas area of an image, while keeping the crop centered. I then hit `Enter` to apply the crop.

4 I now had the main photograph (with a white border) plus the expanded Polaroid border scan open in Photoshop. I selected the move tool, clicked on the border image and dragged it across to the other photograph. As I did so, I held down the *Shift* key so that the border image was placed as a new layer, centered in the image.

5 I then changed the blending mode of the Polaroid layer to Multiply to merge the border layer with the underlying Background layer. Because the central portion of the layer was filled with white, this part of the layer (and any other white areas) appeared transparent. Once I had done this, I selected Edit ⇒ Free Transform to scale the border image layer so that it neatly overlaid the image below.

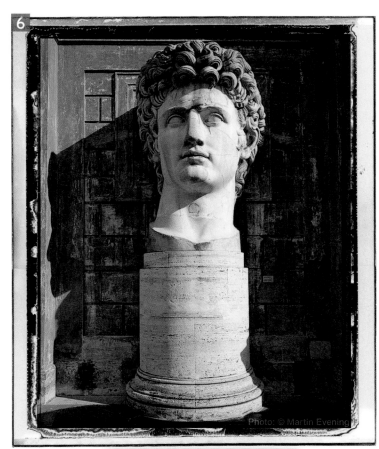

6

Photo: © Martin Evening

6 To remove the surplus border I went to the Image menu and chose Trim... I used the settings shown below to trim the image size based on the Top Left Pixel color (although Bottom Right would have worked just as well). Lastly, I added a Curves adjustment layer that was clipped to the border image layer. I adjusted the color channels in this Curves adjustment so that it colored the border image layer to create a warm sepia color tone that matched the colors in the underlying photograph.

Difference Clouds

The Difference Clouds filter has a cumulative effect on the image. Applying it once creates a cloud pattern based on the inverse color values. Repeating the filter produces clouds based on the original colors, and so on, as the filter effect builds up more cloud contrast.

Adding a Clouds filter border

The Clouds filter is available from the Filter ⇨ Render submenu and can be used to generate a cloud pattern that fills the whole image (or selected area), based on the foreground and background colors. The cloud pattern alters each time the filter is applied, so repeated filtering (using ⌘ F ctrl F) will keep producing a fresh cloud pattern. If you hold down the ⌥ alt key while applying the Cloud filter, the effect will be magnified.

In the example shown here, I made use of the Clouds filter to generate a rough-edged border effect, where the border edge will be different each time you apply this series of steps.

1 I opened an image, added an empty new layer and chose Select ⇨ All, followed by Select ⇨ Modify ⇨ Border, and entered a pixel value that was large enough to create a suitable-sized border.

2 I then feathered the selection by a much smaller percentage. In this example I created a 40 pixel border selection and feathered it by 7 pixels. I reset the foreground/background colors, went to the Filter menu and chose Render ⇨ Clouds.

3 I added another empty new layer and, with the selection still active, filled the selection with black and set the layer blend mode to Multiply.

4 I then deselected the selection, merged the two layers, changed the blend mode of the merged layer to Multiply mode and applied an extreme Levels adjustment that hardened the border edges. As you can see, this combination of steps produced the rough edge border effect shown here. As I mentioned at the beginning, the outcome will be different each time you apply these steps. Don't forget that you can also record this as a Photoshop action, although the Border selection width and Feather Radius settings will need to be adapted for different-sized images.

Ragged borders with the Refine Edge command

The Refine Edge command has certainly improved outlining and silhouetting and other selection work. But as often happens in Photoshop's toolset, if you push the envelope of the tools, you can often achieve unexpected but useful and creative effects. One of the Photoshop engineers, Gregg Wilensky, who worked on improving Refine Edge (along with lots of others) discovered that one of the side-effects of using certain settings can be the creation of interesting ragged-edge borders reminiscent of the old chemical darkroom cut-out negative carrier.

In order to accomplish this you need to make a selection that's less than the entire image and using the Refine Edge command adjust the Edge Detection Radius slider with the Smart Option disabled (wider is often better). After doing that (see Step 2) you'll need to fiddle a bit with the Smooth, Feather, Contrast and Shift Edge settings. For this example I've shown the edges against white, but you can also make black edges (as shown in Step 7).

1 I opened an image, duplicated the Background layer to create a copy, then filled the old Background layer with white. To create the selection, I chose Select ⇨ All, followed by Select ⇨ Modify ⇨ Border, and entered a 150 pixel value to create a suitable-sized border. The actual numbers I've used here were really entirely dependent upon the resolution of the file I was working on. In this example, the image of king penguins was shot on a Canon EOS 1Ds MIII but was downsampled to 3600 x 2505 pixels (12″ x 8.35″ at 300 PPI). After creating the selection border, I went back to the Select menu and chose Inverse to invert the selection, followed by Modify ⇨ Smooth Selection to round out the corners a bit, and used a 50 pixel Sample Radius.

2 With the selection active I went to the Select menu again and selected the Refine Edge command (⌘ ⌥ R / ctrl alt R). For this resolution, I applied an Edge Detection Radius of 25. This meant the command would look 25 pixels on either side of the selection to make image-adaptive adjustments to the edge. Different tones of the image would result in different contours that created the rough edge. This was only the fist adjustment — if you are following these steps using one of your own images, the odds are real good you'll want to revisit this setting after fine-tuning the other settings.

3 The next step was to begin modifying the resulting edges. The detail image above left was the result of Step 2. The detail image on the right was after I had adjusted the Contrast to 50. You'll note that in the right-hand example the middle tones of the edge have now become sharper. I would also adjust the sharpness further in Step 4 on the following page.

4 I next adjusted the Smooth settings. This reduced the complexity of the resulting edge, as shown above left. You'll note, however, that there was still a granular texture, which I removed by adjusting the Feather setting to 1.5. The resulting image, above right, used a 1.5 pixel Feather (which is essentially the same function of adding a 1.5 pixel blur to the edge). I'll also point out that I added a −22 Shift Edge setting to make the resulting white edge border a bit smaller (closer to the penguins).

5 After applying the Adjust Edge settings, I modified the Edge Reduction Radius (typical changing of my mind). In the panel you'll see I adjusted the radius to 30.8 pixels. I also wanted to modify the default edge using the Refine Radius tool. The detail image above left shows me painting with the tool, while the detail image above right shows the results of the new edge. I did this carefully, which is why I zoomed into the image. I ended up painting around the entire image edge. The Refine Radius tool seems to work very well at 'disturbing' the edges and making them appear more spontaneous. However, I've never found the results of using the Erase Refinement tool to be useful for this sort of application.

6 Under the Output options, I selected New Layer with Layer Mask. That way I would be able to preserve the original image in case I wanted to make adjustments. I also selected the option to Remember Settings (you can refer to Step 2 to see the entire dialog).

7 While I liked the results in Step 6, my own personal preference was to use a black edge rather than white. So, I filled the bottom layer with black instead of white and also made the rough edge much smaller. Of course, while working on the image using Refine Edge, I could always have previewed the result against black by changing the View options to display On Black.

Photograph: Martin Evening.
Jeff Schewe portrait | Canon EOS 1Ds Mk III | 40 mm | 1600 ISO | f3.2 @ 1/40th

Chapter 11

Robo Photoshop

Using Photoshop automation to develop an efficient workflow

Perhaps in Fritz Lang's movie *Metropolis*, the Maschinenmensch (German for 'machine-man' or robot) would work tirelessly in Photoshop processing images non-stop at their human's behest. Unfortunately (or fortunately), that isn't our reality. Your Photoshop will just sit there waiting until you make it do something. If you have to sit in front of Photoshop and push every single button for every operation, you'll find that you'll have little life outside Photoshop. Photographers, who must deal with thousands of images, really need to automate as many steps as they possibly can. Photoshop offers some pretty useful tools you can use to develop an automated workflow and that's what this chapter is all about.

Figure 11.1 The figure above is an example of a Pixel Genius capture sharpening action containing 72 individual steps.

Turning Photoshop into a robot

Actions in Photoshop

Photoshop added Actions (recordable macros) back in version 4.0, which was released in November 1996. The original engineer, Sean Parent, first designed the ability to record a series of processing steps to be able to play them back later. Prior to version 4, everything you wanted to do in Photoshop literally had to be done mouse-click by mouse-click. Back then, when imaging artists and photographers usually worked on a relatively small number of image scans, that wasn't too terrible. Today, with photographers producing tens of thousands of digital captures, life without actions and batch processing would be unbearable.

Not everything in Photoshop can be recorded as an action. For example, brush strokes of brush-based tools can't. However, you can record the selection of a brush tool and set the parameters. Fortunately, the functions that can be recorded are extensive and can contain an enormous number of steps. Figure 11.1 shows an example of a long and complicated action originally recorded by Bruce Fraser for the PhotoKit Sharpener automate plug-in. We doubt that we'll be giving too much away by showing this figure – you can't actually see the recorded parameters, just the order of the steps. We're showing this only to illustrate just how complex an action can be. This isn't even the most complicated action that Pixel Genius has created; that action contained just under 200 steps written by Martin for PhotoKit Color 2.

What should you record as an action? Our rule is that any step or series of steps performed manually on a repeated and regular basis should be considered a candidate for an action. A simple example might be recording an action to take an active selection and save it as a channel. How many times have you navigated to the Select menu and used the Save Selection command? Sometimes, you may perform one series of steps which could be recorded followed by some manual steps that must be done by hand, followed by yet additional steps that can be recorded. Actions can be recorded to handle those situations. Ultimately, many actions will be most useful when run on many images in a Batch process. I'll cover recording and batch processing in detail, but first I'll introduce you to running actions you already have. Hopefully, I'll show you how to make your actions speak louder than words!

Playing an action

The Actions panel in Photoshop CS5 already comes with a set of actions called Default Actions. While I wouldn't characterize them as killer effects, they do offer an example of the types of action you can record. Included in Photoshop CS5 are additional actions in the Adobe Photoshop CS5 main folder/Presets/Actions. An easy way to load them is to click on the Actions panel fly-out menu and select them directly. Figure 11.2 shows selecting the Commands action set. If you want to have action sets you've created show up in the fly-out menu, you can save them in the Actions subfolder.

To play an action open an image, select the action (not the action set) and click on the Play button as shown in Figure 11.3. An alternative method of playing an action is to ⌘ ctrl double-click directly on the action. Depending on the steps and options that are recorded in the action you may end up surprised (particularly an action you didn't record). When you open an image to run an action for the first time, we suggest you duplicate the image first (Image ⇨ Duplicate) and close the original image. You can never be too sure what might happen to the image when running an unknown action. While it's unlikely an action would be able to save over your original file by accident, running an action on a copy will mean your original file is completely safe.

When running an action, we strongly suggest you let Photoshop do its work and not interrupt the progress. Martin likes to call this his golden rule and suggests not doing *anything* when an action is running. I'm also cautious but I've actually found that playing an action and then minimizing Photoshop or going to the Finder will actually accelerate the processing of the action because Photoshop will hide all the panels and blank out the document window so Photoshop can apply all its processor clicks to processing, not updating panels and image previews. I do agree with Martin that it's always a bad idea to click on another open image window while an action is already running. Photoshop will quit running the action on the original image and pick up the action steps left and apply them to the second image. We consider this a bug, not a feature.

An action will fail to run if the current state of your image doesn't have the same state that was originally recorded in the action. For example, if your action has a recorded step that modifies a selection such as a feather, you can't run that action

Figure 11.2 Clicking on the Actions panel fly-out menu shows the actions included in the Photoshop CS5 action presets.

Figure 11.3 To play an action, select the action you wish to run and click on the Play button. Alternatively, you can ⌘ ctrl double-click on the action to run it.

Figure 11.4 Photoshop's warning indicating that an action step can't run because the command isn't available.

without a selection being active. Photoshop will display a not terribly helpful warning, shown in Figure 11.4. Remember, dialog windows are designed and written by engineers. As such, what may make sense to an engineer might not make sense to a user. This warning basically means you'll need to figure out what condition is needed in order for the action to be played. We'll cover action troubleshooting in depth on page 414 and show you how to deal with errors and make your recorded action bulletproof.

The Actions panel magic decoder ring

You might think that learning how to use the Actions panel would be fairly easy. Yes, and no. Some of the functions and features are pretty straightforward. Other aspects are not very intuitive. We thought it would be useful though to label everything for you in Figure 11.5.

Figure 11.5 The Actions panel showing various panel indicators and buttons.

A: Action set contains inactive actions.
B: Action contains a pause to reveal a dialog.
C: Action disabled (turned off).
D: Indicates one or more actions steps are inactive and contains a pause.
E: An active action step with a pause to open a dialog box.
F: An action step that is disabled.
G: The Actions panel fly-out menu.
H: An action set expanded.
I: An action with the steps collapsed.
J: The targets action with steps expanded.
K: An action step expanded to show recorded parameters.

The Actions panel fly-out menu

The fly-out menu contains some useful commands not found on the Actions panel. At the top is the command to switch to Button Mode. Because we have so many actions, Button Mode, which makes the Actions panel into a bunch of action buttons, is completely impractical. The next group contains commands that are duplicated on the panel except for the action Duplicate command, which can be useful if you keep a bunch of individual action steps and want to copy them into new actions. The next section also contains a couple of panel-based commands but also has three important commands: Insert Menu Item, Insert Stop and Insert Path. The Insert Menu item allows you to record an action that calls up a command from within the Photoshop menu structure. We use this command a lot. The Insert Stop command allows you to record a series of steps and puts in a stop that shows an informational message and allows the action to continue after the dialog dismissal.

The next two commands, Action Options and Playback Options, are very important. Figure 11.7 shows the two dialogs. The Action Options dialog allows you to rename the action, assign a function key and have the action show in a color in the event you do want to use the Actions panel in Button Mode. The Playback Options allow you to control how an action is played. Usually, you'll want to use the full-speed Accelerated option. However, the Step by Step comes in real handy when trying to troubleshoot an action error. The Pause For option allows you to slow playback down real slow. Slow enough that each step can be displayed on your image so you can watch each step as it is applied to the image.

The fifth section contains commands to load or save action sets as well as reset or replace the sets already loaded. The last two sections contain the action presets and the Close panel or Close Tab Group options.

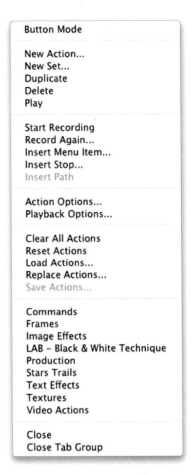

Figure 11.6 The Actions panel fly-out menu.

Figure 11.7 The Action Options and Playback Options dialogs.

Recording a very basic action

Before you can run you must first learn how to walk. So, in this first section, I'm going to show the recording of a very basic action: feathering an active selection. If you are already experienced with recording your own actions, you might wish to skip ahead a bit.

1 To record an action I first needed to add it to an existing set or create a new set. Clicking on the Create new set icon (shown left) launched the New Set dialog shown above. Here, I named the set and clicked OK.

2 Once the new set was created, I clicked on the Create new action button. Note that in this instance there needed to be a selection active which would be the state upon which the feathering would depend. I wouldn't be able to record a feathering step if there wasn't already a selection. Also, I would need to have a selection active for the recorded action to play. Otherwise I would see a warning dialog like the one shown in Figure 11.4.

3 Once I started the action recording, any steps I did in Photoshop would get recorded (except for brush strokes). I navigated to the Feather command from the Select ⇨ Modify submenu. I entered a 2 pixel radius then clicked on the Stop recording button. Note that the action step displays the recorded parameter. In the figure above right, I double-clicked directly on the action step to be able to edit the action step as shown in Figure 11.8.

Basic action editing

Once you've recorded an action, you can edit the parameters originally recorded and rename the action. You can also duplicate the action and modify how the action will play. Figure 11.8 shows how to edit an existing action. Figure 11.9 shows how to duplicate an action and Figure 11.10 shows how to toggle the dialogs and action steps on and off.

Figure 11.8 To edit the recorded parameters in an action step, double-click the action step (not the action itself) as shown above left and enter the revised parameters. In this example I renamed the action to reflect the new parameters (shown above right).

Figure 11.9 While you can select an action and use the Duplicate command from the Actions panel fly-out menu, I prefer to simply drag the action to the Create new action button. This does exactly the same thing and results in a copy of the original action. In addition to duplicating actions, you can duplicate action steps in this manner.

Figure 11.10 If an action step involves some sort of dialog window, you can choose to toggle the dialog on or off (above left). Generally, if you want the specific recorded parameters to be used, I suggest you leave the dialog off. I usually record an action using an Insert menu item in the event I want to manually enter parameters. If you wish to disable an action step (I often decided after I've played an action that one or more steps are less good) you can toggle that step off, as shown above right. If you toggle off an entire action, you'll get the scary-looking warning shown on the far right. Yes, you can't 'undo' the act of toggling, but you can always 'redo' toggling the action back on.

Volatile actions

Once you have recorded an action, the action is only stored temporarily in the Actions panel unless you save it out as part of an action set. As a result, if Photoshop were to crash after recording a lengthy and complicated action it would be gone, gone, gone. We have both been bitten by this, so the first thing we do after recording a complicated action is to save the set immediately.

Recording ruler units

For actions that involve recording the placement of objects or drawing of marquee selections, it is a good idea to record setting the ruler units as part of the action. For example, if you go to the Photoshop preferences and choose Units & Rulers, you can set the rulers to Percentage. By recording this as part of an action, any subsequent placement of Photoshop guides, placement of the type tool or use of the marquee tools can be recorded relative to the proportions of the document. When you then replay an action, the action should work effectively no matter what the size or proportions of the image.

Descriptions of all actions

If you hold down the ⌘ ⌥ ctrl alt keys as you choose Save Actions… this saves the text descriptions of the action steps for every Photoshop action that's currently in the Actions panel.

Troubleshooting actions

If an action doesn't work, first check that the image you are playing it on is in the correct color mode. Many actions are written to operate in RGB color mode only, so if the starting image is in Lab, CMYK or Grayscale mode, any color adjustment commands that were recorded using an RGB file won't work properly. You will also run into issues running actions recorded on 8-bit depth files using filters that aren't available for 16-bit depth.

Recorded actions may make assumptions based on the image containing only a flat, simple *Background* layer. Martin prevents this from being a problem when he records actions by starting each action by using the ⌥ . alt . shortcut (to select the top-most layer), followed by the Merge Visible to new layer shortcut (⌘ ⌥ Shift E ctrl alt Shift E). These two steps will always add a new, flattened merged copy layer at the top of the layer stack. The lack of an actual *Background* layer (as happens when doing a photomerge) can also stop many actions from playing. There's not much you can do about this, other than to create a new layer on the bottom of the layer stack and convert that new layer to a *Background* layer by choosing Layer ⇨ New ⇨ Background from Layer before playing the action.

If you have an action that is producing unexpected results, you can inspect it command by command by selecting the Step by Step option in the Actions panel fly-out menu. Martin's method is to open a test image, expand the action to display all the items, select the first step in the action, hold down the ⌘ ctrl key and click on the Play button. This allows you to play the action one step at a time. You need to have the ⌘ ctrl key held down and keep clicking the Play button to continue playing the remaining steps. If there is a problem with one of the action steps then double-click that action step in the list to rerecord it. You will then need to make sure that action step is selected, keep the ⌘ ctrl key held down again and click on the Play button to continue.

Limitations when recording actions

Most Photoshop operations can be recorded as an action, such as image adjustments, History panel steps, filters, and most Photoshop tool operations. You should be aware that tools such as the marquee are recorded based on the current set ruler unit coordinates (see sidebar on Recording ruler units). Recording actions that include steps that create new layers, channels or paths must be recorded with unique naming so as to avoid the pitfall of ambiguous names. For example, if you have an action that creates a new channel named *Alpha 1* (which is the default name for the first new channel) that action will fail if you try to run that action with another image that already has a channel named *Alpha 1*. When moving layers in a recording, use the main Layer menu or Layer key command shortcuts to reorder the layer positioning. Doing this will make your action more error proof.

When recording an action, only the changed parameters are recorded, not the parameters that may already exist. To solve this potential 'gotcha' you need to intentionally misadjust the parameters before recording the action. Then start recording and enter the desired correct settings. There are other dependencies that can be recorded that may cause errors when playing an action. The recording of an Open or Save step as part of an action hard codes the exact directory path of drive and folder as part of the action. If that drive or folder becomes unavailable, the action will fail. This often happens when you record a Save step to a removable hard drive. If that drive is removed, you'll see an indication of the missing folder in the action step as shown in Figure 11.11. If you remount the missing hard drive the action should find the folder on the original drive. Alternatively, you can create a new folder on a different drive and double-click on the save step and in the Save dialog, navigate to the new folder.

Some people use the technique of recording an action to play another series of recorded action steps – recording an action playing another action. This can be a convenient shortcut when building a complicated series of actions. However, you should be warned that if one of those sub-actions is missing (accidentally deleted or renamed) the main upper level action will fail. Figure 11.12 shows a complicated action named Process Raw Workflow. That upper level action calls upon a series of separately recorded sub-actions. Each of those sub-actions must be available in the action set named Workflow Actions. You'll note that the blue-circled step Ink Jet 360 Sharpen is no longer contained in the Workflow Actions set. Playing the Process Raw Workflow action will fail and display the error message shown in Figure 11.12. This dependency is something we avoid by usually recording each and every step of an action independent of other actions.

Figure 11.11 The action step with a directory path that is not found (top). To fix the path, double-click on the step and find the missing path or create a new directory path (bottom).

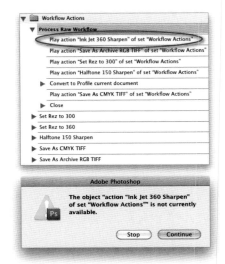

Figure 11.12 The upper level action depends on a series of sub-actions. The first sub-action, named 'Inkjet 360 Sharpen', has been deleted. Trying to run the upper level action will produce the error message above.

Batch processing

The ultimate in Photoshop robotics is the ability to set up and run the Batch process in either Photoshop or Bridge. Once you master the recording of actions, it's a natural progression to use those actions to fully automate image processing on whole bunches of images without you having to be behind the steering wheel. Figure 11.13 shows the Batch dialog as well as the important dropdown menus you'll need to configure.

The Source dropdown menu tells Batch where to get the files to process. The main dialog shows Bridge as the source. The expanded drop-down menu shows the menu options when accessed via Photoshop's File ⇨ Automate. The Bridge option is grayed out because Photoshop can't communicate with Bridge, just Bridge to Photoshop. The Destination drop-down menu lets you select where the processed files are saved. If you have already recorded a save as part of your action, you can chose None. If you want the

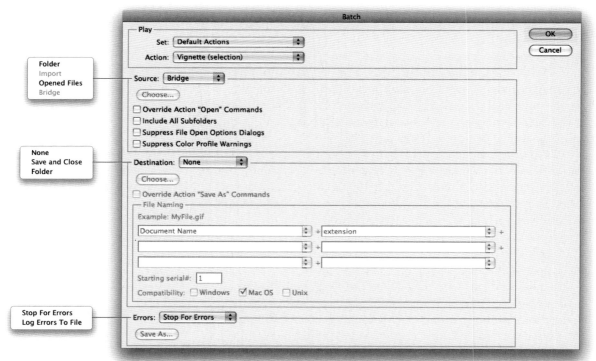

Figure 11.13 The Batch dialog shown above was accessed by choosing the Tools ⇨ Photoshop menu in Bridge.

processed files to save over the originals, Save and Close is useful (but scary). I usually use the Folder option and navigate to the folder I want to have the processed images saved to. Batch does provide the ability to rename files but Bridge CS5's Batch Rename tool has outstripped the functionality provided here. I generally don't rename in a Batch process. The last drop-down menu allows you to control what happens when there are errors. I always have this option set to Log Errors To File. There's nothing so irritating as coming back to the computer after a few hours only to find Batch has halted part of the way through because of an error.

The Batch dialog check boxes offer some obvious and not so obvious options. Figure 11.14 shows all of the options selected. I often have them all checked. The one that you may not use often is the Suppress File Open Options Dialogs. Opening PSD, TIFF and JPEG files won't pop an Open Options dialog, but if you rasterize an EPS file you will get an Options dialog which can be suppressed.

The two confusing options are Override Action "Open" Commands in the Source section and Override Action "Save As" Commands in the Destination section. Can you say 'engineer-speak'? The bottom line is there are two basic rules: one for how to deal with opening files and the other dealing with how to save files. If you have recorded an actual Open step as part of a batch action, the rule states you must check this option otherwise nothing will happen in the Batch. Same deal if you recorded a Save As step. Figure 11.15 shows you the warnings that will appear when selecting either of these options. Confused? Let me try to translate them for you. If you've recorded an Open step in an action you'll generally want to override the file and directory path of the Open step and only use the recorded Open parameters. A typical example would be recording an Open step using Camera Raw and making sure your Workflow Options were set to the correct color space and bit depth. I'll show you a concrete example in the Raw Processing batch workflow section starting on page 419. Similarly, when you record a Save As step and want the Batch Destination to be a different folder than what you recorded in the action, you would record the Save As step for but then check Override Action "Save As" Commands to override the destination recorded in the Save As step. The Save As step would then only play the file format options of the action. Practice makes perfect but know that even we sometimes make mistakes.

Figure 11.14 The Batch dialog Source and Destination check box options.

The warning about Open steps

The warning about Save As steps

Figure 11.15 These are the two difficult to translate warnings when you check either the option to 'Override Action "Open" Commands' on the top or the 'Override Action "Save As" Commands' on the bottom.

Create Droplet tool

Camera Raw's Save Image tool

Image Processor

Figure 11.16 Team Photoshop's automation role players.

Alternative automated processing tools

On any championship sports team, you'll find a few highly paid 'all stars', but the great teams also need to fill out their roster with role players. So it is with Team Photoshop. Actions and the Batch command are the 'all stars'. The role players include Droplets, Camera Raw's Save Image command and the JavaScript named Image Processor. They all fill out Photoshop's automated processing tool set and each provides arguably simplified but useful automation functionality. I don't mean to underplay their importance, I use all three tools on occasion. But since they are simpler to use than Actions and Batch we're only highlighting their existence here. Figure 11.16 shows the three tools.

The Create Droplet tool allows you to take an action and make an executable application (the droplet) that is essentially a saved Batch process. You process files or folders of files by dragging and dropping them on the Droplet to run the process. They can also be cross-platform. If you get a Droplet saved from a Mac, you can convert it to Windows by dragging the Droplet to the Photoshop application icon. The one limiting aspect of Droplets is that they hard code the original action into the Droplet and thus a Droplet is no longer editable.

Camera Raw's Save Image tool is an excellent time-saving feature for saving files directly out of Camera Raw. It's limited to a single file format and destination at a time so it isn't as powerful as a Batch process. But it is simple and can speed up raw processing.

Image Processor, which is actually a JavaScript, was originally 'Dr. Brown's Image Processor'. It is a stripped down batch processing tool available in Bridge via Tools ➪ Photoshop. It's also available in Photoshop via the File ➪ Scripts submenu. Image Processor can be set up to save out JPEG, PSD and TIFF versions of the processed image. The processed files are saved in the destination in separate folders named for the file format. Image Processor has the capability to resize images and you can even have Image Processor include running a Photoshop Action. Photoshop has other JavaScripts you can run for more limited, specific automation functionality. I wish I could learn how to write a JavaScript, but alas, it's beyond my skill set. But take heart, there's a whole community of scripters and third-party creators that offer free or fee-based scripts and actions hosted by Adobe at www.adobe.com/exchange. The Adobe Photoshop Marketplace has its aisles jam-packed with actions, scripts, brushes, shapes, styles and filters.

An automated raw processing workflow

Combining Bridge, Camera Raw and Photoshop

The ultimate payout for learning how to use actions and batch processing is the chance you might get of having a life outside of Photoshop. The chore of selecting images in Bridge, opening them in Camera Raw and processing them through a Batch process can be made far more efficient through automation. In this example of creating an automated raw processing workflow I'll be using images shot while on a photo road trip to the American South West with Martin, where I shot over 5300 raw captures. Figure 11.17 shows only the DNG files selected with two stars or better for a total of 176 files selected for processing. It also shows the Batch process I set up as well as the four folders of about 235 GB of processed files that this produced.

Batch process setup

Processed files saved in folders

Figure 11.17 Above left are the filters used to select the 176 files for processing. The Bridge window shows the image thumbnails. Above is a close-up of the setup for the Batch dialog. To the left is the folder structure that the processed files were saved to on the hard drive. Processing took 1 hour, 4 minutes.

Figure 11.18 To start off recording an Open action, I like to use a sample raw image on my desktop and drag and drop it onto the Photoshop icon to open the image into Camera Raw hosted by Photoshop.

Recording the batch action

In order to show recording the batch action, I'll need to condense some of the steps. Don't worry though, I'll make the action available on the DVD so you can examine everything. I'll also include the Midtone Contrast Actions that include the one sub-action used in the processing. However, the Open and Save As steps will need to be rerecorded to use on your computers. The first and perhaps most important step after creating the set and starting to record the action is to open an image into Camera Raw to capture the Workflow Options settings. Figure 11.18 shows my favorite way of opening an image into Camera Raw.

1 I opened an image via the drag and drop method and clicked on the Workflow Options info button to record setting the Workflow Options. Before I had even started recording the action, I had opened the image and set the Workflow Options to 8-bit sRGB. That way, when recording, I could be absolutely sure that the change to 16-bit ProPhoto RGB at 300 PPI would be recorded. I made sure I didn't make any image adjustments that would also get recorded – this is critical because you don't want the action to override the existing adjustments! To the left is the open step as recorded. I hope Martin doesn't mind me using this self-portrait, which was shot just outside of Moab, Utah. Yes, the camera was on a tripod and I used the self-timer.

2 The next series of steps, which I've combined into one, included changing Photoshop's preferences from Bicubic to Bicubic Sharper (above left), playing the Midtone Contrast 35 pixels action (above right), and adding a Curves and a Hue/Saturation adjustment. I then put both adjustment layers into a layer group named Soft proof setup (above far right). Once that was done, I chose Save As from Photoshop's File menu and navigated to the folder named Archive RGB TIFFs. This saved the full-resolution file with all layers in the correct folder inside the Batch-Output enclosing folder. The action so far would only save out one iteration of each of the 176 files. You can see how this would be useful, but wait, there's more; a lot more! The next step involves recording the conversion of the image from RGB to CMYK and saving that version in a different folder.

3 In order to do a conversion from RGB to CMYK, I used the Convert to Profile command under the Photoshop Edit menu. I used the Convert to Profile command instead of simply doing a mode change to CMYK because not only could I record the exact profile to convert to, but also I could have the file flattened (and I could preview the CMYK conversion while recording). After doing the conversion, I did another Save As command and navigated to the CMYK TIFFs folder. Astute readers may wonder what became of the Soft proof setup layer group. I had actually deleted it before I converted to CMYK because the Soft proof setup was designed for inkjet printing so I didn't want it applied to the CMYK image.

4 The next series of steps actually started by going back in History before the CMYK conversion to the point just before I deleted the Soft proof setup layer group. I had deleted the group for the purpose of doing the conversion to CMYK but wanted the layer group for these recorded steps. This series was intended to downsize the full size and resolution images for 8 x 10″ prints at 300 PPI. Since I had already set Camera Raw to open the images at 300 PPI, I only needed to downsize them. Rather than trying to use the Image Size command, I chose to use Fit Image from the File ⇨ Automate menu. I chose to Constrain Within 3000 x 3000 pixels, which would make horizontal and vertical images 10″ on their longest side. I wish Actions and/or Batch would allow conditional based functions, but alas, it's not there yet. Fit Image is as close as you can get for image sizing. Since I wanted to be able to make prints, I also wanted to do output sharpening. I used PhotoKit Sharpener set to Inkjet 300 Glossy. I also recorded yet another Save As step. I chose TIFF again and saved it to the 8 x 10 Prints folder, making sure to save the layers for later editing. The next series of steps is intended to make web-sized preview images.

5 It was at this stage of the recording that I made my first mistake (I warned you I wasn't perfect). I again used History to go back two steps. Unfortunately, my guess was wrong and I had to go back an additional History state. You can see the steps in the action. This brings up a good point about recording actions – ideally, you would organize all the steps you wanted to record. I have at times hand-written notes about what step to record in what order. Other times I just wing it as I did in this example. If you make a mistake you can do one of two things: stop the recording, undo what you did and delete the step and start recording again, or just correct the error on the fly. If the step involves considerable processing time, I would suggest stopping, making the correction and then starting recording again. In this case, simply stepping back an additional History state would produce no speed penalty so I kept going. After I got back to the correct History state, I used another Fit Image command to downsize the image to 800 x 800 pixels. I also added an Image Size to change the resolution of the image to 72 PPI. You'll note I unchecked the Resample Image option (above right).

6 I once again recorded another Convert to Profile command, this time converting to sRGB for the web. Again I checked the option to Flatten Image to Preserve Appearance. Prior to saving the image, I used the Image ⇨ Mode ⇨ 8-Bits/Channel command to drop down from 16-Bits. I then recorded another Save As command, this time unchecking the option to embed a color profile, and saved the image as a JPEG in the Web sized previews folder. While the image processing steps were now completed, there were two additional steps I recorded, one that is really important: 'Close'. If you don't record an actual Close command, guess what Photoshop will do for you? Yep, it'll keep opening images, processing them and leaving them open. Can you imagine the problems Photoshop would have with 176 images open all at once? After recording that all-important Close command, I also wanted to record another preference change, this time reselecting the Bicubic interpolation option in the Image Interpolation menu.

It's a wrap!

We realize recording actions and doing batch processing isn't very 'visual'. It's pretty technical and rather tedious. However, the payoff is the ability to improve your productivity, increase your consistency and generally make your life a bit easier working with tons and tons of images. You'll note I mentioned consistency; the good thing about having a recorded series of image processing routines is that Photoshop and your computer don't suffer from Monday morning blues (or a hangover). An action played on Monday morning will produce the exact same results on Friday night at midnight.

Figure 11.19 shows the final recorded Batch Process action. Remember, both that action as well as the Midtone Contrast Actions are on the book's DVD. To load them on your own computer, copy them to your hard drive and double-click the .atn file (that's the action format extension). Happy Actioneering!

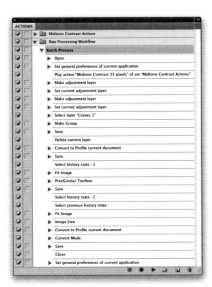

Figure 11.19 The final recorded Batch Process action of the Raw Processing Workflow set.

Chapter 12

Photoshop output

Tips and advice on inkjet and CMYK print output

I t is all very well getting your photographs to look good on screen as you retouch them in Photoshop, but as far as most photographers are concerned, it's how the final print looks that matters most. Getting from screen to print should and can be easy, providing you are using a well-maintained, color-managed workflow. Most of the basic tips and advice on printing are contained in Martin's main *Adobe Photoshop CS5 for Photographers* book. What this chapter does is to provide additional tips and advice on setting up an inkjet printer, combined with instructions on how to make custom profiles, how to soft proof in Photoshop plus how to create CMYK proof prints.

Printing in Photoshop

Inkjet printers

Inkjet printers now dominate the printing market and are especially popular with photographers who are using Photoshop. Inkjet printers come in all shapes and sizes from small desktop devices to huge banner poster printers that are the width of a studio.

The first inkjet devices were manufactured by IRIS and designed for commercial CMYK proof printing on a limited range of paper stocks. It was largely due to the experimentation of country rock musician and photographer Graham Nash that the IRIS evolved to become an inkjet printing device suitable for producing fine-art prints. This costly venture began in the early nineties and thanks to these pioneering efforts, was soon to revolutionize the world of fine-art printing. The IRIS printer stopped production in 2000 and its successor was the IXIA from Improved Technologies. The IRIS/IXIA is still favored by many artists, but in the last decade companies like Epson, Hewlett-Packard (HP), Canon and Roland have developed high quality wide-format inkjet printers that are suitable for large-format printing, including fine artwork applications.

The revolution in inkjet technology began at the high end with expensive wide-format printers, but the technology soon diffused down to the desktop. Epson was one of the first companies to produce affordable high quality desktop printers and Epson has retained its lead in printer and consumables technology, always coming out with new and better printers, inks and papers, although companies like Canon and Hewlett-Packard are now beginning to regain their slices of the printer market with printers to rival Epson's continuing dominance.

How inkjet printers work

Inkjet printers work by spraying very fine droplets of ink as the head travels back and forth across the receiving media/paper. The different tonal densities are generally created by varying the number of evenly sized individual droplets. Epson was one of the first to use variable-sized droplets to avoid the appearance of widely spaced and noticeable fixed-size dots in the highlights; now most of the other manufacturers have followed suit, so that the higher dot density in highlights gives much smoother tones.

Inkjets typically do not have a regular arrangement of their color dots, so more closely follow the results of stochastic printing in the litho world. The latest Epson Stylus Pro models use eight or now 10 color inks and these are capable of producing an even smoother continuous tone output. Figure 12.1 shows Jeff by his Epson 7900 printer. The Epson 4800 printer in my office uses additional light black, light light black, light cyan and light magenta inks to render the paler color tones. The print output is therefore very smooth because there is no discernible dot dithering in the lighter areas. But more significantly, the K3 inks are capable of reproducing richer colors than can be seen on even the wider gamut LCD computer displays, such as the Eizo or NEC models.

Inkjet printers are used for all sorts of printing purposes. An entry-level inkjet can cost as little as $100 and would be suitable for anything from office letter printing to outputting photographs from Photoshop. And you don't have to spend much more than a few hundred dollars to buy an A4 or A3 printer that is capable of producing photo-realistic prints.

Although inkjets use CMYK inks or CMYK plus the additional inks (such as those mentioned above), they work best when they are fed RGB data. This is because a lot of these printers use Quartz rendering (Mac) or GD (PC) drivers as opposed to PostScript. These print drivers can't understand CMYK. So if you send CMYK data to the driver it will convert the data from some form of generic CMYK to RGB before converting the data again to its own proprietary CMYK color. Later on in this chapter we will discuss how it is possible to use an inkjet printer to produce acceptable guide prints for CMYK press color matching. For example, if you perform the color management in Photoshop and disable the printer color management, it is also possible to produce what is known as a cross-rendered CMYK guide print from an RGB file, using the Proof Setup dialog to specify a CMYK space to proof with.

The ideal inkjet

Your first consideration will probably be the print size and how big you need your prints to be. Most desktop inkjet printers are able to print up to A3+ (13″ × 19″), while the Epson 3880 can print up to 17″ × 35″ in size. The wide-format printers like the Epson

Output through a RIP

Some standard print drivers may use a mix of inks to print dark colors. But a good photo RIP like ColorBurst™ will use proper black generation (GCR) control to minimize color shifts in prints.

Figure 12.1 Here is Jeff standing by his Epson 7900 printer (which has recently been replaced with the larger 9900 size). Photo © by Henry Wilhelm.

Hewlett-Packard Z series

The Z series printers include two 12-ink color models. These printers have an incredibly wide color gamut which is achieved by the addition of red, green and blue inks.

Epson x900 class printers

Epson makes the 7900 and 9900 series printers which use 10 color inks. Jeff is particularly impressed with the gamut and D-max of the new UltraChrome HDR inks to the extent that your choice of color workspace in Photoshop is more important than ever if you are to make the most of this latest breed of printer. Only ProPhoto RGB can take advantage of the full range of colors these two printers can achieve.

9900 can print up to 44″ wide and the Hewlett-Packard printers as wide as 96″ (the Hewlett-Packard Z series also has built-in X-Rite calibrators that can help maintain closed-loop color accuracy). Wide-format printers are suitable for all commercial purposes and are particularly popular with fine-art photographers who need to produce extra-large exhibition quality art prints. These bigger printers are designed to be freestanding and therefore require a lot of office space.

Photographic print quality

Almost any inkjet printer can give you acceptable print quality, but some printers are definitely more suited for photographic quality printing than others. The Epson Stylus Pro range of printers is marketed as a good choice for photographic print output because they use specially formulated inks and print with six or more ink colors, which can yield superb results. Printers like these and others can also be adapted to take third-party inks that are specially formulated for black and white or fine-art printing. The Epson 3800 printers are suitable for fine-art printing with longevity and have an extra light black ink which also makes this an almost ideal printer for black and white work (as is the more robust Epson 4880, which also provides you with the ability to use bigger ink cartridges). In recent years, Hewlett-Packard has ramped up its range of photo printers. For example, the PhotoSmart 9180 is simple to set up and also features a built-in calibration device.

Image preservation

The longevity of an inkjet print will be determined by a variety of factors. Mostly it is down to the combination of the inks and media that are used to produce the print, followed by the environment in which a print is kept or displayed and whether it has been specially treated to prevent fading. Light remains the biggest enemy though. If prints are intended for long-term exhibition, then you have to make sure that you use a suitable ink and paper combination, and that the prints are displayed behind UV filtered glass and sited so they are not exposed to direct sunlight every day.

The premium glossy and semi-gloss papers are a popular choice for photographers as these papers match or exceed the quality of a normal photographic print surface, and the print longevity when used with the Epson 4880 is estimated to be close to 100 years. A lot of photographers and artists have enjoyed experimenting with various fine-art paper stocks. When these are combined with the right types of ink, it is possible to produce prints that can be expected to last even longer.

If you are printing to black and white and use the Advanced Black and White Epson print driver (which is available on the higher end models such as the 2880), this will print the photos using just the black, light black and light light black inks with minor amounts of cyan, magenta or yellow. When you print using the Advanced Black and White mode you are using pure carbon pigments and the estimated lifetime for these types of prints is up to 300 years.

Inks and media

To start with I recommend that you explore using the proprietary inks and papers that are 'officially' designated for use with your printer. Firstly, it should be pointed out that the manufacturing engineers have designed these ink and paper products expressly for their printers and, secondly, the printer companies will usually supply canned profiles which these days are often very accurate. Therefore, if you stick to using proprietary inks and papers at the beginning there are fewer variables for you to worry about when you are learning how to print from Photoshop.

There are two types of inks used in inkjet printers. Dye inks were once the most popular because they were capable of producing the purest colors. But the dye molecules in such inks were also known to lack stability. This meant they were prone to deteriorate and fade when exposed to prolonged intense light exposure, high humidity or reactive chemicals. Pigment-based inks have a more complex molecular structure and as a result of this are less prone to fading. But pigmented inks have traditionally been considered less vivid than dye inks and have a restricted color palette (the color gamut is smaller).

Some modern inks use a hybrid combination of dyes and pigments. These specially formulated pigment-based ink and paper combinations will produce bright prints that also have exceptional image permanence. When using the correct paper and inks, the life expectancy is predicted to be over 100 years and may be as long as 200 years with certain paper combinations.

Wilhelm Imaging Research

Henry Wilhelm has conducted much research into the various factors that affect the permanence of inkjet prints. The Wilhelm Imaging Research website contains print permanence reports for several printers. Henry has also coauthored a book: *The Permanence and Care of Color Photographs: Traditional and Digital Color Prints, Color Negatives, Slides, and Motion Pictures*, which offers a definitive account on the subject. For more information go to: www.wilhelmresearch.com

Third-party inks

When ordering ink supplies you need to make sure that the cartridges are compatible with the printer and, if using a custom profile, are of the same type. While it is possible to use third-party inks in some printers, we tend to take the view that the ink technology is often just as important as the printer hardware itself and it may prove a false economy to switch to using non-branded inks.

Inkjet economies

Ink cartridges don't come cheap and once you get into serious print making, you will soon get through a lot of expensive cartridges. We don't recommend you economize by buying ink refill kits as these are very messy to use. In the long run it can work out more economical if you buy a printer that uses single ink cartridges with higher ink capacities (don't forget there are places where you can recycle your used cartridges). Basically, the inkjet manufacturers like to sell their printers cheaply and then make their profit through the sales of proprietary inks designed for their printers. If you care to read the small print, using anything but the manufacturer's own inks may void the manufacturer's guarantee.

Canned printer profiles

These days it is much easier to rely on the canned profiles that ship with most of the current inkjet printers (or at least this is true of the Epson printers that we are most familiar with). There are two key reasons for this. Firstly, now that the printer hardware is more consistent in quality, it is possible to build a profile using one printer and have it work well for every other printer. Secondly, the profiles that are supplied are of better quality anyway. You'll also find that third-party media suppliers such as Hahnemuehle (www. hahnemuehle.com) and Innova (www.innovaart.com) are able to supply ICC profiles for their paper products with various printers and these can be downloaded from their websites. Custom printer profiles should be saved using the following locations: Library/ColorSync/Profiles folder (Mac OS X), Windows XP/System/Color folder (PC). For Windows Vista and Windows 7, just right-click on the profile and choose Install.

Building custom printer profiles

Should you feel the need to create your own custom profiles for non-regular ink and paper combinations then you might want to consider having custom printer profiles made. If you don't have the necessary profiling hardware and software, the most obvious thing to do is to contract the work out to a specialist. For example, Neil Barstow is a UK-based color management consultant who offers a CD containing a manual and test files to help you optimize your printer settings. For more information on this and his UK-based color consultation services, go to: www.colourmanagement.net Our good friend and colleague Andrew Rodney is also a color management expert based in the USA and is the author of *Color Management for Photographers* from Focal Press. Andrew offers consultation services and also makes custom printer profiles. For more info see www.digitaldog.net

DIY custom printer profiles

If you wish to build your own custom profiles, then you'll need to purchase something like an X-Rite Eye-One or ColorMunki device plus the necessary software to read the measured spectral data from which a profile can be built. Whichever approach you choose, you'll need to know how to correctly print a test target image.

Printing a printer test target

The idea of printing the color target is to produce a printed chart of colors in which the color information in the target file (Figure 12.2) is sent directly to the printer without any color management being applied to it. The patch readings that are made subsequently using a spectrophotometer device are then used to build a custom color profile for that particular printer and paper combination that will later be able to convert the image data to produce correct-looking colors. However, printing targets have changed in Photoshop CS5 because the No Color Management (NCM) option in the Photoshop Print dialog has been removed (see Figure 12.3 on the following page). However, if you have Eye-One Match or the ColorMunki, you can simply print the targets directly from the color management software.

Figure 12.2 Here is an example of an X-Rite color target which is used to construct an ICC color profile. The print outputs are then measured using a reflective spectrophotometer and a profile built from these measurements. A third-party profiling service will be able to supply you with the test chart and printing instructions. You mail the color management service provider a print and they will email a printer profile back to you.

Adobe Color Printer Utilty

When the Photoshop engineers decided to remove the No Color Adjustment option from the Photoshop CS5 Print dialog, there was quite a ruckus from the color management geeks. So, the decision was made to offer a free printing application that could be easily set up to offer cross-platform printing of color targets. At the time of this writing, we're not 100% sure of the name, but it'll be something like the 'Adobe Color Printer Utility' and offered as a free download for Mac and Windows on the Adobe Labs site (www.labs.adobe.com).

Why did the Photoshop engineers remove the No Color Management (NCM) option from the Photoshop Print dialog? The NCM option was a non-sanctioned print path that was essentially a program hack to make it work. Current and future versions of operating systems' print pipelines have made that hack very susceptible to breaking with Operating System updates. As a result, Adobe decided to remove the option and in its place offer a free printing utility that can print color targets simply and easily. Figure 12.3 shows the difference between the Photoshop CS4 and CS5 versions of the Color Handling drop-down menu in the Color Management part of the Print dialog.

Figure 12.3 On the left is the Photoshop CS4 Color Handling drop-down menu. On the right is the Photoshop CS5 version.

Target printing workaround

There is actually a sneaky way of correctly printing out color targets in Photoshop CS5 but at this point, it's not a 'sanctioned' method. It works, but it can be tricky and there's no guarantee it will continue to work in the future. But as a matter of addressing your intellectual curiosity, we decided to show you how to do it.

1 The first step was to open the target in Photoshop. Rather than checking the option to 'Leave as is (don't color manage)' you actually want to assign a working color space to the image. In this step, the only critical factor was to make sure I assigned a 'real' RGB working space. For this reason, I suggest using Adobe RGB (1998). You don't want to do a conversion and you don't want to alter the data, just what the data represents.

2 In Step 2, I went to the Photoshop Print command in the File menu. Here, I set the Color Handling setting to Photoshop Manages Colors, so that Photoshop, and the Printer Profile, were in the same color space I had assigned as the target image when I opened the file; in this case, Adobe RGB (1998). The result of setting the Printer Profile to the same profile assigned when opening the image was a null transform. This kept the OS level color management from trying to apply a generic color transform. Don't worry about setting the Rendering Intent; since the working space is considered a 'display space' the only rendering intent to use here would be Relative Colorimetric, which wouldn't actually transform the color data.

3 The next step was to set the print driver settings. Whether you are printing from Mac or Windows, the print driver must be set to your print driver's version of No Color Management. Once I had set up the driver, I clicked Save then Print in the Photoshop CS5 dialog.

433

Getting the most from your printer profiles

There is no such thing as a perfect color management workflow. Allowances will always need to be made for a small margin for error, but if you follow the guidelines carefully you should attain impressive results even from a modest desktop printer. To fully appreciate the printed results you really need an accurate light viewing box to view the prints correctly. Some inkjet prints can take a while to dry after they come off the printer. A print produced on older Epson printers can at first look quite green in the shadows, but after a few hours the ink colors will stabilize and the green cast eventually disappears. This is why you are sometimes advised to wait at least 24 hours before measuring your printed target prints. Then there is the issue of what is often incorrectly described as 'metamerism' (the correct term is metameric failure). This refers to the phenomenon where, when viewing under different lighting conditions, the ink dye/pigment colors will respond differently. This problem can be particularly noticeable when a monochrome image is printed using color inks. Although the color management can appear to be working fine when a print is viewed under studio lighting, if this environment is changed, and the print is viewed in daylight from a window, the print can appear to have a green cast. There was an example of this with the early Epson Ultrachrome 2000 printer where the pigment-based ink suffered from this green shift in daylight problem, but the latest Ultrachrome printers have now managed to resolve this problem.

Despite all your best efforts to produce a perfect profile, you may just find that a specific color on the display does not match exactly. I sometimes see this happening with the skin tones in a portrait. Although I usually obtain a perfect match with a specific ink and paper profile combination, the printed result is sometimes just a fraction out on an item of clothing or in the skin tones, but every other color looks just fine. This could indicate that it is time to recheck the monitor calibration or it could be that you need to adjust the printer profile. If you know what you are doing it is possible to tweak profiles using a program like X-Rite's ProfileMaker Pro™. Another reason why there may be a difference in the colors seen is that the color gamut of the printer is not as large as the gamut of the display on which you are viewing the image (see Figure 12.4).

Original colors plotted against the Apple LCD gamut

Clipped colors plotted against the Apple LCD gamut

Figure 12.4 In this photograph I shot of Jeff, the vibrant colors contained in the ProPhoto RGB master far exceeded what could be displayed on the gamut of an Apple LCD display (represented here by the wire-frame shape). This is an example of where even a calibrated display cannot show the full color potential of an image in print.

Display gamut versus printer gamut

It is important to understand that what you see on the computer display is always going to be a selective view of the colors actually contained in the image. A great many computer displays are effectively sRGB devices, while even the Adobe RGB gamut screens such as the Eizo CG301W and NEC LCD3090 30″ displays may not be able to accurately display every color that your printer can print (although we still recommend these as the best tools for soft proofing). There was a time when this didn't matter so much, but some of the latest inkjet printers such as those made by Epson and HP have color gamuts that well exceed the limits of the average computer display. There is not much you can do to predict the color output of those colors that exceed the gamut limits of your display. If some of the colors you see in an inkjet print don't match those you see on the monitor and you are confident you have color managed everything effectively, this most likely points to the fact that the display isn't able to show some of the colors that will actually show in print (see Figure 12.5). You can't really do anything about this other than to invest in a good quality, large gamut display. But just be aware that what may appear to be color errors don't necessarily point to a failure in color management.

Soft proofing via the display

More often, the colors you see on the display may appear brighter than those you see in print because the tonal contrast range of the display is greater than what you see in print and this can have the opposite effect of making the print image appear dull in comparison to the image displayed on the display. The solution to this is to use soft proofing in Photoshop to simulate the output characteristics of the print output device on the display, as well as CMYK conversions destined to go to the press.

If you are editing an RGB image and go to the View ⇨ Proof Setup menu you'll see a list of proofing options. If you select Working CMYK this will allow you to soft proof an RGB image using the current CMYK space established in the Edit ⇨ Color Settings dialog (using the default rendering intent). If you choose the Custom… option this opens the Custom Proof Condition dialog shown in Figure 12.6 on the following page, where you can select any output profile that's available from your system color

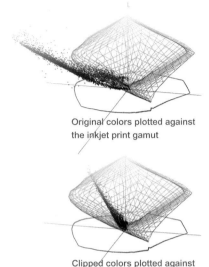

Original colors plotted against the inkjet print gamut

Clipped colors plotted against the inkjet print gamut

Figure 12.5 These two color gamut diagrams really follow on from the Figure 12.4 example because they show the actual colors in the original ProPhoto RGB image plotted against the wire-frame gamut of a glossy inkjet printer profile. Here you can see that while many of the ProPhoto RGB colors are still beyond the gamut of the print output, the print can still reveal much richer blues and shadow detail than can be revealed on the calibrated Apple display. As you can imagine, it's not possible to show in the book the colors that a modern inkjet printer can reproduce, but there was quite a difference.

profiles folder and use this to simulate the tone and color output characteristics of the print device on your monitor using different rendering intents.

You can then save a custom proof setting as a .psf file in the Users/Username/Library/Application Support/Adobe/Color/ Proofing folder (Mac OS X) or the Program Files/Common Files/ Adobe/Color/Proofing folder (PC). This saved proof setting will then be appended to the bottom of the list in the Customize Proof Condition dialog. That way you can quickly access the settings needed for simulated proof printing via the Proof Setup Preset menu in the Print dialog.

You don't have to keep returning to the Customize Proof Condition dialog. Once you have established a custom proof setting you can preview the colors in this space by simply choosing View ⇨ Proof Colors, or use the keyboard shortcut ⌘ Y *ctrl* Y to toggle the preview on and off. This keyboard shortcut makes it very easy for you to switch from Normal to Proof viewing mode. The document window title bar will also display the name of the proofing space after the color mode such as: *RGB/Working CMYK*.

Figure 12.6 Use the View ⇨ Proof Setup menu to select the device or color space you wish to soft proof with, whenever the Proof Colors command ⌘ Y *ctrl* Y is applied. If you click on Custom… this will take you to the Customize Proof Condition dialog, where you can select the profile of your printer or CMYK print output. In this example, I selected a custom CMYK profile for the book printers who are printing this book.

Display simulation options

Once you have established a proof setup and you select the Proof Colors option from the View menu, Photoshop takes the current display view and converts it on-the-fly to the destination color space selected in the Proof Setup. The data is then converted back to the RGB display space to form a preview using the relative colorimetric rendering intent and with black point compensation switched on. In simple terms, the image you see on the display is effectively filtered by the profile space selected in the Customize Proof Condition dialog.

The Proof Colors view provides you with an advance indication of how a file might reproduce after it has been converted to the print output space. The Proof Colors view may make the display image appear muted, but it does more accurately reflect the appearance of the final print output. However, the image on the display will still be optimized to the full contrast range of the display. This is where the Simulate Paper Color and Black Ink options come in (Figure 12.7). These allow you to achieve a more accurate simulation, one that takes into account the color of the paper and the black ink density. The Simulate Paper Color option simulates how the whites in the image will appear, by simulating the color of the paper on the display, and will use an absolute Colorimetric rendering to convert the proof color space data to the display space; it also auto-selects both the color of the paper and the black ink color density. However, the Paper Color simulation only works if the profile used is made on the actual paper stock used for printing, and only if this paper doesn't have too much optical brightener in it (otherwise the results will look bluish on the display – see side panel on page 438).

Turning these options on is equivalent to pressing the 'Make My Image Look Really Bad' buttons. Why? Because a computer display may have a 700 to 1 contrast ratio while a print may only have 200 to 1. Since white will be white and black will be black, the only way to predict the impact that the lowered contrast ratio will have is to make the image look dull and flat. It's accurate, mind you, but it is disappointing unless you know how to use it. So I follow Bruce Fraser's advice and try looking away from the display just prior to checking these press simulation settings. That way I don't see the image die in front of my eyes.

Figure 12.7 The Display Options in the Customize Proof Condition dialog allow you to achieve more authentic on-screen previews that take into account the density of the black in the final output being less black than the maximum black you see on the computer display. When the Simulate Paper Color option is selected the display image will simulate both the color of the paper stock and the black ink color. It is important to note here that while the Proof Condition settings for the Rendering Intent and Black Point Compensation have a bearing on a proof print output, the Simulate Paper Color and Black Ink options will only affect the display preview.

Preserve numbers

You use the Customize Proof condition to preview how a document will look before it has been converted to another color space. The Preserve numbers option can be useful for proofing how a CMYK file in a specific space will print if sent to a known CMYK space. By preserving the numbers you can simulate how a file will print before you consider reseparating it. If the destination space is in the same color mode as the source space (i.e. RGB or CMYK), the Preserve Numbers box allows you to preview how an image would look without a profile conversion.

Inkjet paper optical brighteners

The optical brightener additives contained in many of today's inkjet papers can also bring about quite a noticeable shift in the way a print is perceived under different lighting conditions. If there is a high amount of UV light present the whites will look much brighter, but also bluer compared to a print that has been made using a paper stock such as GMG Premium Proofing papers, which are ideally suited for CMYK proof printing and viewed using controlled lighting with a color temperature of 5000 K.

The Simulate Black Ink option simulates on the display the actual black density of the printing press by turning off the black point compensation in the conversion from the proof color space to the display color space, thus simulating the 'ink on paper black'. Checking both these options allows you to see, as accurately as possible, an on-screen representation of how an image will look when printed. Figure 12.8 shows the results of having the Display Options on and off.

Figure 12.8 On the top is the soft proofed image using the PFP-Medium-GCR proof setup with the Display Options for Paper White and Ink Black off. The figure on the bottom has the options for both turned on.

CMYK output

Color proofing for press output

If you are supplying digital files for CMYK halftone reproduction, then you will want to obtain as much relevant information as you can about the press, paper stock and print process that will be used to print a job. Good luck with that because it doesn't happen often as sometimes the end press and paper won't yet be determined. But if the pre-press people you are communicating with are cooperative and understand what you are asking for, they may be able to supply you with a suitable proofing standard ICC profile, or they can provide you with information about the printing inks and other specifications used for the press. Go to the Edit ⇨ Color Settings ⇨ Working Space ⇨ CMYK ⇨ Custom CMYK dialog, and enter these settings as shown in Figure 12.9. Once you have saved this as a CMYK setting you can convert your RGB image to this custom CMYK color space and save it as a TIFF file.

A CMYK file on its own is not enough to inform the printer how it should look when printed. It is standard procedure to supply a targeted CMYK aim print or proof along with the image, as this will provide a guide as to how you expect the picture to reproduce in print within the gamut of the specific CMYK print process. The term 'contract proof' is used to describe a CMYK proof that has been reproduced using an approved proofing device. These include the Epson x880 and x900 series with a good proofing RIP like the ColorBurst™ RIP. Kodak Approval™ is still much used, and perhaps to a lesser extent DuPont™ Chromalin™.

Inkjet printers are essentially taking over the proofing industry, as many press houses move to Computer to Plate (CTP) technology, thus eliminating the need for film at the proofing stage. The contract proofing devices benefit from having industry-wide recognition, and if the proof that accompanies the file is generated using an approved contract device, a designer can use an aim print to pass off a job to the pre-press company handling the repro. A proof print is more likely to be accepted as a valid target print representing the colors that are achievable on the press.

Realistic proofs

When you supply a CMYK proof you are aiming to show the printer how you envisage the picture should look in print. A proof is a print that has been produced using the same color gamut constraints as the halftone CMYK process. That way the printer will have an indication of what colors they should realistically be able to achieve. However, you should not confuse a really nice fine-art print with a maximum gamut print made from an RGB file as a realistic proof. The colors in such a print simply can't be reproduced on press. Only a cross-rendered CMYK proof will represent a reasonable expectation of what the image will look like when printed.

Figure 12.9 In the Photoshop CS5 Color Settings dialog in the edit menu, click on the CMYK Working Space (top image), select Custom CMYK (bottom image) and enter the numbers provided by the pre-press people.

Contract proof versus aim print

The term 'aim' print most justly describes the appropriateness of a standard profiled inkjet output, when used as a guide for the designer or pre-press person who is determining how the colors in an image will reproduce when using CMYK inks on the actual press.

Rendering intent grayed out

When Proof is selected as the source space, the Rendering Intent will be grayed out and the Black Point Compensation automatically switched off. This is because Photoshop will use the rendering intent that is applied in the custom proof setup.

CMYK proofing with an inkjet

Even a humble inkjet printer is capable of producing 'targeted' CMYK prints that can be used as 'aim' prints or even as contract proofs (if produced via a RIP), because it is possible to simulate the restricted CMYK gamut of the press via the Photoshop Print dialog. Figure 12.10 shows the Photoshop print dialog for a ProPhoto RGB image. When the Proof option is selected as the Print space, the Proof Setup is invoked below and the default Proof Setup will use the current CMYK work space. The Photoshop Manages Colors option should be selected so that you can select a printer profile for the printer. In the Proof Setup you can then also select a saved Customize Proof Condition preset for the print process you wish to simulate (which includes the chosen Rendering Intent) and use the two check boxes below to simulate the press conditions, using: Simulate Paper Color and Simulate Black Ink.

Simulation and rendering intents

The aim here is to produce a print that simulates the output of a CMYK proof printer. We are configuring the Photoshop print dialog settings to utilize the Customize Proof Condition settings (which will already include the device to Simulate and the Rendering Intent) and then applying a further profile conversion from this proof setup space to the printer profile space. Photoshop makes it easy for you to select the right options so that you don't have to do anything more than decide whether you wish to simulate the black ink appearance only or simulate the paper color (in which case the simulate black ink will be checked automatically anyway). So by clicking on one or more of these buttons at the bottom, you can instruct Photoshop to work out for you how the data should be converted and sent to the printer to achieve the desired press simulation.

When Simulate Paper Color is selected, the whites may appear duller than expected. This does not mean the proof is wrong, rather it is the presence of a brighter white border that leads to the viewer regarding the result as looking inferior. To get around this try adding a white border to the outside image you are about to print. When the print is done, trim away the outer paper white border so that the eye does not get a chance to compare the dull whites of the print with the brighter white of the printing paper used.

When you hit the Print button, the same routine should be followed as usual. If you are using Photoshop to manage the colors, the system print settings should have the color management switched off and the Print Settings should match the paper type used, or you should select the saved print preset that was created for use with the custom printer profile.

Figure 12.10 Here, the Print dialog is configured for making a cross-rendered simulated CMYK print. The options for Match Print Colors, Gamut Warning and Show Paper White are selected, but there's not much you can do about the result. Ideally you should take care of that in soft proofing. Note that the Proof not the Document working space is set at the top of the Color Management settings. At the bottom, the Proof Setup is showing the same soft proof setup we previously saved. Before hitting Print, you would need to be sure to click on Print Settings and select the system print driver setting that matches the selected printer profile and media. In this case, I am going to be proofing the image on my Epson 3880 printer using Epson's Semi-matte Proofing Paper.

What flavor of CMYK?

Often photographers are simply told 'give me a CMYK file', but not all CMYK files are really equal. For magazine repro using a web press in the US, Photoshop's default CMYK profile is OK. It really is, but one can do a bit better. If the image is intended for small run sheetfed printing, the problem gets a bit more difficult. You can try to get an ICC profile from the printer (good luck) or the alternative is to have a client specify exactly what proofing system will be used. If you can determine that, then you can separate for the proof and not the press. I have required that clients provide the exact proofing system that will be used on purchase orders before accepting a job. Since I have profiles for pretty much every proofing system out there, I can both soft proof and do the final RGB to CMYK conversions for the actual proof.

Preparing files for output

Any RGB image destined for CMYK halftone reproduction will need to be converted to CMYK by somebody, at some time. The big question is by whom? The photographer? The art director or designer (we doubt that), or the pre-press or printer that will be doing the output? The 'best' answer to the question is whoever can do it in an optimal manner. This could be the photographer or the printer. The circumstances really dictate who will be the most likely.

If the photographer is shooting an assignment where their job is to turn over many images that will end up being selected by somebody way down the road and retouched by somebody else, the odds are it won't be the photographer. Optimizing images for RGB to CMYK conversion takes time and effort to do well. So, unless the assignment is for a few select final images the pre-press provider or printer will probably do the CMYK conversions.

If you are a photographer who can control the final selection of images in concert with the art director or designer (and get paid to do the imaging and final conversions) then you would probably be the best person to do the conversions. You know what the image is supposed to look like and optimizing the RGB images and doing the CMYK conversions isn't really all that hard. It does take some effort and technique. First and foremost is knowing how to use soft proofing to predict what the image will look like and knowing how to take steps to improve the CMYK conversion. That's what we'll try to get across in this section.

The first thing we'll tell you is that it's wise that you never show your clients what your RGB images look like. Since it's a look they'll never be able to get on press, you really should only show them the images after you've already turned on CMYK soft proofing. You can defer the Display Options for paper white and black ink as you wish, but you really should not let them fall in love with the RGB colors from the beginning.

The second thing we'll tell you is that the old Gamut Warning under the view menu is pretty much useless for optimizing CMYK conversions and may actually lead you astray. It has some limited usefulness – most notably as a front end to the ability to select out of gamut colors using Color Range as shown in Figure 12.11. The problem with this approach is that you don't know how much out of gamut a color or tone will be, just that it's out of gamut. It also doesn't show you what the result will look like. For this reason we don't suggest using Gamut Warning but instead suggest learning how to use soft proofing.

We've already talked about using the Customize Proof Condition dialog and how to configure it for your use. The following series of steps shows how to use it to optimize a colorful ProPhoto RGB image for CMYK. There are some hard limits in doing this in the book. For one thing, we can't show you what the ProPhoto RGB image actually looks like because the book is, of course, CMYK. So, the steps show the 'relative' relationship between ProPhoto RGB and the CMYK conversion we are using for the book separations which were provided by Chris Murphy, co-author of Real World Color Management. More info about Chris is at his web site (www.colorremedies.com). However, we will make the original ProPhoto RGB file as well as the CMYK conversions available on the DVD so you can see for yourself how the images were optimized and try it for yourself. The other thing we need to tell people is that the graphic arts industry varies considerably by country and region. Martin has experience in the UK and Jeff in the US, but every country's printing industry operates by slightly different rules and practices. You really need to get to know your own printing industry's expectations and how best to provide them with the optimal CMYK images for their process.

What we'll show you here is what has worked for us over the years. There's no guarantee it'll work for everybody in every situation. The best thing to do is communicate with your client and their printers and gain experience of your own. The big part of learning how to do RGB to CMYK separations is actual practice and experience. We realize that's something that's not always easy to do 'on the job', but everybody had to start at the beginning at some point.

Figure 12.11 The Gamut Warning command is not really recommended. Its primary usefulness is as a method of making a selection based on the out of gamut color in Color Range (middle figure above). The problem of what to do to address the Gamut Warning still remains. Should you reduce the color saturation to the point where the warning essentially goes off, you'll end up with a very weak CMYK image as shown in the bottom figure.

1 I started here by opening an RGB image and making a duplicate. Above, the original ProPhoto RGB image is on the left with soft proofing already turned on. I chose to use Relative Colorimetric as the rendering intent. The copy without soft proofing is on the right. This image is a temp image used to provide a guide to what the image should look like. It will never match the color and dynamic range of this copy because the CMYK gamut is so small and halftone repro is such a lowered contrast range process. But I needed something to aim for.

2 To properly address both the color and contrast range of the CMYK limitations, I needed to use three sets of adjustments. The important tone curve adjustment is shown above. In addition to the Curves adjustment, I made a Hue/Saturation adjustment to tweak the overall saturation of the image up and individually adjust the Yellows: −2 Hue, +10 Saturation and −6 Lightness. The other important color was the Blues, where I did −7 Hue, +14 Saturation and +13 Lightness. The final Selective Color adjustment (the only adjustment for RGB files that give CMYK controls) tweaked the Blues again as well as Black increases in both the Neutrals and Whites drop-down options. Selective Color is a critical tool for doing CMYK style correction on RGB images.

3 The above image shows the actual CMYK file made from the original ProPhoto RGB image without doing any soft proofing tweaks. It looks OK but is flat with dead blues.

Photo: © Jeff Schewe

4 The image above is the one that was soft proofed and with the Curves, Hue/Saturation and Selective Color adjustments. You can see the impact that the adjustments had. No, it doesn't look as 'bad' as the soft proofed image in Step 1. Remember, all we can actually show here in the book are 'relative' differences.

Delivering files for output

You might think that simply saving a CMYK file and giving it to the client is sufficient. It would be in an ideal world, but we live in the real world. You need to take some extra steps to ensure that your carefully prepared CMYK files don't get screwed up.

1 I use Convert to Profile rather than simply doing a mode change. Why? Because Convert to Profile allows explicit confirmation on the profile being used and the Rendering Intent (which I determined should be Relative Colorimetric). When saving, I use the TIFF file format and choose not to embed a profile. Why? Embedding a CMYK profile might lead a printer to do something and most of those things will be wrong. By not embedding the profile, I ensure that the printer will just use it without doing anything (like ignore the embedded profile or convert to some other profile). I also remove any layers and channels.

2 The next thing I do (because clients almost always ask that I also supply RGB files) is that I take the CMYK image and reconvert to back to RGB. Why? Well, we never give clients layered ProPhoto RGB images because most people don't know how to use color management and ProPhoto RGB looks pretty bad unless you use the embedded profile (very dark and green). So, I use the fact that the CMYK image has already undergone the worst color change of its life and preserve that CMYK gamut when converting back to RGB. In this case I used sRGB, but depending on the client I might be inclined to give them Adobe RGB. You'll note I have included the sRGB profile in this file — you really don't want any untagged RGB files around!

3 The last step is to burn a DVD (or CD if the files are small enough) for delivery to the client. The DVD always has a License-ReadMe file outlining use. Why a DVD? Because while expediency may demand a file be uploaded or transmitted via the net, a file delivered in that manner may be altered or otherwise changed (read screwed up) by somebody downstream. If that file is considered your contractual 'deliverable' then it becomes a difficult situation trying to prove exactly who screwed up the file since it has no provenance. By requiring the physical delivery of a read-only medium as the final deliverable, you can always have the client refer back to the DVD as proof of the state of the file when delivered. This has saved me in several situations where the blame game was being played and my client actually appreciated the fact they had a physical file that represented the state of the file prior to giving it to the pre-press provider. It actually saved the client some time and money by being able to prove that neither I nor the client had screwed up the file.

Is CMYK for you?

As you can see, there's more to making a good CMYK image file than just doing an Image ⇨ Mode ⇨ CMYK Color command in Photoshop (although, truth be told, that's the way a lot of people in the graphic arts treat the conversion). Is it worth all the time and hassle? Only you can say… but even if you decide you would rather simply provide sRGB or Adobe RGB files and let the client or the printer deal with the problem (we still don't think you want to give ProPhoto RGB images out), you can still take steps to make sure the images you provide are still the best suited for CMYK conversion down the road. You still need to evaluate the images under relevant CMYK soft proofing conditions and make adjustments for the impact of the CMYK conversion later.

One aspect of the CMYK question is that of economics. Clearly, doing the conversions for free would not be good business – a topic we'll address in the next chapter. But there is an economic incentive to do the work if you can do it well (and be well paid for it).

Process color limitations

A four-color process mix can be used when printing larger sans-serif type using large point sizes, but not when printing fine type and line diagrams, as the slightest misregistration could make the edges appear fuzzy when printed. This is one example of where the use of spot colors is to be recommended.

Spot color channels

Spot colors can be added to images as part of the graphic design when you need to add a specific process color in addition to the standard CMYK printing inks. Photoshop is able to simulate the effect of how a spot color will reproduce in print and how a special color overlay will interplay with the underlying image. Spot colors include a wide range of industry standard colors. The colors available can include those found in the CMYK gamut, but also a whole lot more that are not, including metallic 'specials' (manufacturers' printed book color guides are an accurate reference for how the color will print). Spot colors are mostly used where it is important that the printed color conforms to a known standard and for the printing of small point size type and graphics in color.

1 A spot color channel can be used to add a fifth color to a CMYK file. This master image contained some shape layers based on artwork supplied by the designer, to which I added a drop shadow effect. To add the Spot color channel, I went to the Channels panel fly-out menu and chose New Spot Channel… which popped the New Spot Channel dialog. I clicked on the swatch color to open the Color Picker and then clicked on a button marked Color Libraries. A quick way to select a known Pantone reference color is to rapidly type in the Pantone reference number.

2 I wanted to use the new spot color to add color to the fabric, but not the iron. I drew a path to define the area outside the iron, made an inverse selection and feathered the selection. I activated the new Spot channel and used Image ⇨ Apply Image to blend the selected Cyan channel contents into the Spot color channel using a Normal blend.

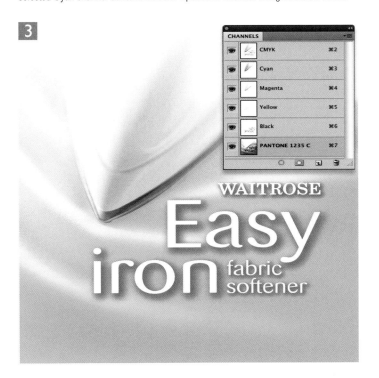

3 Meanwhile, with the selection still active in the Cyan channel, I used ⎇ *Delete* *alt* *Delete* to fill the selected area with white. I then did the same thing in the Magenta channel as well. There now remained a CMYK full color image of the iron, but the fabric and lettering outside of the iron was now using the yellow, black and spot color channels only. To preview all of the color channels combined, I clicked on the composite channel and the Spot color channel eyeball icons. The client wanted the drop shadow lettering to predominantly use the spot color ink. I therefore had to make an inverted selection of the iron in the Black channel and apply a Levels adjustment to substantially lighten the lettering in the Black channel. Here is a screen shot of the image which shows the final result after I had basically taken the image information from the darkest channel (the Cyan channel) and copied this over to the new Spot color channel.

Photograph: Laurie Evans. Designer: Richard Lealan. Client: Waitrose Limited.

Fine-art printing workflow

Opening an image in Photoshop and simply clicking the Print button may get you a reasonably acceptable print, but the odds of that print exhibiting a high degree of craft is pretty low. Making excellent prints from Photoshop is a craft that demands attention to detail and an understanding and appreciation of the process. It's much more than just hitting Print. In this section I'll try to give you the culmination of image processing and printing that we use when making 'serious' prints.

1 The process began in Camera Raw where both the tone and color were optimized for a 'master image' (not yet optimized for output). I also used Camera Raw's capture sharpening and noise reduction to get the initial detail extraction from the capture. I also set the color space to ProPhoto RGB, 16-bits and the native size of the capture. This image was shot in Upper Antelope Canyon just outside Page, Arizona, where I used a Phase One 6 x 4.5 camera with a 28 mm lens and the P 65+ camera back on a tripod with remote release. The exposure was about 8 seconds at f/11.

2 One of the limitations of Camera Raw's Workflow Options is the inability to control image dimensions, just resolution. Therefore, the image was opened into Photoshop at 300 PPI knowing that the height would be wrong since the image height was 29.947″ at that resolution. In this step I used the Image Size dialog to change the height to 20″ while letting the Resolution fall where it may since the Resample Image option was unchecked.

3 The next step was to do a final output sharpening for the print. I used Pixel Genius' PhotoKit Sharpener 2's Inkjet 480 Glossy setting as I was planning on making the print on Epson Exhibition Fiber Paper, which is a glossy type paper. I also added a bit of midtone contrast to punch up the midtone textural detail. I often slightly under-adjust the Clarity slider in Camera Raw so I can add additional midtone contrast in Photoshop, where the radius of the High Pass filter can be adjusted along with the blending options.

4 After getting the tone, color and detail adjusted for our master image, it was time to tweak the image based upon soft proofing the image though the veil of our custom printer/paper profile. It is at this stage where you'll need to evaluate which rendering intent is optimal for your image. In this image, I decided that Relative Colorimetric was better than Perceptual. After clicking OK, the image on-screen flattened out and appeared duller than without the soft proofing. That was because I had the Display Options (On-Screen) turned on.

5 Soft proofing does show you what the image will look like if you print it. However, it doesn't really give you any guidance in terms of adjustments you may need to make to improve the image. For that, I made a duplicate of the image and turned soft proofing off on the duplicate. Above, the original soft proofed image is on the left, on the right is ideally what I want the image to look like. The duplicate was my aim point.

6

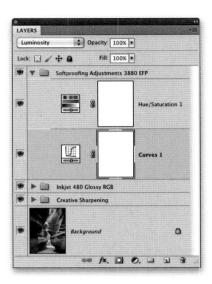

6 Soft proofing shows what the image will look like when the ink hits paper. By using the un-soft proofed image as an guide. I find that there will be at least two tone and color tweaks you'll need to make: a Curves and a Hue/Saturation adjustment, as shown above. The Curve adjustment, set to a Luminosity blend, only changes the image's contrast range to appear less dull. The Hue/Saturation tweak warms up the color and adds saturation. Both of these adjustments are placed inside a layer group named to represent the print and paper the adjustments are intended for. Obviously, you would only turn this layer group visibility on when you wanted to print to this printer/paper combo.

7

7 The image on the left (the soft proofed image) with the tone and color tweaks now appeared to be a better match to the duplicate, un-soft proofed image on the right. Perfect? No. Better? Yes, and that's really what I am striving for, better. At this stage I would normally close the duplicate without saving and go to print out the final image.

8 The Print dialog of Photoshop CS5 has changed visually only a slight amount from CS4 and earlier, yet the change in functionality is significant. The Color Management handling remains essentially the same (minus the NCM option). Here, I selected Photoshop Manages Color and our custom paper profile named 3880-EFP-PK-2880.icc. The big differences in CS5 really come from the elimination of Page Setup in the main File menu and incorporating that functionality in the Print Settings… button.

9 The biggest apparent difference is in the Mac version, shown above left. Since the Photoshop CS5 Print dialog is now 'capturing' the print driver settings, the Mac version has a Save button. The function on the Windows is the same -- setting the parameters for paper and driver settings is stored and sticky in the Print dialog. Hitting the Print button in the CS5 Print dialog now bypasses the print driver and uses the settings already captured. You can even record an action for printing -- it even captures the parameters from the Print Settings dialog!

10 One of the more irritating aspects of some printers is the inability to default to four equal margins. Many inkjet printers need a larger margin where the gripper grabs the paper. In reality this is actually a legacy issue since many printers can make borderless prints. But if your printer has unequal print margins, you can select the custom paper size and create your own size and margin settings. Generally, I prefer to always leave at least a 1″ paper margin for paper handling. In this step I created a custom paper size of 17″ x 22″ and four equal 1″ margins.

11 Even though you can record the print settings and Print dialog parameters in an action, I find it's also useful to create a custom preset for our printers. In this case, I named the preset to indicate the printer and paper. I chose the option to make the preset only available for this printer so I wouldn't accidentally use this preset for any of our other printers. Saving out custom settings is also available in most Windows drivers. The last step? Print!

I am at the stage where about 80% of the time, my first print is a keeper (Martin's not telling). Following these steps to printing won't guarantee you'll become a digital printing master – that takes time and practice. But each of these steps is important to the goal of producing excellent fine-art digital prints.

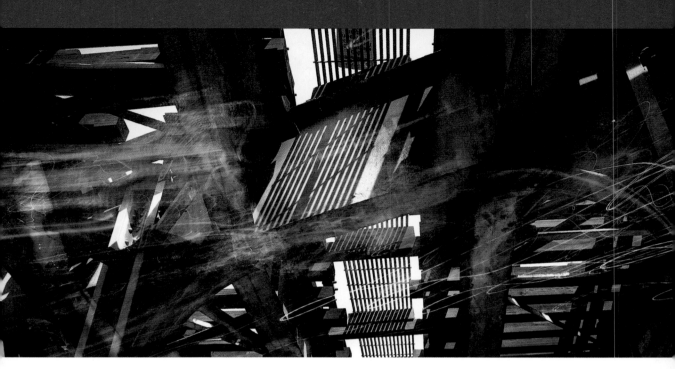

Chapter 13

Minding your own business

Suggestions on how to use Photoshop in your business

For a business to prosper there must be a profit, for if you don't turn a profit you won't be in business for long. Artists have historically been poor business people, in part because there is an assumed conflict of interest – if you do what you do for love how can you put a price on it? But that's exactly what you must learn to do. Ironically, the real value of your work has little to do with how difficult it was to do and more to do with how much perceived value it has by others. That is the key to understanding how to profit by doing what you love to do. And don't be afraid to put a high price on what you do, there's nothing wrong with being a business person as well as an artist. It's what we do… (and we love it, right?)

The keyword and caption detail

Figure 13.1 This figure shows an image shot by me in Downtown Chicago (which is one of the keywords) being displayed in Bridge CS5. Note, the background has been made white for the purposes of this figure.

Adding value to your images

Digital images, on their own, certainly have intrinsic value. But with extensive keywording and captioning, the same image is potentially far more valuable. Many people think of metadata (data about data) as merely an organizational aid without realizing how much value can be added to the image. Our good friend and colleague Seth Resnick strongly advocates extensive keywording and, just as importantly, captioning of the image. Seth does this primarily because he's so anal but also because he depends on the stock sale of images where metadata is an asset when potential buyers are doing image searches. So, for him and many others competing in that industry, adding metadata is a must.

The image shown in Figure 13.1 has 35 keywords (about average for a well-keyworded image intended for stock photo submission) and has almost 150 words in the caption (called Description in Bridge CS5, but we still think of it as a caption). Seth has boasted of having images that needed over 100 keywords for completion. We rarely go that far.

How do you keyword? One of the best tips from Seth is first write the caption (the story) and remember the who, what, when, where and why of journalism. When you write the story many of the keywords will come from the story itself. When adding keywords, be sure to list word variations and alternative spellings, such as color and colour. Use gerunds (verbs that function as nouns) and participles rather than verbs, such as *running* rather than *run*. Try to use the plural rather than the singular form of a word unless the plural spelling is different than merely adding an 's', in which case add that word as well.

Some keywords can be conceptual attributes, but use these very sparingly because overuse will make them useless. Everybody thinks their own work is 'beautiful' so *beautiful* as a keyword is pretty useless. Above all, be consistent in your approach and, if you are a poor speller, keep a dictionary handy. There's nothing quite so embarrassing as misspelling a keyword for the world to see. Using a 'controlled vocabulary' is critical; for more information about developing your own keyword vocabulary, see the website run by photographer David Riecks (www.controlledvocabulary.com).

Identifying your images

It used to be pretty easy to stamp slides with your name and copyright info but doing so with digital images isn't so straightforward (although arguably easier). But for your own sake please be sure to properly embed metadata in the IPTC schema (which stands for International Press Telecommunications Council). While we are still in the relatively early days of extensive metadata development, it's a viable method of identifying your work. If you don't do this you will end up producing what are known as 'orphan works' (see page 473).

You can add metadata using direct text entry in Bridge CS5 or in the File Info panel (see Figure 13.2) in Bridge or Photoshop (or the other applications in the suite – they all support IPTC now). But that's really the slow and inefficient method. We like to use Metadata Templates. Adobe has souped up the XMP (which stands for Extensible Metadata Platform) support in all of their CS5 applications and well they should, since Adobe initiated this free metadata standard. It is based on XML (Google it) and is the basis of the World Wide Web.

The .xmp file icon

Figure 13.2 This figure shows the File Info panel that contains the metadata of the Marina Towers image. Notice that I have marked the status as Copyrighted and added the digital copyright notice – the two most important metadata properties of identification.

File organization methods

The old days of filing cabinets with slide pages are long gone. These days, all of the image organization happens in the computer. If you have good organizational skills and take advantage of using metadata, organizing images is not impossible (just tedious). Jeff does not rename his original image files, he has adopted a logical folder naming convention and relies upon keywords and other metadata to organize his work as shown in Figure 13.3.

Martin's approach is similar to Jeff's except when it comes to client job work, where everything is renamed using a standard naming convention where the abbreviated client name is followed by the capture date (using the YYMMDD format), followed by a four-digit serial number (see Figure 13.4). There are several reasons for adopting this approach. By choosing a regular renaming scheme, it can become easier to identify files by client name and date (it is important to be consistent in the client naming, of course). Four digits is usually enough to cover all the numbers of shots that he might shoot for a client in any year. Martin will start from zero for the first shoot of the year and keep the numbers running consecutively for all subsequent shoots with that client. It is important to carry out such renaming as soon as the files are brought into the computer (see Figure 13.4). So, if a client selects a particular photo via the screen, the name that's referenced is one that stays with the file forever. By including the client name in the renaming scheme this reinforces 'ownership' of the file name.

Figure 13.3 Jeff organizes all captures in an enclosing folder ~Digital Captures and uses upper level folder names such as Events, Portfolio, Studio Shoots and Travel Shoots for the main structure. The Chicago-Shoot was the project shot for this book. You'll note the raw file is still a .CR2 file. Jeff only converts to DNG when he has to deliver a DNG file. All delivery files are renamed using Bridge and the original raw file name is preserved in the metadata.

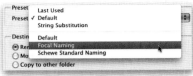

Batch Rename Preset drop-down menu

Figure 13.4 This shows the file renaming method one might apply using the Tools ⇨ Batch Rename… feature in Bridge. Batch Rename in Bridge CS5 now has the ability to save renaming presets to allow consistent Batch Rename settings. Note that the option to Preserve current filename in XMP is checked.

One of the problems Martin found in the early days of shooting digital was that if you didn't rename the images, clients would often rename them for you. There was one client who would ask for prints to be made from 'hairshine-blonde.tif' or some other descriptive name that had been applied to the original retouched images. It all got very complicated trying to work out which exact shots they were talking about.

This is just one way of renaming. In *The DAM Book*, Peter Krogh suggests renaming everything with your name first rather than the client's. This kind of naming scheme immediately makes it clear who is the copyright holder before the image is opened. Peter also suggests using the embedded filename instead of allocating a four-digit serial. The reason for this is that if all your jobs are renamed starting from 0001, your files will all end up renamed within the same low number range. If you use the embedded numbers, fewer of the filename numbers will end up being identical. Hence, if a client can only give you the last four digits you should be able to do a filename search and quickly figure out which image they are referring to.

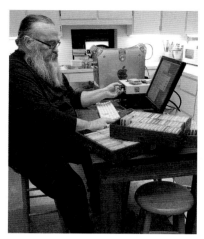

Figure 13.5 Me sitting at the temporary home of my old Mac G4 running System 9.2 and Retrospect 4.2. I was restoring image files from as far back as 1993 for this book that were stored on DAT tape.

Archiving issues

Backing up is not archiving!

Archiving is really the process of long-term conservation and preservation. While you do want to do weekly or daily backups, that process does not ensure long-term viability and availability. In film days, we used to worry about film lasting decades or centuries but with digital the process is complicated by file formats, operating systems and hardware that go out of date and cease to be supported. Unfortunately, at the moment the bad news is there are no good long-term archiving solutions for digital photography. Major institutions such as the National Archives in the US and UK are studying the problem, but there isn't any good news to report. The best advice we can offer about this issue is to maintain multiple copies on multiple media in multiple locations and get into the habit of updating and migrating your image data as new technologies become available.

By multiple media we include tape, hard drives and burnable media like CD or DVD. The long-term prospects of these media are not good. I used to archive first on DAT tape then AIT tape until suffering enough media problems that I gave it up. I still have all of the old DAT and AIT tape archives. For this book I had to resort to pulling up original image files from as early as 1993 (see Figure 13.5). To do so I had to set up an old Mac G4 that I kept around for this purpose. The figure shows me loading a DAT tape while running Retrospect 4.2 and Mac OS 9.2. I've been unable to find SCSI cards that allow me to use the old SCSI DAT drive on any current machines and current DAT drives have problems reading old media that they didn't write.

But the problem going forward is worse than it was back then. Back in the film and scan days, only selected images were actually scanned and you always had the film to fall back on. Now with digital capture, all of the originals are digital objects that must themselves be preserved and maintained – and for long-term considerations the file formats themselves need scrutiny.

Shortly before Adobe shipped the original Creative Suite (CS) Bruce Fraser and I were warned by then Adobe engineer Mark Hamburg (who had since left Adobe but has now returned) that the Photoshop 'native' file format, PSD, wasn't under Photoshop's control anymore and suggested we switch to using TIFF.

The Tagged Image File Format was originally developed by Aldus with input from a few other companies. Ironically, Adobe inherited the format when it acquired Aldus and has done a reasonably good job of moving it forward (although not updating the TIFF 6 spec). But if you want to store processed image files for the long term, we suggest TIFF because it is publicly documented.

But that's for processed files – what about original raw files from a camera? For that we support Adobe's DNG (Digital Negative) file format specification. Adobe has essentially 'given' the DNG file format to the industry and even gone to the extent of offering it (for free) to the ISO for use in an upcoming TIFF-EP specification update (TIFF for Electronic Photography). Ironically, Adobe had already granted the ISO the right to use TIFF in the ISO TIFF-EP specification and it's that spec that pretty much all of the major camera makers such as Nikon and Canon already use. Yet the majority of the camera makers so far have refused to adopt any standard (their use of TIFF-EP is unofficial so they are free to diverge from the spec if they so choose, and they do). Recent camera releases have, however, seen adoption of DNG by some camera manufacturers, notably Pentax by offering a DNG file format writing option and Leica by adopting DNG as its native raw file format.

For the long-term preservation and conservation of digital photography the industry simply must adopt raw file format standards. While traditional chemical photography originals can be accessed from the 19th century, there's a real question whether digital photography since the beginning of this millennium will be so enduring. There are already some early raw file formats that have been orphaned by their original manufacturer.

The United States Library of Congress has studied long-term conservation of digital objects and has identified seven major factors that impact long-term digital preservation and conservation (see sidebar). All of the current proprietary raw file formats (except DNG) violate most, if not all, of these factors. We therefore encourage our readers to support DNG, and wherever possible have your voices heard by the camera makers that proprietary, undocumented raw file formats need to be eliminated. We wish to be clear about one thing: neither of us is suggesting you convert to DNG and toss out your original proprietary raw files. We suggest both using DNG (where appropriate) and keeping your original raws.

The seven sustainability factors

From www.digitalpreservation.gov

Disclosure:
Refers to the degree to which complete specifications and tools for validating technical integrity exist and are accessible to those creating and sustaining digital content.

Adoption:
Refers to the degree to which the format is already used by the primary creators, disseminators, or users of information resources.

Transparency:
Refers to the degree to which the digital representation is open to direct analysis with basic tools.

Self-documentation:
A digital object that contains basic descriptive metadata and incorporates technical and administrative metadata relating to its creation and early stages of its life cycle, will be easier to manage and monitor for integrity and usability and to transfer reliably from one archival system to its successor system.

External dependencies:
Refers to the degree to which a particular format depends on particular hardware, operating system, or software for rendering or use and the predicted complexity of dealing with those dependencies in future technical environments.

Impact of patents:
Patents related to a digital format may inhibit the ability of archival institutions to sustain content in that format.

Technical protection mechanisms:
Content for which a trusted repository takes long-term responsibility must not be protected by technical mechanisms such as encryption, implemented in ways that prevent custodians from taking appropriate steps to preserve the digital content and make it accessible to future generations.

The DAM Book

If you want to find out more about image management using Adobe Bridge, Lightroom and Microsoft Expression Media, we highly recommend that you read: *The DAM Book, Digital Asset Management for Photographers, Second Edition,* by Peter Krogh, ISBN-13: 978-0596523572.

RAID

RAID, which stands for Redundant Array of Independent Disks, is often thought of as some sort of magic bullet for data protection. Not really. RAID level 0 stripes data across multiple drives for speed at the expense of safety. If you lose one drive you lose all your data. RAID 1 (mirrored arrays) is safer but slower. RAID 5 and 6 use one or more of the drives for parity to rebuild the array should a drive fail. But they are sometimes proprietary processes and if you lose the RAID hardware, you can't read the drives, so it's only a risk reduction strategy. NAS or Network Attached Storage is catching on and the units often use RAID 5, but even gigabit Ethernet is much slower than fast eSATA drives, and you are at the mercy of the network and its built-in embedded OS, usually running a Windows variation that may not support fully AFP (Apple File Protocol) connections.

Backing up your data

When managing your digital images, the most important thing is to make sure you have a backup procedure in place that can be relied upon in the event of a disaster, such as a hard drive failure or theft of a computer. If you don't have too big an image library, this could be achieved quite simply by having a single hard drive connected to the computer that you can back up your files to. At a more advanced level, you could invest in a mirrored RAID storage system where the data is mirrored across two or more drives of equal capacity. If one of the drive units were to fail, the data is protected on the backup drive, so you can simply replace the defective drive and the data is mirrored across to the replacement drive again. But be warned that mirroring the data in this way is still not entirely foolproof. However you choose to back up your data, the following points should be borne in mind.

Scheduled backups are most important because it is important to have a buffer between the contents that are on the current working drives and the backup versions. It is all too easy to delete a file or discover you need to revert to an earlier version of a file. If you make a mistake on a mirrored RAID system, the mistake will soon be mirrored to the other drive. But if you also maintain a copy on a separate backup drive system, there should always be a recent backup copy of the data ready for you to access. As a Macintosh user, Martin likes using the Chronosync utility (Figure 13.6) to make regular backups of his computer files. It's a fairly easy program to use and can automatically cross-reference the files on your computer drives with those on the backup drives to auto-synchronize the two. Jeff, on the other hand, has been using Retrospect® from EMC®, originally for writing to tape drives and more recently for doing incremental nightly scheduled hard drive backups using scripts. Jeff has used the searching function of Retrospect extensively either by date or enclosing folder naming.

Where do you store the backup data? If you keep the backup data on separate hard drives, it is not too difficult to keep these backup drives stored in a safe location away from the computer, such as in a fireproof safe, or off-site somewhere. One approach is to use two additional drives for every drive you wish to back up. That way you can keep one backup drive at the office, the other at a separate location, and keep swapping the two backup drives. For absolute security, some people back up all their data over a

Figure 13.6 Chronosync™ from Econ™ technologies (www.econtechnologies.com) is an indispensable tool for carrying out data backups.

fast Internet connection to a remote server. In the writing of this book, the InDesign files and images were constantly backed up to a remote server and updated files were obtained by each author. This allowed Martin and Jeff to work remotely and, given their time zone differences, Jeff would be ending his day by uploading files to the server for the start of Martin's workday. A simple email was used to alert each other to the updated files rather than trying to email actual files.

Hard drives can provide storage space that is fast, cheap and high capacity. But they can still be vulnerable to things like a virus attack. It may take a while to burn copies of your data to CD or DVD, but while such media may not be completely infallible, your data won't be vulnerable to virus attacks. So far, neither author has adopted Blu-ray burners into his scheme. While single layer, 6× 25GB Blu-rays disks have fallen in price (about $3.50), the write speed is still pretty slow compared to 16× for DVDs. Also the price of the Blu-Ray burners remains much higher than DVD burners. We are still on the sidelines and use hard drives.

DVD storage

Recordable DVD drives have become increasingly popular and are often supplied as standard with some computer models. Recordable DVD discs are capable of storing 4.7 GB of data. But again, to be realistic, I would knock that figure down to something more like 4.3 GB as the actual amount of data you can store on a disc. The only problem with a DVD (or CD) is that if it gets damaged you lose everything and that might mean losing a hefty chunk of valuable data. So don't rely entirely on DVD as a backup method. Recordable discs also have a finite life-span. And who is to say if DVD, or the new Blu-ray standard, will not be superseded by some other form of recordable media requiring a different type of hardware device to read the data? Furthermore, if you archive raw camera files without converting them to the DNG format, will you always have the software to interpret these? In this industry a lot can happen in a matter of just a few years. For example, does anyone now remember Syquest disks? We are hoping that Blu-ray may end up as a viable medium, but we certainly hope you didn't back up to HD DVD, the standard Toshiba was promoting that died in early 2008. But then we still don't know about the long-term viability of the media.

Fingerprint plug-ins

Software solutions have been developed to provide better data protection and security, giving suppliers of electronic data the means to identify and trace the usage of their intellectual property. These systems apply an invisible 'fingerprint' or encrypted code that does not spoil the appearance of the image but can be read by the detection software. The code must be robust enough to work at all usage sizes: from screen size to high resolution. It must withstand resizing, image adjustments and cropping. A warning message should be displayed whenever an image is opened up alerting the viewer to the fact that this picture is the property of the artist and a readable code embedded from which to trace the artist and negotiate a purchase.

Two companies have produced such encryption/detection systems: SureSign by Signum Technology and Digimarc by the Digimarc Corporation. Both work as plug-ins for Photoshop. They will detect any encrypted images you open in Photoshop and display a copyright detection symbol in the status bar alongside the file name. You have to pay an annual usage fee to Digimarc to register your individual ID (check to see if free trial period offers are in operation). Anyone wishing to trace you as the author, using the Photoshop Digimarc reader plug-in, will contact their website, input the code and from there read off your name and contact number. SureSign provides a unique author code plus transaction number. In my opinion, the latter is a more adaptable system.

Image protection

Anyone who fully understands the implications of images being sold and transferred in digital form will appreciate the increased risks posed by piracy and copyright infringement. The music industry has for a long time battled against pirates duplicating original disks, stealing music and video sales. Digital music recordings on CD made this problem even more difficult to control when it became possible to replicate the original flawlessly. The issue of piracy is not new to photographers and image makers, but the current scale of exposure to this risk is. It includes not just us Photoshop geeks, but also anyone who has their work published or is interested in the picture library market.

To combat this problem, the first line of defense had been to limit the usefulness of images disseminated electronically by (a) making them too small in size to be of use other than viewing on a screen and (b) including a visible watermark which both identifies the copyright owner and makes it very difficult to steal and not worth the bother of retouching out. The combination of this two-pronged attack is certainly effective but has not been widely adopted. The World Wide Web contains millions of screen-sized images, few of which are protected to this level. The argument goes that these pictures are so small and degraded due to heavy JPEG compression, what possible good are they for print publishing? One could get a better pirated copy by scanning an image from a magazine on a cheap flatbed scanner. Shopping is now replacing sex as the main focus of interest on the Internet, so screen-sized web images do now have an important commercial value in their own right. Furthermore, the future success of digital imaging and marketing will be linked to the ability to transmit image data. The technology already exists for us to send large image files across the world at speeds faster than DSL. Once implemented, people will want to send ever larger files by telecommunications. The issue of security will then be of the utmost importance.

How to make money with Photoshop

How much are you worth?

Creative workers and, in particular freelancers often have difficulty in working out what they're worth and how they should go about charging for the services they provide. Retailers sell goods, taxi drivers sell cab rides, while bankers look after our money. At the end of the day, an employee is simply selling their time and their worth is calculated based on how much their work skills profit the employer. OK, in the case of investment bankers, they screw up the economy and look to the tax payer to bail them out of difficulty, but as far as many workers are concerned, they are essentially all selling their time.

The problem a lot of freelancers have is that they fail to take into account how much time and money is required to run a business. They fall into the trap of confusing freelance income rates with the rates of pay given to full-time employees. There is a big difference. If you work for a company, you cost your boss a lot more than your take home pay check. A company has to provide its workers with premises to work from, light and heating, computer equipment, plus maybe a subsidized canteen, not to mention all the other side-benefits such as a company pension contributions and sickness benefit. So, when you start out on your own and become your own boss, you have to take responsibility for all these added expenses. On top of this you have to fill lots of other roles such as finance director, marketing manager, bookkeeper and coffee maker. So, when calculating how much you need to charge, you first need to work out how you are going to fulfill all these tasks on top of doing the actual work you set out to do as a freelancer.

Let's start with the assumption that you will work a basic 40-hour week. I know most freelancers will work a lot more hours than this, but we need to begin with a sensible business projection that allows us to compare the way you work as a freelancer with the way most other employees are expected to work. Here's how things should break down. If you want to be realistic, you should expect to spend half that time working on freelance commissions and the other working on all the other jobs that are part and parcel of running a self-employed business. So, you might typically only be able to spend 20 hours on average per week working on

Finding an agent

Some people argue that having the right agent can make a tremendous difference to a career. An experienced agent can help nurture creative talents and provide an umbrella that allows the artist to get on doing what they do best, while the agent takes care of managing the job bookings and ensuring that you get paid the best rates, often asking for more money than you might dare ask for yourself. For advertising work, having an agent makes good sense. The fees are substantial enough that everyone usually gains from this type of arrangement. The downside of having an agent is that some agencies will say yes to any kind of job, even if it pays below the market rate. From the agent's point of view, an editorial commission that pays only $150 is still worth $30 to them plus a $30 booking fee. Editorial bookings are usually the simplest ones for them to manage, as all they have to do is pick up the phone and take the booking. The freelancer, meanwhile, is the one who has to do all the work, in order just to make themselves $120. Remember, for an agent to invest their time promoting your talents, they will expect you to be willing to do the work they find for you. An agent can take your career in a whole new direction. This can be a good thing if it gets you good work and earns you decent money. For some people it may mean losing control of the direction they wish to take their career in. So think carefully about what you wish to achieve from such an arrangement.

paying commissions, while the other 20 hours will be spent doing everything else. You don't believe us? Well, think about it for a second. In the early years you will need to spend at least one day a week between sitting down to make calls to make appointments to show your work and going out to see prospective clients. When you get commissioned, you will be asked to send your portfolio in again or spend time making presentations to clients. There will be day-to-day telephone calls to deal with. There will be invoicing work to do as well as bill chasing. Then there are meetings with professionals such as bank managers, accountants and lawyers. What about training? You need to allow time to catch up with the latest news from the forums and attend seminar events to learn more about Photoshop. In fact, shouldn't reading this book count as work? Here is a brief summary of some of the things you might spend time doing:

- Self-promotion: making appointments
- Advertising/website
- Client telephone calls
- Creative research/monitor email forum activities
- Office administration
- Bookkeeping and accounts
- Business meetings
- Seminars and training

If you estimate that you'll spend 20 hours a week on average per week working on commissions, this works out at 1000 billable hours per year. Therefore, if you add up all your likely annual business costs, you can add on to this how much salary you would like to earn, then simply divide this figure by 1000 to calculate what your hourly rate should be. Now, we do realize you'll be offered jobs where the rate offered is a set fee that pays less than this rate, but at least you can use this as a guide to work out what you should be earning. Like most freelancers, you'll probably end up working a lot more than 40 hours per week, which is fine, as long as you are doing so to earn a better living. The above calculation is also based on an individual setting themselves up from scratch as a sole trader. Once you become more established, you can afford to allocate some of the job responsibilities to a personal assistant but then, of course, you'll have to factor in the costs of employing someone and that too will affect how much your hourly rate should be. Here is a brief summary of things that your freelance fees will need to pay for:

- Rent of business premises
- Equipment costs
- Insurance
- Telephone
- Office supplies
- ISP service, including server hosting fees
- Travel
- Training expenses
- Professional fees
- Heating and lighting
- Pension, income protection and health insurance

Your rate is your rate

Once you have worked out your daily and hourly rate, we recommend you stick firmly to it. You have worked out what you should charge based on the minimum amount you need to earn in order to keep your business ticking over, plus what premium you think your skills are worth, and it is therefore in your best interests to hold firm and not waver on that. However, there will come times where you'll be asked to work for less than the going rate. There is a real simple question that you can ask yourself before you take on any job: is it a job for the portfolio or a job for the bank? Most the time the answer will be it's one or the other. Either you want to accept a commission because you reckon it will be a nice job to work on and look good in your portfolio, or you want to do the job because it's a chance to earn some decent money. The best assignments are the ones that provide good money as well as artistic freedom, but you definitely want to avoid cutting your rates to do jobs that pay you less money than you are worth or need to live on, plus do nothing to raise your profile. The reality for some people is that when times are tight you have to swallow your principles and do anything to keep the cash flow ticking over, but whatever you do, be on your guard against those clients who are willing to take advantage. In our experience, the clients who pay the least are the ones who also take the longest to pay (it's true). If you do agree to work for less than the standard hourly rate, then

Editorial rates

Editorial magazines probably offer the lowest rates of pay. In fact, there are a lot of fashion magazines that expect you to work entirely for free, in return for a credit. As we point out, this type of work is only worth doing if it offers a good market place in which to show off your skills and helps you get good published work for your portfolio. We advise you to keep this in mind before taking on these kinds of jobs. We know lots of people who have got sucked into the cycle of working on endless free editorial jobs, where they don't even particularly enjoy the work that they are asked to do.

here's a tip. Never agree to charge less. If you simply invoice the lesser amount, the client will see this as the rate you charge for everything. Instead, you should propose to charge your normal rate, but offer a special discount on the invoice for whatever reason seems appropriate. That way, you make it clear from the start what your rate should be and that the client is getting a special discount this time only. Clients like this kind of arrangement because ultimately they get the saving they wanted and not only that, they feel good because they see the saving shown to them on the invoice. They'll also have more respect for you and are reminded of how much your services are normally worth. When it comes to getting more work from the same client, the starting point for your quote will be the standard day rate again, rather than the lesser amount you actually charged, and you can therefore negotiate from a position of strength if they come back to you with offers of more work.

How to bill for digital

With the advent of digital capture, clients are under the delusion that everything should be cheaper, right? Hey, pixels are free (once you've bought that $8K camera and that $5K computer system and all the other stuff you have to have in order to capture those 'free pixels'). No, in fact while there may be fewer direct costs with digital compared to the old film and processing days, there are actually much higher indirect costs in the equipment needed. So, how can you possibly consider giving your digital services away for free? But it's not up to us to tell you what to charge, just the factors to consider when you do decide.

Seth Resnick makes out a good case for charging a flat fee for all digital work. He'll offer a breakdown whose à la carte totals are more than what he expects to charge and a flat fee that is what he actually wants to charge. Most clients choose the flat fee but he's happy to charge by the service. Jeff on the other hand likes to break things down to their elemental costs. If something costs him something, somewhere, he wants to have an actual price for that cost and pass it along to the client. In Figure 13.7 you'll note that he is proposing to charge $1.25 per capture made. Sure, there will be four shots with 200 captures/shot and the total price would be $1000, but when priced at $1.25 it doesn't seem so high. You'll also note that he is charging for CMYK separations and proofs, burning to DVD (he would charge for digital transmission if needed) and even for storing the files. Figure 13.7 shows Jeff's estimating software built on FileMaker Pro which he uses for all jobs.

Whatever you do decide to charge, just know that as a good business person you are expected to charge something because if you don't, the implication is that there's no value attached – and clients ultimately expect value and will pay.

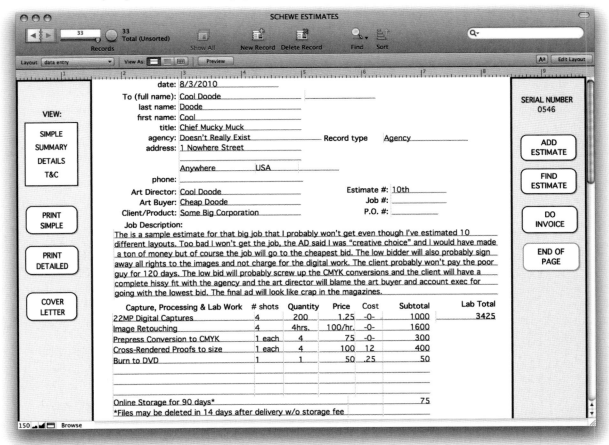

Figure 13.7 This is a sample estimate prepared (in jest if you can read the description) showing an example of how to charge for digital. It should be noted that Jeff is not suggesting you actually charge these rates – these are not Jeff's real rates – they are simply an example of how you might break down the charges to a client. When breaking down the charges, be prepared to explain and, if need be, defend them. Clients fully expect to have to pay for value (sometimes they just like real cheap prices) so you need to be prepared to educate them on the value attached to what you charge.

Protecting your rights

If it was easy to make a living out of photography and working in Photoshop, we could all be rich doing what we enjoy most. The real world provides plenty of obstacles to ensure that only those who are talented enough and persistent enough are able to make a decent living from freelance work. Not everyone is going to be interested in turning their photography into a full-time career, but there are a number of pitfalls that are useful to bear in mind that can help you from being exploited.

Back in the mid-eighties, a fellow photographer, Mike Laye, helped initiate a UK campaign to ensure that photographers were automatically granted copyright ownership of their photographs. I remember Mike enjoyed telling the story of how he first got thinking about the need for photographers to be better protected under the law. A British magazine had asked him to photograph the singer Demis Roussos. 'Demis who?', you ask. Well, he used to be a big star in the seventies, but by the eighties his musical career had all but dried up, which was around the time when Mike was asked to photograph him. A few years later though, and Demis Roussos was one of the passengers on a hijacked TWA flight – the papers were all clambering for recent photos taken of him. That's when Mike saw the photo he had shot a year or two previously appear on the front of nearly every major newspaper. He soon learned that although he had taken the photo, under UK law (as it was then) he was not automatically recognized as the copyright holder. It was the magazine, and not he, who owned the photo. They probably made a killing out of all the syndication fees, while Mike didn't receive so much as a penny (or cent).

Among other things, this story illustrates how the value of any image can be unknown. You never know if a photograph will acquire a greater worth in the future, which is why it is a good policy not to give away your copyright away unless someone rewards you handsomely for it. Freelancers are always going to be pressurized to undersell themselves and assign full copyright, but we have both managed to find work and made good incomes without giving up our copyright. OK, we have also lost some work through being obstinate, but it's not always such a bad thing to lose the odd commission. In the long term we believe you will gain more respect if you stick to your guns and don't sign away your rights.

One thing you should aim to do is to always make sure every photograph you take is marked as being copyrighted. As was mentioned earlier in this chapter, this is a basic means by which you ensure that any photographs you subsequently distribute are seen to be copyrighted. This does not guarantee that no one will edit the copyright status, but it does at least let all the honest users of photography know who owns a particular photograph.

It is also interesting to consider who owns the copyright in a retouched photograph. Is it just the photographer, or does the retoucher have shared rights? We would suggest that in most cases it is the photographer only, but there are instances where a substantial amount of retouching can be considered to be effectively adding completely new content to an image. This could be regarded as work that has a separate copyright ownership.

Orphan works

An orphan work is a copyrighted work whose owner is unknown or impossible to identify. The US Copyright Office has been working to address the issue (which is a real problem) and new legislation governing orphan works is to be introduced that may make it easier for potential infringers to claim they could not identify or find the owner and thus escape some of the penalties of copyright infringement. Without commenting on that issue, we will say it now becomes even more critical that copyright holders avail themselves of the current metadata opportunities and never send out any digital images without having embedded their copyright notice as well as contact information in the file.

Image harvesting

Companies love having the opportunity to get hold of images for free usage and little cost to themselves. It's all down to enticing people to submit photographs through the promise of exposure and in return getting them to sign away the rights associated with those photos. A classic example is the way a TV network might ask you to submit photos of, say, the weather today where you live. If you read the terms and conditions carefully you'll probably note that you are about to provide a free non-exclusive license for the TV network to use the photos you submit, any way they wish.

A more insidious form of image harvesting is photo competitions where the organizers ask photographers to assign full copyright to them as a condition of entry (see sidebar about the Pro-Imaging Bill of Rights for Photography Contests campaign).

Uploading photos and orphan works

Another thing to watch out for is that you don't create an orphan work in the process of uploading photos to a social networking site. It has been pointed out that some sites where you can upload photos to may remove important metadata such as the copyright information. Websites such as Flickr, on the other hand, do appear to preserve all of a file's metadata information. If anything, they expose rather more details than you would expect, such as the software used. For Adobe software testers such as ourselves, this can be potentially rather embarrassing if you are working with prerelease Adobe software that hasn't been officially released yet! What I personally like about Flickr is the fact that all the metadata I regard as important is always preserved.

Pro-Imaging Bill of Rights

Pro-Imaging is a non-profit, web-based organization for people working in the photography and imaging industries, where a condition of entry is that members do not sell royalty-free images. In 2008 they launched a Bill of Rights for Photography Contests campaign, designed to encourage competition organizers to adopt a 'fair business' approach that prevents unfair exploitation of photographs. For more information, go to www.pro-imaging.org. There you will find listings of approved and non-approved photography competitions (specifying onerous clauses in the competition terms and conditions). It is worth checking if you are thinking of entering a photo contest.

473

Index